10687248

STATISTICAL METHODS
FOR EDUCATIONAL AND
PSYCHOLOGICAL RESEARCH

McGRAW-HILL SERIES IN PSYCHOLOGY

Consulting Editors

Norman Garmezy

Richard L. Solomon

Lyle V. Jones

Harold W. Stevenson

ADAMS: Human Memory
BEACH, HEBB, MORGAN, AND NISSEN: The Neuropsychology of Lashley
BERKOWITZ: Aggression: A Social Psychological Analysis
BERLYNE: Conflict, Arousal, and Curiosity
BLUM: Psychoanalytic Theories of Personality
BROWN: The Motivation of Behavior
BROWN AND GHISELLI: Scientific Method in Psychology
BUTCHER: MMPI: Research Developments and Clinical Applications
CAMPBELL, DUNNETTE, LAWLER, AND WEICK: Managerial Behavior, Performance, and Effectiveness
COFER: Verbal Learning and Verbal Behavior
CRAFTS, SCHNEIRLA, ROBINSON, AND GILBERT: Recent Experiments in Psychology
CRITES: Vocational Psychology
D'AMATO: Experimental Psychology: Methodology, Psychophysics, and Learning
DEESE AND HULSE: The Psychology of Learning
DOLLARD AND MILLER: Personality and Psychotherapy
EDGINGTON: Statistical Inference: The Distribution-free Approach
ELLIS: Handbook of Mental Deficiency
FERGUSON: Statistical Analysis in Psychology and Education
FODOR, BEVER, AND GARRETT: The Psychology of Language: An Introduction to Psycholinguistics and Generative Grammar
FORGUS: Perception: The Basic Process in Cognitive Development
FRANKS: Behavior Therapy: Appraisal and Status
GHISELLI: Theory of Psychological Measurement
GHISELLI AND BROWN: Personnel and Industrial Psychology
GILMER: Industrial and Organizational Psychology
GRAY: Psychology Applied to Human Affairs
GUILFORD: Psychometric Methods
GUILFORD: The Nature of Human Intelligence
GUILFORD AND FRUCHTER: Fundamental Statistics in Psychology and Education
GUILFORD AND HOEPFNER: The Analysis of Intelligence
GUION: Personnel Testing
HAIRE: Psychology in Management
HIRSCH: Behavior-genetic Analysis
HIRSH: The Measurement of Hearing
HOROWITZ: Elements of Statistics for Psychology and Education
HURLOCK: Adolescent Development
HURLOCK: Child Development
HURLOCK: Developmental Psychology
JACKSON AND MESSICK: Problems in Human Assessment
KRECH, CRUTCHFIELD, AND BALLACHEY: Individual in Society
LAKIN: Interpersonal Encounter: Theory and Practice in Sensitivity Training
LAWLER: Pay and Organizational Effectiveness: A Psychological View
LAZARUS, A.: Behavior Therapy and Beyond

LAZARUS, R.: Adjustment and Personality
LEWIN: A Dynamic Theory of Personality
LEWIN: Principles of Topological Psychology
MAHER: Principles of Psychopathology
MARASCUILO: Statistical Methods for Behavioral Science Research
MARX AND HILLIX: Systems and Theories in Psychology
MILLER: Language and Communication
MORGAN: Physiological Psychology
MULAIK: The Foundations of Factor Analysis
NOVICK AND JACKSON: Statistical Methods for Educational and Psychological Research
NUNNALLY: Psychometric Theory
OVERALL AND KLETT: Applied Multivariate Analysis
ROBINSON AND ROBINSON: The Mentally Retarded Child
ROSENTHAL: Genetic Theory and Abnormal Behavior
ROSS: Psychological Disorders of Children: A Behavioral Approach to Theory, Research, and Therapy
SCHWITZGEBEL AND KOLB: Changing Human Behavior: Principles of Planned Intervention
SHAW: Group Dynamics: The Psychology of Small Group Behavior
SHAW AND COSTANZO: Theories of Social Psychology
SHAW AND WRIGHT: Scales for the Measurement of Attitudes
SIDOWSKI: Experimental Methods and Instrumentation in Psychology
SIEGEL: Nonparametric Statistics for the Behavioral Sciences
SPENCER AND KASS: Perspectives in Child Psychology
STAGNER: Psychology of Personality
TOWNSEND: Introduction to Experimental Methods for Psychology and the Social Sciences
VINACKE: The Psychology of Thinking
WALLEN: Clinical Psychology: The Study of Persons
WARREN AND AKERT: The Frontal Granular Cortex and Behavior
WATERS, RETHLINGSHAFER, AND CALDWELL: Principles of Comparative Psychology
WINER: Statistical Principles in Experimental Design
ZUBEK AND SOLBERG: Human Development

McGRAW-HILL
BOOK COMPANY
New York
St. Louis
San Francisco
Düsseldorf
Johannesburg
Kuala Lumpur
London
Mexico
Montreal
New Delhi
Panama
Paris
São Paulo
Singapore
Sydney
Tokyo
Toronto

MELVIN R. NOVICK
Professor of Education and Statistics
University of Iowa
Iowa City
Director of Psychometric Research
American College Testing Program
Iowa City

PAUL H. JACKSON
Senior Lecturer in Statistics
University College of Wales
Aberystwyth

Statistical Methods for Educational and Psychological Research

This book was set in Times New Roman.
The editors were Robert P. Rainier and Matthew Cahill;
the cover was designed by Edward A. Butler;
the production supervisor was Thomas J. LoPinto.
The drawings were done by ECL Art Associates, Inc.
The Maple Press Company was printer and binder.

Library of Congress Cataloging in Publication Data

Novick, Melvin R.
Statistical methods for educational and psychological research.

(McGraw-Hill series in psychology)
Bibliography: p. xvii
1. Educational research. 2. Educational statistics. I. Jackson, Paul H., joint author. II. Title.
LB1028.N79 370!.1'82 74-1233
ISBN 0-07-047550-4

STATISTICAL METHODS
FOR EDUCATIONAL AND
PSYCHOLOGICAL RESEARCH

1 2 3 4 5 6 7 8 9 0 MAMM 7 9 8 7 6 5 4

CONTENTS

PREFACE

The transition from classical to Bayesian methods of inference in educational and psychological research has not been taking place as rapidly as some of us had hoped. As early as 1963, a definitive article by Edwards, Lindman, and Savage gained a wide readership among psychologists and educators, but an immediate and dramatic change did not follow in the analysis of behavioral science data. Undoubtedly, there were many reasons for this. Perhaps the most important cause of delay, however, has been the unavailability of methodologically oriented texts at an elementary level which show research workers and practitioners, through the analysis on a very detailed step-by-step basis of real and relevant data in their field, how to use Bayesian methods in their work. Fortunately, this situation is amenable to near-term solution, and it is hoped, a number of books integrating Bayesian and other methods will soon appear, each oriented toward a particular area of application in which a new synthesis of methodology is in demand. This book is meant to be one of that number.

For research in education and psychology, Bayesian techniques are especially relevant. For example, a problem frequently encountered is that of prediction, from scores on selected tests, of the performance of group members on a given task. It is important to be able to specify the particular decisions that must be made and to anticipate where on the performance-criterion scale precise distinctions must be made and where they are superfluous. It is also generally very helpful to be able to incorporate prior experience in predicting performance for similar groups. Typically, we have substantial background information and feel that it would be inappropriate to depend only on sample data unless the sample is very large in size.

Our expectation is that the present book will find use as a text for a second semester, undergraduate or graduate, course in statistical methods and data analysis for students of education, psychometrics, industrial and educational psychology, and the psychology of individual differences, and in a similar position, as part of a methods sequence for mathematical statistics students. Our readers are expected to have had one or two semesters of introductory statistical methods/data analysis. There are many introductory texts that we believe could be used as the basis for a course preliminary to one drawn from this book. We would make the point, however, that the present book is not intended for use in a survey sequence for students who need the second half of a one year *exposure* to statistics. It is meant for those persons who need to develop a basic competency in statistical methods in order to understand critically, and perhaps to contribute to the substantive research literature.

In order to accommodate readers from diverse backgrounds, we have included a good deal more material here than can typically be covered in a single semester so that instructors will have some latitude to tailor the course for their needs. If most of the students in the course have had only a single semester of statistics, not specifically tailored as an introduction to the present text, the instructor will probably want to start at Chapter 1 and proceed carefully through the four chapters of Part 1, doing an ample number of examples in order to lay the groundwork in data analysis and probability for Part 2. If the students have had a more substantial applied background, Chapters 1 and 2 can be read for motivation without spending much time on examples. Similarly, students having a good grounding in probability theory can move quickly through Chapter 3, possibly even skipping it entirely. Chapter 4 has a somewhat different character. While the materials covered there will typically be included in most presentations in probability theory, our emphasis is rather specialized, and we therefore recommend that every reader refresh himself on this chapter and that most readers study it very carefully. The core of the book is contained in Chapters 5 to 8. These chapters should be covered slowly and carefully. Our experience is that Chapters 1 to 8 can be covered in a single semester, though it will be necessary to omit the few optional sections that are not integral to the text but which provide a deeper exposition for the benefit of more highly motivated students. These sections have been indicated in the text by a footnote.

Those instructors who judge their class to be well advanced may wish to start directly with Chapter 4. In such cases, it should be possible to cover Chapter 9 and possibly 10. These chapters will be of particular interest to more advanced students because they include an introduction to modern methods for estimating many parameters.

Our presentation in the core, Chapters 5 to 8, is meant to be detailed and comprehensive. We hope that readers will attain a high degree of mastery of the material in these chapters. It is far more important that readers obtain a real competence in these chapters than that they get a broad overview of a larger number of topics. Whenever there is doubt as to how much material should be covered in a particular course, our standing recommendation is to cover less but to cover it more thoroughly. A reader who has mastered Chapters 5 to 8 should be able to use the materials in Chapter 9 and 10 without great difficulty. The tables given in the Appendix should be adequate for instructional purposes.

The reader will note that a great many detailed numerical examples are given *in the text*, and a few additional exercises are given at the end of each chapter. The numerical examples should be worked through with pencil and paper, verifying our results, particularly where we omit detail. We have tried to exercise enough care so that the numerical work is given in sufficient detail to clearly exhibit the methods, while at the same time leaving a few gaps in the arithmetic to permit the reader to exercise and develop his skills. The exercises should also be considered as integral to the text.

At some point during the reading of this book, we hope that the typical reader will be excited enough by this material to want to investigate other presentations of Bayesian methods. For these readers we have put together a small list of Bayesian books and articles that may be useful. Each of these references, of course, contains its own set of references, and so the interested reader can easily and quickly find himself meandering through the labyrinth of Bayesian literature. Most of the references given here will be readable by persons who have managed to get themselves well into the present book. Others are somewhat more demanding of a mathematical prerequisite; we have placed one asterisk (*) following all but three of these references. Those who are able to function comfortably at a rather higher mathematical level will find these three references—designated by two asterisks (**)—extremely useful.

In teaching this course, we have never given a formal examination nor do we assign, for grading purposes, many numerical exercises. The exercises in the text are suggested to the students with the understanding that if they encounter difficulty, they will receive tutorial assistance. The primary activity of our students involves the preparation of "publication quality" data analyses. Our students have been required to find data appropriate for the analyses they are studying and to actually do a data analysis of a case study and "write it up" in a form suitable for publication. Needless to say, the variation in quality of the initial assignments is very great. However, we encourage our students to seek help from the teaching assistants and other students in addition to the instructor. In effect, these papers are "refereed". We find that by the end of the semester most students have greatly improved their report-writing ability. Some of our students' papers can now be found as case studies in the final sections of Chapters 6, 7, and 8. Not all of these even approach publication quality, but they all represent some displayed competence in Bayesian data analysis.

In developing the present text, we have incurred many debts. The greatest of these is to D. V. Lindley, whose two-volume text of Bayesian methods, *Probability and Statistics from a Bayesian Viewpoint*, was an invaluable reference and guide, and from whom we have learned much over a period of five years through discussion and from his comments on an earlier version of the text. Detailed comments by Lyle V. Jones were very helpful to us. Others who have read the manuscript and helped in a substantial way to debug it include, Ronald Hambleton, Larry Henriksen, James Hickman, Seong-Soo Lee, Jerry Mussio, Kazuo Shigemasu, Hariharan Swaminathan, Charles Lewis, Maurice Tatsuoka, Ming-Mei Wang, Victor Willson, and Dorothy Zorn. We are indebted to Dallas Parry for permission to use some data and text from a report of the Minnesota Statewide Testing Program and to the Psychological Corporation for their policy of permitting material from their Test Service Bulletins to be reprinted.

The computer systems reported here were developed by David Christ (systems programming), Victor Ormsby (sequence programming), and Gerald Isaacs (dialect translation). Each has demonstrated a remarkable ability to translate general suggestions into working programs. Nancy Petersen and Charles Davis have played an invaluable role in preparing or editing many of the exercises and numerical examples and helping to debug the text. They have each also contributed several case studies. Other case studies were contributed by Allan Cohen, Elliott L. Johnson, and Theresa Robinson. We are greatly indebted to Nancy Ralfs, Linda Smith, and Barbara Trigg who took charge of the editing and logistic coordination for the successive drafts of the text. Joanne Armbruster must be commended for her patient typing and retyping of the many revisions of each chapter.

Finally, we wish especially to thank William E. Coffman, E. F. Lindquist, Professor of Education and Director of the Iowa Testing Programs, The University of Iowa, and Leo A. Munday, Vice President, Research and Development Division, The American College Testing Program, whose support made this book possible.

MELVIN R. NOVICK

PAUL H. JACKSON

SELECTED READINGS

Aitchison, J.: "Choice Against Chance" (Reading, Mass.: Addison-Wesley, 1961).

Bayes, T.: An Essay Towards Solving a Problem in the Doctrine of Chances, *Biometrika*, **45**: 293-315 (1958). [Reprinted from the *Philosophical Transactions of The Royal Society of London*, **53**: 370-418 (1763), with a biographical note by G. A. Barnard.]

Blackwell, D.: "Basic Statistics" (New York: McGraw-Hill, 1969).

Box, G. E., and B. Tiao: "Bayesian Inference in Statistical Analysis" (New York: Wiley, 1973).*

De Finetti, B.: Foresight: Its Logical Laws, Its Subjective Sources, reprinted in **H. E. Kyburg, Jr.** and **H. E. Smokler** (eds.), "Studies in Subjective Probability" (New York: Wiley, 1964).*

_____: "Probability and Induction: The Art of Guessing" (New York: Wiley-Interscience, 1973).

De Groot, M. H.: "Optimal Statistical Decisions" (New York: McGraw-Hill, 1970).**

Edwards, W., H. Lindman, and L. J. Savage: Bayesian Statistical Inference for Psychological Research, *Psychological Review*, **70**: 193-242 (1963).

Edwards, W., and A. Tversky: "Decision Making" (Harmondsworth, Middlesex: Penguin Books, Penguin Modern Psychology Readings No. 8, 1967).

Good, I. J.: "The Estimation of Probabilities" (Cambridge, Mass.: The MIT Press, 1965).*

____: "Probability and the Weighing of Evidence" (London: Charles Griffin, 1950).*

Jeffreys, H.: "Theory of Probability", 3d ed. (Oxford: Clarendon Press, 1961).*

Laplace, P. S.: "Essai philosophique sur les probablités", translated by **F. W. Truscott** and **F. L. Ernory**, "A Philosophical Essay on Probabilities" (New York: Dover, 1951).

Lindley, D. V.: " Bayesian Statistics, A Review" (Philadelphia: SIAM, 1972).

____: "Introduction to Probability and Statistics from a Bayesian Viewpoint", vols. I and II (Cambridge: Cambridge University Press, 1965).*

____: "Making Decisions" (London and New York: Wiley-Interscience, 1971).

Meyer, D. L., and R. O. Collier, Jr.: "Bayesian Statistics" (Itasca, Ill.: F. E. Peacock, 1970).

Mosteller, F., R. E. Rourke, and G. B. Thomas: "Probability with Statistical Applications", 2d ed. (Reading, Mass.: Addison-Wesley, 1970).

____, **and D. L. Wallace**: "Inference and Disputed Authorship: The Federalist" (Reading, Mass.: Addison-Wesley, 1964).

Pratt, J. W., H. Raiffa, and R. Schlaifer: The Foundations of Decision under Uncertainty: An Elementary Exposition, *The Journal of The American Statistical Association*, **59**:353-375 (1964).

Raiffa, H.: "Decision Analysis" (Reading, Mass.: Addison-Wesley, 1968).

____ **and R. Schlaifer**: "Applied Statistical Decision Theory" (Boston: Harvard Business School, 1961).*

Ramsey, F. P.: Truth and Probability, reprinted in **H. E. Kyburg, Jr.** and **H. E. Smokler** (eds.), *Studies in Subjective Probability* (New York: Wiley, 1964).

Savage, I. R.: "Statistics—Uncertainty and Behavior" (New York: Houghton-Mifflin, 1968).

Savage, L. J., et al.: "The Foundations of Statistical Inference" (London: Methuen, 1962).*

Savage, L. J.: "The Foundations of Statistics" (New York: Wiley, 1954). Reprinted in paperback (New York: Dover, 1972).**

____: Reading Suggestions for the Foundations of Statistics, *The American Statistician*, **24**: 23-27 (1970).

Schlaifer, R.: "Computer Programs for Elementary Decision Analysis" (Boston: Harvard Business School, 1971).

____: "Probability and Statistics for Business Decisions" (New York: McGraw-Hill, 1959).

Schmitt, S. A.: "Measuring Uncertainty" (Reading, Mass.: Addison-Wesley, 1969).

Winkler, R. L.: The Assessment of Prior Distributions in Bayesian Analysis, *The Journal of The American Statistical Association*, **62**: 776-800 (1967).

Zellner, A.: "An Introduction to Bayesian Inference in Econometrics" (New York: Wiley, 1971).**

PART ONE

Problems, Data, and Probability Models

1
SOME SIMPLE DATA ANALYSIS

In this chapter we present an overview of statistical prediction. First, we illustrate the fitting of a linear prediction function for a simple data set with one predictor and one criterion variable. Next, the concept of loss resulting from errors of prediction is introduced and the most widely known and utilized loss functions are defined. We then extend the prediction model and present an expository discussion of the case of multiple predictor variables. Finally, we illustrate how background information from sources other than our immediate sample can be used to improve prediction.

1-1 ERRORS IN ESTIMATION AND PREDICTION

If we have available a set of pairs of *observations* on n individuals, each pair consisting of one measurement on a *predictor* (independent) variable and one on a *criterion* (dependent) variable, then we are in a position to begin a study of the relation between these variables. Let us use the lowercase letter x to denote an observed value of the predictor variable and the lowercase letter y to denote an observed value of the criterion variable. If we use arabic numerals to index the observations, then our observations consist of the n pairs $(x_1, y_1), (x_2, y_2), \ldots, (x_n, y_n)$.

What we are looking for is some (surely less than perfect) relationship between the x's and the y's. If we know that relationship, and if we are able to obtain the x's for some persons, then we may be able to predict their y values better than if we did not have these x values. Given an x value, we desire a rule for specifying a *prediction function* $\hat{y} = \hat{y}(x)$ so that $\hat{y}$ is a good predictor of the y value corresponding to the known x value. For example, a good prediction function for a particular problem might be the *linear function* $\hat{y} = \hat{y}(x) = .42 + .09x$; then, if x were equal to 1, the predicted value $\hat{y}$ would be $\hat{y} = .42 + .09 = .51$. We shall generally use a hat (^) to indicate an estimator of the kind to be developed in this chapter.

The difference between the predicted value $\hat{y}$ and the actual observed criterion value y is called the *error of prediction*. Thus, we define the error of prediction mathematically as the difference

$$e = \hat{y} - y, \qquad (1\text{-}1.1)$$

which may be either positive or negative. Obviously, we should like to have errors that are generally small in magnitude.

In Fig. 1-1.1, the following 10 hypothetical pairs of (x, y) values relating composite scores on the American College Test (ACT) and grade-point average (GPA) are plotted: (29,4.0), (26,2.8), (25,2.4), (22,3.7), (18,2.9), (18,1.4), (17,1.8), (16,1.5), (15,2.7), (14,2.5). By visual inspection, it appears that the points tend to concentrate along a line running from lower left to upper right. This suggests that if we define our predictor $\hat{y}(x)$ as a linear function $\hat{y} = \alpha + \beta x$ and estimate the unknown parameters α and β accurately, we may find that the errors defined in (1-1.1) are acceptably small on the average. We shall need an explicit method for determining specific values for α and β so that the prediction function is explicitly defined. It is useful, however, to try to develop some skill in fitting points by eye. The reader is, therefore, invited to select one of the following as his guess at the "best-fitting" line for predicting y from x:

1) $.8 + .07x$
2) $-.3 + .10x$
3) $.1 + .10x$
4) $.1 + .12x$
5) $.6 + .10x$

It would be a good idea to actually plot these lines on Fig. 1-1.1 and, perhaps, to supply a sixth line if none of those given above seems satisfactory. Perhaps the easiest way to draw each of these lines is to determine y values for $x = 15$ and $x = 25$. While doing this, the reader should be asking himself just what is meant by saying that a particular line is the "best-fitting" line for a set of points.

On reflection, it should be clear that an error has been committed whether we overestimate y (that is, $\hat{y} - y > 0$) or underestimate y (that is, $\hat{y} - y < 0$). In the latter case, the computation of $\hat{y} - y$ somehow suggests that we have made the negative

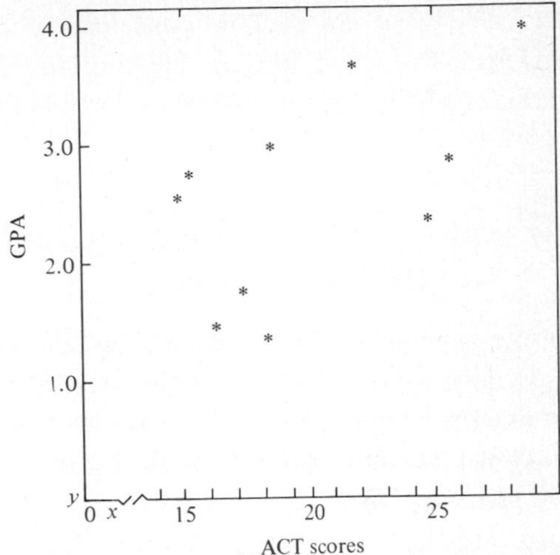

FIGURE 1.1.1
Scatter plot of GPA and ACT scores.

of an error. This does not seem meaningful, since if we were to compute the average error committed, the negative and positive errors would tend to cancel each other. If the optimal prediction function were the mean, we would find the average error to be zero.

If we consider that some sort of loss is involved in either an underprediction or overprediction of y, then as a first approximation, we might think of the loss as being equal to the magnitude of the difference $\hat{y} - y$, but independent of its sign. If we denote by $a(e)$ the loss associated with the error e, we have

$$a(e) = |e|, \qquad (1\text{-}1.2)$$

indicating that the loss is equal to the absolute value of the error. Graphically, $a(e)$ is just the length of the *vertical* line connecting y with the predicted value $\hat{y}(x)$. We might then consider it meaningful to take as the best-fitting linear function the one that minimizes the average of the *absolute-error loss* defined by (1-1.2).

Some of the earliest studies of random phenomena proceeded on this basis. With such a loss function, we are supposing that the direction of the error is irrelevant: Only the magnitude is of consequence. Thus, we are dealing with a loss function that is *symmetric* about zero error. Undoubtedly, in many situations this is a reasonable loss function; in others it may not be so. For example, a tiny error may, in fact, occasion no loss, or perhaps beyond a certain point, errors of all sizes are equally bad. Regardless of this, it is certainly true that the method is not popular, and this is because of the relative difficulty of the computations evolving from it. There is no *simple* method of determining the best-fitting prediction line under absolute-error loss.

Perhaps, we should indicate at the outset that the kinds of losses we are talking about here are not necessarily economic (i.e., involving money or money equivalents).

Basically, what we shall be concerned with is the subjective evaluation of degree of undesirability which in most applications will include, but not be limited to, economic situations. This question will be explored in Chap. 6.

1-2 ABSOLUTE-ERROR, MEAN-SQUARED ERROR, ZERO-ONE, AND THRESHOLD LOSS

In the previous section we studied just one of several possible measures of loss, namely, absolute-error loss. We now study a second measure of loss which has the very desirable symmetry property but which leads to a simpler and more easily interpretable mathematical system. This is the so-called *squared-error-loss function*. With this loss function, we presume that the loss associated with inexact prediction is equal to the square of the error of prediction. Thus, mathematically, we write

$$q(e) = e^2 = (\hat{y} - y)^2. \qquad \text{(1-2.1)}$$

With this loss function, it is desirable to specify a prediction function so as to minimize the average value of the squared errors of prediction. It turns out that the mathematical results flowing from this loss function are particularly simple and elegant, and for this reason, it is the most widely used. Indeed, the standard regression and correlation theories that are the backbone of statistical practice are derived from this assumed loss function.

On reflection, it might seem that the squared-error-loss assumption is somewhat unreasonable. Stating that loss, economic or otherwise, is equal to the square of the error of prediction puts an extremely large penalty on large errors, and this penalty grows with the error. In many problems, one would rather assume that there exists some large value such that errors of this magnitude are expensive, but errors of a larger magnitude are no more expensive. One reason this may not be important is that our observations and, hence, the errors, are typically bounded so that enormous losses are not possible. For the reasons indicated above and those to be discussed in the next section, squared-error loss is one of the four indispensable loss functions, and of these, undoubtedly the most frequently used.

The third loss function of general interest is the so-called *zero-one loss function*. With this loss function, we presume that we have a zero loss if our predicted value does not differ from the actual value by more than some specified constant amount c, but that we lose an amount a (usually taken as 1) if the error is larger than c. Mathematically, we presume that there exists a constant c such that

$$z(e) = \begin{cases} 0 & \text{if } |e| \leq c, \\ a > 0 & \text{if } |e| > c. \end{cases}$$

With this loss function, we are saying that small errors involve no loss whatsoever;

however, beyond a specified point, an error does involve a loss, but the loss is constant for all values of the absolute error beyond that point. Perhaps this situation can best be described by the common expression that "a miss is as good as a mile".

Consider the data used for Fig. 1-1.1 and suppose that for zero-one loss a c value of .5 is considered appropriate; i.e., a prediction is considered accurate provided it does not differ in absolute value by more than .5 from the realized value of y. The following tabulation shows the error, the absolute-error, the squared-error, and the zero-one loss for the first proposed prediction line. The reader should verify these and make a similar tabulation for the four remaining prediction lines.

x	$\hat{y}$	y	e	$a(e)$	$q(e)$	$z(e)$
29	2.83	4.0	−1.17	1.17	1.3689	1
26	2.62	2.8	− .18	.18	.0324	0
25	2.55	2.4	+ .15	.15	.0225	0
22	2.34	3.7	−1.36	1.36	1.8496	1
18	2.06	2.9	− .84	.84	.7056	1
18	2.06	1.4	+ .66	.66	.4356	1
17	1.99	1.8	+ .19	.19	.0361	0
16	1.92	1.5	+ .42	.42	.1764	0
15	1.85	2.7	− .85	.85	.7225	1
14	1.78	2.5	− .72	.72	.5184	1

Again the question may be raised: "Which of the five proposed functions is 'best'?"

A loss function of great interest in educational work is that which we shall call the *threshold-loss function*. Suppose we take a criterion value y_0 as the minimum acceptable level of performance. Our only interest is whether or not the person's performance will be at or above this level, or below it. Thus, we would *dichotomize* the continuous measurement of performance on the criterion value y and define a new variable taking values w such that $w = 1$ if $y \geq y_0$ and $w = 0$ if $y < y_0$. The value $w = 1$, thus, denotes satisfactory performance, and $w = 0$ denotes unsatisfactory performance. Similarly, the estimated value $\hat{y}$ of y can be used to define the variable $\hat{w}$ so that $\hat{w} = 1$ if $\hat{y} \geq y_0$ and $\hat{w} = 0$ if $\hat{y} < y_0$. Thus, $\hat{w} = 1$ denotes a prediction of satisfactory performance and $\hat{w} = 0$ denotes a prediction of unsatisfactory performance. The question of error, then, involves the comparison of $\hat{w}$ with w rather than the comparison of $\hat{y}$ with y. Specifically, the error of prediction of $\hat{w}$ with respect to w is

$$e = \hat{w} - w .$$

Clearly, e will take one of the three values: −1, 0, +1. We can stipulate our losses corresponding to the two kinds of incorrect decisions by letting

$$t(e) = \begin{cases} 0 & \text{if } e = 0, \\ a > 0 & \text{if } e = +1, \\ b > 0 & \text{if } e = -1. \end{cases}$$

Thus, if we predict that a person will be acceptable when he is not, our loss is a; while if we predict that he will not be successful when in reality he is, our loss is b. These two types of incorrect classification are often referred to as *false positives* and *false negatives*, respectively. If we correctly predict the person's performance as being acceptable or not acceptable, the loss is zero.

Consider the data set used before (Fig. 1-1.1) and suppose that y_0 is set at 2.50. Further, assume that $a = 6$, and $b = 3$ and that function (5) is used as the prediction function in this application. The following tabulation shows the threshold loss.

x	$\hat{y}$	y_0	y	$\hat{w}$	w	e	$t(e)$
29	3.50	2.50	4.0	1	1	0	0
26	3.20	2.50	2.8	1	1	0	0
25	3.10	2.50	2.4	1	0	+1	6
22	2.80	2.50	3.7	1	1	0	0
18	2.40	2.50	2.9	0	1	−1	3
18	2.40	2.50	1.4	0	0	0	0
17	2.30	2.50	1.8	0	0	0	0
16	2.20	2.50	1.5	0	0	0	0
15	2.10	2.50	2.7	0	1	−1	3
14	2.00	2.50	2.5	0	1	−1	3

We shall postpone the discussion of how to obtain the *best* estimator under threshold loss and only note here that it does not involve the use of a prediction *line*.

To consider the implications of these four loss functions for statistical practice, let us consider the following problem. We are given the 10 observations on y (GPA) plotted in Fig. 1-1.1 but *not* those on x (ACT), and we are then asked to predict the GPA for one person selected secretly and randomly. Our prediction $\hat{y}$ will not depend on x since we have no information about x; at best, it can be based on our complete knowledge of the population of 10 persons from which this one person was randomly selected. Thus, we want to find the best estimator of the selected person's GPA given a specified loss function. The mathematics is easy if we adopt squared-error loss, so we consider that first; and, since any one of the ten persons could have been selected, we stipulate that we want to determine $\hat{y}$ so that the average squared error over all persons is as small as possible. Symbolically, we wish to minimize the average loss

$$Q(e) = \frac{\Sigma q(e_i)}{n} = \frac{1}{10}\sum_{i=1}^{10}(\hat{y} - y_i)^2, \qquad (1\text{-}2.2)$$

where $q_i(e)$ is the squared-error loss for the ith person. We shall generally use a dot subscript to indicate an average value, so let $y_{\bullet}$ be the average value of the y's. Since $\hat{y}$ is just a number, it must differ from $y_{\bullet}$ by some constant d; that is,

$$\hat{y} = y_{\bullet} - d \qquad (1\text{-}2.3)$$

where d may be positive, negative, or zero. Rewriting (1-2.2), we have

$$Q(e) = \frac{1}{10}\sum_{i=1}^{10}(y_{\bullet} - y_i - d)^2 \qquad (1\text{-}2.4)$$

as the loss that we desire to minimize by a suitable choice of d. We may also write this as

$$Q(e) = \frac{1}{10} \sum_{i=1}^{10} [(y_i - y_\bullet) + d]^2$$

$$= \frac{1}{10}\left[\sum_{i=1}^{10} (y_i - y_\bullet)^2\right] + \frac{2d}{10}\left[\sum_{i=1}^{10} (y_i - y_\bullet)\right] + d^2.$$

If we carry out the summation in the second term, the result is just $2d(10y_\bullet - 10y_\bullet)/10 = 0$, and hence we are left with

$$Q(e) = \frac{\sum_{i=1}^{10} (y_i - y_\bullet)^2}{10} + d^2.$$

To make $Q(e)$ as small as possible, we obviously set $d^2 = 0$ and, thus, discover from (1-2.3) that our estimator is $\hat{y} = y_\bullet$, the sample mean. In our example then, the predicted GPA for the person selected is the sample mean, 2.57. If we look at (1-2.2), we also see that the average loss is just the *variance* of the given population of y scores. Thus, *under squared-error loss, the mean is the best estimator, and the variance is the average loss.* We shall use the symbol s_y^2 to denote the variance

$$s_y^2 = \frac{\sum_{i=1}^{n} (y_i - y_\bullet)^2}{n}$$

of a set of sample observations. Note that the divisor here, and throughout this book, is n rather than $(n - 1)$, as sometimes used in other texts.

If we elect to work *with absolute-error loss, the appropriate estimator is the median*; and if we elect to work *with zero-one loss, the appropriate estimator is approximately equal to the mode* where that quantity is clearly defined. We shall not prove these statements. A few readers may be able to satisfy themselves as to their truth by considering the effect of taking alternative values as estimators. With the data set for Fig. 1-1.1, we would compute a median value as 2.6 (midway between the fifth and sixth ordered values 2.5 and 2.7). Since the sample is small and has no mode, the rule given above for the best estimator under zero-one loss does not apply. In Chapter 3, we shall see that with threshold loss, the prediction $\hat{w}$ of a person's criterion performance w will be based not on the mean, median, or mode, but on the *probability* that a person with a given predictor score will attain a criterion value $w = 1$.

Returning now to our prediction of y given x, we can use the results obtained above to begin to see why we bother observing x in order to predict y. Under squared-error loss, the minimum average loss will be the variance of the distribution. However, suppose we could divide up the population of persons into subpopulations such that "on the average" the variances in the subpopulations were smaller. Then, on the average our loss would be smaller. One way of doing this is to consider each value of x as determining a subset of persons and doing predictions within each subpopulation. In Chapter 4, we shall see that if we subdivide the set of persons in this way, then on the average the variance of y in the subpopulations will be less than in the overall population if there is any relationship at all between the x's and the y's.

Since it may be very useful to base our predictions of y on the x values using a linear prediction function, let us work out the details of fitting a straight line to n pairs of points. The required formulas are easy to derive by entirely algebraic methods. This brief digression will be useful because it will give the reader some understanding of a logical development that underlies many of the methods we shall use.

We desire to find a linear function of x, $\hat{y} = \alpha + \beta x$, so as to minimize

$$\Sigma(\hat{y} - y)^2 = \Sigma(y - \hat{y})^2 = \Sigma[y - (\alpha + \beta x)]^2 = \Sigma[(y - \beta x) - \alpha]^2. \tag{1-2.5}$$

Consider first the case where y and x each have an average value of zero; then so will βx, and hence also $y - \beta x$. Applying the recently established principle that the sum of squared deviations is minimum around the average, we conclude that α must be taken equal to zero. We, therefore, must find β to minimize $\Sigma(y - \beta x)^2$. We can now write (1-2.5) as

$$\Sigma y^2 - 2\beta\Sigma xy + \beta^2\Sigma x^2.$$

We now proceed to "complete the square" and write (1-2.5) as

$$\begin{aligned}\Sigma y^2 + \Sigma x^2 \left[\beta^2 - 2\beta\frac{\Sigma xy}{\Sigma x^2} + \left(\frac{\Sigma xy}{\Sigma x^2}\right)^2\right] - \Sigma x^2\left(\frac{\Sigma xy}{\Sigma x^2}\right)^2 \\ = \Sigma y^2 - \frac{(\Sigma xy)^2}{\Sigma x^2} + \Sigma x^2\left(\beta - \frac{\Sigma xy}{\Sigma x^2}\right)^2.\end{aligned} \tag{1-2.6}$$

The first and second terms do not depend on β, but the third term does, and it surely cannot be negative. Therefore, we minimize (1-2.6) by taking

$$\beta = \frac{\Sigma xy}{\Sigma x^2} \tag{1-2.7}$$

and, thus, making the third term equal to zero. Thus, when y and x both have an average value of zero, the best straight line for predicting y from x is

$$\hat{y} = \frac{\Sigma xy}{\Sigma x^2}x. \tag{1-2.8}$$

It follows from (1-2.6) that the minimum value of the sum of the squared errors is

$$\Sigma y^2 - \frac{(\Sigma xy)^2}{\Sigma x^2} = \Sigma y^2 - \Sigma y^2 \frac{(\Sigma xy)^2}{\Sigma y^2 \Sigma x^2}$$
$$= \Sigma y^2 \left[1 - \frac{(\Sigma xy)^2}{\Sigma y^2 \Sigma x^2}\right], \tag{1-2.9}$$

and this may be written as

$$n s_y^2 (1 - r^2) \tag{1-2.10}$$

where $s_y^2 = \Sigma y^2/n$ is the variance of the y scores (since $y_\bullet = 0$) and r is a quantity called the sample *correlation coefficient* between the x and y values. The *mean-squared error* is just $s_y^2(1 - r^2)$.

More generally, the sample *correlation coefficient* between two sets of observations is defined as

$$r = \frac{\Sigma (x_i - x_\bullet)(y_i - y_\bullet)}{\sqrt{\Sigma (x_i - x_\bullet)^2 \Sigma (y_i - y_\bullet)^2}} \tag{1-2.11}$$

and is a measure, on the range -1 to $+1$, of linear association between the two sets of observations. When $x_\bullet$ and $y_\bullet$ are both equal to zero, this reduces to the form found in (1-2.9). In general, the mean-squared error of predicting y from x is $s_y^2(1 - r^2)$ which has value zero when r is ± 1 and s_y^2 when $r = 0$. In the latter case we say the data are uncorrelated. Thus, we see why the correlation coefficient is, in fact, a measure of association. The correlation of the data from Fig. 1-1.1 works out to $r = .594$.

Returning now to (1-2.5), suppose x and y have average values $x_\bullet$ and $y_\bullet$ not equal to zero. Then, it is a simple matter to get new x's and y's by subtracting $x_\bullet$ and $y_\bullet$ from the old x's and y's. These new variables will have means of zero, and hence the preceding argument will apply. The corresponding substitution of $x - x_\bullet$ for x and $y - y_\bullet$ for y in (1-2.8) gives the best-fitting straight line for predicting y from x as

$$\hat{y} = y_\bullet + \frac{\Sigma (x - x_\bullet)(y - y_\bullet)}{\Sigma (x - x_\bullet)^2} (x - x_\bullet)$$

or, in the standard abbreviated form,

$$\hat{y} = \alpha + \beta x$$

where

$$\beta = \frac{\Sigma (x - x_\bullet)(y - y_\bullet)}{\Sigma (x - x_\bullet)^2} \tag{1-2.12}$$

and

$$\alpha = y_\bullet - \beta x_\bullet. \tag{1-2.13}$$

Now, let us use (1-2.12) and (1-2.13) to fit the data plotted in Fig. 1-1.1. We have $x_\bullet = 20$, $y_\bullet = 2.57$, $\Sigma (x - x_\bullet)^2 = 240$, and $\Sigma (x - x_\bullet)(y - y_\bullet) = 23.7$. Thus,

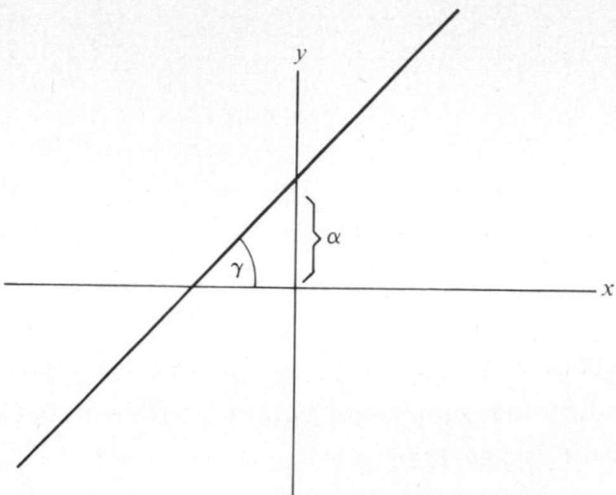

FIGURE 1-2.1
A best-fitting straight line.

$\hat{y} = .6 + .10x$. The reader should now plot this line and compare the fit of this line with the others. Finally, the reader should verify that the averages of the squared deviations of predicted y values from the actual values are, respectively, .59, 1.19, .65, .45, and .43 for the four guessed lines and the actual computed line.

An alternate form for β is $(s_y/s_x)r$, where s_y and s_x are the standard deviations of y and x, respectively. The effect of the division by s_x is to change the scale of the x score to a scale having unit standard deviation; the multiplication by s_y further changes the scale to that of the y scores, and the final factor (the multiplication by r) depends upon the strength of the relationship between the x's and the y's. When x and y are plotted on the same scale, geometrically β is the *slope* (the tangent) of the angle (γ) that the prediction line makes with the x axis, and α, the *intercept*, is the value of y at $x = 0$.

Table 1-2.1 CAREER PLANNING PROGRAM MECHANICAL SKILLS DATA

Person	Mechanical skills (1)	Mechanical skills (2)	GPA
1	75	70	3.0
2	63	67	2.8
3	60	55	2.4
4	56	56	3.5
5	43	40	2.6
6	54	63	2.3
7	47	42	3.1
8	38	54	1.1
9	52	50	1.7
10	37	37	2.3
	$\bar{x}_1$ 52.5	$\bar{x}_2$ 53.4	$\bar{y}$ 2.48
	s_{x_1} 11.2	s_{x_2} 10.7	s_y .66

If the reader will now consider the prediction of the test score from GPA (*postdiction* might be a better word), he will find that the best-fitting line is $\hat{x} = 10.8 + 3.57y$, which is quite different from the other best-fitting line $\hat{y} = .6 + .10x$. Again, it may be useful to plot this directly on Fig. 1-1.1.

Table 1-2.1 gives some representative data relating two administrations of the Mechanical Skills Assessment of the Career Planning Program with each other and with grades in an automobile mechanics course. The correlation between the two administrations of the Mechanical Skills Assessment is .82. The correlation between the first administration of the Mechanical Skills Assessment and GPA is .49. The reader may wish to verify these computations and then, as an exercise, work out the best-fitting straight lines for predicting GPA (y) from the first and from the second administration of the Mechanical Skills Assessment (x_1 and x_2).

1-3 ROBUSTNESS OF LOSS FUNCTIONS

It is relatively easy to work out optimal prediction functions for certain specified loss functions. Mathematicians will always work first with problems which are analytically tractable and only later, and perhaps only if pressed, will they be motivated to consider less convenient formulations. The educational researcher will certainly prefer simple, understandable results and corresponding methods which involve simple computations, since he would rather spend his energies thinking about his data than doing extensive arithmetic calculations. However, he cannot afford to be satisfied with convenient methods, but must be more concerned with the meaningfulness of the individual analysis. For this reason, he must understand, at least as deeply as the mathematician, the substantive nature of the assumptions underlying particular formulas. That is to say, he must have some understanding of both the theoretical background of statistics and the substance of his science even if he requires little or no knowledge of the mathematics of statistics. Given this basic understanding of theory and application, the educational researcher can evaluate the meaningfulness of particular coefficients and their relevance to his problem. If a researcher indiscriminately takes a mathematician's result based on one loss function, and if the actual loss function relevant to the problem is different from this, errors can occur. On the other hand, if the true loss function is different from, but not *too* different from, the assumed loss function, then it will often be the case that satisfactory results will follow.

Specifically, what we would like to have the mathematician study are loss functions which are reasonable for some large class of problems and which also lead to reasonable results when the true loss function differs from them rather widely. Loss functions having these properties are said to be *robust*.

In the previous section, we discussed four loss functions. Most work in educational measurement is based on one or another of these loss functions. Undoubtedly, major reasons for the popularity of results based on these loss functions are their availability and simplicity. Fortunately, however, these four loss functions are also each robust with respect to each other under certain conditions. Furthermore, in their totality, they are relatively inclusive of the kinds of loss functions appropriate to many practical problems. Thus, the study of these four loss functions will provide us with flexible responses with which to face the complexities of the real world. It is a grievous error to believe that *any one* of these loss functions will be adequate for all situations. Squared-error loss is not, as is sometimes suggested, a universally acceptable loss function. The careful worker may often wish to do separate analyses based on two or more of these loss functions and then think hard about the results and the results that might have been obtained if more appropriate but more complex loss functions had been used.

One of the reasons for the relative robustness of these loss functions (and in particular the squared-error-loss function) has to do with the nature of the data that one encounters in educational and psychological work. Such data are typically characterized by the absence of extreme observations. Thus, even when we presume that our data are normally distributed, which would imply the possibility of obtaining both extremely small and extremely large values, we know that, in fact, the values we can obtain are bounded. If we are dealing with a raw test score, then typically it cannot be less than zero or more than the number of items in the test. Even when such scores are scaled, the range of scores is limited. For example, all The American College Testing Assessment scores are two-digit numbers.

In an important special case, three of the four loss functions lead to identical predictions. The squared-error-loss function leads, in its application, to an estimator that is the mean value of the relevant distribution. The absolute-error-loss function leads to the median of the same distribution as an estimator and the zero-one loss function to a mode. When the relevant distribution is symmetric and unimodal (for example, if it is normal), these values will be identical so that the same estimator results from each of the three approaches. In typical applications, these estimators will be close whenever the relevant distribution is nearly symmetric. For this reason, we shall in later chapters choose whichever of these estimators is most easily computed. However, we do so only because of the approximate symmetry of the relevant distribution and because investigations have shown the mean, median, and mode to be approximately equal in these applications.

Again, we would emphasize that this discussion is not meant to sweep the problem of inappropriateness of loss functions "under the rug". Specifically, procedures based on squared-error loss are often very inappropriate. However, we do base our presentation on the position that many problems can usefully employ one of the four loss functions we shall study.

To get a rough idea of the robustness of squared-error loss, we compute the average *absolute* errors of the predictions made for the data in Fig. 1-1.1. These are as follows:

Prediction line	Average absolute error	Average squared error
$\hat{y} = .8 + .07x$	.654	.587
$\hat{y} = -.3 + .10x$	.890	1.187
$\hat{y} = .1 + .10x$	.650	.651
$\hat{y} = .1 + .12x$	.638	.446
$\hat{y} = .6 + .10x$	.630	.431

Thus, we see that the prediction lines that are best (worst) in the minimum mean-squared-error sense are also best (worst) in the minimum average absolute-error sense. Similar exercises might profitably be performed on the data given in Table 1-2.1.

1-4 INFERRING POPULATION CHARACTERISTICS FROM SAMPLE DATA

In the previous section, we have done some relatively simple analysis of data sets. There would be little justification for the educational researcher doing such work unless his interests went beyond the data available there. The historian justifies his efforts to the extent that his study of the past eventually, in some concrete though perhaps only remote way, gives promise that our future actions will benefit from our knowledge of the past. It is beyond our power to influence the past; hence, its study for its own sake has primarily recreational value. Similarly, only if we are interested in future-action problems is there justification for studying available data. If we already have both predictor and criterion data from each member of a population, it is certainly too late to do anything for these people.

Thus, data analysis has meaning only when it has relevance to future-action decisions which may benefit from our present study. If we can presume that our present observations can tell us something about the people and institutions with which we shall be dealing in the future, then we can use this knowledge to make predictions about future performance. If certain assumptions can be satisfied about the nature of the present data, then powerful mathematical techniques can be used.

The initial assumption usually made is that the present observations constitute a random sample from a population, and that future observations will also be a random sample from the same population. Undoubtedly, no such real population exists; but under certain circumstances, we can think of these samples as repeated sets of observations from a relevant hypothetical population.

If a university can assume that one year's applicants are about the same as another year's, then it can act as if any such group constitutes a random sample from which information can be gleaned. However, if a university knows that its applicant group is changing markedly from year to year, or if it knows that it is changing as an institution, then such methods will be useless. Thus, for the work we are doing, temporal stability is a necessary assumption, and one that is too often violated.

Given an initial applicant group to a university and test scores on these applicants, we can compute the average verbal ability score for this "random" sample. The particular value that we obtain, the sample mean, is of interest primarily as the basis for an estimate of the true mean in the hypothetical population. We know that as an estimate of the true "population" value this quantity contains an error which may be either positive or negative, large or small. The process of using such sample information to infer something about population values is the subject matter of statistical inference. Our task is to learn how to use all available information in as efficient a manner as possible.

1-5 THE ESTIMATION AND COMPARISON OF MEANS AND STANDARD DEVIATIONS

A major part of our work in this book will concern the estimation of means and standard deviations for various populations. In illustrating and motivating our methods, the following data sets will be useful. These data were taken from the 1968 and 1969 Basic Research Services of the American College Testing Program. Data were isolated from 22 community colleges emphasizing liberal arts or transfer curricula. Tables 1-5.1 and 1-5.2 give the mean scores, M(1) to M(4), on the four ACT subtests: English, Mathematics, Social Studies, and Natural Sciences. The mean first-year grade-point average for the students is denoted M(0). The corresponding standard deviations are denoted SD(0) to SD(4). College, year, and N refer to the college code number, the year, and the number of students tested. Nationally, the ACT scales have a mean of 20 and a standard deviation of 5. We note here that most of the means are below 20.

Having observed these data and being asked to make an estimate of the mean ACT scores in a 23rd community college identified as being, in other respects, similar to those whose values are listed in Tables 1-5.1 and 1-5.2, it seems reasonable to suppose that the information that we have on the 22 schools should not be ignored. Mean-squared-error theory, in fact, suggests that if we have no observations on the 23rd school, we would do well to use, as an estimate, the mean of the 22 school means. Intuitively, the idea that there is background information for most problems is compelling. We shall devote much of our effort to providing systematic means for quantifying this information.

Let us consider ways in which these tables suggest that background information is often available. Suppose you were given the values M(1) for the 22 colleges and asked to guess whether college 8 or college 2 had a higher M(2) value. Clearly, unless you have masochistic tendencies, you will select college 8, and you will be right. Similarly, suppose you are asked which of these two colleges will have a higher M(1) in 1969. Again, you will guess college 8, and again you will be right (see Table 1-5.2). One can go on at length

Table 1-5.1 SAMPLE MEANS AND STANDARD DEVIATIONS FOR 22 COMMUNITY COLLEGES

College	Year	*N*	M(0)	SD(0)	M(1)	SD(1)	M(2)	SD(2)	M(3)	SD(3)	M(4)	SD(4)
1	68	171	2.11	.85	16.0	5.7	15.1	5.4	17.4	6.3	18.8	5.6
2	68	204	2.05	.62	15.8	5.6	16.1	6.7	17.8	6.9	18.9	6.2
3	68	223	2.40	.79	17.7	4.8	18.7	6.2	19.2	5.9	19.7	5.5
4	68	307	2.22	.78	18.6	5.0	19.8	6.5	19.5	6.1	20.3	6.0
5	68	461	2.20	.70	18.9	4.5	19.1	6.4	19.4	6.0	19.8	5.3
6	68	175	1.69	.87	17.2	5.0	16.5	6.1	18.3	6.1	18.1	4.7
7	68	105	2.28	.90	19.1	5.1	20.5	6.8	20.9	5.2	21.8	5.3
8	68	118	2.21	.86	19.9	4.1	20.7	6.5	21.3	5.6	21.7	5.4
9	68	113	2.05	.84	17.2	4.7	17.1	5.4	18.8	5.9	18.3	5.2
10	68	128	2.25	.92	16.3	5.0	17.5	6.7	17.4	6.5	18.5	6.3
11	68	165	2.46	.78	16.5	5.3	16.9	6.6	17.2	6.4	18.6	5.9
12	68	132	2.37	.64	16.1	5.3	16.3	6.5	16.6	6.7	18.5	5.7
13	68	174	2.15	.69	17.2	5.2	17.9	6.1	18.4	6.4	19.2	6.1
14	68	334	1.99	1.06	17.0	5.3	17.7	6.5	18.0	6.5	18.9	6.1
15	68	167	2.26	.78	18.9	4.2	20.2	6.2	20.4	5.8	22.3	5.6
16	68	327	2.02	.76	18.3	4.1	19.7	6.0	20.1	5.3	21.0	5.4
17	68	739	1.92	.70	17.5	4.8	16.8	6.1	16.8	6.2	17.4	5.5
18	68	235	2.27	.73	16.9	4.5	16.0	5.5	16.4	6.3	17.3	5.3
19	68	117	2.74	.71	19.9	3.8	19.0	6.9	19.8	6.3	20.2	5.7
20	68	209	2.32	.78	16.9	4.3	17.7	5.9	17.8	6.4	18.7	6.2
21	68	394	1.91	.92	19.2	4.4	18.7	6.1	20.9	5.6	20.6	5.7
22	68	410	1.90	.82	17.7	4.5	18.1	6.1	18.5	6.0	19.8	5.5

Table 1-5.2 SAMPLE MEANS AND STANDARD DEVIATIONS FOR 22 COMMUNITY COLLEGES

College	Year	*N*	M(0)	SD(0)	M(1)	SD(1)	M(2)	SD(2)	M(3)	SD(3)	M(4)	SD(4)
1	69	179	2.20	.88	16.3	5.1	15.9	6.3	17.5	6.0	19.0	6.3
2	69	171	2.15	.78	16.9	5.7	16.8	7.1	18.6	6.5	19.3	6.1
3	69	250	2.39	.73	17.8	4.2	18.1	6.4	18.3	5.6	19.2	5.0
4	69	271	2.22	.78	18.1	4.8	18.8	6.2	18.5	5.9	19.7	5.7
5	69	536	2.33	.77	18.9	4.5	18.6	7.1	19.4	5.5	20.0	5.9
6	69	179	1.80	1.07	17.9	4.9	16.6	6.8	18.0	6.2	18.9	5.5
7	69	115	2.32	.75	19.3	4.3	20.3	6.1	21.0	5.1	21.6	4.9
8	69	112	2.20	.75	18.9	5.2	19.2	7.1	20.9	6.1	21.5	6.0
9	69	102	2.27	.82	18.0	4.3	18.1	6.1	18.6	5.9	18.9	6.2
10	69	118	2.48	.69	17.4	4.5	16.8	6.8	18.2	6.4	19.3	6.2
11	69	160	2.49	.92	16.7	5.1	17.1	7.0	18.6	6.0	19.4	6.4
12	69	108	2.49	.72	16.9	4.9	15.5	7.4	17.6	6.3	18.2	6.2
13	69	158	2.17	.86	16.9	4.9	18.0	6.6	17.7	6.3	19.2	5.5
14	69	332	2.28	.90	17.6	4.8	16.7	6.5	18.6	6.1	19.5	5.7
15	69	167	2.34	.71	18.4	4.2	20.1	6.0	20.3	5.6	22.2	5.7
16	69	345	1.95	.88	17.8	4.6	19.2	6.2	19.6	6.0	20.4	5.7
17	69	630	2.19	.69	17.8	4.6	17.0	6.1	17.8	6.1	18.3	5.8
18	69	231	2.10	.99	17.8	4.2	15.6	6.0	16.3	6.1	17.7	5.6
19	69	110	2.25	.96	17.0	5.1	16.5	6.8	18.3	6.0	19.3	5.8
20	69	173	2.11	.77	16.1	5.2	17.0	6.8	17.7	6.3	19.1	6.1
21	69	419	1.89	.97	18.6	4.6	17.4	6.5	19.7	6.3	20.1	6.0
22	69	404	1.88	.73	17.8	4.2	17.9	5.7	18.8	5.8	20.0	5.2

with such illustrations, but the point is really very obvious. In any important research project, we have background information that is important. If we have a very large present sample, perhaps, we can ignore that information; but with small sample sizes, this will be foolish.

Now let us ask ourselves a question about inference from these data. Suppose we are given all of Table 1-5.1 and a sample of size 5 from a 23rd college. If we had *no* information for the 23rd college but desired to estimate $M_{23}(1)$, the mean for variable 1 in college 23, we would use $\overline{M(1)}$, the average value of M(1) in 1968. However, we now have two values—$\widehat{M_{23}(1)}$, the mean based on five observations of variable 1 in college 23, and $\overline{M(1)}$, the average M(1) value. Suppose we had to choose one or the other as an estimate of the true value M(1) for college 23. Which value should we use? The value $\overline{M(1)}$ might well be the better choice, but if this is questioned, consider what we would do with a present sample of size one.

Clearly, with a present sample size of 1, we would value background information higher than direct information. Without experience, it may be difficult for us to judge an exact sample size such that we would equally value present and prior information. However, this does seem to be a meaningful exercise provided great precision is not required.

There is also the implicit suggestion here that both the direct observations and the background information should be used in determining our estimate of the mean for a particular group. The simplest way that both pieces of information can be used is through a weighted average of the two mean values. Thus, our estimate of M(1) in college 23 would be written as

$$W\,\widehat{M_{23}(1)} + (1 - W)\overline{M(1)}$$

where W is the weight (a value between zero and one) assigned to the sample value.

At present we have given no clue as to how the weight W might be rationally determined. In fact, that is the major accomplishment of the theory we shall be describing in later chapters.

1-6 PREDICTION WITH MANY VARIABLES

Our next presentation is based on the same sample described in the previous section taken from the 1968 and 1969 ACT Basic Research Services. Tables 1-6.1 and 1-6.2 give the weights that best combine the test-score variables together with the constant α to provide a single predictor of the criterion, first-year grade-point average. In other words, we are using the linear prediction function of the form

$$\hat{y} = \hat{y}(x_1, x_2, \ldots, x_p) = \alpha + \beta_1 x_1 + \beta_2 x_2 + \cdots + \beta_p x_p \,.$$

which is best, in the squared-error-loss sense, for predicting criterion scores y. The *multiple correlation* between y and the set of values $(x_1, x_2, \ldots, x_p)$ is just the simple correlation between y and $\hat{y}$; that is, it is just the usual correlation coefficient between the criterion and the weighted composite score that is the best linear combination of the predictors. When the variables $(x_1, x_2, \ldots, x_p)$ are subtest scores from a single test, this number is a measure of the *validity of the test* for predicting grades. The individual correlations of the test scales $(x_1, x_2, \ldots, x_p)$ with grades are called the *scale validities.*

The most common way of studying the relationship between test scores on the one hand and academic performance on the other is by means of linear prediction methods. The theory and method for the simple case of one predictor variable will be developed in Chaps. 4 and 9. The theory and computational methods of multiple correlation lie beyond the scope of this book; however, the few simple remarks we have made should help readers understand papers using multiple-correlation methods. For the present, let us simply have a brief look at the data in Tables 1-6.1 and 1-6.2 and try to pinpoint some problems.

Overall, the sample multiple correlations R seem respectably high–ranging from a low of .3823 to a high of .6882. Approximately 75% of these values lie in the interval .44 to .57. The first weight α for each college is the constant needed to correct for the varying mean values of the predictor and the criterion in each college. The four weights β_1 to β_4 are the weights given to each of the four predictors. While most of these values are positive, there are a few negative values scattered about, particularly for the fourth variable.

For example consider Table 1-6.1. For college 2, the observed weight for the fourth predictor variable is negative. A similar result is found for colleges 9, 11, 15, 16, 17, 18, 19, and 21. In total, this phenomenon occurs in 9 of the 22 colleges. If one believed that the true weights were actually negative, this would be rather disturbing for it would suggest that persons with lower scores in the fourth test do better than persons with higher scores. Rather sophisticated theories can be put forward to explain this, but the most parsimonious explanation is simply that the *true* weight is either zero or only slightly positive and that such negative values as are found in *this sample* occur solely by chance. Suppose, in fact, all true β_4's were zero; then we would expect that in repeated samples about half of the observed coefficients would be negative. The fact that less than half are negative, then, should not be surprising. Those who have been exposed to the theory of hypothesis testing in their first course will recognize that there is little, if any, evidence to reject the null hypothesis that these 22 observed values of β_4's are a random sample from some population with a mean value slightly greater than or equal to zero.

If, in fact, the negative values represented true negatives, we would expect to find negatives for data from the following year for the same colleges. In Table 1-6.2, we give the 1969 data and note that there are now 12 negatives out of 22 (our total is now 21 out of 44). Of the 12 negatives, only five occur in colleges with negative values for the 1968

Table 1-6.1 PREDICTION WEIGHTS–MULTIPLE CORRELATIONS–FOR 22 SCHOOLS

College	Year	N	α	β_1	β_2	β_3	β_4	R
1	68	171	.798	.023	.006	.037	.011	.4612
2	68	204	1.172	.042	.011	.006	–.005	.4765
3	68	223	.317	.043	.021	.030	.018	.6234
4	68	307	.925	.009	.036	.003	.016	.4507
5	68	461	.775	.033	.019	.011	.011	.4561
6	68	175	.104	.029	.036	.020	.007	.4865
7	68	105	.287	.069	.025	.007	.001	.5237
8	68	118	.362	.005	.037	.042	.004	.5402
9	68	113	.401	.042	.033	.042	–.023	.5429
10	68	128	.045	.068	.038	.012	.011	.6882
11	68	165	1.087	.060	.006	.022	–.005	.5502
12	68	132	1.205	.048	.005	.012	.007	.5478
13	68	174	.916	.024	.025	.002	.017	.4905
14	68	334	.122	.070	.019	.017	.001	.5095
15	68	167	.215	.070	.031	.026	–.020	.5775
16	68	327	.385	.043	.034	.015	–.006	.4745
17	68	739	.864	.035	.026	.014	–.013	.4317
18	68	235	1.193	.043	.006	.025	–.009	.4105
19	68	117	1.056	.065	.006	.024	–.009	.4756
20	68	209	.892	.053	.007	.010	.012	.4438
21	68	394	–.277	.078	.034	.011	–.008	.5207
22	68	410	.075	.030	.046	.011	.013	.5591

Table 1-6.2 PREDICTION WEIGHTS–MULTIPLE CORRELATIONS–FOR 22 SCHOOLS

College	Year	N	α	β_1	β_2	β_3	β_4	R
1	69	179	.990	.056	–.007	.030	–.006	.4273
2	69	171	.850	.044	.032	.007	–.005	.5506
3	69	250	.845	.041	.034	.009	.001	.4849
4	69	271	.954	.036	.020	.016	–.003	.3832
5	69	536	.760	.048	.015	.024	–.004	.4678
6	69	179	–.393	.105	.029	–.015	.005	.5608
7	69	115	.475	.071	–.004	.010	.016	.4819
8	69	112	.270	.052	.006	.035	.004	.6653
9	69	102	.885	.028	.026	.049	–.027	.4519
10	69	118	1.503	.036	.020	.018	–.016	.3890
11	69	160	.621	.069	.025	.028	–.013	.5846
12	69	108	1.212	.056	.011	.028	–.018	.5442
13	69	158	.640	.070	.023	.012	–.014	.5095
14	69	332	.760	.069	.013	.021	–.016	.4686
15	69	167	1.068	.061	–.005	.007	.005	.4000
16	69	345	.050	.047	.027	.014	.013	.5059
17	69	630	1.053	.039	.010	.022	–.007	.4198
18	69	231	–.390	.111	.017	.015	.000	.5699
19	69	110	.345	.064	.014	.010	.021	.5280
20	69	173	.595	.059	.018	.013	.002	.5756
21	69	419	–.012	.062	.025	.020	–.004	.4846
22	69	404	.166	.037	.032	.011	.014	.5006

weights. Again, there is no evidence whatsoever to suggest that the negatives occur other than by random variation.

The implication of this informal analysis is clear. If we ignore background information, we may do foolish things like using negative weights when substantive theory tells us they should be nonnegative. However, if we fully utilize all background information (in this case the data on the remaining colleges) in a proper manner, this is most unlikely to occur. We shall not, in fact, study the full analysis for this problem since the topic of multiple correlation is beyond the coverage of this book, but the basic problem isolated here is as important in the estimation of means and proportions as it is in the estimation of prediction weights.

In order to provide readers with some interesting data for eyeball examination at this point and for more formal analysis in conjunction with the methods presented in Chap. 9, we have given the basic data for the prediction of grade-point average given only the variable X_1, English score. The required statistics, means, standard deviations, correlations, and the weights and constants of the linear prediction functions are given in Table 1-6.3 for a 25% sample within each of the colleges in Table 1-6.1.

Table 1-6.3 MEANS, STANDARD DEVIATIONS, REGRESSION OF GPA ON ACT ENGLISH SCORE, AND CORRELATIONS FOR 22 COLLEGES

College	N	M(X)	SD(X)	M(Y)	SD(Y)	$\rho(01)$	a	b
1	42	15.0	5.9	1.83	.88	.329	1.09	.049
2	51	15.7	5.7	1.97	.63	.353	1.36	.039
3	55	17.8	4.1	2.21	.84	.500	.41	.101
4	76	17.8	5.2	2.21	.72	.169	1.79	.024
5	115	18.5	4.1	2.15	.73	.429	.75	.076
6	43	18.4	4.9	1.78	.87	.172	1.22	.030
7	26	20.7	4.6	2.30	.77	.590	.25	.099
8	29	19.8	4.0	2.31	.69	.135	1.85	.023
9	28	17.2	4.8	1.99	.94	.701	−.39	.138
10	32	15.4	6.3	2.23	.87	.568	1.03	.078
11	41	16.5	5.1	2.56	.82	.521	1.18	.084
12	33	16.5	5.1	2.52	.61	.673	1.20	.080
13	43	16.5	4.8	1.96	.68	.215	1.45	.030
14	83	17.0	5.4	2.04	1.03	.458	.56	.087
15	41	17.9	3.8	2.10	.68	.384	.87	.069
16	81	18.4	4.1	2.13	.88	.575	−.12	.123
17	184	17.1	5.0	1.89	.70	.388	.97	.054
18	58	16.6	3.7	2.20	.72	.325	1.16	.063
19	29	21.2	3.5	2.88	.75	.446	.88	.094
20	52	16.5	4.8	2.33	.72	.485	1.14	.072
21	98	18.5	4.2	1.86	.90	.423	.19	.090
22	102	18.3	4.3	1.94	.78	.372	.71	.067

1-7 EXERCISES

1 Calculate $s_{\hat{y}}^2$ and the mean-squared error for predicting y from x for the data in Fig. 1-1.1.

2 (*a*) Recompute the correlation for the data in Fig. 1-1.1 after omitting the point (29,4.0).

(*b*) To what extent does this value differ from the r of .59 computed for the 10 pairs of scores?

(*c*) What implications about sampling error are reflected here?

3 (*a*) Recompute the regression of y on x for the data in Fig. 1-1.1, again omitting the point (29,4.0).

(*b*) Does the loss of this one observation have any real impact on the resulting regression equation?

4 (*a*) Recompute the regression of x on y for the data in Fig. 1-1.1, again omitting the point (29,4.0).

(*b*) Do you again observe any real change in the resulting regression equation?

5 (*a*) From Table 1-2.1 compute the correlation between the second administration of the Mechanical Skills Assessment and GPA.

(*b*) How does this value compare with the r of .49 between the first administration and GPA?

6 (*a*) Find the best-fitting straight line for predicting GPA from the first administration of the Mechanical Skills Assessment (Table 1-2.1).

(*b*) Using the scores from the second administration, determine the best-fitting straight line for predicting GPA.

7 (*a*) Compute the average absolute error $\frac{\Sigma|\hat{y} - y|}{n}$ and the average squared error $\frac{\Sigma(\hat{y} - y)^2}{n}$ for the two equations derived in Exercise 1-7.6.

(*b*) Can you decide from this which equation is to be preferred?

2
ANALYSIS OF CATEGORIZED DATA

Our purpose in this chapter is to survey for our readers some simple methods of studying the dependence of one variable on one or more other variables. Simple tabular methods of organizing and presenting data in summary form are described and the use of such tables in certain applications is discussed.

2-1 CONTINGENCY AND EXPECTANCY TABLES

The validity of a test may be thought of loosely as the accuracy with which it measures or predicts that which it is intended to measure or predict. This generic definition is made specific when a particular measure of accuracy or inaccuracy of prediction is selected. The most common specific definition of validity is related to the minimization of the squared error of prediction. In Secs. 1-2 and 1-6, we saw that such a minimization leads to the use of a correlation coefficient (simple or multiple) as the measure of validity. This is the definition which the reader, no doubt, first encountered in his study of statistics. It is not the only meaningful definition of validity.

Validity and prediction data are often summarized in tabular forms loosely referred to as *expectancy tables*. Such tables appear in many formats, and it will prove useful for us to consider several of these. Our purpose is to illustrate some fundamental points in the analysis of educational data and to motivate much of the technical work done in later chapters. We consider first a constructed example relating a criterion variable, grade-point average, to ACT Composite Scaled Assessment Score. The composite assessment score takes integer values on a scale of 1 to 36, but for purposes of this tabulation, the following class intervals were established: 1 to 15, 16 to 20, 21 to 25, 26 to 36. The grade-point average (GPA) criterion was computed by assigning the numerical values 4, 3, 2, 1, and 0 to the course letter grades A, B, C, D, and F; multiplying each numerical value by the number of units of credit earned in the course; summing the results; and dividing the total by the total number of units of credit earned in all courses. For purposes of this tabulation, the following GPA class intervals were established: 0.0 to 1.0, 1.0 to 2.0, 2.0 to 3.0, 3.0 to 4.0. This kind of labeling, though commonly found, is somewhat confusing since it is not clear whether a GPA of 2.0 belongs in the second or third category. We adopt the convention that such integer averages will be placed in the upper category. Thus, a GPA of 2.0 is placed in the class interval 2.0 to 3.0. Table 2-1.1 is an example of a *contingency table* from which an expectancy table will be constructed.

Let us suppose that the college at which these data have been gathered has a clearly delineated (rigid?) student-retention policy. At the end of the first year, those students with a GPA below 1.0 are dropped for poor scholarship. Those with a GPA of at least 1.0 but less than 2.0 are placed on probation and given one further year to raise their average to 2.0. Those with a GPA of 2.0 or above are considered to be making normal progress. Those with a GPA of 3.0 or above are eligible to apply for enrollment in honors sections of various courses.

In this hypothetical situation, losses due to inaccurate prediction are obviously discrete rather than continuous. A very good student will be delighted (zero loss) if his GPA is at least 3.0; and he can, therefore, probably take the honors physics course he desires. If his GPA is 2.75 he will be unhappy (positive loss), and he may be no more unhappy with a GPA of 2.50. The very marginal student, for whom the freshman year has been a trauma, will be ecstatic with a GPA of 1.0, giving him the chance to continue his studies. All GPAs of less than 1.0 have equally disappointing consequences for him. The situation we describe corresponds nicely with what we called threshold loss. It does not correspond with a squared-error-loss function since, in fact, there would be zero loss for a person if the predicted GPA was $\hat{y} = 3.2$ and the obtained GPA was $y = 3.1$.

We presume that the data reported in Table 2-1.1 were gathered over a period of two or three years and that there is reason to believe that they have relevance for at least a few succeeding years. Let us suppose that it is appropriate for prospective students, guidance counselors, and admissions officers to presume that this table can be used to give relevant "probabilities" of success at the college. Thus, given the ACT scaled score,

Table 2-1.1 CONTINGENCY TABLE RELATING ACT SCALED SCORE INTERVALS AND GPA INTERVALS

	ACT scaled scores				
GPA	1–15	16–20	21–25	26–36	*N*
3.0–4.0	15	101	61	32	209
2.0–3.0	40	342	57	15	454
1.0–2.0	71	140	10	4	225
0.0–1.0	38	69	4	1	112
N	164	652	132	52	1,000

each of these persons can determine the chances in a hundred (the probability) that any particular student will attain a GPA in each of the GPA categories. For example, a student with an ACT scaled score of 4 falls in the lowest ACT scaled-score category. His "chances" of attaining a GPA in the interval 2.0 to 3.0 are $\frac{40}{164} = .24$. His chances of attaining a GPA in the interval 3.0 to 4.0 are even smaller, $\frac{15}{164} = .09$. Thus, the probability that he will complete the first year in a normal-progress status ($2.0 \leq \text{GPA} \leq 4.0$) is $\frac{55}{164} = .34$. Unless this student has a compelling desire to attend this college or unless there are special reasons to think that he has a better-than-average probability of success at this institution, he might be well advised to attend a different college.

To facilitate this kind of analysis, the entries in the body of a table such as 2-1.1 are usually divided by the total number in each column to give the relative frequency or proportion of cases in each cell, relative to the column total. The resulting table is called an *expectancy table*. Note that it is important here to retain the column totals because the individual cell values cannot be regained from the given percentages and the total sample size. This will later prove important when we inquire as to the usability of some of these numbers for predictions.

By examining the entries in the column relevant to a particular student, the chances

Table 2-1.2 EXPECTANCY TABLE OF GPA GIVEN ACT SCALED SCORE*

	ACT scaled scores				
GPA	1–15	16–20	21–25	26–36	
3.0–4.0	.09	.15	.46	.61	
2.0–3.0	.25	.52	.43	.29	
1.0–2.0	.43	.22	.08	.08	
0.0–1.0	.23	.11	.03	.02	
N	164	652	132	52	1,000

*The careful reader will note that strict rules of rounding have not been followed. Necessary minor adjustments have been made to assure that percentages add up to one. For final reporting to a consumer this is probably desirable in that it reduces confusion without materially altering the data being presented.

or probability of the student attaining a given criterion category can be estimated. Thus, one very important piece of information is made available to the student, his guidance counselor, and the admissions officer. It would be very poor practice to use this as the only basis for making an application or selection decision, but given the student-progress policy in effect at this college, it would seem foolhardy to proceed without this information.

One point may usefully be made here: It is not always worth the effort to gather information. Suppose that a student will want to enroll in a college only if the probability of his getting a B average or better (required for medical school) is at least .75. If Table 2-1.1 was relevant, the student could compute a probability of $\frac{209}{1000}$ or about .21 for a random student attaining a B average. He has a chance to take the ACT (not required), and if he does, he will receive a class-interval score appropriate for Table 2-1.2 (very fictitious scenario). Studying Table 2-1.2, the student decides that taking the ACT Assessment would be a waste of time; for even if he did blow the top off the test, his probability of a B average would only be reckoned to be .61. This, of course, points up a major failing of contingency tables, namely, that distinctions of performance within groupings cannot be made, and this can be important. We suspect that if regression methods were used, the probability of a B average or better given an ACT score of 36 would, indeed, be at least .75. However, even with sophisticated statistical methods, it is often not worth the effort to gather certain kinds of information.

Expectancy tables are often given in other forms to suit the particular needs of an institution and its prospective students. For example, it is often useful to present the probabilities of getting a "B average or better" and of a "C average or better". The results given in Table 2-1.2 have been reworked to give the desired probabilities as in Table 2-1.3. We shall shortly see some real (rather than hypothetical) tables of this form.

In terms of the degree of relationship between predictor and criterion, the data in Table 2-1.1 may be considered realistic, though the median degree of association found with the ACT Assessment is typically somewhat higher than that illustrated here.

What is somewhat unusual about these data is the regularity in Table 2-1.3. Note that the probability of a C average or better increases steadily as we move up through the

Table 2-1.3 REVISED EXPECTANCY TABLE OF GPA GIVEN ACT SCALED SCORE

	ACT scaled scores				
GPA	1–15	16–20	21–25	26–36	
B average or better	.09	.15	.46	.61	
C average or better	.33	.67	.89	.90	
N	164	652	132	52	1,000

various predictor categories. Real data are not always so neat. It will be worth our while to have a look at some typical real data.

A table similar to Table 2-1.1 is given below based on students enrolling at the University of Wyoming in 1968. A relatively high degree of relationship between test scores and GPA is evident in Table 2-1.4. Notice that no student with an ACT scaled score in the interval 0 to 15 obtained a GPA in the interval 3.0 to 4.0. If one used this past experience to make predictions for the future, a natural reaction would be to state that the probability is zero that a student with an ACT composite score in the interval 0 to 15 will get a GPA greater than 3.0. Such a prediction obviously makes little sense. Our prior beliefs, based on information available to us outside this study, suggest that this is not so. Surely this information should not be ignored. We pass this question for the present, but it should not be ignored by the practitioner. Readers may find it useful to transform the data in Table 2-1.4 into an expectancy table similar to Table 2-1.3.

The uses of contingency and expectancy tables are far too numerous to catalog, but some examples may be useful. In Table 2-1.5, we study the relationship between GPA and curriculum at Northern Illinois University. A total of 2,899 students were cross-tabulated according to their academic curriculum and their GPAs in five GPA intervals. These are the raw data used for study and analysis. The most convenient way of studying and analyzing the data is not in the contingency-table form as given initially, but in the form of the expectancy table that follows. The clear differences in the pattern of proportions for communications and for business is something that both university administration and students will want to know.

One needs to be very careful here. It is not necessarily true that the communications curriculum is easier than the business curriculum. The differences in grading practices could be due to differences in the academic level of the students entering the two programs. Without much closer study, it would be foolhardy to make a blanket statement to students that they would on the average do better in communications than in business. One thing that must be recognized is that students now in these programs are there to a large extent by choice. They were not randomly assigned to programs; rather, they largely self-selected themselves into these programs. It is a mistake not to recognize that students have much information about themselves that is not reflected in test scores.

Table 2-1.4 CONTINGENCY TABLE OF COLLEGE GPA AND ACT COMPOSITE SCALED SCORE

	ACT scaled scores				
GPA	0–15	16–21	22–25	26–36	
3.0–4.0	0	24	92	118	234
2.0–2.9	31	130	299	133	593
1.0–1.9	62	184	157	41	444
0.0–0.9	49	75	75	12	211
Total	142	413	623	304	1,482

Our next example comes from a study, in which one of the authors participated, having to do with the relationship between the Medical College Admissions Test (MCAT) and academic and nonacademic difficulties in medical school. Table 2-1.6 tabulates criterion categories for 680 students who attended one of seven medical schools in the late 1950s. The criterion results are cross-tabulated against three MCAT categories (<430, 430–515, >515) for the average of the verbal-ability and quantitative-ability scales. Table 2-1.7 provides the same tabulation for students from a second set of seven medical schools. The 14 medical schools have been placed in one of the two clusters of schools on the basis of the percentage of entering medical students who completed their medical studies. In the first cluster, the percentages were 88, 84, 82, 88, 81, 87, 89; and in the second, they were 93, 93, 95, 97, 94, 92, 94. The rather definite break in these percentages suggested that two rather different clusters of medical schools could be usefully identified, and the data presented in Tables 2-1.6 and 2-1.7 substantiate this suggestion, in that the percentage of students maintaining regular status in cluster 2 schools is systematically higher over the whole MCAT range.

The purpose of this study was not to provide prognostic information for prospective students, but to assess the usefulness of the MCAT as a selection instrument and to provide some guidance to the medical schools in the use of the instrument as a selection device. Table 2-1.6 does show a definite relationship between test score and criterion. The "probability" of regularity does increase directly with MCAT category, and the probabilities of academic difficulties and academic withdrawal do decrease. Whether the strength of the relationship was as high as we would like it to be, or, more importantly, as high as it could be for a Medical College Admissions Test, is a question we shall not treat here because the present authors do not have the data necessary to make such an evaluation. However, we can discuss possible policy decisions based on that test

Table 2-1.5 NORTHERN ILLINOIS UNIVERSITY

GPA	Science	Soc. Sci.	Communication	Education	Business	Undeclared
			Contingency table for GPA given curriculum of study			
3.0–4.0	76	62	58	69	36	48
2.0–2.9	274	230	212	299	233	221
1.0–1.9	183	143	96	191	167	184
0.0–0.9	38	16	4	10	20	29
Total	571	451	370	569	456	482
			Expectancy table for GPA given curriculum of study			
3.0–4.0	.13	.14	.16	.12	.08	.10
2.0–2.9	.48	.51	.57	.53	.51	.46
1.0–1.9	.32	.32	.26	.33	.37	.38
0.0–0.9	.07	.03	.01	.02	.04	.06
Total	571	451	370	569	456	482

Table 2-1.6 DISTRIBUTION OF STUDENTS WITH ACADEMIC DIFFICULTIES FOR THREE MCAT RANGES (CLUSTER 1)

MCAT range	Regular		Academic difficulties		Academic withdrawals		Nonacademic withdrawals		Total	
	N	%	*N*	%	*N*	%	*N*	%	*N*	%
> 515	158	78	22	11	6	3	16	8	202	30
430–515	224	71	56	18	20	6	16	5	316	46
< 430	89	55	37	23	26	16	10	6	162	24
Total	471	69	115	17	52	8	42	6	680	100

and the stated criterion in schools like those studied. Before doing this, we examine the data from the analysis for the second cluster of medical schools.

Here the picture is nowhere near as clear as in the cluster 1 schools. The observed percentage of regular students does not differ much in the top two MCAT categories; actually, it is slightly lower in the highest category. On the other hand, in the lowest MCAT range, the percentage of regular students is substantially lower and the percentage of academic difficulties and academic withdrawals is substantially higher. (These statements are obviously not independent.) There is, thus, clearly quite a different pattern than in the cluster 1 schools. The careful reader will also have noticed that the smallest percentage of nonacademic withdrawals is in the lowest MCAT category. This could be taken as an indication of a positive correlation between intelligence and emotional instability. The more obvious and probably correct explanation is that the observed frequencies in these cells are too small to indicate any precise effects. Note that the highest percentage of nonacademic withdrawals in cluster 1 was in the highest MCAT group. This supports the previous information; but even when the two are taken together, they are no more than suggestive of a possibility.

Disregarding the last category (nonacademic withdrawal), we might speculate that the observed inversions are due to nothing more than peculiarities of this sample, i.e.,

Table 2-1.7 DISTRIBUTION OF STUDENTS WITH ACADEMIC DIFFICULTIES FOR THREE MCAT RANGES (CLUSTER 2)

MCAT range	Regular		Academic difficulties		Academic withdrawals		Nonacademic withdrawals		Total	
	N	%	*N*	%	*N*	%	*N*	%	*N*	%
> 515	200	91	7	3	6	3	7	3	220	40
430–515	233	92	6	2	3	1	11	4	253	47
< 430	59	83	6	8	5	7	1	0	71	13
Total	492	90	19	3	14	3	19	3	544	100*

*Percentages are strictly rounded in this table. As a result they do not necessarily add to 1.

random fluctuation. One of the greatest dangers of amateur data analysis is the overinterpretation of data. One function of formal statistical analysis is to inhibit this. Before finishing this book, many readers may find that their beliefs concerning how much information is required to estimate a binomial proportion need to be revised drastically.

Suppose that it is suggested that an average verbal ability–quantitative ability score of 430 be required for admission to medical school. Are the consequences of this action beneficial? The answer to this question may well depend on whether or not equivalent applicants with higher MCAT scores are available to replace those *outselected*. Suppose first that replacements are not available. In cluster 1, 162 fewer students would be selected, and this would certainly help lower the overall expenditures in the medical schools, though probably nowhere near in proportion to the percentage outselected. At the same time, the percentage of regular students would increase from 69 to 74%, and this has some desirability. However, 126 fewer doctors would be graduated, and, considering the chronic, acute shortage of doctors, this is very undesirable and probably overshadows all other considerations. Expensive as medical education is, we are sure that many people would feel that if a place is available, an applicant should be accepted even with a probability of success as low as .78, again provided no more promising applicants are available. On the other hand, whether such a student wishes to accept a 45% chance of failure or academic difficulty is something that only he can evaluate. The present authors are not unaware that in high-prestige professions such as medicine, status-conscious parents often pressure their offspring to undertake programs for which they are not qualified. One beneficial effect of such expectancy tables, if they are made available to students and their parents, is to make the dangers of such decisions clear to all concerned.

Suppose now that other qualified and comparable candidates can be found to replace those not selected because of an MCAT score below 430. In cluster 1 schools there would seem to be a rather large potential gain. The percentage of graduated physicians (no academic difficulties) would apparently rise from 69 to 74%. In fact, this would yield approximately seventeen additional doctors. If the cost of getting the additional 162 qualified applicants is not too great, this is probably a good thing to do. (There may, of course, be better things to do.)

In cluster 2 schools, there would seem to be much less potential gain. The data in Table 2-1.7 suggest that only about six additional doctors would be obtained in this way. The decision as to whether to use an MCAT score or not would be much more difficult. One would surely want to investigate other predictive measures for this cluster.

In order to keep the arithmetic of our examples simple, we have so far presented only rather small tables. At this point, it will be useful to give one larger table (Table 2-1.8) which gives a rather more accurate picture of the relationship between test scores and college grades.

Table 2-1.8 DISTRIBUTION OF COLLEGE GPA FOR DIFFERENT VALUES OF ACT COMPOSITE SCORE

	ACT composite scores																				
GPA	13	14	15	16	17	18	19	20	21	22	23	24	25	26	27	28	29	30	31	32	*N*
3.51–4.0	0	0	0	0	0	0	4	0	3	0	9	1	14	27	27	23	41	26	12	1	188
3.01–3.5	0	0	0	0	2	1	5	12	7	22	44	43	58	60	67	69	19	34	12	0	455
2.51–3.0	1	3	11	7	19	16	17	27	32	58	80	72	62	76	71	48	32	4	7	4	647
2.01–2.5	3	4	6	13	21	33	43	43	64	92	76	82	69	69	37	33	6	6	0	0	700
1.51–2.0	7	11	10	12	25	34	32	62	35	45	33	38	24	21	21	14	3	0	3	0	430
1.01–1.5	2	2	7	6	10	15	13	22	18	18	12	4	17	2	1	2	1	0	0	0	152
0.51–1.0	3	1	2	5	0	0	0	3	6	14	2	3	3	0	1	0	1	0	0	0	44
0.01–0.50	0	2	0	0	0	0	2	0	1	0	3	9	0	2	0	0	0	0	0	0	19
0	0	0	0	0	0	1	1	1	0	0	1	1	1	0	0	0	1	0	0	0	7
N	16	23	36	43	77	100	117	170	166	249	260	253	248	257	225	189	104	70	34	5	
Mean GPA	1.68	1.83	2.07	1.88	2.20	2.08	2.18	2.11	2.19	2.27	2.52	2.45	2.61	2.79	2.91	2.95	3.21	3.41	3.28	3.00	
SD of GPA	.57	.61	.61	.66	.52	.50	.63	.60	.61	.61	.63	.67	.67	.61	.60	.59	.71	.43	.64	.40	

There are several points worthy of note concerning Table 2-1.8. First, we note that despite a very large overall sample size there are only five students with a composite score of 32. Thus, we must suppose that the mean GPA for that subgroup may not be representative of potential performances for such persons since random sample errors may be large. Second, we note that the distribution of ACT composite scores is roughly bell-shaped, though moderately negatively skewed. Third, the relationship between test scores and grades seems to be very high. Fourth, the standard deviations in the 20 ACT composite categories are very similar–homoscedasticity (common subgroup variance) is a very reasonable assumption. Perhaps the most interesting feature is the value for GPA in the ACT levels 23, 24, and 25. Note that the GPA values here are not in increasing order despite the relatively large sample sizes.

2-2 THE USE OF EXPECTANCY TABLES IN GUIDANCE

Now let us examine some expectancy tables that have actually been used for guidance purposes. In the spring of 1961, the University of Minnesota *Office of the Dean of Students Research Bulletin*, Vol. 3, No. 2, entitled "Expectancy Tables for Freshmen Entering Minnesota Colleges", was published and distributed through the Minnesota State-Wide Testing Programs. For each participating college in the state, tables for predicting first-year GPA were provided, one based on high school rank (HSR) and the other based on scores on the Minnesota Scholastic Aptitude Test (MSAT). The predictor variable for each table was divided into quintiles. At each level, the expectancies (chances in 100) of a prospective student earning a first-year GPA of B or higher, C or higher, and D or higher were given, as was the approximate size of the group on which these predictions were based. For most colleges, separate tables were provided for males and females.

In Tables 2-2.1 and 2-2.2, we combine and reproduce the four Minnesota expectancy tables for the University of Minnesota General College. The first of these tables refers to males and the second to females. The first parts of these tables are based on HSR as the predictor, and the second parts are based on MSAT as the predictor.

A brief examination of these tables is enough to convince us that MSAT score and HSR are both useful predictors of "success". In the female group, only 33% of those in the bottom MSAT quintile attained a C average or better while more than 80% of those in the top quintile did this well. Similarly, in the HSR for females, only 25% of the bottom quintile attained a C average or better while 99% in the top quintile did this well. This pattern of higher expectations in the higher-predictor-variable groups occurs almost throughout these tables.

There is an exception to this trend in the top quintile of HSR for males. Here, the percentage of D or better drops to 90 from 99% in the next highest quintile, and the percentage of C or higher drops to 60 from 61% in the next highest quintile. Another small inversion is found at the fourth quintile level of MSAT scores for men and yet another in the third quintile level of MSAT scores for women.

Are these inversions "real", or are they due to ordinary random fluctuations found in any sample? The answer to this seems clear when we note that most of the inversions occur where the size of the sample group is small. In no case does such an inversion occur with a sample size of over 100. This phenomenon of "random" inversions occurs in many of the Minnesota expectancy tables, but there does not seem to be any discernable pattern.

In Table 2-1.7, we saw that the percentage of students in a regular status is slightly higher in the middle MCAT category than in the upper MCAT category (92 as opposed to 91%). When this is found, and the finding is not infrequent, it is then suggested by some that our universities are such as to penalize and repress the really bright student, who may be other than acquiescent in class. The contention is that these students receive poorer grades than they should, and that some actually leave college because of friction with their instructors. Unfortunately, it is usually difficult to decidc in such situations whether or not the observed difference with the wrong sign is due to anything more than chance.

Table 2-2.1 UNIVERSITY OF MINNESOTA GENERAL COLLEGE EXPECTANCY TABLES [for First-year GPA Based on Freshmen (Male) Entering College in the Fall of 1959 and the Fall of 1961]*

Quintile group		Chances in 100 of a freshman obtaining an average grade of: D or higher	C or higher	B or higher	Group size
		Predictions based on HSR			
> 80		90	60	10	10–20
60–79		99	61	9	50–100
40–59		95	52	7	> 100
20–39		91	43	5	> 100
< 19		79	27	1	> 100
		Predictions based on MSAT			
Raw score	% ile				
51–78	> 80	99	57	21	10–20
42–50	60–79	94	47	9	20–50
34–41	40–59	97	50	5	> 100
27–33	20–39	92	49	5	> 100
1–26	< 19	87	36	4	> 100

*Size of total group = over 500.

A very good case could be made, we think, for "smoothing the data", i.e., adjusting the reported expectancies to eliminate such inversions. In fact, this is precisely what is done when one decides to use linear regression as opposed to curvilinear regression. With linear regression and a positive correlation, the predicted value of the criterion always increases with the value of the predictor variable.

Actually, with the Minnesota tables, the number of inversions is small; and with one delightful exception, they are not large in magnitude. For this reason, one would not want to quibble with the Minnesota people for not smoothing their data, particularly since these tables were distributed through the statewide testing program and not directly to students, and since a careful discussion of random fluctuation was given in the text introducing the tables. When predictions such as these are reported directly to students, and particularly when guidance-counseling facilities are limited, some smoothing or other device would seem very desirable.

The really delightful inversion occurs in Table 2-2.3, the MSAT expectancy table for women for Macalester College. Here the probability of getting a C or higher for the first quintile of MSAT scores is given as .99, whereas the probabilities for the second, third, fourth, and fifth quintiles are, respectively, .50, .82, .77, .90. Since the size of the

Table 2-2.2 UNIVERSITY OF MINNESOTA GENERAL COLLEGE EXPECTANCY TABLES [for First-year GPA Based on Freshmen (Female) Entering College in the Fall of 1959 and the Fall of 1961]*

Quintile group		Chances in 100 of a freshman obtaining an average grade of: D or higher	C or higher	B or higher	Group size
Predictions based on HSR					
> 80		99	99	40	10–20
60–79		99	69	6	20–50
40–59		93	48	2	> 100
20–39		93	38	1	> 100
< 19		77	25	—	> 100
Predictions based on MSAT					
Raw score	% ile				
51–78	> 80	99	80	40	< 10
42–50	60–79	99	79	7	10–20
34–41	40–59	92	54	2	50–100
27–33	20–39	95	48	2	> 100
< 26	> 19	87	33	1	> 100

*Size of total group = 300–400.

first quintile MSAT group is given as "less than 10"; it is just possible that this group contains precisely one student, and she had a C average!

A further word about observed inversions should be said with reference to the lowest group on the predictor variable. It often happens that colleges adopt a policy of admitting any student with a test score above a certain level but carefully screening students with scores below that level. Also, students at these lower levels on the predictor scores are often directed into remedial courses where they are not in competition with students with higher predictor scores.

If the screening is indeed effective and/or if there is a difference in the courses taken by such students, the results will *often* be that the "probability" of success for students at the lowest-predictor-variable level will be higher than for those at the next-to-lowest level. A similar phenomenon can occur at the upper levels of test scores where it is often the case that students take many of the most difficult courses and thus tend to get slightly lower grades than they would obtain if they took the courses that their friends with lower test scores take. Thus, we see that much care must be exercised in the interpretation of predictive data for these reasons. Both in the guidance of students and in the evaluation of a test as a predictor, the nature of the criterion must be clearly understood.

It would be beyond the intended scope of this book, and certainly beyond the competence of the present authors, to detail precisely how predictive information should be used in a counseling situation. However, the following three paragraphs from the introduction to the Minnesota tables provide a healthy caution.

> Counselors should recognize that the personal meaning of the probability figures in these tables will vary for different students. For a student who wants very much to attend a certain college a 50-50 chance of being at least a "C" student may be encouraging. For the student who is looking for more assurance, a 50-50 chance of being at least a "B" student may be seen as too large a gamble. The decision to

Table 2-2.3 MACALESTER COLLEGE EXPECTANCY TABLES [for First-year GPA Based on Freshmen (Female) Entering College the Fall of 1959 and the Fall of 1961]*

MSAT quintile group:		Chances in 100 of a freshman obtaining an average grade of:			
Raw score	% ile	D or higher	C or higher	B or higher	Group size
51–78	> 80	99	90	39	> 100
42–50	60–79	99	77	11	50–100
34–41	40–59	99	82	12	20–50
27–33	20–39	99	50	5	20–50
1–26	< 19	99	99	—	< 10

*Predictions based on MSAT. Size of total group = 300 to 500.

> make application for a specific college must, of course, rest with the student whose aspirations, motivation, and willingness to assume various levels of risk will temper the probability figures.
>
> There is nothing in these tables that can be used legitimately as a basis for informing any student that he *cannot* achieve a given grade level in any specific college nor for informing him that he *will* achieve at least at a specified level. These tables provide counselors and their students with a summary of the grade-getting experiences of previous Minnesota high school graduates who have attended Minnesota Colleges. That such information can be misunderstood or misinterpreted cannot be too strongly emphasized.
>
> The person in the school who works with students on post-high school plans in a professional manner will study these tables until he understands both the value of the information provided and its limitations. The person who cannot find or take time for such study of these tables should refrain from their use.

One purpose of this book is to provide the training necessary for the interpretation of tables such as these and for the use of more sophisticated methods of obtaining and presenting predictive data.

To continue this section in a less pontifical tone, we point out some facts which are useful and perhaps enlightening. To highlight these results, we combine and present two more Minnesota expectancy tables, those giving predictions based on MSAT for males and females at the University of Minnesota at Duluth.

The striking feature one observes on comparing these two tables is that at almost

Table 2-2.4 UNIVERSITY OF MINNESOTA AT DULUTH EXPECTANCY TABLES [for First-year GPA Based on Freshmen Entering College the Fall of 1959 and the Fall of 1961]

MSAT quintile group		Chances in 100 of a freshman obtaining an average grade of:			
Raw score	% ile	D or higher	C or higher	B or higher	Group size
		Sex: Male; group size, over 500			
51–78	> 80	97	72	23	> 100
42–50	60–79	99	49	5	> 100
34–41	40–59	95	45	3	> 100
27–33	20–39	87	33	2	> 100
1–26	< 19	83	25	1	> 100
		Sex: Female; group size over 500			
51–78	> 80	99	83	31	> 100
42–50	60–79	99	72	12	> 100
34–41	40–59	99	62	7	> 100
27–33	20–39	95	42	3	> 100
1–26	< 19	91	26	1	50–100

any level of MSAT, the probability of a female attaining any specified criterion level is higher than that for a male. Furthermore, the rate of increase of these probabilities with MSAT level is greater for females than for males, indicating a higher correlation between test score and GPA for females. We might summarize these findings by saying that in a university-academic environment, females are overachievers relative to males, and they are also, contrary to folklore, more predictable. This might be explainable by the fact that college instructors are predominantly male or the fact that females excel in verbal skills which are particularly relevant in a university setting. More accurate explanations are probably less simplistic.

While the Duluth data exhibit these phenomena more clearly than the Minnesota General College data, one has no difficulty in seeing them in the first set of tables and, indeed, in most of the Minnesota tables. These phenomena are found regularly in such work, and indeed, their existence is the reason why expectancy tables are constructed separately for males and females whenever sample sizes permit.

The decision that the measurement technician faces is whether or not to divide a given group into subgroups in order to discover and use different prediction functions in the subgroups. If he can accurately estimate the correct prediction function for each group and if these functions are really different, a substantial gain can be had. However, if they are not different and if the smaller sample sizes in the two groups result in poorer estimation of the prediction function in each group, then there will be a loss. The Bayesian methods presented later in this book provide some rational strategy for making this decision, but the question is not a simple one.

2-3 DOUBLE-ENTRY EXPECTANCY TABLES

We hope some of our readers have already noted that it is possible to have two quite different expectancy values for students in the University of Minnesota General College, depending on whether these expectancies are based on HSR or MSAT. It is possible, for example, for a male student to have an HSR in the second quintile and an MSAT score in the top quintile. The probability of getting B or higher for such a student would then depend on which piece of information was used, the respective chances in 100 being 5 and 21. This is a large difference, and it may not be entirely clear to the student which piece of information most accurately gauges his aptitudes and abilities and, hence, will most accurately predict his college performance.

It is, of course, possible to construct expectancy tables using two predictor variables. These are called double-entry expectancy tables. The following description of double-entry expectancy tables is taken from *Test Service Bulletin No. 56*, The Psychological Corporation, May, 1966.

As one illustration of the construction and contribution of double-entry expectancy tables, we have utilized data from the records of college freshmen at a large midwestern university. For each student there were available rank in high school class and scores on the *College Qualification Tests (CQT)*; first semester grade-point averages[1] served as the criterion of success to be predicted. There were 1340 men students and 1053 women for whom complete data were supplied by the university. To make the data manageable for our purposes, the high school ranks, test scores, and college grade-point averages were each grouped into three categories: high, middle, and low. Table 1 shows these groupings. Thus, a high school rank of the 70th percentile or better was called "high," ranks from the 30th to the 69th percentile were called "middle," ranks from the 29th percentile down were called "low." *CQT* total scores were similarly classified. College grade-point averages were grouped by letter grade: A and B as the high group, C as the middle, and D and F as the low.

Table 1 MEANING OF GROUP DESIGNATIONS

Group	HSR % ile	CQT total score % ile	Coll. GPA
High	70-99	70-99	A & B
Middle	30-69	30-69	C
Low	0-29	0-29	D & F

If we construct simple expectancy tables using these categories, we have the data shown in Tables 2 and 3 for the men and in Tables 4 and 5 for the women.

Table 2 RELATIONSHIP BETWEEN CQT TOTAL SCORE AND COLLEGE GPA [Men ($N = 1340$)]

	Grade-point average:			
CQT total	D & F	C	A & B	
High	16	45	39	100
Middle	43	50	7	100
Low	80	19	1	100

Table 3 RELATIONSHIP BETWEEN HIGH SCHOOL RANK AND COLLEGE GPA [Men ($N = 1340$)]

	Grade-point average:			
HSR	D & F	C	A & B	
High	19	49	32	100
Middle	52	41	7	100
Low	72	27	1	100

The number appearing in each cell is the percent of students in each predictor category row who earned the indicated average grade. Table 2, for example, shows that among the men who scored "high" on *CQT* total, 16 percent earned averages of D or F, 45 percent earned C's, and 39 percent earned B or A averages. These results are in sharp contrast to the performance of those men

[1] For ease of reading, letter grade equivalents of the grade-point averages are used in the tables.

Table 4 RELATIONSHIP BETWEEN CQT TOTAL SCORE AND COLLEGE GPA [Women ($N = 1053$)]

	Grade-point average:			
CQT total	D & F	C	A & B	
High	6	43	51	100
Middle	25	60	15	100
Low	57	41	2	100

Table 5 RELATIONSHIP BETWEEN HIGH SCHOOL RANK AND COLLEGE GPA [Women ($N = 1053$)]

	Grade-point average:			
HSR	D & F	C	A & B	
High	14	52	34	100
Middle	50	47	3	100
Low	64	36	—	100

who scored "low" on test: 80 percent with grades D or F, 19 percent with C's, and only one per cent with a grade of A or B. Similar expressions of the probability of earning satisfactory grades are recorded in the cells of Tables 3, 4, and 5.

Obviously, these data are meaningful and useful—to student, counselor, parent, and admissions officer alike. They reveal that despite the considerable relationship between high test scores and college success, some men and women in the top test-score group do fail; they reveal also that despite heavy adverse odds, some low-scoring men and women do pass though few achieve distinguished grades. The information may well serve to motivate both kinds of student at the same time that it reports to the admissions officer the odds for or against success of any candidate. Each table contributes to wisdom in guidance or selection procedures.

It is appropriate to consider, however, how judgments might differ if *both* test score and rank in class were taken into account for each student. Does a good test score compensate for poor previous academic performance? How much are a student's chances of success enhanced if, although he is in the low group or rank in high school, he scores high on the test? Suppose John Jones is at the 78th percentile on test score and at the 52nd percentile on high school rank. The first fact suggests his chances of earning a grade-point average of C or better are 84 percent; the second fact indicates his chances to be 48 percent. The difference is dramatic; it would clearly be more satisfying as well as more accurate to have a statement which combines these probabilities. We can accomplish this by preparing double-entry expectancy tables, as shown below. Table 6 presents probabilities associated with test score and class rank simultaneously, for men; Table 7 presents a parallel display for women.

The data in Tables 6 and 7 reveal the predictions which can be made when *CQT* test score and high school rank are considered jointly, rather than singly. Thus, from Table 2 we learn that 16 percent of the men who scored high on *CQT* failed to earn a better grade from D or F; from Table 3, we see that 19 percent of the men who were admitted with high standing in high school rank similarly failed to earn a grade average higher than D.

Table 6 RELATIONSHIP BETWEEN CQT TOTAL SCORE, HIGH SCHOOL RANK, AND COLLEGE GPA [Men (N = 1340)]

CQT total score		High school rank: Low		Middle		High	
High	GPA	A & B	6	A & B	15	A & B	45
		C	47	C	48	C	45
		D & F	47	D & F	37	D & F	10
Middle	GPA	A & B	0	A & B	4	A & B	10
		C	33	C	44	C	58
		D & F	67	D & F	52	D & F	32
Low	GPA	A & B	0	A & B	2	A & B	0
		C	3	C	21	C	29
		D & F	97	D & F	77	D & F	71

Table 6, however, informs us that if the male freshman came from the top group of his high school class *and* scored high on *CQT*, the likelihood that he will earn a grade-point average lower than C is reduced to a mere 10 percent. On the other hand, if he scored high on *CQT* but came from the low group of his high school class, his likelihood of earning no better than a D or F grade-point average is a sizable 47 percent.[1] Let us return now to John Jones, who was average in high school rank but scored high on *CQT*. If we predicted solely on the basis of his rank in school (Table 3), we would estimate his chances of earning an average grade higher than D at 48 percent. Table 6 reveals that if we also consider his high score on the test, we raise our estimate to a more promising 63 percent (15 percent for A or B plus 48 percent for C).

Table 7 RELATIONSHIP BETWEEN CQT TOTAL SCORE, HIGH SCHOOL RANK, AND COLLEGE GPA [Women (N = 1053)]

CQT total score		High school rank: Low		Middle		High	
High	GPA	A & B	0	A & B	6	A & B	57
		C	100	C	70	C	39
		D & F	0	D & F	24	D & F	4
Middle	GPA	A & B	0	A & B	4	A & B	19
		C	33	C	50	C	64
		D & F	67	D & F	46	D & F	17
Low	GPA	A & B	0	A & B	0	A & B	4
		C	22	C	30	C	55
		D & F	78	D & F	70	D & F	41

[1] As one would expect, relatively few students in the bottom ranks in high school score high on *CQT*; in this instance, the 47 percent represents eight men out of seventeen admitted with low rank and high score.

Table 7 shows a double-entry expectancy table for the women's data reported in Tables 4 and 5. It, too, is a statement of joint probabilities, taking into account both high school record and test score. Thus, if Mary Smith came from the middle group on high school rank we would estimate her chances of earning an average grade better than D at 50 percent (Table 5); if, however, her score on *CQT* was high we would raise the probability estimate to 76 percent. The additional reassurance represented by the higher estimate might be crucial to Mary's willingness to undertake a college education—at least, at this institution. It might also make her, in the eyes of the admissions officer, a superior candidate rather than a mediocre one. It is noteworthy, too, (Table 6) that there were seventeen men admitted whose low high school rank would have predicted their earning an average grade of C or better as 28 percent; their high scores on *CQT* force reappraisal of these odds—nine of the seventeen with low high school rank but high *CQT* score earned at least C grade averages. Test information *can* make a difference.

The development of double-entry expectancy tables separately for men and women permits an interesting observation, one which relates to the qualities which favor women over men in the obtaining of grades. While this phenomenon may be observed by comparison of several analogous cells in Tables 6 and 7, it is perhaps most dramatically displayed by the figures in the lower right-hand cells, which report the expectancies for students who were in the top group of their high school class, but who scored low on the *College Qualification Tests.*

Among men who were admitted from this group, 71 percent (twenty out of twenty-eight) failed to achieve a satisfactory grade; and none of those who did manage to pass earned higher than a C grade-point average. For women, however, the figures are quite different; of seventy-seven low-scoring, high-rank-in-class females who were admitted, only thirty-two (41 percent) failed to achieve a satisfactory grade-point average—55 percent achieved successfully and another four per cent even earned an A or B average. It appears that whatever characteristics were effectively employed by these women to earn good grades in high school—in spite of low scholastic aptitude (as measured by tests)—stood them in equally good stead in college.

The difficulties involved in the use of double-entry expectancy tables become apparent on noting that, in the given example, the student could fall in one of nine classifications, three levels of test score, and three of high school rank. Since the total sample number was 1,053 for women, the average sample size for the categories is 117. Many of the two-way categories such as high CQT and low HSR will have very few students indeed, and thus the estimation of the probability of attaining GPAs in the ranges A and B, C, and D and F will be very imprecise. The estimate of a probability of 1 of attaining a C average for high CQT, low HSR students in Table 7 can hardly be taken seriously. Unfortunately, row-sample sizes were not retained so that we cannot know how precise any of these values are as estimates of the true situation.

The point, of course, is that as a population is divided into finer and finer subclassifications, it is in theory possible to do better and better prediction in the subpopulations. Tradeoffs are possible with relatively fewer classifications being used when a greater number of variables are used. In practice, however, where the sample size is limited, it may very quickly come to the point where the loss due to the decrease in sample size in the subgroups outweighs any gain due to adding classicatory variables. The problem here is analogous to the problem encountered in multiple regression, where, as the result of fitting too many variables, sample estimates of some regression weights may be unrealistic. We found this in Tables 1-6.1 and 1-6.2. We do not suggest here that a solution to either of these problems is to be found in this book, but some simpler problems of this nature are treated here together with the groundwork for future consideration of of such problems.

2-4 EXERCISES

1 Table 2-1.8 is large and not particularly informative to the student.
(*a*) Give three different ways of collapsing the GPA categories and a situation for which each procedure would be appropriate.
(*b*) Give three different ways of collapsing the ACT categories and a situation for which each procedure would be appropriate.

2 Snap College is not highly selective, but does require applicants to take the ACT battery. The college provides an excellent guidance program, one function of which is to help prospective students in determining their chance of success at this institution. Over a period of several years, the guidance program has collected data for predicting first-year GPA based on ACT scores.

Place yourself in the role of a guidance counselor at Snap College. A prospective student asks you to help him make a decision as to his chance of success at this institution. Describe the student in terms of his ACT score and his desire to attend Snap College. (For example, John Doe is not willing to attend Snap College unless his probability of attaining at least a C average is 60%.) Collapse the GPA and ACT categories in Table 2-1.8 in a manner appropriate to the situation you have described. Construct the new version of the table. How would you advise the student?

3 Consider Tables 6 and 7 from the Psychological Corporation data of Sec. 2-3. Devise one or more scenarios in which it would be appropriate to present these data differently, either as one-way tables or as different two-way tables. Question: Would it make sense in Table 7 to combine grade categories A, B, and C for the students who are low on HSR *and* on CQT, and at the same time combine the C, D, and F categories for the students who are high on both of the predictors? If this seems reasonable, discuss the general implications of this idea. If it does not, present a clear case why it is not.

4 With the exception of the lowest category, the class intervals for the y variable (college GPA) in Table 2-1.8 are of equal length. If we consider every y observation to be at the midpoint of its interval, and omit the bottom y category, we can code these values as with the successive integers 1 through 8. It is then possible to code and compute the correlation between the x and y scores, and to determine the best-fitting line for predicting y from x. It will be informative to do this for the entire population (persons with criterion scores $y = 0$ omitted) and for subpopulations restricted to persons with x scores above specified x values. Specifically we recommend that these computations be made in the following populations:

1) $y > 0,\ x \geq 13$
2) $y > 0,\ x \geq 17$
3) $y > 0,\ x \geq 22$
4) $y > 0,\ x \geq 28$

Write a brief description of the results of these computations.

3
PROBABILITY MODELS

In the mathematical theory of probability, a formal model is developed which enables us to discuss (among other things) the relation between population values and their estimates based on sample data. As is the case whenever mathematics is applied to real-life situations, the concept under study—here probability—acquires two aspects. One of these aspects is the formal meaning of "probability" within the mathematical system. This is defined by axioms, and once the definition is made, any quantities which satisfy the axioms are entitled to be called "probabilities". The theory of probability develops the axioms in two ways: by supplementing them with additional definitions, and by deriving their consequences in accordance with the rules of mathematical logic. Such axioms, definitions, and derivations are appropriately called *syntactic*; since they are concerned only with the correct formulation of mathematical sentences (equations, theorems), not with the meaning or interpretation of those sentences outside the mathematical system. It is quite possible to have a mathematical system with an elaborate and perfectly developed syntax for which no real-world interpretation can be found.

The second aspect of the concept of probability is its meaning or interpretation in the real world. Most of us find it meaningful to speak of the *chance* that a tossed coin will fall heads, the *likelihood* of rain tomorrow, the *probability* of our being involved in a serious automobile accident; and the idea that these concepts can be quantified is by now an accepted part of our daily lives. Provided that the quantification can be made in such a way as to satisfy his axioms, the mathematician will regard these real-world meanings as *semantic interpretations* of his syntactically defined concept. Chronologically, of course, the movement is usually in the opposite direction: The axioms adopted by the mathematician are suggested by certain real-world problems. In the case of probability theory, the initial impetus was given by the problems facing European aristocrats as they gambled on games of chance. It will be important for us to maintain the distinction between the syntactic and the semantic aspects of probability, and, in fact, we shall develop more than one semantic interpretation of the syntactic model. This dual semantic interpretation is a source of much controversy. The matter will be taken up more fully in Chap. 6, but meanwhile, a brief statement may help the reader begin to think concretely about probabilities.

One interpretation of probability proceeds in terms of long-term relative frequency: What would happen if a certain experiment (e.g., tossing a coin) were repeated a large number of times. With this interpretation, to say that the probability of heads is one-half means (semantically) that heads would be expected to occur on very nearly one-half of all tosses in such a series of repeated trials. There can be no doubt that this interpretation is the one which concerned the European aristocrats—they played their games of chance so frequently that the Chevalier de Mère could detect by long-term observation the difference between probabilities of .491 and .518. Many classical statisticians would regard a probability statement as meaningful only if it were, at least conceptually, interpretable in this sense.

An alternative interpretation is that probability is a measure of strength of belief. Thus, to say that the probability of "heads" is one-half is to say that my belief that heads will occur on the next toss is no stronger (and no weaker) than my belief that "tails" will occur. If it is asked how my real beliefs can be pinned down, one answer is to suppose that I am offered the choice of betting on "heads" or "tails" with advantage to me if I choose correctly. If I am indifferent to this choice, this indicates equal strength of belief in the two outcomes and corresponds to a probability, for me, of one-half for both "heads" and "tails".

For the remainder of this chapter, controversies over interpretation will be played down as much as possible while relevant areas of the syntactic development of probability theory are surveyed. The critical reader may wish to review the illustrations used here again after studying Chap. 6.

3-1 PROBABILITY MEASURES

Two systems of probability axioms, associated with the names of Kolmogorov and Renyi, respectively, are in common use. The Kolmogorov system is a little easier to understand initially, and we introduce it first. The axioms can be stated, with slight redundancy, as follows (the terms used are defined in the subsequent discussion).

With each *event* A is associated a number Prob (A), called the *probability* of A, having the following properties:

$K(i)$ $0 \leq \text{Prob}(A) \leq 1$; the probability of any event is not less than zero nor more than one.

$K(ii)$ If U is a *universal* event, Prob $(U) = 1$, the probability of a universal event is 1.

$K(iii)$ If A and B are *exclusive* events, then

$$\text{Prob}(A \text{ or } B) = \text{Prob}(A) + \text{Prob}(B),$$

the probabilities of exclusive events add up (are additive). More generally, if $A_1, A_2, \ldots$ are *mutually exclusive* events, then $\text{Prob}(A_1 \text{ or } A_2 \text{ or } \ldots) = \text{Prob}(A_1) + \text{Prob}(A_2) + \cdots$.

The mathematician has a strict definition of the word "event" in terms of the algebra of sets, but for our purposes it will be sufficient to understand it in its everyday sense of an occurrence and to note that we shall be interested in events such as "John's GPA lies (will lie) between 1.5 and 2.5" or "exactly 3 of the 50 students in this class (will) fail the end-of-course test". Events will often be spoken of as the outcome of experiments. Here "experiment" is used in a very broad sense. Conducting a test, making measurements, and recording observations on a random sample are all examples of experiments. The event "pedestrian death by automobile accident" would be regarded as a result of the experiment of allowing pedestrians and vehicles to occupy the same traffic area.

A universal event is an event that must occur whenever the experiment is performed, for example, "John's GPA lies between 0.0 and 4.0 inclusive". (Benjamin Franklin said that, for humans, only death and taxes are universal events.) Axioms K(i) and K(ii), thus, stipulate the scale on which probabilities are to be measured (0 to 1) and an event whose probability lies at one end of that scale. An immediate consequence of the third axiom is that an event which cannot occur (immortality) has probability zero, thus specifying an event at the other end of the scale. (It must be pointed out at once that the converse is false. If an event has probability zero it does *not* follow that it is logically impossible for it to result from the experiment. This point will be clarified in later discussion.)

The first two axioms are little more than conventions: for certain purposes (e.g., the rigorous treatment of the improper probability densities to be discussed in Chap. 6) other conventions might be preferred. The "meat" of the axioms is K(iii), the additivity axiom, which depends on the following definition:

Two events are called exclusive if the occurrence of one excludes the possibility of the occurrence of the other in the same experiment.

For example, it cannot be true that "exactly 3" and "exactly 4" students fail a particular examination, and so these events are exclusive: The same would not be true of the events "at least 3" and "at least 4".

A number of events are said to be mutually exclusive if the occurrence of any one of them excludes the possibility of the occurrence of any other. The fundamental property of probabilities is that the probabilities of mutually exclusive events are additive.

At this point, we may note that all of us are familiar with quantities which satisfy the probability axioms, namely, actual (as opposed to long-term-hypothetical) relative frequencies or proportions (recall the expectancy tables of Chap. 2). For example, if A_i $(i = 1, 2, 3, 4)$ is the event "placed in grade i in the statistics examination"; the proportions of students in a particular class who are placed in each grade could formally be called "probabilities" since, as is readily verified, they satisfy the axioms. Such a renaming would be of little interest. Suppose, however, that random selection of an individual from such a class is defined to mean a procedure which reproduces the relative-frequency structure of the population (the whole class) as a probability structure for the individual chosen (this is usually regarded as a consequence of random sampling rather than a definition). Then we have a way of obtaining numerical probabilities to which either of the previously discussed semantic interpretations can be applied.

3-2 CONDITIONAL PROBABILITY

The Kolmogorov axioms have to be supplemented by the definition of conditional probability before they lead to results of statistical interest. If B is an event with nonzero probability and AB is written as shorthand for the event "both A *and* B occur", then the *(conditional) probability of A given B,* written Prob $(A|B)$, is defined by

$$\text{Prob}\,(A|B) = \frac{\text{Prob}\,(AB)}{\text{Prob}\,(B)}, \qquad (3\text{-}2.1)$$

where Prob (AB) is the probability of the event "A and B". *Semantically, the conditional probability of A given B is the probability of A when it is known (or supposed) that B has occurred.* Equivalently, we may say that the conditional probability of A given B is *the probability of A in the subset or subpopulation in which B holds.* The motivation for the definition will be clear if we consider the grades example at the end of the previous section. Suppose that in a class of 100, totals of 16, 24, 45, and 15 students obtain grades 1 (highest), 2, 3, and 4 (lowest), respectively. If we know only that a student has been selected at random from this class, we will assign probabilities .16, .24, .45, and .15 to his having each of the four grades. If someone now tells us that the student has, in fact, one of the two highest grades, the situation changes. We could return to our basic data, argue that the student is in effect randomly selected from the two highest grades, and conclude that the probability of his grade being 2 is 24/(16 + 24) = .60. Alternatively, we can use the definition of conditional probability (3-2.1), taking B to be the event "A_1 or A_2". By K(iii) we have Prob (B) = Prob (A_1) + Prob (A_2) = .40. Also, the event "A_2 and B" is in this case simply the event A_2. Hence, we have Prob$(A_2|B)$ = Prob(A_2)/Prob(B) = .24/.40 = .60 as before.

The Kolmogorov axioms are framed in terms of unconditional or absolute probabilities. It seems clear that, strictly speaking, no such entities exist in the real world. The simple assignment of the probability one-half to "heads" on the toss of a coin is conditional on my knowing that the coin in question is a two-sided, apparently symmetric object and will be tossed in a manner which does not obviously prejudice the outcome. Even so, a history of previous tosses of the same coin (a conditioning event) might cause me to revise my probability. (When conditioning events are being considered, "outcome of an experiment" is too narrow a way of making concrete the concept of an event. It needs to be replaced by "concomitant of an experiment"—any circumstance attending the particular performance of the experiment.)

The above suggests that an axiom system framed in terms of conditional probabilities might be preferable from the point of view of semantic interpretation. Such a system would also have a slightly greater syntactic generality. It is beyond the scope of this book to explain why this is so, except to hint that it provides a way of circumventing the restriction Prob $(B) \neq 0$, which was required in our previous definition of conditional probability. Conditional probabilities are the basic entities in the Renyi axiom system, which can be stated as follows:

With a pair of events (A, C) is associated a number Prob $(A|C)$ called the probability of A given C and having the following properties:

$R(i)$ $0 \leq \text{Prob}\,(A|C) \leq 1$.

$R(ii)$ Prob $(C|C) = 1$.

$R(iii)$ If events $A_1, A_2, \ldots$ *are mutually given* C, then

$$\text{Prob}\,(A_1 \text{ or } A_2 \text{ or } \ldots | C) = \text{Prob}\,(A_1|C) + \text{Prob}\,(A_2|C) + \cdots.$$

$R(iv)$ Prob $(A|BC)$ Prob $(B|C)$ = Prob $(AB|C)$.

The only new term introduced here is "mutually exclusive given C". Two events are exclusive given C if the occurrence of one excludes the possibility of the other when it is known that C has occurred. For example, the events "priest" and "husband" are, in theory, exclusive given "Roman Catholic", but are not exclusive in general. (A more symmetrical view of the statement "A and B are exclusive given C" is that A, B, and C cannot all occur simultaneously.) A number of events are mutually exclusive given C if, when C is known to have occurred, the occurrence of any one of them excludes the occurrence of any other; e.g., "priest", "husband", "wife", "spinster", are mutually exclusive given "Roman Catholic".

The letter C has been used to suggest a conditioning event, which may, of course, be any event concomitant to the experiment being considered. A case of particular interest is when C is taken to be U, a universal event. Since a universal event must occur whenever the experiment is performed, conditioning on it is redundant. To put it another way, if a probability is conditional on U, we may drop the U from the notation; and if no other conditioning event remains, we may treat the resulting probability as absolute. The reader can verify that applying these rules to axioms R(i) to (iv) with C taken to be U yields axioms K(i) to (iii) and definition (3-2.1). There can, therefore, be no inconsistency between the two axiom systems, though the Renyi system may allow for additional results not obtainable in the Kolmogorov system. The semantic advantage of the Renyi system is that it makes explicit at the outset the population over which a probability is defined.

The main purpose of the previous paragraph is not, however, to demonstrate consistency between the two systems, but to introduce a convention. There is no limit to the number of conditioning events that an ingenious person can dream up. One could argue, for example, that coin-toss probabilities are conditional on the coin falling to the ground/table; since if it rose to the ceiling, it would be debatable which face should be recorded. In our notation, we shall usually suppress reference to conditioning factors which are assumed to be universally present in *any* performance of the experiment. The assumption may be made because any reasonable man would make it (the coin will fall), or it may be explicitly stated in the description of the experiment (a student is chosen at random). If we write an absolute probability, it is to be understood that the only conditioning factors are those universally assumed in the experiment. This will help keep notation within bounds. However, a word of warning is necessary. When a formal statistical analysis is complete, the wise man will take little for granted and will review his "universal assumptions", since the net result of his investigation could be to cast doubt on them. (Were those students *really* chosen at random? Was the coin tossed in a spaceship in flight?) In our example illustrating mutually exclusive events given C, there was the further unuttered condition "1974". These events may or may not be exclusive given $(C,1984)$.

Bayes' Theorem Taking a very short step from the definition of conditional probability (3-2.1), or R(iv) with the C notation suppressed, we can write

$$\begin{aligned} \text{Prob}\,(A|B)\,\text{Prob}\,(B) &= \text{Prob}\,(AB) \\ &= \text{Prob}\,(BA) && \text{(from the meaning of } AB) \\ &= \text{Prob}\,(B|A)\,\text{Prob}\,(A) && \text{(using (3-2.1), with } A \text{ and } B \text{ reversed).} \end{aligned}$$

Hence, if $\text{Prob}\,(B) \neq 0$,

$$\text{Prob}\,(A|B) = \frac{\text{Prob}\,(B|A)\,\text{Prob}\,(A)}{\text{Prob}\,(B)}. \qquad (3\text{-}2.2)$$

This may be regarded as an embryonic form of *Bayes' theorem* and is probably the most useful form to remember. We illustrate the use of Bayes' theorem for inference by an example which is, hopefully, noncontroversial.

A certain country has two political parties, D and R, whose popular support is shown by current opinion polls to be 45 and 55%, respectively (it is assumed here that everybody supports either D or R.) A controversial issue has split the country across party lines into those (F) who favor a proposed reform and those (A) who are against it. The polls also show that 60% of party D supporters and 40% of party R supporters favor the reform. A foreign visitor hears a fellow guest at a party speak in favor of the reform. What is the probability that the guest supports party D? In an obvious notation, we have $\text{Prob}(D) = .45$, $\text{Prob}(R) = .55$, $\text{Prob}(F|D) = .60$, and $\text{Prob}(F|R) = .40$, all of these being derived from the corresponding proportions by a random-selection assumption.

Now those favoring the reform can be divided into two subgroups, those who support D and those who support R. Notationally, these groups are FD and FR and these two groups, by their definition, are mutually exclusive. Thus, we can write

$$\begin{aligned}\text{Prob}(F) &= \text{Prob}(FD) + \text{Prob}(FR)\\ &= \text{Prob}(F|D)\,\text{Prob}(D) + \text{Prob}(F|R)\,\text{Prob}(R)\\ &= (.60)(.45) + (.40)(.55)\\ &= .49\,.\end{aligned}$$

Hence, using Bayes' theorem (3-2.2) with D and F replacing A and B, respectively, we have

$$\text{Prob}(D|F) = \frac{\text{Prob}(F|D)\,\text{Prob}(D)}{\text{Prob}(F)} = \frac{(.60)(.45)}{.49} = .55 \quad \text{(approximately)}.$$

Thus, the additional knowledge that the guest favors the reform has increased the probability that he supports party D from .45 *a priori* (before the "experiment") to .55 *a posteriori* (after the "experiment").

The result could, of course, have been obtained without resorting to Bayes' theorem. A simple calculation shows that 27% of the total electorate support party D and favor the reform while 22% support party R and favor the reform. The conditions of the problem imply that the guest is randomly selected from among those who favor the reform, and so the probability that he supports party D is 27/49. What Bayes' theorem does is to provide a formal mechanism for carrying out this sort of calculation in situations so complex that intuition would fail us. We shall shortly give a form of Bayes' theorem incorporating the computation of $\text{Prob}(F)$.

If our example is, indeed, noncontroversial, it is so because it was framed in such a way that any reasonable person would take .45 and .55 for the probabilities $\text{Prob}(D)$ and $\text{Prob}(R)$ that the guest was a supporter of party D or R before the guest opened his mouth. To this end, a foreign visitor, who would have no previous knowledge of regional variations or sex differences in the support for the two parties, was introduced as the observer. The context of the "experiment" was chosen to suggest that the observer had no previous personal knowledge of the speaker and no hint as to the kind of person to be expected at the party, and so on. It requires little imagination to appreciate how controversial the values of Prob (D) and Prob (R) might be in a real-life situation where different observers will typically have different background knowledge, though one might hope that if they pooled their knowledge, they would then agree. Such controversy as still exists about Bayesian methods is basically over whether, and if so how, prior probabilities can be assessed in the sorts of situations with which statistics deals. We return to the subject in Chap. 5.

The form to which the name Bayes' theorem is usually given is obtained by supposing that events $A_1, A_2, \ldots$ are mutually exclusive and also *exhaustive*, that is, exhaust all possible "outcomes" (concomitant circumstances) of the experiment; thus, exactly one of the A_i must "occur". The event B is then the same as the event "(BA_1) or (BA_2) or . . .", and the events (BA_1), (BA_2), etc., are clearly mutually exclusive. Hence, by K(iii),

$$\begin{aligned}\text{Prob}\,(B) &= \text{Prob}\,(BA_1) + \text{Prob}\,(BA_2) + \cdots \\ &= \text{Prob}\,(B|A_1)\,\text{Prob}\,(A_1) + \text{Prob}\,(B|A_2)\,\text{Prob}\,(A_2) + \cdots .\end{aligned}$$

Substituting this expression for Prob(B) in the denominator of (3-2.2) and replacing A by A_1, we obtain Bayes' theorem in the usual form

$$\text{Prob}\,(A_1|B) = \frac{\text{Prob}\,(B|A_1)\,\text{Prob}\,(A_1)}{\sum_i \text{Prob}\,(B|A_i)\,\text{Prob}\,(A_i)}, \qquad (3\text{-}2.3)$$

with similar results for Prob $(A_2|B)$, and so on.

Suppose that in a particular Minnesota college, the proportion of male students is .55 and the proportion of female students is .45. Denote the event "male" by A_1 and the event "female" by A_2. Then for a randomly selected student Prob $(A_1) = .55$ and Prob $(A_2) = .45$. Let B be the event that a student attains a B average or better, and suppose we know that 40% of the females and 30% of the males attain this average. Then, in terms of conditional probabilities, we have Prob $(B|A_2) = .40$ and Prob $(B|A_1) = .30$.

We are now in a position to revise our judgment as to whether a particular unidentified student is male or female when we are given the information that he (she) has a B average. The computation is based on Bayes' theorem written:

$$\begin{aligned}\text{Prob}\,(A_2|B) &= \frac{\text{Prob}\,(B|A_2)\,\text{Prob}\,(A_2)}{\text{Prob}\,(B|A_2)\,\text{Prob}\,(A_2) + \text{Prob}\,(B|A_1)\,\text{Prob}\,(A_1)} \\ &= \frac{(.40)(.45)}{(.40)(.45) + (.30)(.55)} \\ &= .52 .\end{aligned}$$

On an a priori basis we have Prob $(A_1) = .55$ and would thus have been inclined to guess that the student was male, but on an a posteriori basis given the event B, we have Prob $(A_1|B) = .48$. Thus given the information that this is a B-average student, we are inclined to believe that the student is female. Bayes' theorem has made that revision in our judgment precise.

Consider now the data in Table 2-1.7 and suppose that the categories academic withdrawal and nonacademic withdrawal have been combined to form an overall withdrawal category. Then the data can be summarized as shown in the new contingency table, Table 3-2.1.

From the table, we see that for a randomly selected student the probability that he is in the lowest MCAT category is $\frac{71}{544} = .13$. However, given the fact that he maintains regular status through his medical school years, we can determine the conditional probability of his being in the lowest MCAT category. Bayes' formula is

$$\text{Prob (low MCAT|regular)} = \frac{\text{Prob (regular|low MCAT) Prob (low MCAT)}}{\sum_{\text{MCAT}} \text{Prob (regular|MCAT) Prob (MCAT)}}$$

$$= \frac{\frac{59}{71}\,\frac{71}{544}}{\frac{59}{71}\,\frac{71}{544} + \frac{233}{253}\,\frac{253}{544} + \frac{200}{220}\,\frac{220}{544}}.$$

Since the probabilities are available to us here as fractions, we see that the computations can be simplified through division of common terms. Thus we have

$$\text{Prob (low MCAT|regular)} = \frac{59}{59 + 233 + 200} = \frac{59}{492} = .12,$$

which, of course, could have been obtained directly by remembering that a conditional probability is just a probability in a subpopulation. More typically, we will have probabilities available as decimals, whence we would compute

$$\begin{aligned}\text{Prob (low MCAT|regular)} &= \frac{(.831)(.131)}{(.831)(.131) + (.921)(.465) + (.909)(.404)}\\ &= \frac{.1089}{.1089 + .4283 + .3672}\\ &= \frac{.1089}{.9044}\\ &= .12\end{aligned}$$

Thus, the knowledge that the student maintained regular status has not substantially altered our evaluation of the probability that he had a low MCAT score.

Since there is still a residue of controversy regarding the use of Bayesian methods in statistics, it should be emphasized that there is no dispute whatever about the correctness of Bayes' theorem, considered as part of the syntactic development of probability theory. The dispute centers on the semantic interpretation to be given to the various probabilities entering into Eqs. (3-2.2) or (3-2.3). The interpretation we shall wish to give is that Prob (A_1) is my personal probability of A_1 *prior* to certain additional information B becoming available. Then, Prob $(A_1|B)$ is my personal *posterior* probability of A_1, posterior, that is, to the information B becoming available. The use of a time sequence is a concession to human thought patterns: a computer might "think" it a matter of *where* within itself the information lay, rather than *when* it was used.

Recall also the discussion at the end of Chap. 1. If we look carefully at the data in Tables 1-6.1 or 1-6.2, we would probably decide that the negative regression weights that do appear are, in probability, solely the result of sampling fluctuation. Specifically, if we look at Table 1-6.1 and consider college 2, we would decide that the weight β_4 is probably better estimated as .000 than as −.005. We do this as a result of our study of the data from the remaining 21 colleges. Since these data were collected at the same time as the data for college 2, it seems inappropriate to speak of it as prior information. The discussion, however, is entirely semantic. Bayes' theorem has no time factor. When we learn how to use the data from the remaining 21 colleges, it will be irrelevant that it was not gathered ahead of the data from college 2. In order to introduce some semantic clarity, it may be useful to call such information *collateral information*, but again the benefit is entirely semantic. This point can even be taken further. Suppose we had the data from Table 1-6.2 and the single line for college 2 from Table 1-6.1; again we could argue as before and prefer the estimate .000 to −.005 for β_4 even though the *collateral information* occurred later in time than the event of interest.

One thing that Bayes' theorem does for us is to help us to keep an eye on the right probability. It is common practice in validating a test to proceed in something of the following manner. First, people are classified as having high (H_T) or low (L_T) test scores and then classified as being successes (S) or failures (F) academically. Then, if Prob $(H_T|S)$ > Prob $(L_T|S)$, the test is called valid. The implication is that there is a tendency for successful students to get high scores on the test and a much lesser tendency for them to get low scores. To put it another way, it is said that the high-test-score students are more like the successful students than are the low-test-score students.

Table 3-2.1 REDUCED CONTINGENCY TABLE FOR MCAT DATA

MCAT range	Regular	Academic difficulties	Withdrawals	Total
> 515	200	7	13	220
430–515	233	6	14	253
< 430	59	6	6	71
Total	492	19	33	544

Let us use Bayes' theorem and write

$$\text{Prob}\,(S|H_T) = \frac{\text{Prob}\,(H_T|S)\,\text{Prob}\,(S)}{\text{Prob}\,(H_T)}$$

and

$$\text{Prob}\,(S|L_T) = \frac{\text{Prob}\,(L_T|S)\,\text{Prob}\,(S)}{\text{Prob}\,(L_T)}$$

and then see if it is possible to have Prob $(S|L_T) >$ Prob $(S|H_T)$ even though Prob $(H_T|S) >$ Prob $(L_T|S)$. Comparing the expressions for Prob $(S|H_T)$ and Prob $(S|L_T)$, and dividing by Prob (S), we see that the required condition is

$$\frac{\text{Prob}\,(L_T|S)}{\text{Prob}\,(L_T)} > \frac{\text{Prob}\,(H_T|S)}{\text{Prob}\,(H_T)}\,.$$

This condition will be satisfied if Prob (L_T) is small enough and Prob (H_T) is large enough, in which case it is possible to "observe" that Prob $(H_T|S) >$ Prob $(L_T|S)$ and yet find that Prob $(S|L_T) >$ Prob $(S|H_T)$. For example, consider the following:

$$\text{Prob}\,(H_T|S) = .656 \text{ and Prob}\,(L_T|S) = .344.$$

Now suppose

$$\text{Prob}\,(L_T) = .20, \quad \text{Prob}\,(H_T) = .80, \quad \text{and Prob}\,(S) = .50\,.$$

Then,

$$\text{Prob}\,(S|H_T) = \frac{(.656)(.50)}{.80} = .41,$$

$$\text{Prob}\,(S|L_T) = \frac{(.344)(.50)}{.20} = .86.$$

One could, of course, claim validity for this test but only in a negative and unacceptable sense. What is important here is not the comparison of Prob $(H_T|S)$ and Prob $(L_T|S)$ but the comparison of Prob $(H_T|S)$ with Prob (H_T). We note, however, that this discordant result is obtained only when Prob $(H_T) \neq$ Prob (L_T). If these two quantities are equal or nearly so, then Prob $(H_T|S) >$ Prob $(L_T|S)$ will imply Prob $(S|H_T) >$ Prob $(S|L_T)$. We thus see that the fact that successful people score more highly on a test than do unsuccessful people does not necessarily imply that the test is a valid predictor of success.

The major source of difficulty here arises, as we have suggested, because of a lack of care in interpreting conditional probabilities. The climate for this error is created by an unfortunate condensation of the data. We are misled if we are only given Prob $(H_T|S)$ and Prob $(L_T|S)$. The analysis given above might well have been based on the contingency table on page 55, which, if examined even casually, would never suggest an incorrect interpretation.

	L_T	H_T	
S	172	328	500
F	28	472	500
	200	800	1,000

3-3 INDEPENDENCE

Much of statistical work is concerned with the study of the dependence or lack of dependence of one event on another. We might ask: "What is the probability of snow in Iowa City next Sunday?" A meaningful reply would be: "It depends on what time of the year it is". If W denotes winter and S denotes snow, then the probability of S is different given W and $\overline{W}$ (not W). Notationally, this assertion is that $\text{Prob}\,(S|W) \neq \text{Prob}\,(S|\overline{W})$; that is, the two conditional probabilities differ.

The formalization of this idea is done in the following way. Two events A and B are said to be *independent given C* if

$$\text{Prob}\,(AB|C) = \text{Prob}\,(A|C)\,\text{Prob}\,(B|C)\,. \qquad (3\text{-}3.1)$$

If C is a universal event, this reduces to

$$\text{Prob}\,(AB) = \text{Prob}\,(A)\,\text{Prob}\,(B)\,, \qquad (3\text{-}3.2)$$

which is usually taken as the definition of independence for absolute probabilities. On dividing both sides of (3-3.2) by $\text{Prob}\,(B)$ and using (3-2.1), we obtain

$$\text{Prob}\,(A|B) = \text{Prob}\,(A)\,, \qquad (3\text{-}3.3)$$

which has the interpretation that the additional knowledge that B has occurred does not cause us to revise our probability for A in any way. If (3-3.3) is true, then it must also be true that

$$\text{Prob}\,(A|\overline{B}) = \text{Prob}\,(A) = \text{Prob}\,(A|B)\,.$$

This explains the use of the term independence to describe a situation of nondependence. The same interpretation of nondependence of our probability for A on information about B could be given to the equation obtained by dividing (3-3.1) by $\text{Prob}\,(B|C)$ and using R(iv), namely,

$$\text{Prob}\,(A|BC) = \text{Prob}\,(A|C)\,. \qquad (3\text{-}3.4)$$

Consider the data in Table 3-2.1. Each student has been classified in one of three MCAT categories and one of four progress categories. Let A be the event "regular progress" and C be the event "MCAT range < 430". Then, $\text{Prob}(A) = .904$ and $\text{Prob}(A|C) = .831$; thus the events A and C are not independent. Now let B be the event "MCAT > 515". Then, $\text{Prob}(A|B) = .909$, and $\text{Prob}(A) = .904$ Hence, A and B are not independent. They are, however, more nearly independent than A and C, since the knowledge that B has occurred has changed very little our evaluation of the probability that A has occurred. Now consider the event $\bar{C}$, signifying MCAT $\geqslant 430$, and the probabilities $\text{Prob}(A|\bar{C})$ and $\text{Prob}(A|B\bar{C})$, which are, respectively, .915 and .909. [Note $\text{Prob}(A|B\bar{C}) = \text{Prob}(A|B)$.] Thus, given the information $\bar{C}$, the events A and B are again nearly but not strictly independent.

Readers may find it strange that (3-3.1) is taken as a definition of "independence". Without very careful thought, it is difficult to see how this definition can be fit to the real world–indeed, this is seen only when the equivalent statement (3-3.4) is derived. Semantically, (3-3.4) is the preferable definition of independence, but syntactically (3-3.1) is preferable because of its neater generalization to more than two events. Thus, events $A, B, C, \ldots$ are *mutually independent* if

$$\text{Prob}(ABC \ldots K) = \text{Prob}(A)\,\text{Prob}(B)\,\text{Prob}(C) \ldots \text{Prob}(K), \qquad (3\text{-}3.5)$$

and a similar equation holds for all subcollections of events from the set $A, B, C, \ldots, K$. Thus, A, B, and C are mutually independent if

$$\begin{aligned} \text{Prob}(ABC) &= \text{Prob}(A)\,\text{Prob}(B)\,\text{Prob}(C), \\ \text{Prob}(AB) &= \text{Prob}(A)\,\text{Prob}(B), \\ \text{Prob}(AC) &= \text{Prob}(A)\,\text{Prob}(C), \\ \text{and} \quad \text{Prob}(BC) &= \text{Prob}(B)\,\text{Prob}(C). \end{aligned}$$

However, A, B, C are *not* mutually independent if $\text{Prob}(ABC) = \text{Prob}(A)\,\text{Prob}(B)\,\text{Prob}(C)$ but $\text{Prob}(AB) \neq \text{Prob}(A)\,\text{Prob}(B)$, which is possible, or $\text{Prob}(AB) = \text{Prob}(A)\,\text{Prob}(B)$ but $\text{Prob}(ABC) \neq \text{Prob}(A)\,\text{Prob}(B)\,\text{Prob}(C)$, which is also possible.

In statistical applications, independence is usually an assumption (part of the model) rather than a deduction. One justification for such an assumption would be that two events appear to be unconnected; for example, if the pass level for an examination is fixed in advance, the probabilities of passing for any two students selected at random would be taken as independent. This would not be true of a competitive examination in which only a specified number of students can "pass", since the knowledge that one student has passed reduces the probability that the other has–to zero if only one student was to be selected.

An alternative justification for assuming independence is that all factors which connect two events are explicitly included in the conditioning event; for example, if a mathematics test exists in two alternative forms, the probabilities of my scoring more than 50% of the possible score points on each of the tests might be taken as independent *given my ability in mathematics*. To put it another way, in the subpopulation of individuals having the same mathematical ability as myself, the probabilities of scoring more than 50% on each test are independent. What is being assumed here is that one's score is determined by one's ability and by certain disturbing factors, and that the disturbing factors for the two tests are unconnected.

Frequently in statistical writing, one finds references to independence without a conditioning event being mentioned. This can be justified on the grounds of economy when the only conditioning events are universal events or are clear from the context. However, failure to specify the conditioning event(s) is a rather fertile source of confusion both in one's reading and in one's thinking. It is always worth asking: "Independent? Conditional on what?" We fervently hope that scores on the two mathematics tests are not independent but rather are highly correlated in the entire population of examinees. Again, this emphasizes the point that the answer to the question "conditional on what?" is just the specification of the precise set of experimental units (the population) in which the statement holds.

3-4 RANDOM VARIABLES

The "experiments" with which statistics is chiefly concerned are those which result in the observation of one or more numbers; for example, administration of a battery of educational tests results, for each individual tested, in a set of numerical test scores. The set of scores is an "event" in the sense already discussed. Even categorical criteria of the pass-fail type can often be expressed in numerical form (see Chap. 5 for details).

Consider the case of a single test. For each individual to whom it is administered, we observe a test score x. We shall call the conceptual entity "test score" a *random variable* and denote it by X. Then the statement "we observe a particular test score x" can be expressed as "we observe that X takes the value x" or simply as "$X = x$". We shall want to consider the probabilities of observing various possible test scores, such as 17, 18, . . . ; and the notation Prob $(X = 17)$, Prob $(X = 18)$, . . . and in general Prob $(X = x)$ will give us a convenient way of referring to these.

The name *random variable* is a little unfortunate, since it suggests a connection with random selection or random sampling. There is no direct connection. The "random" means only that the variation in the observed value from experiment to experiment cannot be completely explained on deterministic grounds—at least part of it is probabilistic. Wherever possible, we shall use uppercase letters for random variables, the entities themselves, and lowercase letters for the particular values they take. A time will come when this expenditure of available symbols appears profligate. By then, however, the reader should be sufficiently familiar with the operations involved to make a condensed notation acceptable.

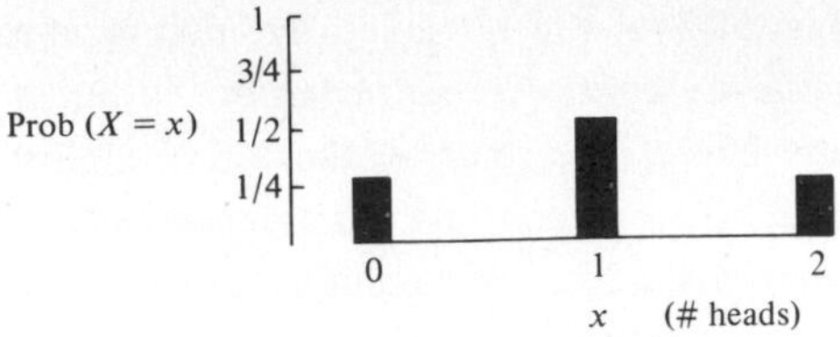

FIGURE 3-4.1
Probability mass function for the number of heads in two tosses of a coin.

An enumeration of all possible observed values x together with their probabilities Prob ($X = x$) is called a *probability distribution*. The probabilities themselves are sometimes referred to as *probability mass elements*. The idea here is that the values x may be thought of as points plotted on a line (the x axis). Then the total available probability of amount (mass) unity has been shared out (distributed) between these points, each receiving a certain element of mass. If we toss a coin twice and the probability of heads on each toss is one-half, independently of the result of the other toss, then the probability of two heads is one-fourth, of two tails is one-fourth, and of one head and one tail is one-half. Now suppose we score a head as one point and a tail as zero; then the probability distribution for the result of this experiment is as given in Fig. 3-4.1.

The enumeration of a probability distribution can, clearly, be set out in tabular form. If the number of possible values of X is at all large, however, such a table becomes very unwieldy. Moreover, it is difficult to bring general mathematical methods to bear on such tables. For these reasons, we first study hypothetical situations in which the probabilities Prob ($X = x$) can be specified by a formula which involves x and certain other quantities called *parameters*. From these situations, we derive standard probability distributions to which we give names and which then become tools in the statistician's workbox. When we come to study real-life situations, we examine whether the conditions are such that one of the standard probability distributions is appropriate, at least to a sufficiently high degree of approximation.

As an example of how a standard distribution is derived, consider the following. An executive who interviews candidates for secretarial positions knows from past experience that a proportion π (the Greek letter corresponding to the first letter in "proportion") of candidates will satisfy him as appearing suitable for the job. On one occasion only one such position is vacant and the candidates are to be interviewed in random order and the job awarded to the first candidate who appears suitable. How many candidates will he have to interview?

Let X be the number of candidates interviewed. Clearly X is a random variable. We shall have $X = 1$ if the first candidate interviewed appears satisfactory. This event has probability π. Thus, Prob ($X = 1$) $= \pi$. The probability that the first interviewee appears unsatisfactory must be $(1 - \pi)$ since "satisfactory" and "unsatisfactory" are two exclusive events, one of which must happen and whose probabilities therefore sum to 1.

We shall have $X = 2$ if the first interviewee appears unsatisfactory and the second satisfactory, and because of the random order of interviewing, these two events are independent. Hence, we can apply (3-3.2) and obtain

$$\begin{aligned}\text{Prob}\,(X = 2) &= \text{Prob (1st unsatisfactory) Prob (2nd satisfactory)} \\ &= (1 - \pi)\pi.\end{aligned}$$

In general, for any integer x, we shall have $X = x$ if the first $(x - 1)$ interviewees appear unsatisfactory and the xth appears satisfactory. Thus,

$$\text{Prob}\,(X = x) = \underbrace{(1 - \pi)(1 - \pi)\ldots(1 - \pi)}_{(x - 1)\text{ terms}}\pi = (1 - \pi)^{x-1}\pi. \tag{3-4.1}$$

We have, thus, achieved our objective of finding a formula for Prob $(X = x)$ in terms of x and the parameter π. The probability distribution it describes is named the *geometric distribution* because successive probabilities are members of the so-called geometric series. It will economize on notation if we write (3-4.1) as $p(x) = (1 - \pi)^{x-1}\pi$. Here, $p(x)$ is a function of the possible values of the random variable which gives the probabilities associated with these values. Alternatively, it is the function which gives the heights of the columns in diagrams such as Fig. 3-4.1. When we come shortly to discuss continuous random variables, $p(x)$ will again give the height of a function though it will not itself be a probability.

So far, the proportion π has been thought of as some known number. If π is unknown or we wish to consider different values of π, then the value of π becomes a conditioning event for the probability that $X = x$, and it will be appropriate to write

$$p(x|\pi) = \text{Prob}\,(X = x|\pi) = (1 - \pi)^{x-1}\pi, \tag{3-4.2}$$

making explicit the dependence on the parameter π.

Expectation

A concept of fundamental importance in studying random variables is that of *expectation* (also called *expected value*). The expectation $\mathcal{E}(X)$ of a random variable X is defined by

$$\mathcal{E}(X) = \sum_{\substack{\text{all}\\\text{possible}\\x}} x\,\text{Prob}\,(X = x) = \Sigma x p(x), \tag{3-4.3}$$

that is, the sum of the products of each possible x with its probability of occurring. Another way to consider this is as the weighted average of x values, weighted according to the probability function $p(x)$.

If we consider a set of data at hand as constituting an entire population, we can easily plot out the probability distribution and compute the expectation. For example, given the population of GPA scores in Table 1-2.1 and associating these scores with the random variable Y, we have

$$\text{Prob}\,(Y = y) = \begin{cases} .1 & \text{for } y = 1.1, 1.7, 2.4, 2.6, 2.8, 3.0, 3.1, 3.5 \\ .2 & \text{for } y = 2.3\,. \end{cases}$$

We also have

$$\begin{aligned} \mathcal{E}(Y) &= (1.1)(.1) + (1.7)(.1) + (2.3)(.2) + (2.4)(.1) + (2.6)(.1) \\ &\qquad + (2.8)(.1) + (3.0)(.1) + (3.1)(.1) + (3.5)(.1) \\ &= 2.48. \end{aligned}$$

The name "expectation" derives from the gambling situation discussed at the beginning of this chapter. If X stands for "winnings", and Prob $(X = x)$, the probability of winning an amount x on one play of the game, is interpreted in the long-term relative-frequency sense, then in a long series of plays of the game, $\mathcal{E}(X)$ is one's average winnings per play. In terms of loss functions, the importance of the expectation arises from the fact that the mean-squared-error loss in predicting X is minimized by taking $\mathcal{E}(X)$ as our prediction. Physically, the point with coordinate $\mathcal{E}(X)$ would correspond to the center of gravity of the mass elements of a probability distribution.

Consider again the geometric distribution developed in the preceding subsection. Several mathematical methods are available to sum the series which is obtained when the probabilities (3-4.1) are substituted into the definition of expectation—Eq. (3-4.3). The result is $\mathcal{E}(X) = \pi^{-1}$. One interpretation of this result is that the average number of candidates interviewed to fill any one vacancy is the reciprocal of the proportion of candidates who are satisfactory, which is intuitively plausible. Because of the possibility of this type of interpretation, the expectation of a random variable is also known as the mean of its distribution. The mean is obviously of some interest to the interviewer in planning his overall work load though, on any particular occasion, he might be more interested in the probability that he will have to miss lunch because no suitable candidate has yet appeared before him. Again, if we wish to emphasize the dependence on the parameter π, we shall write $\mathcal{E}(X|\pi) = \pi^{-1}$ and say that the *conditional expectation* of X *given* π is π^{-1}.

An Aside[1]

A few readers may be curious to see how the expected value π^{-1} can be obtained; and since a simple and possibly useful method is available, we digress for a moment. We have the probability mass function

$$p(x) = (1 - \pi)^{x-1}\pi \qquad \text{for } x = 1, 2, \ldots,$$

and by definition

[1] Reading of this subsection may be deferred without loss of continuity.

$$\mathcal{E}(X) = \sum_{x=1}^{\infty} x(1-\pi)^{x-1}\pi .$$

Now let $y = x - 1$; then, after substituting $y + 1$ for x and distributing the summation, we have

$$\mathcal{E}(X) = \sum_{y=0}^{\infty} y(1-\pi)^y \pi + \sum_{y=0}^{\infty} (1-\pi)^y \pi$$

$$= \left[(1-\pi)\sum_{y=0}^{\infty} y(1-\pi)^{y-1}\pi\right] + \left[(1-\pi)\sum_{y=0}^{\infty}(1-\pi)^{y-1}\pi\right]$$

Consider the first term. In the summation therein, the first term ($y = 0$) is zero, and hence the summation can be written from one to infinity. However, save for the fact that the summation is indexed by the letter y rather than x, this summation is just $\mathcal{E}(X)$. Hence, the first term is $(1 - \pi)\mathcal{E}(X)$. Now consider the second term. The first term of the summation therein ($y = 0$) is $\pi/(1 - \pi)$, and the remaining terms are just the probability mass function of X and, hence, sum to one. Therefore, we have

$$\mathcal{E}(X) = (1-\pi)\mathcal{E}(X) + (1-\pi)\left(\frac{\pi}{1-\pi} + 1\right)$$

and so

$$\mathcal{E}(X) = \pi^{-1}.$$

Discrete and Continuous Random Variables

So far, we have been assuming that the "possible" values of the random variable form a discrete set; that is, if they were plotted as points on a line they would be separated by spaces in which no possible value of the random variable lay. (In practice, the values are often the nonnegative integers.) By contrast, if our "experiment" is that of measuring a person's height, the set of possible values forms a continuum; that is, any point on the line which represents a height between, say, 30 inches for dwarfs and 108 inches for giants will correspond to a possible outcome of the experiment, granted only that we have a sufficiently finely graduated measuring device. We thus have two types of random variables, known as *discrete* and *continuous*, respectively.

Even when, as in the case of test scores, the "possible" observations form a discrete set we may well feel that this reflects a certain crudeness in our measuring instruments, comparable to measuring height "to the nearest inch" rather than reflecting the essence of the measurement being made. From this point of view, we might prefer to regard our random variable as "really" continuous and to interpret a score of 22 as meaning "the random variable" has fallen between $21\frac{1}{2}$ and $22\frac{1}{2}$. (It would be absurd to interpret "three candidates interviewed" as "between $2\frac{1}{2}$ and $3\frac{1}{2}$ interviewed". "Number of candidates interviewed" is a genuinely discrete random variable.)

Carrying these ideas a little further, we obtain a method of writing formulas to express the probability distribution of continuous random variables. Suppose that the possible values of X lie between a and b (see Fig. 3-4.2) and that we can find a function $p(x)$ defined for continuous values of x with the property that the probability of X falling between any two values x_1 and x_2 is given by the shaded *area* under the graph of $p(x)$ between these two points. In particular, the probability that X falls in a small interval of length dx centered at the value x_0 is approximately $p(x_0)\,dx$, that is, the approximate height of the function throughout the interval times the length of the interval. Clearly, since probabilities are nonnegative, we must have $p(x)$ nonnegative at all points between a and b; and since X must fall *somewhere* between a and b, the total area under the graph of $p(x)$ must be unity.

The integral calculus uses the notation $\int_{x_1}^{x_2} p(x)\,dx$ to express the area under the graph of $p(x)$ between x_1 and x_2. The integral sign is merely a variety of S (for sum), and the notation expresses the fact that the area between x_1 and x_2 is the sum of small elements of area of the type $p(x_0)\,dx$ which we have already considered. Availing ourselves of this notation, we can summarize the above discussion by writing

$$\text{Prob}\,(x_1 < X \leq x_2) = \int_{x_1}^{x_2} p(x)\,dx \qquad (3\text{-}4.4)$$

where $\quad p(x) \geq 0$

and $\quad \displaystyle\int_a^b p(x)\,dx = 1.$

In circumstances where the conditions of (3-4.4) are satisfied, we shall call $p(x)$ a *probability density function*. The word density again derives from the idea that a unit mass of probability is distributed along the x axis from a to b. Since we have already noted that the interval dx at x_0 receives an amount $p(x_0)\,dx$ of this mass, $p(x_0)$ is the probability mass per unit length or probability density at the point x_0. An interesting feature of this formulation is that if the interval is reduced to a point, the value $dx = 0$ and thus the probability of any specific point is zero. However, as we indicated previously, this does not imply that specific point values are impossible.

In a manner analogous to (3-4.3), we define the expected value of a continuous random variable X by

$$\mathcal{E}(X) = \int xp(x)\,dx, \qquad (3\text{-}4.5)$$

with interpretations precisely as in the discrete case. Specifically, it is a weighted average of x values, continuously weighted by the function $p(x)$.

The Tabulation of Standard Probability Distributions

In the tabulation of standard probability distributions, and for certain theoretical purposes, the probability Prob $(X \leq x)$ is of particular importance. It is known as the *(cumulative) distribution function* and denoted by $P(x)$. In the case of a continuous random variable, it is the area under the density function to the left of the point x. Thus, if the point $x = x_0$ is specified, then

$$P(x_0) = \int_{-\infty}^{x_0} p(x)\, dx. \qquad (3\text{-}4.6)$$

Note that we use an uppercase P for the cumulative distribution and a lowercase p for the probability mass or density function. In the case of a discrete random variable, $P(x)$ is just the sum of the probabilities of values less than or equal to x:

$$P(x_0) = \sum_{x \leq x_0} \text{Prob}\,(X = x) = \sum_{x \leq x_0} p(x). \qquad (3\text{-}4.7)$$

The obvious properties of the cumulative distribution function are that

$$0 \leq P(x) \leq 1 \quad \text{for all } x$$

and that

$$P(x_2) \geq P(x_1) \quad \text{when } x_2 > x_1.$$

The value x_{mdn} of x such that $P(x_{mdn}) = \frac{1}{2}$, that is, such that the random variable has a 50-50 chance of falling on either side of x_{mdn}, is called the *median* of the distribution. Use of x_{mdn} as our estimate of X minimizes the expected absolute-error loss of prediction. [For a discrete variable, since $P(x)$ increases by "jumps" of amount Prob $(X = x)$, there may be no value of x for which $P(x) = \frac{1}{2}$ exactly. In this case, some additional convention has to be adopted for choosing between, or averaging, the two values most nearly satisfying the equation.]

Many continuous distributions used in statistics are similar to that shown in Fig. 3-4.2, in that the density function increases from zero to a maximum at a point x_{mod} and then falls away to zero again. Such a distribution is called *unimodal*, and the point x_{mod} at which the maximum is attained is called its *mode*. If we have a zero-one loss function, and the length $2c$ of the acceptable (zero-loss) interval is fairly small, it can easily be seen that taking x_{mod} as our estimate of X minimizes the expected loss, since it maximizes the area under the graph which lies within an acceptable distance from the estimate; that is, it maximizes the probability of zero loss. (In Chap. 5, we illustrate some distributions whose density functions are *not* of the form shown in Fig. 3-4.2.) For a discrete distribution, the value of x having the highest probability is taken as the mode. Sometimes the mode of a distribution lies at an extreme value of the variable. However, when the mode lies strictly between the largest and smallest possible values, it is called an interior mode.

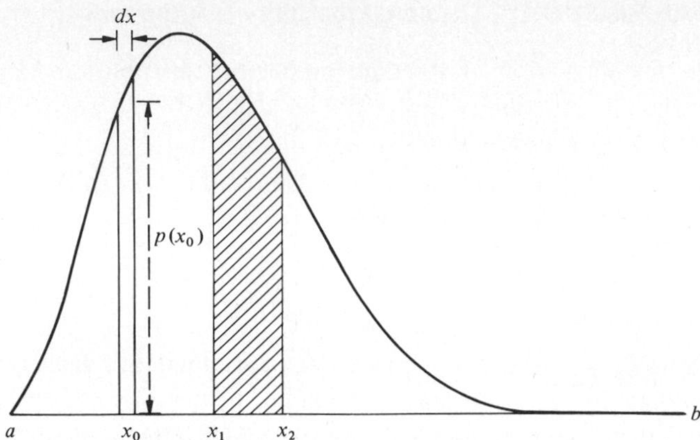

FIGURE 3-4.2
A probability density function.

The reader unfamiliar with the integral calculus will be pleased to learn that while we shall use the integral sign, we shall spare him from having to make any formal operations with it. Earlier in this section, we have explained how the meaning of an integral can be visualized. We now indicate the strategy we shall use in the next few chapters. When new concepts are introduced, they will be discussed first in relation to discrete random variables. In such a context only the summation sign Σ can arise. The reader is then asked to accept that where a formulation for discrete variables involves Σ, the corresponding formulation for continuous variables will involve $\int$. Specifically, to Σ, a summation with respect to x, will correspond $\int \ldots dx$, an integral with respect to x. We have already seen an example of this parallelism in Eqs. (3-4.6) and (3-4.7). In the majority of statistical applications, the sums and integrals will be for all possible values of x, and we shall then not mention the limits of summation/integration.

Actually, we have nearly finished with our use of the integral sign. In applications when we want the probability of an event, we shall simply go to the appropriate set of tables. For example, suppose X is normally distributed with mean zero and variance one, and we are interested in the event A that X lies in the interval $(-1, +1)$. To get Prob (A), we would simply get from Table A.1

$$\text{Prob}\,\{X \leq 1\} = \int_{-\infty}^{1} p(x)\, dx = .8413,$$

where $p(x)$ is the standard normal density function, and subtract from it

$$\text{Prob}\,\{X \leq -1\} = \int_{-\infty}^{-1} p(x)\, dx = .1587,$$

to get Prob (A) = Prob $(-1 \leq X \leq 1) = .8413 - .1587 = .6826$. This example shows that the applied statistician does not really need to be concerned with integrals. He only needs to be able to recognize standard forms and to look things up in tables. It also shows how useful the idea of the random variable is. Imagine trying to write down the probabilities for all of the possible events associated with a continuous random variable. Obviously, it cannot be done explicitly. There are infinitely many possible events, but the probabilities for each of these are theoretically computable by the methods we have described.

Transformations[1]

We shall sometimes be interested in the following problem: If X is a random variable with density function $p(x)$, and Y is some mathematical function of X, can we determine the density function, $g(y)$, of Y? The following are some simple examples:

1) A change of scale:

$$Y = cX,$$

where c is a positive constant.

2) Change of location:

$$Y = X - b,$$

where b is a constant.

3) Standardizing a score:

$$Y = \frac{X - \mu}{\sigma},$$

where μ is the mean of X and σ is the standard deviation of X. This is a combination of (1) and (2).

4) Logarithmic transformation:

$$Y = \ln X$$

where ln denotes the natural or Napierian logarithm.

In each of these cases Y is an increasing function of X. We shall restrict ourselves to such situations for the present.

When X lies between x_1 and x_2, then Y lies between the corresponding values of y_1 and y_2 and vice versa. [For example, in case 1, when X lies between x_1 and x_2, Y lies between cx_1 and cx_2.] Thus, generally, we must have

$$\text{Prob}\,(x_1 < X \leq x_2) = \text{Prob}\,(y_1 < Y \leq y_2).$$

Consider the special case where $x_2 = x_1 + \delta x_1$, with δx_1 small. Then if the scales of X

[1] Reading of this subsection may be deferred without loss of continuity.

and Y are not drastically different, $y_2 = y_1 + \delta y_1$, where δy_1 is also small; and reading $\doteq$ as approximately equal, we have

$$\begin{aligned} p(x_1)\,\delta x_1 &\doteq \text{Prob}\,(x_1 < X \leq x_1 + \delta x_1) \\ &= \text{Prob}\,(y_1 < Y \leq y_1 + \delta y_1) \\ &\doteq g(y_1)\,\delta y_1\,, \end{aligned}$$

or

$$g(y_1) \doteq \frac{p(x_1)}{\delta y_1/\delta x_1}. \tag{3-4.8}$$

Now, imagine that the length δx_1 of the interval we are considering becomes smaller and smaller—in mathematical jargon, "tends to zero". Then, $\delta y_1/\delta x_1$ becomes the instantaneous rate of change of y with x at the point x_1; that is, for a very small region on either side of x_1, it measures the rate at which y increases with x. Such instantaneous rates of change are the subject matter of the differential calculus, which would denote the one under discussion by

$$\left(\frac{dy}{dx}\right)_{x=x_1},$$

and call it the derivative of y with respect to x at the point x_1. Since Eq. (3-4.8) holds at any point x_1, we can drop the subscripts and the reference to the point at which the derivative is to be evaluated and obtain the general equation

$$g(y) = \frac{p(x)}{dy/dx} \tag{3-4.9}$$

which is now exact, not approximate as (3-4.8) was.

The reader who has not studied differential calculus is asked only to note the form of this result; namely, that when one random variable Y is defined as a mathematical function of a random variable X, the density function of Y can be obtained from that of X by a simple process. It is, of course, understood that we shall express the answer in terms of y, using the known relation between y and x. A significant portion of a course in the differential calculus is devoted to learning how to determine the derivatives dy/dx for various functions $y = f(x)$.

Consider again the four examples discussed earlier.

1) A change of scale:

$$Y = cX,$$

where c is a positive constant, $dy/dx = c$. Hence,

$$g(y) = \frac{p(x)}{c} = \frac{p(y/c)}{c}. \tag{3-4.10}$$

2) Change of location:

$$Y = X - b,$$

where b is a constant, $dy/dx = 1$. Hence,

$$g(y) = p(x) = p(y + b).$$

3) Standardizing a score:

$$Z = \frac{X - \mu}{\sigma}, \quad \frac{dz}{dx} = \frac{1}{\sigma}.$$

Hence,

$$g(z) = \sigma p(x) = \sigma p(\mu + \sigma z). \tag{3-4.11}$$

4) Logarithmic transformation of a variable:

$$Y = \ln X, \quad \frac{dy}{dx} = \frac{1}{x}, \quad \text{where } x \geq 0.$$

Hence,

$$g(y) = x\,p(x) = e^y p(e^y). \tag{3-4.12}$$

The results, so far, were obtained assuming that Y increases with X. If Y decreases as X increases, the only change required is to replace dy/dx in (3-4.9) by its absolute value $|dy/dx|$. For example,

$$Y = \frac{1}{X}, \quad \frac{dy}{dx} = -\frac{1}{x^2}.$$

Hence,

$$g(y) = x^2 p(x) = \frac{1}{y^2}\, p\left(\frac{1}{y}\right). \tag{3-4.13}$$

3-5 JOINT DISTRIBUTIONS

Section 3-4 dealt with the situation where each repetition of an experiment results in a single numerical observation. We did note, however, that the result might instead be a set of numbers, e.g., scores on a battery of tests. This is the situation to which we now address ourselves. Of course, each score separately can be considered as a random variable in the manner of the previous section, but this usually throws away valuable information. Indeed, in most of the applications in this book, the "what-goes-with-what" aspect of the data is precisely what we wish to study.

To fix the ideas, consider again the contingency table, Table 2-1.1. For each person, two scores have been observed, a predictor X (ACT score) and a criterion Y (GPA). If we divide the frequency in each cell of the table by the total number of persons (1,000), we obtain the relative frequency of persons having scores corresponding to that cell. When an individual is drawn at random from the population covered by the table, the table of relative frequencies becomes a table of probabilities for that individual's scores: for example, Prob ($1 \leq X \leq 15$ and $2.0 \leq Y \leq 3.0$) = 40/1,000 = .040. The table of probabilities is an example of a *joint probability distribution*. It serves the same purpose for a pair of variables considered jointly that the probability distributions we discussed previously serve for a single variable. A joint probability distribution involving two variables is frequently called a *bivariate* distribution and one involving more than two variables a *multivariate* distribution.

The totals in the margins of the contingency table clearly give, when divided by 1,000, the probability distributions of X and Y separately (for the randomly chosen individual). If we wish to refer to these in a context where the joint distribution is also under discussion, we call them the *marginal distributions* of X and Y, respectively, naming them from their position in the contingency table. For example, the marginal probability that $1 \le X \le 15$ is $164/1{,}000 = .164$.

In the illustration below, the predictor and criterion scores were grouped into class intervals. More generally, we can imagine a (much larger) contingency table in which each possible x is a class on its own, likewise each possible y; and the entries in the cells are the corresponding probabilities. This is the mathematician's joint probability distribution. To obtain a table of manageable size for illustrative purposes, we suppose that in Table 2-1.1 each person with predictor score in the class interval $1 \le X \le 15$ has a score exactly equal to the class mid-value, namely, 8, and similarly for other intervals. If, in addition, we write the relative frequencies in place of the actual frequencies, we obtain the following example of a joint distribution for a randomly sampled person.

Table 3-5.1 SIMPLIFIED JOINT PROBABILITY DISTRIBUTION DERIVED FROM TABLE 2-1.1

$Y \backslash X$	8	18	23	31	$p(y)$
3.5	.015	.101	.061	.032	.209
2.5	.040	.342	.057	.015	.454
1.5	.071	.140	.010	.004	.225
0.5	.038	.069	.004	.001	.112
$p(x)$	.164	.652	.132	.052	1.000

From the way the marginal totals are formed, we evidently have

$$\text{Prob}\,(Y = y) = \sum_x \text{Prob}\,(X = x \text{ and } Y = y). \qquad (3\text{-}5.1)$$

Alternatively, we can view this as a case of axiom K(iii) of Sec. 3-1, since the events ($X = x$ and $Y = y$) for fixed y and varying x are exclusive and together make up the event ($Y = y$). The notation in (3-5.1) is already becoming too cumbersome for use. We simplify it by writing $p(y)$ for Prob ($Y = y$), as in Sec. 3-4, and also writing $p(x, y)$ for Prob ($X = x$ and $Y = y$). Then we have

$$p(y) = \sum_x p(x, y) \qquad (3\text{-}5.2)$$

and similarly

$$p(x) = \sum_y p(x, y). \qquad (3\text{-}5.3)$$

A moment's thought shows that we cannot reconstruct the joint distribution of X and Y from the two marginal distributions, confirming that, in general, the joint distribution contains more information than the collective information in the marginals. An exception would be if we had

$$p(x, y) = p(x)p(y) \quad \textit{for all } x, y. \qquad (3\text{-}5.4)$$

In such a case, we shall say by analogy with (3-3.2) that X and Y are *independent random variables*. Note, however, that independence of two random variables is a much stronger condition than independence of two events, since it asserts that the events $X = x$ and $Y = y$ are independent *for all possible pairs* (x, y).

Now, suppose that we are told the predictor score x of our randomly chosen person. Our situation is completely changed. We are no longer interested in the whole contingency table (the joint distribution) but only in that column which corresponds to the subpopulation consisting of persons with predictor score $X = x$ or to some grouping of x scores, for example, $16 \leq X \leq 20$. In this subpopulation, the probability that a person's criterion score is y is clearly obtained by dividing the frequency in the (x, y) cell by the marginal frequency for x or, what comes to the same thing, dividing the probability $p(x, y)$ for the (x, y) cell of the joint distribution by the marginal probability $p(x)$. Thus, for example, if we are told that $X = 18$, the probability that $Y = 1.5$ is $.140/.652 = .215$.

The probability just referred to is a conditional probability, conditional on our knowledge that $X = 18$. What we have noted is that

$$\text{Prob}\,(Y = y|X = x) = \frac{\text{Prob}\,(X = x \text{ and } Y = y)}{\text{Prob}\,(X = x)}, \qquad (3\text{-}5.5)$$

or, extending our reduced notation to conditional probabilities,

$$p(y|x) = \frac{p(x, y)}{p(x)}. \qquad (3\text{-}5.6)$$

If we go back to Eq. (3-2.1) which defined conditional probability and take A to be the event $Y = y$, B the event $X = x$, we obtain (3-5.5). However, two things are new here. First, the contingency table provides a way of visualizing the meaning of conditional probability which many people find very useful. Second, (3-5.5) is not just one statement but a whole series of statements. If we keep x fixed (stay in one column of the table), considering each possible value of Y in turn gives us a complete set of probabilities

Prob $(Y = y|X = x)$ or $p(y|x)$. In fact, it gives us a probability distribution, the *conditional distribution of* Y *given* x. Similarly, by fixing y (staying in one row of the contingency table), we obtain for the conditional distribution of X given y

$$p(x|y) = \frac{p(x, y)}{p(y)}. \qquad (3\text{-}5.7)$$

Notice that if X and Y are independent, Eqs. (3-5.4) and (3-5.6) give us $p(y|x) = p(y)$ for all x; that is, our probability distribution for Y is unaltered by the information that $X = x$, and so, that information is irrelevant to problems concerning Y.

The concept of independence of random variables can be extended to any number of variables. Random variables $X, Y, Z, \ldots$ are said to be *mutually independent* if

$$p(x, y, z, \ldots) = p(x)p(y)p(z) \ldots, \qquad (3\text{-}5.8)$$

for all $x, y, z, \ldots$. Note that it is not necessary here to include as part of the definition the condition that this equation hold for all subsets of variables—this can be shown to follow from the basic definition. Thus, $p(x, y, z) = p(x)p(y)p(z)$, for all x, y, z, implies $p(x, y) = p(x)p(y)$, etc.

3-6 BAYES' THEOREM FOR RANDOM VARIABLES

In Sec. 3-2 we introduced Bayes' theorem for events. Applications of this theorem show how prior probabilities for events should be modified by data to yield posterior probabilities for these events. In that section we dealt only with experiments that had a very limited number of possible outcomes. Now we wish to extend the theorem to situations in which there are many, perhaps infinitely many, possible outcomes. We have laid the groundwork for this by introducing the concept of the random variable and by defining joint and conditional probabilities for random variables. The derivation of Bayes' theorem for random variables is now very easy.

From (3-5.6) and (3-5.7), we have

$$p(x, y) = p(y|x)p(x) = p(x|y)p(y), \qquad (3\text{-}6.1)$$

and so,

$$\begin{aligned} p(y|x) &= \frac{p(x|y)p(y)}{p(x)} \\ &= \frac{p(x|y)p(y)}{\sum_y p(x, y)} \quad \text{(by 3-5.3)} \qquad (3\text{-}6.2) \\ &= \frac{p(x|y)p(y)}{\sum_y p(x|y)p(y)} \quad \text{(by 3-5.7).} \qquad (3\text{-}6.3) \end{aligned}$$

A comparison with (3-2.3) shows that this is simply Bayes' theorem extended from events to probability distributions. This theorem is the basis of all the remaining work we shall be doing. We shall discuss its interpretation in Chap. 5.

Meanwhile, we may note one feature which we shall use repeatedly. For the reasons given in Sec. 3-4, the case which is of real interest is not when the joint distribution is given by a table, but when it can be represented by a formula. In that case, it is clear that the formula for the marginal distribution $p(x)$ will involve x only, not y. Thus, when we are interested only in the way that $p(y|x)$ varies with y, we can write (3-6.2) as

$$p(y|x) \propto p(x|y)p(y), \qquad (3\text{-}6.4)$$

where $\propto$ indicates proportionality rather than equality. The implication is that equality can be obtained by multiplying the right-hand side by something that does not depend on y. What is more, we can always recover the constant of proportionality, if necessary, by recalling that $p(y|x)$ is a probability function for Y; and so the sum $\Sigma p(y|x)$ of all the probability mass elements is equal to unity.

In practice, what we hope to do is to recognize that the form of $p(y|x)$, as a function of y, is that of one of the several standard probability distributions that we shall be studying in later chapters.

A further word should be said about the marginal densities $p(y)$ and $p(x)$. Equation (3-5.2) shows that

$$p(x) = \sum_y p(x, y).$$

However, from (3-5.7), we have

$$p(x, y) = p(x|y)p(y).$$

Hence,

$$p(x) = \sum_y p(x|y)p(y), \qquad (3\text{-}6.5)$$

as seen, for example, in the denominator of (3-6.3). This equation makes clear the fact that the marginal probability function of X is the average of the conditional probability functions of X given y, averaged with respect to the marginal probability function of Y.

In the continuous case, a bivariate distribution is expressed by means of its density function $g(x, y)$. There are two useful ways of thinking about this density. One is to imagine the total unit mass of probability spread on the (x, y) plane in such a way that the probability mass falling in a rectangle $dx\,dy$ centered at the point (x, y) is approximately $g(x, y)\,dx\,dy$. Alternatively, we may extend the idea that probability for a single continuous random variable can be thought of as area under its density curve. For a bivariate distribution, we imagine a density surface, which will look like a hill or mound with the (x, y) plane for its base. The value of $g(x, y)$ gives the height of the mound above

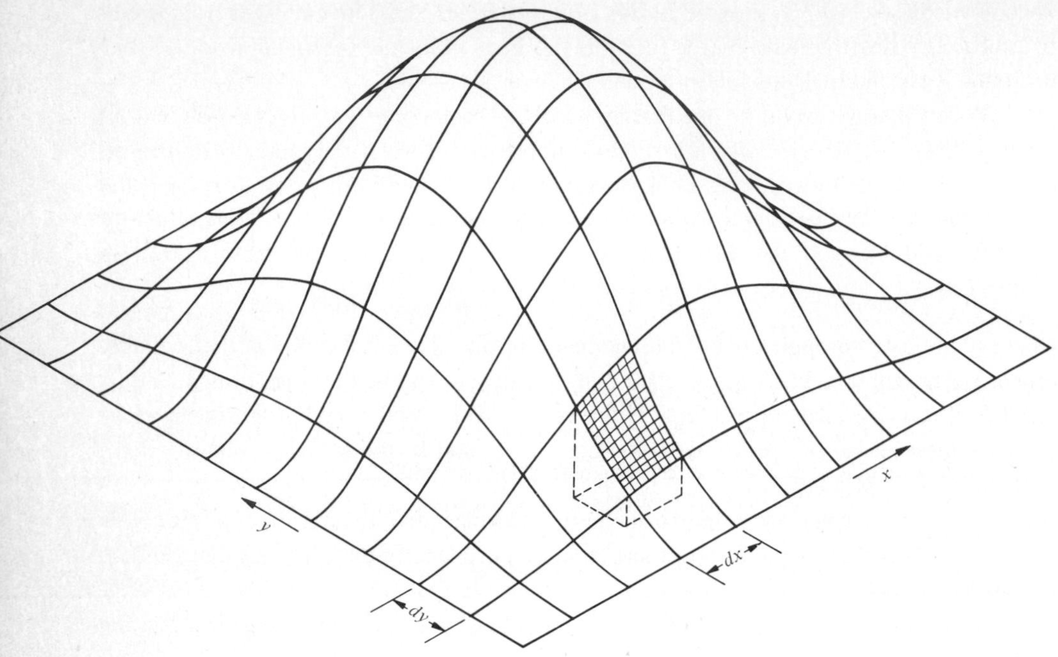

FIGURE 3-6.1
Bivariate continuous density function.

the point (x, y) of the base, and the probability falling in the rectangle $dx\,dy$ corresponds to the volume of the mound which stands vertically above that rectangle.

For making formal operations with continuous joint densities, we shall adopt the same strategy as in Sec. 3-4. There, we used the same symbol $p(x)$ for the probability $\text{Prob}(X = x)$ in the discrete case and for the probability density function in the continuous case. Similarly, $p(x, y)$ will stand for $\text{Prob}\,(X = x \text{ and } Y = y)$ in the discrete case and for the density which we called $g(x, y)$ above in the continuous case. Initially, this convention may seem more a source of confusion than a simplification. In the discrete case $p(x, y)$ is a probability, while in the continuous case, it is $p(x, y)\,dx\,dy$ which is a probability; and one must recall which meaning is relevant before interpreting the symbols. However, the gain far outweighs this inconvenience as is readily seen in regard to the equations developed in this section and the previous one. Adopting our convention, it can be shown that (3-5.2), (3-5.3), (3-6.3), and (3-6.5) are true for continuous densities, subject only to the replacement of the summation by an integration; and that (3-5.4), (3-5.6), (3-5.7), (3-5.8), (3-6.1), (3-6.2), and (3-6.4) are true without any alteration at all.

In concluding this chapter it is important to note that we have not attempted to give any sort of complete treatment of probability theory. Rather, we have selected for presentation just those topics necessary for use in succeeding chapters together with minimum necessary further material to provide an integrated treatment of these topics. Some very basic concepts in probability theory, including Chebyshev's inequality, the laws of large numbers (weak and strong), and the Central Limit Theorem have not even been mentioned. We hope that some of our readers will be intrigued enough by probability theory and its application as seen in the remainder of this book to devote some time to a thorough study of this topic. If so, they should find that the overview that they have received here will provide a useful framework for this detailed study.

3-7 EXERCISES

1 You give a friend a letter to mail. The probability that he mails it is .99. The probability that the post office fails to deliver it, given that it was mailed, is .10. Find Prob (letter mailed *and* post office fails to deliver it).

2 Consider the political party example of Sec. 3-2. Suppose $\text{Prob}(F|D) = p$ and $\text{Prob}(F|R) = p/2$. Find $\text{Prob}(D|F)$ and note that it does not depend on p.

3 Training methods A, B, and C are used, respectively, on 20, 30, and 50 percent of a certain school population. Suppose the probability of a student being found unqualified after training in the respective methods is .01, .02, and .04, respectively, for methods A, B, and C. What is the probability that a person taken at random was given training method C, given that he is found to be unqualified?

4 A certain disease is present in about 2 out of 1,000 persons in a given population, and a program of testing is to be carried out using a detection device which gives a positive reading with probability .98 for a diseased person and with probability .04 for a healthy person. Find the probability that a person who has a positive reading actually does have the disease.

5 In a large midwestern school, 1% of the student body participates in the music program; 40% of these people have a grade point of 3 or better (out of 4) whereas 20% of the remainder of the student body have a grade point of 3 or more. What proportion of the total student body have a grade point of 3 or more? Suppose we select one student at random from the student body and find that he has a grade point of 3.45. What is the probability that he participates in the music program?

6 From Table 3-2.1 compute the probability that a student is in each of the MCAT categories, given that he withdraws from medical school. Why is the probability that the student is in the lowest MCAT category lower than the probability that he is in either of the other two categories? Wouldn't some people think that the fact that a student withdraws is more supportive of the thesis that he is in the low MCAT category rather than in the higher one?

7 Construct a contingency table along the lines of the one at the end of Sec. 3-2 so that $\text{Prob}(L_T) < \text{Prob}(H_T)$, $\text{Prob}(H_T|S) > \text{Prob}(L_T|S)$, $\text{Prob}(S) = .50$, and $\text{Prob}(S|H_T) = \text{Prob}(S|L_T)$.

8 Suppose $\text{Prob}(AB|C) = k\,\text{Prob}(C|A)$ and $\text{Prob}(B|C) = m\,\text{Prob}(C)$ with $k < m$. For what value of Prob (A) will A and B be independent given C? [*Hint:* Use (3-2.1).]

9 Consider the points (1,0,0), (1,1,0), (1,1,1), (0,1,1), (0,0,1), and (0,0,0) in a three-dimensional coordinate system and suppose that the probabilities of these points are, respectively, $\frac{1}{8}$, $\frac{1}{4}$, $\frac{1}{8}$, $\frac{1}{8}$, $\frac{1}{4}$, and $\frac{1}{8}$. Let A_1 be the event: "A one occurs in the first coordinate position". Let A_2 be the event: "A one occurs in the second coordinate position". Let A_3 be the event: "A one occurs in the third coordinate position". Calculate:
(*a*) Prob (A_1), Prob (A_2), Prob (A_3)
(*b*) Prob (A_1, A_2, A_3).
Demonstrate that although

$$\text{Prob}(A_1, A_2, A_3) = \text{Prob}(A_1)\,\text{Prob}(A_2)\,\text{Prob}(A_3)$$

the events are not mutually independent.

10 In one of Mendel's experiments with peas, he encountered this joint distribution:

	Color:	
Texture	Yellow	Green
Smooth	9/16	3/16
Wrinkled	3/16	1/16

What is the conditional distribution of color for wrinkled peas?

4
REGRESSION AND CORRELATION WITH APPLICATION TO THE ESTIMATION OF ABILITY

In Chaps. 1 through 3, we have discussed the concepts of error, estimation, and prediction. We shall now present a general theory encompassing these concepts and underpinning the specific methods to be developed in later chapters. We will also, in Secs. 4-5 through 4-7, use these concepts to build the basis for a coherent theory of measurement, by discussing the estimation of true-score and error variation in measurement. The general theory presented also provides the basis of more advanced methods such as analysis of variance, which we shall not study specifically in this text. Throughout this chapter, we deal with the syntactic development of a mathematical system, though we give a number of direct applications to data to show the semantic uses to which the system will be put.

4-1 THE ALGEBRA OF EXPECTATIONS

In this section, we extend the idea of expectation to functions of random variables, discuss some cases of special importance, and list a number of results having frequent application. Proofs generally are not given. They consist of algebraic manipulation of the definitions, and the algebraically minded reader, wishing to verify some of the results for himself, should have little difficulty in doing so.

For discrete random variables, we have defined the expectation of X as $\Sigma xp(x)$, this being a weighted average of the valued of X with respect to the probability function $p(x)$. We can similarly consider the expectation of X^2 which would be written $\mathcal{E}(X^2) = \Sigma x^2 p(x)$, and we can consider the function $[X - \mathcal{E}(X)]^2$ and its expectation

$$\mathcal{V}(X) = \mathcal{E}\{[X - \mathcal{E}(X)]^2\} = \Sigma [x - \mathcal{E}(X)]^2 p(x) \qquad (4\text{-}1.1)$$

which is the *variance* of X. The variance is the smallest attainable value of the expected squared-error loss in predicting X when the distribution $p(x)$ is known, and is attained by using $\mathcal{E}(X)$ as estimate. We gave an example of this in Sec. 1-2 where the population in which the random variable was defined was the particular sample at hand. Note that at times in this chapter we shall use $\mathcal{E}$ and $\mathcal{V}$, respectively, to denote the taking of an expectation and a variance. At other times we shall use μ and σ^2, respectively, to denote certain expected values and variances.

The square root of the variance, the *standard deviation*, is used as a measure of the dispersion or spread of a distribution. With a normal distribution, for example, 50% of the observed values may be expected to fall within .6745 standard deviations on either side of the mean. Similar results hold for other distributions. In general, the smaller the standard deviation of a distribution the more probability is concentrated around the mean (the expected value) of the distribution.

More generally, we can consider arbitrary functions $\psi(X)$ and their expectations written

$$\mathcal{E}[\psi(X)] = \Sigma \psi(x) p(x) . \qquad (4\text{-}1.2)$$

We think of this as the weighted average of $\psi(x)$ with respect to the probability function $p(x)$. Two special and useful results arise when $\psi(X)$ is a linear function of X. First we have

$$\mathcal{E}(a + bX) = a + b\mathcal{E}(X) . \qquad (4\text{-}1.3)$$

Thus, $\mathcal{E}(2 + 3X) = 2 + 3\mathcal{E}(X)$, and if $\mathcal{E}(X) = 2$, then $\mathcal{E}(2 + 3X) = 8$. Now consider the same linear function $a + bX$. Its variance, $\mathcal{V}(a + bX)$, is

$$\mathcal{E}\left\{[(a + bX) - \mathcal{E}(a + bX)]^2\right\} .$$

Some algebra yields the result

$$\mathcal{V}(a + bX) = b^2 \mathcal{V}(X) . \qquad (4\text{-}1.4)$$

Thus, *the variance of a random variable is unaffected by the addition of a constant, but it is multiplied by the square of any constant multiplying the scale of measurement of the random variable*. Thus,

$$\mathcal{V}(2 + 3X) = 9\mathcal{V}(X).$$

For a function $\psi(X, Y)$ of two random variables with a joint distribution $p(x, y)$, the expected value is defined as

$$\mathcal{E}[\psi(X, Y)] = \sum_{\substack{\text{all}\\ y}} \sum_{\substack{\text{all}\\ x}} \psi(x, y) p(x, y) .$$

An important special case of this is when $\psi(X, Y) = X + Y$. It can then be shown that

$$\mathcal{E}(X + Y) = \mathcal{E}(X) + \mathcal{E}(Y) , \qquad (4\text{-}1.5)$$

the expectation of a sum is equal to the sum of the expectations, which is true even if X and Y are dependent.

Another important joint expectation is the *covariance*

$$\mathcal{C}(X, Y) = \mathcal{E}\left\{[X - \mathcal{E}(X)][Y - \mathcal{E}(Y)]\right\} . \qquad (4\text{-}1.6)$$

Note that $\mathcal{C}(X, Y) = \mathcal{C}(Y, X)$ and $\mathcal{C}(X, X) = \mathcal{V}(X)$. If Y has a general tendency to increase as X increases, Y will be larger (smaller) than its expected value on most occasions when X is larger (smaller) than its expected value. Hence, the covariance will be positive. Conversely, a negative covariance indicates that Y tends to decrease as X increases. If X and Y are independent, $\mathcal{C}(X, Y) = 0$; however, if $\mathcal{C}(X, Y) = 0$, X and Y are not necessarily independent.

A useful property of covariances is that they satisfy the distributive law; that is to say, if U, V, and W are any functions of X and Y,

$$\mathcal{C}(U, V + W) = \mathcal{C}(U, V) + \mathcal{C}(U, W) , \qquad (4\text{-}1.7)$$

a result which extends to covariances involving sums of more than two terms. As a particular case, note that

$$\begin{aligned} \mathcal{V}(X + Y) &= \mathcal{C}(X + Y, X + Y) \\ &= \mathcal{C}(X, X) + \mathcal{C}(X, Y) + \mathcal{C}(Y, X) + \mathcal{C}(Y, Y) \\ &= \mathcal{V}(X) + 2\mathcal{C}(X, Y) + \mathcal{V}(Y) . \end{aligned}$$

This result also extends in an obvious way to the variance of a sum of more than two terms. Note that in the special case of independent variables, the variance of the sum is the sum of the variances. Another property of covariances is that they are unaffected by changes in location, that is, $\mathcal{C}(X + a, Y + b) = \mathcal{C}(X, Y)$.

We have so far considered expectations with respect to marginal distributions and with respect to joint distributions. We now turn to the conditional distribution $p(y|x)$. Recall that this is, for fixed x, a probability distribution for Y, and so definitions (3-4.3) and (4-1.1) apply. No completely satisfactory notation for the resulting expectation and variance exists. The choice lies between a totally consistent notation which clutters the symbols $\mathcal{E}$ and $\mathcal{V}$ with a variety of subscripts indicating the distributions to which they refer and a much simpler but slightly inconsistent notation which relies on the common sense of the reader to use it correctly. We adopt the second choice and denote the mean and variance of the conditional distribution by $\mathcal{E}(Y|x)$ and $\mathcal{V}(Y|x)$.

The two fundamental results involving these quantities are

$$\mathcal{E}(Y) = \mathcal{E}\left[\mathcal{E}(Y|x)\right] \qquad (4\text{-}1.8)$$

and

$$\mathcal{V}(Y) = \mathcal{V}\left[\mathcal{E}(Y|x)\right] + \mathcal{E}\left[\mathcal{V}(Y|x)\right]. \qquad (4\text{-}1.9)$$

Loosely speaking, Eq. (4-1.8) states that the mean of Y is the weighted average of the conditional means of Y given x. That common sense requires (4-1.8) to be read in this way can be seen as follows. The inner expectation on the right-hand side is taken with respect to the conditional distribution; the result is a function of X, and so the outer expectation must be with respect to the marginal distribution of X (though we would obtain the same result evaluating it with respect to the joint distribution). More technically, the first equation states that the expectation of Y, evaluated with respect to the marginal distribution of Y, is the same as the expectation, evaluated with respect to the marginal distribution of X, of the expectation of Y evaluated with respect to the conditional distribution of Y given x.

Equation (4-1.9) expresses the variance of Y as the sum of two distinct components. The first component, $\mathcal{V}\left[\mathcal{E}(Y|x)\right]$, is the variance of the conditional means of Y given x. This is referred to as the between-group variance in the simple one-way analysis of variance model. The second component, $\mathcal{E}\left[\mathcal{V}(Y|x)\right]$, is the average or expected value of the variances for each subpopulation of Y as given by x. In analysis-of-variance terminology, this is referred to as the average within-group variance. Thus, loosely speaking, Eq. (4-1.9) states that the total variance is equal to the variance between groups plus the expected variance within groups.

The meaning of Eqs. (4-1.8) and (4-1.9) can best be understood through application. Consider the probabilities given in Table 3-5.1. Now, analogously to (4-1.8), we can write

$$\mathcal{E}(X) = \mathcal{E}\left[\mathcal{E}(X|y)\right]. \qquad (4\text{-}1.10)$$

To verify (4-1.10), first evaluate the left-hand side of the equation. The marginal probabilities for the values 8, 18, 23, and 31 of X are .164, .652, .132, and .052, respectively. Thus,

$$\begin{aligned} \mathcal{E}(X) &= \Sigma x p(x) \\ &= (.164)(8) + (.652)(18) + (.132)(23) + (.052)(31) \\ &= 17.696. \end{aligned}$$

The evaluation of the right-hand side of Eq. (4-1.10) proceeds by systematically calculating $\mathcal{E}(X|y)$ for each of the possible values of y and then averaging these values with respect to the marginal density of Y.

Step 1 Computation of $\mathcal{E}(X|y)$, for the various values of y:

(*a*) Computation of $\mathcal{E}(X|Y = 3.5)$

$$P(X = 8|Y = 3.5) = \frac{.015}{.209} = .072, \quad \text{approximately}$$

$$P(X = 18|Y = 3.5) = \frac{.101}{.209} = .483, \quad \text{approximately}$$

$$P(X = 23|Y = 3.5) = \frac{.061}{.209} = .292, \quad \text{approximately}$$

$$P(X = 31|Y = 3.5) = \frac{.032}{.209} = .153, \quad \text{approximately}$$

$$\begin{aligned}\mathcal{E}(X|Y = 3.5) &= (.072)(8) + (.483)(18) + (.292)(23) + (.153)(31)\\ &= 20.729.\end{aligned}$$

If a greater number of digits are carried in the computation we obtain $\mathcal{E}(X|Y = 3.5) = 20.732$.

(*b*) Computation of $\mathcal{E}(X|Y = 2.5)$

$$P(X = 8|Y = 2.5) = \frac{.040}{.454} = .088$$

$$P(X = 18|Y = 2.5) = \frac{.342}{.454} = .753$$

$$P(X = 23|Y = 2.5) = \frac{.057}{.454} = .126$$

$$P(X = 31|Y = 2.5) = \frac{.015}{.454} = .033.$$

$$\begin{aligned}\mathcal{E}(X|Y = 2.5) &= (.088)(8) + (.753)(18) + (.126)(23) + (.033)(31)\\ &= 18.176, \quad \text{if sufficient digits are carried.}\end{aligned}$$

We now omit parts of the computations—some readers may wish to do these themselves.

(*c*) $$\begin{aligned}\mathcal{E}(X|Y = 1.5) &= (.316)(8) + (.622)(18) + (.044)(23) + (.018)(31)\\ &= 15.298.\end{aligned}$$

(*d*) $$\begin{aligned}\mathcal{E}(X|Y = 0.5) &= (.339)(8) + (.616)(18) + (.036)(23) + (.009)(31)\\ &= 14.902.\end{aligned}$$

Step 2 Computation of the expected value of $\mathcal{E}(X|y)$:

$$\begin{aligned}\mathcal{E}[\mathcal{E}(X|y)] &= \sum_i \mathcal{E}(X|Y = y_i)p(y_i)\\ &= (20.732)(.209) + (18.176)(.454)\\ &\qquad + (15.298)(.225) + (14.902)(.112)\\ &= 17.696, \quad \text{which verifies (4-1.10)}.\end{aligned}$$

The verification of (4-1.9) is more tedious but proceeds in a similar manner.

Analogously to (4-1.9), we can write

$$\mathcal{V}(X) = \mathcal{E}[\mathcal{V}(X|y)] + \mathcal{V}[\mathcal{E}(X|y)]. \quad (4\text{-}1.11)$$

To verify (4-1.11), first evaluate the left-hand side of the equation. By (4-1.1), note that

$$\mathcal{V}(X) = \mathcal{E}\{[X - \mathcal{E}(X)]^2\} = \mathcal{E}(X^2) - [\mathcal{E}(X)]^2.$$

Recall that $\mathcal{E}(X) = 17.696$. For $\mathcal{E}(X^2)$, we have

$$(.164)(64) + (.652)(324) + (.132)(529) + (.052)(961) = 341.544.$$

Thus,

$$\mathcal{V}(X) = 341.544 - (17.696)^2 = 28.396.$$

The evaluation of the right-hand side of (4-1.11) proceeds as follows:

Step 1 The within-group variances are

$$\begin{aligned}
(a)\quad \mathcal{V}(X|Y = 3.5) &= \frac{.015}{.209}(8 - 20.732)^2 + \frac{.101}{.209}(18 - 20.732)^2 \\
&\quad + \frac{.061}{.209}(23 - 20.732)^2 \\
&\quad + \frac{.032}{.209}(31 - 20.732)^2 \\
&= 32.885 \\
(b)\quad \mathcal{V}(X|Y = 2.5) &= 17.502 \\
(c)\quad \mathcal{V}(X|Y = 1.5) &= 28.369 \\
(d)\quad \mathcal{V}(X|Y = 0.5) &= 26.731.
\end{aligned}$$

Step 2 The average within group variance is

$$\begin{aligned}
\mathcal{E}[\mathcal{V}(X|y)] &= \sum_i [\mathcal{V}(X|y_i)]p(y_i) \\
&= (.209)(32.885) + (.454)(17.502) \\
&\qquad + (.225)(28.369) + (.112)(26.731) \\
&= 24.196.
\end{aligned}$$

Step 3 The variance of the conditional expectations is

$$\begin{aligned}
\mathcal{V}[\mathcal{E}(X|y)] &= \sum_i [\mathcal{E}(X|Y = y_i) - \mathcal{E}(X)]^2 p(y_i) \\
&= (20.732 - 17.696)^2(.209) + (18.176 - 17.696)^2(.454) \\
&\qquad + (15.298 - 17.696)^2(.225) \\
&\qquad + (14.902 - 17.696)^2(.112) \\
&= 4.200.
\end{aligned}$$

Step 4 The unconditional (total) variance is equal to the expected conditional (within) variance plus the (between) variance of the conditional expectations.

$$\begin{aligned}\mathcal{V}(X) &= \mathcal{E}[\mathcal{V}(X|y)] + \mathcal{V}[\mathcal{E}(X|y)] \\ &= 24.196 + 4.200 \\ &= 28.396, \qquad \text{which verifies (4-1.11)}.\end{aligned}$$

Thus, we have shown that the mean and variance of X can be computed from the bivariate frequency table in two ways. First, they were computed using the marginal distribution on X. Second, they were computed using the conditional distributions of X for each value of Y. As an exercise, the reader may wish to compute the mean and variance of Y from Table 3-5.1 using both procedures illustrated above.

4-2 REGRESSION FUNCTIONS AND CORRELATION RATIOS

In this section, we consider a way of describing the nature and extent of the relation between two random variables having a joint distribution. While reading this section, readers are asked to hold in suspense any previous knowledge they have of regression *lines* and correlation *coefficients*.

Consider the joint distribution in Table 3-5.1, and suppose that we are told x and asked to predict Y. In Sec. 3-5, we saw that the relevant distribution is $p(y|x)$. The expected squared-error loss in predicting Y is minimized by taking as our estimate the conditional mean of Y in the subpopulation $X = x$, which we have denoted by $\mathcal{E}(Y|x)$.

For example, suppose we are told that $X = 18$. The conditional probabilities for $Y = 0.5, 1.5, 2.5$, and 3.5 are, respectively, $.069/.652 = .106$, $.140/.652 = .215$, $.342/.652 = .524$, and $.101/.652 = .155$ (check that these sum to 1). Hence, the conditional expectation is

$$\begin{aligned}\mathcal{E}(Y|X = 18) &= (.106)(.5) + (.215)(1.5) + (.524)(2.5) + (.155)(3.5) \\ &= 2.228.\end{aligned}$$

Proceeding in this way, we find the set of conditional expectations

x	8	18	23	31
$\mathcal{E}(Y\|x)$	1.695	2.228	2.826	3.000

. (4-2.1)

The function $\mathcal{E}(Y|x)$ giving the various conditional expectations is known as the *regression function*: It gives our "best" estimates of the criterion using squared-error loss.

How good is our "best"? The natural way to assess this is to see how much we have gained by being told x. Without that information, we would have used $\mathcal{E}(Y)$ as estimate, and our expected loss would have been $\mathcal{V}(Y)$. Knowing x, we use $\mathcal{E}(Y|x)$; and our expected loss is $\mathcal{V}(Y|x)$, a "reduction" of $\mathcal{V}(Y) - \mathcal{V}(Y|x)$ for the particular value of x. However, this is only the "gain" for one particular value of x. What really interests us is the average gain, $\mathcal{V}(Y) - \mathcal{E}[\mathcal{V}(Y|x)]$ resulting from knowledge of the whole regression function. Expressing this gain as a fraction of the original expected loss $\mathcal{V}(Y)$, we obtain the *correlation ratio*

$$\eta^2 = \frac{\mathcal{V}(Y) - \mathcal{E}[\mathcal{V}(Y|x)]}{\mathcal{V}(Y)} = 1 - \frac{\mathcal{E}[\mathcal{V}(Y|x)]}{\mathcal{V}(Y)} \tag{4-2.2}$$

$$= \frac{\mathcal{V}[\mathcal{E}(Y|x)]}{\mathcal{V}(Y)}, \quad \text{using (4-1.9)}. \tag{4-2.3}$$

Perhaps it is worth noting that for some values of x we may have $\mathcal{V}(Y) < \mathcal{V}(Y|x)$, but we will always have $\mathcal{V}(Y) \geq \mathcal{E}[\mathcal{V}(Y|x)]$.

Since variances are nonnegative, η^2 lies between zero and one. It takes the value one when Y is an exact function of X, and so $\mathcal{V}(Y|x)$ in (4-2.2) is zero for all x. In this case, we have perfect prediction. The correlation ratio is zero when all the conditional means $\mathcal{E}(Y|x)$ in (4-2.3) are the same, and so, by (4-1.8), are equal to $\mathcal{E}(Y)$. In this case, knowledge of X is of no value for squared-error-loss prediction. Intermediate values of η^2 indicate the degree of predictability of Y from knowledge of X. For the distribution given in Table 3-5.1, $\eta^2 = .148$.

4-3 LINEAR REGRESSION AND CORRELATION COEFFICIENTS

The regression function, as defined in the previous section, may or may not be linear. A graph of the regression function (4-2.1) shows that in that case the function is approximately, but not exactly, linear. As we have previously indicated, our real interest lies in the case where the joint distribution is given not by a table, but by a formula involving x and y. In this case, the regression function $\mathcal{E}(Y|x)$ will be given by a formula involving x, and the regression will be linear if that function is of the form $\mathcal{E}(Y|x) = \alpha + \beta x$.

Several different lines of thought lead to the consideration of regression *lines*. Since considerable confusion often exists at this point, it is worth enumerating some of them. First, in several of the standard joint distributions in common use, the regression function $\mathcal{E}(Y|x)$ *is* linear. This is true of the bivariate normal distribution and of the trinomial distribution, a special case of the multinomial distribution discussed in Chap. 10. In such cases, the concepts of regression function and regression line coincide.

Second, we frequently use a "regression model", which specifies certain properties of the conditional distributions $p(y|x)$, including the fact that the regression function is linear, without completely specifying the joint distribution.

Third, it is conceivable that we might have a joint distribution in which the regression function is not or not known to be linear, but still demand to use a linear-prediction function on the ground that the gain in simplicity outweighs any possible loss in predictive efficiency. We then require to determine the linear function

$$R(Y|x) = \alpha + \beta x \tag{4-3.1}$$

which "best" predicts Y. The expected squared-error loss using $R(Y|x)$ is

$$\mathcal{E}(Y - \alpha - \beta X)^2 \qquad (4\text{-}3.2)$$

and "best" will mean choosing α and β so as to minimize this.

The calculations needed to determine the values of α and β which minimize (4-3.2) are closely analogous to those used in Sec. 1-2 to find the straight line which best predicts y values from x values in the sample. The result is that (4-3.2) is minimized by taking

$$\beta = \frac{\mathcal{C}(X, Y)}{\mathcal{V}(X)} \quad \text{and} \quad \alpha = \mathcal{E}(Y) - \beta\mathcal{E}(X), \qquad (4\text{-}3.3)$$

and that the expected loss is then

$$\mathcal{V}(Y) - \frac{[\mathcal{C}(X, Y)]^2}{\mathcal{V}(X)}. \qquad (4\text{-}3.4)$$

Thus, by using the linear-prediction function, we are able to reduce our squared-error loss by $[\mathcal{C}(X, Y)]^2/\mathcal{V}(X)$. Expressing this as a fraction of the original expected loss $\mathcal{V}(Y)$, we obtain the squared *correlation coefficient,*

$$\rho^2 = \frac{[\mathcal{C}(X, Y)]^2}{\mathcal{V}(X)\mathcal{V}(Y)}. \qquad (4\text{-}3.5)$$

(The reader will have noted a close parallel between the development in this section and the previous one. Unfortunately, although η^2 and ρ^2 are the analogous quantities, long-established custom calls η^2 the correlation ratio but calls ρ the correlation coefficient.) In taking the square root of (4-3.5), ρ is taken to have the same sign as $\mathcal{C}(X, Y)$. The result always lies in the range from -1 to $+1$. For the distribution in Table 3-5.1, we have $\rho = +.372$ and $\rho^2 = .138$. Note that ρ^2 is only slightly lower than η^2, showing that in this case the regression *line* is almost as good for prediction as the regression *function*; the true regression is almost linear. If the true regression were exactly linear, the correlation coefficient and the correlation ratio would be equal.

A reduced notation is useful for discussing regression and correlation (and in other contexts also). We write $\mu_X = \mathcal{E}(X)$, $\mu_Y = \mathcal{E}(Y)$, chosing the letter "mu" to correspond to the first letter of "mean". We also write $\sigma_X = \sqrt{\mathcal{V}(X)}$, $\sigma_Y = \sqrt{\mathcal{V}(Y)}$, and call these quantities *standard deviations* (again choosing "sigma" to correspond to the first letter of standard deviation).

If the *linear-regression function* $R(Y|x)$ is plotted as a graph, the equation of the *regression line* will be $y = \alpha + \beta x$, which becomes, using (4-3.3),

$$(y - \mu_Y) = \beta(x - \mu_X), \qquad (4\text{-}3.6)$$

showing that the line passes through the point whose coordinates are the means of the X and Y distributions. This point is conveniently referred to as the *centroid*. It is the center of gravity when the joint distribution is thought of as a distribution of probability mass on the (x, y) plane.

The slope of the regression line is β, which is called the *regression coefficient of* Y *on* x, indicating that it pertains to the line appropriate for estimating Y from x. From (4-3.5), we have

$$\mathcal{C}(X, Y) = \rho\sigma_X\sigma_Y, \tag{4-3.7}$$

and so

$$\beta = \frac{\rho\sigma_Y}{\sigma_X}. \tag{4-3.8}$$

There will be a different line appropriate for estimating X from y, and its slope will be the regression coefficient of X on y given by the formula $\beta = \rho\sigma_X/\sigma_Y$. Where it is not clear from the context which regression slope is meant, the notations $\beta_{Y \cdot x}$ and $\beta_{X \cdot y}$, respectively, are used to indicate the regression coefficient for Y on x and for X on y. The expected loss given by (4-3.4) can be written

$$\sigma_Y^2(1 - \rho^2) \tag{4-3.9}$$

and is known as the *residual* variance because it is what remains after we have reduced the original variance σ_Y^2 by using the predictor X.

To check that the regression function and the linear-regression function are identical when the regression function is indeed linear, we have only to note that $\mathcal{E}(Y|x)$ is then a linear function which minimizes the expected squared-error loss for *each* x separately, and thus certainly minimizes the mean of these quantities with respect to the distribution of X. The equivalence of Eqs. (4-2.3) and (4-3.5) is established by noting that when $\mathcal{E}(Y|x) = \alpha + \beta x$, we have

$$\begin{aligned} \mathcal{V}[\mathcal{E}(Y|x)] &= \beta^2\mathcal{V}(X) && \text{by (4-1.4)} \\ &= \rho^2\sigma_Y^2 && \text{by (4-3.8).} \end{aligned}$$

Finally, we note a line of thought which arrives at the correlation coefficient without referring to regression. In Sec. 4-1, we pointed out that the covariance is positive (negative) if the tendency is for Y to increase (decrease) as X increases. The same discussion suggests that the larger the covariance is in size, the more consistent is the tendency to mutual increase. The covariance itself, however, is unsuitable as a measure of this consistency, since it depends on the scale in which X and Y are measured. We can obtain a standardized covariance by first transforming our measurements to what are sometimes called *standard scores*, having zero means and unit variances:

$$X' = \frac{X - \mu_X}{\sigma_X}, \quad Y' = \frac{Y - \mu_Y}{\sigma_Y}.$$

We then have

$$\mathcal{C}(X', Y') = \frac{\mathcal{C}(X, Y)}{\sigma_x \sigma_y} = \rho .$$

Thus, we arrive at a standardized measure of association between X and Y which is symmetrical with respect to the two variables (which the correlation *ratio* is not if the regression is nonlinear). However, our previous discussion warns us that the correlation coefficient is really a measure of the degree of *linear* relation between the variables. It is possible for the correlation ratio to be unity, implying perfect prediction, when the correlation coefficient is zero, implying no linear association. However, the behavioral scientist will seldom, if ever, encounter such a situation.

If the correlation between two variables is sufficiently high, then the use of the observation on one variable to predict the value of the other variable will be helpful. The residual variance and its square root, the residual standard deviation, will be smaller and hence the observations will tend to cluster more nearly around the predicted values. All of this, however, assumes that the parameters α and β are known precisely. We shall discuss the situation in which they are not in Chap. 9.

4-4 THE CONCEPT OF ERROR

An educational test is given to *measure* a person's aptitude, ability, or degree of skill with respect to tasks that are deemed relevant to the educational process. Because persons differ in these regards and because these differences are important in the prognosis of individual growth under differing learning and work conditions, the accurate estimation of these quantities is of major importance in education.

Unfortunately, these measurements cannot be made without error. If we give a group of persons two forms of the ACT examination on successive days, not all persons will obtain precisely the same composite score on each day. This is an empirical fact many times verified. If we were to compute the correlation over persons of the ACT composite scores for the two occasions in a population containing a broad spectrum of ability levels, we would expect to find a correlation somewhat greater than .90 for these scores.

It is clear, then, that whatever is being measured is being measured with error, since the contrary would imply a correlation of 1.0 for such scores. In fact, we know that there is much error in such measurements and, indeed, many sources of this error. These sources include, but are not limited to, day-to-day variations in the performance level of examinees, variations in testing conditions, differences in the test forms, and other factors that are unknown to us and are, therefore, called "random" error.

Having accepted the concept of an *observed score* x and an error component with which we can associate an *error score* e (not yet precisely defined), the concept of a *true-score* $\tau = x - e$ has seemed compelling to many writers. If we remove the error component from the observed score, what would appear to be left is the measurement without error, the true-score. Both the error score e and the true-score τ are hypothetical quantities that have precise meanings only when they are given precise definitions.

Let us consider an observed measurement on a person to be a particular realization of a random variable corresponding to repeated independent, identical measurements, called *replications*, on this person. By independent, identical measurements, we mean that the probabilistic structure of the experiment does not change from one observation to the next and the observation of any particular value x on one measurement in no way affects succeeding measurements. We are obviously speaking of a sequence of measurements which could, in theory, be made but which, in practice, typically cannot be made because persons are seldom unaffected by repeated measurements and because they do not remain unchanged over time.

Even though we cannot operationally make an *unlimited* number of repeated independent observations on any person, we can often make at least two such measurements, and for practical purposes of estimation, this is typically sufficient. Therefore, it makes sense to think of a random variable defined with respect to replications and to study its simple properties. If X_a is the random variable corresponding to the observations on person a, we can write $\tau_a = \mathcal{E}(X_a)$ for the expected observed score over (hypothetical) replications for this person. Psychometric tradition has blessed this entity with the name true-score, though it has no theoretical or empirical properties to suggest this terminology. It is an expected value, nothing more or less. The error in an individual observation is then defined as the difference between the observed score and the true score, viz.,

$$e_a = x_a - \tau_a. \qquad (4\text{-}4.1)$$

For a given person, e_a is the realization of a random variable E_a, which clearly has expectation zero since $\mathcal{E}(X_a) = \tau_a$ and since the quantity τ_a is a constant. The error variable E_a has a variance which we denote by $\sigma^2(E_a)$ and which we refer to as the *error variance for examinee a*. The quantity $\sigma(E_a)$ is called *the standard error of measurement for examinee a*. As always, the standard deviation is a measure of spread or variability of the distribution.

Since τ_a is a constant, we have $\sigma(X_a) = \sigma(E_a)$; thus the error of measurement is an index of the degree of accuracy of the measurement X_a. If $\sigma(E_a)$ is small, we can expect the observed score x_a to be near the true-score (expected value) τ_a. If $\sigma(E_a)$ is large, we must realize that x_a might be far from τ_a. The magnitude of $\sigma(X_a)$ has meaning, however, only in relation to the scale of measurement of X, for if $Y_a = cX_a$, then $\sigma(Y_a) = c\sigma(X_a)$.

It is typically true that for examinees a, b, and a given test, the standard errors $\sigma(E_a)$ and $\sigma(E_b)$ are unequal. Usually, this is a function of the nature of the measuring instrument rather than a characteristic of the persons involved. For many models, the disparity between $\sigma(E_a)$ and $\sigma(E_b)$ will be related to the true-scores τ_a and τ_b.

4-5 THE BASIC RELATIONS OF THE CLASSICAL TEST THEORY MODEL

Most discussions of testing theory do not center on the distribution for a given person, but deal instead with the distribution of scores in some population of persons. The statement of such a population is a conditioning event, and we therefore recognize how important it will be to keep our population in mind throughout our further work in this chapter. All statements we make will have relevance only in the context of the specified population. Looked at the other way around, the distribution of scores for a fixed person is a special case of the distribution for a whole population where that population has been defined (conditioned) to include only the single person.

Given a population of examinees each of whom has a true-score τ_a, we can define a random variable T and associate it with the distribution of such true-scores in the specified population (possibly a specific group of students who have been or might be tested). We assume that this distribution has a mean μ_T, which we shall call the *mean true-score*, and a variance σ_T^2, which we shall call the *true-score variance.* The individual true-scores, the mean true-score, and the true-score variance are unobservable quantities.

In a similar manner, we can consider the error scores e_a made on a single replication by the persons in the specified population. We consider such values to be realizations of an error random variable. The mean of the distribution of this variable taken over persons (and hence, implicitly also over replications for each person) will be zero since the mean value of the errors for each person is zero. (This follows from 4-1.8.) The variance of this distribution σ_E^2 will be equal to the average value across persons of the variances $\sigma^2(E_a)$. This can be seen from (4-1.9) and by noting that the variance across persons of $\mathcal{E}(E_a)$ is zero, since $\mathcal{E}(E_a) = 0$ for all persons a.

Finally, we can consider the observed scores x made on a single replication by these same persons. The mean μ_X of the *observed scores* will be equal to the mean of the true-scores μ_T, because each person's true-score is the expected value, over replications, of his observed score. The variance σ_X^2 of these observed scores is called the *observed-score variance*.

Since $x_a = \tau_a + e_a$ for *each* person, it must follow that $X = T + E$ in the population of persons. This is the basic equation of classical test theory; *observed score equals true-score plus error score*. Because we have assumed that the expected error for any person is zero, it must, therefore, be true that the expected error is zero not only in the entire population but also in the subpopulation of persons having *any* specified true-score τ_a. Symbolically, $\mathcal{E}(E/T = \tau_a) = 0$. This implies that the regression coefficient of E on τ is zero, and this in turn implies that in the overall population or any subpopulation the correlation $\rho(E, T)$ between E and T is zero. This relationship is important in itself and also immediately tells us that $\sigma_X^2 = \sigma_T^2 + \sigma_E^2$; that is, *observed-score variance equals true-score variance plus error variance*. The covariance term to be found in the evaluation of $\sigma^2(T + E)$ is zero because $\rho(E,T) = 0$. Again, since for fixed τ, $X = \tau + E$ and since $\mathcal{E}(E|\tau) = 0$, it must be true that $\mathcal{E}(X|\tau) = \tau$;

and thus the regression of observed score on true-score is linear. The reader should be cautioned that the regression of true-score on observed score is generally not linear.

We have now completed our development of the basic relations in classical test theory. A summary will be useful. We have

$$X = \mathrm{T} + E, \qquad (4\text{-}5.1)$$

observed score equals true-score plus error score;

$$\mathcal{E}(E) = 0, \qquad (4\text{-}5.2)$$

the expected error score is zero;

$$\rho(E, \mathrm{T}) = 0, \qquad (4\text{-}5.3)$$

the correlation between error and true-score is zero;

$$\mu_{\mathrm{T}} = \mu_{\mathrm{X}}, \qquad (4\text{-}5.4)$$

the mean true-score equals the mean observed score; and

$$\sigma_X^2 = \sigma_{\mathrm{T}}^2 + \sigma_E^2, \qquad (4\text{-}5.5)$$

observed-score variance equals true-score variance plus error variance.

Also,

$$\mathcal{E}(E|\tau) = 0, \qquad (4\text{-}5.6)$$

the regression of error score on true-score is linear with constant value zero;

$$\mathcal{E}(X|\tau) = \tau, \qquad (4\text{-}5.7)$$

the regression of observed score on true-score is linear with a value equal to the true-score.

The variance σ_E^2 of the error distribution across persons is a measure of the average imprecision of the measurements in the specified population. Since $\mathcal{E}(E) = 0$, if σ_E^2 is small, the errors will themselves tend to be small; if σ_E^2 is large, the errors will tend to be large. Again, as with $\sigma^2(E_a)$, the magnitude of the error variance will depend upon the scale of measurement. The standard error of measurement cannot be used to compare tests having different scales, even in the same population. In order to make this kind of comparison, it is necessary to have an index that does not depend on the scale of measurement. Given a fixed population, the most common index is the *reliability coefficient*, defined as $\rho^2(\mathrm{X}, \mathrm{T})$, the square of the correlation between observed scores and true-scores. The reliability coefficient can be shown to be equal to the ratio $\sigma_{\mathrm{T}}^2/\sigma_{\mathrm{X}}^2$ of true-score variance and observed-score variance, and from this, we can see that reliability will be zero only if true-score variance is zero. This statement underlines the dependence of the reliability coefficient on the population of persons.

4-6 EXPRESSING PARAMETERS OF UNOBSERVABLES IN TERMS OF PARAMETERS OF OBSERVABLES

The parameters discussed in the previous section are typically unobservable, but two of them, μ_X and σ_X^2, are parameters of a distribution of observable scores. The true-score and error-score parameters μ_T, σ_T^2, and σ_E^2 are parameters in distributions of unobservable scores. It will be useful to express each of the parameters of unobservable variables and the reliability coefficient algebraically as a function of parameters of observable variables. In fact, we already have the relationship $\mu_T = \mu_X$. In order to proceed further with this task for the other parameters, we shall need to deal with the bivariate distribution of two measurements.

The first idea we require is that of *experimental independence*. Conceptually, two measurements are experimentally independent if the taking of one measurement in no way affects the results we get when we take the second measurement. Denoting the first and second measurements on a person by X_{1a} and X_{2a} and denoting the true-scores by τ_{1a} and τ_{2a} for a person a, this can be given mathematical form, for our purposes, by taking the following two conditions as implications of experimental independence. First,

$$\mathcal{E}(E_{1a}|e_{2a}) = \mathcal{E}(E_{2a}|e_{1a}) = 0. \qquad (4\text{-}6.1)$$

The *expected error score for one variable is zero for any given error score on the second variable*. An implication of (4-6.1) is that E_1 and E_2 are uncorrelated in the given population. The second condition is

$$\sigma^2(E_{1a}|e_{2a}) = \sigma^2(E_{1a}), \qquad (4\text{-}6.2)$$

$$\sigma^2(E_{2a}|e_{1a}) = \sigma^2(E_{2a}). \qquad (4\text{-}6.3)$$

The *conditional error variances on each variable are the same for any given value of the error score on the other variable* and, indeed, are equal to the error variances when the other errors are not given. More precisely, experimental independence is defined by the condition $p(E_{2a}|e_{1a}) = p(E_{2a})$; that is, the fact that $E_{1a} = e_{1a}$ in no way affects the distribution of E_{2a}.

Classical test theory deals only with first-order and second-order properties, means, variances, and correlations of measurements. It is, therefore, convenient to have a definition of replications with respect to these first-order and second-order properties. Suppose we have experimentally independent measurements X_1 and X_2 such that for every person a is a specified population

$$\tau_{1a} = \tau_{2a}$$

and

$$\sigma^2(E_{1a}) = \sigma^2(E_{2a});$$

then X_1 and X_2 are said to be *parallel measurements* in that population. This is to say that whether we use measurement X_1 or measurement X_2, the expected values, the true-scores for each person, are the same and the error variances for each person are the same.

The following are some implications of this definition. In the entire population of persons

$$\sigma^2(E_1) = \sigma^2(E_2), \qquad (4\text{-}6.4)$$

the *error variances of parallel measurements are equal;*

$$\sigma^2(\mathrm{T}_1) = \sigma^2(\mathrm{T}_2), \qquad (4\text{-}6.5)$$

the *true-score variances of parallel measurements are equal;*

$$\sigma^2(X_1) = \sigma^2(X_2), \qquad (4\text{-}6.6)$$

the *observed-score variances of parallel measurements are equal;* and

$$\mu(\mathrm{T}_1) = \mu(\mathrm{T}_2), \qquad (4\text{-}6.7)$$

the *mean true-scores of parallel measurements are equal*. Thus, we see that measurements that are parallel in a population are equivalent in that population, at least as far as means and variances are concerned.

If good test-construction procedures are followed carefully, it is not difficult in most applications to construct two or more forms of a test that will yield approximately parallel measurements in most populations. Also in many applications, it is possible to obtain two measurements on each of a group of persons without any material changes occurring in the person. We shall in due course see that this is all that is necessary to provide for the estimation of the various parameters of interest.

Consider experimentally independent measurements X_1 and X_2 and their covariance, which we shall write as $\sigma(X_1, X_2)$. Then, we find that

$$\sigma(X_1, X_2) = \sigma(\mathrm{T}_1 + E_1, \mathrm{T}_2 + E_2) = \sigma(\mathrm{T}_1, \mathrm{T}_2), \qquad (4\text{-}6.8)$$

the *covariance between observed scores is equal to the covariance between true-scores*. The first step in this derivation follows from the relation $X = \mathrm{T} + E$, and the second step follows on noting that the experimental independence of X_{1a} and X_{2a} implies that the covariances $\sigma(\mathrm{T}_1, E_2)$, $\sigma(\mathrm{T}_2, E_1)$, and $\sigma(E_1, E_2)$ are all zero. If X_{1a} and X_{2a} are parallel measurements, denoted by X and X', it follows that the values of T and T′ are identical and that

$$\sigma(X, X') = \sigma(\mathrm{T}, \mathrm{T}') = \sigma_{\mathrm{T}}^2$$

the *covariance between parallel measurements is equal to the true-score variance.*

Now consider the correlation $\rho(X, X')$, between two parallel measurements. We have

$$\rho(X, X') = \frac{\sigma(X, X')}{\sigma(X)\sigma(X')} = \frac{\sigma^2(\mathrm{T})}{\sigma^2(X)}.$$

Next consider

$$\rho^2(X,T) = \frac{\sigma^2(X,T)}{\sigma^2(X)\sigma^2(T)} = \frac{\sigma^2(T,T)}{\sigma^2(X)\sigma^2(T)} = \frac{\sigma^4(T)}{\sigma^2(X)\sigma^2(T)} = \frac{\sigma^2(T)}{\sigma^2(X)}. \qquad (4\text{-}6.9)$$

Therefore, we have

$$\rho^2(X,T) = \frac{\sigma_T^2}{\sigma_X^2} = \rho(X,X'). \qquad (4\text{-}6.10)$$

We have thus accomplished two things. First, we have expressed a parameter involving T in terms of a parameter involving only observables. Specifically, we have shown that the reliability of a test is equal to the correlation between parallel measurements. We have also shown that the reliability of a test defined as $\rho^2(X,T)$ is equal to the ratio of the variance of true-scores to the variance of observed scores.

Algebraically, no new techniques are required to establish the following important relations:

$$\sigma_E^2 = \sigma_X^2(1 - \rho_{XX'}), \qquad (4\text{-}6.11)$$

$$\sigma_T^2 = \sigma_X^2\rho_{XX'}, \qquad (4\text{-}6.12)$$

where we now write $\rho(X,X')$ as $\rho_{XX'}$ and $\rho^2(X,T)$ as ρ_{XT}^2. In theory, then, if σ_X^2 and $\rho_{XX'}$ were well estimated, we could use $\rho_{XX'}$ to estimate ρ_{XT}^2 and use (4-6.11) and (4-6.12) to estimate σ_E^2 and σ_T^2. If σ_X^2 and $\rho_{XX'}$ are not very well estimated, this procedure can be substantially less than optimally efficient.

Consider the fictitious data reported in Table 4-6.1 which might consist of ACT scores for 10 students on two administrations of the test. We shall treat these observations as constituting an entire population consisting of $r = 2$ replications on each

Table 4-6.1 FICTITIOUS ACT SCORES ON TWO OCCASIONS FOR TEN PERSONS

	Occasion			
Persons	1	2	τ_a	$\sigma^2(E_a)$
1	22	23	22.5	$\frac{1}{4}$
2	21	22	21.5	$\frac{1}{4}$
3	20	19	19.5	$\frac{1}{4}$
4	19	20	19.5	$\frac{1}{4}$
5	19	19	19	0
6	17	18	17.5	$\frac{1}{4}$
7	18	15	16.5	$2\frac{1}{4}$
8	15	16	15.5	$\frac{1}{4}$
9	14	15	14.5	$\frac{1}{4}$
10	13	14	13.5	$\frac{1}{4}$

of $n = 10$ examinees. Thus, we can compute some of the quantities we have been discussing.

Proceeding with the computations, we get

$$\tau_1 = (r_1^{-1}) \sum_{j=1}^{r_1} x_{1j} = (2)^{-1}(22 + 23) = 22.5,$$

$$\sigma^2(E_1) = (r_1^{-1}) \sum_{j=1}^{r_1} (x_{ij} - \tau_1)^2$$
$$= (2)^{-1}[(22 - 22.5)^2 + (23 - 22.5)^2] = \tfrac{1}{4},$$

and continuing in a like manner, we obtained the results given in Table 4-6.1. To compute the mean true-score μ_T, we write

$$\mu_T = n^{-1} \sum_{i=1}^{n} \tau_i$$
$$= \frac{1}{10}(22.5 + 21.5 + 19.5 + 19.5 + 19 + 17.5 + 16.5 + 15.5 + 14.5 + 13.5)$$
$$= 17.95.$$

The average variance for the 10-person population is

$$\sigma^2(E) = \frac{\Sigma\sigma^2(E_a)}{n}$$
$$= \frac{1}{10}\left(\frac{1}{4} + \frac{1}{4} + \frac{1}{4} + \frac{1}{4} + 0 + \frac{1}{4} + 2\frac{1}{4} + \frac{1}{4} + \frac{1}{4} + \frac{1}{4}\right)$$
$$= \frac{17}{40}$$
$$= .425.$$

The observed-score variance for the 20 scores is

$$\sigma_X^2 = \frac{\sum_i \sum_j (x_{ij} - \mu_X)^2}{nr} = (20^{-1})[(22 - 17.95)^2 + (23 - 17.95)^2 + \cdots + (13 - 17.95)^2 + (14 - 17.95)^2]$$
$$= 8.35.$$

The true-score variance can be computed as

$$\frac{\Sigma(\tau_i - \mu_T)^2}{n} = (10)^{-1}[(22.5 - 17.95)^2 + (21.5 - 17.95)^2 + \cdots + (13.5 - 17.95)^2]$$
$$= 7.92.$$

Table 4-6.2 REPLICATE MEASUREMENTS ON SIX PERSONS

Replications (Persons)	Persons (reading methods) 1	2	3	4	5	6
1	145	140	195	45	195	120
2	40	155	150	40	230	55
3	40	90	205	195	115	50
4	120	160	110	65	235	80
5	180	95	160	145	225	45

The reader will want to compare carefully what we have done here with the extensive computations in Sec. 4-1. The similarity is real. In fact, the computations done here could have followed the pattern of Sec. 4-1 simply by recognizing that the τ_a and $\sigma^2(X_a)$, etc., are the conditional mean and variance in the subpopulation defined by the single person a. Thus, (4-1.8) and (4-1.9) become

$$\mathcal{E}(X) = \mathcal{E}\left[\mathcal{E}(X|a)\right] = \mathcal{E}(\tau_a) = \mu_T = \mu_X$$

and

$$\mathcal{V}(X) = \mathcal{V}\left[\mathcal{E}(X|a)\right] + \mathcal{E}\left[\mathcal{V}(X|a)\right] = \sigma_T^2 + \mathcal{E}[\sigma^2(X_a)]$$

or

$$\sigma_X^2 = \sigma_T^2 + \mathcal{E}[\sigma^2(E_a)].$$

The decomposition of observed scores into their true and error components is not something unique to (educational) measurement theory. More generally, it is known as *the Analysis of Variance* (ANOVA), or more precisely as the simplest application of the general ANOVA method. In other applications, the analysis will involve the comparison of, for example, 10 treatment groups with 3 persons being treated with each treatment. In this kind of application, persons play the role of replications, and (treatment) groups are the units whose average values (true-scores) are sought.

Consider the data shown in Table 4-6.2. These data could be scores on five administrations of an IQ test to each of six people, or they could be observations of post-training reading scores for five people in each of six different treatment groups. (Actually, the data were yields of dyestuff.) The reader may wish to assume that this constitutes an entire population of persons and replications and compute μ_T, $\sigma^2(E)$, $\sigma^2(T)$, and $\sigma^2(X)$ as an exercise.

4-7 THE ESTIMATION OF TRUE-SCORE

If we are required to estimate the true-score for a single person, an obvious approach is to use the observed score x_a as the estimate of the true-score τ_a. Since $\mathcal{E}(X_a) = \tau_a$, we say that x_a is an *unbiased estimate* of τ_a. The expected squared error of measurement for person a, associated with the estimator X_a, is the error variance $\sigma^2(E_a) = \sigma^2(X_a)$. If this procedure is followed for a random sample from a population of people, the expected average squared error will be σ_E^2, the expected value over persons of the person-error variances $\sigma^2(E_a)$. This quantity has been called the error variance over persons.

One might think that on the average this would be a good way to proceed, but when simultaneous estimation is required for a group of m persons, and we desire to minimize expected *average* squared error, it definitely is not. Following the strategy used in the previous section, we can begin to see this by formal manipulations in the mathematical model, reserving for Sec. 9-5 a more satisfactory treatment of how this problem should be handled for anything but large samples.

As noted in a previous section, the regression of true-score on observed score is typically nonlinear; however, substantial improvement in predictions can often be made by using a linear-regression function for predictive purposes. The minimum expected squared-error linear-regression function for predicting τ given x has the form

$$R(\mathrm{T} \mid x) = \alpha + \beta x,$$

where the regression coefficient is given by

$$\beta = \rho_{X\mathrm{T}} \frac{\sigma_\mathrm{T}}{\sigma_X} = \frac{\sigma_\mathrm{T}}{\sigma_X} \frac{\sigma_\mathrm{T}}{\sigma_X} = \rho_{X\mathrm{T}}^2 = \rho_{XX'}.$$

The *linear-regression coefficient of true-score on observed score is equal to the reliability of the test*. The intercept in the regression function is given by

$$\alpha = \mu_\mathrm{T} - \beta\mu_X = \mu_X(1 - \rho_{XX'}),$$

and the linear-regression function is, thus,

$$R(\mathrm{T} \mid x) = x\rho_{XX'} + \mu_X(1 - \rho_{XX'}). \qquad (4\text{-}7.1)$$

Statistically, this formula due to Kelley (1927) provides the link between classical test theory and the Bayesian methods we shall study in the remainder of the book. Bayesian estimates will often have similar forms; and it is, therefore, important to study this formula carefully. The Kelley estimate is the weighted average of observed score and the population mean observed score, the weights being, respectively, the reliability and one minus the reliability of the test. Estimates obtained from the Kelley formula are often referred to as *regressed estimates*. (They are regressed from the usual estimate x toward the population mean μ_X.) If the measurement is highly reliable, relatively high weight is put on the observed score. If the measurement is very unreliable, great weight is put on the mean observed score, which would, in fact, be the minimum expected squared-error estimate when no information is available on the individual units (a measurement with reliability zero, which can occur only when $\sigma_\mathrm{T}^2 = 0$ or when no measurement is actually taken).

The improvement, on the average, using the Kelley regression estimate as compared to the observed score can be seen by comparing the root of the expected squared error of the Kelley procedure (the standard error of estimation σ_ϵ) with the previously derived standard error of measurement. The two quantities are

$$\sigma_E = \sigma_X\sqrt{1 - \rho_{XX'}} = \sigma_T(1 - \rho_{XX'})^{\frac{1}{2}}(\rho_{XX'})^{-\frac{1}{2}}$$

and, by (4-3.9),

$$\sigma_\epsilon = \sigma_T(1 - \rho_{XX'})^{\frac{1}{2}} \qquad (4\text{-}7.2)$$

and thus

$$\sigma_\epsilon = \sigma_E\sqrt{\rho_{XX'}}\ .$$

Since $0 \leq \sqrt{\rho_{XX'}} \leq 1$, it is clear then $\sigma_\epsilon < \sigma_E$ unless the test is completely reliable. The standard error of estimation will be substantially smaller than the standard error of measurement whenever the reliability is small.

There are some interesting and important implications of the Kelley formula. First, we note that if we are dealing with a single population of persons, the ordering of scores on the persons is the same for the regressed scores as for the original observed scores. The effect of the Kelley formula is to regress the observed score a fixed percentage of its distance from the mean observed score. Scores further from the mean regress more than scores closer to the mean, but the ordering is unaffected. Obviously then, if our sole interest is in selecting a fixed number or percentage of examinees with the highest estimated true-scores, it is immaterial whether we use the observed score or the estimated true-score, provided we are dealing with a single population.

However, if we choose to treat our examinees as coming from two distinct populations, the application of the Kelley formula becomes more meaningful. Suppose first that we are dealing with two populations having different mean observed scores. Let us call these μ_1 and μ_2, with $\mu_1 > \mu_2$, and let us suppose that the reliability of the test is the same in each population. Now consider all persons from both populations who obtained a particular observed score. On the basis of their observed scores alone, each will have the same estimated true-score. However, if we identify each person with one of the two groups, his estimated score will be higher or lower depending upon the group with which we identify him. In fact, it can easily occur that a person from one group will have his estimated true-score lowered and a second person from another group have his estimated true-score raised, so that the estimated true-scores are in the opposite order to the observed scores. If in such a situation, the second person is selected for admission and the first is not, we would have a hard time convincing that student, his parents, and his lawyer that he had been treated fairly. This important problem can be resolved, but only by relating the test scores to the decisions for which they have been obtained.

4-8 EXERCISES

1 Using the data in Table 4-6.1 for occasion 1, multiply each person's score by 2 and add 3.

(*a*) Show that $\mathcal{E}(2X + 3) = 2\mathcal{E}(X) + 3$.

(*b*) Show that $\mathcal{V}(2X + 3) = 4\mathcal{V}(X)$.

Thus, (4-1.3) and (4-1.4), respectively, are verified.

2 In Table 4-6.1, let the scores on occasion 1 be represented by X and the scores on occasion 2 by Y. Add 2 to each person's score on occasion 1 and add 3 to each person's score on occasion 2. Show that $\mathcal{C}(X + 2, Y + 3) = \mathcal{C}(X, Y)$.

3 Using the data in Table 3-5.1, show that $\mathcal{E}(Y) = \mathcal{E}[\mathcal{E}(Y|x)]$ and that $\mathcal{V}(Y) = \mathcal{V}[\mathcal{E}(Y|x)] + \mathcal{E}[\mathcal{V}(Y|x)]$, thus verifying Eqs. (4-1.8) and (4-1.9), respectively.

4 In the notation of Sec. 4-5, we have $\mathcal{E}(E|\tau) = 0$. Show the following.

(*a*) This implies that the regression of E on τ is linear.

(*b*) The regression coefficient is zero. [*Hint*: $\mathcal{E}(E|\tau) = R(E|\tau) = \alpha + \beta\tau = 0$.]

(*c*) The correlation between E and T is zero. [*Hint*: Write the formula for the regression in terms of the correlation and the variances and assume that the variances are not zero.]

5 Compute μ_{T}, $\sigma^2(E)$, $\sigma^2(\mathrm{T})$, and $\sigma^2(X)$ for the data given in Table 4-6.2.

PART TWO

Elementary Bayesian Methods

5

BAYESIAN ANALYSIS OF BINARY DATA

In this chapter we shall provide the skeleton framework for Bayesian inference with the binomial model. After first defining and describing the model, we then proceed to show how Bayesian inference is done with this model. Our purpose here is to give the reader an appreciation of the scope and concrete requirements of the Bayesian method, without treating every facet in complete detail. By the end of this chapter, the reader should be able to handle the gross mechanics of this kind of analysis even though there may be a few features that he feels require a greater depth of understanding on his part. This deeper insight will be provided in a more abstract and detailed discussion in Chap. 6, where we shall give the final working details and case studies on estimating binomial proportions.

5-1 BINARY DATA

The term *binary data* describes the situation where each possible observation falls into one of two categories. Thus, switches may be "on" or "off", statements may be "true" or "false", students may "pass" or "fail", answers to test items may be "right" or "wrong". In each of these examples it is, of course, possible that there might be more than two categories of interest–for example, the "pass" category for a course is commonly divided into grades. Multicategory situations are discussed in Chap. 10; in this chapter, we presume that multicategories have been reduced by combination to just two categories.

With binary data, the two categories are logical opposites: "fail" means the same as "not-pass", "wrong" the same as "not-right". In general, we shall denote the characteristic which defines one category by A (pass, right) and its opposite by $\bar{A}$ (fail, wrong). A set of observations will consist of a sequence of A's and $\bar{A}$'s. Established usage refers to A as a "success" and $\bar{A}$ as a "failure", even when this has the ghoulish effect of making "killed in a road accident" a "success".

We have seen that the theory of statistics is developed in terms of random variables whose values are real numbers. It is, therefore, convenient to describe the observation of an A by saying we observe $X = 1$ and of an $\bar{A}$ by $X = 0$. Such a description is clearly arbitrary–in technical language it establishes a *nominal scale*. We could alternatively describe A by $X = +7.3$ and $\bar{A}$ by $X = 22.6$; all we require is two distinct numbers to be used as x values for the two categories. However, the choice of $X = 1$ for A and $X = 0$ for $\bar{A}$ has the advantage of having a simple interpretation: X is the number of times we observe an A at the particular observation we are making (which must be 0 or 1). Hence, if we make a sequence of observations $x_1, x_2, \ldots, x_n$, then, $\sum_1^n x_i$ is the total number of A's which we observe. With this convention, a set of observations is simply a sequence of 0s and 1s.

5-2 THE BINOMIAL MODEL

Consider the following simplified description of a spelling test. There are a large number (n) of items (words). For any particular student in the group to which the test is administered, each word is equally difficult to spell. The students have different spelling abilities. The effect of a student's ability is that as he spells each word in turn, there is a probability π ("pi" for probability) that he will spell it correctly (success) and $(1 - \pi)$ that he will spell it incorrectly (failure), independently of whether he has spelled other words in the test correctly or incorrectly (independently, that is, given his ability). Different students will have different π values. Since larger values of π indicate better spellers, we may take π itself as a measure of spelling ability. Question: "How many words on this test will a student of ability π spell correctly?"

We are not here discussing the plausibility of the model. The description given above is to be taken at its face value and its consequences examined. Since π can be interpreted as the long-term proportion of words spelled correctly, one answer to the question posed is "roughly πn". To answer the question more precisely, we must recognize that the number we seek is a random variable X (not completely determinate even when π is known), and that we require its probability distribution. This is not difficult to find.

We shall have $X = x$ if our series of observations contains exactly x successes and $(n - x)$ failures. For example, using our zero-one convention for recording observations, one sequence which gives $X = 7$ when $n = 10$ is:

Observation	1	1	0	1	1	0	0	1	1	1
Probability of that observation	π	π	$1-\pi$	π	π	$1-\pi$	$1-\pi$	π	π	π

Underneath each observation, we have written its individual probability. Since the observations are stated to be independent, the probability of the whole sequence is simply the product $\pi^7(1 - \pi)^3$ of all these probabilities. This is also the probability of *any* sequence containing seven successes and three failures, since any other sequence of seven successes and three failures results in the same product, $\pi^7(1 - \pi)^3$.

In the general case, any particular sequence containing exactly x successes has probability $\pi^x(1 - \pi)^{n-x}$. Considered as outcomes of the whole test, any two different sequences of this type are exclusive events. Hence, the probability that $X = x$ is the sum of their separate probabilities, namely, the probability of any one multiplied by the number of different sequences which contain x successes. The number of such sequences is given the symbol representation C^n_x, ${}^nC_x$, or $\binom{n}{x}$, by mathematicians and is conveniently read as "n choose x", since it is the number of ways in which we can choose x words to be spelled correctly out of a total of n. The numerical value of $\binom{n}{x}$ is known to be $n!/x!(n - x)!$ where $n! = n(n - 1) \cdots 2 \cdot 1$ is read as n factorial. Thus for $n = 10$, $x = 7$, we have

$$\binom{10}{7} = \frac{10!}{7!3!} = \frac{10 \cdot 9 \cdot 8}{3 \cdot 2 \cdot 1} = 120 .$$

Generally then, the probability distribution of the number of words spelled correctly by a student of ability π is

$$p(x|\pi) = \binom{n}{x} \pi^x(1 - \pi)^{n-x}, \quad x = 0, 1, 2, \ldots, n. \tag{5-2.1}$$

We make explicit the dependence on π since we may wish to consider students of different abilities.

The distribution (5-2.1) is called the *binomial distribution* with *parameter* π and *index* n. The name is derived from the fact that if we write $\kappa = (1 - \pi)$ and expand $(\kappa + \pi)^n$ algebraically using the binomial theorem,

$$
\begin{aligned}
(\kappa + \pi)^n = \kappa^n &+ n\kappa^{n-1}\pi + \frac{n(n-1)}{2!}\kappa^{n-2}\pi^2 \\
&+ \frac{n(n-1)(n-2)}{3!}\kappa^{n-3}\pi^3 + \cdots \\
&+ \frac{n(n-1)(n-2)\cdots(n-r+2)}{(r-1)!}\kappa^{n-r+1}\pi^{r-1} + \cdots \\
&+ n\kappa\pi^{n-1} + \pi^n,
\end{aligned}
$$

we can obtain the probabilities as the successive terms of the expansion. For $n = 7$, the coefficients 1, n, $n(n-1)/2$, etc., of these terms are 1, 7, 21, 35, 35, 21, 7, 1. Thus, the probabilities of 0, 1, ..., 7 successes, respectively, are $1\kappa^7\pi^0$, $7\kappa^6\pi^1$, $21\kappa^5\pi^2$, $35\kappa^4\pi^3$, $35\kappa^3\pi^4$, $21\kappa^2\pi^5$, $7\kappa^1\pi^6$, $1\kappa^0\pi^7$. If $\pi = \frac{1}{4}$, then $\kappa = \frac{3}{4}$; and the numerical values (rounded to three decimal places) of the probabilities are .133, .311, .311, .173, .058, .012, .001, .000. Save for rounding errors, these probabilities sum to 1.

It may be useful to remind some readers that the coefficients of a binomial expansion can be obtained from Pascal's triangle,

$$
\begin{array}{ccccccccc|c}
 & & & & 1 & & & & & n = 0 \\
 & & & 1 & & 1 & & & & n = 1 \\
 & & 1 & & 2 & & 1 & & & n = 2 \\
 & 1 & & (3) & & (3) & & 1 & & n = 3 \\
1 & & 4 & & (6) & & 4 & & 1 & n = 4,
\end{array}
$$

which can be expanded by bordering the triangle with ones and getting each interior entry as the sum of the entries diagonally above. The reader may wish to compute the values for $n = 5$, 6, and 7 and verify those given by us above.

For the binomial distribution, the expectation and variance are, respectively,

$$\mathcal{E}(X|\pi) = n\pi \quad \text{and} \quad \mathcal{V}(X|\pi) = n\pi(1-\pi). \qquad (5\text{-}2.2)$$

The first of these equations can be viewed in two ways. It gives a more precise meaning to our intuitive answer that the number correct will be "roughly $n\pi$": we can now say that our best estimate of the number correct using squared-error loss is $n\pi$. Also, thinking of π as varying from student to student, we can say that the regression of "number correct" on "spelling ability" is linear with regression coefficient n. It is, perhaps, worth pointing out that this linearity of regression is not a startling new discovery in the the psychology of spelling; it is simply a consequence of the way in which we have defined "spelling ability". This point is relevant in many contexts other than the present one. From the second of the equations (5-2.2), it is worth noting that the variance of X given π is a maximum when $\pi = \frac{1}{2}$ and decreases away from this value, approaching zero as π approaches zero or one.

Referring to (4-1.3) and (4-1.4), we see that

$$\mathcal{E}\left(\frac{X}{n} \mid \pi\right) = \pi \quad \text{and} \quad \mathcal{V}\left(\frac{X}{n} \mid \pi\right) = \frac{\pi(1-\pi)}{n}. \qquad (5\text{-}2.3)$$

Thus, we see that the sampling variation of the proportion X/n is small for large n. In fact, X/n concentrates around the mean value π and its sampling variation tends to zero as n increases. This is precisely why, from a sampling-theory point of view, one wants one's estimate x/n of π to be based on as large a value of n as "costs" will permit.

5-3 NUMERICAL VALUES FOR BINOMIAL PROBABILITIES[1]

The probability distribution given by formula (5-2.1) provides the mathematical answer to the question posed earlier: "How many words will a student of ability π spell correctly?" However, the making of such computations rapidly becomes tedious, and can often be avoided by the use of the tables and the approximations which we now describe. The approximations are also of theoretical interest and will be used again in Chap. 9.

Some events concerning the student with ability π in which we might be interested are:

A–he spells x_0 words correctly.
B–he spells at least x_0 words correctly,
C–he spells x_0 or less words correctly,
D–he spells between x_1 and x_2 (inclusive) words correctly.

One approach to finding the probabilities of these events would be to write a computer program for which the input would consist of n, π, and the smallest and largest number of successes included in the event. Thus, for event A, the input would be (n, π, x_0, x_0); for B, it would be (n, π, x_0, n); for $C, (n, \pi, 0, x_0)$; and for $D, (n, \pi, x_1, x_2)$. The computer would evaluate (5-2.1) for each x in the required range and sum the results to give the probability of the event. For continuing use, this might be the simplest procedure with due allowance being made for the fact that many of the individual terms are very small, and those which are not arise as the product of a large binomial coefficient with a small term $\pi^x(1-\pi)^{n-x}$.

For occasional use, tables are available which serve the same purpose, for example, "Tables of the Binomial Probability Distribution," issued by the National Bureau of Standards in 1950. This volume uses the symbols n, p, r for n, π, x. For values of n from 2 to 49 and values of π by steps of .01 from .01 to .50, two tables are given: (1) the "individual terms" of the probability mass function (5-2.1); and (2) the "partial sums"

[1] Reading of this section can be deferred until the end of Sec. 5-4 without loss of continuity. This may be preferable for many readers.

Prob $(X \geq x)$. In each case and for all possible values of x, the entries are given to seven decimal places. It would have been more in line with modern statistical practice to tabulate the cumulative distribution function, $P(x) = \text{Prob}(X \leq x) = 1 - \text{Prob}(X \geq x + 1)$. The reason that it is unnecessary to include values $\pi > .50$ is that the event "x successes each with probability π" is the same as "$(n - x)$ failures each with probability $(1 - \pi)$". Thus, if $\pi > .50$, we rephrase our event in terms of failures. An example is given below.

The probabilities for the events A and B are given directly by the appropriate entries in the National Bureau of Standards Tables 1 and 2, respectively. The probabilities for the events C and D are easily deduced from Table 2, since

$$\text{Prob}(C) = \text{Prob}(X \leq x_0) = 1 - \text{Prob}(X \geq x_0 + 1),$$

and

$$\begin{aligned}\text{Prob}(D) &= \text{Prob}(x_1 \leq X \leq x_2) \\ &= \text{Prob}(X \geq x_1) - \text{Prob}(X \geq x_2 + 1).\end{aligned}$$

Suppose, for example, that a student has ability .8, and we require the probability that he spells between 18 and 22 (inclusive) words correctly on a 25-word test. This is case D with $n = 25$, $\pi = .80$, $x_2 = 22$, $x_1 = 18$. However, $\pi > .50$, and so we rephrase the event in terms of the number $Y = 25 - X$ of incorrectly spelled words. Thus,

$$\begin{aligned}\text{Prob}(18 \leq X \leq 22) &= \text{Prob}(X \leq 22) - \text{Prob}(X \leq 17) \\ &= \text{Prob}(Y \geq 3) - \text{Prob}(Y \geq 8).\end{aligned}$$

Entering Table 2 with $n = 25$ and a π value of .20 (the probability of a *mis*spelling), we find Prob $(Y \geq 3) = .9018$ and Prob $(Y \geq 8) = .1091$ (to four decimal places), giving a value .7927 for the required probability.

Similar tables for values of n from 50 to 100 are given by Romig, "50-100 Binomial Tables" (New York: Wiley, 1953). His notation uses n, p, x for our n, π, x. The entries are the individual probabilities Prob $(X = x)$ and the cumulative distribution function $P(x) = \text{Prob}(X \leq x)$, and are given side by side in a single table. Probabilities are given to six decimal places, "the last doubtful"; and the size of the tables is greatly reduced by omitting entries when the probabilities are effectively zero or unity. These instances become very numerous as n increases.

The difficulty about tables of the binomial distribution is that they require three-way classification by n, π, and x. A bulky volume is therefore needed to contain them (the Bureau of Standards tables cover 387 pages), and it becomes impossible to reproduce a useful portion of them in a book like this. When n is "large", approximations are available which greatly reduce the amount of tabulation necessary. Just what constitutes a "large" value of n is something for which one gains a feel by experience rather than something which can be prescribed by rule. This is so because the adequacy of an approximation depends not only on n itself but also on the value of π, the part of the distribution which it is required to approximate (near the mean or out in the tails), and the degree of accuracy demanded.

The Normal Approximation

The most useful approximation is based on the fact that *if X is a variable having a binomial distribution with index n and parameter* π, *then* $Z = (X - n\pi)/\sqrt{n\pi(1 - \pi)}$ *has approximately a standard normal distribution.* Several comments will help clarify this statement:

1) Since the mean and standard deviation of the binomial distribution are $n\pi$ and $\sqrt{n\pi(1 - \pi)}$, Z is just the "standard score" form of X, as discussed in Sec. 4-3.

2) The standard normal distribution is the most commonly tabulated of all the distributions used in statistics. It has mean zero and variance unity. It is given as Table A.1 here and is discussed in detail in Chap. 6. For the moment, it is only necessary to note that the table gives the cumulative distribution function Prob $(Z \leq z)$, usually denoted by $\Phi(z)$ in the case of normal distribution; and that the distribution is symmetrical about its mean, zero, so that Prob $(-z < Z \leq 0)$ = Prob $(0 < Z \leq z)$. (See comment 4 in regard to this notation.)

3) The normal distribution applies to (some) *continuous* variables. When we use it to approximate a discrete variable, such as number of words spelled correctly, we are clearly using a convention. The easiest way to think of this convention is as follows. Imagine that the possible values of the discrete variable are "nearest-integer" approximations to an underlying continuous variable X, in the sense discussed in Sec. 3-4. Do this even if you can make no sense of the idea of "$27\frac{3}{4}$ correctly spelled words"–the mathematics is still all right! Thus, "exactly 28 correct" will be interpreted as $27\frac{1}{2} < X \leq 28\frac{1}{2}$, "between 18 and 22 correct" as $17\frac{1}{2} < X \leq 22\frac{1}{2}$, and so on. Find the standard scores z_1 and z_2 corresponding to the limits x_1 and x_2 obtained in the previous sentence, and use the normal distribution table to determine Prob $(z_1 < Z \leq z_2)$. This is the required probability.

4) One distinction between discrete and continuous distributions needs to be emphasized here in order to explain a notation which might otherwise seem puzzling. If X is a *discrete* integer-valued random variable and x is an integer, Prob $(X \leq x)$ means the probability that X takes on the value x or less, whereas Prob $(X < x)$ means the probability that X is less than x. Clearly, the two will differ by an amount Prob $(X = x)$, the probability that X actually takes on the value x.

When X is a *continuous* variable, however, Prob $(X = x)$ is always zero. This is clear on referring to Fig. 3-4.2, since Prob $(X = x_0)$ is the limit of the area in the thin column at x_0 as its width tends to zero. If the result appears paradoxical, it is probably because the reader is interpreting a zero probability as meaning that an event cannot happen. We warned against this interpretation in Sec. 3-1. Speaking very loosely, a continuous random variable has an infinite number of possible values to choose from, so each value separately has probability zero. Only certain collections of values, such as intervals $x_1 < X \leq x_2$, have nonzero probabilities.

The purpose of this digression is to point out that for a continuous variable, it does not matter whether we write Prob $(x_1 \leq X \leq x_2)$ or Prob $(x_1 < X \leq x_2)$, since Prob $(X = x_1) = 0$. The usual convention is to write a "<" sign with the lower limit of the interval and a "≤" sign with the upper limit, since we then have, strictly, for both discrete and continuous variables,

$$\begin{aligned}\text{Prob}\,(x_1 < X \leq x_2) &= \text{Prob}\,(X \leq x_2) - \text{Prob}\,(X \leq x_1) \\ &= P(x_2) - P(x_1)\,.\end{aligned}$$

5) If π is close to .5, the approximation is adequate for many purposes with n as small as 10: individual probabilities are then correct to the second decimal place. For $\pi = .1$ and $\pi = .9$, one would usually not wish to use the approximation for $n < 50$. A very rough rule of thumb might be that if $\kappa = (1 - \pi)$ is less than π, $n\kappa/(1 - \kappa)$ should be greater than 5 if one is working near the mean of the distribution and greater than 10 if one is working in the tails; if π is less than κ, the corresponding relations should hold for $n\pi/(1 - \pi)$. However, this rule is intended to supplement, not supplant, the user's experience.

Let us use the normal approximation to determine the probability that between 18 and 22 words of a 25-word test are spelled correctly by a student of ability .8. We previously obtained the value .7927 for this, correct to four decimal places. Here, the mean $n\pi = 20$, and the variance $n\pi(1 - \pi) = 4$, giving a standard deviation of 2. In accordance with our convention, the X event of interest is $17.5 < X \leq 22.5$, to which corresponds the Z event $-1.25 < Z \leq 1.25$. Using the normal-distribution table, we find

$$\text{Prob}\,(0 < Z \leq 1.25) = \Phi(1.25) - \Phi(0) = .8944 - .5000 = .3944\,.$$

Because of the symmetry of the normal distribution, the required probability is twice this, namely, .7888. The discrepancy from the exact value is about .004.

The Poisson Approximation

When n is "large" but π or $(1 - \pi)$ is "small", the binomial distribution is very asymmetrical, and so the normal approximation is poor. A better approximation is then given by the Poisson distribution with parameter $\mu = n\pi$. A rough indication of what is meant by "large" and "small" is the suggestion that the Poisson approximation may be adequate and preferable to the normal when $n > 30$, $\pi < .1$, and $n\pi < 10$.

The Poisson distribution is discrete with probability mass function

$$p(x|\mu) = \text{Prob}\,(X = x|\mu) = \frac{e^{-\mu}\mu^x}{x!}, \qquad x = 0, 1, \ldots \quad \mu > 0\,. \tag{5-3.1}$$

Both its mean and its variance are equal to μ. Theoretically, the possible values of X are all the nonnegative integers, but in practice, the probabilities for values of $x > \mu + 9$ are small. Successive values of (5-3.1) are

$$e^{-\mu}, \quad \mu e^{-\mu}, \quad \frac{\mu^2 e^{-\mu}}{2!}, \quad \frac{\mu^3 e^{-\mu}}{3!} \ldots$$

and are very simple to calculate, even by hand. The value of $e^{-\mu}$ is available in Table A.21 and one has only to multiply successively by μ, $\mu/2$, $\mu/3$, etc., to find the required probabilities.

A table giving the individual probabilities Prob $(X = x)$ to six decimal places, for values of μ from .1 to 15.0 by steps of .1 is found in E. S. Pearson and H. O. Hartley "Biometrika Tables for Statisticians", part I, table 39 (Cambridge University Press, 1966). To find the sum of a number of terms, one can take advantage of the following interesting relation between the Poisson and chi-square distribution. The *Poisson probability* Prob $(X < x|\mu)$ *is equal to the probability that a chi-square variable with* $2x$ *degrees of freedom exceeds the value* 2μ. A table of chi-square is given as Table A.5, and its use is discussed in more detail in Chap. 7.

Without suggesting that the Poisson approximation is appropriate, let us use it for the spelling example already discussed. Since the approximation is for *small* π, we work with the probability .2 of *mis*spelling. The event of interest is "between 3 and 7 (inclusive) misspellings". Using the Biometrika table with $\mu = (25)(.2) = 5$, we find for the individual probabilities, with $x = 3, 4, 5, 6, 7$, the entries (to four decimal places) .1404, .1755, .1755, .1462, .1044. This gives a total probability of .7420 for the event. The discrepancy from the exact value is about .05. Thus, in this example, the Poisson approximation .7420 to the true value of .7927 is considerably worse than that given by the normal approximation .7888.

In addition to its use as an approximation to the binomial distribution, the Poisson distribution is of great importance when incidents occur randomly in time or space: telephone calls reaching an exchange, flying bombs falling on London, deaths from horse-kick in the Prussian cavalry. It has found some limited use in psychological measurement.

5-4 INFERENCE FOR THE BINOMIAL MODEL

So far, all probabilities in this chapter have been conditional on the spelling ability π, defined as the probability of a student's spelling any one word of the test correctly. That is to say, for *known* values of π, we have calculated the probabilities of various events concerning the number X of words spelled correctly.

In a practical testing situation, the problem which confronts us is the opposite one, namely, to infer the value of π given an observation x of the variable X. Clearly, the knowledge we obtain of π in this way cannot be exact: 20 words correct out of 25 is quite a probable score for students with abilities anywhere in the range from .65 to .90 and a *possible* score for *any* student. Nevertheless, the observation that the student spelled 80% of the words correctly makes an ability around .8 more likely for him than an ability of, say, around .2. Indeed, a plausible intuitive argument would say that since we observe 80% of words spelled correctly, we should estimate π as .8 (we shall see later how this argument could be formalized). A moment's reflection, however, shows that the argument is plausible only if nothing else is known about the student. If, for instance, we know that .8 is an unusually high ability (on the test used) for the group to which the student belongs, we would be more inclined to think that his ability is less than .8, and luck has favored him on the test.

The prior discussion can be formalized as follows. So far, we have studied the (binomial) probability distribution $p(x|\pi)$. When π is unknown, and we observe $X = x$, that observation enables us to form probabilistic ideas about π. The complete and formal expression of those ideas would be a probability density $p(\pi|x)$ for the random variable Π, conditional on the observed value x. Clearly, Π is a continuous variable falling in the interval $0 \leq \Pi \leq 1$. We have noted, however, that $p(\pi|x)$ will depend not only on what we observe but also on what we knew about Π before making the observation, e.g., that .8 was an unusually high value. Let us suppose that we are able to express this previous knowledge by a *prior probability* density $p(\pi)$. In writing this as an unconditional probability, we are using our convention that knowledge assumed throughout the problem (the definition of π, the number of words in the test, the model for the number of correct spellings, prior knowledge about likely values of Π) will not be mentioned explicitly. If we were being more formal, we would denote all this knowledge by, say, H, writing $p(\pi)$ as $p(\pi|H)$ and the density $p(\pi|x)$ which we are seeking as $p(\pi|H \text{ and } x)$.

How do we determine $p(\pi|x)$ from the prior density $p(\pi)$ and the model density $p(x|\pi)$? The answer is given immediately by replacing y by π in Bayes' theorem (3-6.4), thus giving

$$p(\pi|x) \propto p(x|\pi)p(\pi). \qquad (5\text{-}4.1)$$

As was explained in Sec. 3-6, the constant of proportionality can be found, if necessary, from the fact that $p(\pi|x)$ is a density function for Π, and so

$$\int_0^1 p(\pi|x)\, d\pi = 1.$$

Putting the known value of $p(x|\pi)$ into (5-4.1) and dropping the binomial coefficient (which is not a function of π and so can be absorbed into the constant of proportionality), we have

$$p(\pi|x) \propto \pi^x(1-\pi)^{n-x}p(\pi) \qquad 0 \leq \pi \leq 1. \qquad (5\text{-}4.2)$$

Before proceeding to discuss $p(\pi)$, we note a point which will be of increasing importance in later models. Strictly speaking, the outcome of our "experiment" (test) is not the total number x of correctly spelled words but the actual sequence 1, 0, 1, 1, ... of conventional scores indicating whether each word is correctly or incorrectly spelled. Suppose we had used Bayes' theorem in the form

$$p(\pi|\text{sequence}) \propto p(\text{sequence}|\pi)p(\pi). \tag{5-4.3}$$

While deriving the binomial mass function, we noted that the probability of any particular sequence which contains x "correct" and $(n - x)$ "incorrect" words is $\pi^x(1 - \pi)^{n-x}$. On substituting this value for $p(\text{sequence}|\pi)$ in (5-4.3), we obtain the same result for $p(\pi|\text{sequence})$ as we have in (5-4.2) for $p(\pi|x)$. Thus, in obtaining the posterior distribution of Π (posterior to our observations), it makes no difference whether we use the actual sequence of observations or the summary of them given by the total number x correct. The latter, being a single number, is more economical to work with. In such circumstances, we shall say that the number correct, x, is a *sufficient statistic*. As in ordinary speech, the word "sufficient" invites the question: "sufficient for what?" The answer is "sufficient for finding the posterior distribution of Π" or, more briefly, "*sufficient for* Π".

We now return to Eq. (5-4.2) and note how extraordinarily convenient it would be if our prior density $p(\pi)$ were of the form

$$p(\pi) \propto \pi^{a-1}(1 - \pi)^{b-1} \quad 0 \leq \pi \leq 1,\ a > 0,\ b > 0, \tag{5-4.4}$$

since the posterior density would then be

$$p(\pi|x) \propto \pi^{a+x-1}(1 - \pi)^{b+n-x-1} \quad 0 \leq \pi \leq 1 \tag{5-4.5}$$

which is of the same form as (5-4.4) with $(a + x)$ replacing a and $(b + n - x)$ replacing b. There *is* a standard density of the form (5-4.4) known as the *beta distribution* because the constant of proportionality required to ensure that $\int_0^1 p(\pi)\,d\pi = 1$ is the reciprocal of a well-known mathematical function called the beta function. Indeed, the beta function $B(a, b)$ is *defined* to be the integral of the right-hand side of (5-4.4). Since this definition was already established by the time statisticians began to use beta distributions, the form (5-4.4) with the exponents $(a - 1)$ and $(b - 1)$ was adopted as standard rather than the more natural-looking form with exponents a and b. [Readers referring to Lindley (1965) are cautioned that he adopts a standard form with exponents a and b, contrary to common custom.]

The beta distribution has two parameters, a and b. By giving various positive values to these, we obtain a family of density functions of the form (5-4.4), each of which when used as a prior density combines in a very convenient way with the probability mass function of our model—the binomial distribution. (Because of the great similarity of functional form of the two distributions, it is worth reminding oneself that they are totally different things. The model density is a discrete distribution for X—the prior density is a continuous distribution for Π.) When this state of affairs exists between a model distribution and a family of prior distributions, we refer to the family of prior distributions as the family of *natural conjugate distributions* for the model distribution. Such distributions exist for all the models studied in this book. A piece of folk etymology (unsupported, alas, by the dictionary) would relate "conjugate" to "conjugal", noting that a conjugate distribution is a suitable mate for the model distribution and produces offspring of its own kind. The word "natural", however, must be admitted to owe more to rhetoric than to logic—"natural" sounds so much more scientific than "convenient"!

We do, in fact, intend to propose the use of beta prior distributions in making inferences for the binomial parameter. At the present stage of the discussion, a few very perceptive readers will probably feel that we have abandoned our principles for mere expediency. The fact that a certain procedure would be mathematically convenient is a rather poor argument for adopting it. We reserve our defense while we consider briefly semantic interpretations of the prior density $p(\pi)$. A fuller and more general discussion of this question and a more precise definition of natural conjugate densities are given in the next chapter.

The meaning of $p(\pi)$ would be clear to all of our readers if the student tested had been drawn randomly from a population in which the (relative-frequency) distribution of abilities was known to be closely approximated by the density function $p(\pi)$. In such circumstances almost everyone would agree that probability statements about the student's ability (e.g., that it is less than .5) *before* he is tested should be made by finding the area under the relevant portion of the density curve for $p(\pi)$. The requirement of random selection is useful mathematically (syntactically) to enable probabilities to be calculated. In real life, it is rather rare for individuals to be chosen literally at random to be tested. However, the randomness requirement has a more natural, negative interpretation: What is really demanded is that the method by which the student under study was selected from the population should not provide any information about his ability additional to what is contained in our knowledge of $p(\pi)$. He should not, for example, have been chosen because he looked intelligent, or, conversely, because his appearance suggested non-English-speaking parentage. The reader may care to ponder the following question: "If I am told that a student has been chosen from a group in which ability is distributed according to the density function $p(\pi)$, but I am told (literally) *nothing* about how he was selected, should I proceed differently than I would if told that he was randomly selected?" The demonstration that the answer should, under certain clearly specified conditions, be in the negative rests on the exchangeability theorem due to De Finetti, and Hewitt and Savage. It is clear to the present authors that these results and another due to Savage, to be discussed in detail later, are precisely those needed to make Bayesian inference possible.

A different interpretation of $p(\pi)$ would arise if before testing I made a subjective assessment of the student's ability. ("I" may be the reader or one of the authors; the change in pronoun is made because the statement "*we* made a subjective assessment" raises some presently extraneous questions about agreement between assessors.) In making this assessment, I would obtain whatever available information I deemed relevant from school records, by interview, and so on. Then I could quantify my impressions as follows: "I think his ability is around .8; I would be willing to bet at even odds that it lies between .7 and .85; I think it is very unlikely—say 1 chance in 50— that his ability is less than .3 or greater than .95". In this way I could build up a density curve $p(\pi)$ such that the areas under the relevant portions of it correspond to my pretest beliefs about the student's ability.

Something like this is done, in an informal manner, by most teachers who have the same students in their care for any length of time. A perennial debate rages about whether they should use this prior assessment in conjunction with the "objective" but chancy test results, and if so, how. We claim that Bayes' theorem shows how, and that the answer to "whether?" is clearly "yes" if all that is required is to obtain the teacher's posttest (subjective) assessment of the student's ability. If that assessment is to be used by third parties, the problem of subjectivity looms larger and will be discussed in the next chapter.

We now return to the defense of beta prior distributions for the binomial model and produce as "exhibit A" Fig. 5-4.1, which shows a selection of forms which the beta distribution can take. We then address the jury as follows: "Do you really suppose that your knowledge of the population from which a student was selected, or your prior assessment of his ability, would ever be so exact that you could not approximate it by one of the types shown?" Note the word *approximate*. Prior knowledge is typically somewhat imprecise, and many people seem to feel that this is a hindrance in adopting Bayesian methods. This is really not the case. If one is uncertain about the prior distribution, one can consider the effects of several different distributions which approximate one's prior knowledge/beliefs. In the presence of any substantial amount of data, probability statements derived from the corresponding posterior distributions will often be almost identical. If this is *not* the case, it indicates that one's observations are contributing rather little to one's final state of knowledge as compared with one's initial knowledge, and one should weigh the alternatives of (1) trying to pin down more accurately one's prior knowledge or (2) obtaining more observations. A clear exception to this argument is the situation in which our prior beliefs are bimodal. In this case, we would need a mixture of beta densities and a rather more complicated analysis.

Assuming ourselves acquitted of the charge of opportunism, we now summarize the procedure evolved in this section as follows. In making inferences for the parameter of a binomial distribution, we shall express our prior knowledge/beliefs by a beta probability

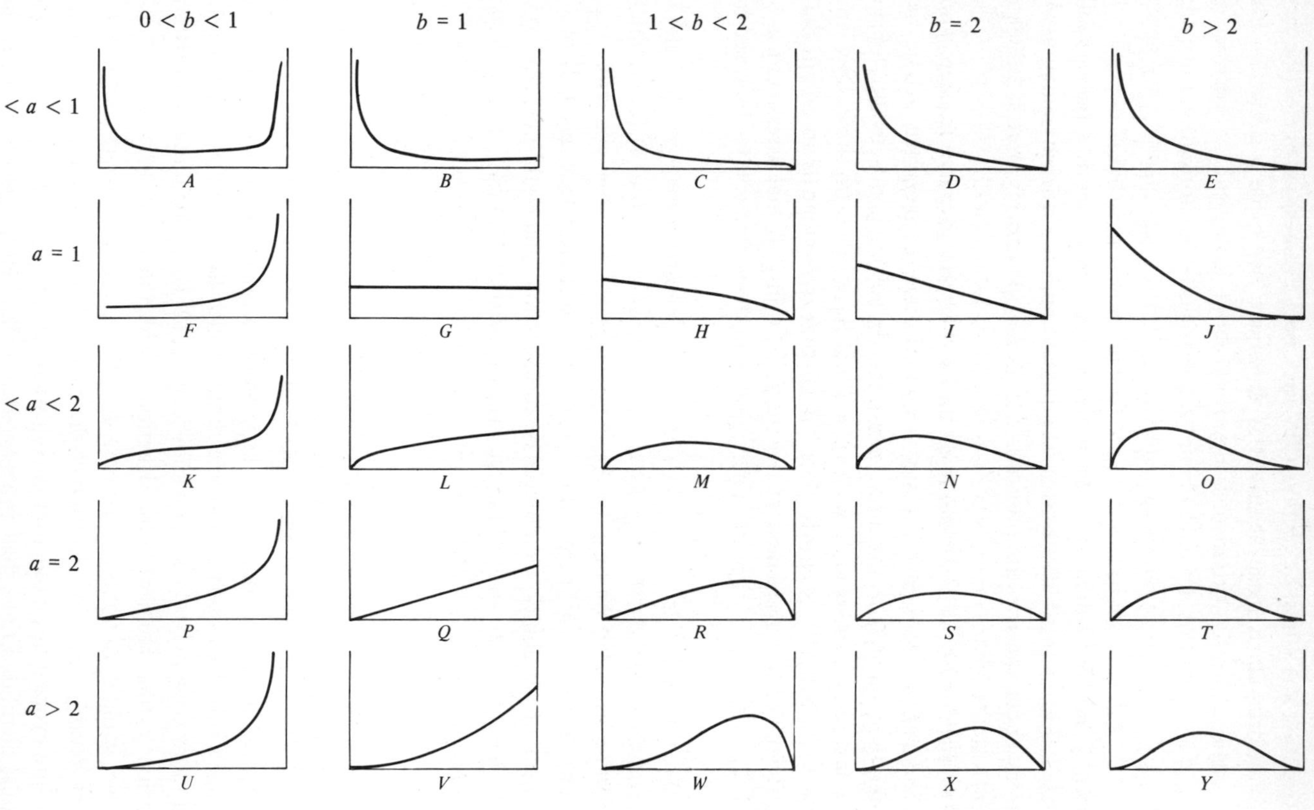

FIGURE 5-4.1
Varieties of beta distributions.

density of the form (5-4.4) with appropriately chosen values of a and b. If we then observe x successes and $(n - x)$ failures, our posterior distribution for Π will also be of beta form with parameters $a + x$ and $b + (n - x)$.

5-5 POINT AND INTERVAL ESTIMATES OF A BINOMIAL PARAMETER

To a Bayesian, the posterior distribution of a parameter *is* the full probabilistic solution to the problem of making inferences about that parameter. It incorporates both his prior knowledge/beliefs/assumptions and the evidence provided by his observations. Any computation we shall make here *after reporting* the posterior distribution will be directed to one of two goals: (1) bringing out those features of the distribution which are relevant to specific problems or decisions or (2) describing the distribution in ways which will be understood by persons to whom a statement such as "Π has a beta posterior distribution with parameters 21 and 6" fails to convey substantial meaning.

As an example of the first goal, consider prediction. It will be convenient to use p and q for the parameters of a general beta distribution, reserving a and b for the prior distribution. Thus, our general density is

$$\frac{\pi^{p-1}(1 - \pi)^{q-1}}{B(p, q)} \quad \text{for } 0 \leq \pi \leq 1, \quad p, q > 0, \tag{5-5.1}$$

where

$$B(p, q) = \frac{(p - 1)!(q - 1)!}{(p + q - 1)!}.$$

For the prior, we have $p = a$ and $q = b$; and for the posterior, $p = a + x$ and $q = b + n - x$. When p or q are not integers the factorials $(p - 1)!$ and $(q - 1)!$ are defined by the relation $(p - 1)! = \Gamma(p)$, where $\Gamma(p)$ is the well-known gamma function. The beta function $B(p, q)$ and the gamma functions $\Gamma(p)$ and $\Gamma(q)$ thus satisfy the relation

$$B(p, q) = \frac{\Gamma(p)\Gamma(q)}{\Gamma(p + q)}.$$

The descriptive characteristics of the beta distribution with parameters (p, q) are

$$\text{Mean} = \frac{p}{p + q}, \tag{5-5.2}$$

$$\text{Variance} = \frac{pq}{(p + q)^2(p + q + 1)}, \tag{5-5.3}$$

and

$$\text{Mode} = \frac{p - 1}{p + q - 2} \quad p > 1, \ q > 1. \tag{5-5.4}$$

We have already noted that the relevant feature of the posterior distribution in prediction depends on the loss function which we are using. With squared-error loss for π, our best estimate is the mean, and the expected loss is then equal to the variance. With zero-one loss, we would use the mode as our estimate. On substituting the appropriate values of p and q in (5-5.2) and (5-5.4), it can be shown that the mean and the mode of the posterior distribution never differ by more than $1/(n - 2)$. This illustrates the remark made in Sec. 1-3 that our procedures are often robust with respect to choice of loss function.

With absolute-error loss, we would use the median of the posterior distribution as our estimate. This is not given by any explicit formula but can be found from tables in the same manner as described below for interval estimates. The median lies between the mean and the mode, so our comment on robustness extends to this loss function also. A useful general approximation for the median as a function of the mean and the mode is given in (7-2.2). That approximation will work well for all beta distributions for which the mode is neither 0 nor 1.

Suppose that in our prior distributions we had taken $a = b = 1$. In Fig. 5-4.1, the corresponding density curve is shown to be a horizontal line. Alternatively, putting $a = b = 1$ in (5-4.4), we can see that $p(\pi)$ is a constant. We call such a distribution *uniform* or *rectangular* on the interval $[0, 1]$. Using it as a prior implies that before we made our observations, all Π intervals of equal length were equally likely. The posterior distribution then has parameters $x + a = x + 1$, $n - x + b = n - x + 1$; and its mode is just x/n, the observed proportion of successes. We have, thus, found a formalization of the intuitive argument, discussed at the beginning of Sec. 5-4, to the effect that if we have no prior knowledge about likely or unlikely values of Π, the fact that we observe 80% of words correctly spelled will incline us to regard .8 as the most likely value of Π. If we were to interpret "no prior knowledge" as "all values of Π equally likely, a priori" (a controversial point) and "most likely value of Π" as "posterior mode for Π", our mathematics confirms our intuition.

The posterior mode using a uniform prior is known as a *maximum-likelihood estimate*. The reason for singling it out from other posterior modal estimates is that it can be arrived at by a non-Bayesian argument, and it is, therefore, extensively used by statisticians of the classical school. The classical argument asserts that one should choose as the estimate that value of π which makes one's observations most likely. In the present context, it implies that one should find the value of π which maximizes $p(x|\pi)$, considered as a function of π. Since the posterior mode maximizes $p(\pi|x) = p(x|\pi)p(\pi)/p(x)$, it follows that if $p(\pi)$ is taken to be a constant, the posterior mode is the same as the maximum-likelihood estimate, since $p(x)$ does not involve π.

We turn now to the second goal—easily comprehensible description of the posterior distribution. The mean, median, and mode can play a role here also since they have simple interpretations; the mean is the average value of the random variable; the median is the value which the variable has a 50-50 chance of exceeding; and the most likely values of the variable lie around the mode. Such quantities are often referred to as *point estimates* because they select a single value (a point on an axis representing the variable) which is from some point of view a good estimate of the variable. They are also called *measures of central tendency* or *position*, since they lie at what can loosely be called the center of the distribution. Point estimates are contrasted with interval estimates such as the credibility intervals described later in this section.

A measure of central tendency alone is inadequate to describe a distribution. It must be supplemented by a *measure of variability* or *spread* which tells us whether the density curve is fairly sharply peaked at the center with the probable values of the variable clustered closely together or is relatively flat with probable values spread over a wide range. The most common such measure is the variance or its square root, the standard deviation. For a great many distributions, most of the probability (area under the density curve) lies within a range of three standard deviations on either side of the mean.

Writing the mean and variance of the posterior beta distribution as

$$\frac{x + a}{n + a + b} \quad \text{and} \quad \frac{(x + a)(n - x + b)}{(n + a + b)^2(n + a + b + 1)}$$

and then as

$$\frac{x/n + a/n}{1 + (a + b)/n} \quad \text{and} \quad \frac{1/n(x/n + a/n)(1 - x/n + b/n)}{[1 + (a + b)/n]^2[1 + (a + b + 1)/n]},$$

we can see what happens as the number of sample observations gets larger. Since a and b are constants, the quantities a/n and b/n approach zero, while x/n approaches the true population proportion. Thus, the mean of the posterior beta density approaches the true population proportion and the variance approaches zero. This means that as n gets larger, all of the posterior probability concentrates around the true parameter value regardless of what prior distribution is determined by specifying the prior parameters a and b. It is also then evident that two persons having possibly quite different prior distributions determined by parameters (a_1, b_1) and (a_2, b_2) will have almost identical posterior distributions given a sufficiently large sample. This result is a general property of Bayesian methods.

Perhaps the most directly meaningful way of describing a posterior distribution is to derive one or more probability statements from the tables of its cumulative distribution function. For each tabulated value of π, the entry $P(\pi) = \text{Prob}\ (\Pi \leq \pi)$ in such a table gives the probability that the variable Π is less than or equal to π. Reversing the procedure, we may choose a probability [a $P(\pi)$ value] of interest and obtain from the table the corresponding value of π. For example, if we take $P(\pi) = .5$, the corresponding value is by definition π_{mdn}, the median of the distribution.

Some probability levels [values of $P(\pi)$] are used so frequently that the corresponding values of the variable have been given names. The more important ones are:

$P(\pi) = \frac{1}{2}$ Median

$P(\pi) = \frac{1}{4}$ 1st or lower quartile

$P(\pi) = \frac{3}{4}$ 3rd or upper quartile

$P(\pi) = \frac{1}{8}$ 1st octile

$P(\pi) = \frac{3}{8}, \frac{5}{8}, \frac{7}{8}$ 3rd, 5th, 7th octile

$P(\pi) = \frac{1}{10}$ 1st decile

$P(\pi) = \frac{k}{10}$ kth decile ($k = 1, 2, \ldots, 9$)

$P(\pi) = \frac{1}{100}$ 1st percentile

$P(\pi) = \frac{k}{100}$ kth percentile ($k = 1, 2, \ldots, 99$) or percentage point.

The distribution function needed for making probability statements about a variable which has a beta distribution is extensively tabulated in "Tables of the Incomplete Beta Function", K. Pearson, ed., 2d edition (Cambridge: University Press, 1968). The importance of such tables to statistics was recognized by Karl Pearson as far back as 1894, but computational difficulties in those days were immense, and it was not until 1933 that the first edition appeared under his editorship. Apart from their direct use in contexts like the present one, the tables are valuable because other distributions can be derived from them; for example, the National Bureau of Standards binomial tables were obtained in this way.

The quantity tabulated, which is there referred to as the incomplete beta function ratio and denoted by $I_x(p, q)$, is just the cumulative distribution function $P(x) =$ Prob $(X \leq x)$ of a beta random variable with parameters (p, q). Tables are given for values of q in steps of .5 from .5 to 11 and, then, in steps of 1 to 50, for values of p by the same steps from q to 50, and each table gives entries for values of x from .01 to 1.00 by steps of .01 (suppressing rows where the entry would be zero or unity to 7 decimal places). There is a standard abbreviation for the previous sentence: We say the tables are for $q = .5(.5)11(1)50$, $p = q(.5)11(1)50$, $x = .01(.01)1.00$. In such statements, the quantities in parentheses are the steps by which the corresponding variable proceeds between the limits on either side.

Tables are given only for $p \geq q$, because if $p < q$, the problem can be rephrased in a similar manner to that employed for the binomial distribution. Specifically, *if we have a* *problem in which a probability π of "success" has a beta distribution with* p < q, *we rephrase it in terms of the probability $\kappa = 1 - \pi$ of "failure"; then κ has a beta distribution with parameters* (q, p). *Since the first parameter is now the larger, the required entries are available in the tables.*

Suppose that we have observed 20 words spelled correctly in a test of 25 words: Thus, $x = 20$, $n - x = 5$. Suppose that our prior knowledge was "all values of π equally likely" which we have seen implies $a = b = 1$. Hence, our posterior distribution for π is beta, with parameters (21,6). To find the median, we turn to the beta table with $p = 21$, $q = 6$ and look for a value of π (the table's x is our π) for which the entry $P(\pi) = .5$. We find for $\pi = .78$, $P(\pi) = .477$ and for $\pi = .79$, $P(\pi) = .527$. A rough interpolation gives us $P(\pi) = .5$ at $\pi = .785$, approximately. Thus, our median value of π is .785. This compares with a mode of $\frac{20}{25} = .80$ and a mean [using (5-5.2)] of $\frac{21}{27} = .778$, approximately. In the same way, taking $P(\pi) = .25$ and $P(\pi) = .75$ in turn, we find the lower and upper quartiles to be .728 and .835, respectively.

An Example Involving Threshold Loss

Applications in which the computation of one value of $I_x(p, q)$ will definitely be required are those having a threshold-loss assumption (see Sec. 1-2). In such applications, there will be a threshold value π_0, and the loss will depend on whether or not the person's π value is correctly assessed as being above or below that value. Suppose, in the example above, that given the prior information and the observations, it is then necessary to *decide* whether the person's π value is equal to or greater than $\pi_0 = .728$ or, alternatively, below that value. As in Sec. 1-2, let $\omega = 1$ if, in fact, $\pi \geq \pi_0$, and $\omega = 0$ otherwise; and let $\tilde{\omega} = 1$ if our decision is that $\pi \geq \pi_0$ and $\tilde{\omega} = 0$ otherwise. We use the symbol $\tilde{\omega}$ here, replacing the $\hat{w}$ used in Sec. 1-2, to indicate that we are using a Bayesian procedure incorporating both prior and sample data rather than a classical procedure using only sample data.

Now suppose further that if the events $(\omega = 0, \tilde{\omega} = 0)$ or $(\omega = 1, \tilde{\omega} = 1)$ occur, there is no loss; but that if $(\omega = 1, \tilde{\omega} = 0)$ occurs, there is a loss c; and if $(\omega = 0, \tilde{\omega} = 1)$ occurs, there is a loss $4c$. Thus the loss for incorrectly deciding that a person's π value is above .728 is taken to be four times as great as for incorrectly deciding that it is below that value. The question is, given the data, which decision should we make? Note the mean, median, and mode are all well above the critical value .728.

Since we do not actually know the true value of π, we are unable to guarantee a minimum (zero) loss. Therefore, the rational thing to do is to minimize the expected loss. Suppose on the basis of the data that we take $\tilde{\omega} = 0$; then there will be a loss only if $\omega = 1$, and that loss will be c. The expected value of the loss will then simply be c times the probability of that loss or more explicitly c times the a posteriori probability that π is greater than .728. Since Prob $(\pi \geq .728) = .75$, we find that the expected loss, if we decide that the person's π value is below .728, is $.75c$ for any value of c. In a similar manner, we compute the expected loss of the decision $\tilde{\omega} = 1$ as $(.25)(4c) = c$ and conclude that for any value of c we had better decide that the person's π value is below .728. We do this not because we have high posterior probability that $\pi < .728$, but because the opposite decision is too risky.

If some of the language of the preceding example is confusing (even if it is standard), perhaps it will be useful to replace the statement that we decide that the person's π value is below .728 with the statement that we shall *act as if* . . . . Of course, until an action is actually imminent, no decision is required, and one can continue to accumulate data and to revise posterior assessments accordingly. Also, it is only when the losses for the two incorrect decisions differ greatly, as they do in this example, that we are going to end up with a statement apparently in conflict with the statements about the mean, median, and mode. Robustness of estimates, as suggested in Chap. 1, is common but not ubiquitous.

Let us now set out formally the comparison made in deciding whether $\pi \geq .728$ or $\pi < .728$. The expected loss associated with the decision that $\pi \geq .728$ is the (weighted) average loss over the two possible outcomes–incorrect decision, correct decision. That expected loss is $a[\text{Prob}\ (\pi < .728)] + 0[\text{Prob}\ (\pi \geq .728)]$ or

1) $a[\text{Prob}\ (\pi < .728)]$;

and, the expected loss associated with the decision that $\pi < .728$ is

2) $b[\text{Prob}\ (\pi \geq .728)]$.

Taking $a = 4c$ and $b = c$ (see Sec. 4-1), our decision is based on whether *1)* or *2)* is the larger. This comparison, however, is equivalent to the comparison of the ratio

3) $$\frac{a}{b} = \frac{4c}{c} = 4$$

to the ratio

4) $$\frac{\text{Prob}\ (\pi \geq .728)}{\text{Prob}\ (\pi < .728)} = \frac{\text{Prob}\ (\pi \geq .728)}{1 - \text{Prob}\ (\pi \geq .728)}$$

This spotlights the fact that the experimenter need not stipulate a and b in any absolute scale. He need only stipulate the ratio a/b. In this example, since $\text{Prob}\ (\pi \geq .728) = .75$, the person will be classified as having spelling ability *less* than .728 unless the ratio $a/b \leq 3$.

This type of analysis is particularly relevant to certain new instructional modes involving the individualization of instruction in which the student proceeds sequentially through a set of training modules. At the completion of each module a decision must be made as to whether or not the student has attained some prespecified mastery level π_0. Threshold loss is assumed and the analysis proceeds as above. Those who have "mastered" a module advance to new material; those who have not are given remedial work.

Credibility Intervals

Percentile values immediately enable us to make probability statements which describe our posterior distribution, e.g.: "The probability that the tested student's ability is less than .835 is 75% (or .75)". While these statements are sometimes the most useful and relevant ones to make, it more typically happens that a statement of limits *between* which the quantity of interest lies with a stated probability are more suggestive. For example, the two quartile values obtained above enable us to state: "The probability that the tested student's ability lies between .728 and .835 is 50% (75% minus 25%)". The interval (.728,.835) is called a *50% credibility interval* for the ability π because the 50% is the measure of the strength of our belief, taking account of our prior knowledge and our observation, that the student's ability lies in that interval. There is, of course, nothing unique about the 50% credibility interval we have chosen. We might have chosen the interval from $\pi = 0$ up to the median, or the interval between the 2nd and 7th deciles. However, the 50% interval between the 25th and 75th percentiles is often a very useful one in describing the posterior distribution. In general, we shall call the interval which contains the central C% of the posterior probability, leaving an amount $\frac{1}{2}(100 - C)$% on each side, a *C% credibility interval*. If, in any context, it is necessary to draw attention to the particular interval we have chosen, we may call it a *central*, or *equal-tailed* (because equal areas are left under the two tails of the density curve) credibility interval. The *length* of the central 50% interval (the distance between the two quartiles) is called the *interquartile range* and is used as a measure of variability of distributions.

Central credibility intervals may be somewhat misleading if the posterior distribution is very skewed as will be the case if p is small and q is large, or vice versa. For example, when $p = 2$ and $q = 12$, the central 50% credibility interval is (.074,.196) and the mode is .083. Thus, the mode is close to one end of the central interval, and the picture conveyed by that interval alone is somewhat misleading. (We shall later meet a distribution in which the mode actually lies outside the central 50% interval when one of the parameters is small!)

In these circumstances, it may be preferable to compute a C% highest-density interval or *highest-density region*—in brief, a C% HDR. This is the C% credibility interval having the property that the value of the density function is larger at all points inside the interval than at any point outside it: speaking very loosely, points inside the interval correspond to more probable values of Π than points outside it. The HDR is most easily visualized in terms of the density curve. This is higher at points inside the interval than at those outside. A little reflection shows (1) that the ordinates at the end of the interval must be equal, (2) that any C% HDR contains the mode, and (3) that for a given C the HDR is the shortest possible C% credibility interval. This last property gives it a certain uniqueness which might also be considered a reason for preferring it to the somewhat arbitrarily chosen central interval. Of course, if the distribution is *symmetric* (and unimodal), the central C% interval and the C% HDR coincide.

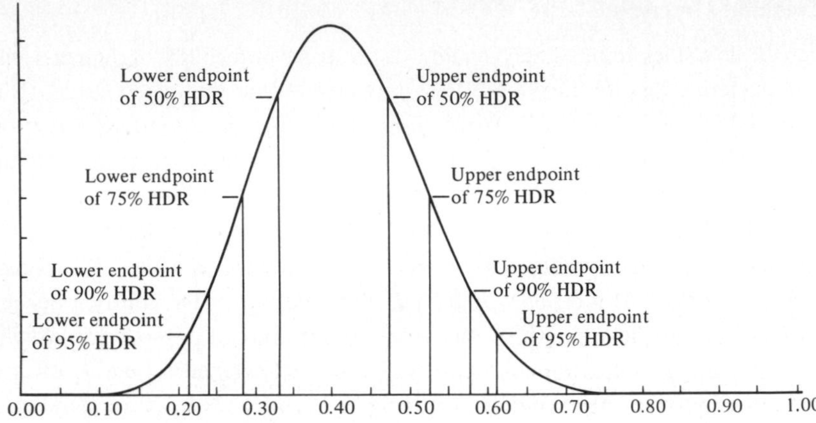

FIGURE 5-5.1
Highest-density regions of a beta distribution.

Figure 5-5.1 displays the beta distribution $\beta(9,13)$. The 50, 75, 90, and 95% HDR credibility intervals are contained within the indicated vertical lines.

A drawback to the use of HDRs is that they cannot be calculated from standard tables of percentage points. However, for all distributions which commonly occur as posterior distributions, formulas exist which generate HDRs (of unspecified C), and a simple iterative procedure exists that enables the particular HDR containing the specified C% probability to be selected using an electronic computer. In the example given above with $p = 2$ and $q = 12$, the 50% HDR is (.040, .148), which is more evenly spaced about the mode .083 than the central 50% interval. The tables of HDRs given in the Appendix were generated in this manner. Table A.15 gives HDRs for the beta densities.

A second drawback to HDRs is that they do not possess an invariance property that, at first, might seem desirable. Thus in the usual analysis, if we compute the endpoints of a C% HDR for a normal standard deviation, they will not correspond exactly with the square root of the endpoints of the C% HDR for the variance. Actually, there is no compelling reason why they should. What is important is that each C% HDR corresponds to some C% interval on the transformed parameter.

(Some readers may already be familiar with the idea of a "confidence interval" in classical statistics. It would take us too far afield to compare this idea in detail with that of the credibility interval defined above. Two brief comments must suffice. First, in a, say, 90% credibility interval, the 90% is a probability which attaches to the particular interval obtained. In a 90% confidence interval the 90% attaches to the method by which the interval is obtained, not to the particular application of it at hand. Second, in many but not all cases where the prior distribution reflects "prior ignorance", the intervals obtained by the two methods will be very similar, though their logical interpretation will still be different.)

Tables of the beta distribution, like those of the binomial distribution, require three-way classification—by the parameters p, q, and the variable values π. As a result, they are very extensive—the Biometrika tables cited occupy 430 pages. If our main purpose in using the tables is to find central $C\%$ credibility intervals, and we can agree upon a suitable set of values of C for regular use, then the amount of tabulation can be drastically reduced, and the tables made simpler to use at the same time.

Suppose, for example, that we are content to be able to find the median, and central 50, 80, 90, 98, and 99% credibility intervals. (The reason for the stress on percentages in the high nineties is twofold: they represent "near certainty", and the increase in length from a 98 to a 99% interval is much greater than that from, e.g., an 80 to an 81% interval.) Then all we require is a set of tables which give, for varying values of p and q, the .5, 1, 5, 10, 25, 50, 75, 90, 95, 99, and 99.5 percentage points. This is so because the upper and lower limits of a central $C\%$ credibility interval are just the $(50 - \frac{1}{2}C)$ and $(50 + \frac{1}{2}C)$ percentage points. What is more, we need only to have tables with $q \geq p$, since *the* $(50 + \frac{1}{2}C)$ *percentage point of a beta distribution with parameters* (p, q) *is found by subtracting from unity the* $(50 - \frac{1}{2}C)$ *percentage point of the beta distribution with parameters* (q, p).

Tables of the percentage points listed above, for $p, q = 2(1)25, q \geq p$, are given as Table A.14. To illustrate the use of the tables, let us find a 90% credibility interval for the ability of our student for whom we have a posterior distribution with parameters $p = 21$, $q = 6$. Since here $p > q$, we reverse the parameters and use the table with $p = 6, q = 21$. We find that the 95 and 5% points are .3626 and .1056, respectively. Subtracting each of these from unity, we obtain the 5 and 95% points of our actual posterior distribution as .6374 and .8944. Rounding these off we find the central 90% credibility interval to be (.64,.89).

Any reader who has frequent occasion to derive credibility intervals from beta distributions and can tolerate a possible error of about .01 in the limits obtained should make himself familiar with the ingenious chart reproduced here in abbreviated form from Table 17 of "Biometrika Tables for Statisticians" (Fig. 5-5.2). By the use of this chart and the scale provided on the end paper of this text, credibility intervals for a wide range of values of p and q and choices of credibility level C can be read straight off from the scale. The use of the chart is fully explained below. Once understood, it yields "instant credibility intervals".

Description and use of the chart in Figure 5-5.2

On the top edge of the chart a scale of q is provided which is split into three sections: A, $1 \leq q \leq 4$; B, $4 \leq q \leq 15$; C, $15 \leq q \leq 60$. These scales form the upper margins of the three corresponding chart sections A, B, and C. Each section

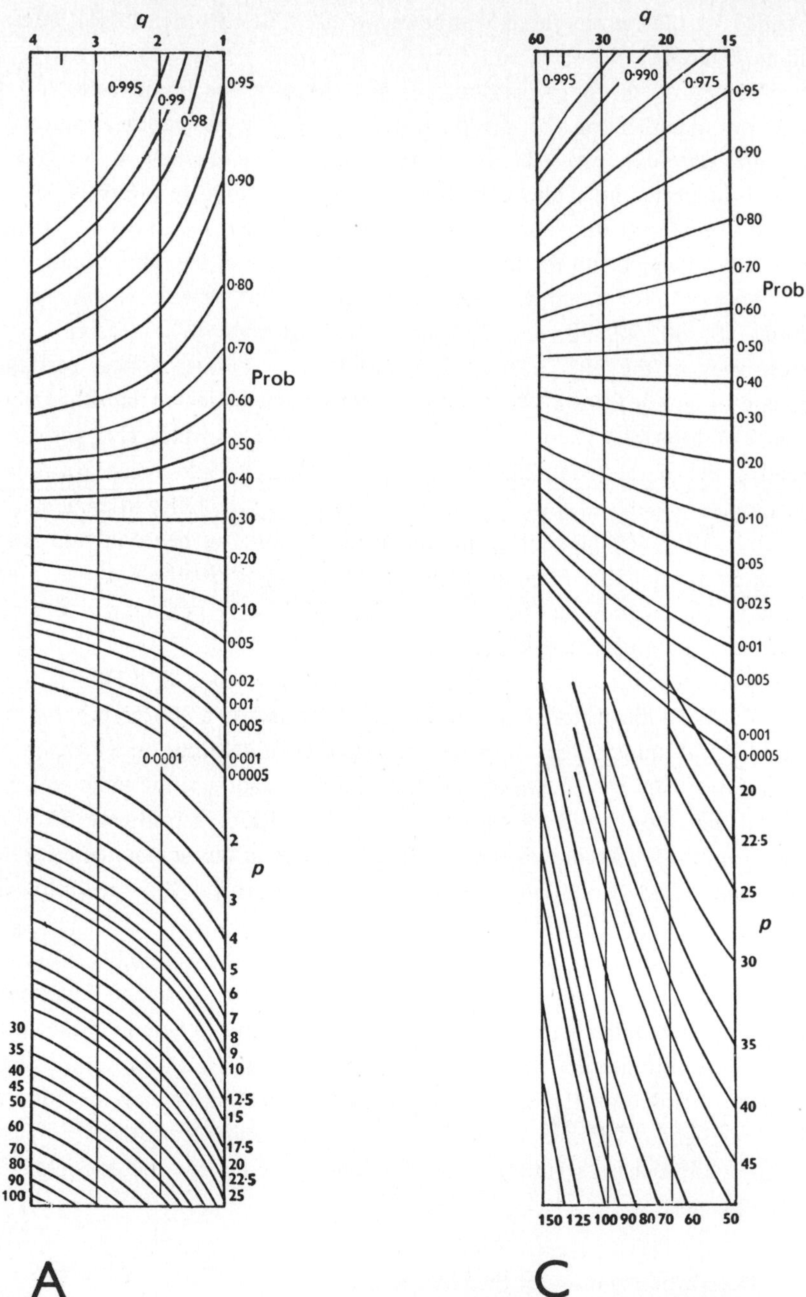

FIGURE 5-5.2
Chart for determining approximate percentage points of the beta distribution. [From E. S. Pearson and H. O. Hartley (eds.), *Biometrika Tables for Statisticians*, 3d ed., vol. 1, University Press, Cambridge, 1966. Reproduced with the permission of the authors and the Trustees of *Biometrika*.]

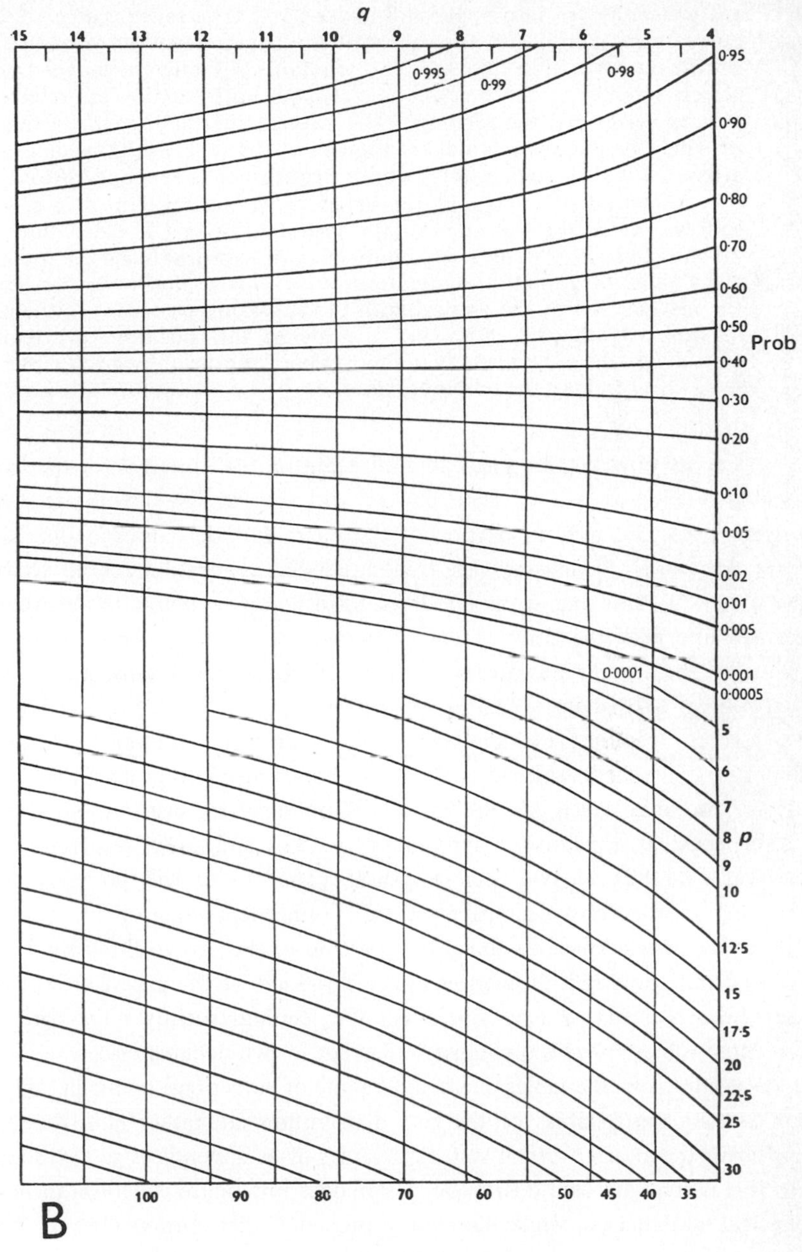
q
15
14
13
12
11
10
9
8
7
6
5
4
0·995
0·99
0·98
0·95
0·90
0·80
0·70
0·60
0·50
Prob
0·40
0·30
0·20
0·10
0·05
0·02
0·01
0·005
0·0001
0·001
0·0005
5
6
7
8 p
9
10
12·5
15
17·5
20
22·5
25
30
100
90
80
70
60
50
45
40
35

B

is further divided into upper and lower parts. The lower part contains a family of curves corresponding to the values of the parameter p shown at the right-hand end of the curves, while the top part contains a family of curves corresponding to selected values of the probability $I_x(p, q)$. Both families are referred to the same abscissa scale q at the top edge. The two families are linked by the aid of x scales provided on the ruler printed at the end of the text. Each x scale is marked with an arrow (→) at the "pivot point", whose significance is explained below.

To find $P = I_x(p, q)$ for given p, q, and x, with $p \geq q$, we proceed as follows. Choosing the appropriate scale (A, B, or C), place the ruler vertically on the chart so that its x scale intersects the abscissa scale (at top of chart) at the given value of q. Slide the rule up or down this vertical until its pivot mark (→) is at the intersection of the vertical with the curve corresponding to the given value of p in the bottom part. With the x scale in this position, the required value of $P = I_x(p, q)$ can be read off in the top part opposite the given x. When $p < q$, find $I_{1-x}(q, p)$ and use the relation $I_x(p, q) = 1 - I_{1-x}(q, p)$.

Let us now use the chart to find a central 90% interval for the beta distribution with $p = 21$ and $q = 6$. Here $p > q$, and we can go directly to the chart. Since $4 \leq q \leq 15$, the relevant portion of the chart and the corresponding sliding scale are those marked B. We lay the scale B alongside the vertical line of the chart marked with the q value 6, and slide it up and down until its arrow points to the intersection of that vertical line with the curve in the lower part of the chart representing the p value 21. Actually, there is no drawn curve for $p = 21$, but we can interpolate by eye between the curves for $p = 20$ and $p = 22.5$.

Next, keeping the sliding scale in place, we turn our attention to the upper part of the chart. The curves marked at their right-hand ends with probabilities $P = .95$ and $P = .05$ are the ones which give the 95 and 5% points of the distribution. These intersect the sliding scale at x values of approximately .893 and .638, respectively, giving a 90% interval (.64,.89) to two decimal places. (The reader will probably obtain x values differing in the third decimal place from ours, depending on just how the "eyeball" interpolation was made in fixing the position of the arrow. Professor E. S. Pearson has pointed out to us that differences in the shrinkage of the papers on which the chart and the scales are printed may also affect the readings slightly.) The agreement with the tabulated values above is very close, and exact to two decimal places.

Aside from the tables cited, and a table of percentage points in "Biometrika Tables for Statisticians", tables of the beta distribution are rather rare—they usually do not appear in the smaller sets of statistical tables or as appendices to textbooks. The reason for this is that the beta distribution itself does not figure largely in the computations of classical statisticians, while the closely related F distribution does. If it is necessary to make inferences from a beta distribution when only tables of F are available, the following fact may be used: *If X has a beta distribution with parameters (p, q), then $Y = qX/p(1 - X)$ has an F distribution with $(2p, 2q)$ degrees of freedom, and $Z = p(1 - X)/qX$ has an F distribution with $(2q, 2p)$ degrees of freedom.* (The "degrees of freedom" of an F distribution are its parameters, usually denoted by (ν_1, ν_2). The reason for the name will be clearer when we come to consider variance ratios.)

Tables of percentage points of the F distribution are included in almost all sets of statistical tables, and appear in this book as Table A.13. For a reason which will become clear in the example below, it is not necessary to tabulate percentage points above *and* below 50%, and the custom is to tabulate those above 50%. [Readers referring to sets of tables other than ours will often find them constructed in terms of "*upper P%* points", by which is meant the value *exceeded* with probability P%, corresponding to what we call the $(100-P)$th percentile or $(100-P)$% point.]

Let us once again find a 90% credibility interval for the beta distribution with parameters (21,6). We require first the 95% point of the F distribution with parameters $\nu_1 = 42$, $\nu_2 = 12$. To obtain this we must interpolate between the tabulated value with $\nu_1 = 40$, $\nu_2 = 12$ (namely 2.426), and with $\nu_1 = 50$, $\nu_2 = 12$ (namely 2.401). This gives us the value 2.42 approximately for the 95% point of the variable Y defined above. To find the corresponding value of X, we solve the equation $6X/21(1 - X) = 2.42$, whence $X = .89$. We also note that Y increases as X increases. Hence,

$$\text{Prob}\,(X \leq .89) = \text{Prob}\,(Y \leq 2.42) = .95\,,$$

showing that .89 is the 95% point of the beta distribution.

To find the 5% point we make use of the variable Z defined above. With $\nu_1 = 12$, $\nu_2 = 42$, the 95% point for Z is found, after interpolation, to be 1.99. Solving for the corresponding value of X, we obtain $X = .64$. However, in this case Z decreases as X increases. Hence,

$$\text{Prob}\,(X \leq .64) = \text{Prob}\,(Z \geq 1.99) = 1 - .95 = .05\,,$$

showing that .64 is the 5% point of the beta distribution. Putting the two results together, we again have (.64,.89) as the 90% credibility interval.

Finally, having seen how interval estimates are obtained from a posterior distribution, we are in a position to consider the reverse process—choosing a prior distribution to fit our initial subjective assessments. In Sec. 5-4 we gave an example of such an assessment. In our new terminology, that example can be interpreted to mean that the prior mode or mean is about .80, the interval (.70,.85) is a 50% (prior) credibility interval, and (.30,.95) is a 98% credibility interval. What we wish to do is to find values of p and q such that the beta distribution with parameters (p, q) has the stated properties. If this has to be achieved by search through the tables, the problem is formidable. However, with the chart, it requires only a few moments work.

For a start, let us consider the 50% interval. Generally speaking, subjective assessments are more accurate for credibility intervals such as 50 and 80% than for extremely high probability levels like 98%. We slide the scale around on the chart until the values $x = .70$, $x = .85$, on its edge, lie over the .25 and .75 probability curves on the chart (these particular curves are not in fact drawn, but again they can easily be interpolated by eye between the .20 and .30, and .70 and .80 lines, respectively). Reading the corresponding values of the parameters, we obtain $p = 10, q = 3$. We now check how well this agrees with our other subjective assessments. The mode is $\frac{9}{11} = .82$, the mean $\frac{10}{13} = .77$, agreeing well with our idea that the student's ability is "about .8". The values .30 and .95 are found from the chart to correspond to the 0.02 and 98% points of the distribution. This does, indeed, give roughly a 98% credibility interval, but not a central one. On reflection we might feel that in contemplating a value as low as .30 for the ability, we were being unduly pessimistic. On the whole, we would be inclined to accept $p = 10$, $q = 3$ as giving a beta distribution which satisfactorily approximates our prior beliefs. The subjective assessments we have used for our illustration were written down without reference to beta tables, and have not been "doctored" to provide an ideal example. The degree of agreement obtained here with a beta approximation may, therefore, be fairly representative of real-life situations.

If we use this prior and observe, as before, 20 successes and 5 failures, the posterior distribution is beta with parameters (30,8). (Note that the data is in this example confirming our prior belief that $\pi = .8$, approximately.) The posterior mean is .789, the median .795, and the mode .806. The central 50% credibility interval is (.75,.84) and the 90% interval is (.67,.89). On comparing these estimates with those obtained using the uniform prior, we note that the mode has increased slightly, the mean and median have moved closer to it, and the credibility intervals are somewhat shorter—the interquartile range is now .09 as compared with .11 before. None of these changes can be called dramatic. There would have been more noticeable changes if our observations had to some extent failed to support our prior beliefs.

There is another way of viewing the effect of our prior distribution. The posterior distribution with $p = 30$, $q = 8$ is the same as if we had started with the all-π-are-equally-likely prior, $p = q = 1$, and then observed 29 successes and 7 failures. Having this prior (instead of the all-π-are-equally-likely prior) is, thus, equivalent to having made an *additional* 11 observations. We shall put this fact to use presently.

5-6 EXERCISES

1 Suppose for the binomial model that $n = 9$ and $\pi = \frac{1}{3}$. Using the binomial expansion, what is Prob $(X \geq 5)$?

2 Suppose for the binomial model that $n = 25$ and $\pi = .40$. Compute $\mathcal{V}(X/n)$ and find Prob $(X/n > .50)$.

3 Given the situation described in Exercise 2, compute Prob $(X/n > c)$ for $c = .50$, .60, .70, .80, and .90 using (*a*) the binomial table and (*b*) the normal approximation.

4 Suppose for the binomial model that $n = 35$ and $\pi = .05$. Compute Prob $(X = 0)$ using (*a*) the binomial table, (*b*) the normal approximation, and (*c*) the Poisson approximation. Give the formula for the Poisson approximation. Repeat for Prob $(X = 1)$.

5 The posterior standard deviation of a beta distribution can be written as

$$\sqrt{\left(\frac{p}{p+q}\right)\left(1-\frac{p}{p+q}\right)\left(\frac{1}{p+q+1}\right)}$$

which is a function of $p/(p+q)$ and $(p+q)$. Taking the mean of the beta distribution successively as equal to .3, .5, .7, and .9, graph the standard deviation as a function of $(p+q)$. Write a brief verbal summary of what these graphs show.

6 On a certain unit of individually prescribed instruction, the a posteriori distribution of a person's mastery score is $\beta(17, 2)$. A person is considered a master if his mastery score is greater than or equal to .80. If we falsely classify the person as a master, our loss will be five times as great as our loss if we were to falsely classify him as a nonmaster. Should this student be classified as a master? Suppose the ratio of the two losses were 10, how should he be classified? In the latter case, is the "estimate" of π consistent with the estimates obtained under any of the three basic loss functions?

7 Given a beta distribution with parameters (4,18), find the mode, the interquartile range, and the 50% HDR. Which interval is the more evenly spaced about the mode?

8 Find a 90% credibility interval for the beta distribution with parameters (8,9) using (*a*) the *F* table, (*b*) the beta table, and (*c*) the Pearson-Hartley chart.

6

THE LOGICAL BASIS OF BAYESIAN INFERENCE

The purpose of this chapter is to pin down a number of concepts which, explicitly or implicitly, will find repeated application in the remainder of this book. The reader has already met specific examples of many of these concepts in previous chapters. Here we shall examine them in greater generality, and develop notations and abbreviations which will clarify and simplify later work. In the final sections of this chapter, we shall bring theory and application together for the analysis of four realistic case studies using some methods of *Computer-assisted Data Analysis* (CADA).

6-1 BAYES' THEOREM FOR SEVERAL PARAMETERS

We recall that our fundamental inference procedure is based on Bayes' theorem in the form

$$p(\theta|x) \propto p(x|\theta)p(\theta)\,, \qquad (6\text{-}1.1)$$

where the constant of proportionality can be determined from the fact that $p(\theta|x)$ is a density (or mass distribution) for θ and so integrates (or sums) to unity over the range (or set of possible values) of θ. Here we may think of x as an observation (e.g., a score on a test) and of θ as a parameter to which x is related (e.g., an ability). The use of parenthetic expressions to cover both continuous and discrete cases is tedious, and we abandon it forthwith, using the language for the continuous case and leaving the reader to translate it, when necessary, into the language for the discrete case. Recall that we remarked in Chap. 3 that if one were prepared to call a probability mass function a density function, a single language would suffice.

One attractive feature of Bayes' theorem is the simplicity with which it generalizes to the case where there are several observations and, possibly, several parameters. All that is needed is to write $\mathbf{x} = (x_1, x_2, \ldots)$ for the set of observations and $\boldsymbol{\theta} = (\theta_1, \theta_2, \ldots)$ for the set of parameters. Bayes' theorem then becomes

$$p(\boldsymbol{\theta}|\mathbf{x}) \propto p(\mathbf{x}|\boldsymbol{\theta})p(\boldsymbol{\theta}). \qquad (6\text{-}1.2)$$

It is customary to refer to $\mathbf{x}$ and $\boldsymbol{\theta}$ as *vectors* of observations and parameters, respectively. We shall also refer to $\mathbf{x}$ as the *data*. The vector $\mathbf{x}$ typically contains the observations from a random sample of people. In this chapter, the vector $\boldsymbol{\theta}$ will contain no more than two elements, e.g., the binomial proportion π or the normal mean and variance (θ, ϕ). In (6-1.2), $p(\boldsymbol{\theta})$ denotes the *joint* density of the parameters $\theta_1, \theta_2, \ldots$ prior to the vector $\mathbf{x}$ of observations becoming available, $p(\boldsymbol{\theta}|\mathbf{x})$ the joint density posterior to obtaining data $\mathbf{x}$, and $p(\mathbf{x}|\boldsymbol{\theta})$ the joint density of the random variables being observed, conditional on the values of the parameters. We now study these components in more detail.

6-2 MODEL DENSITY, LIKELIHOOD, SUFFICIENT STATISTICS

The starting point for statistical inference, classical or Bayesian, is a *model* which describes the probabilistic relationship between the observables and the parameters of interest. For example, in Chap. 5, we discussed the binomial model which relates the number X of successes (correct spellings) to a parameter π which we interpreted as ability. In that instance, it was possible to derive the probability model from more basic assumptions about the probability of spelling correctly each individual word. More typically, the model to be used is itself the basic assumption of the analysis.

The most frequently used model for a continuous random variable is the so-called normal distribution. The name was coined by Karl Pearson in an attempt to be neutral between the Germans who called it Gaussian and the French who called it Laplacean. Pearson himself came to recognize that the name was dangerous since "normal" might be taken to mean "appropriate in most circumstances", and "nonnormal" might be equated with "abnormal". In a slightly different sense, however, the name does reflect the fact that the distribution is used as a "norm" when a symmetrical, unimodal, continuous-probability model is required. When there is doubt about the exact form of model which is appropriate, a common approach is to solve the problem using a normal model and then attempt to evaluate how sensitive the conclusions would be to changes in the model. Frequently, the conclusions are robust with respect to such changes.

Several different factors combine to give the normal distribution this central role as a statistical model. The most prominent of these is mathematical tractability—one can usually do the necessary mathematics if one starts with a normal model. (It would take us far beyond the scope of this book to explain why this is so. Some of the more obvious reasons are the symmetry and the fact that the normal density involves only two parameters—one of which is a measure of location and the other a measure of scale. However, these two properties are shared by densities which are, in other respects, disturbingly intractable.) Tractability would be regarded by the pure mathematician as a sufficient reason for using the model. The statistical practitioner, however, may well feel that it is a rather disreputable reason. An immediate counterargument runs as follows. Surely it is better to get some results using a model which is only approximately relevant than to sit twiddling one's thumbs in front of a model which is felt to be more accurate but which one is unable to manipulate. This argument loses a bit of its force each year as we make progress in the computer analysis of complex models.

However, there are more direct arguments from experience and theory. When Francis Galton (his name being linked with University College, London) collected the masses of anthropometric and biometric data whose analysis gave the initial impetus to the growth of modern statistics (and psychometrics), a large number of the variables which he measured were found to have normal distributions. Much earlier, the normal distribution had been found appropriate for errors of measurement in astronomy and surveying. Possibly accounting for these observed normal distributions are theoretical results known as *central-limit theorems* which say, roughly speaking, that where an observed variable is itself the average or *sum* of a large number of other variables (as an anthropometric variable may be the sum of many hereditary causes, or a total error may be made up of many different types of error), then that observed variable may be expected to have approximately a normal distribution. We saw a concrete example of this in Sec. 5-3 where the large sample distribution of the total number of successes in a binomial sample was given.

The normal distribution with mean μ and variance σ^2 is usually denoted by $N(\mu, \sigma^2)$ where σ denotes the standard deviation. One of the many convenient features of the distribution is that if X is a variable with distribution $N(\mu, \sigma^2)$, then the standard score $Z = (X - \mu)/\sigma$ has distribution $N(0, 1)$, known as the *standard normal distribution*. Thus, a single table can give all the information required for making probability statements about *any* normally distributed variable. The cumulative-distribution function $\Phi(z)$ for the standard normal distribution is given in Table A.1. Almost all the probability (area under the density curve) lies in the range $-3 < Z < +3$, and so tabulation beyond this range is not usually necessary. Also, the symmetry of the distribution makes it unnecessary to list negative values of z since

$$\begin{aligned}\Phi(-z) &= \text{Prob}\,(Z \leq -z) = \text{Prob}\,(Z \geq z) \quad \text{(by symmetry)}\\ &= 1 - \Phi(z).\end{aligned}$$

In other words, to find the probability that Z is less than $-z$, we subtract from unity the probability (given by Table A.1) that Z is less than $+z$.

Hence, if we are interested in the probability that a normally distributed variable X falls in any interval (x_1, x_2), we find the corresponding range (z_1, z_2) for the standard score Z and use Table A.1 to determine $\text{Prob}(z_1 < Z \leq z_2) = \Phi(z_2) - \Phi(z_1)$, making use of the symmetry if one or both of z_1, z_2 are negative. An example of the use of the table was given in Sec. 5-3 where the normal distribution was used as an approximation to the binomial.

In Table A.2 we give percentage points of the standard normal distribution, that is, values of z such that $\text{Prob}\,(Z \leq z) = P\%$, for $P = 75, 80, 85, 87.5, 90, 95, 97.5, 99, 99.5$. These are useful for finding credibility intervals for normally distributed variables and, more generally, for thinking concretely about the implications of the statement that a variable is normally distributed with stated mean and variance. The most widely known percentage point is the value $z = 1.96$ (often approximated to $z = 2$), corresponding to $P = 97.5$. Because of the symmetry, it follows that the probability of a standard normal variable lying between -1.96 and $+1.96$ is 95%. Translating this back in terms of the unstandardized variable, the probability of any normal variable lying within about two (precisely 1.96) standard deviations of its own mean is 95%.

Suppose now that our model for a variable X is the normal distribution $N(\theta, \phi)$ with mean θ and variance ϕ. (The change of notation is made to emphasize the fact that θ and ϕ are now regarded as *unknown* parameters.) For typographical clarity, we shall adopt a common notation and denote $e^{f(x)}$ by $\exp\,[f(x)]$, where $f(x)$ is an arbitrary function of x. When $f(x)$ is itself a ratio, this helps keep the alignment within the expression clear. In the equation that follows $f(x) = -(x - \theta)^2/2\phi$. The normal density function is thus

$$p(x|\theta, \phi) = m_{\theta,\phi}(x) = \frac{1}{(2\pi\phi)^{1/2}} \exp\left[\frac{-(x - \theta)^2}{2\phi}\right]. \tag{6-2.1}$$

Here we have introduced the first of our notational cues—the use of $m(x)$, with the relevant parameters as subscripts, to denote the *model* density of a random variable X. Of course, the new notation does not in any way alter the syntactic properties of the density—it is still the probability density for X conditional on θ and ϕ. The notation does, however, indicate a number of things about the semantic interpretation we are placing on the density, as follows:

1) The model will be treated as fixed or known with certainty for the duration of the analysis. The justification for this approach was discussed above in relation to the normal model.

2) The parameters listed as subscripts are those which are being regarded as unknown. For example, we shall find it convenient in this chapter to use as an illustrative example a normal model with *known* variance which we shall revert to calling σ^2. We shall then write the model density as

$$m_\theta(x) = \frac{1}{(2\pi\sigma^2)^{1/2}} \exp\left[\frac{(x - \theta)^2}{-2\sigma^2}\right], \qquad (6\text{-}2.2)$$

indicating that only the mean θ is regarded as unknown.

3) The model density is thought of as having, at least conceptually, an interpretation in terms of relative frequency. For example, if the normal model with mean zero is used for the error which occurs in making a certain physical measurement, we shall understand it to imply that if a large number of measurements of the same quantity were made independently of each other, about 95% of them would be found to lie within two standard deviations of the true value, and so on. Later, we shall apply the model to an individual's score on a psychological test, regarding this as being composed of a "true" value and an error. Clearly, there are difficulties in considering *actual* repeated applications of the same test, but, at least *conceptually*, we can consider frequency properties which such repeated measurements would have if it were possible to arrange that one testing had no influence on a subsequent testing.

Most classical statisticians are willing to use only probability densities which are frequency-interpretable in the above sense. For them, the parameter θ in (6-2.2) is simply a number which indexes a particular member of the family of normal distributions (with known variance σ^2). They may, indeed, try to estimate θ, but they would regard it as meaningless to talk of a probability density for θ since this does not seem to have any plausible frequency interpretation. It follows that classical statistics is concerned with the manipulation of model densities (only). The remainder of this section would be acceptable to a classical statistician; but later sections, requiring the use of densities for parameters, which can only plausibly be interpreted in terms of strength of belief, would not be acceptable.

Likelihood Function

It is unusual for inference to be based on a single observation. More typically, one obtains a vector $\mathbf{x} = (x_1, x_2, \ldots, x_n)$ of observations in such a manner that the joint density of the X_i, $i = 1, 2, \ldots, n$, can be deduced from the basic model. While many schemes are possible, the one of practical importance is that in which the X_i are independent (given θ) random variables, each having the same model density. Another way of expressing this is to say that the vector $\mathbf{x}$ constitutes a *random sample* from the model distribution. In this case, the joint density [see (3-5.4)] is simply the product (Π) of the model densities for each X_i

$$m_\theta(\mathbf{x}) = \prod_{i=1}^{n} m_\theta(x_i). \tag{6-2.3}$$

This joint density also can be regarded as a model density since it derives directly from the model in use—that is, from the densities for the individual X_i *and* their independence.

For example, if each X_i has the normal density (6-2.2), we find using (6-2.3) that the joint density is

$$m_\theta(\mathbf{x}) = \frac{1}{(2\pi\sigma^2)^{n/2}} \exp\left[\frac{\sum_1^n (x_i - \theta)^2}{-2\sigma^2}\right]. \tag{6-2.4}$$

An alternative form of (6-2.4) which we will find useful in subsequent discussions is

$$m_\theta(\mathbf{x}) = \frac{1}{(2\pi\sigma^2)^{n/2}} \exp\left[\frac{\Sigma(x_i - x_\bullet)^2 + n(x_\bullet - \theta)^2}{-2\sigma^2}\right] \tag{6-2.5}$$

where $x_\bullet = n^{-1}\Sigma x_i$, the mean of the observations. The alternative form is obtained by writing $(x_i - \theta) = (x_i - x_\bullet) + (x_\bullet - \theta)$ in the numerator of the exponent in (6-2.4) and examining the terms of the algebraic expansion which results. The reader who trusts our algebra need not investigate the details. The point is worth mentioning, however, because this maneuver and more sophisticated versions of it are used repeatedly with normal models in order to present densities in their most usable forms.

So far we have been thinking of $m_\theta(\mathbf{x})$ as the joint density of the variables $X_1, X_2, \ldots, X_n$, conditional on the value of the parameter θ. When the observations have been collected and their values inserted in (6-2.4) or (6-2.5), we are left with a function of θ only (σ^2 being a known number). Thought of in these terms, the function given by (6-2.4) or (6-2.5) is called the *likelihood* function of θ and will be denoted by $l(\theta)$ or $l_n(\theta)$, the subscript in the latter case indicating the number of observations on which it is based.

The use of different names and symbols for what appears to be the same function viewed from two different angles may initially seem confusing or at least superfluous. It has to be admitted that the reason for it is partly historical. However, the existence of the two names does help to highlight the process by which observations lead to inferences. The joint model density is relevant before the observations are made. It tells us, loosely speaking, the probability of obtaining various possible vectors of observations for a fixed value of θ. The likelihood function becomes relevant after the observations are made. For any particular value of θ, it tells us, again loosely speaking, how probable our actual observations were. If θ were known, the likelihood function would be of no importance; its usefulness lies in relating the actual observations to the possible values of θ.

We have already encountered in Chap. 5 the method of *maximum-likelihood* estimation based on the principle that one should choose as the estimate that value of θ which makes one's actual observations most probable, that is, which maximizes the likelihood function. We noted that this is equivalent to finding the most probable value of θ (the posterior mode) only if the prior distribution for Θ is uniform. For the model with likelihood function given by (6-2.5), the maximum-likelihood estimate can be found without resort to calculus. Note that θ occurs only in the (nonnegative) term $n(x_{\bullet} - \theta)^2$ in the numerator of the exponent. Because of the minus sign in the denominator, the likelihood will be largest when the numerator is smallest which is clearly achieved by putting $\theta = x_{\bullet}$; hence, the maximum-likelihood estimate of θ is $x_{\bullet}$, the mean of the observations.

Sufficient Statistics

In determining the maximum-likelihood estimate, factors of the likelihood which did not involve θ–the constant $(2\pi\sigma^2)^{n/2}$, and the factor $\exp[\Sigma(x_i - x_{\bullet})^2/-2\sigma^2]$ depending only on the observations–were irrelevant and could have been dropped from consideration. The same is true in Bayesian inference. Our basic equation (6-1.2) can be stated in words as; *the posterior density of the parameter(s) is proportional to the product of the likelihood and the prior density*. Any factor of the likelihood which does not involve the parameter(s) can be absorbed into the constant of proportionality. Thus, for example, the only part of (6-2.5) which is needed in making inferences about θ is the factor

$$\exp\left[\frac{n(x_{\bullet} - \theta)^2}{-2\sigma^2}\right]. \qquad (6\text{-}2.6)$$

This relevant factor is sometimes called the *kernel* of the likelihood, the remaining factors being, by implication, mere shell or chaff which can be thrown away without loss. (Other authors use "likelihood" to mean what we call "kernel of the likelihood", discarding the chaff before making the definition.) On examining the kernel (6-2.6), we see that it involves the observations only through their mean $x_{\bullet}$. Thus, the *only* piece of information about the observations relevant to making inferences about θ, in this model, is their mean. We say that the mean $x_{\bullet}$ is a *sufficient statistic* for θ, a statistic (singular) in general being simply a function of the observations. (The mathematically curious reader who wonders what happens to those factors of the likelihood which involve the observations x_i otherwise than through their mean, and which we so gaily discarded, should study the full form of Bayes' theorem analogous to Eq. (3-6.3) and the factorization of the model (6-2.5): it will then be clear that factors not involving the parameter divide out from the numerator and denominator.)

At the risk of becoming tedious, we repeat the fundamental property of a sufficient statistic, that we shall make the same inferences about our parameter whether we are told the whole set of observations x or merely told the value of the sufficient statistic. In our present example, this means that $p(\theta|\mathbf{x}) = p(\theta|x_\bullet)$. If we had been able to discover without examining the likelihood function that, with *fixed* n, $x_\bullet$ was sufficient for θ, we could have treated $x_\bullet$ as an observation and used Bayes' theorem in the form

$$p(\theta|x_\bullet) \propto p(x_\bullet|\theta)p(\theta).$$

Now, it is well known that the mean of n independent random variables, each with distribution $N(\theta, \sigma^2)$, has distribution $N(\theta, \sigma^2/n)$–in classical statistics this is called the *sampling distribution* of $x_\bullet$ and is the basis of inferences about θ. Thus,

$$p(x_\bullet|\theta) = \frac{1}{(2\pi\sigma^2 n^{-1})^{1/2}} \exp\left[\frac{(x_\bullet - \theta)^2}{-2\sigma^2 n^{-1}}\right].$$

Inspection shows that this has the same kernel as (6-2.6), confirming that we shall obtain the same posterior density by either method.

As a second example of the concepts discussed in this section, the reader may find it useful to review the material of Sec. 5-4. There, the observation x_i is the score for the ith word of the test—$x_i = 1$ if the word is correctly spelled, $x_i = 0$ if it is incorrect. The model density for X_i is

$$m_\pi(x_i) = \begin{cases} \pi & \text{if } x_i = 1 \\ (1 - \pi) & \text{if } x_i = 0 \end{cases}$$

which can alternatively be written

$$m_\pi(x_i) = \pi^{x_i}(1 - \pi)^{(1 - x_i)}, \qquad x_i = 0, 1.$$

The joint model density is

$$m_\pi(\mathbf{x}) = \prod_{i=1}^{n} m_\pi(x_i) = \pi^{\Sigma x_i}(1 - \pi)^{n - \Sigma x_i} = \pi^t(1 - \pi)^{n - t} \qquad \text{(6-2.7)}$$

where $t = \Sigma x_i$, the total number correct (which we previously denoted by x). If n is fixed in advance, this shows that t is sufficient for π, as seems intuitively obvious. From (5-2.1), we know that the distribution of t in samples of size n has the binomial mass function

$$\binom{n}{t}\pi^t(1 - \pi)^{n - t}, \qquad t = 0, 1, 2, \ldots, n, \qquad \text{(6-2.8)}$$

which has the same kernel as (6-2.7).

Suppose, however, that instead of administering a fixed number of words, we go on administering words (of equal difficulty) until the examinee has spelled a fixed number t correctly, and record the total number n of words which we have had to use. The likelihood is still (6-2.7), but now t is fixed and n is the sufficient statistic.

By an argument similar to that used to derive the geometric distribution in Sec. 3-4, the probability mass function for the number n of words administered to an examinee of ability π by the time he spells t words correctly can be shown to be

$$\binom{n-1}{t-1}\pi^t(1-\pi)^{n-t}, \quad n = t, t+1, \ldots \tag{6-2.9}$$

which also has the same kernel as (6-2.7).

Thus, we have here an example of the fact that any sets of observations, however obtained, which have the same likelihood function will lead to the same inferences in a Bayesian analysis (presuming the same prior to be used). The assertion that this ought to be so for any credible inference system is known as the *likelihood principle*. Some non-Bayesian or semi-Bayesian procedures also satisfy it, for example, maximum-likelihood estimation. Note, however, that the mass functions (6-2.8) and (6-2.9) are *not* the same, even though their kernels are. Thus, a method such as classical unbiased estimation, which involves a consideration of the whole mass function of the sufficient statistic and not just its kernel, may violate the likelihood principle (as unbiased estimation does in the present instance), leading to different conclusions according to the procedure which was adopted for collecting the data.

6-3 PRIOR AND POSTERIOR BAYES DENSITIES, NATURAL CONJUGATE DISTRIBUTIONS

The feature which chiefly distinguishes Bayesian statistical methodology is that parameters as well as observables are regarded as random variables having a probability distribution. Indeed, the main goal of a Bayesian analysis is to obtain the *posterior distribution* of the parameters of interest—that is, the distribution which takes into account the evidence about the parameter values which has been provided by the observations. However, unlike the model densities for observables which can be given a frequency interpretation, the densities for parameters, which we shall call *Bayes densities* and denote by $b(\theta)$, have to be interpreted as statements of belief about the parameter value(s). [The notation $b(\theta)$ was chosen as a mnemonic for Bayes density, but by a happy coincidence, it is also a mnemonic for belief density.]

In general, a Bayes density indicates a state of belief about a parameter, intermediate between the statements "I know nothing about θ" and "I know the exact value of θ". In Sec. 5-5, we saw that a useful way to think concretely about the beliefs implied by a particular Bayes density is in terms of credibility intervals. A *C% credibility interval* is an interval in which the parameter has probability $C\%$ of lying. When we have available tables of the percentage points of the relevant Bayes distribution, we can immediately construct credibility intervals—for example, a central 50% credibility interval has as its ends the 25 and 75% points of the distribution. Its interpretation is that we believe there is an even chance that the parameter lies inside or outside the interval.

We shall be concerned with two types of Bayes densities: the *prior density*, representing our beliefs about the parameter(s) before the observations are obtained, and the *posterior density*, representing our beliefs after seeing the data. When the body of data under study is clear from the context, we shall denote the prior density by $b(\theta)$ and the posterior density by $b_n(\theta)$ where n is the number of observations. In more complex situations, it may be clearer to denote the posterior density by $b_{\mathbf{x}}(\theta)$. The terms prior and posterior are, of course, relative to a particular body of data. If after deriving the posterior density using one set of data $\mathbf{x}_1$, we then decide to make additional observations $\mathbf{x}_2$, the posterior density $b_{\mathbf{x}_1}(\theta)$ from the first analysis becomes the prior density for the second analysis. If, as is usually the case, $\mathbf{x}_1$ and $\mathbf{x}_2$ are independent given θ, the following formal manipulations establish a fundamental consistency property of Bayesian methods:

$$\begin{aligned} p(\theta|\mathbf{x}_1, \mathbf{x}_2) &\propto p(\mathbf{x}_1, \mathbf{x}_2|\theta)p(\theta) && \text{(Bayes)} \\ &\propto p(\mathbf{x}_2|\theta)p(\mathbf{x}_1|\theta)p(\theta) && \text{(independence of } \mathbf{x}_1 \text{ and } \mathbf{x}_2\text{)} \\ &\propto p(\mathbf{x}_2|\theta)p(\theta|\mathbf{x}_1), && \text{(Bayes)} \end{aligned}$$

or, in our new notation,

$$b_{\mathbf{x}_1, \mathbf{x}_2}(\theta) \propto m_\theta(\mathbf{x}_2)\, b_{\mathbf{x}_1}(\theta).$$

In other words, this says that *the posterior density of Θ starting from prior $b(\theta)$ and observing data $\mathbf{x}_1$, $\mathbf{x}_2$ is proportional to, and, hence, the same as, that starting from the posterior density $b_{\mathbf{x}_1}(\theta)$ and observing data $\mathbf{x}_2$*. The practically minded reader may feel that this is a rather trivial result to italicize—thinking that any system of inference which did *not* possess this property and which, therefore, gave different results when one pooled data collected on two successive days from those which would have been obtained by updating one's Bayes density on the first night and then incorporating the second day's data would not deserve serious consideration. We agree but point out that some systems of inference do not have this property. In Bayesian statistics the actual analysis of data is the same in sequential sampling as in fixed sampling.

Once the prior density and the model density (or the likelihood) are known, the posterior density follows at once from (6-1.2). From it, in turn, can be derived point estimates (mean, median, mode, etc., depending on one's loss function), measures of the uncertainty of estimates such as the posterior variance, and credibility intervals. Thus, conceptually at least, Bayesian inference always follows a single, simple procedure which we shall refer to as "cranking the Bayesian handle". Of course, conceptual simplicity does not guarantee mathematical simplicity. (Vintage car owners will be aware that cranking the handle is a skilled operation in which the unwary can easily sprain a wrist.) Since in this book we do not require the reader to work through the mathematics involved in any but the simplest cases, we content ourselves with a list of some of the mathematical problems which may be encountered and whose solution is part of the "handlecranking".

1) The posterior distribution (of a single parameter) may not be of a form which is well known and tabulated. Some options are (a) tabulate it (if it seems likely to be of continuing usefulness); (b) approximate it by a tabulated distribution; (c) use a computer to find the required features of the posterior distribution by numerical integration, etc.

2) All but the simplest problems involve two or more unknown parameters. Equation (6-1.2) gives their *joint* posterior distribution. In our new notation, Bayes' theorem reads

$$b_n(\boldsymbol{\theta}) \propto m_{\boldsymbol{\theta}}(\mathbf{x})\,b(\boldsymbol{\theta}), \qquad (6\text{-}3.1)$$

or

$$b_n(\boldsymbol{\theta}) \propto l_n(\boldsymbol{\theta})\,b(\boldsymbol{\theta}). \qquad (6\text{-}3.2)$$

Often the values of some of these parameters are of no interest to us—for example, because they are not relevant to the decisions we are about to take. These parameters are called *nuisance parameters*. They are a necessary part of the model, but we do not wish to make inferences about them. In Sec. 3-5, we saw that the (marginal) density of a single variable X is obtained from the joint density of the pair (X, Y) by summing (integrating) the latter with respect to y. The same procedure is applied to the joint posterior density of (Θ_1, Θ_2), where Θ_2 is a nuisance parameter, to obtain the required posterior density of Θ_1. The method extends to the case of more than one nuisance parameter. Mathematical difficulties arise if the integrations cannot be performed explicitly. We must then either approximate or use a computer to integrate numerically.

3) Even when we have "integrated out" the nuisance parameters, there may be many parameters of interest left in the problem. It is arguable that the joint posterior distribution is the proper expression of our posterior beliefs about these parameters. In practice, however, few people can think concretely about distributions of more than two variables, to say nothing of the impossibility of tabulating them. We, therefore, again resort to marginal densities for the individual parameters. It may, however, be possible to calculate some important features of the joint distribution, for example, the joint mode (the set of parameter values for which the posterior density is largest—loosely speaking, the most probable *set* of values). Indeed, in complex problems, the joint mode may be the *only* feature of the joint distribution for which we can obtain an explicit formula.

Natural Conjugate Densities

The price which the Bayesian pays for the conceptual simplicity of his inference procedure is the close attention which he has to give to the specification of his prior distributions. At the end of Chap. 5, we gave an example of how subjective beliefs about a parameter might be reduced to a probability density by reversing the procedure used to find credibility intervals. The method involved approximating one's prior beliefs by a density which is a member of a mathematically convenient family–a so-called *natural conjugate density* (NCD). We now investigate this idea further.

The basic reason why a beta prior proved convenient for a binary model was that, considered as a function of π, the kernel of the prior $\pi^{a-1}(1 - \pi)^{b-1}$ is of the same form as the kernel of the likelihood found at (6-2.7), $\pi^{\Sigma x_i}(1 - \pi)^{n-\Sigma x_i}$. This, in turn, is necessarily the same as the kernel of the distribution of the sufficient statistic $t = \Sigma x_i$ given by (6-2.8). Or to put it another way, if in the kernel of the likelihood we replace the functions of the observations Σx_i and $n - \Sigma x_i$ by constants such as $a - 1$ and $b - 1$, then we obtain the natural conjugate density. Let us try to find a NCD for the normal model with known variance as given by (6-2.2). The kernel of the likelihood was shown in (6-2.6) to be $\exp[n(x_{\bullet} - \theta)^2/(-2\sigma^2)]$. The functions of the observations it involves are $x_{\bullet}$ and n. For the present purpose and for any strictly formal discussion of sufficient statistics, kernels, etc., the number of observations must be regarded as a function of the observations since it is not or need not be known before the observations are made, at which time the prior distribution is to be specified. Thus, strictly speaking, we should say that for the model given by (6-2.2), $x_{\bullet}$ and n are jointly sufficient statistics. We do not find this formalism helpful for expository purposes nor, indeed, for thinking about practical problems; but it lurks in the mathematical background and from time to time rears its ugly head–as now.

Returning from this rather lengthy digression, we replace $x_{\bullet}$ and n by constants a and b and obtain as the kernel of a natural conjugate density for Θ

$$\exp\left[\frac{b(a - \theta)^2}{-2\sigma^2}\right].$$

If we write μ_0 for a and σ_0^2 for σ^2/b, this becomes

$$\exp\left[\frac{(\theta - \mu_0)^2}{-2\sigma_0^2}\right], \qquad (6\text{-}3.3)$$

in which form it can be recognized as the kernel of a normal density corresponding to the statement that Θ is $N(\mu_0, \sigma_0^2)$. Thus, we have shown that the NCD for a normal model with known variance is itself normal.

If we use $N(\mu_0, \sigma_0^2)$, with suitable values of μ_0 and σ_0, as our prior distribution, we anticipate that our posterior distribution will also be normal. To verify that this is actually so, we multiply together the kernel of the prior density given by (6-3.3) and the kernel of the likelihood (6-2.6). This amounts to summing the two exponents, and a little algebra (of the type known as "completing the square" in the solution of quadratic equations) shows that the sum can be written as

$$\frac{(\theta - \mu_n)^2}{-2\sigma_n^2} + \text{a term not involving } \theta$$

where
$$\mu_n = \frac{\sigma_0^{-2}\mu_0 + n\sigma^{-2}x_\bullet}{\sigma_0^{-2} + n\sigma^{-2}}, \qquad (6\text{-}3.4)$$

and
$$\sigma_n^{-2} = \sigma_0^{-2} + n\sigma^{-2}. \qquad (6\text{-}3.5)$$

The exponential of the term not involving θ can be absorbed in the constant of proportionality in Bayes' theorem, leaving as the kernel of the posterior density

$$\exp\left[\frac{(\theta - \mu_n)^2}{-2\sigma_n^2}\right], \qquad (6\text{-}3.6)$$

which shows that the posterior distribution is $N(\mu_n, \sigma_n^2)$ of the anticipated normal form.

Those readers who enjoy algebraic exercises may wish to verify the following general formula:

$$a(\theta - \alpha)^2 + b(\theta - \beta)^2 = (a + b)\left(\theta - \frac{a\alpha + b\beta}{a + b}\right)^2 + \frac{ab}{a + b}(\alpha - \beta)^2, \qquad (6\text{-}3.7)$$

which can then be used to verify the result given above and later be used to obtain further, more complicated results of this type.

The form of Eq. (6-3.4) is very interesting and exhibits a feature of Bayesian results which will recur frequently in this book. Note that the posterior mean μ_n is a weighted average of two quantities: μ_0, the prior mean of Θ; and $x_\bullet$, the mean of the observations, which can be regarded as a "natural" estimate of θ from the sample (more formally, we have seen that it is the maximum-likelihood estimate). The weights given to the two components are, respectively, σ_0^{-2}, the reciprocal of the variance of the prior distribution, and $n\sigma^{-2}$, the reciprocal of the variance σ^2/n of the sampling distribution of the sufficient statistic $x_\bullet$. Now, the reciprocal of the variance of a distribution tells us how closely the variable values cluster around the mean and is, therefore, sometimes called the *precision* of the distribution. The prior precision is a measure of how much is known about θ before the observations are made—the larger the precision, the closer we are able to pin θ down as being "near μ_0". The precision of the sampling distribution indicates how close the statistic is expected to lie to the mean θ of its distribution. As one would expect, this precision increases with the number n of observations made. Thus, Eq. (6-3.4) illustrates in a rather dramatic, and to us intuitively appealing, way how the use of Bayes' theorem strikes a compromise between prior knowledge and sample information.

It may be useful to collect together our results for this model.

In the problem of making inferences about the mean θ of a normal distribution with known variance, the sample mean $x_\bullet$ is a sufficient statistic. The natural *conjugate density is also normal. Using it as prior, the posterior distribution is normal with mean a weighted average of the prior mean and* $x_\bullet$, *the weights being the precisions (reciprocals of variances) of the prior distribution and the sampling distribution of* $x_\bullet$, *respectively, (6-3.4). The posterior precision is the sum of the prior precision and the sampling precision (6-3.5).*

6-4 PREDICTIVE DENSITIES

In Sec. 3-5, we saw that when two random variables (in the present context X and Θ) have a joint density, this gives rise to two marginal densities, one for X and one for Θ; and to two sets of conditional densities, one set for X given θ and another for Θ given x. In the application to Bayesian inference, the conditional density of X given θ is the model density $m_\theta(x)$ which is supposed known; and the marginal density of Θ is the prior Bayes density $b(\theta)$, chosen to reflect prior knowledge or lack of it. As is seen from (3-5.7), the product $m_\theta(x)\,b(\theta)$ is the joint density of X and Θ. From it, we can obtain the conditional density of Θ given x which is simply the posterior density $b_1(\theta)$ after obtaining a single observation x.

We can also obtain the density we have not so far discussed—the marginal density of X, which we call the *(prior) predictive density* and denote by $p(x)$ (p for predictive). By analogy with (3-6.5), we have

$$p(x) = \int m_\theta(x)\,b(\theta)\,d\theta\,. \qquad (6\text{-}4.1)$$

The interpretation of this density is as follows. Suppose that, knowing the model and the prior density of Θ but not yet having made any observations, we are asked to make predictions about X, the first observation we are about to make. What is the density which expresses our beliefs about X? Fairly obviously, just as the marginal density of Θ expresses our present beliefs about Θ, the marginal density $p(x)$ of X expresses our present beliefs about X. The only difference is that we can make a direct observation on X, whereas we cannot (usually) make a direct observation on Θ.

Another approach to the predictive density is useful. The model density is, of course, a function of both x and θ. However, we can think of the whole density curve (or density function) as a single entity which changes as θ changes. In this sense, it is a function of θ (we did the same in talking about the likelihood). Then, since $b(\theta)$ is the density of Θ, Eq. (6-4.1) says that $p(x)$ is the expectation of the model density; or to put it a more expressive way, $p(x)$ is the weighted average of the set of model densities (one for each value of θ), weighted according to their relative probabilities. This certainly seems an intuitively reasonable way of obtaining, for the situation where θ is unknown, the analog of what the model density would tell us if θ were known.

Now consider the situation when n observations have been made, and we wish to predict the $(n + 1)$st. The only real change in the situation is that our beliefs about Θ

have been updated from $b(\theta)$ to the posterior density $b_n(\theta)$. The model is unchanged. Hence, analogous to (6-4.1), we have the *posterior predictive density*

$$p_n(x_{n+1}) = \int m_\theta(x_{n+1})\, b_n(\theta)\, d\theta\,, \qquad (6\text{-}4.2)$$

the subscript to p denoting the number of observations already made, and the (strictly speaking, redundant) subscript to x reminding us that we are predicting the $(n + 1)$st.

There are certainly situations where prediction of X is more important than estimation of some underlying parameter θ—predicting tomorrow's stock prices springs to mind. Indeed, this type of prediction was the real concern of early workers such as Bayes, and Laplace, with his Rule of Succession. This fact is rather obscured because they were concerned with the binary model in which the model density is $m_\pi(1) = \pi$, $m_\pi(0) = 1 - \pi$, "1" and "0" as usual standing conventionally for success and failure. Now we have seen that the predictive density is the expectation of the model density. Thus, $p_n(1) = \mathcal{E}\,[m_\pi(1)] = \mathcal{E}(\Pi)$ and $p_n(0) = \mathcal{E}[m_\pi(0)] = 1 - \mathcal{E}(\Pi)$, the expectation in each case being taken with respect to the posterior distribution of Π. There is, thus, in this model no difference between finding the posterior predictive probability that $X = 1$ and finding the posterior mean of Π. It is hardly surprising, therefore, that it is not always clear which aim an author had in mind.

Suppose two persons have different prior distributions for Π; for the first, the distribution of Π is $\beta(5, 5)$, and for the second $\beta(10,10)$. For each person, $\mathcal{E}(\Pi) = .5$, and so Prob $(X = 1) = .5$. Thus, each would just be willing to bet at even odds that the defining event would occur. That event might be "rain tomorrow", or "Malcolm successfully completes his first semester at Junior College". The personal probabilities of the event occurring are identical for the two persons [Prob $(X = 1) = .5$], yet surely the second person is more certain of his statement than the first. There is no inconsistency here, but it must be recognized that the statement of the probability of an event is always a statement involving an expectation; and thus, that statement does not convey all of the information about the relevant parameter conveyed in the Bayes distribution.

Turning to the normal model discussed in Sec. 6-3, where $m_\theta(x)$ is a $N(\theta, \sigma^2)$ density with σ known and $b(\theta)$ is a $N(\mu_0, \sigma_0^2)$ density, the joint distribution of X and Θ is what is known as bivariate normal. It has the property that all the conditional and marginal distributions are (univariate) normal. In particular, the prior predictive distribution is $N(\mu_0, \sigma_0^2 + \sigma^2)$. Note that its mean is the same as that of the prior density of Θ, but its variance is the sum of the prior variance and the model variance. If we interpret a variance as a measure of imprecision or uncertainty, this says that our uncertainty about X is the sum of our uncertainty about X when θ is known and our uncertainty about Θ—an intuitively pleasing result.

The parameters of the predictive density can also be regarded as an example of the use of the basic Eqs. (4-1.8) and (4-1.9) in the algebra of expectations. We have

$$
\begin{aligned}
\mathcal{E}(X) &= \mathcal{E}[\mathcal{E}(X|\theta)] && \text{(generally)},\\
&= \mathcal{E}(\Theta) && \text{(in this model)},\\
&= \mu_0 && \text{(from the prior)},
\end{aligned}
$$

and

$$
\begin{aligned}
\mathcal{V}(X) &= \mathcal{V}[\mathcal{E}(X|\theta)] + \mathcal{E}[\mathcal{V}(X|\theta)],\\
&= \mathcal{V}(\Theta) + \mathcal{E}(\sigma^2), && \text{(from the model)},\\
&= \sigma_0^2 + \sigma^2, && \text{(from the prior, and because } \sigma^2 \text{ is a constant)}.
\end{aligned}
$$

In the same way, the posterior predictive density is $N(\mu_n, \sigma_n^2 + \sigma^2)$, where μ_n and σ_n^2 are the posterior mean and variance of Θ given by (6-3.4) and (6-3.5). Recalling that $\sigma_n^{-2} = \sigma_0^{-2} + n\sigma^{-2}$, we see that, a posteriori,

$$\mathcal{V}(X) = \sigma^2 \left[\frac{\sigma^2 + (n+1)\sigma_0^2}{\sigma^2 + n\sigma_0^2} \right].$$

Then, if σ_0^2 is very large,

$$\mathcal{V}(X) = \sigma^2 \left(1 + \frac{1}{n} \right).$$

To understand what this means, consider the problem of estimating the value of the $(n + 1)$st observation from a normal distribution with known variance. If the mean of the model density is also known, then it is the best estimate under squared-error loss, and the expected loss is the variance σ^2. If the mean of the model density is unknown, the best estimate is the mean μ_n of the posterior predictive density and the variance is $\sigma^2[1 + (1/n)]$, assuming a very large prior variance. In the second case, we have had to guess a good point estimate knowing that the point μ_n would not be at the optimum value μ. The result of this inaccuracy, of course, is that we pay the price of having a larger squared-error loss, $\sigma^2[1 + (1/n)]$ rather than σ^2, associated with the procedure. As n increases, the variance of the predictive density decreases, ultimately reaching the value σ^2, as it should, since the value μ_n being used will get closer and closer to the true value μ as n increases.

When we consider the regression models used, for example, for predicting college grade-point average Y from an aptitude test score x, it is clear that the density of real interest is the predictive density of Y for given x (if it can be found) rather than, what customarily receives most of the attention, the posterior densities of the regression slope and intercept.

6-5 BELIEF PROBABILITIES: SUBJECTIVE AND LOGICAL

At the beginning of Sec. 6-3, we drew a sharp distinction between those probability densities (such as our model densities) which can be interpreted in a relative-frequency sense and are acceptable to all statisticians, and those (such as our Bayes densities) whose only plausible interpretation is in terms of beliefs. This dichotomy is useful to clarify thinking, but it is a good deal less than absolute. For instance, when a Bayesian accepts as appropriate a model density which has long-term relative-frequency implications for his observations, that same density must presumably also reflect his beliefs about each of those observations.

From the other side, a classical statistician might claim that the dichotomy misrepresents his position. This type of disagreement is possible because once we begin to talk about interpretations, we have left the ivory tower of mathematics (the probability axioms) and entered the real world of competing philosophies, or, to quote a well-established if lighthearted usage, competing (statistical) religions. There is, indeed, a striking parallel between the issue now under discussion and the famous dichotomy between "faith" and "works" in Christianity. The Epistle of James poses the challenge as follows: "Show me your faith apart from your works, and I by my works will show you my faith." In similar vein the classical statistician might say: "I too think that probability is a measure of belief. But I hold a statement of belief to be void unless there are 'works' by which the reality of that belief can be put to the test. I for my part am clear what those works should be—a long series of repeated trials which will reproduce my alleged probability (density) as a relative frequency (density). I will regard a statement of belief as meaningful only when it is possible at least to conceive of such a set of trials. You claim to have beliefs when this sort of verification is not even conceptually possible. What 'works' do you propose to offer as evidence of your 'faith'?"

One simple answer to this challenge is: "I would be willing to take on bets in accordance with my belief probabilities. Thus, if I say that the probability of an event is one-third, I will be just willing to accept a bet in which I gain 20 cents if the event occurs and lose 10 cents if it does not, that is, a bet at odds of 2:1. I shall be very happy to accept a bet on this event at more favorable odds but unwilling to accept a bet at less favorable odds than 2:1."

With this view, to name a $C\%$ credibility interval is to say that one would be just willing to bet at odds of $(100 - C)$: C that the parameter lies in the stated interval. This interpretation of probability is known as *subjective probability* and is associated with the names of Ramsey, De Finetti, and Savage. Since one can consider betting on any "event", a subjective interpretation can be given to any quantity which qualifies as a probability in terms of the basic axioms. It is straightforward, though tedious, to verify that probabilities defined in terms of betting odds do satisfy the axioms. The reader may refer to Lindley (1965, vol. I, sec. 1.6), where he will also find an interesting discussion of many of the matters raised here.

The Necessity of Gambling

Several objections have been raised against the use of subjective probability. One of these is that the idea of betting is irrelevant to the process of scientific inference. A more extreme form of the same argument is to say that betting is immoral and, therefore, cannot be contemplated. Only from the most remote ivory-tower position (scientific or moral) can this objection be sustained. If any action is to be taken as a result of our inferences, now or at some future date (and if not, why make them?), a little reflection shows that we are inescapably involved in a betting situation.

This is perhaps clearest when the inferences are used by a businessman who has to decide, in an uncertain situation, whether to embark on a particular enterprise. The success of the enterprise will bring him a profit; its failure will bring him a loss. The decision to go ahead is equivalent to accepting a bet at odds calculated from these potential profits and losses and must clearly depend on his assessment of the probability of success. However, the same is true of almost any aspect of everyday life. The decision to marry is, presumably, taken in anticipation of certain benefits. However, only the very naive or the very self-confident can ignore the possibility that the outcome will be the opposite of beneficial. One possible view of dating and courtship is as an information-gathering process in the search for a partner with whom the probability of success is sufficiently high to make the gamble acceptable. Even in the most trivial matters such as the decision to eat a meal, the anticipation of "satisfaction" must be tempered by the possibility of indigestion or even food poisoning so that the wise man may find the gamble unacceptable with respect to certain foods or certain eating places.

In the educational context, the decision to admit student A to an institution rather than student B, on the basis of his aptitude test scores, is a gamble on the part of the institution that student A will achieve more of the goals which the institution deems desirable (whether this be bringing credit to the institution or making contributions to the life of the nation) than would student B. Again, one would have to be very naive to think that this was certain. Similarly in the guidance situation, the choice by a student of one institution rather than another is a calculated gamble. We must, therefore, reject the argument that gambling is irrelevant to our purpose.

The "Objectivity" of Science

A second objection to the use of subjective probability is precisely the fact that it is subjective—since there is no compelling reason why the odds at which I would be willing to bet should be the same as those at which you are willing to bet on the same event, it becomes necessary to speak of "my probability" and "your probability". This is felt by some to be the antithesis of science, whose aim is to be "objective"—to make statements to which all will assent. We suggest that this is a misunderstanding of the nature and history of science, a misunderstanding which statistical reasoning can help to clear up.

It is widely recognized that the philosophy of controlled experimentation as expounded, for example, by Sir Francis Bacon prepared the way for the scientific revolution of the last three centuries. Now experimentation is analogous to the statistical procedure of obtaining a sample of n observations rather than making inferences on the basis of a single observation. Thus, for example, the normal model discussed in Sec. 6-3 can serve to illustrate what happens when a scientist determines the value of a physical constant. θ will now stand for the constant and σ for the standard deviation of the errors of measurement (assumed normally distributed with mean zero). Controlled experimentation has two implications: first, the conditions of the experiment will be so designed as to make the errors, and hence, their standard deviation, as small as possible; and second, the experiment will be repeated until a firm conclusion is reached.

If we now refer to Eqs. (6-3.4) and (6-3.5), we can see what the effect of such controlled experimentation will be. As n increases, the terms which do not involve n will become unimportant in comparison with those which do have n as a factor. Furthermore, since n always appears in conjunction with σ^{-2}, itself a large quantity because we have arranged for σ to be small, this dominance by the terms involving $n\sigma^{-2}$ will occur very rapidly. Thus, even a relatively small number of experiments will result in a posterior distribution which has, for all practical purposes, mean $x.$ and (large) precision $n\sigma^{-2}$. Note that the parameters μ_0 and σ_0 of the prior distribution do not appear in that statement—prior beliefs have been swamped by sample evidence. To put it another way, any reasonable man, no matter what his prior beliefs about the value of the constant, will now accept that for all practical purposes it is equal to the sample mean $x.$ (the posterior variance σ^2/n being so small that even the endpoints of a 99% credibility interval will differ from $x.$ only in the later significant figures).

Thus, what characterizes scientific results is not "objectivity" but sample precision. The division between "exact" and "nonexact" (e.g., social) sciences lies chiefly in the extent to which repeated measurements with small error are an operational possibility. In the absence of such measurements, it is not possible to "swamp" the effect of prior subjective judgments.

Similar considerations apply to scientific "laws" which express the relationships between physical quantities. The nonexact sciences use regression techniques for the same purpose. Again, the difference is a matter of the extent to which observational error can be controlled and the precision with which the constants of the relational equations can be estimated rather than any fundamental difference between "objective" and "subjective" inference.

Cash Benefit and Utility

A more serious difficulty in interpreting probabilities as betting odds is illustrated by the following. Suppose two coins are to be tossed, we judge them to be for all practical purposes symmetrical, and we judge the tosses to be independent. If H stands for heads and T for tails, an almost inescapable conclusion from the symmetry is that our belief "ought" to be Prob $(H, H) = \frac{1}{4}$. In such a situation, most of us would be just willing to accept a bet which pays us 30 cents if (H, H) occurs and loses us 10 cents if any other result occurs. Some of us would be willing to stake a dollar on this bet. Fewer would stake ten dollars, and probably only a few nonmillionaires would stake $1,000. Yet, the betting odds are the same in each case (3 to 1). How then can we possibly use just-acceptable betting odds to determine probabilities?

This objection is not as insuperable as it at first appears. A little reflection shows the source of the anomaly to be the equating of "benefit" with cash gain. When large sums are at stake, while winning might be pleasant, losing might be disastrous, and the real odds are not the cash sums but "great pleasure" and "disaster". The behavior of most people is consistent with Pushkin's dictum "never risk the necessary to gain the superfluous". The word used to express the real (as opposed to cash) value of the outcome of a bet is *utility*. If we decline to bet at even odds on the toss of a coin which we judge symmetrical, the implication is that the increment in utility to us of winning the amount at stake is not as great as the decrement in utility as a result of losing it, and so the expected change in utility of the bet (in the formal sense of expectation) is negative. If we can establish a scale of utility measured in units called *utiles* rather than in dollars cash, it can be shown (making assumptions about consistent behavior which it is hard to fault) that the betting behavior of a rational man would serve to determine his personal (subjective) probabilities, no matter what the size of the stakes. Such a scale would also have the advantage that it could incorporate the effect of noncash benefits or losses such as are typically the chief concern of educators.

A utility scale is clearly a personal thing. Even in respect of cash gains and losses, it will depend on one's current assets and responsibilities—for example, a man might very properly take a more serious view of losses when married than when single. When nonfinancial changes of status are considered, it is quite conceivable that what one man regards as a loss another might regard as a gain. The crucial question is as follows: "Can a scale of utility be constructed for each person?"

A detailed discussion of this question at present would lead us too far afield. Briefly, the answer is "Yes, and typically this is done by considering how the person would act in gambling situations with known probabilities". The reader with a keen nose will scent a circular argument here: Utilities, if known, serve to determine probabilities via betting behavior; probabilities, if known, serve to determine utilities via betting behavior.

Two simple ways out of this dilemma immediately suggest themselves. First, there are certain situations, such as the tossing of a symmetrical coin, where there seem to be probabilities which one "ought" to assign to the possible outcomes on grounds of symmetry. If 43 red and 57 white balls, identical except for color, are to be shaken up in a bag and one drawn at random, it is difficult to make a case for assigning any number except .43 to the probability that the ball drawn will be red. (It is also difficult, however, to know how one would convince a person who insisted that red was his lucky color and that the probability of red turning up for him was greater than .43.) Granted the existence of such "objective" probabilities, they can be used to frame hypothetical betting situations and establish a scale of utilities for a particular person. The utility scale can then be used to determine the person's subjective probabilities for events to which no such "objective" argument applies.

An alternative approach argues that when the stakes are small, cash gain/loss can be equated with utility gain/loss. Thus, a person may determine his subjective probability for any event by considering betting on that event with small stakes. Having determined the probability, he may then construct his utility scale by considering bets with larger stakes on the same event. There is a real problem here, however, because when monetary bets are small, psychological variables become of dominant importance and monetary considerations become almost meaningless.

Whose Probability?

We have presented a spirited defense of subjective probability. In many respects the theory has a strong ring of reality to it. Different persons *do* have different probabilities for the same event–sometimes wildly different. The tangle of probability with utility is also entirely realistic. When my neighbor, a man as rational as myself, takes risks which I would not take, is it because he assesses the probabilities involved differently than I do, or because the utilities of the outcomes are different for him than for me?

Those who participate actively in the game of science soon lose any illusions they originally may have had about what constitutes scientific "proof". Science is seldom if ever a pleasant, cooperative search for truth. Rather, it is often a brutal battle between opposing theorists each struggling to prove the correctness and value of one theory as opposed to a competing one, with some very ill-defined community of scholarly peers sitting in judgment. This can only be described as an adversary situation not unlike the American system of trial by jury.

Every good attorney, prosecutor or defense counsel, knows that *his* prior beliefs are irrelevant to the judgment that the jury will render. If the jury is predisposed on behalf of his case, he knows that all he needs to do is counter the evidence presented by opposing counsel. He will avoid going deeply into areas in which he feels that the jury already believes what he wants them to believe. However, if the jury is predisposed against his client, he knows that he must present a weight of evidence that will swamp the jury's prior belief. The appropriate strategy then is to dig deep and take rather larger risks. In a criminal proceeding, each juror is instructed by law to begin with a prior belief weighted heavily on innocence. No defense counsel is so naive as to believe that this will always be the case. Rather, he tries to gauge accurately the prior beliefs and prejudices of the jury in an attempt to determine the substance and weight of evidence he must present. Such judgments are not easily made; however, successful attorneys and scientists invariably display this skill.

Our point of view is that personal probability is as valid for science as it is for business. However, the wise scientist will recognize that his prior distribution may be shared by no one and that some very strong evidence, indeed, may be necessary to offset the bias of prior beliefs held by his peers, who may even at times be right.

Logical Probability

There is another side to the story, however. When people have very different probabilities for the same event, it usually turns out on closer examination that this is because they have different information on which to base their judgments. The probability of the event E, "at the time these lines are being written the President of the United States is sitting at his desk in the White House", will be assessed very differently by the authors, by a member of the President's household staff, and by the President himself (for whom it will be either 0 or 1). However, that is simply because the different assessors are not talking about the same probability. All probabilities are conditional, and one should not talk about the probability Prob (E) of the event E but about the probability Prob $(E|H)$ of E conditional on evidence or knowledge H. We have agreed to suppress reference to H when it is taken for granted by all parties to the discussion; but in the present context, it is precisely the differences in H which are causing the differences in the probability assessments.

Now comes the haunting question. *At least in matters of scientific inference, ought it not to be true that if two rational beings have exactly the same evidence available, they should make the same (probabilistic) inferences which could, therefore, be called objective or logical inferences?* (Our earlier argument was not that science *ought* not to do this, but that the techniques which have given it a reputation for objectivity *do* not do this.)

Clearly, the answer we give to this question will depend on considerations far outside the field of statistics. The philosopher will no doubt wish to know what the word "ought" in the question means; the psychologist may query in what sense two people can ever have exactly the same evidence available. A school of thought which answers the question in the affirmative is associated with the names of Keynes and Jeffreys. This school endeavors to specify what inferences *ought* to be when all the available evidence is explicitly stated.

To see how the theory works, consider again the binary model discussed in Chap. 5, which is essentially the model considered by Thomas Bayes in his original (1763) paper. Suppose the *only* available evidence about a student's spelling ability π is the fact that he spelled x words correctly on the n-word test; that is, we have no prior information whatever about this student. What we are seeking is universal agreement on the posterior density $b_n(\pi)$. Since there is universal agreement on the correctness of Bayes' theorem, and the density $m_\pi(x)$ is determined by the model, a glance at Bayes' theorem in the form (6-3.1) shows that we shall achieve our object if (and only if) we can obtain universal agreement on the appropriate prior $b(\pi)$ to use when we have no information whatever about Π.

It is reasonably clear from Bayes' paper (1) that the above was his own line of reasoning, (2) that he regarded a uniform prior ("all π equally likely") as the appropriate expression of ignorance in this context, and (3) that he did not see his way to obtaining universal agreement on this prior and that this led him to defer publication (the paper was published posthumously). The uniform prior assumption has long been known as Bayes' postulate. It corresponds to taking $a = b = 1$ in the beta prior (5-4.4). There are two objections which can be raised against it. (1) Use of a uniform prior implies that before the test is administered $\text{Prob}\left(\Pi < \frac{1}{2}\right) = \frac{1}{2}$, and so I should be willing to bet at even odds that the student's ability is less than $\frac{1}{2}$. Is this consistent with the statement that I know nothing about his ability? (2) It is easily shown that using a uniform prior for Π is not consistent with using a uniform prior for Π^2; but if I am ignorant about Π, I am just as ignorant about Π^2, and I should express my ignorance in the same way for both.

The astute reader will foresee the next stage in this development—criteria will be established to determine what is the correct density to express prior ignorance in any particular situation. He might not foresee that the resulting theory will be called *logical probability*. Considered as a ploy in the game of statistical rhetoric, this name must be reckoned a winner. L. J. Savage often used to comment on the psychological advantage classical statisticians gained by calling one of their estimates "unbiased". "Who," he asked, "can stand up in public and state that he prefers to use *biased* estimates?" In similar vein, who can stand up and assert that he prefers illogical probabilities? The only consolation is that if the Reverend Thomas Bayes himself had christened the method, he would almost certainly have called it "moral probability"! (We have seen that the word logical really expresses an *aim* of the method—*if* universal agreement can be obtained on an ignorance prior, then there will be universally agreed posteriors which would qualify as "logical".)

It may be of interest to consider where logical probability stands in the "faith" versus "works" controversy. Astonishingly—considering the known cast of mind of many who espouse it—it could appear to line up with the "fundamentalist" or authoritarian view of religion; that is to say, it focuses all subjectivity on a single principle (e.g., the inerrancy of scripture). Accept the principle and one will know what one *ought* to believe. This belief, in turn, will determine how one ought to act (one's betting behavior, for instance); but any consideration of the implied acts is excluded while the beliefs are being determined. The danger of demanding rigid adherence to such principles is well known. It requires but one instance where the belief one "ought" to have or the act one "ought" to perform is (subjectively) unacceptable, and one has no choice but to throw the principle overboard. Whereas, if a lesser claim is made for the principle, one might be happy to use it as a general guide. The authors wish the principles of logical probability suggested in this book to be understood as useful guides rather than as touchstones for excommunication!

More than one set of criteria has been proposed for determining the proper expression of prior ignorance, and so there are competing theories of logical probability. In this book we adopt the criteria which lead to a prior known as an *indifference prior*. For example, the indifference prior for the binary parameter is a beta distribution with parameters (0,0). To the practical investigator who finds controversy among supposed experts unsettling, we offer the following crumbs of comfort:

1) The different principles advanced for determining ignorance priors often lead to the same conclusions, and these conclusions can often also be reached by more intuitive arguments.

2) Even when different principles lead to different priors, the order of difference is very small—roughly equivalent to one or two extra observations in the sample.

3) In the presence of any substantial amount of data bearing directly on the parameter of interest, these small differences between priors are completely swamped in the posterior distribution.

4) Many subjectivists, while inclined to doubt whether one ever starts from a position of total ignorance, accept that in order to develop general solutions, it is useful to reason "as though" one started from such a position, and they use the same ignorance priors (though a different terminology).

5) In this book ignorance distributions are never used as actual prior distributions. They are used only as foundations for building an acceptable prior distribution, in which case the choice of indifference prior has a scarcely perceptible effect on the final analysis.

So far, we have discussed indifference priors as the "proper" starting point in a state of actual ignorance or when it is desired to proceed "as though" one started in such a state. Their more practical use, however, is as reference points with which to compare (subjective) priors expressing knowledge. For example, at the end of Chap. 5, we used the credibility-interval method to approximate our prior knowledge by a beta distribution with parameters (10,3). This is the same as the posterior distribution we would have reached starting with the indifference prior and obtaining a sample of 13 observations made up of 10 successes and 3 failures. Our assessed prior, in effect, asserts that our prior knowledge is equivalent to having observed such a sample, and this provides an additional check on its reasonableness. Alternatively, we can bypass the credibility-interval argument completely and make a (subjective) assessment of a sample to which our prior knowledge is equivalent. Combining this with the indifference density by Bayes' theorem, we obtain the proper prior density which incorporates our knowledge. (If we had taken Bayes' postulate as our reference point, the implied sample in our example would instead have contained 9 successes and 2 failures. It would be unusual for our prior knowledge to be so accurately assessable as to allow us to distinguish clearly between the two possibilities.)

Disentangling Probability and Utility

It is evident from our previous discussions that in the theory of personal probability, the concepts of personal probability and utility are tightly, almost inextricably, interwoven. Neither can be measured unless the other is held constant, and that is typically a difficult task. Much work has been done to untangle the two concepts by defining personal probabilities on the basis of preferences rather than utilities. However, one may well feel that preferences are just reflections of ordinally measured utilities and that, therefore, the operational independence of the two concepts has not been entirely attained.

On the other hand, we note that if in estimating a parameter, a person is asked to specify an interval for that parameter so that he is willing to bet at even odds on the parameter truly being within or without that interval, the utility aspect of the bet is completely neutralized regardless of the size of the bet. This simple fact will be the basis of the method for determining prior distributions that we shall develop later in the text. However, the two events defined by the person's 50-50 bet must be "ethically neutral" in Ramsey's terminology. That is to say, the person must not have any sort of emotional involvement in either event. For example, loyal hometown fans of a team in last place may be willing to bet at even odds on their team winning on a given day. However, this probably only means that there is a real (if not economic) loss to them in demanding better than even odds. Statisticians have seldom analyzed anything but economic losses. This is unfortunate.

Those persons having backgrounds in educational testing also know that human responses are variable from day to day even on such purely factual things as ability-test items. On such admittedly subjective notions as personal probability and utility, reliability in the sense of stability over time cannot be expected to be very high. Thus, one may wish to pursue the possibility of finding quite different methods of determining and evaluating prior distributions.

The logical-probability approach to Bayesian inference is attractive to the present authors because without invoking notions of utility, it provides a basis point for prior probability evaluations, and, as we shall see, a means of evaluating prior distributions in terms of their influence, relative to any sample, on the posterior distribution. If readers find this method of evaluation useful, then they will react favorably to logical probability because of its "works". There is, of course, no reason why a statistician cannot use the assessment methods of both the personal and logical-probability theories to evaluate prior distributions. (We shall, in fact, do this.) The two theories are not incompatible. Indeed, L. J. Savage has described the necessary view (i.e., logical probability) as a limiting case of personal probability in which so many criteria of consistency have been specified as to leave the individual no choice among priors. That limit will never be reached in practice, but consistency (or coherence) is a virtue to be practiced whenever and to the extent feasible.

Regardless of what approach one adopts to specify prior distributions, the exercise should not be taken lightly. We use statistics (Bayes' theorem) because man is a fallible inference-maker. If he were infallible in this regard, the question of competing statistical religions (Bayesian or classical) would disappear—neither would be necessary. He would need no formal statistical system. For a Bayesian, man's fallibility is a double problem. Bayes' theorem can help man evaluate current data, but to do so there must exist an evaluation of prior experience expressed in a prior distribution. Surely, this second evaluation is the more difficult. The data on which it must be based are obscure, perhaps intangible.

Stable Estimation

A final word should, perhaps, be said to temper an argument previously given in support of Bayesian methods. It was implied earlier that, ultimately, Bayesian inference does not depend on the prior used. Edwards, Lindeman, and Savage (1963) have formalized this in the principle of *stable estimation*, giving specific and quite reasonable conditions on the prior distribution which would guarantee the ultimate (i.e., for a sufficiently large sample size) agreement of all persons using Bayes' theorem. In mathematical language, the result is the "asymptotic convergence" of the Bayes densities for any reasonable prior distribution. John Maynard Keynes, however, noted that "asymptotically, we shall all be dead". It does seem important to reach scientific consensus before that occurs. The careful evaluation of prior distributions may be helpful. Perhaps the way to do this is to apply Bayes' theorem to the evaluation of prior "data".

A contrary view, however, is common where the principle of stable estimation is used to justify prior distributions characterizing little prior information with the knowledge that, ultimately, the result will not differ from that obtained from an analysis using a more concentrated prior distribution. Despite the fact that there is a sound mathematical basis for this strategy, we think that it will not be effective. If we accept science as an adversary proceeding and argumentation as its practice, then it may be useful to devise a "winning" strategy. Suppose scientist A wishes to convince scientist B, whose prior beliefs are quite different from his own. It will do scientist A little good to present an analysis based on his prior distribution or one based on a no information prior. Scientist B will reject either analysis and justify this rejection because of the "unreasonableness" of the prior. But, suppose A presents an analysis based on B's prior; then if B accepts the model, he must either accept the analysis or subject himself to the charge of committing the one heresy of Bayesian statistics–the heresy of incoherence.

Coherence

The function of Bayesian statistics is to help make our probability assessments *coherent*. If we say that our Bayes distribution for a binomial proportion is of the beta form with a mean of 7/17, a 50% HDR of (.3210, .4827), and a mode of 6/16, we are incoherent. Only one beta distribution has the given mean *and* 50% HDR and its mode is 6/15. If we insist on a member of the beta class for our prior and the stipulated value for the mean and 50% HDR, then we must accept 6/15 as the mode of our Bayes density and specifically accept $\beta(7,10)$ as our prior or we will not be coherent (consistent). If we accept this prior and then obtain 10 binomial observations of which 5 are successes and state that our new 50% HDR is (.3926,.5251), we would again be incoherent. Bayes' theorem states that our posterior is $\beta(12,15)$ which has the 50% HDR (.3759,.5055). If, of course, we insist on the posterior HDR (.3926,.5251), then we must somehow convince ourselves that our prior was $\beta(7,9)$ and that, therefore, our posterior is $\beta(12,14)$. This would be a coherent specification if we were able to accept a mean value of 7/16 for our prior. By compelling us and others to be coherent, Bayesian inference provides a framework for constructive discussion. But it does mean that we shall have to look carefully at "all" of our statements to see that they are coherent and that all of the coherent implications of these statements are acceptable to us.

6-6 SOME NOTES ON LOGICAL PROBABILITY*

Let us see how far common sense can take us toward specifying prior densities which represent ignorance. One argument is that such a prior should not enable us to make a meaningful estimate of the value of the parameter. A slightly reduced argument would be that if the prior does permit such an estimate (its mean or mode, for example), this prior estimate should receive no weight in determining the corresponding posterior estimate. On examining (6-3.4), we see that for the normal model, the value given to μ_0 (which is mean, median, and mode of the prior) will receive no weight in the posterior if we allow the prior precision σ_0^{-2} to tend to zero. This also seems intuitively reasonable–information with very low precision is barely distinguishable from ignorance.

If we let σ_0^{-2} tend to zero (or let σ_0^2 tend to infinity) in the kernel (6-3.3) of the prior, the limiting form is a uniform density for Θ which can be denoted by $b(\theta) = c$, a

*Reading of this section may be deferred without loss of continuity.

constant. Now, however, we encounter a difficulty. The range of θ is from $-\infty$ to $+\infty$; and so, there is no value of c which will make the density $b(\theta)$ *proper*, that is, which will make the area under the density curve $b(\theta) = c$ equal to unity. The uniform density $b(\theta) = c$ on the whole real line is an example of an *improper density* (a slightly less blunt term is *unnormed density*). Note that we have no difficulty in using such a density in Bayes' theorem since we do not need to know the value of c—we simply take the density in the form $b(\theta) \propto 1$.

Is the use of improper densities legitimate? Broadly, the answer is that, while from a practical point of view, it is probably a bad thing to do, there are usually no mathematical/technical problems. An intuitive explanation of why this is so might run as follows. While there is no proper density $b(\theta) = c, -\infty < \theta < +\infty$, there is a density $N(\mu_0, 10^{10})$ which for all practical purposes is indistinguishable from a uniform density; and which when used as a prior yields a posterior density practically indistinguishable from that obtained using the improper prior (unless the measurement errors have a very large standard deviation σ, in which case replace 10^{10} by 10^{100} and so on). The improper density may, therefore, be thought of as a convenient approximation to a proper density with very small precision. Notice in passing that while we set out to find a prior density which might have a mean-median-mode μ_0 but which would give no weight to that prior "estimate" of θ, we actually finished up with a density which has no mode since it is uniform and has no mean or median since these cannot be defined for improper densities.

Let us attempt to use the same intuitive arguments for our binary model [the notation is that of Eqs. (5-4.4) and (5-4.5)]. Suppose that the prior has mode λ_0 which we assume not to be zero or one. Thus, by (5-5.4),

$$\lambda_0 = \frac{a-1}{a+b-2} = \frac{a-1}{(a-1)+(b-1)}, \qquad (6\text{-}6.1)$$

and so

$$(b-1) = (a-1)(\lambda_0^{-1} - 1). \qquad (6\text{-}6.2)$$

The posterior mode is similarly

$$\lambda_n = \frac{(a-1+x)}{(a-1+x)+(b-1+n-x)} = \frac{(a-1)+x}{(a-1)\lambda_0^{-1}+n}, \qquad (6\text{-}6.3)$$

and so the value of the prior mode will carry no weight in determining the posterior mode if we let a tend to unity, in which case it follows from (6-6.2) that b tends to unity. Taking the limiting case $a = b = 1$, we arrive at the uniform density on (0,1) which is proper but has no mode. We have seen that this prior is known as Bayes' postulate.

If we apply the same argument to the prior and posterior *means* (μ_0 and μ_n) using Eq. (5-5.2), we obtain

$$b = a(\mu_0^{-1} - 1) \qquad (6\text{-}6.4)$$

and

$$\mu_n = \frac{a+x}{a\mu_0^{-1}+n} \qquad (6\text{-}6.5)$$

and so the limiting "no weight" prior is that with $a = 0$, and by (6-6.4), this implies $b = 0$. The density having $a = b = 0$ is improper (see Fig. 5-4.1). The two tails of the density curve go off to infinity so quickly that the area under them becomes infinite and the distribution does not have mean, median, or mode though the density does have a minimum at $\frac{1}{2}$.

The two priors to which our intuitive arguments have led are different—but not very different. If we start with $a = b = 0$ and observe one success and one failure, our posterior distribution has both parameters unity. Thus, the two priors differ in that the Bayes' postulate prior effectively includes the equivalent of two additional observations, one success and one failure.

One objection to the prior with $a = b = 0$ for binary data is worth mentioning. Equation (5-5.4) shows that starting with $a = b = 0$ and observing 3 successes in 10 trials, the a posteriori most-likely value (mode) is $\frac{2}{8} = .25$, whereas if we use Bayes' postulate $a = b = 1$, the mode has the "natural" value $\frac{3}{10} = .30$. Of course, in regard to means [see (5-5.2)], the situation is reversed—the prior with $a = b = 0$ leads to .30 while Bayes' postulate leads to $\frac{4}{12} = .33$. However, the intuitive meaning of the posterior mean is much less clear than that of the posterior mode. The authors cannot explain why, starting from a state of ignorance and observing 3 out of 10 successes, they should not say that the most likely values of the success probability lie around .30.

The original objective of arguments such as the ones just given was to pinpoint a unique specification of "no prior information", often called an *indifference prior*, with the idea that this prior should be used for most statistical work. This would, it was argued, "let the data speak for itself". For the binomial model, we would take the beta prior with $a = b = 0$ as the indifference prior if for no other reason than that it is logically antecedent to the Bayes postulate prior in the sense already discussed.

However, the idea of using an indifference prior as the actual prior distribution for any analysis now seems undesirable for two reasons. First, though substantial effort was expended by many statisticians, no universally acceptable specification of the state of "no prior information" has been provided. Second, even if a consensus were reached, it would probably not be a good idea to use such distributions in most applications where, in fact, we and other interested persons typically have prior information or beliefs.

6-7 A WORKED EXAMPLE OF A SIMPLE BAYESIAN BETA-BINOMIAL ANALYSIS

The various approaches and techniques that we have been discussing can now be brought together and exemplified in a structured example that exhibits important aspects of typical applications. We state the problem and outline a line of analysis and then later provide the details of this analysis. The reader would certainly profit by working through much of this on his own before referring to our detailed analysis.

Consider the data from the 22 community colleges (Table 1-5.1) for the year 1968 assuming that these colleges represent a random sample of a certain type of community college. We are interested in doing a study of community colleges of this type that have mean ACT English scores [M(1)] of 19.0 or better. Four such colleges (7, 8, 19, and 21) appear to be available from the present sample. Suppose we feel that we need four more colleges that meet our criterion. Suppose also that before looking at these data you would have expected about 33.3% to have a mean of 19.0 or better, and you feel that your prior beliefs should weigh about .8 as heavily as the present data. Let π be the true proportion of colleges with mean English scores of 19.0 or better.

1) From the given information, state a prior distribution in the beta class for Π and give the mean, mode, and variance of that distribution.

2) Find an interval having upper and lower tail areas having equal probability and such that you would be just willing to bet at odds of 9:1 that π lies in the interval. If this result does not seem reasonable, adjust your prior.

3) State the posterior distribution of Π and the mean, mode, variance, and standard deviation of this distribution.

4) There is no right answer to this question, but it will be useful for the reader to state whether he would choose mean-squared-error or zero-one loss as being appropriate for this problem in light of the remaining parts of the problem.

5) For the loss function you have selected, state the appropriate estimator and its value as determined from the posterior Bayes density.

6) Determine an approximate 50% credibility interval with 25% being on each side of this point.

7) Using your posterior point estimate as if it were the true value of π, give the expected number of further colleges you would need to sample (one-by-one) to get the four additional colleges you require.

8) Again, assuming that your point estimate is the true value of π, determine the minimum odds that you would require to bet on the next four colleges satisfying your requirement.

The problem has been structured so as to exhibit most of the issues and methods we have been discussing. The model for the analysis is the binomial model (5-2.1), and for convenience, we take our prior distribution to be a member of the beta class (5-5.1), viz,

$$b(\pi) = \frac{\pi^{p-1}(1-\pi)^{q-1}}{B(p,q)}.$$

The indifference or no-prior-information beta distribution has $p = q = 0$. In the posterior density of Π, the constant p will have the same effect as the number of observed "successes"–x in the sample–and $p + q$ will have the same effect as the number of observations n. Thus, we can think of a prior hypothetical experiment consisting of p

successes in $p + q$ trials. Since we wish our prior information to weigh about .8 as heavily as the sample information $(n = 22)$, we could take $(p + q) = 18$ which would give us a weight of .8181 and an integer value for $p + q$. The expected value of the beta distribution is $p/(p + q)$, and our prior expectation of Π is .333. Hence, we require $p/(p + q) = .333$, which implies that $p = 6$ and $q = 12$. The mode of the beta density is

$$\frac{p - 1}{p + q - 2} = .313$$

which does not differ much from the mean. The variance is

$$\frac{pq}{(p + q)^2(p + q + 1)} = .012 \, .$$

The standard deviation is roughly .1. Clearly, we have not been dogmatic in our prior estimate of π.

If we are prepared to bet at odds of 9:1 that π lies in a certain interval, that interval must be a 90% credibility interval (the odds on its containing π are 90:10 or 9:1). Table A.14 enables us to find a 90% equal-tailed credibility interval directly since its endpoints will be the 5 and 95% points of the distribution $\beta(6,12)$, namely, .1664 and .5219.

At this point, the researcher and the statistician must carefully evaluate whether all of the above statements are acceptable. Is the stated 90% credibility interval too large (or too small)? The interval could be shortened by taking a larger value for $p + q$, but this would mean that the prior distribution would weigh more heavily relative to the observations. Are the investigators prepared to state that their prior information is worth more than the sample data? There is no answer to this question outside of the context of a well-defined experimental situation.

The remaining sections of this problem require the use of a point estimate as if it were the true value of the parameter. As long as the posterior distribution is unimodal, the mode, the most probable value, is generally the best estimate to use. This, of course, implies a zero-one loss which on its own seems most appropriate.

Given the prior and the data, the posterior density is seen to be a beta density with parameters

$$p' = p + x = 6 + 4 = 10 \quad \text{and} \quad q' = q + n - x = 12 + 18 = 30 \, .$$

The a posteriori mode is, thus, $(p' - 1)/(p' + q' - 2) = \frac{9}{38} = .237$. This is a very substantial change from our prior modal estimate of .313. However, this value is well within our prior 90% credibility interval.

A 50% credibility interval, 25% credibility being on each side of the modal estimate .237, is most easily obtained from chart B of Fig. 5-5.2. Here, $p = p' = 10$ and $q = q' = 30$. Since this chart gives values for $p \geq q$, we must use the relationship $I_x(p, q) = 1 - I_{1-x}(q, p)$. At the mode we have $1 - x = .763$. By placing the x scale associated with chart B vertically along the line indicating $q = 10$ with the pivot ($\rightarrow$) at the point of intersection between the curve $p = 30$ and the line $q = 10$, we note that $I_{.763}(30, 10) = .55$, approximately. Since we wish to have a 50% credibility interval with 25% on each side of the point estimate, we now find y where $I_y(30, 10) = .80$ and z where $I_z(30, 10) = .30$. By following the proper probability curve to its intersection with the x scale, we find $y = .805$ and $z = .714$, approximately. Upon reversing the transformation, we get the interval (.19,.29).

The number of colleges one would expect to need to test to find one with a mean 19.0 or greater is $1/\pi$. To get n schools with the required score one would expect to need to test n/π. For example, if $n = 4$ and $\pi = .237$ (the modal estimate obtained above), one would expect to test about 17 schools to get the required 4 additional schools with the required scores. Since the probability of getting 4 out of 4 colleges with mean 19.0 or greater is $(\pi)^4(1 - \pi)^0 = \pi^4$ (or, in the case of the modal estimate of .237, approximately, .003), one would wish odds of about 997:3 to bet on the first four colleges being acceptable.

To get some further idea of how important prior information is, the problems involved in obtaining prior information, and the care required in interpreting results from a Bayesian analysis, we now consider a very simple analysis. Educator I is concerned with the success rate of a remedial instruction program. His prior best guess is .40, and he thinks his information is worth $m = 10$ observations. If .40 is interpreted as the mode of his prior distribution, then fitting these beliefs to a beta we get $\beta(4.2,5.8)$, which has a mean of .42 and the 50% HDR credibility interval (.30,.51). This seems reasonable to the educator and so he proceeds to the posterior analysis. In the sample $n = 20$ and $x = 7$, so that the sample proportion is .35, and the posterior distribution is $\beta(11.2,18.8)$. The posterior mean is .37; the posterior mode is .36; and the posterior 50% HDR credibility interval is (.31,.43). All of this seems very sensible—or is it?

Suppose the prior best guess (.40) is taken to be the mean of the prior distribution. Then, the prior distribution is $\beta(4,6)$; the mode is .38; and the 50% HDR credibility interval is (.27,.48). There is just enough difference in these two results to suggest that it might be important to be sure of whether the best guess is the person's prior mean or prior mode. The posterior distribution is $\beta(11,19)$, and it has a mean of .37; a mode of .36; and the 50% HDR credibility interval (.30,.42). This differs just a little from the original result.

Suppose educator II believes a priori that the success rate is .30, and he takes $m = 14$. If .30 is taken as his prior mode, then his distribution is $\beta(4.6,9.4)$; his prior mean is .33; and his prior 50% HDR credibility interval is (.22,.39). A posteriori, his distribution is $\beta(11.6,22.4)$; his mean is .34; his mode is .33; and his 50% HDR credibility interval is (.28,.39). Note that educators I and II still have some difference of opinion, but this difference is much smaller than it was a priori.

Finally, suppose educator II really intended .30 to be the mean of his prior distribution. Then, his prior is $\beta(4.2,9.8)$. The prior mode is .27 and the 50% HDR credibility interval is (.19,.35). A posteriori, his Bayes distribution is $\beta(11.2,22.8)$, which has a mean of .33; mode of .32; and 50% HDR credibility interval (.27,.38). The differences between educators I and II here are probably big enough to suggest that some careful attention needs to be given to the specification of the prior distribution, but that if care is exercised, we can have confidence in our results.

6-8 COMPUTER-ASSISTED DATA ANALYSIS

We have seen that Bayesian inference follows a very straightforward outline which we believe that our readers can follow using the various tables and charts given in the Appendix and in the text. Nevertheless, Bayesian inference is complicated and the computations can become tedious as one systematically checks on the coherence of one's prior distribution. This is unfortunate; professionals should not expend their energy doing computations. Statistics courses should not be courses in arithmetic.

For the professional in the field, the problem is even more difficult. Few scientific investigators can maintain expertise in statistical methods. They may have had substantial training in, understanding of, and competence in statistical methods; but they are unlikely to exercise these skills often enough to maintain them at a high level of proficiency. For all investigators, the tedium of computation, or, alternatively, the maintenance of esoteric computer expertise, is a regrettable hindrance to their function of extracting meaning from data.

One solution to this problem is a computer-based interactive conversational language system for assisting investigators on a step-by-step basis in the use of Bayesian methods. This system for *Bayesian Computer-Assisted Data Analysis*[1] (CADA) interacts with the investigator in the English language. The investigator need not be familiar with computer languages or with the internal workings of the computer. He need only learn how to sign in and sign off the terminal and to make simple numeric responses. We now exhibit the use of part of the CADA program PRIORB for the analysis of binomial data. Later we shall exhibit the use of PRIORX for the analysis of normal data.

Suppose that an administrator, in trying to evaluate the admissions policies of the University of Iowa, needs an estimate of the proportion of students enrolled at Iowa who received ACT composite scores of 19 or better. Furthermore, assume that although he has no "summary data" on ACT scores of Iowa students per se, he does have the following three pieces of pertinent information.

1) He knows that a 1966 report which placed the national proportion (N = 238,145) at 67% indicated that 77% of a sample (N = 77,383) of those enrolled at midwestern colleges had ACT composite scores at or above 19.0.

[1] Melvin R. Novick, "Bayesian Computer-Assisted Data Analysis", *ACT Technical Bulletin No. 3*, The American College Testing Program, 1971.

2) He knows that this year a 10% national sample indicated that the proportion of those enrolled scoring at or above 19.0 is .66 ($N = 55{,}702$).
3) In similar kinds of studies, Iowa typically falls near the average for midwestern colleges. He also, of course, has a variety of impressions gained during his years of experience.

Turning to the computer for help in evaluating his prior, our administrator signs on the terminal, loads CADA, and receives the following:

computer-assisted data analysis

if you wish an explanation type 1, else type 0.
?
1

[A question mark indicates that a response is required from the analyst who in this case desires a listing of available routines.]

this packet of programs provides a grounding in the fundamentals of bayesian methods of statistical inference. these routines are designed to guide the researcher who has only a minimal acquaintance with bayesian methods, step-by-step through a complete bayesian analysis. a list of the routines follows:

1 prior beta-binomial model
2 posterior beta-binomial model
3 prior two-parameter normal—marginal distribution for standard deviation
4 prior two-parameter normal-conditional distribution for mean
5 posterior two-parameter normal
6 prior m-group proportions
7 posterior m-group proportions
8 evaluate student-distribution
9 evaluate beta-distribution
10 evaluate inverse chi-distribution
11 evaluate normal distribution

if you want to run one of the above routines, type its number. otherwise, type a zero.
?
1

bayesian statistical analysis for the beta-binomial model

this program will assist you in specifying a prior distribution in the beta class for a binomial parameter (proportion), pi. after arriving at a satisfactory specification for the prior, sample data from your experiment will be used to compute the posterior distribution.

considering your prior information, what do you feel to be the most probable value for pi? pi must be greater than .05 and less than .95.
?
.75

[Recognizing that the Midwest sample includes colleges in such states as Illinois, Indiana, Minnesota, Michigan, etc., our administrator decided upon a modal estimate of $\Pi = .75$.]

now considering your prior information as if it were the results of an experiment of sample size (m), how many sample observations do you feel your prior information to be worth? this m value is the amount of weight that will be given to your prior information and must be 6 or greater.
?
25

[Since the 1966 report is rather old and since, on reflection, our administrator realizes that he really has no idea of how many of the major midwestern schools participated in the ACT assessment, he decides upon an initial $m = 25$.]

your modal estimate of pi .750 and the m value 25.000 you selected imply that you would be willing to give even odds that the true value of pi will be in the 50.0% hdr credibility interval which extends from .688 to .806.

please consider this interval. it may or may not be satisfactory to you. you may increase it by selecting a smaller m value, or decrease it by selecting a larger m value. however, any change will affect the relative weight you will be giving to your prior information.
if you are satisfied with the interval, please type a zero. otherwise, type your new m value.
?
50

[In view of the stability of the national proportion, it seems reasonable to presume that the midwestern proportion would also remain relatively stable. Consequently, our administrator places little probability on the belief that the true proportion lies outside the interval (.688,.806). Therefore, incrementing m is clearly indicated.]

your modal estimate of pi .750 and the m value 50.000 you selected imply that you would be willing to give even odds that the true value of pi will be in the 50.0% hdr credibility interval which extends from .707 to .790.
if you are satisfied with the interval, please type a zero. otherwise, type your new m value.
?
100

[For the same reasons given above, our administrator must also reject this interval and proceed to increment m once again.]

your modal estimate of pi .750 and the m value 100.000 you selected imply that you would be willing to give even odds that the true value of pi will be in the 50.0% hdr credibility interval which extends from .720 to .779.
if you are satisfied with the interval, please type a zero. otherwise, type your new m value.
?
150

[When evaluating these intervals, the reader must keep in mind that they are *50%* HDR's. This means, of course, that once you select one of these even-odds betting intervals, you must be willing to let someone else select which side of the bet he wishes to take. You must be *indifferent* when betting whether the true proportion is within or outside the interval chosen. With this in mind, our administrator rejects the above interval as too broad and again increments his *m* value.]

your modal estimate of pi .750 and the m value 150.000 you selected imply that you would be willing to give even odds that the true value of pi will be in the 50.0% hdr credibility interval which extends from .726 to .773.
if you are satisfied with the interval, please type a zero. otherwise, type your new m value.
?
200

[Our administrator is convinced that even this interval is too large and increments *m* again.]

your modal estimate of pi .750 and the m value 200.000 you selected imply that you would be willing to give even odds that the true value of pi will be in the 50.0% hdr credibility interval which extends from .729 to .770.
if you are satisfied with the interval, please type a zero. otherwise, type your new m value.
?
0

[Although our administrator would like the 50% HDR to be slightly tighter, he recognizes that the last 50 hypothetical observations did not significantly change his interval estimate and that additional changes will require more hypothetical observations than he is willing to specify. Therefore, he decided to accept this as a reasonable description of his prior beliefs about the proportion of University of Iowa students with ACT composite scores above 19.0.]

your prior distribution for pi is a beta distribution with a mode of .750 a mean of .747 and a standard deviation of .031. the 50% hdr credibility interval extends from .729 to .770. it has parameters 149.500 and 50.500.

if you wish to respecify your estimate of pi, please type that estimate. otherwise, type a 0.
?
0

if you want to see any other hdr, type the percent desired. type it as a decimal. for example, a 75% hdr would be .75. otherwise, type a zero.
?
.99

[As a final check on his prior, our administrator decides to look at the 99% HDR.]

your modal estimate of pi is .750 and m is 200.000. the 99.0% hdr extends from .666 to .823.

if you want to see any other hdr, type the percent desired. type it as a decimal. for example, a 75% hdr would be .75. otherwise, type a zero.
?
0

Looking at this interval, he feels comfortable with the assertion that almost all of his probability lies between .666 and .823. Satisfied that a $\beta(149.5,50.5)$ adequately describes his prior beliefs, our administrator is now ready to collect some data. Going to his files, our administrator randomly selects 100 student folders and finds that 77 of the 100 students have ACT composites at or above 19.0. He is now ready to evaluate his posterior.

do you want to run a posterior analysis?
if you do then type a one. otherwise, type a zero.
?
1

this part of the program will combine your prior distribution with the sample data, and describe the posterior distribution. please type in the two parameters from your prior, in order. enter first parameter, please.
?
149.5
enter second parameter, please.
?
50.5

please type in the number of observations in your sample.
?
100

finally, please type in the number of successes in the sample.
?
77

the posterior distribution for pi is a beta distribution with a mode of .757 a mean of .755 and a standard deviation of .025. it has parameters 226.500 and 73.500. a 50% hdr credibility interval extends from .740 to .773.
if you wish to further evaluate this posterior distribution please type 1. otherwise, type 0 (zero).
?
1

Now if the administrator had wanted only a point estimate under either squared-error or zero-one loss, the analysis would have been terminated at this point. If he had wanted an estimate under absolute-error loss, a good approximation for the median of a unimodal, moderately asymmetric distribution is:

$$\begin{aligned}\text{Median} &= \tfrac{1}{3}[2 \times \text{mean} + \text{mode}]\\ &= \tfrac{1}{3}[2(.755) + .757]\\ &\doteq .756\end{aligned}$$

However, in order to demonstrate some of the other features of the CADA programs, we shall let the computer display some of the descriptive characteristics of his $\beta(226.5,73.5)$ posterior.

this program evaluates a beta distribution. you have the following options: (1) you may ask to see any p% hdr credibility interval, (2) you may ask the probability that pi is less than or greater than any particular point, or (3) you may ask the probability that pi is between any two points. please indicate which of the above options you wish by typing I, 2, or 3.
if you wish to exit the program type a zero.
?
2

what are the parameters of the beta distribution you wish to evaluate? please type in the first parameter.
?
226.5

now, input the second parameter.
?
73.5

at which point do you wish to evaluate the beta distribution? please type this point as a decimal. (for example, .65).
if you do not wish to evaluate this type a zero.
?
.756

the probability that pi is less than .756 is .507. the probability that pi is greater than .756 is .493.

if you wish to evaluate another point, type that point. otherwise, type 0 (zero).
?
.755

[Although this is very close to the median, our administrator decreases his estimate slightly to see if he can do better.]

the probability that pi is less than .755 is .491. the probability that pi is greater than .755 is .509.

[Clearly, .756 is our best three-digit estimate of the median.]

if you wish to evaluate another point, type that point. otherwise, type 0 (zero).
?
.66 [The national proportion]

the probability that pi is less than .660 is .000. the probability that pi is greater than .660 is 1.000.

if you wish to evaluate another point, type that point. otherwise, type 0 (zero).
?
.75 [The prior mode]

the probability that pi is less than .750 is .412. the probability that pi is greater than .750 is .588.

if you wish to evaluate another point, type that point. otherwise, type 0 (zero).
?
.77 [The sample proportion]

the probability that pi is less than .770 is .722. the probability that pi is greater than .770 is .278.

if you wish to evaluate another point, type that point. otherwise, type 0 (zero).
?
0

this program evaluates a beta distribution. you have the following options: (1) you may ask to see any p% hdr credibility interval, (2) you may ask the probability that pi is less than or greater than any particular point, or (3) you may ask the probability that pi is between any two points. please indicate which of the above options you wish by typing 1, 2, or 3.
if you wish to exit the program type a zero.
?
1

what are the parameters of the beta distribution you wish to evaluate? please type in the first parameter.
?
226.5

now, input the second parameter.
?
73.5

what p% hdr interval do you wish to see? type the p% as a decimal. for example, a 75% hdr would be typed .75.
?
.95

the 95% hdr interval extends from .706 to .803.
if you wish to see an additional hdr, type the p%, again as a decimal. otherwise, type a 0 (zero).
?
.75

the 75% hdr interval extends from .727 to .784.
if you wish to see an additional hdr, type the p%, again as a decimal. otherwise, type a 0 (zero).
?
0

this program evaluates a beta distribution. you have the following options: (1) you may ask to see any p% hdr credibility interval, (2) you may ask the probability that pi is less than or greater than any particular point, or (3) you may ask the probability that pi is between any two points. please indicate which of the above options you wish by typing 1, 2, or 3
if you wish to exit the program type a zero.
?
0

end of program
computer-assisted data analysis

if you wish an explanation type 1, else type 0.
?
0

if you are finished with cada type 0.
if you wish to run another program type its number.

```
if you wish a list of programs type 999.
?
0
9999, normal exit from prog.¹
```

The example given here is atypical in that an unusually large amount of prior information is assumed ($m = 200$). In more typical examples an m value of substantially less than 100 is usually appropriate. On the other hand, this example shows that an investigator who puts high probability on a short interval (say .73 to .77) must recognize that this is equivalent to a very large hypothetical sample number. Put another way, it takes a very large sample indeed (real or hypothetical) to assign high probability, say .95, to so short an interval. The reader should not fail to work out just how large $a + b$ must be if the posterior standard deviation is to be less than .01 when the posterior mean is .75. The answer is a four-figure number.

An alternative method of fitting a beta distribution is with a fractile assessment procedure (FASP). In this procedure, the investigator specifies fractiles of his Bayes distribution and these statements are used to determine a specific distribution from the beta class. As in previous methods, the interrogation can be such as to overspecify the prior distribution and, thus, require adjustment for coherence. Some theory useful for this method follows.

Let q_i be the ith quartile, for $i = 1$ or $i = 3$, let q_2 be the median, and let

$$d_i = \left\{[q_2(1 - q_i)]^{1/2} - [q_i(1 - q_2)]^{1/2}\right\}^2.$$

The parameters of the beta distribution are then given approximately by

$$a = c_i q_2 + \tfrac{1}{3} \quad \text{and} \quad b = c_i(1 - q_2) + \tfrac{1}{3}$$

where

$$c_i = \frac{z_i^2}{4d_i} \doteq \frac{.114}{d_i}.$$

Here Prob $(Z \leq z_i) = .25i$ and z is a standard normal variate, so that $|z_i| = .6745$ for $i = 1$ or 3. Thus, the beta distribution can be easily fit either by specifying q_1 and q_2 or q_2 and q_3.

If values of q_1, q_2, and q_3 have all been specified, approximate values of a and b are given by

$$a = cq_2 + \tfrac{1}{3} \quad \text{and} \quad b = c(1 - q_2) + \tfrac{1}{3}$$

[1] The above annotated output was obtained from a run of The CADA Monitor described by David E. Christ in ACT *Technical Bulletin No. 12*, The American College Testing Program, 1972.

where $$c = .057(d_1^{-1} + d_3^{-1}).$$

Again the values of a and b obtained from this method will only approximately reproduce the specified values of q_1, q_2, and q_3, and hence some adjustment will be required. [This method was suggested by J. W. Pratt, H. Raiffa, and R. Schlaifer, "Introduction to Statistical Decision Theory" (New York: McGraw-Hill, 1965).]

We note that this procedure of fitting a and b by quartile specifications is derived using the result that when Π is distributed as $\beta(a, b)$, the quantity

$$2\left[\pi\left(b - \tfrac{1}{3}\right)\right]^{1/2} - 2\left[(1 - \pi)\left(a - \tfrac{1}{3}\right)\right]^{1/2}$$

is distributed as $N(0, 1)$ approximately. This approximation is accurate for large a and b. In practice, it is considered sufficient to have $a + b \geq 10$. For extremely small a and b, the approximation will not be adequate. Thus, this procedure will be less than perfect when the specified quantities actually fit a beta with small parameters a and b. For example, consider the quartile specifications (.25,.50,.75); FASP will fit it to $\beta(1.184,1.184)$ with revised quartiles (.27,.50,.73). However, it is easy to see that $\beta(1,1)$ fits perfectly to the quartiles (.25,.50,.75). Thus, if a, b given by FASP are relatively small, they may be considered as crude estimates of the parameters. Nevertheless, as long as the fitted a, b is rounded off to the nearest integers for the prior distribution, the fitting of FASP will be reasonably satisfactory provided both a and b are greater than 1. Note that since beta is a two-parameter density function, there always exists a member in the beta family which will reproduce exactly any two specified fractiles. Therefore, it is important to check against some other specified characteristics of one's prior distribution for coherence. This is usually done by specifying other fractiles or the mean or mode to compare with their reproduced values by the fitted beta. In contrast, if one tries to fit beta to three specified fractiles (e.g., the three quartiles), it is likely a perfect fit cannot be obtained. Consequently, one would have to adjust his specifications until a satisfactory fit is achieved.

Suppose we ask an investigator to specify all three values and obtain as his response $q_1 = .11$, $q_2 = .20$, and $q_3 = .30$. We begin by finding a and b given q_2 and q_3. We have

$$d_3 = \left\{[q_2(1 - q_3)]^{1/2} - [q_3(1 - q_2)]^{1/2}\right\}^2$$

$$= \left\{[(.2)(.7)]^{1/2} - [(.3)(.8)]^{1/2}\right\}^2$$

$$= .013394.$$

thus, $$c_3 = \frac{.114}{d_3} = \frac{.114}{.013394} = 8.5113$$

and finally,

$$a = c_3 q_2 + \tfrac{1}{3} = (8.5113)(.2) + \tfrac{1}{3} = 2.0356$$

$$b = c_3(1 - q_2) + \tfrac{1}{3} = (8.5113)(.8) + \tfrac{1}{3} = 7.1424\,.$$

For all practical purposes, we can take the specification to be $\beta(2,7)$, and for this density, the value of q_1 is .12. Clearly, the initial specification is mildly incoherent and an adjustment should be made. The easy way out would simply be to adjust the estimated value of q_1 to .12. This is certainly appealing since, by now, the investigator has remembered that unless it has mean equal to .5, a beta density is not symmetric. The reader will, however, want to check the exact values for q_3 and q_2 for $\beta(2,7)$ from the beta tables.

If, for any reason, this did not seem satisfactory, a fresh start could be made using the given values of q_1 and q_2 which yield $d_1 = .015688$ and $c_1 = 7.2667$. These values give $a = 1.787$ and $b = 6.147$. For this density, the value of q_3 is .31 and again a mild incoherence is found. The easy adjustment here is to take $q_3 = .31$.

In accepting the specification $\beta(1.787,6.147)$, the investigator must realize that his posterior distribution will also contain decimal values, which will result in a bothersome interpolation in cumulative probability and HDR tables. Considering the typically inexact nature of prior information and the force of the law of stable estimation, there may be little point to choosing noninteger-valued beta densities as priors. Rounding off the computed values of a and b given q_1 and q_2 would give a beta density $\beta(2,6)$, the characteristics of which would then be studied carefully by the investigator.

Since the investigator has actually specified all three values q_1, q_2, and q_3, the third set of formulas can be used to specify a and b. The computed value of c is

$$\begin{aligned} c &= .057\,(d_1^{-1} + d_2^{-1}) \\ &= .057\,[(.015688)^{-1} + (.013394)^{-1}] \\ &= 7.8890\,, \end{aligned}$$

and hence the implied values of a and b are

$$a = (7.8890)(.2) + \tfrac{1}{3} = 1.9111$$

and

$$b = (7.8890)(.8) + \tfrac{1}{3} = 6.6445\,.$$

To illustrate the approximate nature of these techniques, we note that the actual values of q_1, q_2, and q_3 for $\beta(1.91,6.64)$ are .119, .201, and .306.

The third set of computations have again suggested the beta densities $\beta(2,6)$ and $\beta(2,7)$. The final selection of one of these two densities would depend upon the comparative evaluation of other characteristics of these densities: means, modes, etc.

The FASP seems to do sensible sorts of things even with rather pathological input.

Consider the quartiles specification (.24,.30,.36) which FASP fits to $\beta(8.272,18.858)$. This density, in turn, has actual quartiles (.243,.300,.362). This must certainly be considered to be a good fit despite the fact that the initial specification was for symmetric quartiles in a situation in which a beta distribution cannot yield them. Now suppose the initial specification is (.24,.30,.50) which FASP fits to $\beta(4.483,10.017)$. This density, in turn, has actual quartiles (.223,.300,.386). We note that FASP has fit a beta density to the median and to that quartile that is closest to the median. This is the typical behavior of FASP. For example, the prior specification (.24,.30,.40) yields the density $\beta(5.628,12.688)$ which, in turn, has quartiles (.231,.300,.376), and the prior specification (.24,.30,.60) yields the density $\beta(4.262,9.499)$ which has quartiles (.221,.300,.389). We note that as the third quartile here moves further away from the median, the total number of degrees of freedom $(a + b)$ of the beta density is reduced, but the fitted values for the first quartile and the median are changed very little and that of the third quartile only slightly more. Now let us consider the prior quartile specification (.24,.30,.33). This specification cannot possibly be coherent since it is skewed in the wrong direction. The FASP, however, does fit a coherent specification to these values, namely, the density $\beta(20.470,47.318)$ which has quartiles (.263,.300,.339). Again, we see that the median has been held constant and the density has been further determined largely by whichever of the other two quartiles is closest to the median. In most situations, this should work out well. FASP, as a procedure, should work well provided some additional checks for coherence are made. The easiest of these would be the assessment of the total number of degrees of freedom $(a + b)$ as the hypothetical prior sample size.

As we demonstrate in this book, prior distributions can be fit in a variety of ways. While various techniques have been subject to study and comparison, it is not at all clear that any available method is best for all people, in all situations. What we have stressed here are some general principles of specification, coherence testing, and adjustment. While we demonstrate several possible sequences of questions, we recognize that some investigators may wish to adopt quite different sequences. What is of primary importance, however, is that a prior distribution be specified that accurately specifies the investigator's prior beliefs. For reasons discussed at some length in this chapter, and others that require a depth of mathematical analysis beyond the scope of this book, it is seldom acceptable to use uniform indifference priors for parameters.

6-9 CASE STUDIES IN BETA-BINOMIAL ANALYSIS

We now present four case studies done by our students. The depth and sophistication of the analyses vary, but with the addition of our comments, these should provide a guide to acceptable performance.

Case Study 6-9.1 TMR Physical Fitness[1]

In 1953 the Kraus-Weber test for minimum muscular fitness showed 44% of American children passing the test.[2] The Kraus-Weber test consists of six items which must be passed to pass the test. Failure of any item means failure of the test. The test consisted of items to measure fitness in the (1) low back, (2) psoas, (3) upper back, (4) abdominal minus psoas, (5) abdominal plus psoas, and (6) flexibility.

Purpose The purpose of this study was to determine the success in passing the Kraus-Weber test of muscular fitness by trainable mentally retarded (TMR) children.

Prior distribution Trainable mentally retarded students can gain up to one-half the knowledge of the normal student. Mimicking a physical skill should be easier than learning by traditional methods. TMR children have muscles that can be as strong as normal children; however, they are more awkward because of the lack of intelligence and coordination. For these reasons, the data analyst believes that the success rate of the trainable mentally retarded student will be 25% or just greater than one-half of the normal child's success rate. The estimate is regarded as equivalent to 15 observations.

The investigator's prior beta distribution for π has a mode of .25, a mean of .2833, a variance of .0127, and a 50% highest-density-region credibility interval of (.1784,.3321). He therefore believes that the true value of the success rate for the TMR has a 50-50 chance of lying between 18% and 33%.

A second observer may believe even more strongly that TMRs can be as physically fit as children with normal intelligence. Suppose that he believes that 30% of the children will pass based on an equivalency of 15 observations. His prior beta distribution for π has a mode of .30, a mean of .3267, a variance of .0137, and a 50% HDR credibility interval of (.2232,.3851). Thus, he believes that the true value of the success rate for the TMR has a 50-50 chance of lying between 22 and 39%.

Discussion of prior The prior distribution of the investigator and the second observer differ in that the mean, the mode, and the variance for the second observer are higher than for the investigator. The range of the second observer's 50% HDR is .16, compared to the first investigator's range of .15. The two prior distributions differ because the one analyst believes the physical fitness of TMR children is higher than the other analyst believes is true, although each analyst has the same confidence in their separate estimates.

[1] Data taken from a study done by Joe Brown, Comparative Performances of Trainable Mentally Retarded on the Kraus-Weber Test, *Research Quarterly*, **38**:348-354 (1967).

[2] Hans Kraus and Ruth Hirschland, Muscular Fitness and Health, *Journal of Health, Physical Education and Recreation*, **24**:17 (1953).

Procedures The sample was 38 boys and girls at Blue Grass School for the Retarded in Lexington, Kentucky. Their ages ranged from 8 to 16 and their IQ scores ranged from 30 to 55. This school is a typical sample of TMR children because they have a full range of TMR intelligences and a range of all ages.

Each child was shown how to do each item correctly. He was then tested and either success or failure recorded. This is the method for the Kraus-Weber test. All six items of the test must be passed to pass the test. The children tested showed a success rate of 21%.

Results The investigator's posterior beta distribution has a mode of .2206, a mean of .2311, and a variance of .0033. The 50% HDR credibility interval extends from .1936 to .2709. These results show 22 to 23% of TMR children passing the Kraus-Weber test. There is a 50-50 chance, however, that the true success rate will be outside the interval .19 to .27.

The second observer has a posterior beta distribution with a mode of .2333, a mean of .2434, and a variance of .0034. The 50% HDR credibility interval extends from .2051 to .2838. These results show 23% of TMR children passing the Kraus-Weber test. The second observer would be willing to bet with even odds that the true success rate will be in the interval (.2051,.2838).

Discussion The investigator's posterior mean is .2311 and the mode is .2206. The central 50% credibility interval is (.1936,.2709). When comparing these results with the prior information we see that the mode has decreased and the mean has gotten closer to the mode. The credibility interval has become shorter. The length of the 50% interval is now .0773 compared to the prior length of .2333.

The second observer's posterior mean is .2434 and the mode is .2333. The posterior variance is .0034 and the 50% HDR credibility interval extends from .2051 to .2838. When comparing these results with the prior information, the mode has decreased and the mean has gotten closer to the mode. The credibility-interval length has decreased from .1619 to .0787.

1) The investigator's probability is .998 that the true success rate for TMR children is less than .44, the success rate for normal children.

2) The investigator's probability is .50 that the true success rate for TMR children lies in the interval from .19 to .27.

3) The investigator's probability is .95 that the true success rate for TMR children lies in the interval from .15 to .34.

Authors' comment: This mid-term effort is a neat organization of prior, sample, and posterior information. However, by the end of a one-semester course, we would expect a somewhat sharper depth of analysis and clearer picture of the motivation for the study, and an understanding of how these results are relevant to the reasons for undertaking the study.

Case Study 6-9.2 The Need for Remedial Instruction

The mathematics staff at West Junior High School has long contended that the school's mathematics program fails to meet the mathematical needs of those students who failed to learn the basic skills in the elementary school. The staff argues that the junior high mathematics program assumes that all seventh graders have mastered the basic skills before grade 7, thus denying a large percentage of the seventh graders the opportunity to acquire these skills. The absence of this opportunity deprives many students of the chance to learn the basic facts necessary to achieve success in junior high mathematics courses.

To solve this problem the West teachers are asking that the school administration provide the resources necessary for a program of remedial mathematics instruction. The resources would include additional staff and increased purchase of teaching aids. The staff estimates that this change in program would cost $16,000.

In presenting this request to the school's principal, the teachers are contending that the remedial instruction is needed by a large number of the school's seventh graders. The mathematics supervisor points to a recent poll of the school's four seventh-grade teachers which shows that, in the opinion of the teachers, there are 52 of the school's 294 seventh-graders (18%) needing remedial instruction. Examination of these students' test scores on the school's seventh-grade diagnostic test reveals that each student has a score of 24 or less.

The district superintendent, when presented with this information, has requested that a careful study be made to determine the proportion of students entering all junior high schools of the district with basic skill deficiencies. He points out that West Junior High School has consistently shown high mean achievement in mathematics, as compared to other junior high schools of the district; thus, the district's needs may be even greater than anticipated by the West faculty.

Considering the information about West Junior High from the superintendent and the 18% of West seventh-graders making 24 or below in the school's diagnostic test, the district mathematics supervisor speculates that the district percentage is nearer to 28%. He further concludes that this information is reasonably reliable and that it is worth a sample of 40 randomly selected seventh-graders.

Applying a Bayesian data analysis, we find that our prior distribution is a beta distribution with a mode of .2800, a mean of .2910, and a variance of .0050. The 50% credibility interval extends from .2335 to .3299. This is a reasonable interval since an examination of the school records has shown West to have had consistently higher mean achievement than other schools in the district.

Testing the school district's 1,247 seventh-grade students is not feasible at this time; hence, the supervisor decides to randomly select 48 seventh-graders and administer the diagnostic test to them.

The test results for these 48 seventh-graders show that 13 of the 48 students have scores less than or equal to 24.

Again combining our prior information with the sample data we find that our posterior distribution is a beta distribution with a mode of .2749, a mean of .2800, and a variance of .0023. The 50% credibility interval extends from .2485 to .3126.

We conclude that the proportion of the schools' seventh-graders is, with even odds, between .2485 and .3126, thus justifying a modification of the junior high mathematics program to meet the needs of some 300 students.

Questions

1) Suppose someone on the staff did not believe, a priori, that the overall percentage needing remedial work in the district was different from that at West Junior High. State a reasonable prior distribution for that person, and determine his posterior distribution. Suppose the district superintendent was willing to fund a remedial program only if "everyone involved was at least 50% sure that at least 22% of the students from the other junior high schools required remedial work". What action should be taken assuming that the persons whose priors we have used represent extreme positions?

2) What would happen if the analysis were based on an indifference prior?

3) Using the three priors discussed above, what would happen if the sample size had been 24, 12, 6, or 3 and the number of students with scores of 24 or less was (to the nearest integer) such as to give the same sample proportion as we observed on the sample of 48?

Case Study 6-9.3 Marijuana on a University Campus

The apparent widespread use of marijuana by University students inevitably leads to an occasional confrontation between law officers and students. Unofficially all local law-enforcement agencies avoid, whenever possible, pressing charges for simple possession. In some situations, however—when a citizen's complaint is filed or another crime is involved, for example—law officers are left without an option regarding filing charges for marijuana possession.

This uncertainty about the enforcement of the law has prompted certain student groups to advocate an official moratorium by peace officers on arrests for simple possession. Such a moratorium, they feel, would both reduce anxiety among students and serve as a political lever to persuade the legislature to consider liberalizing the laws on marijuana.

An important consideration in this issue is the proportion of the University student body who use marijuana. Information supporting the hypothesis that a high percentage of the students are "users" would add considerable weight to the arguments presented by these student groups. Evidence suggesting that the true proportion of users is over one-half–i.e., nonusers are actually in the minority–would perhaps be the most cogent argument that these groups could present.

Purpose of the study The purpose of this study is to estimate by means of Bayesian statistical analysis the "true" proportion of the University student body who have used marijuana.

Procedure While it is perhaps unfair to classify an individual who has "tried" or "experimented" with marijuana only once as a "user", this simple dichotomy does avoid the complications of deciding how much usage is needed to be a "user" and consequently will be the basis for classification in this study.

Estimates of marijuana use on campuses vary widely with the date of the particular survey cited and the campus studied. A high is probably the 90% usage reported at Stony Brook by Goode (1971). Cross and Davis (1972) cite a recent Gallup Poll which found 42% of college students have used marijuana. This poll will be the basis for the prior distribution in the present study.

PRIOR DISTRIBUTION The question of assigning a modal value to the University prior distribution based on the Gallup Poll involves comparing the University student body with others in the country. Numerous factors would have to be considered in this comparison, but it appears to this investigator that the local University students are slightly more "liberal", "left", and "non-status-quo" than the national average. There is only a small proportion of students on campus in the traditionally conservative technical/engineering and undergraduate education major areas. There is a relatively high proportion of graduate students in the humanities, with the resulting "liberalizing" effect on the student body. Finally, the University has been the scene of probably more than an average number of political demonstrations, and several left-leaning organizations have thrived here. This is not to say that liberalism or revolution are perfectly related to marijuana use, but it does suggest that the local University has a lower proportion than many schools of conservative, rigid, or authoritarian students who would be less likely to experiment with marijuana. Consequently, this investigator has assigned the value .52 to the mode of the prior distribution with a 50% HDR credibility interval extending from .45 to .59. This interval reflects this investigator's uncertainty about his estimate, implying he would bet at even odds that the true value of π (proportion of "users") lies within or outside of this interval. It implies also that the prior distribution is worth 22 observations. The beta density, $\beta(11,10)$, was found to fit these values reasonably well.

SAMPLE In the spring of 1971 a random sample of juniors at the University were contacted by graduate student interviewers and questioned about a variety of opinions, attitudes, behaviors, and background data. One of the inquiries made concerned whether the student had used marijuana. A total of 101 students were contacted, representing approximately 80% of the original sample selected. The remaining 20% could not be located. Of the students contacted, 61 (60%) said that they had used marijuana at least once.

This sample might be criticized because it consists entirely of juniors and is not sampled from the student body at large. The opinion of this investigator, however, is that the juniors represent a compromise between the lower-level undergraduates and the seniors and graduate students, and that the proportion of juniors who have used marijuana very closely approximates the proportion of the total student body who have smoked marijuana.

Results

POSTERIOR DISTRIBUTION The modal value of π in the posterior beta distribution is .59 with a mean of .59 and a variance of .002. The 50% HDR credibility interval extends from .56 to .62. This beta distribution has parameters $a = 72$, $b = 50$.

The best estimate of the true proportion of the student body who have used marijuana is then .59. The true value of π lies with 50% certainty in the interval .56 to .62. The probability that π is greater than .50 is, for this beta distribution, .977.

We can thus say with an extremely high degree of certainty that the majority of the local University students have used marijuana at least once, and that nonusers are thus in the minority.

Authors' comment: The opinions, conclusions, and implications of this study are those of the data analyst; and they are not identical with those of the authors. We would say, however, that the analysis is clear and thus a good basis for discussion, which is, of course, the very nature of good data analysis.

References

Cross, H. J. and G. L. Davis: College Students' Adjustment and Frequency of Marijuana Use, *Journal of Counseling Psychology,* **19**: 65-67 (1973).

Goode, E.: Drug Use and Grades in College, Paper read at American Education Research Association, New York, February, 1971, from *Journal of College Student Personnel Abstracts*, **7**(2): 248-249 (1972).

Case Study 6-9.4 Bayesian School Administrators[1]

The problem to be analyzed involves a decision to be made by the superintendent of a city school system. The principal of an elementary school contends that the population of children which feed into his school are, on the whole, below normal in intelligence and as a result it is almost impossible to attain the same educational standing as the other elementary schools. The principal denies that the low standing of his school is due to any lack of effort from his staff. To improve the educational level of his pupils, the principal desires special funds for construction of special classrooms, for engaging additional specialized instructors, and for purchase of special equipment and materials for the slow learner.

The superintendent undertook a statistical investigation of the intelligence characteristic of the principal's elementary school population. The IQ score yielded by the Wecshler Intelligence Scale for Children (WISC) was used as a measure of intelligence. Since the WISC must be administered individually, only a small sample ($n = 50$) of children could be selected.

The superintendent views the population as a dichotomous one, consisting of children who are either below or not below normal intelligence. If the population is like the usual one, the proportion of its members with IQs less than 100 is 0.50. The principal believes that the proportion of the population with IQs less than 100 is greater than 0.50. Let us assume that the principal feels that the most probable proportion is 0.55 for the population. The analysis will attempt to determine whether or not the principal should receive special funds.

Before looking at the data, the superintendent expected 0.50 of the pupils to have IQs less than 100. Because of his past teaching and administrative experience, the superintendent felt that his prior beliefs should weigh as heavily as the present small sample. The principal expected 0.55 of the pupils to have IQs less than 100. He also felt that his prior beliefs should weigh as heavily as the sample data. Let π be the true proportion of the population with IQs less than 100.

A prior distribution will be chosen from the beta class since it is usually possible, due to the great variety of beta distributions, to chose a beta distribution which will approximate one's prior knowledge of the population. The first step in the specification

[1] The article used as a reference for this illustration of Bayesian binomial analysis is Paul Blommers and E. F. Lindquist, The Problem of the Principal and the Superintendent, *Elementary Statistical Methods,* chap. 10, (New York: Houghton-Mifflin, 1960).

The original Bayesian analysis of "The Problem of the Principal and the Superintendent" is given by Donald L. Meyer, A Bayesian School Superintendent, *American Educational Research Journal,* 1(4): 1964.

of the prior is to ask what is the most likely value for π. The second step involves evaluating the amount of prior information available relative to sample information. Suppose the experimenter decides that the prior information is equivalent in amount to the present sample of size 50. Let p equal the number of successes in $p + q$ trials. Prior beliefs weighted as heavy as the sample information ($n = 50$) implies that the prior information is worth $(p + q) = 50$ observations. Let the principal's and the superintendent's prior estimates of π represent the mode of their respective prior distributions.

Prior distribution for the superintendent The superintendent's prior estimate (or mode) of the beta density was suggested to be 0.50 and the value of his prior information was to be $m = (p + q) = 50$. The mode of the beta density is $(p - 1)/(p + q - 2)$. Thus, the mode of 0.50 implies $p = 25$ and $q = 25$. The form of the prior density is

$$b_0(\pi) = \frac{\pi^{p-1}(1 - \pi)^{q-1}}{B(p, q)} = \frac{\pi^{24}(1 - \pi)^{24}}{B(25, 25)}.$$

The mean is $p/(p + q) = .50$. The variance of the prior is $pq/(p + q)^2(p + q + 1) = .0049$ with standard deviation .07. This standard deviation is not overly strict considering the weight given to the prior information.

With the prior distribution on π established, it is desired to find a credibility interval such that one would be willing to bet at even odds that the true value of π lies in this interval. The 50% HDR credibility interval is (.4522,.5478). Although the credibility interval is quite small, the superintendent feels it is acceptable. In order to have a larger interval the prior information would have to be assigned less weight than the superintendent is willing to approve.

Prior distribution for the principal The principal suggested the prior estimate (or mode) of the beta density to be 0.55 and he also valued his prior information to be worth $(p + q) = 50$ observations. The mode of the beta density is $(p - 1)/(p + q - 2) = 0.55$, implying $p = 27.4$ and $q = 22.6$. The form of the prior density is

$$b_0(\pi) = \frac{\pi^{p-1}(1 - \pi)^{q-1}}{B(p, q)} = \frac{\pi^{26.4}(1 - \pi)^{21.6}}{B(27.4, 22.6)}$$

The prior density has a mean of .5480, a variance of .0049, and a standard deviation of .07. The 50% HDR credibility interval is (.5021,.5973). Although this credibility interval is quite small, it is acceptable to the principal.

Posterior distribution for the superintendent Let $p' = (p + x)$ and $q' = (q + n - x)$, where n is the sample size and x is the number of sample successes (number of children with IQs less than 100). The sample data is $n = 50$ and $x = 30$. Then, $p' = 55$ and $q' = 45$. The posterior density from the beta class is

$$b_n(\pi) = \frac{\pi^{p'-1}(1-\pi)^{q'-1}}{B(p',q')} = \frac{\pi^{54}(1-\pi)^{44}}{B(55,45)}$$

The mean is $p'/(p'+q') = .5500$. The mode is $(p'-1)/(p'+q'-2) = .5510$. The variance is $p'q'/(p'+q')^2(p'+q'+1) = .0025$ with standard deviation .05.

Both the mean and the mode are a substantial change from the prior estimates. Note that they are not contained within the prior 50% HDR credibility interval. The smaller standard deviation should imply that a 50% HDR credibility interval based on the posterior distribution should be tighter about the modal estimate of π. The 50% HDR credibility interval is (.5165,.5833). As expected, this interval is tighter. It is interesting to note that this interval does not include either the prior or the sample estimate. The substantial shifting of the mean, mode, and 50% HDR credibility interval indicates that the posterior distribution is quite different from the prior distribution.

Posterior distribution for the principal Again, let $p' = (p + x)$ and $q' = (q + n - x)$, where n is the sample size and x is the number of sample successes. The sample data is $n = 50$ and $x = 30$. Then, $p' = 57.4$ and $q' = 42.6$. The posterior density from the beta class is

$$b_n(\pi) = \frac{\pi^{p'-1}(1-\pi)^{q'-1}}{B(p',q')} = \frac{\pi^{56.4}(1-\pi)^{41.6}}{B(57.4,42.6)}$$

The mean is .5740, the mode is .5755, the variance is .0024, and the standard deviation is .049.

Neither the mean nor the mode have changed substantially from the prior estimates, and both lie in the prior 50% HDR credibility interval. The posterior 50% HDR credibility interval is (.5407,.6070). This interval includes both the prior and the sample estimate for π.

RESULTS ($m = 50$; $n = 50$; $x = 30$)

	Prior			Posterior		
	Mode	50% HDR	SD	Mode	50% HDR	SD
Superintendent	.50	(.4522,.5478)	.07	.5510	(.5165,.5833)	.050
Principal	.55	(.5021,.5973)	.07	.5755	(.5407,.6070)	.049

After the analysis of the data, the superintendent and the principal are in closer agreement as to the true proportion of the elementary population with IQs less than 100. Their estimates of π are each contained within the other's 50% HDR credibility interval. The 50% HDR credibility intervals overlap considerably and neither contains the value .50. The a posteriori probability that $\pi > .50$ is .84 for the superintendent and .98 for the principal. It would appear that the true value of π is greater than .50 and the superintendent should allocate special funds for the principal's elementary school.

For purposes of illustration, I will now present the results of two other analyses for the superintendent and the principal situation. Both examples will use a smaller sample size ($n = 25$), retaining the original sample proportion (.60) of success requiring $x = 15$.

The first analysis will illustrate the effect of a smaller sample and lesser prior information. The superintendent's and the principal's prior estimates of π (.50 and .55, respectively) will not change. The prior information is now taken to be worth $(p + q) =$ 25 observations.

The superintendent's prior distribution for π is a beta distribution with mean of .5000, mode of .5000, variance of .0096, and standard deviation of .098. The 50% HDR credibility interval is (.4322,.5678).

The prior distribution for the principal is a beta distribution with mean of .5460, mode of .5500, variance of .0095, and standard deviation of .097. The 50% HDR credibility interval is (.4819,.6169). The sample data is $n = 25$ and $x = 15$.

For the posterior analysis, the superintendent has a beta distribution with mean of .5500, mode of .5521, variance of .0049, and standard deviation of .07. His 50% HDR credibility interval is (.5029,.5967), and his a posteriori probability that $\pi > .50$ is .76.

The principal's posterior distribution for π is a beta distribution with mean of .5730, mode of .5760, variance of .0048, and standard deviation of .069. His 50% HDR credibility interval is (.5260,.6193), and his a posteriori probability that $\pi > .50$ is .85.

RESULTS ($m = 25; n = 25; x = 15$)

	Prior			Posterior		
	Mode	50% HDR	SD	Mode	50% HDR	SD
Superintendent	.50	(.4322,.5678)	.098	.5521	(.5029,.5967)	.070
Principal	.55	(.4819,.6169)	.097	.5760	(.5260,.6193)	.069

Referring back to the original analysis, one sees that decreasing the sample size increases the variance and thus increases the length of the 50% HDR credibility interval. The mode has also increased slightly in the posterior analysis.

Again, the principal's and the superintendent's modal posterior estimates for π are much closer than their prior estimates. The credibility intervals still overlap considerably and neither contains 0.50. In this example also, it would appear that the principal's request for special funds should be granted.

The last analysis illustrates the effect of the weight given one's prior beliefs. Let us assume that the superintendent has very serious doubts as to the validity of the principal's claim. He now wishes to weight his prior beliefs 20% heavier than the sample data. His prior beliefs are then worth $(p + q) = 1.20(25) = 30$ observations. Assume the principal feels that his prior estimate of π (.55) is very tentative. He wishes to weight his prior beliefs only 80% as much as the sample. The principal's prior beliefs are now worth $(p + q) = .80(25) = 20$ observations.

The superintendent's prior distribution for π is a beta distribution with mean of .5000, mode of .5000, variance of .0081, and standard deviation of .09. The 50% HDR credibility interval is (.4382,.5618).

The principal's prior distribution for π is a beta distribution with mean of .5450, mode of .5500, variance of .0118, and standard deviation of .109. The 50% HDR credibility interval is (.4737,.6248). The sample data are $n = 25$ and $x = 15$.

The posterior beta distribution for π for the superintendent has a mean of .5455, mode of .5472, variance of .0044, and standard deviation of .066. His 50% HDR credibility interval is (.5005,.5901), and his a posteriori probability that $\pi > .50$ is .75.

Notice, compared to the previous analysis, that the variance has decreased due to the added weight of the prior beliefs. This also caused the 50% HDR to shift closer to the prior estimate of π(.50). The posterior estimate of π shifted closer to the prior estimate. In light of all three analyses, for the superintendent's posterior estimate of π not to differ greatly from his prior estimate would require an unreasonable heavy weighting of his prior beliefs.

The principal's posterior beta distribution for π has a mean of .5756, a mode of .5791, a variance of .0053, and a standard deviation of .073. His 50% HDR credibility interval is (.5261,.6243), and his a posteriori probability that $\pi > .50$ is .85.

RESULTS ($n = 25; x = 15$)

	Prior			Posterior		
	Mode	50% HDR	SD	Mode	50% HDR	SD
Superintendent ($m = 30$)	.50	(.4382,.5618)	.090	.5472	(.5005,.5901)	.066
Principal ($m = 20$)	.55	(.4737,.6248)	.109	.5791	(.5261,.6243)	.073

Notice, compared to the previous analysis, that the variance has increased due to the lesser weight of the prior belief. This has increased the posterior estimate of π and increased the length of the credibility interval. This also caused the credibility interval to shift nearer to the sample proportion.

Even in this example, the superintendent and the principal have come to a closer agreement as to the true value of π after the posterior analysis. Both estimates are still substantially larger than .50. I would still suggest that the principal receive his special funds.

It might be mentioned at this time that this decision is contradictory to the decision reached by the superintendent in the original classical statistical analysis presented in the reference problem.

Authors' comment: This is, of course, much more than a data analysis. Rather it is a compelling demonstration of why Bayesian methods are to be preferred to the classical methods of significance testing. The original article by Meyer must be regarded as a classic of educational statistics literature. The amplification presented here is a model of what a highly motivated student can accomplish, though some further work in paragraph structuring is clearly indicated.

6-10 EXERCISES

1 A researcher indicates that his modal estimate of a binomial proportion π is .4. He further claims that the mean of his prior distribution is .38. Will it be possible to fit his prior beliefs to a beta distribution? If not, why not? If possible, are there any values for the mean for which this will not be possible?

2 A researcher indicates that his modal estimate of a binomial proportion is about .30 and that the mean of his prior distribution is about .31. He thinks that a beta prior distribution might be reasonable, but thinks that his prior information is not great and thus would like to take a value of m (hypothetical prior observations) less than 20. Can a coherent specification be obtained under these restrictions?

3 After observing a sample of size 10 containing 4 successes, a researcher states that his posterior distribution is beta with mean .65 and mode .68. Can you determine his prior beta distribution and state how many observations it was worth? Now consider what you would consider his prior to be if he had stated unrounded values of .6452 for the mean and .6849 for the mode, instead of the rounded values given above.

4 An eminent visiting statistician once stated a beta prior distribution having the following properties:

Percentile	π value
25th	.30
50th	.35
75th	.40

If you judge this (non-Bayesian) statistician to be reasonably coherent in this instance, find a beta distribution that closely fits these values. If this fit were exact, is there any other beta distribution that would also fit these three values? Suppose that only two of the three values were given. Would it then be possible to find two *quite different* betas to fit these *two* values?

5 A researcher gives π values .097 and .182 as his .05 and .95 percentage points of a beta distribution. What is the value of the median of his beta distribution (.136)?

7 BAYESIAN INFERENCE FOR THE NORMAL MODEL

The normal distribution plays a central role in statistical applications, and it is, therefore, important that Bayesian methods for analyzing normal data be described in some considerable detail. In almost all applications both the mean and the variance of the normal distribution are unknown so that a *joint* posterior distribution on these parameters is the first desired outcome of a Bayesian normal law analysis. In order to facilitate the presentation of a method for making the joint prior specification, we first study the two one-parameter normal models (mean unknown, variance known, and mean known, variance unknown, respectively). This is done in Secs. 7-1 to 7-5. The two-parameter normal analysis is then a simple putting together and natural extension of the two one-parameter analyses. This is begun in Sec. 7-6.

Section 7-7 presents a simplified method of fitting a slightly restricted class of conjugate priors and is presented largely for pedagogical purposes. Sections 7-8 and 7-9 present the details of the complete, general, two-parameter normal analysis in a self-contained package. Sections 7-10 and 7-11 present some useful supplementary material; however, reading of these sections can easily be deferred. In Sec. 7-12, we give two case studies that we believe illustrate in some detail how Bayesian two-parameter normal analysis should be done.

7-1 REVIEW OF THE KNOWN-VARIANCE MODEL

All the inference procedures to be discussed in this chapter use as a basic model the normal distribution $N(\mu, \sigma^2)$ with mean μ and variance σ^2, whose density function is

$$\frac{1}{(2\pi\sigma^2)^{1/2}} \exp\left[-\frac{\frac{1}{2}(x-\mu)^2}{\sigma^2}\right], \qquad -\infty < x < \infty.$$

From this point onward, we shall usually abandon, with respect to *parameters*, the convention of using uppercase letters when thinking of them as random variables and lowercase letters when thinking of particular values they may take. The reader may already in Chap. 6 have begun to find this convention more of a hindrance than a help. Also, some uppercase Greek letters are easily confused with Roman letters while others are required for special purposes—e.g., uppercase sigma. In this chapter, it will be convenient to continue using θ in place of μ for a normal mean which we are regarding as unknown and ϕ in place of σ^2 for an unknown variance.

The concepts developed in the previous chapter enable the Bayesian analysis of any model to be laid out in a concise and logical manner. We enumerate the stages below, giving, in brackets, a recapitulation of the results for the normal model with known variance which we previously used as an illustration.

Step-by-step Procedure of Bayesian Analysis

1) State the model. [X is $N(\theta, \sigma^2)$, σ^2 known.]

2) Find the likelihood and/or its kernel. [See (6-2.5) and (6-2.6).]

3) Note the sufficient statistics. [$x_{\bullet}$—or, strictly, n and $x_{\bullet}$.]

4) Determine the family of natural conjugate densities. [Normal distributions.]

5) Choose a prior distribution from the natural conjugate family. [$N(\mu_0, \sigma_0^2)$]

6) Evaluate this choice of prior in terms of hypothetical prior observations [$m = \sigma^2/\sigma_0^2$, see details in example following] and make any necessary revisions in (5).

7) Find the (joint) posterior density of parameter(s)[$N(\mu_n, \sigma_n^2)$] the and any of their features (e.g., mode) which are of interest.

8) Find the posterior marginal distributions of the parameters and any of their features (mean, median, mode, variance, credibility intervals) which are of interest. [$N(\mu_n, \sigma_n^2)$, where $\sigma_n^{-2} = \sigma_0^{-2} + n\sigma^{-2}$ and $\sigma_n^{-2}\mu_n = \sigma_0^{-2}\mu_0 + n\sigma^{-2}x_{\bullet}$.]

A detailed worked example following this paradigm was given at the end of the previous chapter. In this chapter, we shall provide further worked examples with somewhat greater emphasis on (6), which is shown in Sec. 7-4 to be useful in verifying the coherence of an experimenter's prior beliefs.

With regard to (5), it is not, of course, suggested that if one's prior knowledge/belief cannot be adequately approximated by a member of the conjugate family, one should still force it into that mold—one would have to obtain some other representation of it and attempt a solution. The results will not typically be expressible in terms of tabulated distributions so that complex numerical methods will be required. With the availability of adequate computer facilities, the work can be done by a qualified computer specialist. Without such facilities the solution will not be practical.

Also, when there are more than two unknown parameters, the conjugate density is a multivariate one which may be difficult to match to a subjective assessment of potential betting behavior or prior knowledge. In this case, it may be convenient to solve the problem using the indifference prior and adopting the hypothetical-preliminary-sample method of quantifying one's prior knowledge. This will be discussed in Sec. 7-7.

EXAMPLE 1 Consider the data from the 22 junior colleges (Sec. 1-5). Suppose we are now studying a 23rd such college which, because of our limited knowledge, is indistinguishable from the others. We wish to estimate the mean ACT English score of the entering freshman class [M(1)]. Only a very small sample will be available, so we must consider our prior distribution for the mean very carefully. Scanning the 1969 junior college data (Table 1-5.2), we find an average mean college ACT English score of 17.5. It seems correct then to center our prior distribution at this value, that is, $\mu_0 = 17.5$. The standard deviations in the colleges are running from 4.2 to 5.7, and we decide to proceed as if we knew the standard deviation for this college was 5. Further, it seems to us that we are a little more than 95% sure that the mean is actually between 15 and 20.

Accepting a natural conjugate density for the prior distribution $[N(\mu_0, \sigma_0^2)]$, the central 95+% prior credibility interval is obtained as follows:

$$\mu_0 - 2\sigma_0 = 15, \qquad \mu_0 + 2\sigma_0 = 20.$$

From this, we conclude that the stated length for our prior credibility interval implies a value $\sigma_0 = \frac{5}{4}$. Thus, our prior distribution is normal with mean $\mu_0 = 17.5$ and variance $\sigma_0^2 = \frac{25}{16}$; a statement we abbreviate to θ: $N(17.5, \frac{25}{16})$.

Now suppose we have nine observations with mean $x_{\bullet} = 18.0$. Since we are assuming the variance to be known, the sufficient statistics are $(n, x_{\bullet})$. Our posterior distribution is $N(\mu_n, \sigma_n^2)$, where

$$\sigma_n^{-2} = \sigma_0^{-2} + n\sigma^{-2} = \tfrac{16}{25} + \tfrac{9}{25} = 1 \qquad (7\text{-}1.1)$$

and

$$\begin{aligned} \mu_n &= \sigma_n^2(\sigma_0^{-2}\mu_0 + n\sigma^{-2}x_{\bullet}) \\ &= 1\left[\tfrac{16}{25}(17.5) + (9)\left(\tfrac{1}{25}\right)(18)\right] \qquad (7\text{-}1.2) \\ &= 17.7\,. \end{aligned}$$

Thus, a posteriori, θ: $N(17.7, 1)$ and a 95+% central credibility interval for θ is 15.7 to 19.7.

Clearly, nine observations have not changed our beliefs very much. Apparently, these observations are not as important as our prior information. From (7-1.2), we see that, in determining the posterior mean, the prior mean ($\mu_0 = 17.5$) receives a weight of 16 (observations) as compared with the sample mean ($x. = 18.0$) which was calculated from 9 observations. Indeed, an alternative way to view our assessed prior is that it is equivalent to having started with the indifference prior ($\sigma_0^{-2} = 0$) and having obtained from our model with known $\sigma = 5$ a hypothetical preliminary sample of size 16 and mean 17.5. In that case, we would have had altogether 25 observations with sample sum $16(17.5) + 9(18.0)$ and mean μ_n as given by (7-1.2). Also, our posterior precision would have been $\sigma_n^{-2} = 0 + 25(5)^{-2}$, agreeing with (7-1.1). Yet another way to express this equivalence is to say that our prior estimate, 17.5, of θ is "worth" 16 observations. The number of observations m "contained" in the prior distribution is given, in general, by

$$m = \frac{\sigma^2}{\sigma_0^2}$$

which in this example is $25/\frac{25}{16} = 16$.

7-2 THE CHI-SQUARE DISTRIBUTION

Our next objective is to make inferences when the variance of our basic normal model is unknown. The analysis of this situation will involve the use of three related probability distributions which we have not so far studied and which are of considerable importance in many areas of statistical inference. In order not to interrupt the flow of the discussion in Sec. 7-4 and to facilitate reference to the properties of the distributions when they arise in other contexts, we treat them separately—the chi-square distribution in this section and the inverse chi-square and inverse chi distributions in the next.

A random variable Y is said to have a chi-square (χ^2) distribution on (or with) ν degrees of freedom if its density function is proportional to

$$y^{[(\nu/2)-1]} \exp\left[\frac{-y}{2}\right], \quad 0 < y < \infty, \ \nu > 0. \qquad (7\text{-}2.1)$$

The distribution occurs in various contexts. In Sec. 5-3, for example, we saw that it can be used to find the sums of terms of the Poisson distribution.

When $\nu > 2$, the distribution is unimodal but asymmetrical with a long upper tail and a short lower tail. The mean is ν, and the variance is 2ν. For $\nu \geq 2$, the mode is $\nu - 2$, and for $\nu \geq 5$, the median is, approximately, $\nu - \frac{2}{3}$. Note that, approximately,

$$\text{Mean} - \text{mode} = 3(\text{mean} - \text{median}),$$

or

$$\boxed{\text{Median} = \tfrac{1}{3}(2 \text{ mean} + \text{mode})}, \tag{7-2.2}$$

a relationship which has been found empirically to hold for a wide variety of unimodal, moderately asymmetric distributions.

The usual form of tabulation of the chi-square distribution is that used in Table A.5 where for each of the values $\nu = 4(1)30(10)100$, a selection of percentage points is given. Ordinary (linear) interpolation is adequate for intermediate values of ν. Because of the asymmetry, it is necessary to tabulate percentage points in both tails.

For large values of ν, the following approximation is useful. *If Y has a chi-square distribution,* $[(2Y)^{1/2} - (2\nu - 1)^{1/2}]$ *is approximately a standard normal variable.* To obtain some idea of how "large" ν needs to be, consider the case $\nu = 50$. Using the approximation, the 95% point y is given by $(2y)^{1/2} - (99)^{1/2} = 1.64$ (the normal 95% point), hence $y = 67.16$. This compares with the value 67.50 obtained from Table 5. Proceeding in this manner, we obtain the following values for $\nu = 50$:

P(%)	.5	1	2.5	5	10	25	50	75	90	95	97.5	99	99.5
Exact	28.0	29.7	32.4	34.8	37.7	42.9	49.3	56.3	63.2	67.5	71.4	76.2	79.5
Approximate	27.2	29.0	31.9	34.5	37.6	43.1	49.5	56.4	63.1	67.2	70.9	75.4	78.5

Expressing the error as a percentage of the mean, we see that it is about 2% in the tails and less than .5% in the interquartile interval. Similar calculations, with $\nu = 100$, show that this percentage error is halved.

The chi-square distribution for a given number of degrees of freedom is a standardized distribution in the same sense that the standard normal distribution $N(0, 1)$ is a standardized form of any normal distribution $N(\mu, \sigma^2)$. The type of statement we shall usually wish to make is not that the random variable Y of interest has a chi-square distribution on ν degrees of freedom, but that a random variable W of interest is such that $Y = W/\omega$ has that chi-square distribution on ν degrees of freedom, where ω is a constant. It will be convenient to have a reduced notation similar to $N(\mu, \sigma^2)$ for expressing this.

Clearly, ω is simply a scale factor. Hence, we shall say that W has a chi-square(χ^2) distribution on ν degrees of freedom with scale factor ω and abbreviate this to W is $\chi^2(\nu, \omega)$. The reader is warned that this notation is not standard but is peculiar to this book. However, it saves a considerable amount of circumlocution and enables one to focus one's attention on the fact that a random variable of interest is, apart from a constant divisor which may in applications be complex in form but does not really alter the situation, a standard χ^2 random variable $\chi^2(\nu, 1)$ on ν degrees of freedom. An example of the use of the notation will be given in Sec. 7-4.

If we wish to find explictly the density function of the $\chi^2(\nu, \omega)$ variable W, we make use of the result (3-4.10) for constant multiples of a random variable to transform the density of Y given in (7-2.1). The result is that W has a density proportional to

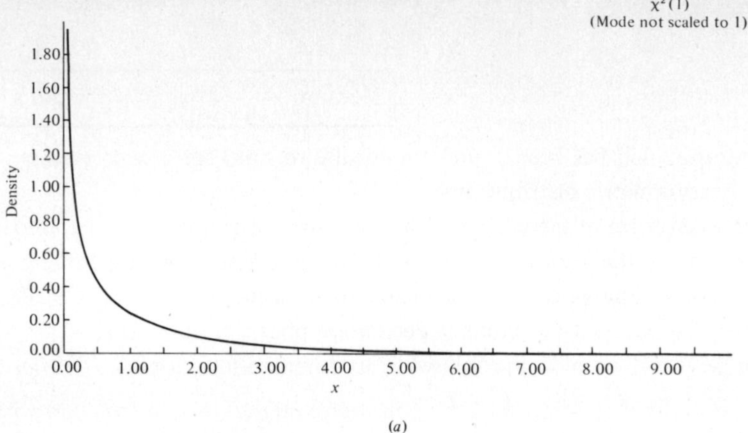

(*a*)

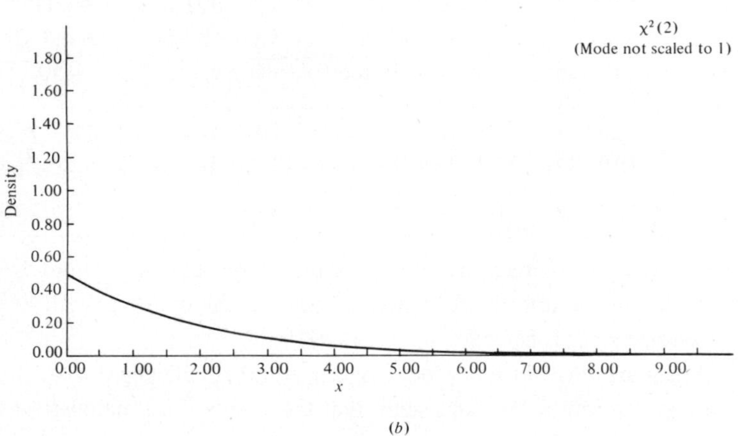

(*b*)

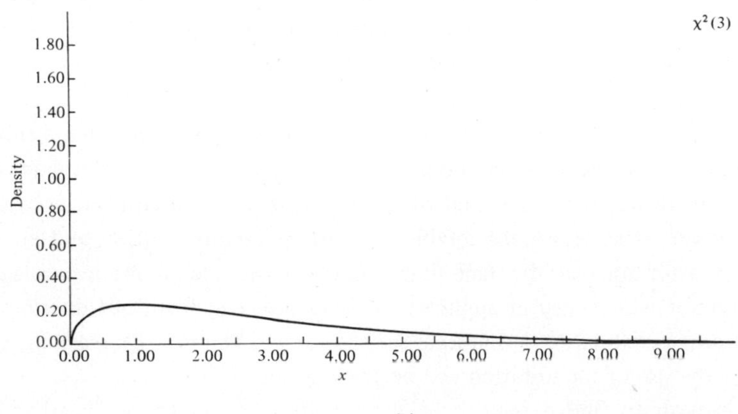

(*c*)

FIGURE 7-2.1
Chi-squared distributions.

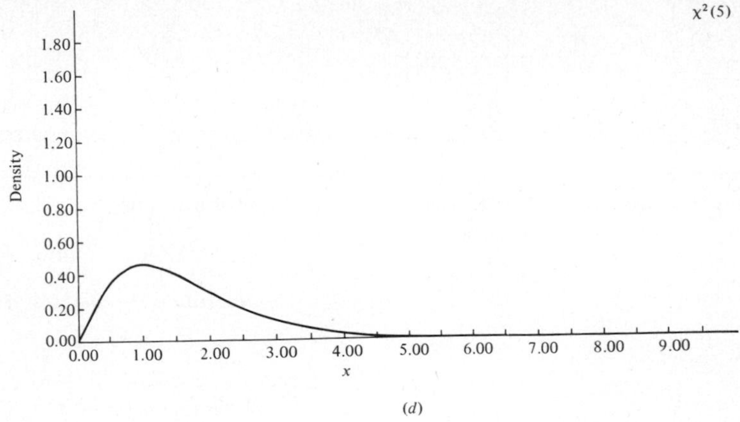

(d)

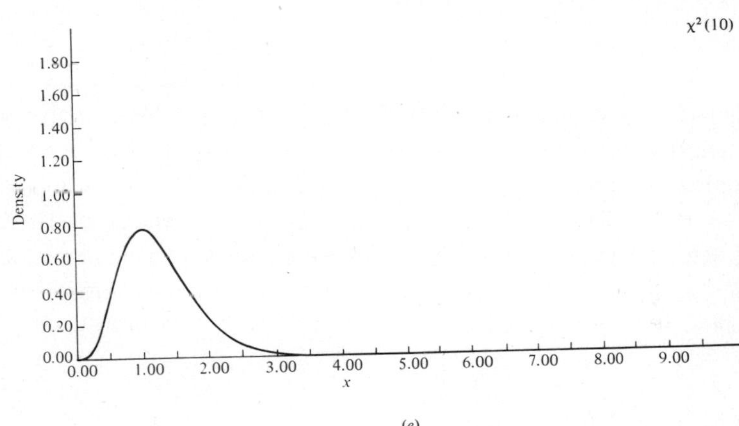

(e)

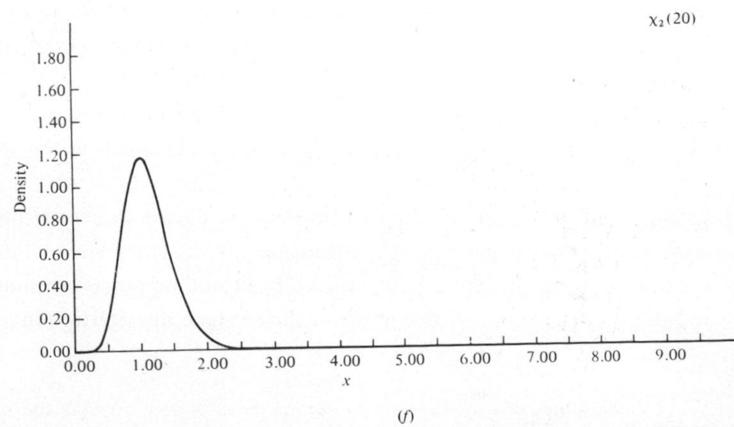

(f)

FIGURE 7-2.1 (*Continued*)

$$\frac{W^{(\nu/2)-1}}{\omega^{\nu/2}} \exp\left[\frac{-W}{2\omega}\right], \quad W > 0, \ \nu > 0, \ \omega > 0, \qquad (7\text{-}2.3)$$

the constant of proportionality being simply a number, that is, not depending on ω or W.

The descriptive characteristics of the $\chi^2(\nu, \omega)$ distribution are

$$\text{Mean} = \omega\nu, \qquad (7\text{-}2.4)$$

$$\text{Variance} = 2\omega^2\nu. \qquad (7\text{-}2.5)$$

If $\nu \geq 2$,

$$\text{Mode} = \omega(\nu - 2); \qquad (7\text{-}2.6)$$

otherwise it is not defined. If $\nu \geq 5$, the approximate

$$\text{Median} = \omega\left(\nu - \tfrac{2}{3}\right). \qquad (7\text{-}2.7)$$

In Fig. 7-2.1*a* to *f*, we give plots of $\chi^2(\nu)$ for $\nu = 1, 2, 3, 5, 10$, and 20.[1] From these figures, we see that χ^2 becomes more nearly normal as ν increases. For $\nu = 1$, the density function approaches infinity as χ^2 approaches zero. For $\nu = 2$, the density has a mode at zero. For $\nu = 3$, the density has a height of zero at $\chi^2 = 0$. When ν reaches 5, we begin to see the standard pattern of the χ^2 distribution, namely, a unimodal, asymmetric distribution that is positively skewed. This skewness decreases as ν increases, which can be seen in the plots for $\nu = 10$ and 20.

7-3 THE INVERSE CHI-SQUARE AND INVERSE CHI DISTRIBUTIONS

Bayesian inference for a normal variance ϕ frequently leads to the conclusion that "λ/ϕ is a chi-square variable on ν degrees of freedom", where λ is a positive constant. Note that this is the reverse (or more precisely, the inverse) of the situation discussed above—here ϕ, the variable of interest, occurs in the denominator of the fraction, and λ is simply a scale factor for ϕ which is equal to the reciprocal of the scale factor in the χ^2 density of ϕ^{-1}.

Again, in order to avoid the circumlocution of the phrase in quotation marks, we shall say that ϕ has an inverse chi-square distribution on ν degrees of freedom with scale parameter λ and abbreviate this to ϕ is $\chi^{-2}(\nu, \lambda)$. It should be remarked that a standard nomenclature has not yet evolved. Some writers call the same distribution inverse gamma,

[1] For values of $\nu = 3$ and above, ω has been chosen so that the mode of each distribution is at $\chi^2 = 1$.

while Lindley (1965) takes a different form for the parameter λ. We believe our nomenclature to be the simplest for practical use.

In Sec. 3-4, we saw how, when we know the density function of one random variable, we can find the density function of its inverse (3-4.13) and of a constant multiple of it (3-4.10). In the present context, $Y = \lambda/\phi$ has the chi-square density (7-2.3). Successive application of the two results just quoted shows that $\phi = \lambda/Y$ has a density function proportional to

$$\frac{1}{\phi^{\frac{1}{2}\nu + 1}} \exp\left[\frac{\lambda}{-2\phi}\right], \quad 0 < \phi < \infty, \ \lambda > 0, \ \nu > 0. \qquad (7\text{-}3.1)$$

Hence, to state that ϕ is $\chi^{-2}(\nu, \lambda)$ is to say that its density function is a constant multiple of (7-3.1) and that the distribution of ϕ^{-1} is $\chi^2(\nu, \lambda^{-1}) = \chi^2(\nu, \omega)$.

The descriptive characteristics of the $\chi^{-2}(\nu, \lambda)$ distribution are:

$$\text{Mean} = \frac{\lambda}{\nu - 2} \qquad (7\text{-}3.2)$$

if $\nu > 2$; otherwise it is not defined.

$$\text{Mode} = \frac{\lambda}{\nu + 2}; \qquad (7\text{-}3.3)$$

in particular, if $\nu = 1$, λ is equal to three times the mode;

$$\frac{\lambda}{\nu - \frac{1}{2}} < \text{median} < \frac{\lambda}{\nu - \frac{2}{3}}, \qquad (7\text{-}3.4)$$

if $\nu \geq 1$, with the upper limit approached closely when $\nu > 5$. And

$$\text{Variance} = \frac{2\lambda^2}{(\nu - 2)^2(\nu - 4)} \qquad (7\text{-}3.5)$$

if $\nu > 4$; otherwise it is not defined (is infinite). Note that the reciprocal of the approximate median for $\nu > 5$ is equal to the approximate median (7-2.7) for the (chi-square) density of ϕ^{-1}, namely, $\chi^2(\nu, \lambda^{-1})$.

Percentage points of the inverse chi-square distribution can be obtained directly from tables of χ^2. For example, if ϕ_{95} denotes the 95% point of a $\chi^{-2}(\nu, \lambda)$ variable ϕ,

$$.05 = \text{Prob}\,(\phi > \phi_{95}) = \text{Prob}\left(\frac{\lambda}{\phi} < \frac{\lambda}{\phi_{95}}\right),$$

and so λ/ϕ_{95} is the 5% point of the χ^2 distribution with ν degrees of freedom. Thus, to

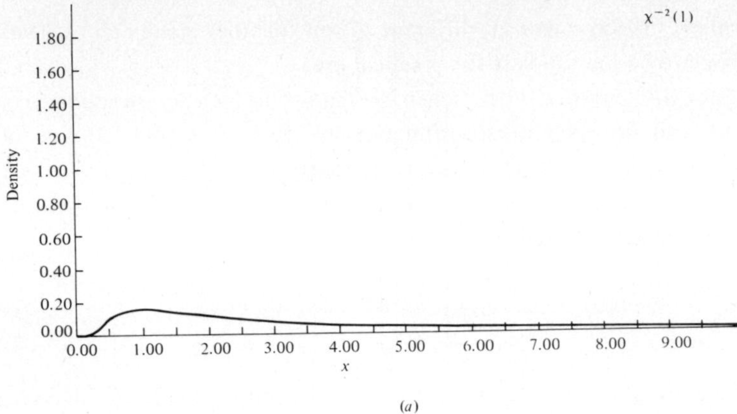

(a)

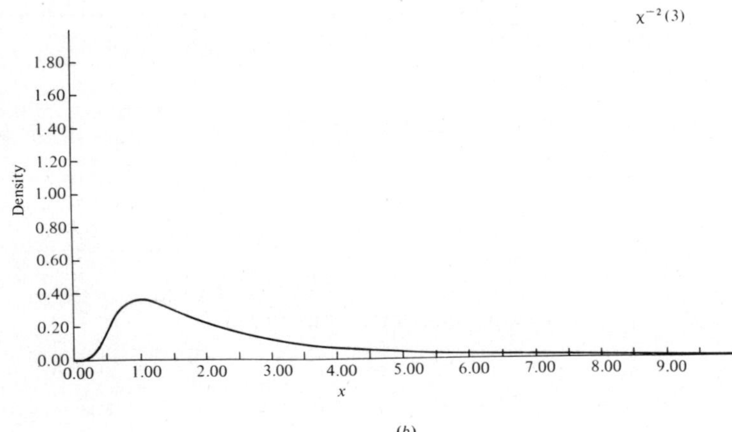

(b)

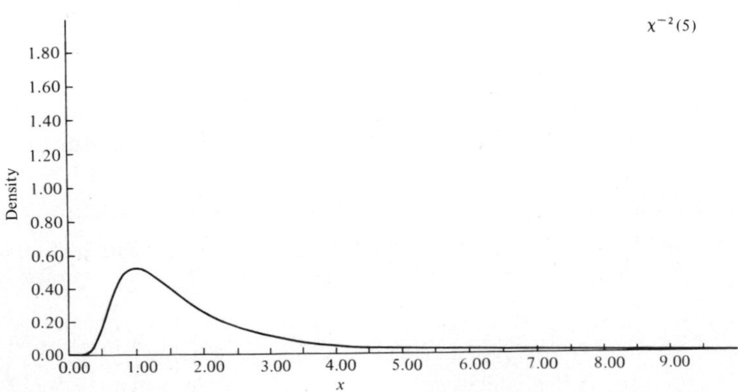

(c)

FIGURE 7-3.1
Inverse chi-squared distributions.

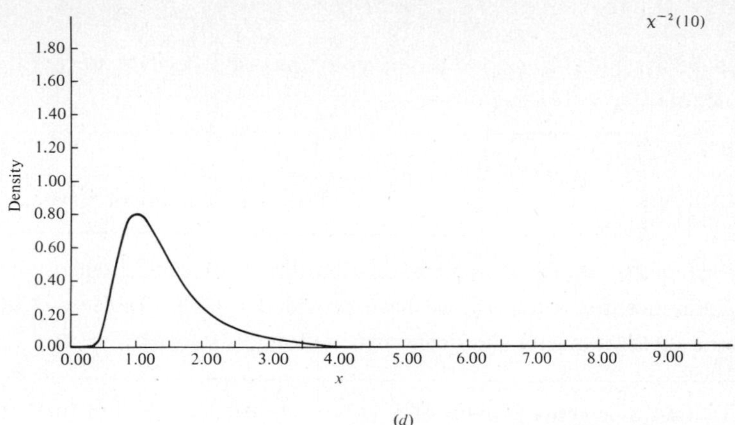

(*d*)

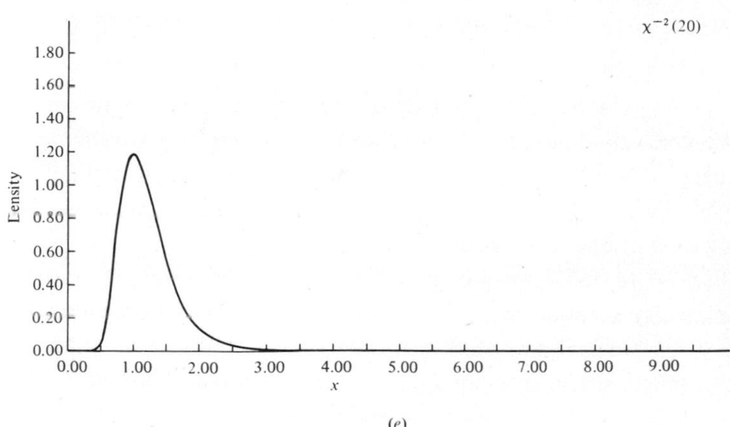

(*e*)

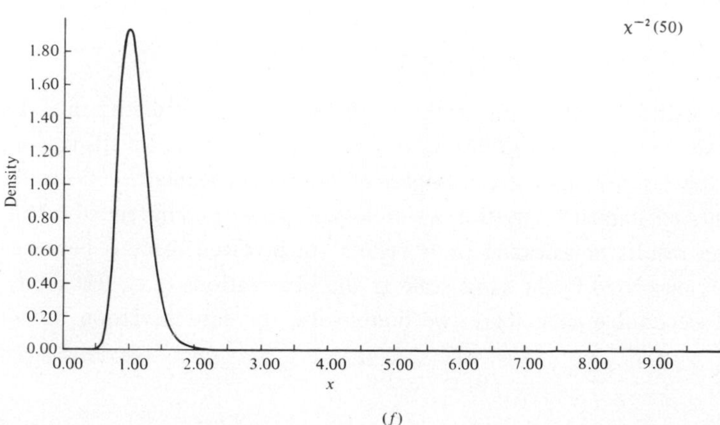

(*f*)

FIGURE 7-3.1 (*Continued*)

obtain the 95% point for ϕ: $\chi^{-2}(\nu, \lambda)$, you find the 5% point of $\chi^2(\nu, 1)$, which is typically denoted by $\chi^2(\nu)$, and divide λ by it; i.e.,

$$P\% \text{ point of } \chi^{-2}(\nu, \lambda) = \frac{\lambda}{(100 - P)\% \text{ point of } \chi^2(\nu)} \cdot \tag{7-3.6}$$

However, since the inverse chi-square distribution is of such frequent occurrence in Bayesian inference for variances, we have provided a table (Table A.7) of percentage points of the *standard* inverse chi-square distribution $\chi^{-2}(\nu)$ with $\lambda = 1$.

To find a percentage point of a $\chi^{-2}(\nu, \lambda)$ distribution, find the entry in the standard table for ν degrees of freedom and multiply it by λ.

$$P\% \text{ point of } \chi^{-2}(\nu, \lambda) = \lambda\,[P\% \text{ point of } \chi^{-2}(\nu)]$$

For values of ν beyond the limits of the table, a simple approximation is to take $\phi^{1/2}$ to be normally distributed with mean $[\lambda/(\nu - 1)]^{1/2}$ and variance $\lambda/2(\nu - 2)^2$. The adequacy of this approximation is examined below. HDR credibility intervals for $\chi^{-2}(\nu, 1)$ are given in Table A.8. Corresponding values of $\chi^{-2}(\nu, \lambda)$ can be obtained by multiplying each of the tabled values by λ.

In Fig. 7-3.1*a* to *f*, we give plots of $\chi^{-2}(\nu)$ for $\nu = 1, 3, 5, 10, 20, 50$.[1] For $\nu > 0$, the density function has a height of zero at $\chi^{-2} = 0$. Comparing this distribution with that of χ^2 for the same number of degrees of freedom (the comparisons $\nu = 3, 5, 10$, and 20 are possible here), we find that χ^{-2} is much more positively skewed than is χ^2.

Inverse Chi

The mathematics by which statistical results (e.g., posterior distributions) are derived is usually easiest to carry out using the variance as the measure of dispersion or spread of our observations. We shall see examples of this in subsequent sections. However, most people find the standard deviation a simpler measure to comprehend when questions of interpreting results or assessing prior beliefs are involved. This is because the standard deviation is measured in the same scale as the observations (e.g., test scores) themselves; that is, if we double each score, we double the standard deviation but *quadruple* the variance.

[1] These have been scaled so that each has a mode at $\chi^{-2} = 1$.

Thus, it will be useful to be able to make a priori and a posteriori statements about the standard deviation $\phi^{1/2}$, which, since, we are running short of Greek letters, we shall for the remainder of this section denote by σ without thereby implying that it is known.

When ϕ is $\chi^{-2}(\nu, \lambda)$ as defined above, we shall say that $\sigma = \phi^{1/2}$ has an *inverse chi distribution* with ν degrees of freedom and scale parameter $\lambda^{1/2}$, and abbreviate this to σ is $\chi^{-1}(\nu, \lambda^{1/2})$. The form $\lambda^{1/2}$ is retained for the scale parameter so as to make explicit the relationship with the inverse chi-square distribution. [Again there is no standard nomenclature: Schmitt (1969) calls *this* distribution inverse gamma.] Applying our standard results on transformations to the transformation $\sigma = \phi^{1/2}$ it follows that σ has density function proportional to

$$\frac{1}{\sigma^{\nu+1}} \exp\left(\frac{-\lambda}{2\sigma^2}\right), \quad 0 \leq \sigma < \infty. \qquad (7\text{-}3.7)$$

With the exception of the mode, the descriptive characteristics of the distribution have rather complicated forms, and so we list, in addition, useful approximate formulas.

CHARACTERISTICS OF THE INVERSE CHI DISTRIBUTION

Exact value	Approximate value	
Mean: $\frac{[(\nu-3)/2]!}{[(\nu-2)/2]!}\left(\frac{\lambda}{2}\right)^{1/2}$ provided $\nu > 1$.*	$\left(\frac{\lambda}{\nu - 3/2}\right)^{1/2}$, with error < 1% for $\nu \geqslant 5$.	(7-3.8)
Median: $\left(\frac{\lambda}{\text{median of } \chi^2(\nu, 1)}\right)^{1/2}$	$\left(\frac{\lambda}{\nu - 2/3}\right)^{1/2}$, with error < 1% for $\nu \geqslant 4$.	(7-3.9)
Mode: $\left(\frac{\lambda}{\nu+1}\right)^{1/2}$	$\left(\frac{\lambda}{\nu+1}\right)^{1/2}$ (exact)	(7-3.10)
Variance: $\frac{\lambda}{\nu-2} - \left(\begin{matrix}\text{exact}\\ \text{mean}\end{matrix}\right)^2$, provided $\nu > 2$.	$\frac{\lambda}{2(\nu-2)(\nu-5/3)}$, with error approximately 1% for $\nu \geqslant 4$.	(7-3.11)

**Note*: $\left(-\frac{1}{2}\right)! = \sqrt{\pi}$. Thus, for $\nu = 6$, $\left(\frac{\nu-3}{2}\right)! = \left(\frac{3}{2}\right)! = \left(\frac{3}{2}\right)\left(\frac{1}{2}\right)\left(-\frac{1}{2}\right)! = \frac{3\sqrt{\pi}}{4}$.

The exact formula for the median is a particular case of a general procedure for obtaining probability statements about σ, using the fact that λ/σ^2 has a standard

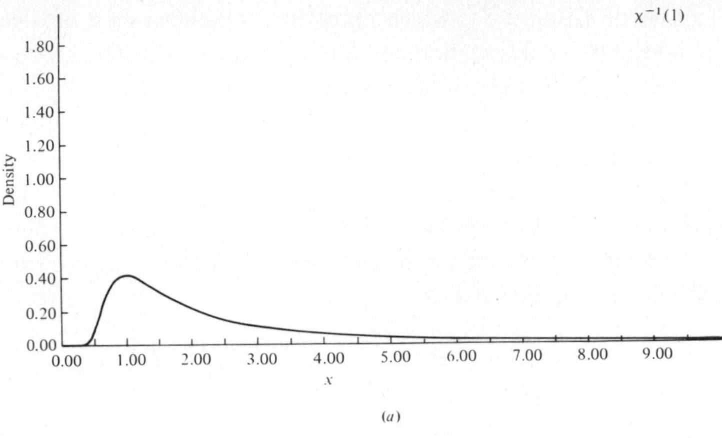

(a)

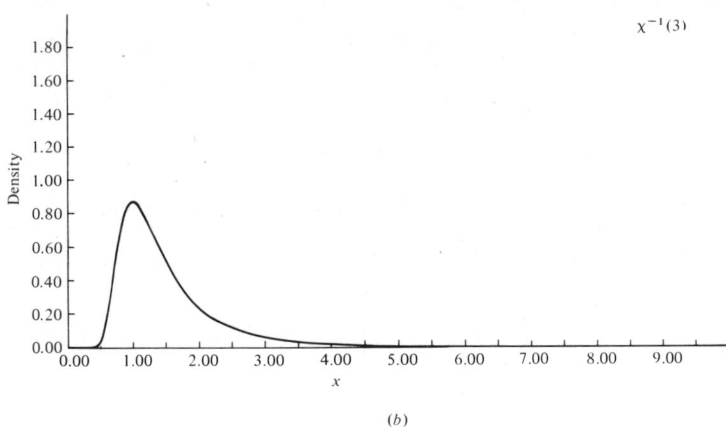

(b)

FIGURE 7-3.2
Inverse chi distributions.

chi-square distribution on ν degrees of freedom. To obtain the P% point for σ, find the $(100 - P)$% point of standard chi-square on ν degrees of freedom, divide λ by it, and take the square root. (This procedure is, of course, exactly the same as finding the P% point of $\phi = \sigma^2$ and then taking the square root.)

$$\boxed{P\% \text{ point of } \chi^{-1}(\nu, \lambda^{1/2}) = \sqrt{\frac{\lambda}{(100 - P)\% \text{ point of } \chi^2(\nu)}}} \tag{7-3.12}$$

Thus, percentage points, and in particular the median, transform in a natural manner

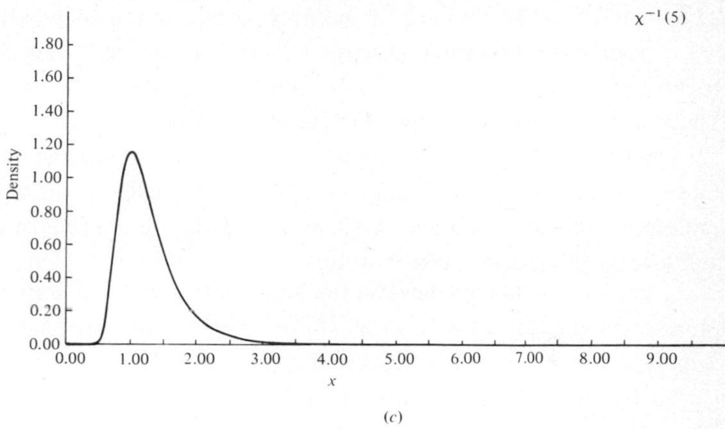

(c)

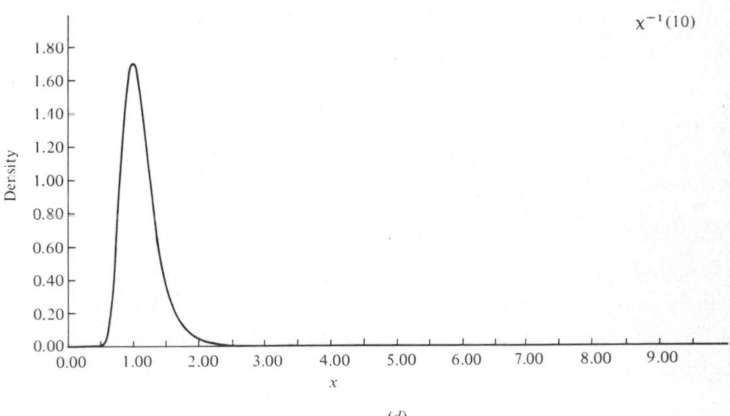

(d)

FIGURE 7-3.2 (*Continued*)

when one transforms the variable under study, e.g., from ϕ to $\phi^{1/2}$. Note, however, that one *cannot* find the mean or mode of $\phi^{1/2}$ by finding the mean or mode of ϕ and taking the square root.

Since the inverse chi distribution will be frequently used in this text, we have included a table (Table A.9) of percentage points of the *standard* inverse chi distribution [that is, $\chi^{-1}(\nu, 1)$]. In order to find the percentage points of the nonstandard inverse chi distribution, $\chi^{-1}(\nu, \lambda^{1/2})$, it will be necessary to multiply the tabled value by $\lambda^{1/2}$.

$$P\% \text{ point of } \chi^{-1}(\nu, \lambda^{1/2}) = \lambda^{1/2}[P\% \text{ point of } \chi^{-1}(\nu, 1)] \qquad (7\text{-}3.13)$$

HDR credibility intervals for $\chi^{-1}(\nu, 1)$ are given in Table A.10. Corresponding values for $\chi^{-1}(\nu, \lambda^{1/2})$ can be obtained by multiplying each of the tabled values by $\lambda^{1/2}$.

Both the distributions discussed in this section are skewed and, when ν is small, have very long upper tails. Hence, the central $C\%$ credibility intervals to describe them may be unsatisfactory. For example, when $\nu < 7$, the mode of the inverse chi-square distribution lies outside (below) the interquartile range (the central 50% interval). Thus, for smallish values of ν, the use of HDRs, as discussed in Sec. 5-5, may be preferable. In Tables A.8 and A.10, we give HDRs for the standardized inverse chi-square and inverse chi densities, respectively.

For large values of ν beyond the limits of tables, a simple approximation is to take σ as normally distributed with mean $[\lambda/(\nu - 1)]^{1/2}$ and variance $\lambda/2(\nu - 2)^2$. This is the same approximation as was suggested above for finding percentage points of the variance ϕ. To obtain some idea of how "large" ν needs to be, consider the case $\nu = 50, \lambda = 1$. Using the approximation, the 95% point y is given by $(y - .1429)/.01473 = 1.64$ (the normal 95% point), hence $y = .1671$. This compares with the value .1696 obtained from Table A.9.

Proceeding in this manner, for $\nu = 50, \lambda = 1$, we obtain the following values:

P (%)	1	5	10	25	50	75	90	95	99
Exact	.1146	.1217	.1258	.1332	.1424	.1526	.1629	.1696	.1835
Approximate	.1085	.1186	.1240	.1329	.1429	.1528	.1617	.1671	.1772

Expressing the error as a percentage of the mean, we see that it ranges from 5% in the extreme tails to less than .5% in the interquartile range. Thus, this approximation will be fairly satisfactory when ν is outside the range of our tables.

In Figs. 7-3.2a to d, we give plots of $\chi^{-1}(\nu)$ for $\nu = 1, 3, 5, 10$. Each of these is plotted with λ chosen so that the mode of the density is at $\chi^{-1} = 1$. Comparing this density with that of χ^{-2}, we find that it is less positively skewed (but more than χ^2), but it also tends to be rather highly peaked with virtually no left tail. Generally, we would judge this distribution to be nicer (i.e., more nearly normal) than χ^{-2}.

7-4 THE NORMAL MODEL WITH KNOWN MEAN AND UNKNOWN VARIANCE

The model discussed in this section, where the normal mean μ is known but the variance is unknown, will find limited direct application, but will be useful in evaluating prior distributions. In addition to this use, the discussion of this model will exemplify the strategy of Bayesian inference in a context which, while still relatively simple, requires the use of the important distributions introduced in Secs. 7-2 and 7-3 in essentially the same way as they will be used in more realistic (and complex) situations.

A rationalization of the model might be that in order to determine the precision of some new measuring instrument (physical or psychological), we use it to make measurements of some *known* quantity. *If the measurements are unbiased*, it will be reasonable to assume the observations have a $N(\mu, \phi)$ distribution where ϕ^{-1} is the precision which we wish to determine. The difficulty about the model lies in the italicized phrase: *Can we know in advance that our new instrument is unbiased?*

The Model

The model density is

$$m_\phi(x) = \frac{1}{(2\pi\phi)^{1/2}} \exp\left[\frac{(x-\mu)^2}{-2\phi}\right], \quad 0 < \phi < \infty, \quad -\infty < x < \infty, \tag{7-4.1}$$

where, as the notation $m_\phi(x)$ indicates, ϕ is the parameter about which inference is to be made and μ is a known constant.

The Likelihood Kernel

If n independent observations are obtained, the kernel of the likelihood is

$$\frac{1}{\phi^{n/2}} \exp\left(\frac{T^2}{-2\phi}\right), \tag{7-4.2}$$

where $T^2 = \sum_{i=1}^{n} (x_i - \mu)^2$, the sum of squared deviations from the (known) mean μ. This result is obtained by multiplying together the expressions for $m_\phi(x_i)$ obtainable from (7-4.1). From (7-4.2), we see that T^2 and n are the sufficient statistics for ϕ since the observations enter into the likelihood kernel only through these quantities.

Bayes' Theorem and the Sufficient Statistics

A well-known sampling-theory result states that *given ϕ and n, the distribution of T^2/ϕ is standard chi-square on n degrees of freedom*. In our abbreviated notation, T^2 is $\chi^2(n, \phi)$. Note that since we are talking about the conditional distribution given ϕ, ϕ is a constant and T^2 is the random variable. From (7-2.3), we see that T^2 has a density proportional to

$$\frac{T^{n-2}}{\phi^{n/2}} \exp\left(\frac{T^2}{-2\phi}\right), \quad 0 \leq T^2 < \infty. \tag{7-4.3}$$

Comparing this with (7-4.2), we see that it differs only in having the factor T^{n-2}. Recall that in obtaining the likelihood kernel for ϕ, we can drop factors not involving ϕ. Thus, we have here another illustration of the fact that the likelihood kernel can be found from the sampling density of the sufficient statistic by dropping irrelevant factors, and, hence, inferences using Bayes' theorem will be the same whether we work with the full set of observations x or the sufficient statistic T^2.

Natural Conjugate Densities

The family of natural conjugate densities is obtained by replacing the sufficient statistics n and T^2 in the likelihood kernel (7-4.2) by constants κ and λ. If we take $\kappa = \nu + 2$ for convenience, we find that a density in the conjugate family is proportional to

$$\frac{1}{\phi^{\frac{1}{2}\nu + 1}} \exp\left(\frac{\lambda}{-2\phi}\right), \quad 0 < \phi < \infty. \tag{7-4.4}$$

However, this is exactly the form of an inverse chi-square distribution given in (7-3.1), which is the reason for our having discussed that distribution. Thus, we have shown that the *family of densities which is natural conjugate to our present model is the inverse chi-square family*. Specifically, ϕ: $\chi^{-2}(\nu, \lambda)$.

Indifference Prior

The indifference prior, whose general nature and purpose we discussed in Sec. 6-6, is in this instance obtained by letting ν and λ go to zero in the general form of the conjugate density (7-4.4), giving

$$b(\phi) \propto \phi^{-1}, \quad 0 < \phi < \infty. \tag{7-4.5}$$

Notationally, (7-4.5) may be written ϕ: $\chi^{-2}(0, 0)$.

From the discussion of the transformation $Y = \ln X$ given at Eq. (3-4.12), it can be seen that if Y has a uniform density $f(y)$ = constant, then X has a density $f(x) \propto x^{-1}$ and vice versa. Thus, the density (7-4.5) for ϕ corresponds to $\ln \phi$ having a uniform density. For this reason, we shall describe the density by saying that *ϕ has a log-uniform distribution, meaning that its (natural) logarithm has a uniform distribution*. Note that the range of $\ln \phi$ is from $-\infty$ to $+\infty$.

The situation we have here is fairly typical. The indifference prior for a variable with a restricted range (here, $\phi \geq 0$) will not be uniform but will correspond to taking a uniform prior on some function of the original variable which has an unrestricted range.

The Posterior Distribution

Let us suppose that the prior beliefs about ϕ can be described by an inverse chi-square distribution with selected parameters ν_0 and λ_0. The choice and evaluation of this prior will be discussed shortly. We know that having chosen a conjugate prior, we shall obtain a posterior distribution of the same form; and on multiplying the likelihood kernel (7-4.2) by the prior kernel (7-4.4) with $\lambda = \lambda_0$ and $\nu = \nu_0$, we see that the posterior distribution is $\chi^{-2}(\nu_n, \lambda_n)$, where

$$\nu_n = \nu_0 + n, \qquad (7\text{-}4.6)$$

and

$$\lambda_n = \lambda_0 + T^2 \qquad (7\text{-}4.7)$$

with $T^2 = \Sigma(x_i - \mu)^2$ as before. To obtain the posterior corresponding to use of the indifference prior, we have only to put $\nu_0 = 0$, $\lambda_0 = 0$, obtaining

$$\nu_n = n, \quad \lambda_n = T^2. \qquad (7\text{-}4.8)$$

Equations (7-4.6) and (7-4.7) strongly suggest the interpretation that our prior distribution is equivalent to having additional (hypothetical) data, namely, ν_0 extra observations with sum of squared deviations λ_0. (This same phenomenon was observed in the normal model with unknown mean and known variance.) Our indifference prior gives formal expression to this suggestion. Starting with the indifference prior $\chi^{-2}(0, 0)$ and being given the stated hypothetical observations, we obtain a posterior $\chi^{-2}(\nu_0, \lambda_0)$ which we then use as prior for the second stage—the actual data. This line of reasoning provides an alternative way of choosing a prior distribution or a way of evaluating a prior assessed by the credibility interval method. I ask myself: "Can I equate my prior knowledge to ν_0 observations from the model under study with sum of squares λ_0?" In the present instance, a useful way to proceed would be first to ask oneself what is the most likely value of ϕ, giving the modal value $\lambda_0/(\nu_0 + 2)$, and then to ask how many observations one's previous knowledge is worth, giving ν_0.

If we temporarily refer to the value λ/ν, intermediate between the mean $\lambda/(\nu - 2)$ and the mode $\lambda/(\nu + 2)$ of the $\chi^{-2}(\nu, \lambda)$ distribution, as its "center" and denote it by γ, we can exhibit the "averaging" effect of Bayes theorem. Equation (7-4.7) can then be written as

$$\nu_n \gamma_n = \nu_0 \gamma_0 + n \frac{T^2}{n} \qquad (7\text{-}4.9)$$

or

$$\gamma_n = \frac{\nu_0 \gamma_0 + n(T^2/n)}{\nu_0 + n}. \qquad (7\text{-}4.10)$$

By differentiating the likelihood kernel (7-4.2) with respect to ϕ, we find that the maximum-likelihood estimate of ϕ is T^2/n. Thus, the "center" of the posterior distribution is a weighted average of the "center" of the prior distribution and the maximum-likelihood estimate of ϕ. Note that in (7-4.10), the degrees of freedom play the role occupied by the precision in the analysis for a normal mean—that is, more observations (hypothetical or real) correspond to more information.

EXAMPLE 2 Consider again the English scores in the 1969 junior college data (Table 1-5.2), with a 23rd college being studied with the assumption that this college is indistinguishable from the others. We are interested in a "quick" estimate of the variance in the new college. To simplify the computations, we proceed as if we knew the mean to be some fixed value μ. Suppose that, a priori, our "best guess" at ϕ is 25; and we feel that our estimate (garnered from our experience in the first 22 colleges) is based upon rather little information, perhaps the equivalent of about seven direct observations from the 23rd college. We suppose that our prior beliefs can be fitted by an inverse chi-square (χ^{-2}) distribution with parameters (ν_0, λ_0). From (7-3.3), we have

$$\lambda_0 = (\nu_0 + 2)(\text{mode})$$

and from our specifications, this gives

$$\lambda_0 = (9)(25) = 225,$$

where we have here interpreted "best guess" to mean the mode of the prior distribution. We then proceed to draw a sample of size $n = 16$ and observe $T^2 = 449.44$. Then, a posteriori,

$$\phi : \chi^{-2}(\nu_n, \lambda_n)$$

where

$$\nu_n = \nu_0 + n = 7 + 16 = 23,$$

$$\lambda_n = \lambda_0 + T^2 = 225 + 449.44 = 674.44.$$

Thus, a posteriori, $\phi : \chi^{-2}(23, 674.44)$. Our posterior estimates of ϕ are, thus,

$$\text{Modal estimate} = \frac{\lambda_n}{\nu_n + 2} = \frac{674.44}{25} = 26.98,$$

$$\text{Mean estimate} = \frac{\lambda_n}{\nu_n - 2} = \frac{674.44}{21} = 32.12,$$

as compared with a prior estimate of 25.

This analysis is not at all as satisfactory as we have implied it to be. We have taken our prior modal estimate to be 25 with $\nu_0 = 7$ yielding $\lambda_0 = 225$. However, from (7-3.2), we see that this implies a prior

$$\text{Mean estimate} = \frac{225}{5} = 45.$$

The square root of this value (an estimate of the standard deviation) is nearly 7 and this seems inconsistent with the standard deviations given in Table 1-5.2. We must start over and see if we can get out something that is coherent, i.e., something that makes sense when looked at from every angle. Obviously, one way of avoiding this problem is to take ν_0 very much larger, but we may not wish to do this as we do not wish to put very much weight on our prior information.

Suppose we repeat the analysis, equating our prior guess to the a priori mean, which we take to be 25. This conflicts with the idea that our prior modal estimate should be 25, and we shall need to satisfy ourselves as to which is more acceptable. We then have

$$\text{Mean} = 25 = \frac{\lambda_0}{\nu_0 - 2} = \frac{\lambda_0}{5}$$

or

$$\lambda_0 = 125.$$

Then, a posteriori, $\phi: \chi^{-2}(23, 574.44)$. The a posteriori mean is

$$\frac{\lambda_n}{\nu_n - 2} = \frac{574.44}{23 - 2} = 27.35.$$

The a posteriori mode is

$$\frac{\lambda_n}{\nu_n + 2} = \frac{574.44}{23 + 2} = 22.98$$

as compared with the prior mode

$$\frac{\lambda_0}{\nu_0 + 2} = \frac{125}{9} = 13.89.$$

The square roots of the two posterior estimates are 5.23 and 4.79, consistent with our prior information.

The 5% point of the χ^2 distribution with 23 degrees of freedom is 13.1. Thus, ϕ_{95}, the 95% point of $\chi^{-2}(23, 574.44)$, is

$$\frac{574.44}{13.1} = 43.85 \quad \text{[see (7-3.6)]}.$$

Thus, we can state that, a posteriori, the probability that $\phi \leq 43.85$ is .95. The more direct way of obtaining this value would be by direct reference to the inverse chi-square table. A priori given $\nu_0 = 7, \lambda_0 = 125$, the corresponding statement was

$$\text{Prob}\ (\phi \leq 57.68) = .95.$$

The square root of 57.68 is about 7.6. Thus, our prior statement was that we were willing to give odds of 19:1 against the standard deviation in the 23rd college being greater than 7.6, clearly a favorable gamble. However, it would be embarrassing if we were asked to accept these odds. The present authors would not accept these odds, suggesting that for them the prior is not yet what it should be. In order to get a really coherent prior distribution, one would need to increase ν_0. This, however, might raise howls of protest about our putting too much weight on the prior information. The protests would, of course, be wrong. At this point, we shall let the reader find a value of ν_0 that is satisfactory for him. We shall come back to this problem later.

7-5 STUDENT'S DISTRIBUTION

The predictive density $p_n(x_{n+1})$ for an $(n + 1)$st observation from the model of the previous section is obtained by combining two pieces of knowledge: (1) given ϕ, the distribution of X_{n+1} is $N(\mu, \phi)$; and (2) the (posterior) distribution of ϕ is $\chi^{-2}(\nu_n, \lambda_n)$. As we saw in Sec. 6-4, the predictive density of X_{n+1} is obtained by multiplying together the densities for (1) and (2) to find the joint distribution of X_{n+1} and ϕ, and then integrating with respect to ϕ to find the marginal density of X_{n+1}.

The result of carrying out this procedure is

$$p_n(x_{n+1}) \propto \frac{1}{[(x_{n+1} - \mu)^2 + \lambda_n]^{\frac{1}{2}(\nu_n + 1)}}. \tag{7-5.1}$$

At first sight, it would appear that a table of this distribution will require three-way classification to allow for all possible values of ν_n, μ, and λ_n. However, we can standardize the distribution by writing

$$t = \frac{\nu_n^{1/2}(x_{n+1} - \mu)}{\lambda_n^{1/2}}. \tag{7-5.2}$$

Then,

$$p_n(t) \propto \frac{1}{(1 + t^2/\nu_n)^{\frac{1}{2}(\nu_n + 1)}}, \qquad -\infty < t < \infty, \tag{7-5.3}$$

and thus we need only tabulate percentage points for possible values of ν_n. The density (7-5.3), with ν in place of ν_n in the general case, is that of *Student's t distribution on ν degrees of freedom*.

The t distribution is defined for $\nu > 0$. It is symmetrical about $t = 0$, which is therefore its median, and where it also has a mode. While it might seem "obvious" that the mean is also zero, this is true only when $\nu > 1$. The case $\nu = 1$, a proper symmetric density which just fails to have a properly defined mean, is known as the *Cauchy distribution*. The variance of the t distribution is $\nu/(\nu - 2)$ provided that $\nu > 2$; otherwise it is undefined.

Table A.4 gives percentage points of the t distribution for $\nu = 1(1)10(2)30(10)60, \infty$. Because of the symmetry, it is only necessary to tabulate percentage points between 50 and 100%. For $P < 50$, the P% point is the negative of the $(100 - P)$% point. As ν becomes large, the t distribution is approximated by the standard normal distribution—the entries in the table for $\nu = \infty$ are the normal percentage points and are included partly to show the closeness of the approximation. As can be seen from the table, the P% point is further from the median in the t distribution than in the normal distribution—very substantially so for small values of ν. This is also reflected by the fact that the variance $\nu/(\nu - 2)$ is greater than unity. In appearance, a t distribution has

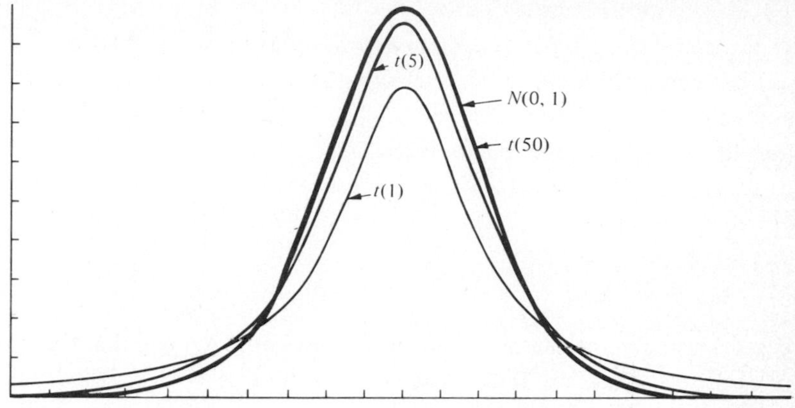

FIGURE 7-5.1
Graphs for densities $t(1)$, $t(5)$, $t(50)$ and $N(0, 1)$.

longer, fatter tails than the normal. In Fig. 7-5.1 "t" densities with 1, 5, and 50 degrees of freedom are drawn together with a normal density. Note that the $t(50)$ and normal densities are visually indistinguishable.

In reporting the predictive density, we noted that it was not X_{n+1} itself but a standardized form of X_{n+1}, namely, $\nu_n^{1/2}(X_{n+1} - \mu)/\lambda_n^{1/2}$, which has Student's t distribution on ν_n degrees of freedom. This is typical of results involving the t distribution. In the general case, the usual form of report is: *"The distribution of Y is such that $\nu^{1/2}(Y - \zeta)/\kappa^{1/2}$ has Student's t distribution on v degrees of freedom".* (Various algebraic rearrangements of the defining fraction are found.) It will be convenient to abbreviate this sentence to "Y is $t(\nu, \zeta, \kappa)$", this abbreviated statement having exactly the same meaning as the italicized one above. The reader is again warned that this is a convenient shorthand peculiar to this book, not standard notation.

The descriptive characteristics of the $t(\nu, \zeta, \kappa)$ distribution are

$$\text{Mean} = \text{median} = \text{mode} = \zeta, \tag{7-5.4}$$

and

$$\text{Variance} = \frac{\kappa}{\nu - 2}. \tag{7-5.5}$$

The standard t distribution, as tabulated in Tables A.3 and A.4, is thus $t(\nu, 0, \nu)$.

Cumulative probabilities for $t(\nu, \zeta, \kappa)$ can be obtained from those of $t(\nu, 0, \nu)$, the standardized t distribution, by noting that

$$\text{Prob}\,(Y > c) = \text{Prob}\left[T > \frac{\nu^{1/2}(c - \zeta)}{\kappa^{1/2}}\right].$$

Thus, if $\nu = 10$, $\zeta = 105$, and $\kappa = 5533.2$,

$$\begin{aligned}\text{Prob}\,(Y > 110) &= \text{Prob}\,(T > .213)\\ &= 1 - \text{Prob}\,(T < .213)\\ &= 1 - .58\\ &= .42\,.\end{aligned}$$

To get a specified percentage point p for Y use Table A.4 and find that percentage point, say t, for T. Thus, we find t such that $\text{Prob}\,(T \leq t) = p$. Then, the corresponding percentage point c for Y will be given by

$$c = \zeta + \left(\frac{\kappa}{\nu}\right)^{1/2} t\,.$$

In the above example, the 75th percentile for T is $t = .6998$; hence, the 75th percentile for Y is 121.46. The central 50% credibility interval is then 105 ± 16.46 or (88.54, 121.46).

7-6 THE NORMAL MODEL WITH UNKNOWN MEAN AND VARIANCE

A much more realistic model than those so far discussed in this chapter for repeated measurements subject to error is the normal distribution $N(\theta, \phi)$ with unknown mean *and* variance. In this model, the n observations are used to provide information about both θ and ϕ. We would, therefore, expect that the information we obtain about either is less precise.

The model density is

$$m_{\theta,\phi}(x) = \frac{1}{(2\pi\phi)^{1/2}} \exp\left[\frac{(x - \theta)^2}{-2\phi}\right]. \tag{7-6.1}$$

Multiplying together the model densities for each of the n independent observations x_i, we obtain the likelihood whose kernel can be expressed by means of the algebraic rearrangements discussed after (6-2.5) in the form

$$\frac{1}{\phi^{n/2}} \exp\left[\frac{n(x_{\bullet} - \theta)^2 + S^2}{-2\phi}\right], \tag{7-6.2}$$

showing that sufficient statistics are the sample size n, sample mean $x_{\bullet} = n^{-1}\Sigma x_i$, and $S^2 = \Sigma(x_i - x_{\bullet})^2$, the sum of squared deviations from the sample mean.

This is an appropriate point at which to comment on the phrase *degrees of freedom*. In Sec. 7-4, where the degrees of freedom were n, the sufficient statistic T^2 was the sum of the squares of n mathematically unconnected quantities $(x_i - \mu)^2$; unconnected because μ was simply a known number, and the values x_i arose as observations. There were, thus, n "free" terms in the sum. In the present case, S^2 is the sum of the squares of n quantities $(x_i - x_\bullet)$, but only $(n - 1)$ of them are "free" since they are connected by the relation

$$\sum (x_i - x_\bullet) = \sum x_i - nx_\bullet = 0$$

by the definition of $x_\bullet$. This relation is called a constraint. One way of looking at it is that if $(n - 1)$ of the quantities $(x_i - x_\bullet)$ are known, the nth can be determined using the constraint. Generally speaking, the number of degrees of freedom is the number of quantities which enter (usually squared) into the statistic used minus the number of constraints connecting these quantities. It will never be necessary for us to calculate the number of degrees of freedom in this way, and we could simply regard "degrees of freedom" as a rather cumbersome name for one of the parameters of our distributions. However, for purposes of heuristic interpretation, the notion that the degrees of freedom are the number of distinct pieces of information employed is a useful one.

Prior Distributions

If we replace n, $x_\bullet$, and S^2 in (7-6.2) by constants a, b, and c, we obtain a natural conjugate density for this model. A brief examination suffices to show that it cannot be factorized as the product of two terms, one a function of θ only and the other a function of ϕ only, and so θ and ϕ are not independent in the conjugate density. Hence, we cannot reach a conjugate prior by applying to θ and ϕ, separately, the techniques discussed in previous sections. We therefore defer to the next two sections the problem of assessing prior information and present here an analysis using the indifference prior. An added benefit of this approach is that we can keep the formulas relatively simple while studying the first *joint* posterior distribution we have met.

The joint indifference prior is obtained by taking "independent" indifference priors of the forms used previously on θ and ϕ. The word "independent" is so written to indicate that a certain degree of mathematical caution (which need not concern the reader) is needed when talking of the independence of improper priors. For our purposes, the word will simply mean that the joint density is (as usual for independent variables) the product of the individual densities. Thus,

$$\begin{aligned} b(\theta, \phi) &= b(\theta)\, b(\phi) \\ &\propto \phi^{-1}, \quad -\infty < \theta < \infty, \phi > 0 \end{aligned} \tag{7-6.3}$$

since $b(\theta)$ is uniform, that is, has a constant value, and $b(\phi)$ has the log-uniform distribution given by (7-4.5).

The argument for assuming "independence" runs as follows. If I start from ignorance of θ and ϕ, and then someone tells me the value of θ, is the nature of my ignorance about ϕ in any way changed? Conversely, if I am told the value of ϕ, is the nature of my ignorance of θ in any way changed? In many educational and psychological applications, a negative answer can be returned to both these questions, implying that the conditional distributions are the same as the marginal ones, that is, that the variables are independent.

The Joint Posterior Density

Multiplying the prior (7-6.3) by the likelihood kernel (7-6.2), we obtain the joint posterior density

$$b_n(\theta, \phi) \propto \frac{1}{\phi^{(n/2)+1}} \exp\left[\frac{n(\theta - x_\bullet)^2 + S^2}{-2\phi}\right]. \qquad (7\text{-}6.4)$$

This is the first *joint* posterior density we have met. Before going on to obtain the marginal densities of θ and ϕ, we consider what features of the joint density itself may be worth reporting. There would be no point in reporting the joint means (expectations of θ and ϕ with respect to the joint density) or the variances from the joint distribution since these are identical with the marginal means and variances. Also, no useful definition of joint median seems possible. The joint mode, however, has several properties which make it worth reporting.

1) It has a clear meaning. It locates the point of the (θ, ϕ) plane around which the probability is concentrated–loosely speaking, it gives the map reference of the "peak", the highest point of the probability surface "hill".

2) It is relatively easy to determine by use of the differential calculus (as contrasted, e.g., with the mean, which requires use of the integral calculus).

3) When the posterior distribution is based on a considerable number of observations, the density "hill" is typically very steep-sided, and so all the probability is clustered around the joint mode; also, the joint mean will be close to the joint mode, a fact which is useful when the mean cannot be found analytically.

4) The coordinates of the joint mode are *not*, in general, the same as the marginal modes.

Property (4) may raise a question in the reader's mind. If the joint modal values are not the same as the marginal modal values, which are the correct ones to report? We recall that the measures of central tendency we report serve two purposes: (a) they may be optimal estimates with respect to some loss function, and (b) they are descriptive features of the posterior distribution. With regard to (a), the loss function in use will determine which is/are the appropriate modal values—if our loss function is zero-one in θ, the marginal mode for θ is obviously the relevant one; if it is zero-one in θ and ϕ jointly, the joint mode is relevant. In case (b), the question becomes: "Which posterior distribution is the relevant one?" The answer will depend on the focus of our interest. If our *real* interest centers on the mean θ (the "true value" of the measurement) and ϕ is simply a *nuisance parameter*, then the posterior distribution of θ alone is relevant. If, however, θ and ϕ are the mean and variance of the abilities of a class of students, the wise teacher will be concerned with both of them, and the joint distribution may be relevant.

In the present model, the joint mode of the pair (θ, ϕ) is $[x_{\bullet}, S^2/(n+2)]$. We shall see below that the marginal modes are $x_{\bullet}$ and $S^2/(n+1)$. The joint maximum-likelihood estimate, which is the same as the joint posterior mode if we take $b(\theta, \phi) =$ constant in place of (7-6.3), is $(x_{\bullet}/S^2/n)$.

Another feature of the joint density which is not captured by the marginal densities and which is, therefore, worth reporting separately is the posterior covariance or correlation. In the present model, the *posterior covariance is zero*, and so θ and ϕ are a posteriori uncorrelated. Since it is clear from (7-6.4) that the parameters θ and ϕ are *not* independent, this may come as something of a surprise. The reason for it will become clear later; meanwhile, it serves to underline the warning we gave in Sec. 4-1 that while independence implies zero correlation (or covariance), zero correlation does not, in general, imply independence.

The Posterior Marginal Densities

We now turn to the posterior marginal densities, dealing first with ϕ since its density under this model is similar to that when the mean is known. Specifically, *the posterior marginal distribution of ϕ is inverse chi square on $(n-1)$ degrees of freedom with scale parameter S^2.* In brief, ϕ is $\chi^{-2}(n-1, S^2)$. This result is obtained by integrating the joint density (7-6.4) with respect to θ. The characteristics of the distribution follow immediately from the general discussion in Sec. 7-3 by putting $\lambda = S^2$ and $\nu = n - 1$; for example, the posterior mode is $S^2/(n+1)$ and the posterior mean is $S^2/(n-3)$. Note that the mean does not exist unless n is at least 4.

The result of integrating the joint density (7-6.4) with respect to ϕ is the posterior marginal density for θ,

$$b_n(\theta) \propto \frac{1}{[n(\theta - x_{\bullet})^2 + S^2]^{n/2}} \cdot \tag{7-6.5}$$

This expression is reminiscent of the density (7-5.1) which we were able to standardize to a Student's t form. On examining (7-6.5), we note that if we write $\nu = n - 1$ as in the previous paragraph and define

$$t = \frac{\nu^{1/2}(\theta - x.)}{n^{-1/2}S}, \tag{7-6.6}$$

then

$$b_n(t) \propto \frac{1}{(S^2t^2/\nu + S^2)^{n/2}} \propto \frac{1}{(1 + t^2/\nu)^{\frac{1}{2}(\nu+1)}} \tag{7-6.7}$$

which is precisely Student's t distribution (7-5.3) on $\nu = n - 1$ degrees of freedom. (In deriving (7-6.7), the derivative of t with respect to θ, which is a constant, and the factor S^2 removed from the denominator, have been absorbed into the constant of proportionality.)

Thus, we have shown that in the customary format: "*The posterior (marginal) distribution of θ is such that*

$$\frac{\theta - x_{\bullet}}{\sqrt{\dfrac{S^2/\nu}{n}}}$$

has a t distribution on $\nu = n - 1$ degrees of freedom". In the shorthand notation introduced in the previous section, this statement reads: "θ is $t(\nu, x_{\bullet}, n^{-1}S^2)$". It follows that the posterior density of θ is symmetric and unimodal, with mean, median, and mode at $\theta = x_{\bullet}$, and with variance $n^{-1}S^2/(\nu - 2)$.

The reader may be puzzled by our use in the previous two paragraphs of both the symbols n and $\nu = (n - 1)$. However, if one traces how the two quantities came into the expression for t, the n is associated with $x_{\bullet}$ and the ν with S^2. We shall shortly meet examples where this general pattern is preserved, but the relation between the two is no longer the simple one that $\nu = (n - 1)$. It will then appear that the notation has been wisely chosen.

The Posterior Conditional Densities

At (7-6.4), we gave the joint posterior density of θ and ϕ. So far, we have considered the joint distribution itself and the marginal distributions. It is natural to ask ourselves: "Of what interest, if any, are the conditional distributions of θ given ϕ and ϕ given θ?" One immediate answer is that (assuming indifference priors throughout) the work presented in Secs. 7-1 and 7-4 for the known mean and known variance cases was mathematically unnecessary (though, we hope, pedagogically useful) since the posterior distributions for these cases can be deduced directly from the joint density of which they are simply the conditional distributions.

To see that this is so, one has only to note the semantic equivalence of the phrases (1) "conditional on ϕ", (2) "given that ϕ takes a particular value–i.e., σ^2", (3) "assuming that $\phi = \sigma^2$ where σ^2 is known". Perhaps more directly meaningful in terms of making inferences from data is to suppose that after carrying out the calculations detailed in this section, someone informs us that in point of fact, the variance ϕ is known to be equal to σ^2. We are then no longer interested in the marginal density of θ but in its density conditional on this known value of ϕ. From an alternative point of view, the firm *knowledge* that $\phi = \sigma^2$ completely overrides any attempts at *inference* about ϕ expressed by the posterior distributions and puts us right back to the known variance case.

Let us find the posterior conditional distribution

$$b_n(\theta|\phi) = \frac{b_n(\theta, \phi)}{b_n(\phi)} \cdot$$

Considered only as a function of θ, $b_n(\theta|\phi)$ is proportional to $b_n(\theta, \phi)$. Suppose we are given that $\phi = \sigma^2$. Substituting this value in (7-6.4) and discarding constant factors, we obtain

$$b_n(\theta|\phi = \sigma^2) \propto \exp\left[\frac{n(\theta - x_{\bullet})^2}{-2\sigma^2}\right]. \tag{7-6.9}$$

This is recognizable as the kernel of a $N(x_{\bullet}, n^{-1}\sigma^2)$ distribution and is the same as the result for the known variance case obtained at (6-3.6) when we give σ_0^{-2} in (6-3.4) and (6-3.5) the indifference value zero.

The reader may like to verify that if in (7-6.4) we put $\theta = \mu$ and find $b_n(\phi|\theta = \mu)$, the result is the inverse chi-square density which we found in Sec. 7-4 with the parameters of the prior given the indifference values $\nu_0 = 0$, $\lambda_0 = 0$. [Equations (6-2.4) and (6-2.5) and the discussion around them will save algebra!]

We are now in a position to see why θ and ϕ are uncorrelated, a posteriori, even though they are not independent. The mean of the conditional distribution of θ, given *any* value of ϕ is $x_{\bullet}$; thus the regression function of θ on ϕ (Sec. 4-2) is the straight line $\theta = x_{\bullet}$. As shown in Sec. 4-3, it follows that the *linear*-regression function is also $\theta = x_{\bullet}$, a line of slope zero since it does not contain a ϕ term. It then follows from (4-3.8) that the correlation must be zero (since the variance is not).

The Posterior Predictive Density

The predictive distribution for an $(n + 1)$th observation in the present unknown mean and variance model is

$$t\left[n - 1, x_{\bullet}, (1 + n^{-1})\sum(x_i - x_{\bullet})^2\right]. \tag{7-6.10}$$

Its properties follow immediately from those of the *t* distribution; in particular, its mean is the sample mean $x_{\bullet}$ as one would expect in the absence of prior knowledge about θ. In the final indicator of the distribution, the factor $(1 + n^{-1})$ can be, roughly, attributed to two causes. The 1 represents uncertainty associated with the next observation while the n^{-1} represents uncertainty about how close $x_{\bullet}$ is to the true mean θ.

7-7 QUANTIFICATION OF PRIOR INFORMATION

In this section, we discuss, in the context of the model of the previous section, one approach to quantifying prior information when it exists. The formulation we present at this point is appropriate *only* when the amounts of prior information we have on the mean and on the standard deviation are equal. A more general and more complex formulation will be given in the next section. We have seen that there are difficulties in applying the credibility-interval method to the parameters separately. However, if we are able to equate our prior state of knowledge to that which we would have reached by starting from a state of ignorance and making a set of m preliminary observations $\mathbf{w} = (w_1, w_2, \ldots, w_m)$ with mean $w_{\bullet}$ and sum of squares $R^2 = \Sigma(w_i - w_{\bullet})^2$, it follows that the required prior density is given by the joint density (7-6.4) with m for n, $w_{\bullet}$ for $x_{\bullet}$, and R for S. We shall not need to rework our analysis using this new prior since the fundamental consistency property of Bayesian inference discussed in Sec. 6-3 shows that the result of combining the new prior with the observations $\mathbf{x} = (x_1, x_2, \ldots, x_n)$ of our actual experiment will be the same as that obtained using the indifference prior and taking the data to consist of $(m + n)$ observations

$$(\mathbf{w}, \mathbf{x}) = (w_1, \ldots, w_m, x_1, \ldots, x_n).$$

It then requires only a little algebra to show that the effect of replacing the indifference prior (7-6.3) used in our previous analysis by the new prior expressing knowledge is that in (7-6.4); and in all subsequent results derived from it, we must replace

$$\boxed{\begin{array}{lll} n & \text{by} & m + n, \\ x_{\bullet} & \text{by} & \dfrac{mw_{\bullet} + nx_{\bullet}}{m + n} \\ S^2 & \text{by} & R^2 + S^2 + \dfrac{mn(x_{\bullet} - w_{\bullet})^2}{m + n} \end{array}}$$

and (the last line above).

It is, perhaps, worth commenting that the Bayesian method uses not only the within-sample information R^2 and S^2 in estimating ϕ but also the between-sample information $(x_{\bullet} - w_{\bullet})^2$. If $x_{\bullet}$ and $w_{\bullet}$ are close together, this would suggest that ϕ is small; we can hardly ignore this information.

How practical a proposition is it to quantify prior knowledge in this way? If one is prepared to assume that one's knowledge can, indeed, be equated to that gained from a preliminary sample, one might interrogate oneself as follows:

1) What is the most likely value of θ? This will be the mode $w_{\bullet}$ of our prior marginal distribution for θ.
2) What is the most likely value of ϕ? This, similarly, will be $R^2/(m+1)$.
3) What is a 50% central credibility for θ (its center must be the previously estimated $w_{\bullet}$ if the method is to work)? If $2l$ denotes the length of this interval and $t_{75}(m-1)$ the 75% point of a t distribution on $(m-1)$ degrees of freedom, we must have

$$l = [m(m-1)]^{-1/2} R t_{75}(m-1). \tag{7-7.1}$$

Writing ν for $m-1$, we can write the approximate equality

$$\frac{t_{75}(\nu)}{\nu^{1/2}} \doteq \frac{l}{[R^2/(m+1)]^{1/2}}. \tag{7-7.2}$$

Since the numerator and denominator of the right-hand side of (7-7.2) have already been estimated, one can scan the 75% point column of the table of t, dividing the tabulated values by the square root of the degrees of freedom until one finds a value ν for which the equation is satisfied. Then, $m = (\nu + 1)$ which, in turn, allows R^2 to be deduced from the answer to (2) above. If the value of ν obtained is small, in view of the approximation made in obtaining (7-7.2) from (7-7.1) it will be worth checking whether increasing ν by 1 gives better agreement in (7-7.1). Having found m, $w_{\bullet}$, and R^2 in this manner, one should then obtain a series of credibility intervals for θ and ϕ using the $t(m-1, w_{\bullet}, m^{-1}R^2)$ and $\chi^{-2}(m-1, R^2)$ distributions and check that these are in reasonable agreement with one's prior knowledge. This may lead one to modify m and possibly R^2.

The procedure in the previous paragraph is not claimed to be optimal (though it is probably safer than, for example, obtaining both R^2 and m by considering ϕ alone). It is offered as a demonstration that the hypothetical preliminary sample method can be made to work under the conditions stated at the beginning of the section. That is, a reasonable approach to prior knowledge is to perform the analysis with an indifference prior and then try to match one's prior knowledge with the posterior (marginal) distributions for a hypothetical sample. Even when the method is not used to *determine* the prior, it provides a useful way of *interpreting* any proposed prior in the conjugate class. Our experience is that most people are cautious in quantifying prior knowledge and tend to make it equivalent to a rather small number of hypothetical observations. However, if we find someone using a prior equivalent to 500 observations, we shall certainly demand that he justify it.

An alternative version of the preliminary sample method makes direct use of the number of preliminary observations one feels one's prior knowledge to be "worth". For instance, having learned from the example in Sec. 7-4 that we probably have more prior information about the variance than we thought we had, we may decide to reassess the whole situation more carefully. First, it may strike us that we have as much prior information about the variance as we do about the mean, at least in terms of hypothetical prior observations. So we decide to take $m = 16$, the number of observations which we found our prior information on the mean to be worth in Sec. 7-1. We take the same prior estimate of θ and so set $w_\bullet = 17.5$. Now we equate our prior estimate of the variance to the *mean* of the (marginal) prior distribution for ϕ. Thus,

$$\text{Mean} = \frac{R^2}{m - 3} = 25$$

which gives us $R^2 = (25)(13) = 325$. Now let us see what we can do treating both θ and ϕ as unknown. In the notation of the two-parameter normal model, we have $m = 16$, $w_\bullet = 17.5$, and $R^2 = 325$. The joint posterior density of θ and ϕ is given by (7-6.4), with n, $x_\bullet$, and S^2 replaced by $(m + n)$; $(mw_\bullet + nx_\bullet)/(m + n)$; and

$$\left[R^2 + S^2 + \frac{mn(x_\bullet - w_\bullet)^2}{m + n}\right]$$

The joint posterior mode is

$$\left[\frac{mw_\bullet + nx_\bullet}{m + n}, \frac{R^2 + S^2 + mn(x_\bullet - w_\bullet)^2/(m + n)}{m + n + 2}\right]$$

Now suppose we observe $n = 16$; $x_\bullet = 17.2$; $s^2 = 29.16$; and, therefore, $S^2 = 466.56$. Then the joint posterior mode is

$$\left(\frac{16(17.5) + 16(17.2)}{16 + 16}, \frac{325.00 + 466.56 + 0.72}{16 + 16 + 2}\right) = \left(17.35, 23.30\right),$$

and we note that $\sqrt{23.30} = 4.83$ which seems a reasonable estimate of the standard deviation. Marginally, in the basic notation of (7-6.4), θ has the t distribution $t(\nu, x\ , n^{-1/2} S)$. Making the substitutions previously indicated, we take

$$\nu = 31,$$
$$x_\bullet = 17.35$$

and $$S = \sqrt{325.00 + 466.56 + 0.72} = \sqrt{792.28} = 28.15\,.$$

Looking at Table A.4, we find a line for $\nu = 30$ but not for $\nu = 31$. However, we can extrapolate. The 97.5% points for $\nu = 28$ and 30 are, respectively, 2.048 and 2.042, which, differing by .006, suggest that for $\nu = 31$, the 97.5% point will be 2.039. Thus,

$$\text{Prob}\left(-2.039 \le \frac{\nu^{1/2}(\theta - x_\bullet)}{n^{-1/2} S} \le 2.039\right) = .95\,,$$

or $$\text{Prob}\left(x_{\bullet} - \frac{(2.039)n^{-1/2}S}{\nu^{1/2}} \le \theta \le x_{\bullet} + \frac{(2.039)n^{-1/2}S}{\nu^{1/2}}\right) = .95,$$

or $$\text{Prob}\,(15.53 \le \theta \le 19.17) = .95.$$

The preliminary sample method in its present form will clearly fail if our knowledge about each of the parameters is of a different caliber—if it is, in effect, based on different numbers of preliminary observations. One extreme case of practical importance, which can be treated by making only minor modifications to the existing analysis, arises when we use an instrument with which we have some previous experience to measure a quantity about which we know nothing—a case intermediate between the results of Sec. 7-6 where ignorance about both θ and ϕ was assumed and those in Sec. 7-1 where ϕ was completely known. We will then wish to take the indifference prior for θ (zero preliminary observations) and a $\chi^{-2}(m - 1, R^2)$ prior to ϕ (the natural conjugate prior). The latter can be assessed either by the credibility-interval method or by equating one's knowledge to a preliminary sample of size m. Note that if our prior knowledge arises from the previous measurements made with the instrument, it will *already* be expressed in inverse chi-square form (the postpreliminary distribution). That is, the preliminary observations will be actual, not hypothetical.

The effect of this prior knowledge is to increase by $(m - 1)$ the degrees of freedom associated with the total sum of squares $(R^2 + S^2)$ while leaving unchanged the number of observations used in calculating the mean. The posterior marginal distribution of θ is, therefore, $t[m+n-2, x_{\bullet}, n^{-1}(R^2+S^2)]$ and that of ϕ is $\chi^{-2}(m+n-2, R^2+S^2)$.

The posterior conditional distribution of θ given ϕ is $N(x_{\bullet}, n^{-1}\phi)$, exactly as with the indifference prior, because our previous experience with the instrument is irrelevant if we are *told* the value of ϕ. The predictive density for X_{n+1} is $t[m + n - 2, x_{\bullet}, (1 + n^{-1})(R^2 + S^2)]$.

In summary, when we are ignorant about θ and have previous information about ϕ, and assuming $m \ge 2$, the results are as follows:

Distribution of	*a priori*
θ (marginal)	uniform
ϕ (marginal)	$\chi^{-2}(m - 1, R^2)$
Distribution of	*a posteriori*
θ (marginal)	$t[m + n - 2, x_{\bullet}, n^{-1}(R^2 + S^2)]$
ϕ (marginal)	$\chi^{-2}(m + n - 2, R^2 + S^2)$
θ given ϕ	$N(x_{\bullet}, n^{-1}\phi)$
X_{n+1}	$t[m + n - 2, x_{\bullet}, (1 + n^{-1})(R^2 + S^2)]$.

EXAMPLE 3 Suppose we wish to estimate the mean and variance of the freshman ACT English scores in a new junior college (Table 1-5.2). Assume we have no previous information about the mean; however, from past experience with the ACT battery, we have prior information on the variance. Our "best guess" at ϕ is 25 and we feel our estimate is equivalent to $m = 16$ observations.

We equate our prior estimate of the variance to the mean of the (marginal) prior distribution for ϕ. Thus,

$$\text{Mean} = \frac{\lambda}{\nu - 2} = \frac{\lambda}{m - 3} = 25$$

which gives $R^2 = (13)(25) = 325$. Now, suppose we observe $n = 16$, $x_{\bullet} = 17.2$, and $S^2 = 464.6$. Marginally, the posterior modal estimate of the variance is

$$\frac{R^2 + S^2}{m + n} = \frac{789.6}{32} = 24.675\,,$$

and we note that $(24.675)^{1/2} = 4.97$ which seems a reasonable estimate of the standard deviation. The posterior marginal distribution for the mean is $t(30, 17.2, 49.35)$; thus, $(30)^{1/2}(\theta - 17.2)/(49.35)^{1/2}$ has a t distribution on 30 degrees of freedom. Looking at Table A.4, we find that the 97.5% point for $\nu = 30$ is 2.042. Thus

$$\text{Prob}\left(-2.042 \leq \frac{(30)^{1/2}(\theta - 17.2)}{(49.35)^{1/2}} \leq 2.042\right) = .95$$

or

$$\text{Prob}\left(17.2 - \frac{2.042\,(49.35)^{1/2}}{(30)^{1/2}} \leq \theta \leq 17.2 + \frac{2.042\,(49.35)^{1/2}}{(30)^{1/2}}\right) = .95$$

or

$$\text{Prob}\,(14.58 \leq \theta \leq 19.82) = .95.$$

In the above example and preceding discussion, we were thinking of m and R^2 as coming from a hypothetical sample, and of n, $x_{\bullet}$, and S^2 as coming from an actual sample. However, we can go one step further and suppose that *both* sets of sufficient statistics come from hypothetical samples. This leads to an interesting discovery: It is perfectly reasonable to suppose that one has prior knowledge which can be expressed as a conjugate prior and that one's information on the mean is worth a different number of observations from one's information on the variance. (We noted earlier that this could not happen if we restricted ourselves to a *single* hypothetical sample.) This discovery will be exploited in the next section.

7-8 COMPUTER-ASSISTED DATA ANALYSIS–THE TWO-PARAMETER NORMAL MODEL

In Sec. 6-9, we saw how the CADA programs greatly simplified the numerical work necessary in specifying a prior and in carrying out the Bayesian analysis with a binomial model. In the present section, we illustrate other parts of the CADA package. These programs should be of help when your model is from the normal family with unknown mean and variance.

We shall illustrate the use of the CADA program for a specific problem that is typical of a type of problem that arises with high frequency. An investigator needs to get a pretty good idea of the level of attainment of college-bound graduating high school students in the state of Iowa. He needs this information quickly. To get information, he looks at some data obtained from a published report with the hope that he will not have to get further data.

The information he has consists of scores on the ACT Assessment for 20 students who participated in a statewide survey. He has examined the process by which these students were selected and finds no evidence to challenge the assertion that this is a random sample of current college-bound students. More specifically, he has no information to distinguish these students from other students in the population.

The background information available to him is as follows: He knows that nationally the mean ACT score is 20, and the standard deviation is 5. He knows that the state of Iowa has a very high literacy rate and a very high per pupil expenditure on schools. This leads him to expect a mean value greater than 20. Also, as a statistician, he expects, on the average, a greater homogeneity in one state than across states.

Undoubtedly, some investigators will have more specific prior information, and thus we must expect that different investigators will wish to use different prior distributions. Our task is to assist each investigator in quantifying *his* prior beliefs. We shall follow our investigator through the CADA program, annotating the output where some explanation seems useful.

computer assisted data analysis

if you wish an explanation type 1. otherwise, type 0.
?
1

this packet of programs provides a grounding in the fundamentals of bayesian methods of statistical inference. these routines are designed to guide the researcher who has only a minimal acquaintance with bayesian methods, step-by-step through a complete bayesian analysis. a list of the routine follows:

1 prior beta-binomial model
2 posterior beta-binomial model

3 prior two-parameter normal—marginal distribution for standard deviation
4 prior two-parameter normal—conditional distribution for mean
5 posterior two-parameter normal
6 prior m-group proportions
7 posterior m-group proportions
8 evaluate student-distribution
9 evaluate beta-distribution
10 evaluate inverse chi-distribution
11 evaluate normal distribution

if you want to run one of the above routines, type its number. otherwise, type a zero.
?
3

this program will assist you in specifying a prior distribution on the standard deviation.

considering your prior information, what do you feel is the most probable value of the standard deviation?
?
4.9

now viewing your information about the standard deviation as if it were the result of an experiment of a certain sample size (n), how large an n-value do you feel your prior information to be worth? this n-value is the amount of weight that will be given to your prior knowledge and should be greater than 6.
?
7

[Inexperienced investigators are typically very conservative in their specification of *n*. When they see the length of the 50% credibility interval implied by their value, they typically increase this value.]

the value of n and your estimate of the standard deviation imply that you would be willing to give even odds that the true standard deviation will lie in the 50% hdr credibility interval from 4.029 to 6.117. this is the shortest possible 50% credibility interval for this value of n.

consider the above interval. it may or may not be satisfactory to you. you may increase the interval by selecting a smaller n, or decrease the interval by selecting a larger n.
if you think you may be able to improve this interval by selecting a new value of n, please type that value. otherwise, type zero.
?
20

the new 50% credibility interval, based on an n of 20.00 extends from 4.390 to 5.494. the old 50% credibility interval based on an n of 7.00 extends from 4.029 to 6.117.
if you think you can improve this interval by selecting a new value of n, please type that value. otherwise, type 0.
?
25

the new 50% credibility interval, based on an n of 25.00 extends from 4.452 to 5.428. the old 50% credibility interval based on an n of 20.00 extends from 4.390 to 5.494.
if you think you can improve this interval by selecting a new value of n, please type that value. otherwise, type 0.
?
0

on the basis of the information so far given, the prior marginal distribution of the standard deviation is an inverse chi with 24.00 degrees of freedom and a scale parameter of 24.500. this distribution has a mode of 4.900 a median of 5.072 and a mean of 5.165. a 50% credibility interval extends from 4.452 to 5.428.

[The value of n typically settled on is one that implies a somewhat longer interval than the investigator would have initially specified. By requiring the investigator to balance two judgments against each other, we hope to arrive at a coherent and realistic assessment.]

if you think you may be able to obtain a better prior distribution by respecifying your modal estimate of the standard deviation, please type your new estimate. otherwise, type 0.
?
4.7

[This is one of several points at which the investigator can change his mind about some aspect of his prior beliefs. This is a particularly useful point. Most investigators are inappreciative of the assymmetry of the inverse chi density, and thus, are surprised by the length above the mode required to obtain a 50% HDR interval. A typical desire, at this point, is to lower the modal estimate slightly.]

now viewing your information about the standard deviation as if it were the result of an experiment of a certain sample size (n), how large an n-value do you feel your prior information to be worth? this n-value is the amount of weight that will be given to your prior knowledge and should be greater than 6.
?
20

the value of n and your estimate of the standard deviation imply that you would be willing to give even odds that the true standard deviation will lie in the 50% hdr credibility interval from 4.211 to 5.269. this is the shortest possible 50% credibility interval for this value of n.

consider the above interval. it may or may not be satisfactory to you. you may increase the interval by selecting a smaller n, or decrease the interval by selecting a larger n.
if you think you may be able to improve this interval by selecting a new value of n, please type that value. otherwise, type zero.
?
0

on the basis of the information so far given, the prior marginal distribution of the standard deviation is an inverse chi with 19.00 degrees of freedom and a scale parameter of 21.019. this distribution has a mode of 4.700 a median of 4.909 and a mean of 5.025. a 50% credibility interval extends from 4.211 to 5.269.

if you think you may be able to obtain a better prior distribution by respecifying your modal estimate of the standard deviation, please type your new estimate. otherwise, type 0.
?
0

do you wish to specify a prior on the mean at this time? if so type 1. otherwise, type 0.
?
1

this program will, given your modal estimate of the standard deviation and the number of observations it is worth, assist you in fitting your prior conditional distribution on the mean to a normal distribution.

what is your modal estimate of the standard deviation?
?
4.7

how many observations is your estimate worth?
?
20

now considering your prior information about the mean and assuming your modal estimate of the standard deviation is the actual true value, what is your best estimate of the true value of the unknown mean?
?
21

suppose i estimated a certain mean to be 100 and was willing to give even odds that the true mean would be between 95 and 105, then my central 50% credibility interval would be 10 units long.

how long would a central interval around your estimate of the mean for the present problem need to be for you to be willing to give even odds that the true mean will lie in this interval?
?
2

considering your prior knowledge as if it were the result of an experiment of a certain sample of size m, how many observations do you feel your prior knowledge about the mean to be worth?
?
5

the value of m you selected implies a 50% credibility interval extending from 19.582 to 22.418 (m = 5.00). the original interval specified, which implies m = 10.00, extends from 20.000 to 22.000.

Having treated the investigator gently in the first part of the program, we now attempt to show him that coherence in prior specifications is difficult to attain. The present investigator displays a rather high degree of coherence at this point compared with others who have used this program.

please compare these two intervals. if your original interval is longer than the interval resulting from your selection of m, you may wish to select a smaller value of m. if your interval is smaller, you may wish to select a larger value of m. however such changes will affect the weight you will be giving to your prior information.
if you are satisfied with the interval extending from 19.582 to 22.418 (m = 5.00), please type 0. otherwise, select a new value for m. presumably you will want to select some value between m = 5.00 and m = 10.00 although you are free to select any positive value you wish.
?
8

the new interval around your estimated mean with m = 8.00 extends from 19.879 to 22.121.
your original interval around the mean with m = 10.00 extends from 20.000 to 22.000.
if you think you can improve your present interval by selecting a new value for m, please type that value. otherwise, type 0.
?
10

the new interval around your estimated mean with m = 10.00 extends from 19.998 to 22.002.
your original interval around the mean with m = 10.00 extends from 20.000 to 22.000.

if you think you can improve your present interval by selecting a new value for m, please type that value. otherwise, type 0.

?

0

your prior conditional distribution for the mean (given that the true standard deviation is 4.700) is normal, with a mean of 21.000 a variance of 2.209 and a standard deviation of 1.486. the 50% credibility interval around the mean extends from 19.998 to 22.002.

your prior marginal distribution on the mean is a students distribution on 19.00 degrees of freedom, with mean, mode and median of 21.000 and standard deviation 1.612 the 50% credibility interval about the mean extends from 19.951 to 22.049.

[The investigator should note here that the *t* interval on the mean is longer than the normal interval.]

if you wish to evaluate the posterior distribution at this time type 1. otherwise, type 0.

?

1

[Having specified his prior, our investigator would probably stop the analysis now and collect some data. He could then reenter the program at this point by selecting program 5.]

posterior analysis for the two-parameter normal model

this program calculates the posterior distribution given the prior modal estimate of the standard deviation and the number of observations it is worth, the prior modal estimate of the mean and the number of observations it is worth, and the mean, standard deviation and number of items from your sample.

what is your prior modal estimate of the standard deviation?

?

4.7

how many observations is it worth?

?

20

what is your prior modal estimate of the mean?

?

21

how many observations is it worth?

?

10

how many observations are there in your present sample?

?

25

what is the mean of your sample?

?

21.3

what is the standard deviation of your sample?
?
5.2

the joint posterior mode for the mean and the standard deviation is (21.214, 4.931). this is the point on the plane around which the probability is most highly concentrated.

the posterior marginal distribution on the population standard deviation is an inverse chi distribution on 44.000 degrees of freedom with scale factor 33.443. the posterior marginal mode is 4.985. the posterior median is 5.080. the posterior mean is 5.130. the 50% hdr credibility interval is from 4.642 to 5.368.

the posterior marginal distribution on the population mean is a student's distribution on 44.000 degrees of freedom. it has a mean, median and mode of 21.214 and a standard deviation of .872. the 50% hdr credibility interval is from 20.635 to 21.794.

if you wish to evaluate the distribution on the mean type 1. if you wish to evaluate the distribution on the standard deviation type 2. otherwise, type 0.
?
1

this program evaluates a non-standard student distribution. you have the following options (1) you may ask to see any p% hdr credibility interval, (2) you may ask the probability that t is less than or greater than any particular point, or (3) you may ask the probability that t is between any two points. please indicate which of the above options you wish by typing 1, 2, or 3.
if you wish to exit the program type 0.
?
2

[As you can see, our investigator has great flexibility here. He has many important descriptive statistics at his fingertips.]

what is the degree of freedom of the student distribution you wish to evaluate?
?
44

what is the standard deviation of the student distribution?
?
.872

now, what is the mean of the student distribution?
?
21.214

at what point do you wish to evaluate the student distribution?
?
21.00

the probability that t is less than 21.000 is .401. the probability that t is greater than than 21.000 is .599.

if you wish to evaluate another point type 1. otherwise, type 0.
?
0

this program evaluates a non-standard student distribution. you have the following options (1) you may ask to see any p% hdr credibility interval, (2) you may ask the probability that t is less than

```
or greater than any particular point, or (3) you may ask the probability that t is between any two
points. please indicate which of the above options you wish by typing 1, 2, or 3.
if you wish to exit the program type 0.
?
1

what is the degree of freedom of the student distribution you wish to evaluate?
?
44

what is the standard deviation of the student distribution?
?
.872

now, what is the mean of the student distribution?
?
21.214

what p% hdr interval do you wish to see? type the p% as a decimal. for example, a 75% hdr would be
typed .75.
?
.95

the 95% hdr interval extends from     19.497 to     22.931.
if you wish to see an additional hdr, type the p%, again as a decimal. otherwise, type 0 (zero).
?
0

     this program evaluates a non-standard student distribution. you have the following options (1)
you may ask to see any p% hdr credibility interval, (2) you may ask the probability that t is less than
or greater than any particular point, or (3) you may ask the probability that t is between any two
points. please indicate which of the above options you wish by typing 1, 2, or 3.
if you wish to exit the program type 0.
?
0

                              end of program
```

7-9 TWO-PARAMETER NORMAL ANALYSIS—THE GENERAL FORM

The mathematics underlying the computer program presented in the previous section can be described quite simply. The user supplies a modal estimate $\tilde{\sigma}$ of the standard deviation and the number of observations m_S (called n in the program) which he feels it to be worth. Taking his prior distribution for σ to be inverse chi, its degrees of freedom will be $\nu = (m_S - 1)$ and its scale parameter, from (7-3.10), is $\lambda^{1/2} = (\nu + 1)^{1/2}\tilde{\sigma}. = m_S^{1/2}\tilde{\sigma}$. A check on the acceptability of this specification can be obtained by finding a 50% HDR for this distribution, and adjusting m_S and $\tilde{\sigma}$ until one is willing to bet at even odds that the true value of the parameter is either inside or outside the interval.

Next the user supplies the mean $w_{\bullet}$ of the conditional distribution of θ, given that σ takes his modal value $\tilde{\sigma}$; he also states the number of observations m_M (called m in the program) which he feels his estimate to be worth. Taking the conditional distribution to be normal, it will be $N(w_{\bullet}, m_M^{-1}\tilde{\sigma}^2)$. It also follows that the marginal distribution for θ is $t(\nu, w_{\bullet}, m_M^{-1} m_S \tilde{\sigma}^2)$–see (7-11.2) for a general statement of the result used here. Again a 50% HDR can be computed and adjustments in m_M made until the user is satisfied.

Assuming that the joint prior distribution can be adequately represented by a member of the conjugate family (or, equivalently, that prior knowledge can be equated to a sample from the present model together with an additional sample from another population with the same variance), the quantities m_M, $w_{\bullet}$, m_S, and $\tilde{\sigma}$ are sufficient to specify that joint distribution. Finally, this is combined with a sample having sufficient statistics n, $x_{\bullet}$, and S^2 as usual. The results are as follows:

General Form for the Natural Conjugate Density of θ and σ

Joint mode $\left[h, \left(\dfrac{\lambda}{\nu + 2}\right)^{1/2}\right]$

Distribution of

θ (marginal) $t(\nu, h, k^{-1}\lambda)$

σ (marginal) $\chi^{-1}(\nu, \lambda^{1/2})$

θ given σ $N(h, k^{-1}\sigma^2)$

σ given θ $\chi^{-1}\left\{\nu + 1, [\lambda + k(\theta - h)^2]^{1/2}\right\}$

where the a priori and a posteriori values of the constants are

	a priori	*a posteriori*
h	$w_{\bullet}$	$\dfrac{m_M w_{\bullet} + n x_{\bullet}}{m_M + n}$
k	m_M	$m_M + n$
λ	$m_S \tilde{\sigma}^2$	$m_S \tilde{\sigma}^2 + S^2 + \dfrac{m_M n (x_{\bullet} - w_{\bullet})^2}{m_M + n}$
ν	$m_S - 1$	$m_S + n - 1.$

The results given at the beginning of Sec. 7-7 are, of course, the special case of the above for which $m_M = m_S = m$ and $R^2 = m\tilde{\sigma}^2$. In Sec. 7-7, the joint distribution considered was that of the population mean and *variance*. Here we consider the joint distribution of the mean and *standard deviation*. This accounts for the joint mode involving the quantity $\nu + 2$ rather than $\nu + 3$ as previously.

EXAMPLE 4 Consider again the 1969 junior college data (Table 1-5.2), with a 23rd college being studied with the assumption that this college is indistinguishable from the others. We are interested in an estimate of the mean and standard deviation for the freshman English ACT scores in the new college. Suppose that we have prior knowledge which can be expressed as a conjugate prior and that our information on the mean is worth fewer observations than our information on the standard deviation. We feel that we have additional information on the standard deviation stemming from our previous experience with the ACT battery.

We decide to take $m_M = 16$, the number of observations which we found our prior information on the mean to be worth in Sec. 7-1. We take the same prior estimate of θ and, so, set $w_{\bullet} = 17.5$. We decide to take $m_S = 26$ and set $\tilde{\sigma} = 4.9$. We equate our prior estimate of the standard deviation to the mode of the (marginal) prior distribution for σ. Thus,

$$\text{Mode} = \left(\frac{R^2}{m_S}\right)^{1/2} = 4.9$$

which gives us $R^2 = m_S(4.9)^2 = (26)(24.01) = 624.26$. Now, suppose we observe $n = 32$, $x_{\bullet} = 17.35$, and $S^2 = 793.61$. Then the joint posterior mode is

$$\left\{\frac{m_M w_{\bullet} + n x_{\bullet}}{m_M + n}, \left[\frac{R^2 + S^2 + m_M n(x_{\bullet} - w_{\bullet})^2/(m_M + n)}{m_S + n + 1}\right]^{1/2}\right\}$$

$$= \left[\frac{16(17.5) + 32(17.35)}{16 + 32}, \left(\frac{624.26 + 793.61 + .24}{26 + 32 + 1}\right)^{1/2}\right]$$

$$= (17.4, 4.9026).$$

Marginally, the posterior modal estimate of the standard deviation is

$$\left(\frac{\lambda}{m_S + n}\right)^{1/2} = \left(\frac{1418.11}{58}\right)^{1/2} = 4.9447.$$

This seems a reasonable estimate of the standard deviation. In the notation of this section, the posterior marginal distribution of θ is $t(\nu, h, k^{-1}\lambda)$. Thus, $\nu^{1/2}(\theta - h)/k^{-1/2}\lambda^{1/2}$ has a t distribution on ν degrees of freedom. Making the necessary substitutions, we take

$$\begin{aligned} k &= 48 \\ \nu &= 57 \\ h &= 17.4 \\ k^{-1}\lambda &= 29.5440, \quad (k^{-1}\lambda)^{1/2} = 5.435\,. \end{aligned}$$

Looking at Table A.4, we can find a line for $\nu = 50$ and for $\nu = 60$ but not for $\nu = 57$. However, we can interpolate. The 75% points for $\nu = 50$ and 60 are, respectively, .6794 and .6786, which suggests that for $\nu = 57$ the 75% point will be approximately .6788. Thus,

$$\text{Prob}\left(-.6788 \le \frac{\nu^{1/2}(\theta - h)}{k^{-1/2}\lambda^{1/2}} \le .6788\right) = .50$$

or $$\text{Prob}\left(h - \frac{(.6788)\,k^{-1/2}\lambda^{1/2}}{\nu^{1/2}} \le \theta \le h + \frac{(.6788)\,k^{-1/2}\lambda^{1/2}}{\nu^{1/2}}\right) = .50$$

or $$\text{Prob}\,(16.91 \le \theta \le 17.89) = .50\,.$$

7-10 COMPARISON OF THE RESULTS FOR THE VARIOUS MODELS[1]

It is instructive to compare the results obtained in Sec. 7-6 for the case when the normal mean and variance are both unknown with those given in Secs. 7-1 and 7-4 for the cases where the variance and the mean, respectively, are known. To effect a comparison, we shall, of course, use indifference priors in the latter two cases, which is equivalent to putting $\sigma_0^{-2} = 0$ in Sec. 7-1 and $\nu_0 = 0$, $\lambda_0 = 0$ in Sec. 7-4. To make the comparison meaningful, we must have some idea of what value of S^2 we would be likely to observe if the variance σ^2 of the model distribution $N(\mu, \sigma^2)$ were known. From well-known facts about the relation of the sampling distributions of T^2 and S^2 to the chi-square distribution and the value of the mean of that distribution, it follows that

$$\mathcal{E}[T^2|\mu,\sigma^2] = \mathcal{E}\left[\sum_1^n (x_i - \mu)^2|\mu, \sigma^2\right] = n\sigma^2 \qquad (7\text{-}10.1)$$

and

$$\mathcal{E}[S^2|\sigma^2] = \mathcal{E}\left[\sum_1^n (x_i - x_\bullet)^2|\sigma^2\right] = (n-1)\,\sigma^2\,. \qquad (7\text{-}10.2)$$

[1] Reading of this section may be deferred without loss of continuity.

We shall take the expectations as the "likely values" of the quantities themselves in the next two paragraphs–it need hardly be mentioned that the discussion is heuristic and suggestive, not demonstrative.

When σ^2 is known, the posterior distribution for θ is $N(x_\bullet, n^{-1}\sigma^2)$ and so

$$\frac{n^{1/2}(\theta - x_\bullet)}{\sigma} \quad \text{is} \quad N(0, 1)\,.$$

When σ^2 is unknown, the posterior distribution for θ is $t[n - 1, x_\bullet, n^{-1}\Sigma(x_i - x_\bullet)^2]$, and, replacing the last identifier by its expected value given in (7-10.2), we find that

$$\frac{n^{1/2}(\theta - x_\bullet)}{\sigma}$$

has the standard t distribution on $(n - 1)$ degrees of freedom. The comparison between the two posterior distributions is, thus, essentially that between the standard normal and standard t distributions which we have already discussed. Both are symmetrical with median zero (implying median $x_\bullet$ for θ), but because the percentage points of t are farther out than those of the normal distribution, credibility intervals for θ will be longer when the variance is unknown than when it is known–markedly so if n is small. One way of viewing this is that if only a small number of repeated measurements of some quantity are to be made, additional information about the precision of the measuring instrument will be valuable.

To illustrate the above discussion, let us take $n = 10$, $x_\bullet = 30$, $\sigma^2 = 25$, and $\Sigma(x_i - x_\bullet)^2 = k$. Thus, when σ^2 is known, the posterior distribution for θ is $N(30, 2.5)$ and so $(\theta - 30)/(2.5)^{1/2}$ is $N(0, 1)$. Using this transformation and Table A.2, we find that a 95% credibility interval for θ is (26.9,33.1). Now, when σ^2 is unknown, the posterior distribution for θ is $t(9, 30, k/10)$; and so, using the expected value for k [see (7-10.2)], $(\theta - 30)/(2.5)^{1/2}$ is standard t on 9 degrees of freedom. Using the transformation and Table A.4, we find that a 95% credibility interval for θ is (26.42,33.58). The credibility interval for θ is shorter when σ^2 is known than when σ^2 is unknown. Thus, when one wants to estimate the mean, additional information about the variance is beneficial.

When μ is known, the posterior distribution for ϕ is $\chi^{-2}[n, \Sigma(x_i - \mu)^2]$; and when μ is unknown, it is $\chi^{-2}[n - 1, \Sigma(x_i - x_\bullet)^2]$. The most instructive comparison is between the known mean case with n observations and the unknown mean case with $(n + 1)$ observations. Replacing the scale parameters by their expectations (7-10.1) and (7-10.2), with $(n + 1)$ for n in the latter, we see that in either of these cases, the posterior distribution is $\chi^{-2}(n, n\sigma^2)$. Thus, knowledge of the mean is equivalent to a single additional observation. This suggests that, in many applications, when the object is to estimate the variance, it will not be worth obtaining additional (external) information about the mean since the same effect can be achieved by making one more observation. This contrasts with the result for the mean above.

For purpose of illustration, let us take $n = 25$ and $\sigma^2 = 25$. Then $\mathcal{E}[\Sigma(x_i - \mu)^2] = 625$, but $\mathcal{E}[\Sigma(x_i - x_\bullet)^2] = 600$. Using these as the values for T^2 and S^2 respectively, we have an a posteriori distribution which, in the first instance (known mean) is $\chi^{-2}(25, 625)$ and in the second instance (unknown mean) is $\chi^{-2}(24, 600)$. The corresponding central 95% credibility intervals are (15.38,47.64) and (15.24,48.38). The closeness of these results exemplifies the fact that assuming the mean to be unknown is equivalent to the loss of only one observation and that the effect of this will be very small unless n itself is very small.

We can also compare the predictive densities under the models. When the variance is known, the predictive density using the indifference prior for μ is $N[x_\bullet, (1 + n^{-1})\sigma^2]$, obtained from Sec. 6-4, with $\sigma_0^{-2} = 0$. When the variance is unknown, replacing $\Sigma(x_i - x_\bullet)^2$ in (7-6.10) by its expected value gives a predictive density which is $t[n - 1, x_\bullet, (1 + n^{-1})(n - 1)\sigma^2]$. The comparison here is, thus, of the same nature as that for the posterior distribution of θ, the difference being that credibility intervals in the unknown variance case are based on a t distribution with $(n - 1)$ degrees of freedom, and, hence, are longer.

Finally, to establish a comparison of the predictive density with the known mean case, we take a "likely value" of $x_\bullet$ to be its expectation in sampling from the model distribution, namely, μ, in addition to taking "likely values" of T^2 and S^2. Also, as we did when comparing the posterior distributions of the variance, we shall suppose that we take an additional observation to compensate for our ignorance of the mean μ. The resulting comparison is between a predictive distribution $t\{n, \mu, [1 + (n + 1)^{-1}]n\sigma^2\}$ when the mean is unknown and $t(n, \mu, n\sigma^2)$ when the mean is known. Thus, for predicting X_{n+1}, taking an additional observation does not completely compensate for ignorance of μ—credibility intervals are still longer by a factor $[1 + (n + 1)^{-1}]^{1/2}$ when the mean is unknown.

7-11 TWO IMPORTANT DISTRIBUTIONAL RESULTS[1]

In the course of this chapter, we have met examples of two types of distributional results which have great generality. By stating the results formally now, we shall be able to reduce the amount of mathematical manipulation necessary to obtain the results of the next chapter. First:

> *If sets of conditionally independent observations are obtained from two or more normal distributions having a common unknown variance ϕ and means which are either known or are nonidentical unknown parameters, and the analysis of each set separately using (independent) indifference priors yields a posterior distribution*

[1] Reading of this section may be deferred without loss of continuity.

$\chi^{-2}(\nu_i, \lambda_i)$ for ϕ, then the analysis of the whole set of data using independent indifference priors yields a posterior distribution $\chi^{-2}(\Sigma\nu_i, \Sigma\lambda_i)$ for ϕ. (7-11.1)

The requirement of nonidentical unknown means—that is, that we do *know* that $\theta_i \neq \theta_j$ for any $i \neq j$—is mathematically necessary because it affects the degrees of freedom; however, it is not a practical restriction because if we know $\theta_i = \theta_j$, we can simply combine the ith and jth sets of data.

An example of the use of this result occurred at the end of Sec. 7-7 where we discussed the possibility of incorporating prior knowledge about ϕ gained from previous measurements with the same instrument. If the previous data were obtained starting from a state of ignorance about ϕ, the postpreliminary distribution of ϕ will be $\chi^{-2}(m - 1, R^2)$ in two situations: (1) m measurements were made of an *unknown* quantity with sum of squared deviations from the sample mean equal to R^2; (2) $(m - 1)$ unbiased measurements were made of a known quantity μ with sum of squared deviations from μ equal to R^2. The result (7-11.1) applies to either situation.

If the current data similarly lead, when analyzed using the indifference priors, to a $\chi^{-2}(n - 1, S^2)$ posterior, the result of combining preliminary data with current data is a $\chi^{-2}(m + n - 2, R^2 + S^2)$ posterior, as previously noted.

The second general result is as follows:

If the distribution of a variable θ conditional on ϕ is $N(h, k^{-1}\phi)$ with h and k known, and the marginal distribution of ϕ is $\chi^{-2}(\nu, \lambda)$, then the marginal distribution of θ is $t(\nu, h, k^{-1}\lambda)$; and the conditional distribution of ϕ given θ is $\chi^{-2}[\nu + 1, \lambda + k(\theta - h)^2]$. (7-11.2)

The reader can verify that, taking $h = x_{.}$, $k = n$, $\nu = (n - 1)$, $\lambda = S^2$, this result is a concise statement of the relationship between the posterior distributions in the model discussed in Sec. 7-6, and the notation was used explicitly in describing the mathematics underlying the interactive computer program. An earlier example was the predictive density in the known mean case, Sec. 7-5. There X_{n+1} was $N(\mu, \phi)$ by the model and ϕ was $\chi^{-2}(\nu_n, \lambda_n)$ from the posterior distribution. Thus, X_{n+1} comes in place of θ in (7-11.2); $h = \mu$ (known), $k = 1$, $\nu = \nu_n$, and $\lambda = \lambda_n$. Hence, the predictive distribution, which is the marginal distribution of X_{n+1}, is $t(\nu_n, \mu, \lambda_n)$, as already noted.

7-12 CASE STUDIES IN NORMAL ANALYSIS

Case Study 7-12.1 A Curriculum Evaluation

To demonstrate an application of Bayesian analysis for the normal model, consider the following hypothetical situation. An elementary school system desires to use a standardized achievement test as an aid in evaluating curriculum strengths and weaknesses. The school system lacks the necessary financial resources to administer the test to the entire student body. The school administration wants a method for estimating each grade's standing on the achievement test based on the results of a small sample. The administration does not feel that the financial situation is likely to improve, so it would be beneficial if the method used was easily adaptable from year to year.

To illustrate a solution to this problem, the results for the Iowa City Community School System on the Iowa Test of Basic Skills (ITBS) for the years 1969-1971 were used. In particular, only the results on Test V (vocabulary) of the ITBS for grade 3 were considered. The test results are in terms of grade equivalents. The Iowa City Community School System was chosen for two reasons. First, I am familiar with the community. This is beneficial in establishing suitable prior distributions for the mean and standard deviation for grade 3 Test V results. Second, and most important, test results for the years 1969-1971 on the ITBS were available for each student and for the mean of grade 3. This was necessary for selecting random samples. And, it was essential in order to compare the results from the Bayesian normal analysis, using a small sample, with the actual outcome for the entire population.

Now, for purposes of the situation under consideration, assume that the Iowa City Community School System had not previously administered the ITBS before 1969. Also assume the school system cannot afford to administer the ITBS to more than 10% of the student body. To ensure that the sample of grade 3 students used for each year was a random sample, a number from 1 to 10 was chosen from a table of random digits. This number was used to designate the first student selected, then each consecutive tenth student was chosen. This also ensured appropriate representation in relation to size for each grade 3 class in the school system.

The analysis will attempt to determine the mean on Test V of the ITBS for grade 3 in the Iowa City Community School System for the years 1969-1971.

Quantification of prior information All of the computations will be made by use of a computer program entitled PRIORX. The first step is to ask what is a most likely value for the mean θ and for the standard deviation $\phi^{1/2}$. The convenient prior distribution is from the normal-gamma class. The relevant model is $N(\theta, \phi)$ with sufficient statistics sample size n, sample mean $x_{\bullet}$, and sample variance S^2/n.

Even though there exists no past information about θ and $\phi^{1/2}$ for the Iowa City Community School System, prior information is available. The results from the national standardization of Test V for grade 3 of the ITBS, based on a sample of more than 18,000 students, are known. For grade 3 midyear, the mean is 34.6 and the standard deviation is 11.65. The Iowa City community is quite homogeneous. It is a university town with no heavy industry. Basically, Iowa City is a middle- to upper-middle-class community. A large segment of the population is presently enrolled at the university or already have college degrees. Due to the great supply, the staff for the school system tends to be of higher than average quality.

Due to the homogeneity of the Iowa City community and the small size of the school system in relation to the sample used for the national standardization of the ITBS, one would expect the standard deviation to be slightly smaller than 11.65. Let us use $\tilde{\sigma} = 10$ as a prior modal estimate for $\phi^{1/2}$: $\tilde{\sigma} = 10$ would imply that approximately two-thirds of the students in grade 3 would have test scores in the interval extending from one year below the class mean to one year above the class mean. This would appear to be a reasonable assumption. Due to the high educational level of the community and the quality of the school staff, one would expect the grade 3 midyear vocabulary average to be somewhat higher than 34.6. Let us use 36.8 as a prior estimate for θ. This would imply that the average grade 3 student in the Iowa City Community School System is already proficient at handling vocabulary materials that the average grade 3 student will not have mastered for approximately 10 more weeks. This would appear to be a reasonable assumption. Our prior distribution is then normal-gamma with the marginal mode of θ as $w_{\bullet} = 36.8$ and of $\phi^{1/2}$ as $\tilde{\sigma} = (m^{-1}R^2)^{1/2} = 10$.

It is now necessary to determine how many observations m my prior information is worth. The interactive computer program **PRIORX** was used to assess my prior values. I supplied a modal estimate of $\phi^{1/2}$ and the number of observations m_S I felt it to be worth. Taking the prior distribution for $\phi^{1/2}$ to be inverse chi, its degrees of freedom will be $\nu = m_S - 1$ and its scale parameter is $R = m_S^{1/2}\tilde{\sigma}$. The computer prints out a 50% HDR from this distribution. I then adjusted my specifications until satisfied, satisfaction implying that I was willing to bet at even odds that the true value of $\phi^{1/2}$ was either inside or outside this interval.

Next, I supplied the $w_{\bullet}$ of the conditional distribution of θ, given that $\phi^{1/2}$ takes on the modal value of 10. I also stated the number of observations m_M which I felt my estimate of θ to be worth. The conditional distribution will be $N(w_{\bullet}, m_M^{-1}\tilde{\sigma}^2)$. The marginal distribution for θ is $t(\nu, w_{\bullet}, m_M^{-1} m_S \tilde{\sigma}^2)$. The computer prints out 50% HDRs for these distributions and I made adjustments until satisfied.

I then reconciled my values of m_S and m_M so that $m_S = m_M = 50$. Then, $w_{\bullet} = 36.8$ and $R^2 = m\tilde{\sigma}^2 = 5{,}000$.

The following prior marginal distributions, their properties, and 50% HDR for $\phi^{1/2}$ and θ were obtained.

For $\phi^{1/2}$: $\chi^{-1}(\nu, R) = \chi^{-1}(49, 70.7107)$

$$\text{Mode} = \left(\frac{R^2}{\nu + 1}\right)^{1/2} = 10.0000$$

$$\text{Median} \doteq \left(\frac{R^2}{\nu - 2/3}\right)^{1/2} = 10.1710$$

$$\text{Mean} \doteq \left(\frac{R^2}{\nu - 3/2}\right)^{1/2} = 10.2598$$

50% HDR is (9.3504, 10.7285).

For θ: $t(\nu, w_{\bullet}, m^{-1}R^2) = t(49, 36.8, 100)$

$$\text{Mode} = \text{median} = \text{mean} = w_{\bullet} = 36.8000$$

$$\text{Standard deviation} = \left(\frac{m^{-1}R^2}{\nu - 2}\right)^{1/2} = 1.4586$$

50% HDR is (35.8290, 37.7710).

The data to be used in the posterior Bayesian normal analysis were now collected. The data are listed in the Appendix at the end of this case study.

Posterior distributions for 1969 The joint posterior density is

$$b_n(\theta, \phi^{1/2}) \propto \frac{1}{\phi^{(n+m)/2}} \exp\left\{\frac{(m+n)\left(\theta - \dfrac{mw_{\bullet} + nx_{\bullet}}{m+n}\right)^2 + R^2 + S^2 + \left[\dfrac{mn(x_{\bullet} - w_{\bullet})^2}{m+n}\right]}{-2\phi}\right\}.$$

The prior information is

$$m = 50 \quad w_{\bullet} = 36.8 \quad R^2 = m\tilde{\sigma}^2 = 5{,}000.$$

The sample data are

$$n = 84 \quad x_{\bullet} = 36.18 \quad S^2 = 84(107.55) = 9034.20.$$

Quantification of prior information and sample data establishes the following posterior marginal distribution for $\phi^{1/2}$ and θ.

$$\text{For } \phi^{1/2}: \ \chi^{-1}\left\{\nu = m + n - 1, \left[R^2 + S^2 + \frac{mn(x_{\bullet} - w_{\bullet})^2}{m+n}\right]^{1/2}\right\}$$

$\phi^{1/2}$: $\chi^{-1}(133, 118.5122)$
Mode = 10.2379
Median = 10.3022
Mean = 10.3348.

$$\text{For } \theta: \quad t\left\{\nu, \frac{mw_{\bullet} + nx_{\bullet}}{m+n}, (m+n)^{-1}\left[R^2 + S^2 + \frac{mn(x_{\bullet} - w_{\bullet})^2}{m+n}\right]\right\}$$

θ: $t(133, 36.4113, 104.8145)$
Mode = median = mean = 36.4113
Standard deviation = 0.8945
50% HDR is (35.8109, 37.0118).

Since the distribution function is symmetric, the school administration's best point estimate for the true value of θ is 36.4. The probability that θ is larger than 34.6, the mean for the national standardization of Test V for grade 3 on the ITBS, is:

$$\begin{aligned}
\text{Prob}(\theta > 34.6) &= \text{Prob}\left[\frac{(\theta - \zeta)\nu^{1/2}}{\kappa^{1/2}} > \frac{(34.6 - \zeta)\nu^{1/2}}{\kappa^{1/2}}\right] \\
&= \text{Prob}\left[t_{(133)} > \frac{(34.6 - 36.4)\sqrt{133}}{\sqrt{104.8145}}\right] \\
&\doteq \text{Prob}(z > -2.04) \\
&= 0.9793.
\end{aligned}$$

Thus, the school administration can feel very confident in assuming that the average level of performance in vocabulary for grade 3 is above the national average.

It might be remarked that the true mean in the population from which the sample was drawn was 37.1; thus, the prior beliefs in combination with the sample data gave a somewhat better estimate (36.4) than the sample mean (36.2) alone.

Posterior distributions for 1970 The school administration would now like to estimate the actual value of θ for 1970. The curriculum for grades 1 and 2 has not changed in the last several years and there has been no noticeable change in the composition of the Iowa City community. It would be reasonable, then, to assume that the 1969 sample of students in grade 3 was a random sample from the population of future grade 3 students. Thus it would be desirable if the sample information from 1969 could be used in estimating the true value of θ for 1970. This is possible when using Bayesian analysis. In Bayesian analysis, if after deriving the posterior distribution for one set of data $\mathbf{x}_1$, we then make additional independent observations $\mathbf{x}_2$, the posterior density $b_{\mathbf{x}_1}(\theta, \phi^{1/2})$ from the first analysis becomes the prior density for the second analysis.

Thus, for 1970, the prior information is:

$$m = 134 \qquad w_{\bullet} = 36.41 \qquad \tilde{\sigma} = 10.24.$$

The sample data are:

$$n = 83 \qquad x_{\bullet} = 35.27 \qquad \left(\frac{S^2}{n}\right)^{1/2} = 12.38.$$

The posterior marginal density for $\phi^{1/2}$ is an inverse chi distribution on 216 degrees of freedom with scale parameter 163.8245. The posterior marginal mode is 11.1211, the median is 11.1641, and the mean is 11.1858.

The posterior marginal density for θ is a t distribution on 216 degrees of freedom. It has a mode, median, and mean of 35.9740, and a standard deviation of 0.7602. The 50% HDR extends from 35.4627 to 36.4852.

For 1970, the school administration's best point estimate for the true value of θ is 36.0. The probability that θ is larger than 34.6 is 0.9649. For the Iowa City schools, the average level of performance in vocabulary for grade 3 is above the national average.

The sample mean was 35.27, the posterior mean was 35.97, and the true mean was 36.5. Again, the use of Bayesian analysis helped us to make a more accurate assessment of the true value of θ.

In 1969, the discrepancy between the posterior mean (36.41) and the true mean (37.1) was –0.69. For 1970, the discrepancy is –0.53. Also, the standard deviation for θ has decreased from 0.8945 in 1969 to 0.7602 in 1970. Being able to incorporate the 1969 data into the prior distribution for 1970 helped to increase our ability to estimate the true value of θ.

Posterior distributions for 1971 The posterior density for 1970 will be used as the prior density for the 1971 analysis.

The prior information is:

$$m = 217 \quad w_{\bullet} = 35.97 \quad \tilde{\sigma} = 11.12\,.$$

The sample data are:

$$n = 75 \quad x_{\bullet} = 37.91 \quad \left(\frac{S^2}{n}\right)^{1/2} = 11.42\,.$$

The posterior marginal density on $\phi^{1/2}$ is an inverse chi distribution on 291 degrees of freedom with scale parameter 191.8958. The posterior marginal mode is 11.2299, the median is 11.2620, and the mean is 11.2782.

The posterior marginal density on θ is a t distribution on 291 degrees of freedom. It has a mode, median, and mean of 36.4683, and a standard deviation of 0.6606. The 50% HDR extends from 36.0237 to 36.9129.

The best point estimate for the true value of θ for 1971 is 36.4683. The probability that θ is larger than 34.6, the mean from the national standardization of the ITBS, is 0.9977.

The true value of θ for 1971 was 36.8. The posterior estimate for the mean is 36.5. The sample mean was 37.9. The use of Bayesian analysis enabled us to make a considerable improvement in our estimation of θ.

The standard deviation for θ has decreased from 0.7602 for 1970 to 0.6606 for 1971. The discrepancy between the true mean and the posterior mean for 1970 was −0.53. For 1971, the discrepancy is −0.33.

It is now obvious that the incorporation of prior information and past data in the Bayesian estimation procedure proves extremely beneficial.

Caution should be taken in accumulating prior information over a period of two or more years. After a period of several years, the weight given to the prior information will override the present sample data. Also, the composition of the population of interest will not usually remain static for more than a few years, making it necessary to respecify the prior information based only on the data from the previous year. In fact, whenever a shift in the composition of the population is noticed, the prior information should be respecified.

Alternative situation for future study Suppose the elementary school system had, previous to 1969, been using a standardized achievement test to aid in the evaluation of curriculum strengths and weaknesses. In 1969, due to a lack of funds, the school system could administer the test to only a small sample of students.

If this had been the original problem, the 1968 results for grade 3 could have been used in establishing the prior distribution for 1969. It would be interesting to compare the results of the Bayesian normal analysis model for these two situations.

Appendix

	1969	1970	1971
Total enrollment in grade 3:	830	779	762
Grade 3 mean:	37.1	36.5	36.8
Sample size n:	84	83	75
Sample mean $x_{\bullet}$:	36.18	35.27	37.91
Sample variance S^2/n:	107.55	153.35	130.51
Sample standard deviation:	10.37	12.38	11.42

Case Study 7-12.2 Learning to Juggle[1]

In a previous study of juggling (Knapp and Dixon, 1950), it was found that senior male students at the University of Illinois who were majoring or minoring in physical education could learn to juggle in an average time of 69.86 minutes. The students used a practice situation of 5 minutes per day for a total of 200 minutes. The criterion for learning was

[1] Data taken from a study done by Clyde G. Knapp, W. Robert Dixon, and Murney Lazier, Learning to Juggle, III, A Study of Performance by Two Different Age Groups, *Research Quarterly*, (1958).

100 consecutive catches. Only those students who met the criterion were used as subjects. Ninety-four percent of the college students who attempted to juggle were successful.

Purpose The purpose of this study is to determine the learning abilities of random male high school freshmen when learning to juggle. The same practice situation and criterion for learning will be used.

Prior distribution College seniors in physical education are more mature than high school students and should have more ability to perform tasks involving complex sensory motor skills. Therefore, college seniors specializing in physical education should show substantial superiority to randomly selected high school students in the ability to attain a standard of proficiency in juggling. Espenschade (1940), for example, found that during the adolescent years there is a continual improvement in athletic performance. Thus, the mean training time to proficiency required by the high school students should be higher than the mean of 69.86 for the college students. The data analyst believed the high school students would have a mean value of about 79 minutes.

Because of the difficulty of the criterion of 100 consecutive catches, the maturity and greater ability of the college student should make it possible for more college students to learn to juggle. The slower-learning college student may be able to meet the criterion, while the slower-learning high school student probably will not. Any student who cannot juggle after 200 minutes will be taken out of the study. This will cause the range of scores for the high school group to be less than the range for the college group. Because of the decreased range of scores, the standard deviation for the high school students will be lower than the college group's standard deviation of 48.20. The data analyst believed the high school students would have a standard deviation of 43. The n value that the analyst felt his prior information was worth is 18 observations.

The prior marginal distribution on the standard deviation is an inverse chi with 17 degrees of freedom and scale parameter 182.4335. It has a mode of 43, a median of 45.1406, and a mean of 46.3382. The analyst believed the true value of the standard deviation had a 50-50 chance of lying between 38.37 and 48.64.

The investigator feels his prior information on the mean is worth $m = 15$ observations. His prior conditional distribution for the mean, given the standard deviation of 43, has a mean of 79, a variance of 123.2667, and a standard deviation of 11.1026. There is a 50% chance that the true mean value lies in the interval extending from 71.51 to 86.49.

The prior marginal distribution on the mean is a t distribution with 17 degrees of freedom. It has a mean, mode, and median of 79, a standard deviation of 12.1622, and a 50% credibility interval extending from 71.13 to 86.87.

Procedure The sample was a random selection of male freshmen high school students enrolled in physical education classes at Evanston Township High School. The novel skill of juggling was demonstrated, rules and suggestions were given to each subject, and any questions were answered concerning the procedure. The criterion for learning to juggle was 100 consecutive catches. Each student practiced juggling three paddle-tennis balls for 5 minutes a day, 5 days a week, for 8 weeks in a physical education class. It was assumed that the students who could not juggle after 200 minutes would never be able to juggle.

The 19 boys who met the criterion had a mean of 83.53 minutes and a standard deviation of 40.12. Fifty-seven percent of the boys who tried to learn to juggle succeeded.

Results The joint posterior mode for the mean and the standard deviation is (81.5315,41.0509). This is the point around which the probability is most highly concentrated.

The posterior marginal distribution for the population standard deviation is an inverse chi distribution with 36 degrees of freedom and scale parameter 253.0547. The posterior marginal mode is 41.6019, the posterior median is 42.5718, and the posterior mean is 43.0829.

The posterior marginal distribution on the population mean is a t distribution with 36 degrees of freedom. The posterior marginal distribution has a mean, median, and mode of 81.5315, and a standard deviation of 7.4428. The 50% credibility interval extends from 76.60 to 86.46.

Conclusion In teaching freshmen males to juggle three paddle-tennis balls by practicing 5 minutes per day, the probability is .5 that the population mean number of trials to mastery is between 76.6 and 86.5, and the probability is .95 that the mean is between 66.4 to 96.6.

Bibliography

Espenschade, Anna: *Motor Performance in Adolescence*, Society for Research in Child Development, National Research Council, Washington, 1940.

Knapp, Clyde G., and W. Robert Dixon: Learning to Juggle, I, A Study to Determine the Effect of Two Different Distributions of Practice on Learning Efficiency, *Research Quarterly*, 21: 331-336 (1950).

——, ——, **and Murney Lazier**: Learning to Juggle, III, A Study of Performance by Two Different Age Groups, *Research Quarterly*, 29: 32-36 (1958).

7-13 EXERCISES

1 Find the 25th, 50th, and 75th percentiles for χ^2 (49,.014). Where, in Case Study 7-12.1, would this distribution be relevant?

2 Consider the distribution $\chi^{-2}(10,100)$. Find the 75th percentile by reference to the χ^{-2} table, the χ^2 table, the χ^{-1} table, and by using the normal approximation.

3 Reread the example in Sec. 7-1.

(*a*) Assuming that we wish to estimate the mean ACT mathematics score [M(2)] of the entering freshman class in our 23rd college, specify a prior distribution on that mean and justify this specification.

(*b*) Suppose we *know* the standard deviation of ACT mathematics scores in this college is 6 and obtain the following 10 observations:

$$26, 15, 12, 14, 27, 25, 13, 17, 24, 27.$$

Using your prior in part *a*, describe your posterior beliefs on the location of the mean ACT mathematics score for this class.

4 Consider Example 2 in Sec. 7-4. Suppose we wish to estimate the variance of ACT mathematics scores in a 23rd college which is indistinguishable from the other 22. Proceed as if you knew the mean for that college to be 18. Assume that, a priori, your best guess for ϕ is 36. Further assume that this estimate is based upon prior knowledge which you consider to be the equivalent of eight hypothetical observations.

(*a*) Specify your prior on ϕ.

(*b*) Using the sample data from Exercise 7-13.3*b*, specify your posterior on ϕ.

5 Continuing with this example, now obtain the predictive density. In particular, obtain from this density the probability that X will be greater than 20. State verbally the interpretation and application of this probability statement.

6 Assuming the joint indifference prior on μ and ϕ, work right through Sec. 7-6 using the data in Exercise 7-13.3*b*. For each probability density you explicitly determine, state verbally the interpretation of probability statements that can be made from it.

7 Now redo this analysis after using the methods of Sec. 7-7 to quantify a joint prior distribution on the unknown mean and variance.

8 Consider carefully the sequence of interrogation used in the CADA example in Sec. 7-8. Suggest *at least* one other sequence of questioning and describe in some detail where and why the sequence you suggest may (or may not) be as convenient for you as the one used in the text.

9 Again, redo the analysis of the mean ACT mathematics score in our 23rd college. This time use the techniques of Sec. 7-9. You will again need to use the data in Exercise 7-13.3*b*.

10 Finally, using the techniques of Sec. 7-9, redo the analysis one more time. For this analysis, assume that the sample mean and standard deviation are those which you computed from the data in Exercise 7-13.3*b* but that the sample size upon which they were based is 25 instead of 10.

11 A new method is proposed for teaching remedial reading in secondary schools. It is known that the method currently being used will, on the average, raise a student's reading grade level by 2.5 years with a standard deviation of one year, for each year in the program. Seven students are randomly assigned to the new method. After one year, the increments in their reading levels are the following:

$$2.5, 2.7, 2.2, 2.1, 2.0, 3.5, 4.0$$

(*a*) Assuming that your initial state of knowledge about the new method can be adequately described by a normal prior with mean 2.5 and variance .25 and further assuming a normal likelihood, describe your state of knowledge concerning the location of the population mean after seeing the data.

(*b*) The following year you assign seven more students to the new method and obtain the following increments:

$$2.7, 2.9, 2.5, 1.9, 2.0, 3.5, 4.0.$$

Using the posterior distribution from part *a* as your prior, determine your distribution of belief posterior to these data.

(*c*) Although a change would be expensive in both money and effort, you want to change teaching methods if the new method can be shown to be a significant improvement over the old one. Specifically, assume your loss function may be approximated by the following:

True Average Increment	*Action*	*Loss*
Below 2.5	Change	5
2.5-3.0	Change	3
3.0 and higher	No change	7
All other combinations have zero loss.		

After seeing the data in parts *a* and *b*, would you recommend a change in the teaching method?

(*d*) Indicate a 50% HDR betting interval for the posterior distribution in part *b*.

12 Two researchers have beliefs about some parameter θ which are

$$N(\mu_i, \sigma_i^2) \quad \text{for } i = 1, 2,$$

respectively. On discussing the reasons for their beliefs, they decide that the separate pieces of information which led them to their beliefs are independent. What should be their common beliefs about θ if their knowledge is pooled?

13 A civil rights trial alleges discrimination against minority races in a particular county in the selection of juries. All minority races make up 24 percent of the adult population of the country. The current jury panel has 65 members of whom 10 are from minority races. Discuss this situation from a Bayesian viewpoint. What kinds of collateral information would be useful in evaluating your degree of belief that there is "substantial" discrimination?

14 The results of an investigation indicate that a posteriori a parameter θ has a normal distribution with mean 80 and variance 16. The investigator further reports that he had drawn a sample of size 5 from a normal population with variance 160. Can you determine the investigator's prior distribution? If you are unable to determine the prior distribution, explain what additional information will be needed.

PART THREE

Bayesian Methods for Comparing Parameters

8
BAYESIAN INFERENCE FOR TWO NORMAL DISTRIBUTIONS

In this chapter, we discuss a number of situations where our observations are drawn not from a single population to which a normal model applies but from two such populations. One desire will be to compare mean levels in two populations. Another will be to compare the two variances. The techniques to be described here are meant to deal with the most commonly encountered research questions. This chapter relies heavily on the methods developed in the previous chapter.

8-1 COMPARISON OF TWO NORMAL MEANS

Suppose we wish to *compare* the level of achievement in mathematics of two different high schools. A natural, if unsophisticated, procedure is to administer a common achievement test to the graduating classes of both schools. It is often the case that achievement test scores in large, relatively homogeneous groups are normally distributed.

An adequate model of the situation might, therefore, be obtained by supposing that the first school is characterized by a $N(\theta_1, \phi_1)$ distribution for scores on the test, and that the scores $\mathbf{x}_1 = (x_{11}, x_{12}, \ldots, x_{1n_1})$ of the n_1 students actually tested constitute a random sample from this distribution. Similarly, at the other school, we have a sample $\mathbf{x}_2$ of size n_2 from a $N(\theta_2, \phi_2)$ distribution. In this formulation, θ_1 and θ_2 are natural quantities to take as measures of the overall level of achievement at the two schools. (Note, however, that one can never really avoid a consideration of loss structure. A university fed by the two high schools might be little interested in the means for the two schools, but very interested in the proportions of students attaining a certain level of achievement which it regarded as minimal for participation in one of its courses—a case of threshold loss.)

Our object then is to "compare" θ_1 and θ_2. What does this mean? Since we cannot hope that our readers will pass through life unsullied by acquaintance with classical hypothesis testing, we place that approach in the pillory first. The procedure starts by setting up the hypothesis that $\theta_1 = \theta_2$—this is a sort of straw man which one typically hopes to knock down. Next, one searches for a statistic whose distribution is known completely, given that the hypothesis is true. In the present instance, if it is reasonable to assume that $\phi_1 = \phi_2$ (same measuring instrument), students showed that the distribution of

$$\frac{x_{2\bullet} - x_{1\bullet}}{\sqrt{(n_1^{-1} + n_2^{-1})(S_1^2 + S_2^2)/(n_1 + n_2 - 2)}},$$

given that $\theta_1 = \theta_2$, is

$$t(n_1 + n_2 - 2),$$

where

$$x_{i\bullet} = n_i^{-1} \sum_j x_{ij}$$

the mean score for school i $(i = 1, 2)$, and

$$S_i^2 = \sum_j (x_{ij} - x_{i\bullet})^2,$$

the sum of squares for the ith school. Armed with this sampling distribution, one declares the observations significant at the 5% level if the observed value of $(x_{2\bullet} - x_{1\bullet})$ lies below the $2\frac{1}{2}\%$ point or above the $97\frac{1}{2}\%$ point of its sampling distribution. One also says that the hypothesis is rejected at the .05 level. The logic of this procedure is a simple disjunction. Either the hypothesis is false or an unlikely event has happened. If the data do not lead one to reject a hypothesis (at some chosen significance level), one "accepts" it.

It is possible to imagine circumstances where the hypothesis-testing framework parallels one's perception of the real situation. For example, I am a member of a scientific expedition to the moon. The rocks in the region where we have landed are rather large, and I cannot fragment them. I am considering two rocks for inclusion in a sample to take back to earth. If the two have a different chemical composition, it will be valuable to take both; if they have the same composition, taking both will be a waste of millions of dollars worth of payload which another member of the expedition could have used profitably. I am provided with an instrument which makes quick but not too accurate assessments of molecular weight. If the rocks are chemically identical, their molecular weights will be also (no isotopes allowed!). When I have made as many repeated determinations of the molecular weights of the two rocks as time allows, I am as near as I shall ever get to being in the hypothesis-testing situation. This example also allows us to pin down the meaning of the probabilities involved in hypothesis testing. Suppose I reject at the 1% level the hypothesis that the rocks are identical and so bring both back to earth. On detailed examination, they turn out to be identical. When called to account for my actions, I am fully entitled to bemoan my luck—only one time in a hundred would I bring back two identical rocks.

While we may concede the relevance of a hypothesis-testing framework (without endorsing the usual analysis of it) in one of the exact sciences where objects are either "the same" or "different", in the social sciences, it would hardly be an exaggeration to describe hypothesis testing as a method of giving a misleading answer to a question which nobody is asking! Taking the second half of this denunciation first, it is almost an axiom of the social sciences that no two individuals are identical, no two groups are identical, and that the object of the exercise is to discover what generalizations can usefully be made in the absence of such identity. In the situation of the high schools, my prior assessment of the probability that $\theta_1 = \theta_2$ is zero, by which I mean that if there were some way in which θ_1 and θ_2 could be determined to an accuracy of several decimal places (for example, in a time of social and educational stability, by pooling the scores of several year's graduates), I would be willing to bet at almost any odds that $\theta_1 \neq \theta_2$. The hypothesis $\theta_1 = \theta_2$ is, thus, virtually certain to be false before we start the analysis. The question, "Is θ_1 equal to θ_2?" is one which nobody is asking. To reject the hypothesis is superfluous; to accept it is grotesque.

Secondly, the language of hypothesis testing is seriously misleading. It is but a short verbal step from saying that the observed difference $(x_{2\bullet} - x_{1\bullet})$ is significant to saying that the means θ_1 and θ_2 are significantly different. There are two points here: (1) The step from a probability statement about $(x_{2\bullet} - x_{1\bullet})$ given $(\theta_2 - \theta_1)$ to one about $(\theta_2 - \theta_1)$ given $(x_{2\bullet} - x_{1\bullet})$ can only logically be made if we have a prior distribution for $(\theta_2 - \theta_1)$; it, therefore, is not legitimate to make it in a classical analysis. (2) Even when we have a prior and so can conclude, say, that the posterior probability is .95 that θ_2 is greater than θ_1, it is still misleading to say that θ_1 and θ_2 are significantly different. Suppose our achievement test is scored on a 1,000-point scale, and we have such a mass of data available that 99% credibility intervals for θ_1 and θ_2 are $713 \pm \frac{1}{4}$ and $714 \pm \frac{1}{4}$, respectively. It is, thus, almost certain that θ_2 is greater than θ_1, the difference being of the order of one scale point. Are the schools significantly different? Very few people would say so. The difference is clearly established, but it is of a size which for any practical purpose is unimportant. One might hope that scientifically trained workers would avoid this sort of linguistic confusion, but a glance through a selection of papers dealing with educational measurement is enough to shatter that hope. Indeed, many writers seem to think that when a statistical technique yields a "significant" difference, one may conclude that there is, in the ordinary sense of the words, a significant difference between the entities being compared. Nonsense!

The main purpose of the previous two paragraphs was not to lambast the classical hypothesis test but to elucidate what we really have in mind when we say we wish to compare two means. If the arguments of these two paragraphs are accepted, then we clearly are not interested in testing point hypotheses. Classical statistics also provides a method for making confidence-interval statements of the form, "The probability that the random interval (c_1, c_2) covers the true mean is .95". However, despite the brainwashing done by classical statistics which results in researchers talking about random intervals covering a difference between two means, researchers, in fact, are interested in *and think* in terms of the probability that the difference falls in some specified interval, i.e., *probabilities of events* such as $(\theta_2 - \theta_1 > d)$ where d is a difference which would be judged important (significant in the everyday sense of the word). Less specifically, researchers typically wish to form an idea of the probable size of the difference $(\theta_2 - \theta_1)$; more specifically, they may be using a loss function which depends on that difference. In most of these circumstances, what is required initially is the posterior distribution of $(\theta_2 - \theta_1)$, and so to a Bayesian finding this distribution will be the essential part of comparing two means.

In our presentation, it will be useful to distinguish three cases:

1) $\phi_1 = \sigma_1^2, \phi_2 = \sigma_2^2$; both variances are known,
2) $\phi_1 = \phi_2$; variances equal but unknown,
3) ϕ_1, ϕ_2, both unknown and possibly different.

We shall initially use indifference priors throughout and indicate after each case what types of prior information can be incorporated in the analysis without changing its basic form, and we shall show in detail just how this can be done. We use indifference priors initially only to simplify the presentation. In applications, it is essential to incorporate prior information, and we shall provide explicit formulas making this possible and, indeed, relatively easy. In the remainder of this section, we are treating the variances as nuisance parameters which we eliminate in order to concentrate on the real parameters of interest, the θ_i.

Variances Known

We are assuming the two sets of observations, $\mathbf{x}_1$ and $\mathbf{x}_2$, to be independent random samples from $N(\theta_1, \sigma_1^2)$ and $N(\theta_2, \sigma_2^2)$ distributions, respectively. If we feel that knowledge or information about θ_1 provides no knowledge or information about θ_2, then we will have independent priors for θ_1 and θ_2, and the posterior distributions will also be independent. This is intuitively obvious–the analyses for the two high schools are quite independent of one another–but it can be formally established as follows:

$$\begin{aligned}
p(\theta_1, \theta_2 | \mathbf{x}_1, \mathbf{x}_2) &\propto p(\mathbf{x}_1, \mathbf{x}_2 | \theta_1, \theta_2) p(\theta_1, \theta_2) && \text{(Bayes)} \\
&= p(\mathbf{x}_1, \mathbf{x}_2 | \theta_1, \theta_2) p(\theta_1) p(\theta_2) && \text{(independent priors)} \\
&= p(\mathbf{x}_1 | \theta_1, \theta_2) p(\mathbf{x}_2 | \theta_1, \theta_2) p(\theta_1) p(\theta_2) && \text{(independent samples)} \\
&= p(\mathbf{x}_1 | \theta_1) p(\mathbf{x}_2 | \theta_2) p(\theta_1) p(\theta_2) && (\mathbf{x}_1 \text{ does not depend on } \theta_2) \\
& && (\mathbf{x}_2 \text{ does not depend on } \theta_1) \\
&\propto p(\theta_1 | \mathbf{x}_1) p(\theta_2 | \mathbf{x}_2). && \text{(Bayes)}
\end{aligned}$$

We already know that, using indifference priors, θ_1 is a posteriori $N(x_{1\bullet}, n_1^{-1}\sigma_1^2)$ and θ_2 is $N(x_{2\bullet}, n_2^{-1}\sigma_2^2)$. We now make use of the important result that *if θ_1 and θ_2 are independent normal variables and a_1 and a_2 are constants, then $(a_1\theta_1 + a_2\theta_2)$ is also a normal variable*. The parameters of the resulting distribution are easily found using (4-1.5) and (4-1.7). Thus,

$$\mathcal{E}(a_1\theta_1 + a_2\theta_2) = \mathcal{E}(a_1\theta_1) + \mathcal{E}(a_2\theta_2) = a_1\mathcal{E}(\theta_1) + a_2\mathcal{E}(\theta_2) \tag{8-1.1}$$

and

$$\begin{aligned}
\mathcal{V}(a_1\theta_1 + a_2\theta_2) &= \mathcal{V}(a_1\theta_1) + 2\mathcal{C}(a_1\theta_1, a_2\theta_2) + \mathcal{V}(a_2\theta_2) \\
&= a_1^2\mathcal{V}(\theta_1) + a_2^2\mathcal{V}(\theta_2),
\end{aligned} \tag{8-1.2}$$

the covariance term vanishing because θ_1 and θ_2 are independent. Putting $a_1 = -1$, $a_2 = +1$, we find that the posterior distribution of $\delta = \theta_2 - \theta_1$ is

$$N(x_{2\bullet} - x_{1\bullet}, n_1^{-1}\sigma_1^2 + n_2^{-1}\sigma_2^2).$$

The reader is by now thoroughly familiar with the normal distribution, and no comment seems necessary beyond noting that the most likely value (mode) of δ is the "natural" value–the difference of the observed means, since a normal distribution is symmetric.

Prior knowledge of either mean can be incorporated by the method summarized in Sec. 7-1 using a normal (conjugate) prior. The generalized result is that the posterior distribution of δ is normal, with mean the difference of the posterior means of θ_1 and θ_2 and variance the *sum* of their posterior variances–see Sec. 7-1, Step 8, for the values.

Suppose we wish to compare the mean achievement level in mathematics of high schools I and II by administering a common mathematics achievement test to the graduating class of both schools. School I and school II both used the mathematics achievement test last year. The variance on the mathematics achievement test for school I was 25, and the variance for school II was 16. To simplify the analysis, we will proceed as if these values are the true values of the variance for each school; that is, $\sigma_1^2 = 25$ and $\sigma_2^2 = 16$.

Last year, the mean on the mathematics achievement test for school I was 30. Thus, we assume our best guess at the mean for school I is $w_{1\bullet} = 30$ and we feel that our estimate is worth $m_1 = 15$ observations. This year, we had $n_1 = 25$ observations for school I with a mean of $x_{1\bullet} = 34$. Assuming the variance to be known, the posterior distribution for school I is normal, with mean of 32.5 and variance of .625; that is, a posteriori, θ_1: $N(32.5, .625)$. (Refer to Sec. 7-1.)

Last year, the mean on the mathematics achievement test for school II was 28. Thus, we assume our best guess at the mean for school II is $w_{2\bullet} = 28$ and again we feel that our estimate is worth $m_2 = 15$ observations. This year, we had $n_2 = 21$ observations for school II with a mean of $x_{2\bullet} = 32$. Assuming the variance to be known, a posteriori, θ_2: $N(30.33, .444)$.

The quantity of interest is the difference in the mean achievement level in mathematics for high schools I and II. Let $\delta = \theta_1 - \theta_2$ represent this difference. The posterior distribution of δ is normal with mean of $32.5 - 30.33 = 2.17$ and variance of $.625 + .444 = 1.069$. The 50% HDR credibility interval for δ extends from 1.47 to 2.87. The probability that δ is greater than 0 is .982, but this is not a particularly significant finding. What is more significant is that the odds are 3:1 that students presently emerging from school I will have mathematics achievement scores on the average of at least 1.5 points higher than those from school II.

Variances Equal but Unknown

In comparing high schools, this model would be appropriate if the schools have similar intakes, and we think that differences in (say) teaching efficiency are likely to affect the achievement level of all students at a school without materially affecting the differences in achievement between students at that school. Incidentally, we must point out that this assumption is often untrue and should not be made casually.

The posterior distributions of θ_1 and θ_2 are no longer independent even when the priors *are*, because the variance ϕ is common to both populations (schools). However, we can make use of previously obtained results to avoid making any fresh computations. Note, first, that using indifference priors, we are in exactly the situation described by the general result (7-11.1). Each school separately gives a $\chi^{-2}(n_i - 1, S_i^2)$ posterior for ϕ, and so the posterior using the combined data from both schools is $\chi^{-2}(n_1 + n_2 - 2, S_1^2 + S_2^2)$.

Next, consider the *conditional* distribution of δ *given* ϕ (that is, assuming ϕ to be known). This is just the known variance case discussed above with $\sigma_1^2 = \sigma_2^2 = \phi$. Hence, conditional on ϕ, δ is $N[x_{2\bullet} - x_{1\bullet}, (n_1^{-1} + n_2^{-1})\phi]$. Now combine this result with that of the previous paragraph using the general result (7-11.2). It follows that *the posterior marginal distribution of* δ *is*

$$t[n_1 + n_2 - 2, x_{2\bullet} - x_{1\bullet}, (n_1^{-1} + n_2^{-1})(S_1^2 + S_2^2)].$$

Again the mode is the "natural" value $(x_{2\bullet} - x_{1\bullet})$.

The reader may already have noted the close similarity between this result for the posterior distribution of δ and that for the sampling distribution of $(x_{2\bullet} - x_{1\bullet})$ on which classical hypothesis tests are based. One practical consequence of this similarity is that, in the absence of prior information, a 95% credibility interval for δ will coincide with what a classicist would call a 95% confidence interval (the set of values of d for which the hypothesis $\theta_2 - \theta_1 = d$ would not be rejected at the 5% significance level). This confluence of the two methods is fortunate since it means that a practical research worker who uses "the rule in the book" to find a confidence interval and then interprets it as though it were a credibility interval (i.e., as though it expresses his beliefs about δ) is "right", but for the wrong reason. It should be stressed that the confluence arises not only from the use of indifference priors but also from the symmetrical way in which $(x_{2\bullet} - x_{1\bullet})$ and $(\theta_2 - \theta_1)$ enter into the sampling distribution of the former. When such symmetry is absent, Bayesian and classical methods will not agree, even using indifference priors. The classical analysis, moreover, is incomplete; it gives no indication of what values within the confidence interval are "more likely". The posterior Bayes distribution provides precisely this information and, in addition, makes it possible to accomplish the necessary task of incorporating prior information.

Prior knowledge about ϕ can be incorporated by the method discussed toward the end of Sec. 7-7 using a $\chi^{-2}(\nu, \lambda)$ prior. The effect on the posterior distribution of δ is to increase the degrees of freedom of t by ν to $n_1 + n_2 + \nu - 2$ and to increase the sum of squares by λ to $S_1^2 + S_2^2 + \lambda$, leaving everything else unchanged. Prior knowledge about the means can also be incorporated. First let us look at a derivation and then at the simple manner in which the fitting can be accomplished.

Suppose first that some information about the measuring instrument has been gathered so that the Bayes distribution for ϕ, posterior to the gathering of this information but prior to the main data gathering, is $\chi^{-2}(\nu, \lambda)$. This puts us in the situation described in the preceding paragraph. Now suppose we have in addition some specific information about each group which we are able to equate, in the way we have learned, to hypothetical prior observations in the two populations. Denoting the sufficient statistics for these hypothetical observations as $(m_1, w_{1\bullet}, R_1^2)$ and $(m_2, w_{2\bullet}, R_2^2)$, the Bayes distribution of δ posterior to the addition of this information and the original information on the variance is t, with $m_1 + m_2 + \nu - 2$ degrees of freedom, with mean $w_{2\bullet} - w_{1\bullet}$, and with scale parameter $[(1/m_1) + (1/m_2)](R_1^2 + R_2^2 + \lambda)$.

Now suppose we have a second (a real) sample from each group with sufficient statistics $(n_1, x_{1\bullet}, S_1^2)$ and $(n_2, x_{2\bullet}, S_2^2)$. Combining these observations with the hypothetical observations and the initial knowledge about ϕ gives us the posterior Bayes distribution of the difference between the means of two normal populations with equal but unknown variances:

$$\delta : t\left[m_1 + n_1 + m_2 + n_2 + \nu - 2,\right.$$
$$\frac{m_2 w_{2\bullet} + n_2 x_{2\bullet}}{m_2 + n_2} - \frac{m_1 w_{1\bullet} + n_1 x_{1\bullet}}{m_1 + n_1},$$
$$\left(\frac{1}{m_1 + n_1} + \frac{1}{m_2 + n_2}\right)\left((R_1^2 + R_2^2 + \lambda) + S_1^2 + \frac{m_1 n_1 (x_{1\bullet} - w_{1\bullet})^2}{m_1 + n_1}\right.$$
$$\left.\left. + S_2^2 + \frac{m_2 n_2 (x_{2\bullet} - w_{2\bullet})^2}{m_2 + n_2}\right)\right]. \tag{8-1.3}$$

We can convince ourselves that this is correct in the following way. Suppose that our prior on the means is uniform and on ϕ is $\chi^{-2}(\nu, \lambda)$, and suppose we observe the combined samples (hypothetical and real) for the two groups. Then the sufficient statistic, the sample number, sample mean, and sample sum of squares in the first group is

$$\left(m_1 + n_1, \frac{m_1 w_{1\bullet} + n_1 x_{1\bullet}}{m_1 + n_1}, R_1^2 + S_1^2 + \frac{m_1 n_1 (x_{1\bullet} - w_{1\bullet})^2}{m_1 + n_1}\right) \tag{8-1.4}$$

with a similar quantity for the second group. The third component, the pooled within-sum-of-squares, is a complicated quantity because it must take account of the difference between the actual sample mean and the hypothetical prior sample mean. After all, if the difference between these two means is great, it may well reflect a large error variation.

Fitting a prior distribution for this analysis is not appreciably more difficult than in the one-population case. Proceeding as in that case, we ask the investigator for his modal estimate of ϕ and equate that to

$$\frac{R_1^2 + R_2^2 + \lambda}{m_1 + m_2 + \nu} \tag{8-1.5}$$

and then determine $m_1 + m_2 + \nu$ by asking the investigator how many hypothetical observations his prior information is worth. These two specifications can then be cross-checked against credibility-interval statements and necessary adjustments made.

Interrogation about each mean, assuming the true variance is given by (8-1.5) as the mode of the Bayes distribution for the variance, proceeds precisely as in the one-population case with the best estimates being equated to $w_{1\bullet}$ and $w_{2\bullet}$ and the amounts of prior information to m_1 and m_2. There is a constraint here in that for coherence, we must have the amount of prior information about ϕ, $m_1 + m_2 + \nu$, greater than or equal to the sum of the information, $m_1 + m_2$, used in specifying the two means. In practice, this restriction causes no discomfort. A model for this was given in Sec. 7-9. Having obtained m_1 and m_2 (prior information on θ_1 and θ_2), and $m_1 + m_2 + \nu$ (prior information on ϕ), we can solve for ν and then solve for $R_1^2 + R_2^2 + \lambda$. In Chap. 9, we discuss a much more general and useful way of expressing the belief that certain parameter values (here, θ_1 and θ_2) are "similar".

Again, suppose we wish to compare the mean achievement level in mathematics of high schools I and II by administering a common mathematics achievement test to the graduating class of both schools. Both schools used the mathematics test last year. Last year, the variance on the test for school I was 25, and the variance for school II was 16. Let us now assume that for the present year, school I and school II actually have a common *unknown* variance ϕ. We will assume that our best modal estimate of ϕ is 16, and we feel this estimate is worth 50 observations. Then,

$$16 = \frac{R_1^2 + R_2^2 + \lambda}{m_1 + m_2 + \nu}$$

and

$$50 = m_1 + m_2 + \nu .$$

From the previous example, for school I, our best prior estimate of the mean θ_1 was $w_{1\bullet} = 30$ and we felt this estimate to be worth $m_1 = 15$ observations. For school II, our best prior estimate of the mean θ_2 was $w_{2\bullet} = 28$, and we felt this estimate was also worth $m_2 = 15$ observations. Substituting $m_1 = 15$ and $m_2 = 15$ in the above equations, we obtain $\nu = 20$ and $(R_1^2 + R_2^2 + \lambda) = 800$.

The sample statistics for school I are $n_1 = 25$, $x_{1\bullet} = 34$, and $S_1^2 = 400$. For school II, the sample statistics are $n_2 = 21$, $x_{2\bullet} = 32$, and $S_2^2 = 525$.

The quantity of interest is the difference in the mean achievement level in mathematics for high schools I and II. Let $\delta = \theta_1 - \theta_2$ represent this difference. The posterior distribution of δ is a t distribution defined by Eq. (8-1.3). Substituting the necessary values and simplifying, a posteriori, we have $\delta : t(94, 2.1667, 106.3472)$. The 50% HDR credibility interval for δ extends from 1.45 to 2.88. The probability that δ is greater than 0 is .98, though again this is not an important statement. It might be more important to note that Prob $(\delta > 1) = .86$. Each of these computations can be made by reference to Table A.1 of the cumulative normal distribution and noting that the standard deviation of the posterior "t" distribution is 1.075.

Both Variances Unknown and Possibly Unequal

This model will be more appropriate if the two high schools have different types of intake (greater selectivity would usually reduce the variance of student ability) or if they employ radically different teaching methods (some methods advance bright students at the cost of leaving the less bright to straggle in the rear, thus increasing the variance; while others help the not-so-bright but fail to stimulate brighter students, thus reducing the variance).

Let us first consider each population separately. From Sec. 7-6 we know that if we use indifference priors, the posterior (marginal) distribution of θ_i is

$$t(n_i - 1, x_{i\bullet}, n_i^{-1}S_i^2), \quad i = 1, 2.$$

Also, in Sec. 7-7, we saw that if we have prior knowledge about the parameters (θ_i, ϕ_i) equivalent to a hypothetical sample $(m_i, w_{i\bullet}, R_i^2)$ from the ith population, the posterior (marginal) distribution of θ_i is

$$t\left\{m_i + n_i - 1, \frac{m_i w_{i\bullet} + n_i x_{i\bullet}}{m_i + n_i}, (m_i + n_i)^{-1}\left[R_i^2 + S_i^2 + \frac{m_i n_i (x_{i\bullet} - w_{i\bullet})^2}{m_i + n_i}\right]\right\}$$

$$i = 1, 2.$$

In either case, or in the further case in which we have more prior information about the standard deviation than about the mean, the posterior distribution of θ_i is of the form $t(\nu_i, \zeta_i, \kappa_i)$.

Assuming that our prior information on the two populations is independent, the same will be true of our posterior information (there is now no common variance connecting the two populations), and, in particular, the posterior distributions of θ_1 and θ_2 will be independent. Hence, the general problem we have to solve is: "Given that θ_1 and θ_2 have independent distributions $t(\nu_1, \zeta_1, \kappa_1)$ and $t(\nu_2, \zeta_2, \kappa_2)$, what is the posterior distribution of $\delta = \theta_2 - \theta_1$?" Obtaining the answer to this question is simply a matter of performing certain integrations and expressing the result in a convenient form for tabulation. It turns out that the distribution depends on five quantities—$\zeta = (\zeta_2 - \zeta_1), \nu_1, \nu_2, \kappa_1, \kappa_2$—but that the necessary tabulation can be reduced to a three-way classification by standardizing δ in a manner similar to that used for standardizing t. Specifically,

$$u = \frac{\delta - \zeta}{\epsilon}$$

has a (standard) Behrens distribution with ν_1, ν_2 *degrees of freedom and angle* ψ *defined by*

$$\tan^2 \psi = \frac{\nu_1^{-1}\kappa_1}{\nu_2^{-1}\kappa_2},$$

where $\epsilon = (\nu_1^{-1}\kappa_1 + \nu_2^{-1}\kappa_2)^{1/2}$. We shall write this as $u : B(\nu_1, \nu_2, \psi)$ in the standardized form, and as $\delta : B(\nu_1, \nu_2, \psi, \zeta, \epsilon)$ in the general form.

Behrens Distribution

The distribution is named after an early investigator (Behrens) of our present model. It is symmetric about zero, and so the posterior density of δ is symmetric about $(\zeta_2 - \zeta_1)$. Since δ is the difference of two independent t variables, its variance is the sum of their variances, namely, $\kappa_1(\nu_1 - 2)^{-1} + \kappa_2(\nu_2 - 2)^{-1}$, and the variance of the Behrens distribution is $(\nu_1^{-1}\kappa_1 + \nu_2^{-1}\kappa_2)^{-1}$ times the variance of δ.

The sudden appearance of an *angle* as a parameter of the distribution is unnecessarily alarming! Clearly, ψ is merely another way of recording the ratio $\nu_1^{-1}\kappa_1/\nu_2^{-1}\kappa_2$, and at first sight, an inconvenient one, since it necessitates having trigonometrical tables at hand. (In the Appendix, we provide a table (Table A.12) of $\arctan\sqrt{x}$ which makes the required transformation from the ratio to the angle.) The notation is, however, the standard one, and it has certain compensations. One is in suggesting a picture of what is taking place. When $\psi = 0^\circ$, the Behrens distribution is t on ν_2 degrees of freedom with the sum of squares coming entirely from the second sample; as ψ increases to 90°, the distribution "swings round" to become t on ν_1 degrees of freedom, with the sum of squares coming entirely from the first sample. Another advantage is that interpolation in the table is more satisfactorily carried out in terms of ψ than in terms of the ratio itself.

The 75, 90, 95, $97\frac{1}{2}$, and 99% points of the distribution for $\nu_1, \nu_2, = 6, 8, 12, 24, \infty$, and $\psi = 0^\circ(15^\circ)45^\circ$ are given in Table A.11. Making use of the symmetry of the distribution, these values enable central 50, 80, 90, 95, and 98% credibility intervals for u (and, hence, for δ) to be found. It is not necessary to consider $\psi > 45^\circ$, corresponding to ratios $\nu_1^{-1}\kappa_1/\nu_2^{-1}\kappa_2 > 1$, because when this is the case, we can renumber the two populations, calling the first the second and vice versa. Ordinary (linear) interpolation in ν_1, ν_2, and ψ is adequate (except for $\nu_1 > 24$ or $\nu_2 > 24$ when it is not possible and must be replaced by interpolation using the reciprocals of the degrees of freedom).

For example, suppose we wish to find a 95% central credibility interval for u when $\nu_1 = 30$, $\nu_2 = 40$, and $\psi = 15^\circ$. It will be necessary to interpolate using the reciprocals of the degrees of freedom. First, interpolate to find the $97\frac{1}{2}$% point for $\nu_1 = 30$, $\nu_2 = 24$, $\psi = 15^\circ$, and for $\nu_1 = 30$, $\nu_2 = \infty$, $\psi = 15^\circ$. Then, interpolate to find the desired $97\frac{1}{2}$% point for $\nu_1 = 30$, $\nu_2 = 40$, $\psi = 15^\circ$. From Table A.11, the $97\frac{1}{2}$% points for $\nu_1 = 24$, $\nu_2 = 24$, $\psi = 15^\circ$, and $\nu_1 = \infty$, $\nu_2 = 24$, $\psi = 15^\circ$, are 2.06 and 2.06, respectively. Thus, the $97\frac{1}{2}$% point for $\nu_1 = 30$, $\nu_2 = 24$, $\psi = 15^\circ$ is 2.06. From Table A.11, the $97\frac{1}{2}$% points for $\nu_1 = 24$, $\nu_2 = \infty$, $\psi = 15^\circ$, and $\nu_1 = \infty$, $\nu_2 = \infty$, $\psi = 15^\circ$, are 1.97 and 1.96, respectively. The $97\frac{1}{2}$% point for $\nu_1 = 30$, $\nu_2 = \infty$, $\psi = 15^\circ$ is

$$1.97 - (1.97 - 1.96)\,\frac{1/24 - 1/30}{1/24 - 0} = 1.968.$$

Now interpolate between $\nu_1 = 30, \nu_2 = 24, \psi = 15°$, and $\nu_1 = 30, \nu_2 = \infty$, $\psi = 15°$, $97\frac{1}{2}\%$ points to find the $97\frac{1}{2}\%$ point for $\nu_1 = 30, \nu_2 = 40, \psi = 15°$. Thus, the $97\frac{1}{2}\%$ point for $\nu_1 = 30, \nu_2 = 40, \psi = 15°$ is

$$2.06 - (2.06 - 1.968)\frac{1/24 - 1/40}{1/24 - 0} = 2.023\,.$$

Since the Behrens distribution is symmetric about zero, a 95% central credibility interval for u extends from -2.02 to 2.02.

Examination of the $97\frac{1}{2}\%$ point table shows that the approximate formula

$$u_{97\frac{1}{2}}(\nu_1, \nu_2, \psi) = t_{97\frac{1}{2}}(\nu_1)\sin^2\psi + t_{97\frac{1}{2}}(\nu_2)\cos^2\psi$$

(where in each case the notation refers to the $97\frac{1}{2}\%$ point of the standardized distribution) reproduces the tabulated values with an error of less than .02, or 1% of the entry. The error in every case is conservative, that is, makes credibility intervals longer than they should be. Unfortunately, this approximation is not as good for other percentage points and cannot be recommended for general use.

Now let us consider again the comparison of the mean achievement levels in mathematics in high schools I and II. Dropping the assumption of equal variances, we need to fit prior distributions for the two populations separately. Prior modal estimates of 25 and 16 would seem appropriate, and m_{S_1} and m_{S_2} values of 25 might seem appropriate. Then, the prior distributions for ϕ_1 and ϕ_2 are respectively $\chi^{-2}(24, 650)$ and $\chi^{-2}(24, 416)$. A posteriori, the distributions are $\chi^{-2}(49, 1200)$ and $\chi^{-2}(45, 1081)$. With natural conjugate prior distributions having parameters $m_{M_1} = 15$, $w_{1\bullet} = 30$, and $m_{M_2} = 15$, $w_{2\bullet} = 28$, the posterior distributions for the means are $t(49, 32.5, 30)$ and $t(45, 30.33, 30.028)$. The angle ψ of the Behrens distribution is

$$\psi = \tan^{-1}\sqrt{\frac{\nu_1^{-1}\kappa_1}{\nu_2^{-1}\kappa_2}} = 43.77 \text{ degrees,}$$

and the scale parameter is

$$\epsilon = (\nu_1^{-1}\kappa_1 + \nu_2^{-1}\kappa_2)^{1/2} = 1.1312.$$

Thus, the difference $\delta^* = \theta_2 - \theta_1$ a posteriori has the Behrens distribution $B(\nu_1, \nu_2, \psi, \zeta, \epsilon) = B(49, 45, 43.77, -2.17, 1.1312)$. Note that δ^* is $\theta_2 - \theta_1$ while in previous examples we have worked with $\delta = \theta_1 - \theta_2$.

So the posterior mean, median, and mode of the distribution of our belief on δ^* is $\zeta = -2.17$, and the posterior standard deviation of δ^* is given by

$$\text{Standard deviation }(\delta^*) = \left(\frac{\kappa_1}{\nu_1 - 2} + \frac{\kappa_2}{\nu_2 - 2}\right)^{1/2} = 1.156\,.$$

Using the probability distribution of u, we are able to derive credibility intervals on δ^*. Since

$$\text{Prob}\,(-B_{100-(P/2)} < u < B_{100-(P/2)}) = \frac{P}{100}$$

where $B_{100-(P/2)}$ is the $(100 - P/2)$ percentile of the standard Behrens-Fisher distribution given in Table A.11, substituting for u we have

$$\text{Prob}\,(\zeta - \epsilon B_{100-(P/2)} < \delta^* < \zeta + \epsilon B_{100-(P/2)}) = \frac{P}{100}\,.$$

Interpolating in Table A.11, we find $B_{75}(49,45,43.77) \doteq .68$, and therefore the posterior 50% credibility interval on δ^* is given by $[-2.17 - 1.1312(.68), -2.17 + 1.1312(.68)]$ or $(-2.94, -1.40)$. Since the Behrens distribution is symmetric, this credibility interval is also an HDR. The corresponding interval for $\delta = \theta_1 - \theta_2$ would be (1.40, 2.94). Note that this interval is slightly larger than the interval (1.45, 2.88) obtained under the assumption of a common unknown variance and that the interval, in turn, is slightly larger than the interval (1.47, 2.87) obtained when the variances are assumed known. In this example, the differences among these interval lengths are not great because of the relatively large *effective* sample sizes (hypothetical plus real).

8-2 COMPARISON OF TWO NORMAL VARIANCES

What does it mean to say we wish to compare two variances? A rather hasty generalization from the previous section would be to answer that it means finding the posterior distribution of $(\phi_2 - \phi_1)$. There is no difficulty in principle in doing this, but the result is frankly a mess. Without necessarily endorsing the pure mathematician's doctrine that the inelegant is unworthy of study, the messiness of the solution does suggest a check on whether we are solving the right problem.

A mean is a measure of location. It tells us where the "center" of the density curve is positioned on the real line. When each mean may take any value, the most sensible—perhaps the only sensible—way to compare them is in terms of their distance apart. A variance is different. It is a measure of variability, of scale, of spread of the density curve. The natural comparison is of the type that distribution A is spread out twice as far as distribution B. The same is true if we think in terms of precision. The natural statement is that instrument A measures twice as precisely as instrument B. Thus, it appears that our natural concern is with the *ratio* ϕ_2/ϕ_1, not with the difference $\phi_2 - \phi_1$. (This is not to say that there will never be situations in which it is the difference that is of interest.)

The mathematics of the problem lends support by being simple and elegant when the ratio is considered. There is also a tieup with the indifference prior. We saw that this was equivalent to taking a uniform prior for $\ln \phi$. Now $\ln \phi_2 - \ln \phi_1 = \ln (\phi_2/\phi_1)$, and so considering the ratio of the variances is equivalent to considering the difference of their logarithms. In both cases, it is the *logarithm* of the variance which takes the place of the mean.

In principle, we should again consider three cases: (1) both means known, (2) means equal but unknown, and (3) both means unknown. However, it turns out that the same analysis will cover cases (1) and (3), while case (2) is of such rare occurrence as not to justify spending time on the rather complicated mathematics to which it leads—in any case, throwing away the information that the means are equal and treating case (2) as case (3) is roughly equivalent (on the average) to losing a single observation.

In both cases (1) and (3) if we take independent conjugate priors for the parameters of the two populations, the posterior distributions of ϕ_1 and ϕ_2 are independent $\chi^{-2}(\nu_i, \lambda_i)$ with suitable values for ν_i and λ_i. In case (3), that of unknown means, and assuming no prior information, we have from Sec. 7-6 that

$$\nu_i = n_i - 1, \quad \lambda_i = S_i^2 = \sum_j (x_{ij} - x_{i\bullet})^2 .$$

If the means are known, the degrees of freedom are both increased by 1, that is, $\nu_i = n_i$, and the sums of squares are calculated from the population mean instead of from the sample mean, that is, $\lambda_i = T_i^2 = \sum_j (x_{ij} - \mu_i)^2$. Modifications to take account of prior information were discussed in Secs. 7-4, 7-7, and 7-8.

In general terms, therefore, our problem is: "Given that ϕ_i $(i = 1, 2)$ are independent $\chi^{-2}(\nu_i, \lambda_i)$ variables, what is the distribution of ϕ_2/ϕ_1?" The distribution depends on the four parameters ν_1, ν_2, λ_1, and λ_2, but it can be standardized by defining

$$F = \frac{\phi_2/(\lambda_2/\nu_2)}{\phi_1/(\lambda_1/\nu_1)} \tag{8-2.1}$$

which has a distribution requiring only two-way tabulation by ν_1 and ν_2. This standard distribution is known simply as the F distribution and is denoted by $F(\nu_1, \nu_2)$. As with previous distributions we have studied, it will be a convenient shorthand to extend this notation and say that *the variance ratio* ϕ_2/ϕ_1 *has an* $F(\nu_1, \nu_2, \lambda_1, \lambda_2)$ *distribution, by which we mean that the quantity* F *defined by (8-2.1) has a standard* $F(\nu_1, \nu_2)$ *distribution*. We shall study the distribution of F in some detail shortly. For the present, we need only note that percentage points are given in Table A.13.

By means of (8-2.1), we can pass from percentage points and credibility intervals for F to those for ϕ_2/ϕ_1. However, central credibility intervals may not be the most useful descriptors of the posterior distribution when our intention is comparison. We may be much more interested in probabilities such as

$$\text{Prob}\,(\phi_2 > \phi_1) = \text{Prob}\left(\frac{\phi_2}{\phi_1} > 1\right) = \text{Prob}\,[F(\nu_1, \nu_2, \lambda_1, \lambda_2) > 1]$$

$$= \text{Prob}\left(F > \frac{\nu_2\lambda_2^{-1}}{\nu_1\lambda_1^{-1}}\right).$$

Since this probability depends on the observed ratio $\nu_2\lambda_2^{-1}/\nu_1\lambda_1^{-1}$ as well as on ν_1 and ν_2, very extensive tabulation would be necessary to enable it to be found directly from tables. However, by examining the F table for ν_1, ν_2 degrees of freedom, we can first note between which percentage points the observed ratio lies and then, if necessary, interpolate between those points to determine that the observed value corresponds approximately to the P% point. The form of the F table which we give as Table A.13 will be found more useful for this procedure than the more conventional form. Having found P, it follows that Prob $(\phi_2 > \phi_1) = (100 - P)$%. Often, we shall not be required to know the value of P exactly. It will suffice to note the first tabulated percentage point P_u that is greater than the observed ratio and the first point P_l that is less than the observed ratio and to conclude either that Prob $(\phi_2 > \phi_1) < (100 - P_l)$% or that Prob $(\phi_2 > \phi_1) > (100 - P_u)$%. Note, in passing, that assuming our ν_i and λ_i to be those obtained using an indifference prior for each parameter, a classical hypothesis test of the hypothesis $H_0 : \phi_1 = \phi_2$ against the alternative $H_1 : \phi_2 > \phi_1$ will extract from the same data the conclusion that H_0 should be rejected at the $(100 - P_u)$% level but not at the $(100 - P_l)$% level—a conclusion which would usually be (mis)understood to mean the same as the Bayesian result in the previous sentence. This confluence of methods again results from the use of indifference priors and an essential symmetry of the quantity F which will be made more explicit in the next paragraph.

Some insight into the meaning of F can be gained by considering the case of prior ignorance and introducing the quantity

$$\xi_i^2 = \frac{S_i^2}{\nu_i} \tag{8-2.2}$$

known as the *mean square*. More generally, we define

$$\text{Mean square} = \frac{\text{sum of squares}}{\text{degrees of freedom}}. \tag{8-2.3}$$

Equation (8-2.1) then becomes

$$F = \frac{\phi_2/\xi_2^2}{\phi_1/\xi_1^2}. \tag{8-2.4}$$

Now, the a posteriori mode of the distribution of ϕ_i differs little from the mean square ξ_i^2. Hence, likely values of ϕ_i are around ξ_i^2, and so "likely values" of F are those around the value one. The above comments hold whether the mean is unknown or known if S_i^2 and ν_i are properly defined.

For an example of the comparison of two normal variances suppose, a posteriori, $\phi_1 : \chi^{-2}(25, 390)$ and $\phi_2 : \chi^{-2}(30, 400)$. Modal estimates of the two variances are 14.444 and 12.5, respectively. The a posteriori distribution of ϕ_2/ϕ_1 is then $F(25, 30, 390, 400)$. To compare ϕ_1 and ϕ_2, we note that

$$\begin{aligned}\text{Prob}\left(\frac{\phi_2}{\phi_1} > \kappa\right) &= \text{Prob}\,[F(25, 30, 390, 400) > \kappa] \\ &= \text{Prob}\left[F(25, 30) > \kappa\,\frac{30\,(400)^{-1}}{25\,(390)^{-1}}\right] \\ &= \text{Prob}\,[F(25, 30) > 1.17\kappa] \\ &= 1 - \text{Prob}\,[F(25, 30) < 1.17\kappa]\,.\end{aligned}$$

Suppose we are interested in the probability that ϕ_2 is 10% greater than ϕ_1. Then $\kappa = 1.1$ and

$$\text{Prob}\left(\frac{\phi_2}{\phi_1} > 1.1\right) = 1 - \text{Prob}\,[F(25, 30) < 1.287]\,.$$

From Table A.13, we find that the 75th percentile of $F(25, 30)$ is 1.291, so that we can state that

$$\text{Prob}\left(\frac{\phi_2}{\phi_1} > 1.1\right) = 1 - .75 = .25\,,$$

approximately.

If $\kappa = 1$, we note that

$$\text{Prob}\,[F(25, 30) < 1.291] = .75$$

and

$$\text{Prob}\,[F(25, 30) < .9955] = .50\,.$$

Thus, $P_l = .9955$ and $P_u = 1.291$ with corresponding percentile values of 50 and 75. Interpolating, we arrive at the value

$$50 + \frac{1.17 - .9955}{1.291 - .9955}\,(75 - 50) = 64.76\,.$$

Thus,

$$\text{Prob}\,[F(25, 30) < 1.17] = .6476\,,$$

approximately, and

$$\text{Prob}\left(\frac{\phi_2}{\phi_1} > 1\right) = 1 - .6476 = .3524,$$

which is equivalent to the statement that

$$\text{Prob}(\phi_1 > \phi_2) = .6476 .$$

Suppose further that we desired

$$\text{Prob}(\phi_1 > 2\phi_2) .$$

This can be written as

$$\begin{aligned}\text{Prob}\left(\frac{\phi_1}{\phi_2} > 2\right) &= \text{Prob}\,[F(30, 25, 400, 390) > 2] \\ &= \text{Prob}\left[F(30, 25) > 2\,\frac{25\,(390)^{-1}}{30\,(400)^{-1}}\right] \\ &= \text{Prob}\,[F(30, 25) > 1.71] \\ &= 1 - \text{Prob}\,[F(30, 25) < 1.71] .\end{aligned}$$

The 95th percentile of $F(30, 25)$ is 1.919 and the 90th percentile is 1.659. Thus, Prob $[F(30, 25) < 1.71] = .91$, approximately, so that

$$\text{Prob}\left(\frac{\phi_1}{\phi_2} > 2\right) = .09 ,$$

approximately. The reader may now wish to verify that Prob $(\phi_1/\phi_2 > 1.1) = .56$, approximately. Interestingly, the probability that $.91 < \phi_2/\phi_1 < 1.1$ is only about .19.

In comparing the mean achievement level in mathematics of high schools I and II in the previous section, we at one point assumed that school I and school II had a common unknown variance. Let us now question the validity of this assumption by examining the variance ratio ϕ_1/ϕ_2.

Since both schools gave the test last year, we will base our prior information on last year's results. We will assume that our prior information on the mean and the variance for each school is worth 15 observations. Our prior information is

	$w_{\bullet}$	m_m	$\tilde{\phi}$	m_s
I:	30	15	25	15
II:	28	15	16	15

The prior distribution for the variance of school I (ϕ_1) is inverse chi square, with

$$\nu_1 = m_{s_1} - 1 = 14$$

and

$$R_1^2 = (m_{s_1} + 1)\tilde{\phi}_1 = 400 .$$

The prior distribution for the variance of school II (ϕ_2) is $\chi^{-2}(14, 256)$.

The sample statistics are

	n	$x_{\bullet}$	S^2
I:	25	34	400
II:	21	32	525

The posterior distribution for ϕ_1 is inverse chi square, with

$$\nu_1 = n_1 + m_{s_1} - 1 = 39$$

and

$$\lambda_1 = R_1^2 + S_1^2 + \frac{m_{m_1} n_1 (x_{1\bullet} - w_{1\bullet})^2}{m_{m_1} + n_1} = 950\,.$$

The posterior distribution for ϕ_2 is $\chi^{-2}(35, 921)$.

The quantity of interest is the variance ratio ϕ_1/ϕ_2. The posterior distribution of ϕ_1/ϕ_2 is $F(35, 39, 921, 950)$. Using the relationship defined in (8-2.1), a 50% central credibility interval for ϕ_1/ϕ_2 extends from .74 to 1.16. The probability that ϕ_1 is greater than ϕ_2 is .41.

Let us now assume that we have prior information on the variance for each school, but that we have no prior information on the means.

The prior distributions for ϕ_1 and ϕ_2 will not be altered. A priori $\phi_1 : \chi^{-2}$ (14,400), and $\phi_2 : \chi^{-2}(14{,}256)$. The modal estimates are 25 and 16, respectively.

Referring to Sec. 7-7, the posterior distribution for ϕ_1 is inverse chi square, with

$$\nu_1 = m_{s_1} + n_1 - 2 = 38$$

and

$$\lambda = R_1^2 + S_1^2 = 800\,.$$

The posterior distribution for ϕ_2 is $\chi^{-2}(34, 781)$.

The quantity of interest is again the variance ratio ϕ_1/ϕ_2. The posterior distribution of ϕ_1/ϕ_2 is $F(34, 38, 781, 800)$. A 50% central credibility interval for ϕ_1/ϕ_2 extends from .73 to 1.15. The probability that ϕ_1 is greater than ϕ_2 is .40. None of these analyses assigns very high probability to either variance being meaningfully higher than the other.

The F Distribution

The symbol F was chosen to commemorate the contributions by Sir Ronald Fisher to the study of variances and variance ratios (Fisher himself worked with the quantity $\frac{1}{2}\ln F$ which he called z). We have already noted in Chap. 5 that a simple transformation enables percentage points of the beta distribution to be derived from those of F, and the same is true for the t and χ^2 or χ^{-2} distributions. However, the basic reason for the importance of the F distribution is its habit of turning up whenever the ratio of variances or variancelike quantities is considered. In Table A.13, we give percentage points 50, 75, 90, 95, and 99% of the distribution for $\nu_1 = 3(1)30(10)50$, $\nu_2 = 3(1)30(10)100$.

The quantity F is always nonnegative. Its density function is proportional to

$$\frac{F^{\frac{1}{2}\nu_1 - 1}}{(\nu_2 + \nu_1 F)^{\frac{1}{2}(\nu_1 + \nu_2)}}, \qquad 0 \le F < \infty, \qquad \text{(8-2.5)}$$

when ν_1 and ν_2 are positive.

If we interchange the subscripts 1 and 2 in all the factors on the right-hand side of the defining ratio (8-2.1)–that is, call the first high school the second and vice versa–symmetry demands that the result have an $F(\nu_2, \nu_1)$ distribution. However, the result of the interchange is simply F^{-1}. Hence, *if a variable has an* $F(\nu_1, \nu_2)$ *distribution, its reciprocal has an* $F(\nu_2, \nu_1)$ *distribution*. We shall return to this point after listing some of the chief characteristics of the distribution.

Characteristics of the F Distribution $F(\nu_1, \nu_2)$

If $\nu_1 > 2$, the density function has an interior mode, rising from zero at $F = 0$ to a maximum at

$$\text{Mode}(F) = \frac{\nu_1 - 2}{\nu_1} \frac{\nu_2}{\nu_2 + 2}, \quad (\doteq 1 \text{ when } \nu_1, \nu_2 \text{ are large}) \quad (8\text{-}2.6)$$

and then falling off to zero as $F \to \infty$. In terms of ϕ_2/ϕ_1 this means that

$$\text{Mode}\left(\frac{\phi_2}{\phi_1}\right) = \frac{\nu_1 - 2}{\lambda_1} \frac{\lambda_2}{\nu_2 + 2}. \quad (8\text{-}2.7)$$

If $\nu_1 < 2$, the function is unbounded (infinite) at $F = 0$ and decreases steadily as $F \to \infty$.

The F distribution has a mean if $\nu_2 > 2$, namely,

$$\text{Mean}(F) = \frac{\nu_2}{\nu_2 - 2}, \quad (\doteq 1 \text{ when } \nu_2 \text{ is large}), \quad (8\text{-}2.8)$$

which rather surprisingly depends only on ν_2. To it corresponds

$$\text{Mean}\left(\frac{\phi_2}{\phi_1}\right) = \frac{\nu_1}{\lambda_1} \frac{\lambda_2}{\nu_2 - 2}, \quad (8\text{-}2.9)$$

which depends on both ν_1 and ν_2. The variance exists for $\nu_2 > 4$ and is given by

$$\text{Variance}(F) = \frac{2\nu_2^2(\nu_1 + \nu_2 - 2)}{\nu_1(\nu_2 - 4)(\nu_2 - 2)^2}, \quad (8\text{-}2.10)$$

or $$\text{Variance}(F) \doteq 2(\nu_1^{-1} + \nu_2^{-1}) \quad \text{when } \nu_1 \text{ and } \nu_2 \text{ are large}. \quad (8\text{-}2.11)$$

A feature of the above results, at first sight disturbing, is the lack of symmetry with respect to subscripts. It follows, for example, that if M is the mode of the distribution of ϕ_2/ϕ_1, the mode for ϕ_1/ϕ_2 is *not* M^{-1}. Similar remarks apply to the mean. There is nothing mysterious about this–it is an inevitable consequence of the processes of differential and integral calculus involved in calculating the mode and mean. Nor is this the first time we have met the phenomenon—the mode of a standard χ^2 distribution on ν degrees of freedom is $(\nu - 2)$, while the mode of a standard χ^{-2} distribution on ν degrees of freedom is $(\nu + 2)^{-1}$. It does warn us, however, not to make the mistake of thinking of the modal (or mean) value of a parameter as its "true" value. It would be nonsensical to say that the true value of ϕ_2/ϕ_1 is M, but the true value of ϕ_1/ϕ_2 is not M^{-1}. The warning is most important when the number of observations is small. For large values of ν_1 and ν_2, if M is the mode of the distribution of ϕ_2/ϕ_1, then M^{-1} will be very close to the mode of the distribution of ϕ_1/ϕ_2.

A fairly extreme case of this problem occurs when we have three observations from each population and the means are unknown, so that $\nu_1 = \nu_2 = 2$. With $\nu_1 = 2$, the density function of ϕ_2/ϕ_1 has its (finite) largest value at zero; and by symmetry, with $\nu_2 = 2$, the density of ϕ_1/ϕ_2 is largest at zero. Thus, if one has to bet on an interval of length 10^{-2} (say) for the ratio ϕ_2/ϕ_1, one should choose to bet on $0 \leq \phi_2/\phi_1 \leq 10^{-2}$, implying that $\phi_1/\phi_2 \geq 100$. However, if one has to bet on an interval of length 10^{-2} for ϕ_1/ϕ_2, one should bet that $\phi_1/\phi_2 \leq 10^{-2}$!! There is no real inconsistency here. The two betting situations are just not comparable, because intervals of equal lengths for one ratio may correspond with intervals of very different lengths for the other ratio. To put it another way, using a zero-one (or a squared-error) loss function with a variable Y is, in general, not consistent with using the same loss function with Y^{-1}. The loss function one is using will determine which mode (mean) is the one that minimizes the expected loss.

The implication of all this for scientific reporting, when the experimenter himself has no particular loss function in mind but wishes to make available a suitable summary of his investigations, is that the posterior distribution itself (and the prior used), not just features of the posterior distribution, should always be reported. This will enable the eventual user to minimize *his* expected loss. Any descriptive features of a posterior distribution which are reported, such as the mean or mode, should be interpreted with caution when the number of observations on which they are based is small. For example, the "most likely value" interpretation of the mode must be recognized for what it is—loose talk! It can really make no sense to say simultaneously that the most likely value of ϕ_2/ϕ_1 is at (or near) zero and also that the most likely value of ϕ_1/ϕ_2 is at (or near) zero.

The problems discussed above are usually greatly alleviated as the number of observations increases and the posterior variance of all parameters becomes small. It can be shown then that the mean of the reciprocal of a variable is approximately the reciprocal of its mean, and a similar result will usually hold for modes. The corresponding result for *medians* always holds, even with small samples, and this might be regarded as a reason for preferring the median as a descriptive measure of central tendency. The main drawback is that medians can usually not be expressed by an analytic formula but must be obtained from the 50% point table of the distribution. However, for $\nu_1 > 5$ and $\nu_2 > 5$, the relationship (7-2.2) will work very well. We also note that our work in Secs. 7-3 and 7-4 strongly suggests that in most applications values of $\nu > 5$ will be required to produce coherent prior distributions.

8-3 CASE STUDIES IN NORMAL ANALYSIS

Case Study 8-3.1 A Bayesian Study of the Use of Programmed Material in Geography

The idea of programming subject material is not new, but in some fields of study comparatively little research has been done with programmed materials. As a result, many educators have doubts concerning the merits of programmed instruction. It has been hypothesized by some educators that students using programmed material will complete the unit of work much faster than students taught in the conventional manner. It has been hypothesized by other educators that both groups will have approximately the same achievement rate. The purpose of this study is to determine, by the use of an objective test, if the level of achievement in geography for seventh grade students using programmed material differs from that of students taught in the conventional manner.

A programmed geography unit on China and a 50-point objective test for the unit were developed. A study had been undertaken to ensure that the objective test was reliable and had subject-matter validity. Permission to conduct a study using the programmed geography unit was granted by a school district in Western Pennsylvania. A seventh grade geography teacher was selected to conduct the study in his classes.

It was decided to use only groups of students of average achievement. The instructor had two classes that were considered of comparable average achievement level. The experimental class had 26 students and the control group had 30 students.

It was agreed that the experimental group would work at their own rate until they had completed the programmed unit. Upon completion of the material the students were immediately given the objective test.

The instructor was to teach the control group in the conventional manner, covering the same material contained in the programmed unit. The students in the control group would then receive the same objective test taken by the students in the experimental group. The maximum obtainable score on the objective test was 50 points. It was felt that the difference in achievement level between the experimental class and the control group must be at least 5 points, 10% of the total, in order to have educational significance.

Bayesian analysis, as applied to the normal model, was used to study the question of difference in average level of achievement between students in both groups.

From the initial study of the objective test, it was known that the distribution of scores should be approximately normal. However, no prior information was available for the mean or the standard deviation of either the experimental group or the control group, and thus it was decided to use indifference priors. More precisely, it might be said that the people involved were unable to quantify their prior information.

The experimental class and the control group were selected for similar achievement level. The same objective test was administered to each group. Thus, it was believed that both groups would have the same standard deviation.

The following sample data were collected:

	n	$x_{\bullet}$	s	S^2
1 Experimental	26	33.04	7.32	1393.1424
2 Control	30	23.93	7.16	1537.9680

Each group separately gives an $\chi^{-2}(n_i - 1, S_i^2)$ posterior distribution for the variance (ϕ). The posterior marginal distribution for ϕ, using the combined data from both groups, is an inverse chi-square distribution on $n_1 + n_2 - 2$ or 54 degrees of freedom with sum of squares $S_1^2 + S_2^2$ or 2931.1104.

The quantity of primary interest is the difference in mean achievement between the experimental class and the control group. Let δ represent the difference $(\theta_1 - \theta_2)$. The marginal distribution of δ is a t distribution on $n_1 + n_2 - 2$ or 54 degrees of freedom. It has a mean, median, and mode of $x_{1\bullet} - x_{2\bullet}$ or 9.11, and a standard deviation of $[(n_1^{-1} + n_2^{-1})(S_1^2 + S_2^2)/(n_1 + n_2 - 4)]^{1/2}$ or 2.01. The 50% HDR for δ extends from 7.79 to 10.43.

Given the difference that was observed (9.11), the probability that the programmed material will produce a difference in level of achievement of at least 5 points, the minimum difference required for educational significance, is

$$\begin{aligned} \text{Prob}\,(\delta > 5) &= \text{Prob}\left[\frac{(\delta - \zeta)\sqrt{\nu}}{\sqrt{\kappa}} > \frac{(5 - \zeta)\sqrt{\nu}}{\sqrt{\kappa}}\right] \\ &= \text{Prob}\left[t > \frac{(5 - 9.11)\sqrt{54}}{\sqrt{210.4387}}\right] \\ &\doteq \text{Prob}\,(z > -2.08) \\ &= 0.9812\,. \end{aligned}$$

The average time needed by the teacher to complete the geography unit taught in the conventional manner was 216 minutes. The average time needed for the students in the experimental group to complete the programmed material was 110 minutes. Since the amount of time saved by using the programmed material was substantial, one would have expected very little difference, perhaps even a negative difference, between the average achievement level for the experimental class and the control group. Thus, a positive difference of 9.11 was indeed surprising.

It was decided to repeat the experiment the following year. Since the difference in achievement level between the two groups was very substantial, it was desirable to discover if the results from the first study were reliable in assessing the gains derived from the use of programmed study materials in seventh grade geography.

The following year, the teacher had four classes that were considered of average achievement level. Two classes with a combined total of 52 students were in the experimental group and two classes with a combined total of 55 students were in the control group. Because there were certain changes in each of the teaching methods, some increase of proficiency of the instructor, and possibly some change in the student body, it seemed necessary to assess very carefully the information from the first experiment as prior information for the second experiment. The original study, with $s_1 = 7.32$ and $s_2 = 7.16$, supported the contention that the two populations have a common standard deviation, and a simple average of these values seemed a reasonable value to take. The sample means for the two treatments from the first experiment were 33.04 and 23.93, and it was decided to take these as the starting values.

The prior estimates used are:

$$w_{1\bullet} = 33.04 \quad w_{2\bullet} = 23.93 \quad \tilde{\phi}^{1/2} = 7.24 .$$

It was now necessary to determine how many observations one felt each piece of prior information to be worth. The interactive CADA computer program was used to assess the prior values. First, the modal estimate of $\phi^{1/2}$ (7.24), and the number of observaitons (m_S) it was felt to be worth, were supplied. Taking the prior distribution of $\phi^{1/2}$ to be inverse chi, the computer prints out a 50% HDR from this distribution. Specifications are then adjusted until one is satisfied, satisfaction implying that one is willing to bet at even odds that the true value of $\phi^{1/2}$ is either inside or outside the given interval. Since the sample values of the standard deviation from the first experiment were very similar, it was felt that an interval of 1 unit around the modal estimate of $\phi^{1/2}$ would be satisfactory for the 50% HDR.

Next, the mean($w_{i\bullet}$) of the conditional distribution of θ_i, given that $\phi^{1/2}$ takes on the modal value of 7.24, and the number of observations (m_{M_i}) which the estimate of θ_i was felt to be worth, were supplied. Taking the prior marginal distribution of θ_i to be a t distribution, the computer prints out a 50% HDR and adjustments are made until satisfied. Since the results for θ_1 and θ_2 from the first experiment were somewhat unexpected, it was felt that an interval of $2\frac{1}{2}$ units would be necessary for the 50% HDR for each mean.

In order to achieve the above specifications, the prior weights assigned to the modal estimates for $\phi^{1/2}$, θ_1, and θ_2 are:

$$m_S = 50 \quad m_{M_1} = 15 \quad m_{M_2} = 15 .$$

Interestingly, the value m_S is almost equal to the full number of degrees of freedom (54) from the first experiment, but the values m_{M_1} and m_{M_2} are substantially less. Perhaps this indicates a certain conservatism on the part of the experimenter in evaluating his prior information on the means, or perhaps an unwillingness to accept the full relevance of the first experiment to the second. Interestingly though, the experimenter does seem to feel that he has much information about the variance.

The following prior marginal distributions, their properties, and 50% HDRs for $\phi^{1/2}$, θ_1, and θ_2 were obtained.

For $\phi^{1/2}$: $\chi^{-1}(49,51.1945)$

Mode = 7.2400

Median = 7.3638

Mean = 7.4281

50% HDR is (6.7696, 7.7674).

For θ_1 : $t(49,33.04,174.7258)$

Mode = median = mean = 33.0400

Standard deviation = 1.9281

50% HDR is (31.7565,34.3235).

For θ_2 : $t(49,23.93,174.7258)$

Mode = median = mean = 23.9300

Standard deviation = 1.9281

50% HDR is (22.6465,25.2135).

The following sample data were collected:

	n	$x.$	s	S^2
1 Experimental	52	32.58	7.25	2743.25
2 Control	55	22.26	7.30	2930.95

Quantification of prior information and sample data established the following posterior marginal distributions for θ_1 and θ_2.

For θ_1 : $t(101,32.68,79.9407)$

Mode = median = mean = 32.6830

Standard deviation = 0.8986

50% HDR is (32.0806,33.2853).

For θ_2 : $t(104,22.62,79.780)$

Mode = median = mean = 22.6179

Standard deviation = 0.8844

50% HDR is (22.0249,23.2108).

The quantity of interest is the difference in mean achievement between the experimental group and the control group. Let δ represent the difference $(\theta_1 - \theta_2)$.

The sufficient statistics are:

	Sample weights		*Sample means*	*Sample sum of squares*
Prior information	$m_{M_1} = 15$	$m_S = 50$	$w_1. = 33.04$	$\lambda = 51.1945$
	$m_{M_2} = 15$		$w_2. = 23.93$	$R_i^2 = 2620.88$
Sample data	$n_1 = 52$		$x_1. = 32.58$	$S_1^2 = 2743.25$
	$n_2 = 55$		$x_2. = 22.26$	$S_2^2 = 2930.95$

The posterior marginal distribution for δ and its properties are:

δ : $t(184,10.065,320.0062)$

Mode = median = mean = 10.0651

Standard deviation = 1.326

50% HDR is (9.1757,10.9545).

The probability that $(\theta_1 - \theta_2)$ is greater than 5, the minimum difference required for educational significance, is 0.9999.

This study indicates that the use of programmed geography material for seventh grade can not only save class time, but greatly increase the level of achievement. It would be desirable then for schools to develop and use more programmed geography materials.

A word of caution should be given. This study involved only seventh grade geography students of average achievement level, and it cannot be readily assumed that a substantial increase in achievement can be obtained by the use of programmed materials in other fields of study, for other grade levels, or for students of low or superior achievement level.

Bibliography

Aven, Samuel D., Lawrence DiRusso, and J. Leonard Azneer, A Study in the Use of a Programmed Geography Unit, *California Journal of Educational Research*, 21:64-67 (1970).

Case Study 8-3.2 Common Variance–A Valid Assumption?

In my study of the use of programmed geography material for seventh grade, I made the assumption of a common variance for the experimental class and the control group when studying the difference in level of achievement between the two groups. This assumption was based on three things. First, both the experimental class and the control group were selected for comparable (average) achievement level. Second, each group had the same instructor and the same geography material was presented to each class. Third, each took the same achievement test. The purpose of this paper is to determine whether the assumption of a common variance for the experimental class and the control group was valid.

The original study was conducted over a two-year period. The first year, due to the absence of previous information regarding the mean θ_1 and the variance ϕ_1 of the experimental class and the mean θ_2 and the variance ϕ_2 of the control group, it was decided to use indifference prior distributions.

The following sample data were collected:

	n	$x.$	s	S^2
1 Experimental	26	33.04	7.32	1393.1424
2 Control	30	23.93	7.16	1537.9680

Each group separately gives an $\chi^{-2}(n_i - 1, S_i^2)$ posterior distribution for the variance ϕ_i. The posterior distribution for the variance ϕ_1 of the experimental group is $\chi^{-2}(25,1393.1424)$. The posterior distribution for the variance ϕ_2 of the control group is $\chi^{-2}(29,1537.9680)$.

The variance is a measure of the dispersion of a distribution. The natural comparison then is of the type that distribution A is spread out twice as far as distribution B. Thus, the quantity of interest is the variance ratio ϕ_2/ϕ_1 for the control group and the experimental class. The variance ratio has an $F(\nu_1, \nu_2, \lambda_1, \lambda_2)$ distribution. The quantity $(\nu_2\lambda_1/\nu_1\lambda_2)(\phi_2/\phi_1)$ has a standard $F(\nu_1, \nu_2)$ distribution. The $F(25,29,1393,1538)$ distribution for ϕ_2/ϕ_1 has a mode of .8190, a median of .95, a mean of 1.0221, and a standard deviation of .4381. The 50% credibility interval extends from .73 to 1.23.

The interval is large due to the small sample sizes, but it is quite symmetrical about 1. These results support the assumption of a common variance for the experimental class and the control group.

The original study was repeated to determine if the observed large difference (9.11) in the mean achievement between the two groups from the first study was reliable. The second year prior information regarding θ_1, θ_2, ϕ_1, and ϕ_2 was available from the first study. I decided to use the observed values from the first study as the prior modal estimates for θ_1, θ_2, ϕ_1, and ϕ_2 for the follow-up study. It was then necessary to determine how many observations I felt each piece of prior information to be worth. The interactive computer program PRIORX was used to assess the prior estimates.

Considering the length of the achievement test (50 items) and the homogeneity of the two groups, I felt that I would be willing to make a bet at even odds if the 50% credibility interval for each standard deviation was 1 unit in length. This implied assigning a weight of $m_{S_i} = 50$ observations to the prior estimate for each standard deviation. Since very little difference had been expected in average achievement between the experimental class and the control group, I felt that an interval of $2\frac{1}{2}$ units would be necessary for the 50% credibility interval for each mean. This implied assigning a weight of $m_{M_i} = 15$ observations to the prior estimate for each mean. For comparison purposes, I am assigning the same prior weights to θ_1 and θ_2 that were used in the original study. Now, however, the weight of 50, assigned to the common ϕ in the original study, is assigned to each ϕ_i.

The sufficient statistics from the hypothetical prior sample are:

	m_M	$w.$	m_S	s
1 Experimental	15	33.04	50	7.32
2 Control	15	23.93	50	7.16

The following prior marginal distributions for the standard deviations $\phi_1^{1/2}$ and $\phi_2^{1/2}$ were obtained.

For $\phi_1^{1/2}: \chi^{-1}(49,51.7602)$

Mode = 7.3200

Median = 7.4451

Mean = 7.5102

50% credibility interval is (6.8445,7.8533).

For $\phi_2^{1/2}: \chi^{-1}(49,50.6288)$

Mode = 7.1600

Median = 7.2824

Mean = 7.3460

50% credibility interval is (6.6949,7.6816).

The following sample data were collected:

	n	$x.$	s	S^2
1 Experimental	52	32.58	7.25	2743.25
2 Control	55	22.26	7.30	2930.95

Quantification of the prior information and sample data established the following posterior marginal distributions for $\phi_1^{1/2}$ and $\phi_2^{1/2}$.

For $\phi_2^{1/2}$: $\chi^{-1}(101,73.5856)$

Mode = 7.2861

Median = 7.3463

Mean = 7.3770.

For $\phi_1^{1/2}$: $\chi^{-1}(104,74.3445)$

Mode = 7.2553

Median = 7.3136

Mean = 7.3432.

Again the quantity of interest is the variance ratio ϕ_2/ϕ_1 for the control group and the experimental group. It is known that $(\nu_2\lambda_1/\nu_1\lambda_2)(\phi_2/\phi_1)$ has a standard $F(101,104)$ distribution.

The $F(101,104,73.6,74.3)$ distribution for the variance ratio (ϕ_2/ϕ_1) has a mode of .9533, a median of .99, a mean of 1.0107, and a standard deviation of .2044. The 50% credibility interval extends from .87 to 1.14.

The mean, median, and mode are very close together and near 1. The 50% credibility interval is quite small and almost symmetrical about 1. Thus, I now feel confident that my assumption of a common variance for the experimental group and the control group was valid.

Case Study 8-3.3 The Difference Between Two Means on a Second-grade Economics Test

This study is part of a larger project undertaken to develop materials for units on economic concepts for grades 2 through 4. As part of the project, it was necessary to develop a test of economic understanding that could be used at all three grade levels. The instrument which was finally constructed, The Primary Test of Economic Understanding (PTEU), was initially developed and normed for third-grade pupils (Davison and Kilgore, 1971). A subsequent analysis was undertaken to establish the level of economic understanding (as measured by the PTEU) of children in grade 2. The results of this latter study indicated that the PTEU could be used in second-grade classrooms. The present study is designed to measure the difference in economic understanding (as measured by the PTEU) between second-grade children in two specific groups of schools. The procedure for designating membership in either one of these groups is such that neither group can be considered as representative of the total population.

The entire project was funded as part of the Joint Council on Economic Education's Project DEEP (Developmental Economic Education Project). One of the responsibilities of this project was to measure the difference in economic understanding (which is defined as the behavior measured on the PTEU) of second-graders in these two specific groups of schools. These groups were designated as "target" and "nontarget" school groups. The distinction between target and nontarget was made on the basis of the school's eligibility for financial aid under Title I of the Elementary and Secondary Education Act (E.S.E.A.). A school was designated as a target school if certain criteria of socioeconomic need and of cultural deprivation (both terms are defined by the Title I provisions of E.S.E.A.) qualified the school for special help under Title I funds.

The PTEU is a 32-item multiple-choice instrument with three foils and one correct response for each item. Each item is read orally by the pupils' classroom teacher in an effort to counter (as much as possible) the effects of poor reading skills on the part of the pupils taking the test. There is no time limit for the test although previous administrations of this test to second-graders indicated that 20 to 30 minutes were sufficient for all pupils to finish every item.

Prior distributions The mean and standard deviation for the PTEU, based on a representative sample of 135 second-grade children, were 12.16 and 4.41, respectively. Since the present study is concerned with two subpopulations of the second-grade population, this author feels that the standard deviations of both subpopulations will be less than that from the total second-grade population. In addition, the variability of scores for one of these subpopulations on several different achievement tests has been observed to be greater than for the other subpopulation. Consequently, this author does not feel that the standard deviation of scores within each of these two subpopulations is the same.

Prior distributions for the target schools Because second-grade children in target schools have generally been observed to be more alike in their performance on several different achievement tests, a value of 4.0 was felt to be the most probable value of the standard deviation for the second-grade target subpopulation. An interval was constructed around this value of 4.0 from 3.65 to 4.41 such that the author felt the probability of the true value of the standard deviation being in this interval was .50. The prior marginal distribution for the standard deviation, for which the interval from 3.65 to 4.41 is a 50% credibility interval, is an inverse chi distribution with 26 degrees of freedom and a scale parameter of 20.78. The mode of this inverse chi distribution is 4.0, the median is 4.13, and the mean is 4.20. (This inverse chi distribution suggests that the estimate of the standard deviation is being weighted as if it were made from the data of a sample of 27 observations.)

Because children in target-area schools have generally been observed to be lower in overall academic achievement as measured on several different achievement tests, the author felt the most probable value for the mean of children in such schools would be lower than the mean for all second-graders. A value of 10.0 was felt to be the most probable value of the mean PTEU score for second-grade children in target-area schools. An interval was constructed around this value of 10.0 from 9.46 to 10.54 such that the author felt the probability of the true value of the mean being in this interval was .50. The prior marginal distribution on the mean, for which the interval 9.46 to 10.54 is a 50% credibility interval, is a t distribution with 26 degrees of freedom and a standard deviation of .82. (This particular t distribution suggests that the prior estimate of the mean PTEU score for children in this subpopulation is being weighted as if it came from a sample of 27 observations–compromise values $m_S = m_M$ were taken here for convenience.) The conditional distribution of the mean, given that 4.0 is the actual value of the standard deviation, is normal, with a mean of 10.0 and a standard deviation of .77. A 50% credibility interval for this conditional distribution extends from 9.48 to 10.52.

Prior distributions for the nontarget schools Second-grade children in nontarget schools have generally been observed to be more variable in their performance on several different achievement tests. Consequently, it was felt by this author that the most probable value for the standard deviation of this subpopulation would be 4.35, a value slightly less than that for the total population but somewhat larger than that for the target subpopulation. An interval was constructed around this value of 4.35 from 3.96 to 4.80 such that the author felt the probability of the true value of the standard deviation for the nontarget subpopulation being in this interval was .50. The prior marginal distribution for the standard deviation, for which the interval from 3.96 to 4.80 was a 50% credibility interval, is an inverse chi distribution with 26 degrees of freedom and a scale parameter of 22.60. The mode of this inverse chi distribution is 4.35, the median is 4.49, and the mean is 4.57. (This particular inverse chi distribution suggests that the estimate of the standard deviation is being weighted as if it were made from the data of a sample of 27 observations.)

Because children in schools which are classified as "nontarget" have generally been found to be higher in overall academic achievement as measured by several different achievement tests, it was felt by the author that the most probable value for the mean PTEU score for these children would be somewhat higher than the overall mean for second-grade children. A value of 14.0 was felt to be the most probable value for the mean PTEU score for this subpopulation. Around this value of 14.0 an interval from 13.40 to 14.60 was constructed such that the author felt the probability of the true value of the mean for this subpopulation being in the interval was .50. The prior marginal distribution on the mean, for which the interval from 13.40 to 14.60, is a 50% credibility interval, is a *t* distribution on 26 degrees of freedom with a standard deviation of .89. (This particular *t* distribution would indicate that this estimate of the mean PTEU score was being weighted as if it were made from the data from a sample of 27 observations.) If the value of the standard deviation of scores for children in this subpopulation is 4.35, the prior conditional distribution on the mean is normal with a mean of 14.0 and a standard deviation of .84. The 50% credibility interval for this conditional distribution extends from 13.44 to 14.57.

Posterior distributions

SUBJECTS The 200 second-grade children who participated in this study were selected in classroom units from two specific subpopulations of schools in a large urban midwestern school system with approximately a 46,000 student enrollment. The two groups of schools were designated as either target or nontarget schools depending on the eligibility of the schools for E.S.E.A. Title I funds. Target schools are those schools which were eligible for these special funds. Within each of these two specific subgroups of schools, four second-grade classrooms (100 pupils in each group composed of 50 boys and 50 girls) were selected. The mean PTEU score for the second-graders in this sample was 13.48 with a standard deviation of 4.49.

Summary table of sufficient statistics

Subpopulation	Prior	Sample
Target	$N = 27$	$N = 100$
	SD = 4.0	SD = 3.96
	50% C.I. = (3.65,4.41)	
	$M = 27$	
	Mean = 10.0	Mean = 9.55
	50% C.I. = (9.46,10.54)	
Nontarget	$N = 27$	$N = 100$
	SD = 4.35	SD = 4.49
	50% C.I. = (3.96,4.80)	
	$M = 27$	
	Mean = 14.0	Mean = 13.48
	50% C.I. = (13.40,14.60)	

Posterior distributions for the target schools The posterior marginal distribution on the target subpopulation standard deviation, given the sample mean of 9.55 and standard deviation of 3.96, is an inverse chi distribution with 126 degrees of freedom and a scale parameter of 44.77. The posterior marginal mode is 3.97, the median is 4.00, and the mean is 4.01.

The posterior marginal distribution on the target subpopulation mean is a t distribution with 126 degrees of freedom. The mean, median, and mode of this distribution is 9.65 with a standard deviation of .36. The 50% credibility interval for the target schools subpopulation mean extends from 9.41 to 9.89.

Posterior distributions for the nontarget schools The posterior marginal distribution on the nontarget subpopulation standard deviation, given the sample mean of 13.48 and standard deviation of 4.49, is an inverse chi distribution with 126 degrees of freedom and a scale parameter of 50.33. The posterior marginal mode is 4.47, the median is 4.50, and the mean is 4.51.

The posterior marginal density on the nontarget subpopulation mean is a t distribution with 126 degrees of freedom. The mean, median, and mode of this distribution is 13.59 with a standard deviation of .40. The 50% credibility interval for the nontarget schools subpopulation mean extends from 13.32 to 13.86.

Posterior distribution of the difference between nontarget and target schools' means The most probable value for δ (where δ is the difference between the mean for the nontarget subpopulation and the target subpopulation) is 3.94 with a standard deviation of .538. The standardized posterior distribution for δ is a Behrens distribution with degrees of freedom $\nu_1 = 126, \nu_2 = 126$, and angle $\psi = 42°$. This distribution has a mean of 0.0 and a standard deviation of 1.008. Transforming back to the scale of δ, an approximate 95% credibility interval for δ extends from 2.89 to 4.99.

Discussion This study was undertaken as part of a larger project to develop materials for units on economic concepts for grades 2 through 4. As part of this project it was necessary to develop an instrument to assess the level of economic understanding for use at these grade levels. The present study was undertaken to measure the difference in economic understanding (as measured by the PTEU) between two subpopulations of the second-grade population. It was necessary, therefore, to ascertain what the value of this difference, δ, was between these two subpopulations. The most probable value for δ between the nontarget and target subpopulations was 3.94. The probability is approximately .95 that the true value of δ is between 2.89 and 4.99. This difference between the two subpopulations is felt to be educationally significant.

An implication of the results of this study is that materials prepared for use in classrooms in target schools may have to be specially adapted to some degree. Such an adaptation would have to take into account the initially lower level of economic understanding (as measured by the PTEU) of second-graders in the target schools. This study provides a basis for adapting the economics materials for use by the target and the nontarget schools.

Bibliography

Davison, Donald G., and John H. Kilgore, "An Evaluation of Second-grade Economic Materials", Bureau of Business and Economic Research, College of Business Administration, University of Iowa, Iowa City, Iowa, 1970.

____ **and** ____, "Examiner's Manual: Primary Test of Economic Understanding", Bureau of Business and Economic Research, College of Business Administration, University of Iowa, Iowa City, Iowa, 1971.

8-4 EXERCISES

1 Consider again variable 2 from Table 1-5.2. We are concerned with the extent of the true difference (on a continuing basis) between the means of colleges 1 and 4 on variable 2. Using the prior distributions developed in the previous chapter now proceed to do a posteriori comparisons of means under the following conditions:

(*a*) Variances assumed known and equal to the sample values.
(*b*) Variances assumed unknown but equal.
(*c*) Variances assumed unknown and unequal.

After stating the posterior distribution of the difference, give the following:

$$\text{Prob}\ (\theta_4 > \theta_1)$$
$$\text{Prob}\ (\theta_4 > \theta_1 + 2)$$

A 50% HDR credibility interval on the difference.

Under case *c* compare the standard deviations σ_4 and σ_1. After stating the posterior distribution, give the following:

$$\text{Prob}\ (\sigma_4 > \sigma_1)$$
$$\text{Prob}\ (\sigma_4 > 2\sigma_1).$$

2 The following two sets of data, *A* and *B*, are from the Miller Analogies Test. Assume that groups A and B differ on some characteristic which has previously been shown to be correlated with scores on the test—such as cultural background, sex, or the like. Further assume that your previous knowledge about the two groups can be summarized by the following statistics.

	Group *A*	Group *B*
$\tilde{\sigma}_o$	15	15
m_S	15	15
$w.$	75	65
m_M	15	10

Group *A*					
85	53	43	77	53	79
51	56	99	57	75	67
80	88	76	84	48	86
77	69	84	83	89	77
56	72	71	27	48	90

Group *B*					
48	66	50	65	75	48
47	53	99	79	53	79
67	75	76	69	75	62
75	54	69	78	48	96
76	75	76	67	89	84
					92

(*a*) Determine the posterior distribution of the difference in means $\delta = \theta_A - \theta_B$, assuming the variances of the two groups are equal but unknown. To determine the prior, combine m_{S_A} and m_{S_B} so that you have a combined hypothetical sample size of 30 for the standard deviation.

(*b*) Determine the 50% HDR for δ posterior to the data.

(*c*) Find the posterior probability that $\delta > 2$.

3 Using the data and the prior of Exercise 8-4.2:

(*a*) Determine the posterior distribution of the difference in means, ignoring the prior information that the variances of the two groups are equal.

(*b*) Determine the 50% HDR for δ in this distribution and compare it with the one obtained in 8-4.2*b*. Which interval is longer and why?

4 Using the data of Exercise 8-4.2:

(*a*) Determine the posterior distribution of the difference in means, assuming uniform priors on θ_A, θ_B, $\ln \sigma_A$, and $\ln \sigma_B$. As in Exercise 8-4.2, assume the variances of the two groups are equal but unknown.

(*b*) Determine the 50% HDR for δ in this distribution and compare it with 8-4.2*b* and 8-4.3*b*. Explain the differences.

(*c*) Determine the posterior probability that $|\delta| > 2$ and compare this result with those obtained in 8-4.2*c*. Explain the differences.

5 Using the data in Exercise 8-4.2:

(*a*) Determine the posterior distribution of the difference in means, as in Exercise 8-4.4, only this time do not assume that the variances are equal.

(*b*) Determine the 50% HDR for δ in this distribution and compare it with 8-4.2*b*, 8-4.3*b*, and 8-4.4*b*. Explain the differences.

6 In Exercise 7-13.11*a* and *b* we presented some evidence about a new method for teaching remedial reading. With the old method, considerable evidence has been gathered over the past 5 years of use. On the basis of this experience, we are able to estimate the average student's increment after one year in the old program by a $t(900, 2.5, .6)$ distribution.

(*a*) On the basis of the data given in Exercise 7-13.11*a* and *b*, estimate the probability that the new method increases the average increment by at least .5 years over the old average. Assume unknown, possibly unequal, variances for the two methods.

(*b*) Using the following loss function, estimate the expected loss under the "change" and "no-change" actions.

$$\text{Loss} = \begin{cases} 5 & \text{if } \delta < 0 \text{ and change} \\ 3 & \text{if } 0 < \delta < .5 \text{ and change} \\ 7 & \text{if } .5 < \delta \text{ and no change} \\ 0 & \text{otherwise.} \end{cases}$$

Compare these estimates with those obtained in 7-13.11*c*. Why should you expect to find differences?

7 The following table gives the values of the cephalic index found in two random samples of skulls.

Sample I: 74.1, 77.7, 74.4, 74.0, 73.8,
79.3, 75.8, 82.8, 72.2, 75.2,
78.2, 77.1, 78.4, 76.3, 76.8

Sample II: 70.8, 74.9, 74.2, 70.4, 69.2,
72.2, 76.8, 72.4, 77.4, 78.1,
72.8, 74.3, 74.7

If it is known that the distribution of cephalic indices for a homogeneous population is normal, test the following points:

(*a*) Is the observed variation in the first sample consistent with the hypothesis that the standard deviation in the population from which it has been drawn is 3.0?

(*b*) Is it probable that the second sample came from a population which has a mean cephalic index of 72.0?

(*c*) Reconsider (*b*) assuming that it is known that the two samples are obtained from populations having the same but unknown variance.

(*d*) Obtain the 90% credibility interval for the ratio (ϕ_2/ϕ_1) of the variances of the populations from which the two samples are derived.

9

REGRESSION AND THE BIVARIATE NORMAL MODEL

In this chapter, we provide methods of Bayesian inference which may be appropriate when the sample data consist of pairs (x, y) of observations on each person or sampling unit. In Sec. 9-1, we discuss the linear-regression model. This requires no random sampling assumption with respect to the x values, and so may also be useful when the x's are predetermined or selected by the experimenter. To study *correlations,* however, we are required to have randomly sampled pairs (x, y) and to use a bivariate model. This is the subject of Sec. 9-2, which is based on the bivariate normal model. In Sec. 9-3, we study the difference of the (population) means of correlated observations, which in some contexts may be interpretable as the mean gain due to training or treatment. The model used is the same as in Sec. 9-2. Finally, in Secs. 9-4 to 9-6, we provide methods for comparing whole sets of normal means, using techniques having their genesis in the classical theory of mental testing as exposited in Sec. 4-7.

9-1 LINEAR-REGRESSION MODEL

In Secs. 1-1 and 1-2, we considered the problem of predicting the value of a *criterion* variable y (say, college GPA) from knowledge of a related *predictor* variable x (say, ACT score). We saw there how to find the linear prediction function which best fits data points $(x_1, y_1), (x_2, y_2), \ldots, (x_n, y_n)$, in the sense of minimizing the mean-squared error of prediction. Then in Secs. 4-2 and 4-3, we studied the idea of *regression* (conditional expectation), and noted that the regression function might, or might not, be linear.

In this section, we bring these two ideas together, and show how to make inferences using a model which asserts that the true regression function of Y on x *is* linear,

$$\mathcal{E}(Y|x) = \alpha + \beta x, \qquad (9\text{-}1.1)$$

and that the regression is *homoscedastic;* that is

$$\mathcal{V}(Y|x) = \phi, \qquad (9\text{-}1.2)$$

where ϕ is the same for all x. We shall also assume that the *residual*

$$Y - \mathcal{E}(Y|x) = Y - (\alpha + \beta x)$$

is normally distributed (for fixed α, β, and x). It follows immediately from (9-1.1) and (9-1.2) that the mean and variance of the distribution of the residual are zero and ϕ, respectively. For this reason, ϕ is often referred to as the (population) *residual variance*.

As with any other model, the reasonableness of the assumptions must be considered in relation to each particular application of the model which we wish to make. In many educational measurement situations, for example that shown in Table 2-1.8, we may feel that the assumptions sufficiently well approximate the underlying state of affairs–note, for example, in Table 2-1.8 that the standard deviations are very similar for most values of ACT composite score x (homoscedasticity) and that a plot of mean college GPA against ACT score is nearly linear. As is often the case, the assumptions are least plausible for extreme values of the predictor variables, but since relatively few persons have scores at these extremes, our inference procedures should be little affected. We may, however, wish to exercise caution when making predicitions for persons with extreme predictor scores.

We shall continue to refer to x as the *predictor* and y as the *criterion*, reflecting the use to which the model is most commonly put. Outside the field of educational and psychological measurement, the names *independent variable* and *dependent variable* are often used for x and y respectively, but in our context, this nomenclature is not useful and may even be misleading since "independent" here has nothing to do with "independence" as applied to random variables.

It is of some importance in data gathering and estimation of parameters to note that the model says nothing whatever about the nature of the variable x. Sometimes x will itself be a random variable, as when our data consist of pairs (x, y) of scores for randomly sampled persons. However, it is also open to us to select certain values of x in advance and sample randomly from among persons having the prescribed x scores to obtain the pairs (x, y) which constitute our data—we shall see later that this may be a more efficient procedure.

It is also important to note that the model may be appropriate for a number of different reasons, making it difficult to reconcile statements on this subject found in different texts. In contexts more commonly encountered in the physical sciences than in the social sciences, there may be a *deterministic* linear relation, $\eta = \alpha + \beta\xi$ between η and a variable ξ which can be measured with no (appreciable) error (e.g., the temperature at which a machine is set to operate); however, η cannot be directly observed and the actual observations are of a random variable Y having "true-score" η and error variance ϕ. In this case, the model will apply to the regression of Y on ξ. For this reason, texts oriented towards industrial applications will often imply (or even state) that the predictor *must* be a variable measured without error if the model is to apply. This statement is imprecise and possibly misleading. The model may apply equally well when the pair (x, y) have a bivariate distribution of the type exhibited in Table 2-1.8. Here the ACT score x is an observed score, not a true-score, and in that sense contains "error". Nevertheless, the regression model looks very reasonable for this situation. The point to bear in mind is that what we obtain from our analysis in this case is a linear prediction function for predicting college GPA from *observed* ACT score, *not* an idealized deterministic relationship between "true-GPA" and ACT true-score. Measurement without error is required only for this second purpose.

The Model and the Indifference Prior

We can state our model in a slightly different form. Conditional on α, β, ϕ, and x,

$$Y : N(\alpha + \beta x, \phi) . \qquad (9\text{-}1.3)$$

Note that the model density and, hence, our inference procedure is conditional on the particular x value(s) we use, whether prescribed or arising randomly. In one sense this is obvious. If we were so foolish as to make observations on Y only for two very similar values of x, it is intuitively clear that our estimates of the regression line would be very imprecise—many different regression lines would provide a good fit to our sample points. However, there is one interesting consequence for Bayesian inference. Since the whole analysis is conditional on the x values used, a Bayesian may take account of these values when specifying his prior distribution for the parameters. Having drawn attention to this fact here, we henceforth suppress reference to the conditioning on x in our notation.

The model density is

$$m_{\alpha,\beta,\phi}(y) = \frac{1}{(2\pi\phi)^{1/2}} \exp\left[\frac{-1}{2\phi}(y - \alpha - \beta x)^2\right], \qquad (9\text{-}1.4)$$

and so the likelihood function for n independent observations at x values $x_1, x_2, \ldots, x_n$ is proportional to

$$\frac{1}{\phi^{n/2}} \exp\left[\frac{-1}{2\phi}\sum (y_i - \alpha - \beta x_i)^2\right]. \qquad (9\text{-}1.5)$$

We shall initially carry out the analysis using independent indifference priors, uniform for α and β (which have range $-\infty$ to ∞) and log-uniform for ϕ (which has range 0 to ∞). Later, we shall show how to incorporate prior information. Thus, we take

$$\begin{aligned} b(\alpha,\beta,\phi) &= b(\alpha)\, b(\beta)\, b(\phi) \\ &\propto \phi^{-1}. \end{aligned} \qquad (9\text{-}1.6)$$

The posterior distribution will be found by multiplying together (9-1.5) and (9-1.6). The analysis can be considerably simplified by making a transformation which is equivalent to a change of origin for x. We write

$$\alpha = \alpha^* - \beta x_\bullet \qquad (9\text{-}1.7)$$

where $x_\bullet = n^{-1}\Sigma x_i$. Thus, α^* is the ordinate of the regression line at the point $x_\bullet$, whereas α is the ordinate at the origin (see Fig. 9-1.1). Then by a series of steps similar to the work we did in Sec. 1-2, we can rearrange the summation in (9-1.5) as follows:

$$\begin{aligned} \Sigma(y_i - \alpha - \beta x_i)^2 &= \Sigma[y_i - \alpha^* - \beta(x_i - x_\bullet)]^2 \\ &= \Sigma[(y_i - y_\bullet) - \beta(x_i - x_\bullet)]^2 + n(y_\bullet - \alpha^*)^2 \\ &= S_y^2 - 2\beta S_{xy} + \beta^2 S_x^2 + n(\alpha^* - y_\bullet)^2 \\ &= n(\alpha^* - y_\bullet)^2 + S_x^2\left(\beta - \frac{S_{xy}}{S_x^2}\right)^2 + S^2 \end{aligned} \qquad (9\text{-}1.8)$$

where

$$\begin{aligned} S_x^2 &= \Sigma(x_i - x_\bullet)^2, \\ S_y^2 &= \Sigma(y_i - y_\bullet)^2, \\ S_{xy} &= \Sigma(x_i - x_\bullet)(y_i - y_\bullet), \\ S^2 &= S_y^2 - \frac{S_{xy}^2}{S_x^2}. \end{aligned} \qquad (9\text{-}1.9)$$

The four steps in the above manipulation are: (1) substitute for α from (9-1.7); (2) use the general result that the sum of the squares of n quantities is equal to the sum of the squares of their differences from their own mean plus n times the square of that mean; (3) expand the term in brackets and perform the summation; (4) "complete the square"–

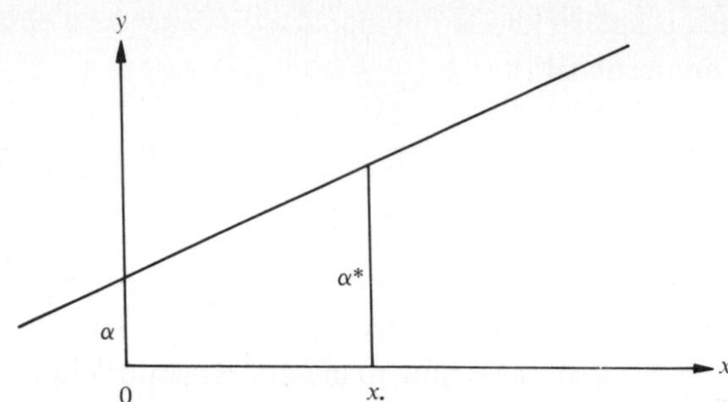

FIGURE 9-1.1
A regression line.

compare (1-2.6). Note, in passing, that we have shown that a set of sufficient statistics is n, $y_\bullet$, S_x^2, S_{xy}, and S_y^2, or equivalently, n, $y_\bullet$, S_x^2, S_{xy}, and S^2.

Next, we note that the prior distribution of α^*, β, and ϕ is also

$$b(\alpha^*, \beta, \phi) \propto \phi^{-1}. \qquad (9\text{-}1.10)$$

The formal proof of this requires an extension of the work on transformations in the starred portion of Sec. 3-4. (Any reader with a knowledge of advanced calculus can verify that the Jacobian of the transformation is constant.) However, a simpler argument is that we could have expressed our model in terms of α^* in the first place.

The Posterior Distributions

Multiplying (9-1.5) by (9-1.10) and making use of (9-1.8), we find the joint posterior density of the three parameters,

$$b_n(\alpha^*, \beta, \phi) \propto \frac{1}{\phi^{(n/2)+1}} \exp\left\{\frac{-1}{2\phi}[n(\alpha^* - y_\bullet)^2 + S_x^2(\beta - \hat{\beta})^2 + S^2]\right\} \qquad (9\text{-}1.11)$$

where for notational convenience we have written

$$\hat{\beta} = \frac{S_{xy}}{S_x^2}. \qquad (9\text{-}1.12)$$

The *joint mode* for the set (α^*, β, ϕ) is

$$\left(y_\bullet, \hat{\beta}, \frac{S^2}{n+2}\right). \qquad (9\text{-}1.13)$$

The *a posteriori correlations* between α^* and β, α^* and ϕ, β and ϕ, are *all zero*:

$$\rho(\alpha^*, \beta) = \rho(\alpha^*, \phi) = \rho(\beta, \phi) = 0. \qquad (9\text{-}1.14)$$

This is one of the benefits gained by expressing the model in terms of α^*.

If we write (9-1.11) as

$$b_n(\alpha^*, \beta, \phi) \propto \frac{1}{\phi^{(n/2)+1}} \exp\left[\frac{n(\alpha^* - y_{\bullet})^2}{-2\phi}\right] \exp\left[\frac{S_x^2(\beta - \hat{\beta})^2}{-2\phi}\right] \exp\left(\frac{-S^2}{2\phi}\right),$$

and then take ϕ to have a *fixed* value, the first and last terms in the product are simply constants. Hence, we find that the joint density of α^* and β, *given* ϕ is proportional to

$$\exp\left[\frac{n(\alpha^* - y_{\bullet})^2}{-2\phi}\right] \exp\left[\frac{S_x^2(\beta - \hat{\beta})^2}{-2\phi}\right].$$

Now this is the product of two terms, one involving the parameter α^* only, and the other involving β only (remember ϕ is fixed). Hence, α^* and β are conditionally independent, given ϕ. Moreover, each term of the product is recognizable as the kernel of a normal density function. Thus we have the following:

Conditional on ϕ, α^* and β are a posteriori independent with

$$\alpha^* : N(y_{\bullet}, n^{-1}\phi) \qquad (9\text{-}1.15)$$

and

$$\beta : N(\hat{\beta}, S_x^{-2}\phi). \qquad (9\text{-}1.16)$$

The simplicity of this result is another benefit of our transformation of the parameters.

The *marginal* distributions of the three parameters are

$$\alpha^* : t(n - 2, y_{\bullet}, n^{-1}S^2), \qquad (9\text{-}1.17)$$

$$\beta : t(n - 2, \hat{\beta}, S_x^{-2}S^2), \qquad (9\text{-}1.18)$$

and

$$\phi : \chi^{-2}(n - 2, S^2). \qquad (9\text{-}1.19)$$

The last result has to be found by integration of the joint distribution. However, some readers may like to verify that, assuming (9-1.19) to be true, the marginal distributions (9-1.17) and (9-1.18) follow from the conditional distributions (9-1.15) and (9-1.16) by using the general result (7-11.2).

From (9-1.17) through (9-1.19), and the properties of the t and χ^{-2} distributions, it follows that the marginal means of α^*, β, and ϕ are $y_{\bullet}$, $\hat{\beta}$, and $S^2/(n - 4)$ and hence the joint mean of (α^*, β, ϕ) is

$$\left(y_{\bullet}, \hat{\beta}, \frac{S^2}{n - 4}\right), \qquad (9\text{-}1.20)$$

which differs not greatly from the joint mode (9-1.13). Thus, for a variety of loss functions our point estimates will be:

For β: $$\hat{\beta} = \frac{S_{xy}}{S_x^2}, \qquad (9\text{-}1.21)$$

For α^*: $$y_{\bullet}, \qquad (9\text{-}1.22)$$

For $\alpha = \alpha^* - \beta x_{\bullet}$: $$y_{\bullet} - \hat{\beta} x_{\bullet}, \qquad (9\text{-}1.23)$$

For ϕ: $$\text{approximately, } n^{-1}S^2. \qquad (9\text{-}1.24)$$

The reader may already have noticed the similarity of these results to those obtained in Sec. 1-2 for the straight line which best fits the data—compare (9-1.21) with (1-2.12), (9-1.23) with (1-2.13). This line is often referred to as the *sample* regression line, in contrast to the line $\alpha + \beta x$ of our model which is the (true) *population* regression line. Thus, our results so far have established that *in the absence of prior information,* our estimate of the population regression line will, for many loss functions, be the sample regression line. Note also that S^2 is just the sum of squared errors about the sample regression line—compare (1-2.9).

A further feature of the posterior marginal distributions is worth comment. The degrees of freedom in each case are determined by the sample size n; also, the scale factor in the distribution of α^* is n^{-1} times the sample residual sum of squares. Thus, the only action we can take to improve our estimates of α^* and ϕ (apart from incorporating prior information) is to increase the sample size n. The case of β is different, however. Here the scale factor of the t distribution is S^2/S_x^2 with $S_x^2 = \Sigma(x_i - x_{\bullet})^2$. We noted earlier that, if our experimental situation permits, we can choose the x values in any way we please. Clearly, for fixed n, we should choose them to make S_x^2 large, that is, take them widely spread. This is the converse of our earlier remark that it would be foolish to choose only two very similar x values. *In theory,* the best estimation of β would be achieved by making half of our observations at each extreme of the range of x. *In practice,* this would be unwise for two reasons. First, we have noted that our model may not hold for such extreme values; and second, our data would then give us no warning if the linear regression assumption was unsatisfactory. Nevertheless, this discussion does suggest that when possible, a planned experiment with the x values well spread from their mean will be more efficient than an experiment where the x values arise randomly, and so will tend to cluster around their mean.

Another posterior distribution which may be of interest is that of the ordinate, α_0 say, of the population regression line at any particular point x_0. We can find it as follows. We have

$$\alpha_0 = \alpha + \beta x_0 = \alpha^* + \beta(x_0 - x_{\bullet}). \qquad (9\text{-}1.25)$$

Conditional on ϕ, α^* and β have the independent distributions given by (9-1.15) and (9-1.16), and so, using (8-1.1), (8-1.2), and the result given there, α_0 is normally distributed with mean

$$\mathcal{E}(\alpha_0) = \mathcal{E}(\alpha^*) + (x_0 - x_\bullet)\mathcal{E}(\beta) = y_\bullet + \hat{\beta}(x_0 - x_\bullet) \quad (9\text{-}1.26)$$

and variance

$$\mathcal{V}(\alpha_0) = \mathcal{V}(\alpha^*) + (x_0 - x_\bullet)^2\mathcal{V}(\beta) = \left[\frac{1}{n} + \frac{(x_0 - x_\bullet)^2}{S_x^2}\right]\phi. \quad (9\text{-}1.27)$$

Combining this result with the marginal distribution (9-1.19) of ϕ by means of the general result (7-11.2), we find that, marginally,

$$\alpha_0 : t\left\{n - 2, y_\bullet + \hat{\beta}(x_0 - x_\bullet), \left[\frac{1}{n} + \frac{(x_0 - x_\bullet)^2}{S_x^2}\right]S^2\right\}. \quad (9\text{-}1.28)$$

In particular, the ordinate α at $x = 0$ has distribution

$$\alpha : t\left[n - 2, y_\bullet - \hat{\beta}x_\bullet, \left(\frac{1}{n} + \frac{x_\bullet^2}{S_x^2}\right)S^2\right]. \quad (9\text{-}1.29)$$

The distribution (9-1.28) enables us to find, for any given x_0, a central 50% (say) credibility interval for α_0. Note that the midpoint of this interval will lie on the sample regression line, and that the length of the interval will be least when $x_0 = x_\bullet$ and increase as x_0 moves away from $x_\bullet$ in either direction [because of the term $(x_0 - x_\bullet)^2$ in the scale factor of the t distribution]. A useful diagrammatic representation of the situation is obtained by drawing the sample regression line R and a selection of curves giving the endpoints B_1, B_2 and A_1, A_2 of C% credibility intervals, as illustrated in Fig. 9-1.2.

The Predictive Distribution

It will often be the case that none of the distributions so far derived is the one of real interest. If our purpose is to *predict* Y from x, the relevant distribution is the predictive distribution for an $(n + 1)$th observation Y_{n+1} made when $x = x_{n+1}$ (some *known* value). By arguments similar in nature to those used to derive (9-1.28), this can be shown to be

$$Y_{n+1}: t\left\{n - 2, y_\bullet + \hat{\beta}(x_{n+1} - x_\bullet), \left[1 + \frac{1}{n} + \frac{(x_{n+1} - x_\bullet)^2}{S_x^2}\right]S^2\right\}. \quad (9\text{-}1.30)$$

Again, the midpoint of a central credibility interval lies on the sample regression line, and such intervals are shortest when $x_{n+1} = x_\bullet$. A diagram similar to Fig. 9-1.2 can be drawn to indicate the accuracy of prediction which we can achieve. Note that because of

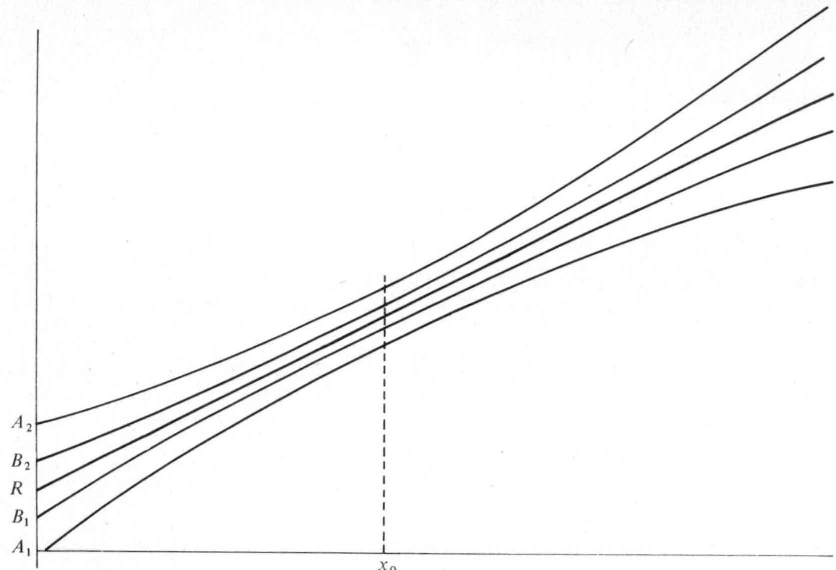

FIGURE 9-1.2
Graph of 75 and 90% credibility intervals for α_0 at various values of x_0. R is the sample regression line at which α_0 is centered. For any value of x_0, α_0 lies with probability .75 between curves B_1 and B_2 at x_0 and with probability .99 between curves A_1 and A_2 at x_0.

the additional term in the scale factor of (9-1.30) as compared with (9-1.28), credibility intervals for Y_{n+1} will be longer than those for the corresponding ordinate of the regression line.

Indeed, for heuristic purposes, the length of the predictive interval can usefully be assigned to various "causes". The fact that we have a t distribution with longer intervals than the corresponding normal distribution is due to our uncertainty about ϕ. The terms S^2/n and $(x_{n+1} - x_\bullet)^2 S^2/S_x^2$ in the scale factor of (9-1.30) arise from our uncertainty about α^* and β respectively—note that they occur also in (9-1.28). The remaining term S^2 in the scale factor represents the inescapable uncertainty about the next observation Y which is still present even when α, β, and ϕ are very precisely estimated and x is observed.

Incorporation of Prior Information

There is a close similarity between some of the results we have obtained while analyzing the regression model using indifference priors and those we obtained in Sec. 7-6 for the two-parameter normal model. Compare, for example, the posterior marginal distributions of ϕ in the two cases, and the posterior conditional distribution (9-1.15) for α^* with that for θ given in (7-6.9). Indeed, it is possible to regard the two-parameter normal model as a limiting case of the regression model in which all the observations are made for a single fixed value x (of course, β cannot then be estimated).

This suggests that it may be possible to extend to the present model the hypothetical-preliminary-sample methods of quantifying prior information which we developed in Secs. 7-7 through 7-9. Before pursuing this suggestion, however, we must give a little more thought to our results concerning ordinates of the regression line. We have seen that, using indifference priors, β and α^* are a posteriori independent, given ϕ. This is *not* true of β and the ordinate α_0 at any point x_0 other than $x_0 = x_{\bullet}$. Indeed, if β and α^* are independent, and hence uncorrelated, we have

$$\begin{aligned} \mathcal{C}(\beta,\alpha_0) &= \mathcal{C}[\beta, \alpha^* + \beta(x_0 - x_{\bullet})] \\ &= \mathcal{C}(\beta,\alpha^*) + (x_0 - x_{\bullet})\mathcal{C}(\beta,\beta) \qquad \text{(by 4-1.7)} \\ &= (x_0 - x_{\bullet})\mathcal{V}(\beta), \qquad [\text{since } \mathcal{C}(\beta,\alpha^*) = 0] \end{aligned}$$

which is not zero except in the case $x_0 = x_{\bullet}$ already noted, or the trivial case $\mathcal{V}(\beta) = 0$ when β does not vary (is completely known) and so nothing can co-vary with it. And if β and α_0 are correlated, they certainly cannot be independent.

The upshot of this discussion is that if we wish to quantify our prior information by saying that β and some ordinate α_0 are a priori independent, given ϕ, we must name the point x_0 at which this is true. It will almost always be inappropriate to make the statement for the ordinate at the origin of an unscaled score x, since such an origin is usually devoid of educational or psychological significance. If the x values are randomly sampled from some distribution, it may often be appropriate to specify the independence of β and the ordinate at the mean of this distribution. On the other hand, we may proceed by first finding the mean $x_{\bullet}$ of the x values in our actual sample (recall that we are fully entitled to do this *before* making our prior specifications for α, β, and ϕ), and then consider whether, in the light of the foregoing discussion, it is in reasonable accord with our prior knowledge to take β independent (given ϕ) of the ordinate α^* at this point. When this is the case, the resulting algebra is considerably simplified, so we treat this case first.

First Procedure

We can use the method of Sec. 7-9 to assess a prior marginal distribution for $\sigma = \phi^{1/2}$, where σ is now the standard deviation of the *residuals* (the vertical distances between sample points and the true regression line). There will be one very slight difference of detail. Since the posterior distribution (9-1.19) for ϕ is equivalent to saying that $\sigma : \chi^{-1}(n - 2, S)$, when we have specified the modal estimate $\tilde{\sigma}$ and the number m_S of observations our prior knowledge is worth, we shall equate this to a prior distribution

$$\sigma : \chi^{-1}(m_S - 2, R)$$

where

$$R^2 = (m_S - 1)\tilde{\sigma}^2 . \qquad (9\text{-}1.31)$$

Next, just as in Sec. 7-9, we assess normal distributions for β and the ordinate α^* at $x_{\bullet}$, assuming that σ has our modal value $\tilde{\sigma}$. Recall that we are here supposing that it is consistent with our prior knowledge to take these two distributions as independent, given σ (or ϕ). Let the assessed distributions be $N(\tilde{\mu}_\beta, \tilde{\sigma}_\beta^2)$ and $N(\tilde{\mu}_\alpha, \tilde{\sigma}_\alpha^2)$, respectively. By analogy with (9-1.15) and (9-1.16), we suppose

$$\tilde{\mu}_\beta = \frac{R_{wv}}{R_w^2} \qquad \tilde{\sigma}_\beta^2 = R_w^{-2}\tilde{\sigma}^2$$

$$\tilde{\mu}_\alpha = v_{\bullet} \qquad \tilde{\sigma}_\alpha^2 = m_\alpha^{-1}\tilde{\sigma}^2$$

and so we define

$$v_{\bullet} = \tilde{\mu}_\alpha \qquad (9\text{-}1.32)$$

$$m_\alpha = \frac{\tilde{\sigma}^2}{\tilde{\sigma}_\alpha^2} \qquad (9\text{-}1.33)$$

$$R_w^2 = \frac{\tilde{\sigma}^2}{\tilde{\sigma}_\beta^2} \qquad (9\text{-}1.34)$$

$$R_{wv} = \frac{\tilde{\mu}_\beta \tilde{\sigma}^2}{\tilde{\sigma}_\beta^2} . \qquad (9\text{-}1.35)$$

If $m_S = m_\alpha = m$, what we have done in Eqs. (9-1.31) through (9-1.35) is to equate our prior knowledge to a hypothetical sample of m pairs (w, v)—note the order—with sufficient statistics

$$m,\ v_{\bullet},\ R_w^2,\ R_{wv},\ \text{and } R^2 .$$

If, on the other hand, we take $m_S > m_\alpha$, we have equated our prior knowledge to a hypothetical sample of size m_α together with additional information about the residual variance ϕ (or σ). The logical basis for this is exactly the same as in the two-parameter normal case—see the end of Sec. 7-7.

With the above prior specification, the various posterior distributions are of exactly the same forms as those already obtained. We need to make certain substitutions. These are given in Table 9-1.1 where all references are to results in *this* section and so we have abbreviated (9-1.17) to (17) and so on.

Now let us proceed slowly and systematically to construct a prior distribution for the analysis of the data given in Fig. 1-1.1 regarding the pairs of observations as relating to ten students randomly sampled from some college of interest. We have not given the kind of background information required to do this with any justification, and as a result, we shall have to introduce some "out of the air" judgments. One way of proceeding is to begin by considering the five parameters σ_Y, σ_X, ρ, β, and σ, and specifying coherence point estimates of these quantities. One might start, for example, with the specifications:

$$\sigma_Y = .7, \quad \sigma_X = 8, \quad \rho = .5, \quad \beta = .08, \quad \sigma = .4 .$$

To test coherence, we consider the relations

$$\beta = \rho \frac{\sigma_Y}{\sigma_X} \quad \text{and} \quad \sigma = \sigma_Y \sqrt{1 - \rho^2},$$

which originally appeared as (4-3.8) and (4-3.9). Substituting, we have

$$.08 \stackrel{?}{=} (.5) \frac{(.7)}{(8)} \quad \text{and} \quad .4 \stackrel{?}{=} (.7)\sqrt{1 - .5^2},$$

which unfortunately yields

$$.08 \neq .044 \quad \text{and} \quad .4 \neq .606 .$$

Clearly, our joint specification is incoherent. Some study indicates that our evaluation of

Table 9-1.1 POSTERIOR VALUES FOR SIMPLE LINEAR REGRESSION WITH PRIOR INFORMATION

Replace	By	In
df $(n - 2)$	$m_S + n - 2$	(17), (18), (19), (28), (29), (30)
$(n + 2)$	$m_S + n + 2$	(13)
$(n - 4)$	$m_S + n - 4$	(20)
n	m_S	(24) *only*
$y_\bullet$	$(m_\alpha v_\bullet + n y_\bullet)/(m_\alpha + n)$	(13), (15), (17), (20), (22), (23), (28), (29), (30)
$\hat{\beta}$	$(R_{wv} + S_{xy})/(R_w^2 + S_x^2)$	(13), (16), (18), (20), (21), (23), (28), (29), (30)
S^2	$R^2 + S^2 + \dfrac{m_\alpha n}{m_\alpha + n}(v_\bullet - y_\bullet)^2 + \dfrac{R_w^2 S_x^2}{R_w^2 + S_x^2}\left(\dfrac{R_{wv}}{R_w^2} - \dfrac{S_{xy}}{S_x^2}\right)^2$	(13), (17), (18), (19), (20), (24), (28), (29), (30)
n^{-1} or $\dfrac{1}{n}$	$(m_\alpha + n)^{-1}$	(15), (17), (28), (29), (30)
S_x^{-2} or $\dfrac{1}{S_x^2}$	$(R_w^2 + S_x^2)^{-1}$	(16), (18), (28), (29), (30)

the correlation is much too low, relative to the values we have selected for the regression coefficient and the residual variance. Reconsideration prompts us to raise this estimate, say to .55. We then substitute this new value into the coherence relations, which gives

$$.08 \stackrel{?}{=} (.55)\frac{(.7)}{(8)} \quad \text{and} \quad .4 \stackrel{?}{=} (.7)\sqrt{1 - .55^2}$$

which yields $$.08 \neq .048 \quad \text{and} \quad .4 \neq .585\,.$$

Clearly, we have not made a substantial movement toward coherence in the first relation, though the situation looks somewhat better in the second relation. On reconsidering the first relation, we decide that our estimate of σ_X may be too high in the restricted population considered, and therefore lower it to $\sigma_X = 6$. We also raise our estimate of ρ to .57 and our estimate of σ to .5. We then have

$$.08 \stackrel{?}{=} (.57)\frac{(.7)}{(6)} \quad \text{and} \quad .5 \stackrel{?}{=} (.7)\sqrt{1 - .57^2}$$

which yields $$.08 \neq .067 \quad \text{and} \quad .5 \neq .575$$

which is a substantial improvement. After some further reflection, which might be described as being of the form of "change your estimates where it hurts the least" we take $\sigma_X = 5$ and $\rho = .59$, which gives us

$$.08 \stackrel{?}{=} (.59)\frac{(.7)}{(5)} \quad \text{and} \quad .5 \stackrel{?}{=} (.7)\sqrt{1 - .59^2}$$

$$.08 \neq .083 \quad \text{and} \quad .5 \neq .565\,.$$

Strict equality has not yet been obtained, but we now decide the slight changes in β and σ are tolerable and so we state our final judgments as $\beta = .083$, $\sigma = .565$, $\rho = .59$, $\sigma_Y = .7$, and $\sigma_X = 5$, which are coherent.

In most applications, our judgment concerning the ordinate at the mean value of x in the population will not depend on our judgment concerning the slope. If the x values are randomly determined–not prespecified–then we can reasonably set our prior distribution for α at $x_\bullet$ independently of β. In the example, $x_\bullet = 20$. We now ask ourselves what level of performance we might expect at this college from a student whose ACT composite score is 20. A value of 2.5 comes to mind–reflecting a performance midway between C and B.

Given this value, we can now determine the intercept, α, at $x = 0$. We have

$$y = \alpha + \beta x_{\bullet\bullet}$$

Substituting the values $y = 2.5$, $x = 20$, and $\beta = .083$, we have

$$2.5 = \alpha + (.083)(20)$$

or $$\alpha = 2.5 - (.083)(20) = .84\,.$$

Our first reaction to this might be that we would not expect a person with an ACT composite score of zero to pass any courses, and hence, we feel quite confident that his GPA would be zero. This might well be true, if indeed such a person were to be admitted to college; however, the behavior of the regression line below the x level required for admission is irrelevant. In fact, one does not expect linearity of regression below that level, for reasons discussed in Chap. 1.

It seems more relevant to consider y values at several values of x that are important for the particular college. Three such values could be $x = 10$, 20, and 30, for which the predicted y values would be $y = 1.67$, 2.5, and 3.33. Perhaps these values are reasonable; perhaps they are not. If they are not, then a decision must be made whether a change in α or a change in β, or both, will be required. A change in α will raise or lower these y values by a constant amount. An increment in β will raise the y value for $x = 30$ and lower the y value for $x = 10$. If a change is made in β, then the specifications for ρ, σ_Y, σ_X, and possibly σ must also be considered. Coherence must be maintained. For the present example, we shall assume that the computed values of y for $x = 10$, 20, and 30 are acceptable, and we therefore consider the task of specifying prior point estimates for the six parameters as being completed.

We might remark that a good way of getting initial estimates of β and α is to plot three y points for carefully selected values of x, adjust these to obtain strict linearity, and then determine α, the intercept at $x = 0$. The slope β is then obtained as the tangent of the angle between the regression line and the x axis. This can be computed given any two pairs of x, y values by the formula,

$$\beta = \frac{y_2 - y_1}{x_2 - x_1}.$$

For the present example, we take the points (30,3.33) and (20,2.5), and thus

$$\beta = \frac{3.33 - 2.5}{30 - 20} = .083.$$

We are now in a position to fit prior distributions to the parameters of the model. We begin with the residual standard deviation. The mode of our a priori distribution is .565. Using (9-1.31), we write

$$\begin{aligned} R^2 &= (m_S - 1)\tilde{\sigma}^2 \\ &= (m_S - 1)(.319225). \end{aligned}$$

A value of 10 comes to mind for m_S, which would give us an inverse chi distribution on 8 degrees of freedom. The 50% HDR credibility interval for a standardized inverse chi distribution on 8 degrees of freedom extends from .2820 to .4023. The value of the scale parameter is

$$\lambda^{1/2} = R = \sqrt{9(.319225)} = 1.695.$$

Thus, the 50% HDR credibility interval for σ extends from (.2820)(1.695) to

(.4023)(1.695), that is, from .478 to .682. This seems reasonable and so we accept $\chi^{-1}(8, 1.695)$ as our prior distribution for σ.

Now let us specify a prior distribution for β conditional on σ being equal to its modal value $\sigma = .565$. The distribution in question is $N(\tilde{\mu}_\beta, \tilde{\sigma}_\beta^2)$ and we have already decided that $\tilde{\mu}_\beta = .083$. To determine $\tilde{\sigma}_\beta^2$, we first specify an interval around $\tilde{\mu}_\beta$ that, for us, has .50 probability content. In this example, such an interval might be (.063,.103). Thus, $.6745\ \tilde{\sigma}_\beta = .02$, and hence $\tilde{\sigma}_\beta = .02965$ and $\tilde{\sigma}_\beta^2 = .000879$. Rounded values would be $\tilde{\sigma}_\beta = .03$ and $\tilde{\sigma}_\beta^2 = .0009$. In the notation of this section, we have

$$\tilde{\sigma}^2 = .319, \quad \tilde{\mu}_\beta = \frac{R_{wv}^2}{R_w^2} = .083, \quad \text{and } \tilde{\sigma}_\beta^2 = R_w^{-2}\tilde{\sigma}^2 = .0009 .$$

Hence,

$$R_w^2 = \frac{\tilde{\sigma}^2}{\tilde{\sigma}_\beta^2} = \frac{.319}{.0009} = 354.44 ,$$

$$R_{wv} = R_w^2\tilde{\mu}_\beta = (354.55)(.083) = 29.42 .$$

Proceeding systematically, we now specify a prior distribution for α^*, the ordinate of $x_\bullet$, conditional on σ. The distribution in question is $N(\tilde{\mu}_\alpha, \tilde{\sigma}_\alpha^2)$ and we have already decided on the value 2.5 for $\tilde{\mu}_\alpha$. A 50% interval around this point might reasonably extend from 2.3 to 2.7. Thus, we have $.6745\ \tilde{\sigma}_\alpha = .2$ or $\tilde{\sigma}_\alpha = .3$, and $\tilde{\sigma}_\alpha^2 = .09$. Again, in the notation of this section, we have

$$v_\bullet = \tilde{\mu}_\alpha = 2.5, \quad m_\alpha = \frac{\tilde{\sigma}^2}{\tilde{\sigma}_\alpha^2} = \frac{.319}{.09} = 3.54 .$$

We note that m_α is substantially smaller than m_S, but we are not inclined to seek a compromise value, nor is there any necessity to insist on an integer value for m_α.

Now, having numerical values for m_S, $v_\bullet$, m_α, R_{wv}, R^2, and R_w^2 and having sample sufficient statistics n, $y_\bullet$, S_{xy}, S, S_x^2, we are prepared to enter Table 9-1.1 to obtain the parameters of our posterior distribution. From Chap. 1, we have $n = 10, y_\bullet = 2.57, S_{xy} = 23.7, S_x^2 = 240, S_y^2 = 6.641$, and $S = 2.073$.

Using the values from Table 9-1.1 in Eqs. (9-1.17) to (9-1.19), we have the following posterior marginal distributions.

For α^* (the intercept at $x = 20$):

$$t\left\{m_S + n - 2, \frac{m_\alpha v_\bullet + n y_\bullet}{m_\alpha + n}, \right.$$

$$\left.(m_\alpha + n)^{-1}\left[R^2 + S^2 + \frac{m_\alpha n}{m_\alpha + n}(v_\bullet - y_\bullet)^2 + \frac{R_w^2 S_x^2}{R_w^2 + S_x^2}\left(\frac{R_{wv}}{R_w^2} - \frac{S_{xy}}{S_x^2}\right)^2\right]\right\} .$$

For β:

$$t\left\{m_S + n - 2, \frac{R_{wv} + S_{xy}}{R_w^2 + S_x^2},\right.$$

$$\left.(R_w^2 + S_x^2)^{-1}\left[R^2 + S^2 + \frac{m_\alpha n}{m_\alpha + n}(v_{\bullet} - y_{\bullet})^2 + \frac{R_w^2 S_x^2}{R_w^2 + S_x^2}\left(\frac{R_{wv}}{R_w^2} - \frac{S_{xy}}{S_x^2}\right)^2\right]\right\}.$$

For ϕ:

$$\chi^{-2}\left\{m_S + n - 2, \left[R^2 + S^2 + \frac{m_\alpha n}{m_\alpha + n}(v_{\bullet} - y_{\bullet})^2 + \frac{R_w^2 S_x^2}{R_w^2 + S_x^2}\left(\frac{R_{wv}}{R_w^2} - \frac{S_{xy}}{S_x^2}\right)^2\right]\right\}.$$

Upon careful substitution, we obtain

$$\alpha^*: t(18, 2.552, .533)$$
$$\beta: t(18, .089, .012)$$
$$\phi: \chi^{-2}(18, 7.219).$$

The 50% central credibility interval for α^* extends from 2.434 to 2.669. The 50% central credibility interval for β extends from .071 to .107. The 50% HDR credibility interval for ϕ extends from .287 to .463. Taking the square root, we obtain $\sqrt{.287} = .536$ and $\sqrt{.463} = .680$. These values seem reasonable for $\phi^{1/2}$. Recall also that throughout this discussion $x_{\bullet}$ denotes the mean x value in the actual sample. We have here no concern with the mean $w_{\bullet}$ of w values in the hypothetical sample since we are, in effect, supposing it to be equal to $x_{\bullet}$. If we had a prior (hypothetical) sample of pairs of observations, we would naturally now take the prior sample mean $w_{\bullet}$ as the point at which our beliefs concerning α and β are independent.

Second Procedure[1]

If the previous subsection is inappropriate because our *prior* beliefs include the independence (given ϕ) of β and the ordinate at some specific point $w_{\bullet}$ different from the mean $x_{\bullet}$ of our actual sample, we must modify our analysis. This will certainly be *required* when the x values are prespecified rather than randomly obtained, for then the value $x_{\bullet}$ is not informative. The assessment of prior knowledge will now include the choice of the appropriate value for $w_{\bullet}$, but otherwise will be made exactly as in the first procedure above. The ordinate whose distribution is assessed will, of course, be the ordinate at $w_{\bullet}$.

[1] Reading of this subsection may be deferred without loss of continuity.

The posterior distributions, however, will not be presented in terms of the ordinate at $w_\bullet$, or in terms of the ordinate α^* at $x_\bullet$, but in terms of the ordinate α^{**} at the mean predictor value in the combined hypothetical and actual samples, namely, the point

$$\frac{m_\alpha w_\bullet + n x_\bullet}{m_\alpha + n}.$$

The forms of the posterior distributions will be exactly the same as previously, but we will need to make the following substitutions:

Replace	By	In
α^*	α^{**}	throughout
df $(n-2)$	$m_S + n - 2$	(17), (18), (19), (28), (29), (30)
$(n+2)$	$m_S + n + 2$	(13)
$(n-4)$	$m_S + n - 4$	(20)
n	$m_S + n$	(24) *only*
$y_\bullet$	$\dfrac{m_\alpha v_\bullet + n y_\bullet}{m_\alpha + n}$	(13), (15), (17), (20), (22), (23), (28), (29), (30)
$\hat{\beta}$	$\dfrac{R_{wv} + S_{xy} + \dfrac{m_\alpha n}{m_\alpha + n}(w_\bullet - x_\bullet)(v_\bullet - y_\bullet)}{R_w^2 + S_x^2 + \dfrac{m_\alpha n}{m_\alpha + n}(w_\bullet - x_\bullet)^2}$	(13), (16), (18), (20), (21), (23), (28), (29), (30)
S^2	$R^2 + S^2 + \dfrac{R_w^2 S_x^2}{R_w^2 + S_x^2}\left(\dfrac{R_{wv}}{R_w^2} - \dfrac{S_{xy}}{S_x^2}\right)^2 + \left[\dfrac{m_\alpha n(w_\bullet - x_\bullet)^2(R_w^2 + S_x^2)}{(m_\alpha + n)\left\{R_w^2 + S_x^2 + \dfrac{m_\alpha n}{m_\alpha + n}(w_\bullet - x_\bullet)^2\right\}} \left(\dfrac{R_{wv} + S_{xy}}{R_w^2 + S_x^2} - \dfrac{v_\bullet - y_\bullet}{w_\bullet - x_\bullet}\right)^2\right]$	(13), (17), (18), (19), (20), (24), (28), (29), (30)
n^{-1} or $\dfrac{1}{n}$	$(m_\alpha + n)^{-1}$	(15), (17), (28), (29), (30)
S_x^{-2} or $\dfrac{1}{S_x^2}$	$\left[R_w^2 + S_x^2 + \dfrac{m_\alpha n}{m_\alpha + n}(w_\bullet - x_\bullet)^2\right]^{-2}$	(16), (18), (28), (29), (30)
$x_\bullet$	$\dfrac{m_\alpha w_\bullet + n x_\bullet}{m_\alpha + n}$	(23), (28), (29), (30)

In spite of their formidable appearance, these substitutions are derived by the relatively straightforward process of taking the joint distribution analogous to (9-1.11) posterior to the hypothetical sample, multiplying it by the likelihood (9-1.5) rewritten using (9-1.8), and patiently applying high school algebra to the resulting exponent, making frequent use of the identity (6-3.7).

The difficulty in choosing an x value at which our beliefs about α and β are independent can be reduced by the following considerations. Let us suppose all of our prior information can be equated to a hypothetical prior bivariate normal sample (with an indifference prior preceding it). Further suppose that the (prior) sample regression line is

$$\hat{y} = v_{\bullet} + b(z - z_{\bullet}).$$

Clearly, for this sample line the only value of z for which the estimate $\hat{y}$ of y does not depend on b is the value $z = z_{\bullet}$. This *suggests* that following the incorporation of our prior information, we would have independence in our joint distribution of α and β only for $\alpha = \alpha(z_{\bullet})$, the intercept at $x = z_{\bullet}$. The meaningfulness of this heuristic argument is apparent on reference to (9-1.14), the statement immediately preceding (9-1.15) and the discussion in the subsection of 9-1 on the incorporation of prior information.

The result of this consideration is that in the presence of any material amount of prior information about θ_X, the mean of X, of the form stated above, it is *theoretically* necessary to take $z_{\bullet}$, our estimate of θ_X, as the x value for which our prior beliefs about β and α are independent. This is what has been done in the second procedure. Note, however, that in this procedure, as $m_\alpha \to 0$, the posterior point of independence tends to $x_{\bullet}$, which is coherent with the result obtained in the first procedure, where there was no prior information concerning θ_X and, in fact, it was not even meaningful to discuss this quantity. Thus, the first procedure can be considered as a useful simplification of the second procedure that will be useful whenever the real sample size is large compared to the hypothetical prior sample size.

9-2 CORRELATION IN THE BIVARIATE NORMAL MODEL

In this section and the following one, we are concerned with the situation in which our observations consist of pairs (x, y) randomly sampled from a bivariate distribution. For example, the data presented in Table 2-1.8 might be regarded as a large sample from the joint distribution of random variables X and Y, where X stands for ACT composite score and Y for college GPA.

A minimum requirement for a general model of this situation is that it shall include location and scale parameters for each of X and Y, and a parameter expressing their co-relatedness. The bivariate normal model which we study here involves *only* these five parameters. Nevertheless, a general treatment of inference using this model is algebraically complex without the use of matrices. We therefore focus attention on those results which are likely to be most useful in educational and psychological research. In this section, the emphasis is on the correlation coefficient.

The Model

The density function of the bivariate normal model depends on five parameters: the means θ_X and θ_Y, and the variances ϕ_X and ϕ_Y, of X and Y respectively, and the correlation ρ between X and Y. In the most usual research situation these parameters are all unknown, and we confine attention to that case. The model density is

$$m_{\theta_X,\theta_Y,\phi_X,\phi_Y,\rho}(x, y)$$

$$= \frac{1}{2\pi\{\phi_X\phi_Y(1-\rho^2)\}^{1/2}} \exp\left\{\frac{-1}{2(1-\rho^2)}\left[\frac{(x-\theta_X)^2}{\phi_X} - \frac{2\rho(x-\theta_X)(y-\theta_Y)}{\phi_X^{1/2}\phi_Y^{1/2}} + \frac{(y-\theta_Y)^2}{\phi_Y}\right]\right\}. \quad (9\text{-}2.1)$$

The algebraic complexity is already apparent, and the reader may find it hard to credit that this is one of the more tractable bivariate models.

As usual, the nature of the bivariate distribution is most easily comprehended in terms of its marginal and conditional distributions and some of its descriptive properties. The marginal distributions are:

$$X: N(\theta_X, \phi_X) \quad (9\text{-}2.2)$$

and

$$Y: N(\theta_Y, \phi_Y)\,. \quad (9\text{-}2.3)$$

The conditional distributions are

Given x, $$Y: N\left[\theta_Y + \rho\phi_Y^{1/2}\phi_X^{-1/2}(x-\theta_X),\ \phi_Y(1-\rho^2)\right] \quad (9\text{-}2.4)$$

Given y, $$X: N\left[\theta_X + \rho\phi_X^{1/2}\phi_Y^{-1/2}(y-\theta_Y),\ \phi_X(1-\rho^2)\right]. \quad (9\text{-}2.5)$$

The marginal distributions need no comment. The conditional distributions, however, have some important features. From (9-2.4) we see that the conditional expectation $\mathcal{E}(Y|x)$ is a linear function of x, in other words, the regression of Y on x is linear. In Sec. 4-3, we noted that when this is the case, the ideas of regression function and linear regression function coincide. Hence, we may use the notation of that section to express the properties of the conditional distributions in a more familiar form.

Analogously to (4-3.8), let

$$\beta_{Y\cdot x} = \rho\phi_Y^{1/2}\phi_X^{-1/2}, \beta_{X\cdot y} = \rho\phi_X^{1/2}\phi_Y^{-1/2}; \qquad (9\text{-}2.6)$$

these are the slopes of the lines of regression of Y on x and X on y, respectively. Then, from (9-2.4) we have

$$\mathcal{E}(Y|x) - \theta_Y = \beta_{Y\cdot x}(x - \theta_X), \qquad (9\text{-}2.7)$$

with a similar equation for $\mathcal{E}(X|y)$; compare this equation with the regression line (4-3.6). Also, let

$$\phi_{Y\cdot x} = \phi_Y(1 - \rho^2)$$

and

$$\phi_{X\cdot y} = \phi_X(1 - \rho^2) \qquad (9\text{-}2.8)$$

be the residual variances—compare (4-3.9). From (9-2.4) we have $\mathcal{V}(Y|x) = \phi_{Y\cdot x}$, which is the same for all x; in other words, the regression of Y on x is homoscedastic. Finally, we note from (9-2.4) that, given x, the *residual*

$$Y - \mathcal{E}(Y|x) \qquad (9\text{-}2.9)$$

is normally distributed with mean zero and variance $\phi_{Y\cdot x}$. Thus, we have seen that *the regression of Y on x is linear and homoscedastic, with normally distributed residuals* (likewise the regression of X on y).

Now linear, homoscedastic regression was precisely the model studied in Sec. 9-1. Hence, if our data are randomly sampled from a bivariate normal distribution, and our real interest lies in the regression of Y on x (or X on y), the regression analysis of the previous section applies and there may be no need to become involved with the more complex analysis required for the bivariate normal model.

One useful way of visualizing the bivariate normal distribution is by drawing contours of the density function, that is, curves in the (x,y) plane for which $m(x, y) =$ constant. An example is given in Fig. 9-2.1. The contours are a set of ellipses all having the same major and minor axes. Their center, the point (θ_X, θ_Y), is both the joint mean and the joint mode. When $|\rho|$ is large, the ellipses are long and thin, and as $|\rho| \to 1$ the contours converge on to the line

$$\frac{y - \theta_Y}{\phi_Y^{1/2}} = \frac{x - \theta_X}{\phi_X^{1/2}}$$

(i.e., the standardized x and y scores are equal), which then gives the exact linear relationship between x and y. The case shown in the Fig. 9-2.1 is for $\rho > 0$; if $\rho < 0$ the ellipses will appear to run from northwest to southeast.

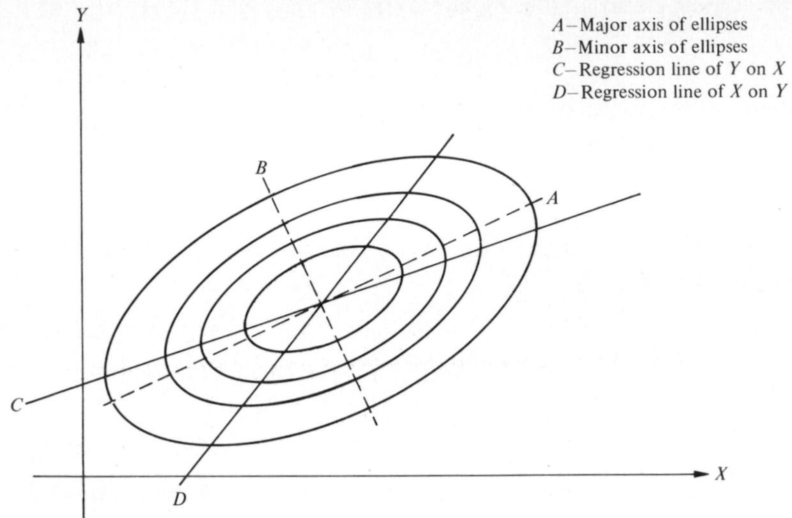

FIGURE 9-2.1
Contours of the bivariate normal distribution.

The regression lines can be determined geometrically on this "contour map" of the distribution. To find the regression line of Y on x, we draw tangents to any one of the ellipses parallel to the y axis. The line joining the points where they touch the ellipse is the required regression line. Similarly, we obtain the regression line of X on y by first drawing tangents parallel to the x axis. The two regression lines meet at the center of the ellipses.

Posterior Distributions Using an Indifference Prior

We shall first present some results of the analysis when an indifference prior is assumed, and then discuss how to incorporate prior information. The indifference prior we use here is equivalent to taking the usual independent uniform and log-uniform priors for θ_X, θ_Y, and ϕ_X, ϕ_Y, respectively, and an independent prior

$$b(\rho) \propto (1 - \rho^2)^{-3/2}. \qquad (9\text{-}2.10)$$

and ρ. Thus,

$$b(\theta_X, \theta_Y, \phi_X, \phi_Y, \rho) \propto \phi_X^{-1} \phi_Y^{-1} (1 - \rho^2)^{-3/2}. \qquad (9\text{-}2.11)$$

The prior (9-2.10) differs very slightly from the ignorance prior $b(\rho) \propto (1 - \rho^2)^{-1}$ proposed by Lindley in a work from which we shall shortly quote. However, the difference is of the order of only one observation on ρ.

Derivation of the joint posterior distribution of the five parameters and their marginal distributions involves much algebra and calculus, but no new matter of principle. We therefore suppress the details and list first some results which we shall require when we come to quantify prior information.

The a posteriori conditional distributions of the means are

Given ϕ_X, $$\theta_X : N(x_\bullet, n^{-1}\phi_X)\,, \qquad (9\text{-}2.12)$$

Given ϕ_Y, $$\theta_Y : N(y_\bullet, n^{-1}\phi_Y)\,, \qquad (9\text{-}2.13)$$

where as usual $x_\bullet = n^{-1}\Sigma x_i$ and $y_\bullet = n^{-1}\Sigma y_i$. These two results are exactly the same as we would have obtained by using indifference priors in the analysis of Sec. 7-1, and paying attention to the x scores (or y scores) only. The a posteriori marginal distributions, however, are

$$\theta_X : t(n - 2,\, x_\bullet,\, n^{-1}S_x^2)\,, \qquad (9\text{-}2.14)$$

and

$$\theta_Y : t(n - 2,\, y_\bullet,\, n^{-1}S_y^2)\,, \qquad (9\text{-}2.15)$$

where $S_x^2 = \Sigma(x_i - x_\bullet)^2$, $S_y^2 = \Sigma(y_i - y_\bullet)^2$. Note that the degrees of freedom here are $n - 2$, as contrasted with $n - 1$ for the marginal distribution of the mean of the two-parameter normal model.

A posteriori knowledge about the variances is most easily expressed in terms of the residual variances $\phi_{Y\cdot x}$ and $\phi_{X\cdot y}$ defined by (9-2.8), and related sample quantities. Let

$$S_{xy} = \Sigma(x_i - x_\bullet)(y_i - y_\bullet) \qquad (9\text{-}2.16)$$

as usual, and let

$$r = \frac{S_{xy}}{S_x S_y} \qquad (9\text{-}2.17)$$

be the *sample* correlation coefficient (compare 1-2.11). The sample residual sum of squares $S_{y\cdot x}^2$ (that is, the sum of squared deviations from the sample regression line of y on x) is given by

$$S_{y\cdot x}^2 = S_y^2(1 - r^2) = S_y^2 - S_{xy}^2 S_x^{-2}\,. \qquad (9\text{-}2.18)$$

This was proved, for the special case $x_\bullet = y_\bullet = 0$, in (1-2.9), and the result generalizes as in the succeeding paragraphs. Also, by comparison with (9-1.9), we see that $S_{y\cdot x}^2$ is just the quantity which we called S^2 in our work on the regression model. Similarly we write

$$S_{x\cdot y}^2 = S_x^2(1 - r^2) = S_x^2 - S_{xy}^2 S_y^{-2}\,. \qquad (9\text{-}2.19)$$

We can now state the a posteriori marginal distributions of $\phi_{Y\cdot x}$ and $\phi_{X\cdot y}$ as follows:

$$\phi_{Y\cdot x} : \chi^{-2}(n - 1,\, S_{y\cdot x}^2)\,, \qquad (9\text{-}2.20)$$

and

$$\phi_{X\cdot y} : \chi^{-2}(n - 1, S^2_{x\cdot y}) \,. \qquad (9\text{-}2.21)$$

Next we turn to the parameter which is our real focus of interest in this section, the correlation ρ. Here we encounter a difficulty. The exact posterior marginal distribution of ρ is not one of the commonly tabulated distributions, nor can its density function be given as an explicit formula. The density function can, however, be expressed as a relatively simple integral, enabling it to be computed numerically. The precise form of the integral is given in equation (5) of section 8-2 of Lindley (1965) ("Introduction to Probability and Statistics from a Bayesian Viewpoint, part 2"), from which source also we take the following results.

Let us write

$$z = \tfrac{1}{2} \ln \frac{1 + r}{1 - r} = \operatorname{arctanh} r \,, \qquad (9\text{-}2.22)$$

the hyperbolic arc tangent of r, so that

$$r = \tanh z \,, \qquad (9\text{-}2.23)$$

the hyperbolic tangent of z. Tables A.20(a) and (b) enable us to pass easily from r to z and vice versa. Similarly, let us define a transformed parameter

$$\zeta = \operatorname{arctanh} \rho \,. \qquad (9\text{-}2.24)$$

Then for large n ($n \geq 50$ seems satisfactory), the posterior distribution of ζ is given approximately by

$$\zeta : N(z, n^{-1}) \,. \qquad (9\text{-}2.25)$$

Lindley has also worked out a somewhat improved approximation

$$\zeta : N\left\{z - \frac{r}{2n}, \left[n - \tfrac{3}{2} + \tfrac{1}{2}(1 - r^2)\right]^{-1}\right\} . \qquad (9\text{-}2.26)$$

He comments that while the change in the variance between (9-2.25) and (9-2.26) is not appreciable, the adjustment of the mean can sometimes be of importance.

Using one of the above approximations, we can find credibility intervals for ζ in the usual way and then transform them into intervals for ρ by applying to their endpoints the transformation inverse to (9-2.24), namely,

$$\rho = \tanh \zeta \,. \qquad (9\text{-}2.27)$$

Table A.20(b) facilitates this operation. We may need to note that $\tanh(-\zeta) = -\tanh \zeta$, and so, when a percentage point of ζ is negative, we find the corresponding point for ρ by using the table with $|\zeta|$ in place of ζ and then putting a minus sign in front of the ρ value obtained.

The transformation (9-2.22) was first studied by Fisher and is often referred to as the Fisher z transformation. He was concerned with the sampling distribution of r, given the model parameters. He showed that this distribution depends only on ρ, and can be approximated, for large n and for $|\rho|$ not too close to unity, by saying that z: $N(\zeta, n^{-1})$. Thus, the result (9-2.25) is the same as we would have obtained had we taken our data to consist simply of n and r, or equivalently n and z, and then used the analysis of Sec. 7-1 with a uniform prior for ζ, assuming z to have its approximate distribution.

Incorporation of Prior Information

The method described here equates prior knowledge to a hypothetical sample from the model distribution together, possibly, with additional prior information about the set ϕ_X, ϕ_Y, ρ [or equivalently about the three "covariances": $\mathcal{C}(X, X) = \phi_X$, $\mathcal{C}(Y, Y) = \phi_Y$, and $\mathcal{C}(X, Y) = \rho\phi_X^{1/2}\phi_Y^{1/2}$]. This introduces certain constraints: We have to suppose the number of observations our prior knowledge is worth to be the same for each of ϕ_X, ϕ_Y, and ρ, and similarly for the conditional distributions of θ_X and θ_Y. This may sometimes seem a less than ideal procedure. We may, for example, feel that we have more information about the variance of ACT score than about the variance of college GPA (though we must remind ourselves that it is the variance of ACT score *in the population under study* which is relevant, not the overall variance of the test). However, to do otherwise would require us to use priors outside the conjugate family, and complex numerical methods would then become necessary in order to find the posterior distributions. What we may have to do in some circumstances is, in effect, to discard some of our prior knowledge for the sake of tractability.

We begin by using the method of Sec. 7-9 to assess prior distributions for the *residual* variances $\phi_{Y \cdot x}$ and $\phi_{X \cdot y}$. In other words, we consider first the *regression* aspects of our model. Exactly as in Sec. 9-1, we quantify our knowledge of the residual variance in the regression of Y on x; then we deal similarly with the regression of X on y. Let $\tilde{\sigma}_{Y \cdot x}$ and $\tilde{\sigma}_{X \cdot y}$ be the modal estimates of the corresponding standard deviations. As noted above, we must reconcile the numbers of observations we feel these estimates to be worth, obtaining a common value m_S. Then, corresponding to (9-2.20) and (9-2.21), we take priors

$$\phi_{Y \cdot x}: \chi^{-2}(m_S - 1, R^2_{v \cdot w}), \quad \phi_{X \cdot y}: \chi^{-2}(m_S - 1, R^2_{w \cdot v}), \qquad (9\text{-}2.28)$$

where

$$R^2_{v \cdot w} = m_S \tilde{\sigma}^2_{Y \cdot x} \quad \text{and} \quad R^2_{w \cdot v} = m_S \tilde{\sigma}^2_{X \cdot y}. \qquad (9\text{-}2.29)$$

Next we consider ρ. Let $\tilde{\rho}$ be our modal estimate and let $\tilde{\zeta} = \operatorname{arctanh} \tilde{\rho}$ be its Fisher transform. In accordance with (9-2.25), our prior distribution for ζ should be approximately $N(\tilde{\zeta}, m_S^{-1})$. We obtain credibility intervals for ζ from this distribution, translate them into intervals for ρ, and see whether these intervals adequately match our prior beliefs about ρ. If not, we may wish to slightly modify the estimate $\tilde{\rho}$ (while the ζ intervals are symmetric about $\tilde{\zeta}$, the ρ intervals will not be symmetric about $\tilde{\rho}$), or we may have to adjust the value of m_S. In the latter case we must then go back and try to reconcile the new m_S with that used in (9-2.28). If this proves impossible, we may have to use for m_S the smallest of the three values which we feel appropriate for $\phi_{Y \cdot x}$, $\phi_{X \cdot y}$, and ρ, thereby, in effect, throwing away some of our prior knowledge. By analogy with (9-2.17) to (9-2.19) and (9-2.25), we see that the work so far has equated our prior knowledge about the "covariances" to a sample of m_S pairs (w, v), with sums of squares

$$R_w^2 = \frac{R_{w \cdot v}^2}{1 - \tilde{\rho}^2} = \frac{m_S \tilde{\sigma}_{X \cdot y}^2}{1 - \tilde{\rho}^2} \tag{9-2.30}$$

and

$$R_v^2 = \frac{R_{v \cdot w}^2}{1 - \tilde{\rho}^2} = \frac{m_S \tilde{\sigma}_{Y \cdot x}^2}{1 - \tilde{\rho}^2}, \tag{9-2.31}$$

and with sum of products

$$R_{wv} = \tilde{\rho} R_w R_v = \frac{m_S \tilde{\rho} \tilde{\sigma}_{X \cdot y} \tilde{\sigma}_{Y \cdot x}}{1 - \tilde{\rho}^2}. \tag{9-2.32}$$

Next we turn our attention to the parameters θ_X and θ_Y. If $\tilde{\sigma}_{X \cdot y}^2$, $\tilde{\sigma}_{Y \cdot x}^2$, and $\tilde{\rho}$ were the *true* values of $\phi_{X \cdot y}$, $\phi_{Y \cdot x}$, and ρ respectively, we would have from (9-2.8)

$$\phi_X = \tilde{\sigma}_{X \cdot y}^2 (1 - \tilde{\rho}^2)^{-1} \quad \text{and} \quad \phi_Y = \tilde{\sigma}_{Y \cdot x}^2 (1 - \tilde{\rho}^2)^{-1}. \tag{9-2.33}$$

Conditional on these values we assess normal prior distributions analogous to (9-2.12) and (9-2.13) for θ_X and θ_Y. We take our modal estimate of θ_X to be $w_\bullet$ and to be worth m_M observations. Then, exactly as with the two-parameter normal model, we examine the implications of this specification in terms of the conditional distribution θ_X: $N(w_\bullet, m_M^{-1} \phi_X)$ and the marginal distribution θ_X: $t(m_S - 2, w_\bullet, m_M^{-1} R_w^2)$—compare (9-2.12) and (9-2.14)—possibly revising m_M in consequence. We repeat the process for θ_Y, with modal estimate $v_\bullet$ also worth m_M observations. Here again we have to reconcile the values of m_M which we might feel appropriate for θ_X and θ_Y separately, or, if necessary, use the smaller.

This completes the specification of the joint prior distribution of the five parameters. We have assessed a set of sufficient statistics

$$m_M,\ w_\bullet,\ v_\bullet, \qquad m_S,\ R_w^2,\ R_v^2,\ R_{wv},$$

for our hypothetical prior sample(s). If $m_S = m_M$, we have equated prior knowledge to a single sample from the model under study; if $m_S > m_M$, we have equated it to such a sample plus additional information on the "covariances". At this point, it will be useful to assume that our various estimates are the true values, calculate the regression lines, and check that these are also to our satisfaction (adequately express our prior knowledge). This may lead us to modify some of the modal estimates.

Using the prior we have assessed, the various posterior distributions will be of the same form as those obtained using indifference priors. To find their parameters we make the following substitutions:

Replace	By	In
df $(n-2)$	$m_S + n - 2$	(14), (15)
df $(n-1)$	$m_S + n - 1$	(20), (21)
n^{-1}	$(m_S + n)^{-1}$	(25) *only*
n	$m_S + n$	(26)
n^{-1}	$(m_M + n)^{-1}$	(12), (13), (14), (15)
$x_\bullet$	$\dfrac{m_M w_\bullet + n x_\bullet}{m_M + n}$	(12), (14)
$y_\bullet$	$\dfrac{m_M v_\bullet + n y_\bullet}{m_M + n}$	(13), (15)
S_x^2	$R_w^2 + S_x^2 + \dfrac{m_M n}{m_M + n}(w_\bullet - x_\bullet)^2$	(14), (17), (18), (19)
S_y^2	$R_v^2 + S_y^2 + \dfrac{m_M n}{m_M + n}(v_\bullet - y_\bullet)^2$	(15), (17), (18), (19)
S_{xy}	$R_{wv} + S_{xy} + \dfrac{m_M n}{m_M + n}(w_\bullet - x_\bullet)(v_\bullet - y_\bullet)$	(17), (18), (19)

The values of r, $S_{y \cdot x}^2$ and $S_{x \cdot y}^2$ obtained from (17), (18), and (19) after making the substitutions shown in the last three rows of the table are the ones to be used in (22) and (26), (20), and (21), respectively. Since the focus of this section has been on the correlation coeffieient, we conclude with an explicit statement concerning its posterior distribution.

With prior information quantified as described above, the posterior distribution of ρ *is such that* $\zeta = \text{arctanh}\,\rho$ *has approximately a normal distribution with mean*

$$\text{arctanh}\frac{R_{wv} + S_{xy} + [m_M n/(m_M + n)](w. - x.)(v. - y.)}{\left[R_w^2 + S_x^2 + [m_M n/(m_M + n)](w. - x.)^2\right]^{\frac{1}{2}}\left[R_v^2 + S_y^2 + [m_M n/(m_M + n)](v. - y.)^2\right]^{\frac{1}{2}}} \qquad (9\text{-}2.34)$$

and variance

$$(m_S + n)^{-1}. \qquad (9\text{-}2.35)$$

The methods of this section closely parallel those of the previous section; hence, we shall only illustrate the computation of the posterior distribution for ζ. To complete the specification of the prior distribution, we need to choose a value m_M, the number of hypothetical prior observations relevant to our information about θ_X and θ_Y.

Our best estimate of θ_Y is $v_{\bullet} = 2.5$ and of $\phi_Y^{1/2}$ is .7. Suppose we set $m_M = \sigma_Y^2/\sigma_{\theta_Y}^2 = 4$, where $\sigma_{\theta_Y}^2$ is the variance of the Bayes' distribution of θ_Y. Then $\sigma_{\theta_Y} = .35$. Now $v_{\bullet} - .6745\,\sigma_{\theta_Y} = 2.26$ and $v_{\bullet} + .6745\,\sigma_{\theta_Y} = 2.74$. This would appear to be a reasonable 50% central credibility interval for θ_Y. Our best estimate of θ_X is 19 and of $\phi_X^{1/2}$ is 5. If $m_M = \sigma_X^2/\sigma_{\theta_X}^2 = 4$, then $\sigma_{\theta_X} = 2.5$. Now $w_{\bullet} - .6745\,\sigma_{\theta_X} = 17.31$ and $w_{\bullet} + .6745\,\sigma_{\theta_X} = 20.69$. This is a satisfactory 50% central credibility interval for θ_X. Let us thus set $m_M = 4$.

From the previous example, we have $m_S = 10$, $\tilde{\rho} = .59$, and $\tilde{\sigma}_{Y \cdot x} = .565$ (previously denoted by $\tilde{\sigma}$). The value of $\tilde{\sigma}_{X \cdot y}$ which is coherent with our previous specification is given by (9-2.33), namely,

$$\begin{aligned} \tilde{\sigma}_{X \cdot y}^2 &= \phi_X(1 - \tilde{\rho}^2) \\ &= 25(.6519) \\ &= 16.2975, \end{aligned}$$

or

$$\tilde{\sigma}_{X \cdot y} = 4.037.$$

Substituting into (9-2.30), (9-2.31), and (9-2.32), respectively, we obtain

$$\begin{aligned} R_w^2 &= \frac{m_S \tilde{\sigma}_{X \cdot y}^2}{1 - \tilde{\rho}^2} \\ &= \frac{10(16.2975)}{.6519} \\ &= 250, \end{aligned}$$

$$\begin{aligned} R_v^2 &= \frac{m_S \tilde{\sigma}_{Y \cdot x}^2}{1 - \tilde{\rho}^2} \\ &= \frac{10(.3194)}{.6519} \\ &= 4.9, \end{aligned}$$

and

$$\begin{aligned} R_{wv} &= \frac{m_S \tilde{\rho} \tilde{\sigma}_{X \cdot y} \tilde{\sigma}_{Y \cdot x}}{1 - \tilde{\rho}^2} \\ &= \frac{10(.59)(4.037)(.565)}{.6519} \\ &= 20.6433. \end{aligned}$$

The set of sufficient statistics for our prior information is then

$$\begin{aligned} m_M &= 4 \quad w_{\bullet} = 19 \quad v_{\bullet} = 2.5 \\ m_S &= 10 \quad R_w^2 = 250 \quad R_v^2 = 4.9 \\ R_{wv} &= 20.6433. \end{aligned}$$

Suppose that our sample data are

$$n = 46 \qquad y. = 2.57 \qquad x. = 20$$
$$S_{xy} = 23.7 \qquad S_y^2 = 6.641 \qquad S_x^2 = 240\,.$$

The posterior distribution of ρ is such that ζ = arctanh ρ has approximately a normal distribution with

$$\text{Mean} = \operatorname{arctanh}\left\{\frac{R_{wv} + S_{xy} + [m_M n/(m_M + n)](w. - x.)(v. - y.)}{\left[R_w^2 + S_x^2 + [m_M n/(m_M + n)](w. - x.)^2\right]^{\frac{1}{2}}\left[R_v^2 + S_y^2 + [m_M n/(m_M + n)](v. - y.)^2\right]^{\frac{1}{2}}}\right\}.$$

Upon careful substitution,

$$\text{Mean} = \operatorname{arctanh}(.5904) = .6783$$

and

$$\text{Variance} = (m_S + n)^{-1} = .02\,.$$

A 50% central credibility interval for ζ extends from .5829 to .7737. Transforming back to ρ, a 50% central credibility interval for ρ extends from .5248 to .6506. The value $\tilde{\rho}$ = .5904 corresponds to the mean estimate $\tilde{\zeta}$ = .6783 for ζ.

A central 50% credibility interval could also have been obtained from Table A.23. For n = 50 and r = .5904, we find that the 25th percentile is .5271 and the 75th percentile is .6536. Thus, the central 50% interval extends from .5271 to .6536. Its length differs from the previously computed interval by .0004. This table of approximate percentiles for ρ was constructed from an approximate formula for the posterior density of ρ given by Lindley (1965). It should be reasonably accurate for values of n or $(n + m_M) \geq 30$.

9-3 THE DIFFERENCE BETWEEN MEANS OF CORRELATED PAIRS OF OBSERVATIONS

In this section we continue to use the bivariate normal model studied in the previous section, but we now focus attention on the posterior distribution of $\delta = (\theta_Y - \theta_X)$, the difference of the two population means. One situation in which this distribution will be of interest is where educational or psychological measurements are made on each person, both before and after he experiences some learning process or treatment, resulting in observations x and y, respectively. Then δ measures the gain in mean performance level of the population due to the treatment.

The random variables X and Y will typically be correlated in the population of persons. None of the methods developed in Sec. 8-1 for the difference of two normal means will apply, since the observations are there assumed to be independent, given the mean and variance of their respective distributions. To take account of the correlation, we must pass to the bivariate normal model.

The result is refreshingly simple. With the notation of the previous section, and using the indifference prior discussed there, the posterior distribution of the difference of the means is

$$\delta : t[n - 2, y_{\bullet} - x_{\bullet}, n^{-1}(S_x^2 - 2S_{xy} + S_y^2)] . \qquad (9\text{-}3.1)$$

We can incorporate prior information by the method discussed in the previous section. The posterior distribution of δ is then obtained from (9-3.1) by making the same substitutions as before [here n^{-1} is replaced by $(m_M + n)^{-1}$, as it was in the closely related results (9-2.14) and (9-2.15)].

The result (9-3.1) could, in fact, have been deduced from (9-2.14) or (9-2.15). If for each person we let $d = y - x$, the pairs (x,d) clearly convey the same information as the pairs (x, y). With a simple linear transformation of this sort, we might well anticipate that the joint distribution of X and D will also be bivariate-normal, and this is indeed the case. [Using the results given in Sec. 4-1 the reader can verify that its parameters are $\theta_X, \delta, \phi_X, \phi_X + \phi_Y - 2\rho\phi_X{}^{1/2}\phi_Y{}^{1/2}$ and $(\rho\phi_y^{1/2} - \phi_x^{1/2})/(\phi_x + \phi_y - 2\rho\phi_x^{1/2}\phi_y^{1/2})$. It follows from (9-2.15) that, a posteriori,

$$\delta : t[n - 2, d_{\bullet}, n^{-1} \Sigma(d_i - d_{\bullet})^2] ,$$

and we have

$$d_{\bullet} = y_{\bullet} - x_{\bullet} ,$$

and

$$\begin{aligned} \Sigma(d_i - d_{\bullet})^2 &= \Sigma(y_i - x_i - y_{\bullet} + x_{\bullet})^2 \\ &= \Sigma[(y_i - y_{\bullet}) - (x_i - x_{\bullet})]^2 \\ &= S_x^2 - 2S_{xy} + S_y^2 \end{aligned}$$

on expanding the square and summing.

To illustrate the methods of this section, consider the data given in Table 1-2.1. We would expect little variability in a student's score on the Mechanical-Skills test from one administration to the next. Thus, let us assume our prior information regarding the mean and variance for each administration of the test is the same. Let our estimate of the variance $\sigma_{X_1}^2 = \sigma_{X_2}^2 = 121$ be worth $m_S = 13$ observations. Let our estimate of the mean be $w_{\bullet} = v_{\bullet} = 53$, also worth $m_M = 13$ observations. These values give a 50% central credibility interval for the mean of (50.94,55.06). This interval is satisfactory. We would expect the correlation between the two sets of scores to be fairly high. Let us assume our best estimate of the correlation coefficient is $\tilde{\rho} = .80$.

Using (9-2.33),

$$\tilde{\sigma}_{X_1 \cdot x_2}^2 = \tilde{\sigma}_{X_1}^2(1 - \tilde{\rho}^2) = 121(.36) = 43.56$$

and

$$\tilde{\sigma}_{X_2 \cdot x_1}^2 = \tilde{\sigma}_{X_2}^2(1 - \tilde{\rho}^2) = 121(.36) = 43.56 .$$

Now substituting into (9-2.30), (9-2.31), and (9-2.32), we obtain

$$R_w^2 = \frac{m_S \tilde{\sigma}^2_{x_1 \cdot x_2}}{1 - \tilde{\rho}^2} = \frac{13(43.56)}{.36} = 1573\,,$$

$$R_v^2 = \frac{m_S \tilde{\sigma}^2_{x_2 \cdot x_1}}{1 - \tilde{\rho}^2} = \frac{13(43.56)}{.36} = 1573\,,$$

and

$$R_{wv} = \frac{m_S \tilde{\rho}\, \tilde{\sigma}_{x_1 \cdot x_2} \tilde{\sigma}_{x_2 \cdot x_1}}{1 - \tilde{\rho}^2} = \frac{13(.80)(6.6)(6.6)}{.36} = 1258.4\,.$$

The set of sufficient statistics for our prior information is

$$m_M = 13 \quad w_{\bullet} = v_{\bullet} = 53$$
$$m_S = 13 \quad R_w^2 = R_v^2 = 1573$$
$$R_{wv} = 1258.4.$$

The sample data are

$$n = 10 \quad x_{1\bullet} = 52.5 \quad x_{2\bullet} = 53.4$$
$$S_{x_1 x_2} = 989 \quad S_{x_1}^2 = 1254.4 \quad S_{x_2}^2 = 1144.9\,.$$

The posterior distribution for δ, the difference between means of correlated observations, is

$$\delta : t\left(m_S + n - 2,\ \frac{m_M v_{\bullet} + n x_{2\bullet}}{m_M + n} - \frac{m_M w_{\bullet} + n x_{1\bullet}}{m_M + n},\right.$$
$$(m_M + n)^{-1}\left\{R_w^2 + S_{x_1}^2 + \frac{m_M n (w_{\bullet} - x_{1\bullet})^2}{m_M + n}\right.$$
$$- 2\left[R_{wv} + S_{x_1 x_2} + \frac{m_M n}{m_M + n}(w_{\bullet} - x_{1\bullet})(v_{\bullet} - x_{2\bullet})\right]$$
$$\left.\left. + R_v^2 + S_{x_2}^2 + \frac{m_M n (v_{\bullet} - x_{2\bullet})^2}{m_M + n}\right\}\right).$$

Upon careful substitution, we obtain

$$\delta : t(21, .391, 45.873).$$

A 50% central credibility interval for δ extends from $-.623$ to 1.405.

9-4 ESTIMATION AND COMPARISON OF A SET OF NORMAL MEANS

In many applications of statistics in education and psychology, we are concerned not with one or two normal distributions but with many. For example, in the situations discussed in Sec. 8-1, where the focus of interest is the mathematics achievement level of high schools, there will typically be several high schools we wish to compare rather than just two, and it may be appropriate to take the model $N(\theta_i, \phi_i)$ for the ith college, where $i = 1, 2, \ldots, m$, the total number of schools. Likewise in educational testing, we are concerned with estimating ability or achievement parameters for large numbers of persons. Here θ_i would denote the ith person's "true-score" and ϕ_i his "error-score variance", and m would be the total number of persons in the group being studied.

Take first the question of estimating the means θ_i. If the inferences we make about θ_i, considered as one of a set of means, are in any way different from those we make about θ_i in isolation (by the methods of Chap. 7), this must be because we are assuming that the set of distributions $N(\theta_i, \phi_i)$, $i = 1, 2, \ldots, m$, have something in common. In this section, we confine attention to the case where the linking factor is a common (but unknown) variance, that is, where $\phi_i = \phi$ for all i. This is the so-called homoscedastic model.

Estimation of a Single Mean with Homoscedastic Errors

The assumption of a common variance ϕ is most easily justified in the case where θ_i denotes the true value of some physical measurement and ϕ_i the variance of errors of measurement, and where a common measuring instrument is used to make all the measurements. It may then be reasonable to regard the variance ϕ_i as being associated exclusively with the measuring instrument and so to take $\phi_i = \phi$. Similarly, in a well-planned agricultural trial where the observations consist of the yields of a number of plots planted with various species, it may be reasonable to assume that the variability in the yields of plots planted with the same species is due to differences in soil, watering, etc.; and that the variance will, therefore, have the same value for all species.

In psychological measurement, it is usually much less clear whether observed variability is to be attributed to the measuring instrument, the individual measured, or both. The validity of the assumption of a common variance or its adequacy as an approximation must, therefore, be justified by empirical investigation.

Granted this assumption, what is the relevance of observations on person h to inference about the mean θ_i for person i? Clearly, it is in providing information about ϕ. We can imagine that (repeated) measurements are made first on all persons except the ith. In this process, a considerable amount of information is gained about ϕ but none about θ_i (under our present assumptions). More specifically, after the observations on the other $(m - 1)$ persons are obtained, we have a posterior distribution for ϕ which can be used as the *prior* distribution for our analysis of the data for the ith person, but our prior distribution for θ_i is unchanged.

Suppose we make n_i independent observations on the ith person $(i = 1, 2, \ldots, m)$. Let x_{ij} denote the jth observation on that person and define

$$x_{i\bullet} = n_i^{-1} \sum_j x_{ij}, \quad \text{the average of observations on person } i, \tag{9-4.1}$$

and

$$S_i^2 = \sum_j (x_{ij} - x_{i\bullet})^2, \tag{9-4.2}$$

the sum of squared deviations from the mean for the ith person.

Assume that we have independent indifference priors for ϕ (log-uniform) and $\theta_1, \theta_2, \ldots, \theta_m$ (uniform). Prior knowledge about ϕ could be incorporated by the simple device of equating it to appropriate observations on a mythical "person zero". If we consider only the observations on person i, by the work of Sec. 7-6 our posterior distribution for ϕ will be $\chi^{-2}(n_i - 1, S_i^2)$. However, this is exactly the situation to which our first general distributional result in Sec. 7-11 applies (7-11.1), with the conclusion that after considering *all* the observations, our posterior for ϕ will be inverse chi square with parameters equal to the sums of the parameters for the separate posterior distributions. Thus, *posterior to obtaining all the observations, the Bayes distribution of* ϕ *is* $\chi^{-2}(N - m, S^2)$, where

$$N = \Sigma n_i, \quad \text{the total number of observations} \tag{9-4.3}$$

and

$$S^2 = \sum_i S_i^2 = \sum_i \sum_j (x_{ij} - x_{i\bullet})^2 . \tag{9-4.4}$$

Next, consider the conditional distribution of θ_i for given ϕ. From the work summarized in Sec. 7-1, with σ_0^{-2} given the indifference value zero, we see that this is $N(x_{i\bullet}, n_i^{-1}\phi)$. We are thus in a position to apply our second general result (7-11.2) with θ_i for θ, $h = x_{i\bullet}$, $k = n_i$, $\nu = N - m$ and $\lambda = S^2$. We conclude that *posterior to obtaining all the observations, the Bayes distribution of* θ_i *is* $t(N - m, x_{i\bullet}, n_i^{-1}S^2)$ *with mean* $x_{i\bullet}$ *and variance* $n_i^{-1}S^2/(N - m - 2)$.

What have we gained by using data on all persons to make inferences about the ith person? If we treat the ith person in isolation, we find in Sec. 7-6 that the posterior distribution of θ_i is $t(n_i - 1, x_{i\bullet}, n_i^{-1}S_i^2)$. This suggests that the gain is in the number of degrees of freedom of the resulting t distribution. That suggestion is correct with regard to average values that we are likely to observe in actual data sets.

We saw earlier that the larger the degrees of freedom, the shorter the credibility intervals or the "tighter" the estimation of θ_i. If the number of observations on each subject (person) is small, as is often the case in educational testing, the increase in precision of estimation by using all the data will be very valuable. If the degrees of freedom for each subject separately is already large, however, the gain in precision will be small since the t distribution tends to a limiting normal form as the degrees of freedom increase; and for degrees of freedom greater than 60, the difference between credibility intervals based on t and those based on $N(0, 1)$ is for most purposes negligible.

Let us consider a data set consisting of what could be five replications on each of six persons, as given in Table 9-4.1. Suppose, for simplicity, that we have no prior information on the means, but that our prior distribution for the common variance is χ^{-2} (6, 11552). This distribution has a mean of 2888, a mode of 1444 and the square roots of these values are respectively 53.74 and 38. Referring to the results on page 215 and denoting the quantity m there by m_S here, to avoid confusion with the number of groups, we are able to specify a prior χ^{-2} distribution having m_S and R^2 values respectively of 7 and 11552. If we consider person one in isolation from the others, assuming the mean and variance are both unknown, we have, a posteriori,

$$\begin{aligned}\theta_1\colon\ & t[m_S + n - 2,\ x_\bullet, n^{-1}(R^2 + S^2)] \\ &= t[7 + 5 - 2,\ 105,\ 5^{-1}(11552 + 15900)] \\ &= t\,[10,\ 105,\ 5490.4]\ .\end{aligned}$$

The central 50% credibility interval for the standardized t distribution on 10 degrees of freedom extends from −.6998 to .6998. Hence, the central 50% credibility interval for θ_1 is (88.60,121.40) (see Sec. 7-5).

Now let us take account of the information about ϕ contained in the observations on persons 2 to 6. Using the data on all six persons to compute the posterior distribution for θ_1, we have

$$\begin{aligned}S^2 &= \Sigma S_i^2 \\ &= (15900 + 4430 + 5770 + 18880 + 10000 + 3850) \\ &= 58830.\end{aligned}$$

Table 9-4.1

	Persons					
Replications	1	2	3	4	5	6
1	145	140	195	45	195	120
2	40	155	150	40	230	55
3	40	90	205	195	115	50
4	120	160	110	65	235	80
5	180	95	160	145	225	45
$x_\bullet$	105	128	164	98	200	70

Hence, the "posterior" distribution for θ_1 is $t(N - m, x_{1\bullet}, n_1^{-1}S^2) = t(24, 105, 11766)$. The central 50% credibility interval for θ_1 now extends from 89.84 to 120.16.

Even now, however, we have not used all of the available information. There still exists the unused prior information on the common value of $\phi - \phi : \chi^{-2}(6, 11552)$, a priori. Adding the degrees of freedom and prior sum of squares from this distribution to the posterior distribution for θ_1 immediately above, we have

$$\theta_1 : t[N - m + m_S - 1, x_{1\bullet}, n_1^{-1}(R^2 + S^2)]$$

or

$$\theta_1 : t(30, 105, 14076.4).$$

For this distribution, the central 50% credibility interval extends from 90.21 to 119.79. As we might expect, the length of the credibility interval decreases as the amount of relevant information increases. However, this can only be expected to happen "on the average". It does not happen, for example, in the estimation of θ_2, as the reader may wish to verify. Just how useful the above gain in precision should be considered cannot be evaluated without looking much more carefully at the problem for which the data were obtained.

The Comparison of Several Means with Homoscedastic Errors

There may be several ways of explicating the general question of comparing several normal means. At this point, we shall consider only the simple answer that we wish to examine the $m(m - 1)/2$ pairwise comparisons between θ_i and θ_j. If the variances ϕ_i and ϕ_j are either known or unrelated, these comparisons will be no different from those described in Sec. 8-1, cases 1 and 3, where the posterior distributions of $(\theta_i - \theta_j)$ were, respectively, normal and Behrens. If, however, we are assuming a common variance ϕ for all the populations, we now have additional relevant information about ϕ from the data for populations other than i and j. Specifically, we showed earlier in this section that the posterior distribution of ϕ is now $\chi^{-2}(N - m, S^2)$. If the reader will review Sec. 8-1, case 2, he will find that this is the *only* change which needs to be made in the argument, and so the posterior distribution of $(\theta_i - \theta_j)$ is

$$t[N - m, x_{i\bullet} - x_{j\bullet}, (n_i^{-1} + n_j^{-1})S^2] . \qquad (9\text{-}4.5)$$

The gain in precision is again that due to the increase in the number of degrees of freedom. One useful way of viewing the situation is that the data for populations other than i and j provide an informative prior distribution for ϕ when we come to consider the ith and jth populations. The idea of pairwise comparisons, in itself, therefore introduces no new ideas in the many mean case.

To exemplify this method, consider again the data in Table 9-4.1. We desire to compare θ_1 and θ_2 under the assumption of a common variance for all six persons. We use (9-4.5) and state the posterior distribution for $\theta_2 - \theta_1$ as $t[N - m, x_{2\bullet} - x_{1\bullet},$

$(n_2^{-1} + n_1^{-1})S^2]$ which works out to be $t[24, 23, 23532]$. The central 50% credibility interval extends from 1.55 to 44.45. Thus, using the additional information on ϕ from the other four persons, we are about 75% confident that θ_2 is at least $1\frac{1}{2}$ points greater than θ_1. The corresponding credibility interval obtained when this information is ignored is (.48,45.52) (see Sec. 8-1.3).

Some shortening of this interval can be accomplished by also using the prior information on ϕ contained in the prior distribution $\phi\colon \chi^{-2}(6, 11552)$. The value of κ is given by $(n_1^{-1} + n_2^{-1})(S^2 + R^2)$, and hence the posterior t distribution on $\theta_2 - \theta_1$ is $t[30, 23, 28152.8]$. For this distribution, the central 50% credibility interval extends from 2.08 to 43.92. Thus, using all of the information we have so far learned to use, we have been able to successively and substantially shorten the central 50% credibility interval.

9-5 CLASSICAL TEST THEORY AND THE ESTIMATION OF MANY MEANS

Suppose that we are in a situation where we need to estimate many means, and suppose that our prior expectation is that they will not be too dissimilar. Then having traveled this far down the Bayesian road, we hope that our reader feels that when m supposedly similar parameters (e.g., normal means) are to be estimated, surely for estimation in the mth group, some information is gained from the data in the remaining $(m - 1)$ groups. If all of the mean values in the $(m - 1)$ groups are high, we would expect the mth mean also to be high. We would be inclined, we hope, to consider the information in the $(m - 1)$ groups either as actual prior information for the mth group, or at least as being equivalent to such information. The fact that such information is not temporally prior is not particularly relevant–Bayes' theorem is independent of any time considerations. To avoid any such semantic difficulties, we can refer to such information as *collateral* information. The technical problem is then to devise a method for using this information efficiently and to do so without assuming that all of the means are exactly equal. Actually, the basis for such a method is available from the material presented in Chap. 4.

Recall that in classical test theory, the observed test score x of a particular person on a specified test is taken to be a realization of a random variable X which has expectation τ, the person's true-score. The error score E is defined by $E = X - \tau$ and, thus, has expectation zero for each person. The variance of E is denoted for the time being by σ_E^2. We then act as though the true-score of each person tested is sampled randomly from a distribution with mean μ_T and variance σ_T^2, these parameters characterizing some population (e.g., a school) with which the person is identified. The true-score variance σ_T^2 measures the extent to which the true-scores of persons randomly selected from the population cluster together. An important theorem known as the *exchangeability* theorem implies that for such an assumption to be reasonable, it is not necessary that the person in question be actually chosen by a random-sampling procedure from the population with which he is identified, but only that, apart from testing, *we are unable to distinguish between persons or groups of persons from that population in respect to their true-scores.*

Treating μ_T, σ_T^2, and σ_E^2 as known, the model developed in the previous paragraph can be summarized as follows. When (we act as though) a person is selected at random, the conditional distribution of observed score X given τ has mean τ and variance σ_E^2, while the (marginal) distribution of T has mean μ_T and variance σ_T^2. These two distributions together determine, when their forms are fully known, a joint distribution for X and T, some of whose properties can be studied even without further specification of the forms. For example, the marginal distribution of X has mean μ_T and variance $\sigma_X^2 = \sigma_T^2 + \sigma_E^2$. The quantity $\rho = \sigma_T^2/\sigma_X^2$ is called the *reliability of the test* (strictly the reliability of the test as applied to the population from which the person is randomly selected).

Of great practical importance in this model is the regression of T on x, since this can be used as an estimate of T when an observation x has been made. This regression will not in general be linear, although it will be so in the important case in which the distributions of T and of X given τ are both normal, since the joint distribution of X and T is then bivariate normal. Even when the regression itself is not linear in x, we can determine a *linear* regression function $R(T|x)$ which is the best linear predictor of T in the sense that it minimizes the expectation (evaluated over the joint distribution) of the square of the difference, $R(T|x) - T$, between the true-score and the linear-regression-function estimate of it. The linear regression function was given in Chap. 4:

$$R(T|x) = \rho x + (1 - \rho)\mu_T \qquad (9\text{-}5.1)$$

$$= \frac{\sigma_T^2 x - \sigma_E^2 \mu_T}{\sigma_T^2 + \sigma_E^2}. \qquad (9\text{-}5.2)$$

This is Kelley's result, which, as he points out, yields an estimate which is a weighted average of the "obvious" estimate x and the mean μ_T of the group from which the person is sampled, giving more/less weight to x depending on whether the error variance σ_E^2 is small/large compared with σ_T^2 (the reliability is high/low). In the case where the joint distribution of X and T is bivariate normal, (9-5.1) and (9-5.2) also give the true regression $\mathcal{E}(T|x)$. Note that everything which has been said so far relates to a single, randomly sampled person.

Kelley's formula cannot usually be applied directly, since μ_T, σ_T^2 and σ_E^2, which have so far been assumed known, are, in fact, unknown and have to be estimated. To estimate σ_E^2, we require repeated measurements on the same person, and to estimate σ_T^2, we require measurements on more than one person. Therefore, suppose that we obtain test scores for m persons randomly sampled from the same population and indexed by $i = 1, 2, \ldots, m$; also that for person i, we obtain n_i independent realizations of the observed-score random variable X_i, denoted by x_{ij}, $j = 1, 2, \ldots, n_i$. Conceptually, these replications (realizations) could be obtained by repeated applications of the same test; this is usually impractical for psychological tests; and the same effect is obtained by the use of parallel tests—tests such that a person's true-score and his error-score variance are the same for each test. The independence of the replications implies that the error scores $e_{ij} = x_{ij} - \tau_i$ are uncorrelated for person i. We also assume that error scores of different persons are uncorrelated.

The model for our observations is, thus,

$$x_{ij} = \tau_i + e_{ij} , \qquad (9\text{-}5.3)$$

where the τ_i are independent realizations of a random variable T with mean μ_T and variance σ_T^2 while the e_{ij} are independent realizations of a random variable E_i which has zero mean and is also uncorrelated with the τ_i [since $\mathcal{E}(E_{ij}|\tau_i) = 0$ for any τ_i]. If we make the further assumption that the variance of e_{ij} has the same value σ_E^2 for all i, j, that is, that the error variance is the same for all persons, then (9-5.3) gives the usual model II (random effects) analysis of variance, except that the "overall effect" μ_T has not been subtracted from the τ_i.

In the most familiar situation, where the number of replications is the same for each person ($n_i = n$), a simple estimate of μ_T is

$$\hat{\mu}_T = x_{\bullet\bullet} = (mn)^{-1}\Sigma\Sigma x_{ij} , \qquad (9\text{-}5.4)$$

and simple estimates of the variances are

$$\hat{\sigma}_E^2 = [m(n-1)]^{-1}\Sigma\Sigma(x_{ij} - x_{i\bullet})^2 \qquad (9\text{-}5.5)$$

where

$$x_{i\bullet} = n^{-1}\sum_j x_{ij} ,$$

and

$$\hat{\sigma}_T^2 = (m-1)^{-1}\Sigma(x_{i\bullet} - x_{\bullet\bullet})^2 - n^{-1}\hat{\sigma}_E^2 . \qquad (9\text{-}5.6)$$

Unfortunately, the equation (9-5.6) can give a negative estimate and, thus, causes theoretical problems. For the present purpose, however, the proper course in that event seems to be to set $\hat{\sigma}_T^2 = 0$ which results in all the τ_i being estimated as $x_{\bullet\bullet}$. The estimates (9-5.4) through (9-5.6) can now be substituted for μ_T, σ_E^2, and σ_T^2 in (9-5.2) to obtain what we shall call *regressed* estimates of τ_i—regressed in the sense that they are pulled back from the "obvious" value x toward the common mean. Of course, since we now have n scores for person i, we shall use their average $x_{i\bullet}$, which has sampling mean τ_i and variance σ_E^2/n, to estimate τ_i using the formula

$$R(T_i|x_{i\bullet}) = \frac{\hat{\sigma}_T^2 x_{i\bullet} + n^{-1}\hat{\sigma}_E^2 x_{\bullet\bullet}}{\hat{\sigma}_T^2 + n^{-1}\hat{\sigma}_E^2} = \frac{\dfrac{x_{i\bullet}}{\hat{\sigma}_E^2/n} + \dfrac{\hat{\mu}_T}{\hat{\sigma}_T^2}}{\dfrac{1}{\hat{\sigma}_E^2/n} + \dfrac{1}{\hat{\sigma}_T^2}} . \qquad (9\text{-}5.7)$$

Consider again the data in Table 9-4.1. We compute

$$\hat{\mu}_T = x_{\bullet\bullet} = (mn)^{-1}\Sigma\Sigma x_{ij} = 127.5$$

$$\hat{\sigma}_E^2 = [m(n-1)]^{-1}\Sigma\Sigma(x_{ij} - x_{i\bullet})^2 = [m(n-1)]^{-1}\Sigma S_i^2$$
$$= [6(4)]^{-1}(58830)$$
$$= 2451.25$$

$$\hat{\sigma}_T^2 = (m-1)^{-1}\Sigma(x_{i\bullet} - x_{\bullet\bullet})^2 - n^{-1}\hat{\sigma}_E^2$$
$$= 2254.3 - 490.25$$
$$= 1764.05$$

$$R(T_i|x_{i\bullet}) = \frac{1764.05x_{i\bullet} + 490.25x_{\bullet\bullet}}{2254.3}$$
$$= \frac{1764.05x_{i\bullet} + 62506.875}{2254.3}$$

$$R(T_1|x_{1\bullet}) = 109.89 \quad R(T_4|x_{4\bullet}) = 104.41$$
$$R(T_2|x_{2\bullet}) = 127.89 \quad R(T_5|x_{5\bullet}) = 184.23$$
$$R(T_3|x_{3\bullet}) = 156.06 \quad R(T_6|x_{6\bullet}) = 82.50\,.$$

When the replication numbers are unequal, recommended estimates for σ_E^2, σ_T^2, and μ_T, are

$$\hat{\sigma}_E^2 = (N-m)^{-1}\Sigma\Sigma(x_{ij} - x_{i\bullet})^2\,, \qquad (9\text{-}5.8)$$

where $N = \Sigma n_i$ and $x_{i\bullet} = n_i^{-1}\Sigma x_{ij}$;

$$\hat{\sigma}_T^2 = (m-1)^{-1}\Sigma(x_{i\bullet} - \bar{x})^2 - m^{-1}(\Sigma n_i^{-1})\hat{\sigma}_E^2 \qquad (9\text{-}5.9)$$

where $\bar{x} = m^{-1}\Sigma x_{i\bullet}$; and

$$\hat{\mu}_T = \frac{\Sigma w_i x_{i\bullet}}{\Sigma w_i} \qquad (9\text{-}5.10)$$

where $w_i = [\hat{\sigma}_T^2 + (\hat{\sigma}_E^2/n_i)]^{-1}$. The estimate of τ_i is then

$$\hat{\tau}_i = R(T_i|x_{i\bullet}) = \frac{\hat{\sigma}_T^2 x_{i\bullet} + n_i^{-1}\hat{\sigma}_E^2\hat{\mu}_T}{\hat{\sigma}_T^2 + n_i^{-1}\hat{\sigma}_E^2}\,. \qquad (9\text{-}5.11)$$

As noted previously, the estimate of the between person variance $\hat{\sigma}_T^2$ may be negative, in which case it should be replaced by zero. The effect will be to completely regress all the τ_i to $x_{\bullet\bullet} = \Sigma\Sigma x_{ij}/\Sigma n_i = \Sigma n_i x_{i\bullet}/\Sigma n_i$.

It is not necessary to make the assumption that each person's error variance is the same. Let us, for typographical reasons, denote the ith person's error variance by ϕ_i

(rather than $\sigma_{E_i}^2$). It can be estimated from the repeated measurements on that person. Of course, if n_i is small, ϕ_i will be rather imprecisely estimated, and this may more than offset the advantage gained by dropping the somewhat unrealistic assumption of a common error variance. A compromise procedure is discussed in Sec. 9-6.

For unequal error variances and possibly unequal replication numbers, the regressed estimate of τ_i is

$$R(T_i|x_{i\cdot}) = \frac{\hat{\sigma}_T^2 x_{i\cdot} + n_i^{-1}\hat{\phi}_i\hat{\mu}_T}{\hat{\sigma}_T^2 + n_i^{-1}\hat{\phi}_i} = \frac{\dfrac{x_{i\cdot}}{\hat{\phi}_i/n_i} + \dfrac{\hat{\mu}_T}{\hat{\sigma}_T^2}}{\dfrac{1}{\hat{\phi}_i/n_i} + \dfrac{1}{\hat{\sigma}_T^2}} . \tag{9-5.12}$$

Here,

$$\hat{\phi}_i = (n_i - 1)^{-1} \sum_j (x_{ij} - x_{i\cdot})^2 , \tag{9-5.13}$$

and

$$\hat{\sigma}_T^2 = (m - 1)^{-1} \Sigma (x_{i\cdot} - \bar{x})^2 - m^{-1} \Sigma n_i^{-1} \hat{\phi}_i , \tag{9-5.14}$$

where, as before, $x_{i\cdot} = n_i^{-1}\Sigma x_{ij}$ and $\bar{x} = m^{-1}\Sigma x_{i\cdot}$. Also,

$$\hat{\mu}_T = \frac{\Sigma w_i x_{i\cdot}}{\Sigma w_i} \tag{9-5.15}$$

where

$$w_i = \left(\hat{\sigma}_T^2 + \frac{\hat{\phi}_i}{n_i}\right)^{-1} .$$

This result includes the equal-replication-numbers case on putting $n_i = n$. Equation (9-5.12) amounts to making a separate estimate,

$$\frac{\hat{\sigma}_T^2}{\hat{\sigma}_T^2 + n_i^{-1}\hat{\phi}_i} ,$$

of the reliability of each person's mean score $x_{i\cdot}$.

Again for the data in Table 9-4.1, we compute

$$\hat{\phi}_i = (n_i - 1) \sum_{j=1}^{m} (x_{ij} - x_{i\cdot})^2$$

$$\hat{\phi}_1 = \frac{15900}{3974} = 3975 \qquad \hat{\phi}_3 = \frac{5770}{4} = 1442.5$$

$$\hat{\phi}_2 = \frac{4430}{4} = 1107.5 \qquad \hat{\phi}_4 = \frac{18880}{4} = 4720$$

$$\hat{\phi}_5 = \frac{10000}{4} = 2500 \qquad \hat{\phi}_6 = \frac{3850}{4} = 962.5 .$$

$$\begin{aligned}\hat{\sigma}_T^2 &= (m-1)^{-1}\Sigma(x_{i\bullet} - \bar{x})^2 - m^{-1}\Sigma n_i^{-1}\hat{\phi}_i \\ &= (5^{-1})(11271.5) - (6^{-1})(2941.5) \\ &= 1764.05\end{aligned}$$

$$w_i = \left(\hat{\sigma}_T^2 + \frac{\hat{\phi}_i}{n_i}\right)^{-1}$$

$$\begin{aligned}w_1 &= (1764.05 + 795)^{-1} = (2559.05)^{-1} \\ w_2 &= (1764.05 + 221.5)^{-1} = (1985.55)^{-1} \\ w_3 &= (1764.05 + 288.5)^{-1} = (2052.55)^{-1} \\ w_4 &= (1764.05 + 944)^{-1} = (2708.05)^{-1} \\ w_5 &= (1764.05 + 500)^{-1} = (2264.05)^{-1} \\ w_6 &- (1764.05 + 192.5)^{-1} = (1956.55)^{-1}\end{aligned}$$

$$\begin{aligned}\hat{\mu}_T &= \frac{\Sigma w_i x_{i\bullet}}{\Sigma w_i} \\ &= \frac{.041031 + .064466 + .079900 + .036188 + .088337 + .035777}{.002704} \\ &= 127.85 .\end{aligned}$$

Then the regression estimates are

$$\begin{aligned}R(T_i|x_{i\bullet}) &= \frac{\sigma_T^2 x_{i\bullet} + n_i^{-1}\hat{\phi}_i\hat{\mu}_T}{\hat{\sigma}_T^2 + n_i^{-1}\hat{\phi}_i} \\ &= \frac{(1764.05)\,x_{i\bullet} + \left(\frac{1}{5}\right)(127.85)\,\hat{\phi}_i}{(1764.05) + \left(\frac{1}{5}\right)\hat{\phi}_i} \\ &= \frac{1764.05x_{i\bullet} + 25.57\hat{\phi}_i}{1764.05 + .2\hat{\phi}_i} .\end{aligned}$$

$$\begin{aligned}R(T_1|x_{1\bullet}) &= 112.10 & R(T_4|x_{4\bullet}) &= 108.41 \\ R(T_2|x_{2\bullet}) &= 127.98 & R(T_5|x_{5\bullet}) &= 184.07 \\ R(T_3|x_{3\bullet}) &= 158.92 & R(T_6|x_{6\bullet}) &= 75.69 .\end{aligned}$$

We see here that the amount of regression from the within-person mean to the grand mean depends heavily on the estimated error variance for that person.

Note that the simultaneous estimation methods developed here cover both applications suggested in the opening paragraph of Sec. 9-4. The assumptions of the "two" models are identical. Whether the experimental unit is the group, and the replications are persons, or the experimental unit is the person, and the replications are repeated measurements on the same person, is unimportant. The model applies equally to both situations.

9-6 REGRESSED ESTIMATES OF ERROR VARIANCES AND MEANS

In Sec. 9-5, we were compelled to take one of two extreme positions about the error variances ϕ_i. We could either assume them all equal, taking $\phi_i = \sigma_E^2$, or we could treat each one in isolation, which in many applications will result in very imprecise estimation. It seems natural to apply the logic of the Kelley formula to the ϕ_i also, treating them as sampled from a common distribution and, hence, regressing them toward a common value. Clearly, this is a compromise between the two extremes mentioned.

Corresponding to each ϕ_i, we have a single "observation",

$$\hat{\phi}_i = (n_i - 1)^{-1} \sum_j (x_{ij} - x_{i\bullet})^2 , \qquad (9\text{-}6.1)$$

which we can use to estimate it. If we assume normality for the observations x_{ij}, that is, that x_{ij}: $N(\tau_i, \phi_i)$ independently for $j = 1, 2, \ldots, n_i$, then for fixed ϕ_i, $(n_i - 1)\hat{\phi}_i/\phi_i$ has a chi-square distribution on $(n_i - 1)$ degrees of freedom with mean $(n_i - 1)$ and variance $2(n_i - 1)$, that is, $\hat{\phi}_i$: $\chi^2[n_i - 1, \phi_i/(n_i - 1)]$. Hence, $\hat{\phi}_i$ is distributed with mean ϕ_i and variance $2\phi_i^2/(n_i - 1)$. Unfortunately, both the mean and the variance of the distribution of $\hat{\phi}_i$ depend on ϕ_i.

We noted in Sec. 9-5 that if the distributions of X given τ and of T are normal, the Kelley formula (9-5.2) is identical with the regression function $\mathcal{E}(T|x)$ and so is more directly meaningful. It, therefore, seems desirable to transform our "observation" $\hat{\phi}_i$ so that it has approximately a normal distribution. It is known that $\ln \hat{\phi}_i$ is more nearly normally distributed than $\hat{\phi}_i$, and the approximate mean and variance are known to be

$$\mathcal{E}(\ln \hat{\phi}_i) = \ln \phi_i - (n_i - 1)^{-1} , \qquad (9\text{-}6.2)$$

and

$$\mathcal{V}(\ln \hat{\phi}_i) = 2(n_i - 1)^{-1} . \qquad (9\text{-}6.3)$$

Let us write

$$\nu_i = (n_i - 1) \qquad (9\text{-}6.4)$$

and define a transformed observation

$$t_i = \ln \hat{\phi}_i + \nu_i^{-1} \qquad (9\text{-}6.5)$$

and a transformed parameter

$$\omega_i = \ln \phi_i . \qquad (9\text{-}6.6)$$

Then we have shown that, approximately,

$$t_i : N(\omega_i, 2\nu_i^{-1}) .$$

The transformation that was used has given us both normality for the statistic and a *known* variance. Thus ω_i, a true log-variance, corresponds to true-score in the Kelley case. When the replication numbers are unequal, we have different but *known* variances for the statistic t_i (which corresponds to x or $x_{i\bullet}$ in the Kelley case).

Now let us assume, as we did for the true-scores, that the ω_i are themselves realizations of a random variable Ω which has a $N(\mu_\Omega, \sigma_\Omega^2)$ distribution. Then, by comparison with Eqs. (9-5.12) through (9-5.14), we obtain directly the regressed estimate of ω_i

$$\hat{\omega}_i = R(\Omega_i | t_i) = \frac{\hat{\sigma}_\Omega^2 t_i + 2\nu_i^{-1}\hat{\mu}_\Omega}{\hat{\sigma}_\Omega^2 + 2\nu_i^{-1}} . \qquad (9\text{-}6.7)$$

Here,

$$\hat{\sigma}_\Omega^2 = (m-1)^{-1}\Sigma(t_i - t_\bullet)^2 - 2m^{-1}\Sigma\nu_i^{-1} , \qquad (9\text{-}6.8)$$

where

$$t_\bullet = m^{-1}\Sigma t_i ,$$

and

$$\hat{\mu}_\Omega = \frac{\Sigma w_i t_i}{\Sigma w_i} \qquad (9\text{-}6.9)$$

where

$$w_i = (\hat{\sigma}_\Omega^2 + 2\nu_i^{-1})^{-1} .$$

Finally, from (9-6.6), we obtain as a regressed estimate of the error variance

$$\hat{\hat{\phi}}_i = \exp \hat{\omega}_i . \qquad (9\text{-}6.10)$$

Note that the regression is, essentially, toward the *geometric* mean of the $\hat{\phi}_i$, and is a geometric weighted average as compared with an arithmetic weighted average in the true-score case.

Having obtained regressed estimates $\hat{\hat{\phi}}_i$ of ϕ_i, we can then use them in place of $\hat{\phi}_i$ in Eqs. (9-5.12) and (9-5.14) when finding regressed estimates of true-score; and in many circumstances, this will be preferable to making the assumption of a common error variance.

For the data in Table 9-4.1, we compute

$$\ln \hat{\phi}_1 = 8.28778 \qquad \ln \hat{\phi}_4 = 8.45956$$

$$\ln\hat{\phi}_2 = 7.00986 \qquad \ln\hat{\phi}_5 = 7.82405$$
$$\ln\hat{\phi}_3 = 7.27413 \qquad \ln\hat{\phi}_6 = 6.86953$$
$$t_1 = 8.53778 \qquad t_4 = 8.70956$$
$$t_2 = 7.25986 \qquad t_5 = 8.07405$$
$$t_3 = 7.52413 \qquad t_6 = 7.11953$$
$$t_{\bullet} = m^{-1}\Sigma t_i = \tfrac{1}{6}(47.2249) = 7.87082$$
$$\begin{aligned}\hat{\sigma}_{\Omega}^2 &= (m-1)^{-1}\Sigma(t_i - t_{\bullet})^2 - 2m^{-1}\Sigma\nu_i^{-1}\\ &= (5)^{-1}(2.24753) - .5\\ &= .449506 - .5\\ &= -.050494\,.\end{aligned}$$

Since the computed value of $\hat{\sigma}_{\Omega}^2 < 0$, we replace the computed value by zero.

$$\begin{aligned}w_i &= (\hat{\sigma}_{\Omega}^2 + 2\nu_i^{-1})^{-1}\\ &= [0 + 2(4)^{-1}]^{-1}\\ &= 2, \quad \text{for all } i\,.\end{aligned}$$
$$\Sigma w_i = 12$$
$$\hat{\mu}_{\Omega} = \frac{\Sigma w_i t_i}{\Sigma w_i} = \frac{2\Sigma t_i}{12} = \frac{\Sigma t_i}{6} = 7.87082$$
$$\hat{\omega}_i = R(\Omega_i|t_i) = \frac{\hat{\sigma}_{\Omega}^2 t_i + 2\nu_i^{-1}\hat{\mu}_{\Omega}}{\sigma_{\Omega}^2 + 2\nu_i^{-1}}\,.$$

But with $\hat{\sigma}_{\Omega}^2 = 0$ this reduces to $\hat{\omega}_i = \hat{\mu}_{\Omega} = 7.87082$ for all i. Then the estimate of ϕ_i is

$$\hat{\hat{\phi}}_i = \exp\hat{\omega}_i = \exp(7.87082) = 2619.71, \quad \text{for all } i\,.$$

Then,

$$\begin{aligned}\hat{\hat{\sigma}}_T^2 &= (m-1)^{-1}\Sigma(x_{i\bullet} - x_{\bullet\bullet})^2 - m^{-1}\Sigma n_i^{-1}\hat{\hat{\phi}}_i\\ &= 2254.3 - 523.942\\ &= 1730.358\,.\end{aligned}$$

Finally,

$$\begin{aligned}R(T_i|x_{i\bullet}) &= \frac{\hat{\hat{\sigma}}_T^2 x_{i\bullet} + n_i^{-1}\hat{\hat{\phi}}_i\hat{\mu}_T}{\hat{\hat{\sigma}}_T^2 + n_i^{-1}\hat{\hat{\phi}}_i}\\ &= \frac{(1730.358)x_{i\bullet} + (.2)(2619.71)(127.5)}{1730.358 + (.2)(2619.71)}\\ &= \frac{(1730.358)x_{i\bullet} + 66802.605}{2254.3}\\ &= .76758x_{i\bullet} + 29.6334\,.\end{aligned}$$

Thus,

$$\begin{aligned} R(T_1|x_1\centerdot) &= 110.23 & R(T_4|x_4\centerdot) &= 104.86 \\ R(T_2|x_2\centerdot) &= 127.88 & R(T_5|x_5\centerdot) &= 183.15 \\ R(T_3|x_3\centerdot) &= 155.52 & R(T_6|x_6\centerdot) & \quad 83.36\,. \end{aligned}$$

A difficulty will arise in applying the formulas of this section if any person i has identical scores on each of the parallel tests, since then $\hat{\phi}_i = 0$, and its logarithm cannot be taken. The risk of this happening will be greatest when we have only two replications. A little reflection shows that the difficulty results from the limited accuracy of the measuring instrument (test).

Suppose that scores are recorded as integers in the range from 0 to 1,000. The statement $x_{i1} = x_{i2}$ means, so far as the statistical model is concerned, that the ith person's scores on the first and second tests are *identical*, to the 100th decimal place if necessary. However, the statement $x_{i1} = 523$, $x_{i2} = 523$, means only that $522.5 \leq x_{i1} < 523.5$ and $522.5 \leq x_{i2} < 523.5$. If in some way we were able to measure to an accuracy of even three decimal places, we would be astonished to find the two scores identical—indeed, we would suspect that a recording error had been made. Conversely, if we measure crudely enough—say to the nearest 100 score points—the great majority of persons will have "identical" scores for each of the parallel tests. Thus, when we record that a person's observed score random variable X takes the value x, what we really mean is that

$$X = x + \epsilon \qquad (9\text{-}6.11)$$

where ϵ is a recording error produced by grouping or by the inaccuracy of the measuring instrument (not to be confused with the error score E which is best thought of as relating to the person—he does not always function at exactly his "true" level τ). One approach to this error when all the observations x_{ij} on person i are equal (to x_i, say) is to assume that each observation "really" has a uniform distribution in the range $(x_i - \frac{1}{2}c,\ x_i + \frac{1}{2}c)$ which is implied by a recorded score of x_i. The quantity c is the class width of the grouping. In the example above, we had $c = 1$.

Making the further assumption that the x_{ij} are independent, conditional on their having fallen in the interval with center x_i, the expected value of $\sum_j (x_{ij} - x_i)^2$, in the sense of the value we would expect to find if we could measure with perfect accuracy, is $(n_i - 1)c^2/12$. If we use this in place of the actual sum of squares in (9-6.1), we obtain the estimate

$$\hat{\phi}_i = \frac{c^2}{12}\,. \qquad (9\text{-}6.12)$$

One might think that the estimate should depend on n_i, the number of observations falling in the range $(x_i - \frac{1}{2}c,\ x_i + \frac{1}{2}c)$, with a large number of observations indicating a smaller variance. This is not so. The larger the number of observations, the more likely that they are "really" spread right across the interval or that their true range is nearly equal to c; and this balances out the increase in the number of degrees of freedom on which the estimate $\hat{\phi}$ is based.

10
FURTHER BAYESIAN ANALYSIS OF DISCRETE DATA

In Chap. 5, we studied, from first principles, the Bayesian analysis of the binary model in which the observations fall into one of two categories. Our main finding was that if the prior distribution for the "success rate" π is of the beta type with parameters (a, b), and we observe x "successes" in a sample of size n, then the posterior distribution is also beta with parameters $(a + x, b + n - x)$. The beta distribution is not very convenient because of the extensive tables required to make available the cumulative distribution functions for all possible combinations of parameter values p and q. For this reason, we now consider various approximate methods which can be used to simplify the analysis of binary data. In Sec. 10-7, we also discuss the multicategory situation and provide a Bayesian analysis for the multinomial distribution. Finally, in Secs. 10-8 and 10-9, we introduce some techniques for the estimation of many binomial parameters and the smoothing of contingency tables.

10-1 INFERENCES ABOUT PROPORTIONS USING THE ARCSINE TRANSFORMATION

One commonly used approximation is to transform our observation x by writing

$$g = \sin^{-1}\sqrt{\frac{x}{n}} \qquad (10\text{-}1.1)$$

where $\sin^{-1}\sqrt{x/n}$ is the angle, measured in radians, whose sine is $\sqrt{x/n}$. This is known as the inverse sine or arcsine transformation. Note that g is measured in radians, not in degrees. Since $0 \leq x \leq n$, we have $0 \leq g \leq \pi/2 = 1.57$, approximately. Values of the arcsine of $\sqrt{p}$ for arguments $p = .000(.001).999$ are given in Table A.18(*a*) and the inverse transformation values, i.e., the values of $\sin^2$, are given in Table A.18(*b*).

The pair (n, g) convey exactly the same information as the pair (n, x) and so must be sufficient statistics for the model. Now it is known that if n is not too small and x not too near zero or n, then for fixed n, g has approximately the distribution

$$N[\sin^{-1}\sqrt{\pi}, (4n)^{-1}] .$$

[A rough criterion for the adequacy of the approximation is $x(1 - x/n) > 5$.] Hence, if we write

$$\gamma = \sin^{-1}\sqrt{\pi}, \qquad (10\text{-}1.2)$$

we have the very useful result that our transformed model is that of a normal distribution with unknown mean γ and *known* variance $(4n)^{-1}$. This is the simplest possible normal model. It was discussed at length in Chap. 6 and reviewed in Sec. 7-1.

Suppose, just to keep things simple for a start, we use a uniform prior distribution for γ. Drawing on the results of Sec. 7-1, we find that the posterior distribution of γ is (approximately)

$$N[g, (4n)^{-1}] .$$

With this result, it is possible to make credibility interval statements about γ and, hence, about π from the table of the cumulative normal distribution, Table A.1. It is not then necessary to consult the massive set of Pearson tables of the incomplete beta function ratio. Note that taking a uniform prior for γ is equivalent to a prior for π of the form

$$b(\pi) \propto \pi^{-1/2}(1 - \pi)^{-1/2}, \qquad (10\text{-}1.3)$$

which is beta with $p = q = \frac{1}{2}$. This is not very different from the indifference prior, $p = q = 0$, used in the original beta-binomial analysis.

It is also possible to compute Prob $(\gamma > \gamma_0)$ for specified values of γ_0 and, thus, to estimate γ and, hence, π under threshold loss. We have

$$\begin{aligned} \text{Prob}\ (\pi > \pi_0) &= \text{Prob}\ (\gamma > \gamma_0) \\ &= 1 - \Phi[(4n)^{1/2}(\gamma_0 - g)] \\ &= \Phi[(4n)^{1/2}(g - \gamma_0)], \end{aligned}$$

where, as usual, Φ denotes the cumulative distribution function of the standard normal variable, and $\pi_0 = \sin^2 \gamma_0$.

Suppose $x = 20$, $n = 30$; then $x[1 - (x/n)] = 20(1 - \frac{1}{3}) = \frac{40}{3} = 13.3$ and we can confidently use the arcsine transformation. Assuming for the moment that we have no prior information, we adopt a uniform prior for $\gamma = \sin^{-1}\sqrt{\pi}$. Then we state that γ is normally distributed a posteriori with mean g and variance $(4n)^{-1}$ where $g = \sin^{-1}\sqrt{x/n}$. From Table A.18(a) we find $g = \sin^{-1}\sqrt{x/n} = \sin^{-1}\sqrt{.667} = .9557$. (Note carefully that the tabulated value is $\sin^{-1}\sqrt{}$, i.e., the square-root operation is built into the table so that the value of the argument is p rather than $\sqrt{p}$.) We thus assert that a posteriori γ has a normal distribution with mean .9557 and variance $(4n)^{-1} = (120)^{1} = .008333$. The standard deviation corresponding to this variance is approximately .0913. Thus, for example, a 95% credibility interval for γ is .9557 ± (1.96)(.091) = .9557 ± (.1789) or (.7768,1.1346). The reader no doubt is perplexed at this point because γ is not a parameter that has any meaning for him and therefore a credibility interval for it has equally little meaning. However, this statement about γ can be transformed into a statement about π. All we need to do is use Table A.18(b) to transform the endpoints of the credibility interval for γ into the endpoints of the credibility interval for π. From Table A.18(b) we see that the values corresponding to the arguments .7768 and 1.1346 are .4916 and .8218. Rounding these values to a more meaningful statement, we assert that π is in the interval (.49, .82) with probability .95. The only point estimate that comes naturally from the procedure is $x/n = .67$. This value corresponds to a γ value of .9557 which is the a posteriori mean, median, and mode of the distribution of γ. Thus, .67 is the correct point estimate of π when we have squared-error, absolute-error, or zero-one loss with respect to γ. It is not immediately clear what point estimate of π is correct but a robustness argument can justify the value .67, unless our loss structure for π is very asymmetric.

One situation in which we would proceed differently is if we had a threshold-loss structure for π. Then to decide whether π was bigger than some value π_0, we would need to compute Prob $(\pi \geq \pi_0)$. Suppose, for example, that the critical value was $\pi_0 = .60$. Entering Table A.18(a) with $p = .60$, we find that the corresponding value of γ_0 is .8861. Then we need to know Prob $(\gamma > .8861)$. Since γ is normally distributed with mean .9557 and standard deviation .0913,

$$\text{Prob}(\gamma > .8861) = \text{Prob}\left(Z > \frac{.8861 - .9557}{.0913}\right) = \text{Prob}(Z > -.762).$$

From Table A.1, using linear interpolation and recalling that Prob $(Z > -.765) =$ Prob $(Z < +.765)$, we find the required probability to be .7770. Thus Prob $(\pi > .60)$ is .7770.

If we have independent samples of sizes n_1 and n_2 from populations with parameters γ_1 and γ_2 and transform the observed proportion in each sample using

(10-1.1) to obtain values g_1 and g_2, respectively, we can quote from Sec. 8-1, case 1, to say that the posterior distribution of $(\gamma_1 - \gamma_2)$ is

$$N[g_1 - g_2, (4n_1)^{-1} + (4n_2)^{-1}] .$$

We could then compute Prob $(\gamma_1 - \gamma_2 > 0)$, which is just Prob $(\gamma_1 > \gamma_2)$ and also Prob $(\pi_1 > \pi_2)$. We shall exemplify this later.

The preceding paragraphs have covered, at what may at first reading seem to be breakneck speed, ground which previously needed several pages of careful discussion. This underlines the purpose of approximations: by converting our model to a normal one, we return to territory which is already familiar and where, moreover, all the necessary statistical tables are readily available. Now let us pause and consider a number of points supplementary to the main argument but important to the careful implementation of these methods.

First, what can be done when prior information is available and so the uniform prior is inappropriate? Any prior information which can reasonably be represented by a beta distribution with parameters (a,b)—in Chap. 5, we argued that this will almost always be the case—is equivalent to having started with the prior (10-1.3) and observed $(a - \frac{1}{2})$ successes and $(b - \frac{1}{2})$ failures. All we need to do, therefore, in order to use our approximate analysis in the standard form presented above is to add these hypothetical observations to the actual observations in our sample before making the transformation (10-1.1). For practical purposes, we may ignore the $-\frac{1}{2}$ and proceed as usual, adding a and b to the observed numbers of successes and failures.

Second, for general use, we recommend the use of the refined approximation due to Anscombe (1948) who showed that if we make the transformation

$$g = \sin^{-1} \sqrt{\frac{x + \frac{3}{8}}{n + \frac{3}{4}}} , \qquad (10\text{-}1.4)$$

then the distribution of g is approximately $N[\gamma, (4n + 2)^{-1}]$ where, as before, $\gamma = \sin^{-1} \sqrt{\pi}$. The transformation (10-1.4) is superior to (10-1.1) in two ways: the error involved in asserting that the variance does not depend on x is smaller, as is the error involved in saying that the mean is γ. (Again, a rough criterion of adequacy is $x[1 - (x/n)] > 5$.) Starting with a uniform prior for γ, the posterior will now be $N[g, (4n + 2)^{-1}]$ where g has the value (10-1.4). For the difference $\gamma_1 - \gamma_2$, the posterior is

$$N[g_1 - g_2, (4n_1 + 2)^{-1} + (4n_2 + 2)^{-1}] .$$

Third, there is a price to pay (in addition to the approximate nature of the results) for the simplicity of the analysis. This is that our results are all expressed in terms of γ which is a parameter with no natural interpretation and for which we have no intuitive "feel". When we are concerned only with a single population, this is not too serious since any probability statement concerning π can immediately be translated into one about γ and vice versa as in the example given previously. However, when we wish to compare the success rates π_1 and π_2 in two populations, the handicap of working with γ becomes more serious. We are likely to be interested in probabilities such as Prob $(\pi_1 - \pi_2 > c)$ or Prob $(\pi_1/\pi_2 > c)$, neither of which can, in general, be expressed in terms of $(\gamma_1 - \gamma_2)$, whose posterior distribution we have found. As indicated previously, there is, however, one important exception. If we are interested simply in the probability that π_1 is greater than π_2, this is

$$\begin{aligned}\text{Prob}\,(\pi_1 > \pi_2) &= \text{Prob}\,(\gamma_1 > \gamma_2)\\ &= \text{Prob}\,(\gamma_1 - \gamma_2 > 0)\\ &= \Phi\left\{(g_1 - g_2)[(4n_1 + 2)^{-1} + (4n_2 + 2)^{-1}]^{-1/2}\right\}.\end{aligned}$$

Suppose we have two populations with beta priors $\beta(5,2)$ and $\beta(4,3)$ for π_1 and π_2, respectively, and sample observations $x_1 = 20$, $n_1 = 30$, and $x_2 = 25$, $n_2 = 30$. We may combine the hypothetical prior samples with the real samples and proceed as if the sample from the first population consisted of 25 successes in 37 trials and the sample from the second population consisted of 29 successes in 37 trials. Then, a posteriori, the distribution of the difference $\gamma_1 - \gamma_2$ is normal, with mean

$$\begin{aligned}g_1 - g_2 &= \sin^{-1}\sqrt{\frac{25 + \frac{3}{8}}{37 + \frac{3}{4}}} - \sin^{-1}\sqrt{\frac{29 + \frac{3}{8}}{37 + \frac{3}{4}}}\\ &= \sin^{-1}\sqrt{.672} - \sin^{-1}\sqrt{.778}\\ &= .9610 - 1.0802\\ &= -.1192\end{aligned}$$

and variance

$$\begin{aligned}(4n_1 + 2)^{-1} + (4n_2 + 2)^{-1} &= (4\cdot 37 + 2)^{-1} + (4\cdot 37 + 2)^{-1}\\ &= .0133\,.\end{aligned}$$

The probability that π_1 is greater than π_2 is

$$\begin{aligned}\text{Prob}\,(\pi_1 > \pi_2) &= \Phi\left\{(g_1 - g_2)[(4n_1 + 2)^{-1} + (4n_2 + 2)^{-1}]^{-1/2}\right\}\\ &= \Phi\left[(-.1192)(.0133)^{-1/2}\right]\\ &= \Phi(-1.0323)\\ &= .1515\,.\end{aligned}$$

10-2 THE LOG-ODDS TRANSFORMATION[1]

In everyday life, probabilities are most often discussed in terms of odds. If an event has probability p, we say that the odds are (in the ratio) $p\colon(1 - p)$ in favor of the event. It is natural to extend this nomenclature to the binary model whether π is thought of as a probability or as a proportion. Thus, we speak of $\pi/(1 - \pi)$ as the odds parameter of the model. We may also speak of the ratio $x/(n - x)$ of observed successes and failures as the sample odds.

In Sec. 5-5, we showed how a beta distribution for π can be transformed when beta tables are not available so as to allow credibility intervals to be obtained from F tables. The essence of the transformation was to consider the odds. Using our standard notation for F defined below Eq. (8-2.1), we can summarize the result as follows. If our prior for π is beta with parameters (a, b), then the prior for the odds $\pi/(1 - \pi)$ is

$$F(2a, 2b, 1, 1)$$

and if we observe x successes and $(n - x)$ failures, then the posterior distribution of the odds $\pi/(1 - \pi)$ is

$$F[2(a + x), 2(b + n - x), 1, 1] .$$

This transformation solves only the problem of availability of tables, not the problem of complexity. The F distribution is simply the beta distribution expressed in a different form, and so the amount of tabulation and the mathematical complexity of the density function are identical for the two distributions. However, in our discussion of the F distribution, we noted that Fisher himself worked with the quantity $z = \frac{1}{2} \ln F$ (where F is a random variable having an F distribution) which is approximately normally distributed. The factor $\frac{1}{2}$ is irrelevant for our present purpose, and so we work directly with the *log-odds*

$$\delta = \ln \frac{\pi}{1 - \pi} = \ln \pi - \ln(1 - \pi) \qquad (10\text{-}2.1)$$

which in the case of the posterior distribution above is approximately normally distributed $N(\mu_n, \sigma_n^2)$, with mean

$$\mu_n = \ln \frac{a + x - \frac{1}{2}}{b + n - x - \frac{1}{2}} \qquad (10\text{-}2.2)$$

and variance

$$\sigma_n^2 = (a + x)^{-1} + (b + n - x)^{-1} . \qquad (10\text{-}2.3)$$

We could, for example, use this transformation to find posterior credibility intervals in the situation discussed on the last page of Chap. 5. There we had, in our present

[1] Reading of this section may be deferred without loss of continuity.

notation, $a = 10$, $b = 3$, $n = 25$, and $x = 20$. Hence, the approximate posterior distribution of δ is $N(1.369,.158)$. The standard deviation is $\sqrt{.158} = .398$. Thus, a 50% credibility interval for δ is $1.369 \pm (.675)(.398)$ or $(1.100,1.638)$.

We have now to transform this back into an interval for π. Using Table A.10(b), the table of inverse log-odds, we find the central 50% credibility interval for π to be (.75,.84), agreeing perfectly to two decimal places with the exact interval obtained from the beta distribution. In like manner, taking values of δ at 1.96 standard deviations from the mean, we find the 95% interval to be (.64,.90): The exact interval was (.65,.90).

As with other transformations, the real payoff comes when we wish to deal with more than one proportion π. Consider again the problem of comparing two proportions, π_1 and π_2, with corresponding log-odds, δ_1 and δ_2. If we have independent priors and independent samples, the posterior distribution of $(\delta_1 - \delta_2)$ is approximately normal, with mean the difference of the posterior means for δ_1 and δ_2 as given by (10-2.2) and variance the sum of the variances given by (10-2.3). Hence, we can find

$$\begin{aligned} \text{Prob}\,(\pi_1 > \pi_2) &= \text{Prob}\,(\delta_1 > \delta_2) \\ &= \text{Prob}\,(\delta_1 - \delta_2 > 0)\,, \end{aligned}$$

the latter probability being found in the usual way from the normal distribution.

We are still confronted with the problem we experienced when studying the arcsine transform, that with the exception of the special case just discussed, neither of the statements $\pi_1 - \pi_2 > c$ or $\pi_1/\pi_2 > c$ translates into a statement about $(\delta_1 - \delta_2)$; and so the posterior distribution we have found does not help in determining their probabilities. However, when π_1 and π_2 are interpretable as probabilities, we can obtain statements which may be useful to persons accustomed to thinking in terms of odds. We have

$$\delta_1 - \delta_2 = \ln \frac{\pi_1/(1 - \pi_1)}{\pi_2/(1 - \pi_2)}\,. \qquad (10\text{-}2.4)$$

Hence, if $\delta_1 - \delta_2 > \ln 2$, say, the odds in the first model are more than twice the odds in the second model, and we can determine the probability that this is so from the posterior distribution of $(\delta_1 - \delta_2)$. This is a useful interpretation and we suspect that the popularity of this kind of analysis will increase as readers become more accustomed to thinking about odds ratios.

Consider the data analyzed in the previous section. Our beta priors were $\beta(5,2)$ and $\beta(4,3)$ and our sample data were $x_1 = 20$, $n_1 = 30$, and $x_2 = 25$, $n_2 = 30$. Analyzing each sample separately, the posterior distribution for δ_1 is approximately normal, with mean

$$\begin{aligned} \mu_{n_1} &= \ln \frac{5 + 20 - \frac{1}{2}}{2 + 30 - 20 - \frac{1}{2}} \\ &= \ln\,(2.1304) \\ &= .7563 \end{aligned}$$

and variance

$$\sigma_{n_1}^2 = (5 + 20)^{-1} + (2 + 30 - 20)^{-1}$$
$$= .1233 .$$

The posterior distribution for δ_2 is approximately normal, with mean

$$\mu_{n_2} = \ln \frac{4 + 25 - \frac{1}{2}}{3 + 30 - 25 - \frac{1}{2}}$$
$$= \ln (3.8000)$$
$$= 1.3350$$

and variance

$$\sigma_{n_2}^2 = (4 + 25)^{-1} + (3 + 30 - 25)^{-1}$$
$$= .1595 .$$

The posterior distribution of $(\delta_1 - \delta_2)$ is approximately normal, with mean

$$\mu = \mu_{n_1} - \mu_{n_2}$$
$$= .7563 - 1.3350$$
$$= -.5787$$

and variance

$$\sigma^2 = \sigma_{n_1}{}^2 + \sigma_{n_2}{}^2$$
$$= .1233 + .1595$$
$$= .2828 .$$

Thus, the probability that π_1 is greater than π_2 is

$$\text{Prob}\,(\pi_1 > \pi_2) = \text{Prob}\,(\delta_1 - \delta_2 > 0)$$
$$= \Phi\,(\mu\sigma^{-1})$$
$$= \Phi\,(-1.0881)$$
$$= .1383 .$$

10-3 THE POISSON APPROXIMATION

In Sec. 5-3, we noted that when π (or $1 - \pi$) is small and n is fairly large, a good approximation to the binomial distribution is provided by the Poisson distribution with mean parameter $\mu = n\pi$ [or $n(1 - \pi)$]. Thus, if we are concerned with inference about success (or failure) rates which are expected to be small, we can approximate the full beta-binomial analysis by the simpler analysis to be presented here. Specifically, this analysis would be very satisfactory if $n > 10$, $\pi < .05$. This is particularly fortunate since it is for precisely these extreme values of π that the arcsine and log-odds approximations are unsatisfactory.

We noted also in Sec. 5-3 that there are occasions when a Poisson model is appropriate in its own right. Any reader who has cause to use such a model will find that the analysis given below applies equally to it on writing $n\pi = \mu$ or $\pi = \mu/n$. The only differences will be the numerical values of the parameters of the prior and posterior distributions and their interpretation in the context of the model.

From (5-3.1) with $\mu = n\pi$, we have the model density

$$m_\pi(x) = \frac{(n\pi)^x e^{-n\pi}}{x!}, \qquad (10\text{-}3.1)$$

for $x = 0, 1, 2, \ldots$. The Poisson distribution (10-3.1) has mean and variance both equal to $n\pi$. The quantity x is the number of times the defining event, such as "success", occurs. Thus, the likelihood is

$$l_n(\pi) \propto \pi^x e^{-n\pi}. \qquad (10\text{-}3.2)$$

Note that if π is small and n is large, the Poisson model assigns very little probability to values of $x > n$, which, in part, helps us retain our belief that the Poisson model may be a good approximation to the binomial model under these conditions.

From (10-3.2) we can, as usual, derive a conjugate density by replacing x and n by constants $(z - 1)$ and m, obtaining

$$b(\pi) \propto \pi^{z-1} e^{-m\pi}. \qquad (10\text{-}3.3)$$

[The reason for taking $(z - 1)$ rather than z will appear in a moment.] Using (10-3.3) as the prior, the posterior distribution has density

$$b_n(\pi) \propto \pi^{z+x-1} e^{-(m+n)\pi}. \qquad (10\text{-}3.4)$$

This is of the same form as the prior, with $(z + x)$ for z and $(m + n)$ for m. The indifference prior is

$$b(\pi) \propto \pi^{-1} \qquad (10\text{-}3.5)$$

which corresponds to putting $z = m = 0$ in (10-3.3). Conversely, the general prior (10-3.3) can be regarded as the result of using the indifference prior and obtaining a hypothetical prior sample of size m containing z successes.

Before naming the conjugate distribution or discussing credibility intervals, we must look at one point concerning the approximation. If μ or $n\pi$ were a general Poisson parameter which could take any positive value, the range of π in the Bayes distributions would be $0 \leq \pi < \infty$. In fact, however, we know that $0 < \pi < 1$ when the Poisson distribution is used to approximate the binomial. We are going to ignore this distinction and act as though the range of π were, indeed, infinite. The justification for doing so is that the Poisson approximation is only appropriate when the true value of π is small. Hence, in any analysis for which it is valid, the posterior probability that π exceeds unity will be negligible. It will, therefore, make no practical difference whether we take the range to be (0,1) or $(0,\infty)$, but taking the latter range will enable standard distributions and tables to be used.

With this understanding about the range, the density (10-3.3) is that of a gamma distribution with *index* z and (scale) *parameter* m. As with beta, the name gamma is taken from a closely related mathematical function which is defined by an integral and was known to mathematicians long before the distribution was used in statistics. The mathematicians' definition had the power $(z - 1)$ for π, hence the adoption of the same form in statistics.

The gamma form is useful because of the simple way (noted above) in which the observations change the parameters. When it comes to finding credibility intervals, however, we note that a gamma density is merely another way of writing a chi-square density. Specifically, if we compare the π of (10-3.3) with W of (7-2.3), we see that π has a χ^2 distribution with $\nu = 2z$ degrees of freedom and scale parameter $\omega = (2m)^{-1}$. Thus, we obtain prior credibility intervals by using χ^2 tables with $2z$ degrees of freedom and dividing the limits so obtained by $2m$. Similarly, for posterior intervals, we enter χ^2 tables with $2(z + x)$ degrees of freedom and divide the limits by $2(m + n)$.

The identification of the posterior distribution as χ^2 also enables us to state its descriptive characteristics. In the case $z = m = 0$ (indifference prior), these are as follows.

Characteristics of the Posterior χ^2 Distribution

$$\text{Mean} = \frac{x}{n};$$

$$\text{Variance} = \frac{x}{n^2};$$

$$\text{Mode} = \frac{x - 1}{n};$$

$$\text{Median} = \frac{x - \frac{1}{3}}{n}, \quad \text{approximately.}$$

Results for a general posterior are obtained by writing $(z + x)$ for x and $(m + n)$ for n, that is, by using a hypothetical prior sample to represent the information contained in the prior distribution.

The form of the posterior distribution also sheds some light on what can easily be a confusing question: Are small success rates easy or difficult to estimate well? We note that the posterior variance x/n^2 decreases as x decreases, and so in an *absolute* sense, smaller values of π, which can be expected to yield smaller values of x, are more precisely estimated. However, the degrees of freedom of the posterior distribution are $2x$ which also decreases as x decreases. We have seen that, in many contexts, the degrees of freedom indicate the amount of information we have available. Thus, it seems that in some *relative* sense we get (for fixed n) less information when π is small. One way to make this relative sense explicit is to calculate the posterior

$$\text{Coefficient of variation} = \frac{\text{standard deviation}}{\text{mean}} = \frac{1}{\sqrt{x}} .$$

Thus, the size of the standard deviation relative to the mean decreases as a function of x, indicating that in this relative sense large π values are more accurately estimated since they will, on the average, yield higher values of x. In other words, whereas in absolute terms small values of π are well estimated, in terms of percentage error they are poorly estimated.

Consider the data in Table 2-1.5. Since the Poisson approximation is most satisfactory when π is very small, let us estimate the percentage of science students (π_1) and the percentage of social science students (π_2) who have GPAs in the category 0.0 to 0.9. A priori, we might expect π_1 and π_2 to be the same. Suppose our prior estimate of π_1 and of π_2 is .05 with $z = 2$ and $m = 40$. Our prior distribution is chi square on $2z = 4$ degrees of freedom with scale parameter $(2m)^{-1} = (80)^{-1}$. A 50% central credibility interval for π_1 and for π_2 extends from

$$\frac{\chi^2_{.25}(2z)}{2m} = \frac{1.923}{80} = .0240$$

to

$$\frac{\chi^2_{.75}(2z)}{2m} = \frac{5.385}{80} = .0673 .$$

The science sample data are $x_1 = 38$ and $n_1 = 571$. The posterior distribution for π_1 is chi square on $2(z + x_1) = 80$ degrees of freedom with scale parameter $[2(m + n_1)]^{-1} = (1{,}222)^{-1}$ and has

$$\begin{aligned}\text{Mean} &= \frac{z + x_1}{m + n_1}\\ &= \frac{2 + 38}{40 + 571}\\ &= .0655 ,\end{aligned}$$

and

$$\begin{aligned}\text{Variance} &= \frac{z + x_1}{(m + n_1)^2}\\ &= \frac{2 + 38}{(40 + 571)^2}\\ &= .0001 .\end{aligned}$$

The 50% central credibility interval for π_1 extends from

$$\frac{\chi^2_{.25}[2(z + x_1)]}{2(m + n_1)} = \frac{71.14}{1222} = .0582$$

to

$$\frac{\chi^2_{.75}[2(z + x_1)]}{2(m + n_1)} = \frac{88.13}{1222} = .0721 \ .$$

The social science sample data are $x_2 = 16$ and $n_2 = 451$. The posterior distribution for π_2 is chi square on $2(z + x_2) = 36$ degrees of freedom with scale parameter $[2(m + n_2)]^{-1} = (982)^{-1}$ and has

$$\text{Mean} = \frac{z + x_2}{m + n_2} = \frac{2 + 16}{40 + 451} = .0367$$

and

$$\text{Variance} = \frac{z + x_2}{(m + n_2)^2} = \frac{2 + 16}{(40 + 451)^2} = .00007 \ .$$

The 50% central credibility interval for π_2 extends from

$$\frac{\chi^2_{.25}[2(z + x_2)]}{2(m + n_2)} = \frac{29.988}{982} = .0305$$

to

$$\frac{\chi^2_{.75}[2(z + x_2)]}{2(m + n_2)} = \frac{41.292}{982} = .0420 \ .$$

The posterior mean for π_1 is .0655 and for π_2 it is .0367. The posterior 50% central credibility intervals for π_1 and π_2 do not overlap. Apparently, more students in science receive GPAs of 0.0 to 0.9 than students in social science.

An advantage of the Poisson analysis is that the posterior distribution obtained is that of the parameter π itself, not of some transform of that parameter. In addition to making the posterior distribution easier to comprehend, this also makes it possible to make direct comparisons between two (small) success rates.

The ratio of two independent χ^2 variables has an F distribution (in generalized form). Thus, if we have independent samples (n_1, x_1), (n_2, x_2) from populations with rates π_1 and π_2 (small) and take independent indifference priors for these two rates, the posterior distribution of π_1/π_2 will be

$$F(2x_1, 2x_2, 2n_1, 2n_2) \ . \qquad (10\text{-}3.6)$$

If we let p_1 and p_2 denote the sample proportions x_1/n_1 and x_2/n_2 and write out, using (8-2.1), what (10-3.6) means in terms of the tabulated (standardized) F variable, we find the intuitively attractive result that

$$\frac{\pi_1/p_1}{\pi_2/p_2} = \frac{p_2}{p_1}\frac{\pi_1}{\pi_2} \tag{10-3.7}$$

has standard F distribution on $(2x_1, 2x_2)$ degrees of freedom. The corresponding results when π_1 and π_2 have (independent) nonindifference priors of conjugate form can be easily obtained by using the hypothetical prior sample technique. Using (10-3.7), we can obtain probabilities of the type Prob $(\pi_1 > c\pi_2)$ = Prob $(\pi_1/\pi_2 > c)$ = Prob $(F > p_2c/p_1)$ where F denotes a standard F variable with $(2x_1, 2x_2)$ degrees of freedom.

Referring to the previous example, the posterior distribution for π_1 (science) was chi square on $2(z + x_1) = 80$ degrees of freedom with scale parameter $[2(m + n_1)]^{-1} = (1{,}222)^{-1}$. The posterior distribution for π_2 (social science) was chi square on $2(z + x_2) = 36$ degrees of freedom with scale parameter $[2(m + n_2)]^{-1} = (982)^{-1}$. Let $p_1 = (z + x_1)/(m + n_1) = .0655$ and $p_2 = (z + x_2)/(m + n_2) = .0367$. Then, the posterior distribution of $(\pi_1/\pi_2)(p_2/p_1)$ is $F(2 \cdot 40, 2 \cdot 18) = F(80, 36)$. The probability that π_1 is greater than π_2 is

$$\begin{aligned} \text{Prob}(\pi_1 > \pi_2) &= \text{Prob}\left(\frac{\pi_1}{\pi_2} > 1\right) \\ &= \text{Prob}\left(F_{(80,\,36)} > \frac{p_2}{p_1}\right) \\ &= \text{Prob}\left(F_{(80,36)} > .56\right) \\ &= .978\,. \end{aligned}$$

10-4 THE NORMAL APPROXIMATION

The Poisson approximation discussed in the last section is appropriate when n is large and either π or $(1 - \pi)$ is small. When n is large but neither π nor $(1 - \pi)$ is small, the binomial distribution of x can be approximated by a normal distribution with mean $n\pi$ and variance $n\pi(1 - \pi)$. This approximation was given in Sec. 5-3, and the reader may have wondered why we have not made use of it rather than resort to transformations to achieve normality.

There are two reasons. First, the arcsine transform leads to a statistic g whose distribution approaches normality much more rapidly (i.e., for much smaller sample sizes) than does that of x itself. Second, while the direct approximation is useful for calculating binomial probabilities, it is not very useful in a Bayesian analysis since both the approximate mean *and variance* depend on π. Thus, even with a very simple prior—say, uniform—the posterior density will not be recognizable as that of a standard distribution. An advantage of the arcsine transformation is its variance-stabilizing property, namely, that the approximate variance does not depend on π.

However, corresponding to the normal approximation to the binomial there is a normal approximation to the beta distribution. In general terms, if π has a beta distribution with parameters (a, b) where neither a nor b is small (say, not < 10), then this distribution can be approximated by a normal distribution with mean $a/(a + b)$ and variance $ab/(a + b)^2(a + b + 1)$. The mean and variance are just those of the beta distribution as given in (5-5.2) and (5-5.3).

Thus, if we use the indifference prior for π and obtain a sample (n, x), our posterior distribution, which is beta with parameters $(x, n - x)$, can be approximated by the distribution

$$N\left[\frac{x}{n}, \frac{x(n - x)}{n^2(n + 1)}\right]. \qquad (10\text{-}4.1)$$

Prior information can again be incorporated by the hypothetical sample method. Given m "prior" observations of which z are successes, the posterior distribution will be given by (10-4.1), with x replaced by $(z + x)$ and n replaced by $(m + n)$.

This normal approximation enables us to make comparisons involving the difference between two binary parameters π_1 and π_2. Let us write $p_i = x_i/n_i$ and $q_i = (n_i - x_i)/n_i$, the observed proportions of successes and failures in the ith sample $(i = 1, 2)$. Then, from (10-4.1), the posterior distribution of π_i is $N[p_i, p_i q_i/(n_i + 1)]$; and so, assuming independent priors and samples, the posterior distribution of $(\pi_1 - \pi_2)$ is

$$N(p_1 - p_2, \epsilon^2) \qquad (10\text{-}4.2)$$

where

$$\epsilon^2 = \frac{p_1 q_1}{n_1 + 1} + \frac{p_2 q_2}{n_2 + 1}. \qquad (10\text{-}4.3)$$

Hence, the posterior probability that $\pi_1 - \pi_2$ is greater than some constant c is

$$\text{Prob}\,(\pi_1 - \pi_2 > c) = \Phi\left[\frac{p_1 - p_2 - c}{\epsilon}\right],$$

where Φ as usual denotes the standard normal distribution function.

Consider again the data in Table 2-1.5. Since the normal approximation is appropriate when neither π nor $(1 - \pi)$ is small, let us estimate the percentage of science students (π_1) and the percentage of social science students (π_2) who have GPAs of at least 2.0. From the examples in the last section, we observed that the percentage of students having GPAs of 0.0 to 0.9 is larger in science than in social science. Thus, we might expect the percentage of students having GPAs of at least 2.0 to be smaller in science than in social science.

Assume our prior estimate of π_1 is .60, with $z_1 = 24$ and $m_1 = 40$. The prior distribution for π_1 is approximately normal, with

$$\text{Mean} = \frac{z_1}{m_1} = \frac{24}{40} = .60$$

and

$$\begin{aligned}\text{Variance} &= \frac{z_1(m_1 - z_1)}{m_1^2(m_1 + 1)}\\ &= \frac{24(16)}{40^2(41)}\\ &= .0059\ .\end{aligned}$$

A 50% central credibility interval for π_1 extends from .548 to .652.

Assume our prior estimate of π_2 is .65 with $z_2 = 26$ and $m_2 = 40$. The prior distribution for π_2 is approximately normal with

$$\text{Mean} = \frac{z_2}{m_2} = \frac{26}{40} = .65$$

and

$$\begin{aligned}\text{Variance} &= \frac{z_2(m_2 - z_2)}{m_2^2(m_2 + 1)}\\ &= \frac{26(14)}{40^2(41)}\\ &= .0055\ .\end{aligned}$$

A 50% central credibility interval for π_2 extends from .600 to .700.

The sample data are:

Science: $x_1 = 350 \quad n_1 = 571$

Social science: $x_2 = 292 \quad n_2 = 451\ .$

The posterior distribution for π_1 is approximately normal, with

$$\begin{aligned}\text{Mean} &= \frac{z_1 + x_1}{m_1 + n_1}\\ &= \frac{24 + 350}{40 + 571}\\ &= .612\end{aligned}$$

and

$$\begin{aligned}\text{Variance} &= \frac{(z_1 + x_1)(m_1 + n_1 - z_1 - x_1)}{(m_1 + n)^2(m_1 + n_1 + 1)}\\ &= \frac{374(237)}{(611)^2(612)}\\ &= .00038\ .\end{aligned}$$

A 50% central credibility interval for π_1 extends from .599 to .625.

The posterior distribution for π_2 is approximately normal, with

$$\text{Mean} = \frac{z_2 + x_2}{m_2 + n_2} = \frac{26 + 292}{40 + 451} = .648$$

and

$$\text{Variance} = \frac{(z_2 + x_2)(m_2 + n_2 - z_2 - x_2)}{(m_2 + n_2)^2(m_2 + n_2 + 1)} = \frac{318(173)}{(491)^2(492)} = .00046\ .$$

A 50% central credibility interval for π_2 extends from .633 to .663.

Now, let $p_1 = .612$, $q_1 = .388$, $n_1 = 611$, $p_2 = .648$, $q_2 = .352$, and $n_2 = 491$. The posterior distribution for $(\pi_1 - \pi_2)$ is normal, with mean

$$p_1 - p_2 = .612 - .648 = -.036$$

and variance

$$\epsilon^2 = \frac{p_1 q_1}{n_1 + 1} + \frac{p_2 q_2}{n_2 + 1} = \frac{.612(.388)}{612} + \frac{.648(.352)}{492} = .00085\ .$$

The probability that π_1 is greater than π_2 is

$$\text{Prob}\,(\pi_1 > \pi_2) = \text{Prob}\,(\pi_1 - \pi_2 > 0) = \Phi\left[\frac{p_1 - p_2}{\epsilon}\right] = \Phi(-1.2336) = .1093, \text{ or } .11, \quad \text{approximately.}$$

Alternatively,

$$\text{Prob}\,(\pi_2 > \pi_1) = .89, \quad \text{approximately.}$$

10-5 DIRECT METHODS OF COMPARING BINOMIAL PROPORTIONS

One goal of the approximate methods discussed in Secs. 10-3 and 10-4 was to facilitate the comparison of binary parameters by providing posterior distributions for either $(\pi_2 - \pi_1)$ or π_2/π_1 which could be referred to standard tables. This goal can also be approached directly when suitable computing facilities are available. Conceptually, there is no difficulty. With independent indifference priors and independent samples (n_i, x_i)–into which any prior knowledge can be incorporated–the posterior distributions of π_1 and π_2 are independent beta distributions with parameters $(x_i, n_i - x_i)$. The remaining problem is mathematical. What is the distribution of the difference, or the ratio, of two independent beta variables? The need for approximations arises because the answer to this question is that for general values of the parameters (k_1, l_1), (k_2, l_2) the distribution is not tabulated.

A simple method exists for computing Prob $(\pi_1 - \pi_2 > c)$ to any desired degree of accuracy, and thus, in effect, obtaining the posterior distribution of $(\pi_1 - \pi_2)$ in numerical (as contrasted with algebraic) form. The method is best illustrated by a diagram. We show the case for $c = .10$.

Figure 10-5.1 shows the region over which the joint posterior distribution of π_1 and π_2 is defined. Since $0 \leq \pi_1 \leq 1$ and $0 \leq \pi_2 \leq 1$, the region is a unit square. The joint density can be imagined, in the manner of Sec. 3-6, as a surface or a "hill" positioned over this square.

We have divided the unit square into 100 small squares by lines parallel to the axes. The choice of 100 was arbitrary. We shall see shortly that the fineness or coarseness of the mesh determines the accuracy with which the posterior probability is calculated.

We have also drawn the diagonal line $\pi_1 - \pi_2 = c = .10$. In the region to the southeast of this line, we have $\pi_1 - \pi_2 > c$; to the northwest, $\pi_1 - \pi_2 < c$. Hence, to find the posterior probability that $\pi_1 - \pi_2 > c$, we have to find the probability that the point (π_1, π_2) falls in the southeast corner.

Consider the blackened square. The point (π_1, π_2) lies in it if $.5 < \pi_1 < .6$ *and* $.1 < \pi_2 < .2$. However, π_1 and π_2 are independent a posteriori. Hence, the probability of both these events occurring is just the product

$$\text{Prob}\ (.5 < \pi_1 < .6)\ \text{Prob}\ (.1 < \pi_2 < .2)$$

of the probabilities of each of them occurring separately. Now the probabilities in this product relate to the (beta) posterior distributions of π_1 and π_2 separately and so can be found from the table of the incomplete beta function in the way described in Sec. 5-6. There are also standard computer programs available which calculate them. Thus, we can find the probability that the point (π_1, π_2) falls in the blackened square.

By repeating this procedure for each complete square in the southeast corner and summing, we obtain a probability, p_1 say, which falls short of Prob $(\pi_1 - \pi_2 > c)$ by the probability that (π_1, π_2) falls in the vertically shaded triangular regions–hopefully a small amount.

Now consider the northwest region. Applying the same procedure and summing over complete squares, we obtain a probability, p_2 say, which is less than Prob $(\pi_1 - \pi_2 < c)$. Hence, $1 - p_2$ is greater than Prob $(\pi_1 - \pi_2 > c)$. Thus, we have

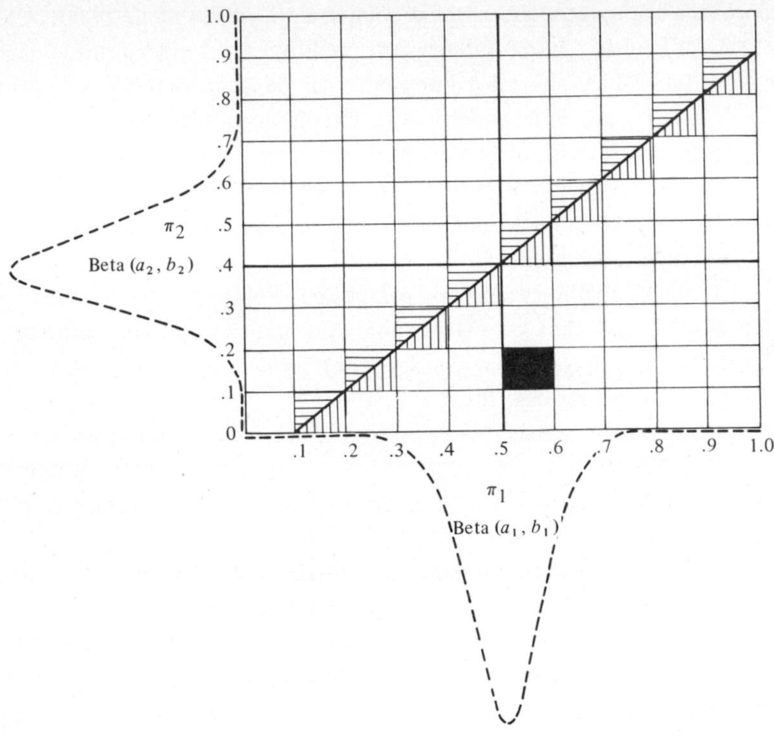

FIGURE 10-5.1
Computation of Prob $(\pi_1 - \pi_2 > .1)$.

sandwiched the probability we wish to compute between two known values:

$$p_1 < \text{Prob}\,(\pi_1 - \pi_2 > c) < 1 - p_2\,.$$

If p_1 and $1 - p_2$ are equal to the order of accuracy at which we wish to operate, we have achieved our goal. Indeed, the simple average of these two quantities will usually be very close to the exact value. If the discrepancy is too great to be tolerated, we must use a finer mesh. This can either be done starting again from scratch, or the fine mesh can be used simply to compute the probabilities in the shaded regions which we have ignored. If one were using a desk calculator, one would clearly choose the latter method. With an electronic computer, the decision is the familiar one of how much programming time it is worth expending to achieve a reduction in computing time.

If the computations are to be made by hand and using published tables of the beta distribution, some small saving can be accomplished by proceeding as follows:

1) Look up Prob $(\pi_1 > .5) = 1 - \text{Prob}\,(\pi_1 < .5)$.

2) Look up Prob $(\pi_2 < .4)$.

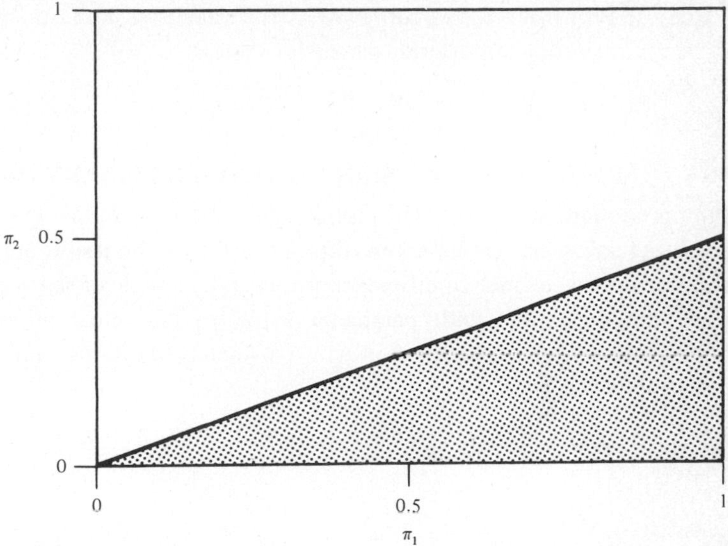

FIGURE 10-5.2
Computation of Prob $(\pi_1/\pi_2 > 2)$.

3) Compute Prob $(\pi_1 > .5, \pi_2 < .4)$ = Prob $(\pi_1 > .5)$ Prob $(\pi_2 < .4)$.

4) Compute Prob $(\pi_2 > .4, \pi_1 < .5)$ = [1 – Prob $(\pi_2 < .4)$][1 – Prob $(\pi_1 > .5)$].

We have now avoided computations of 50 of the cell probabilities required for the tabulation. We continue as follows:

5) Look up Prob $(\pi_1 < .7)$.

6) Look up Prob $(\pi_2 < .6)$.

7) Compute Prob $(.5 < \pi_1 < .7, .6 < \pi_2 < 1.0)$.

This completes the computation for eight cells, and while the gains using this shortcut are small from this point on, the work can be done quite systematically.

The method described above could also be used to compute Prob $(\pi_1/\pi_2 > c)$. This is simply the computation of the probability of the area below the line $\pi_1/\pi_2 = c$. For $c = 2$, we have graphed this function and indicated the relevant area by shading.

Values of $\text{Prob}(\pi_1 > \pi_2) = \text{Prob}(\pi_1/\pi_2 > 1)$ calculated in this manner are given in Table A.16 for a selection of posterior parameter values.

10-6 A SUMMARY OF BAYESIAN METHODS FOR BINARY DATA

In this section, we briefly recapitulate the various methods which can be used when analyzing data which are binary in form. In each case, the results are presented assuming a state of prior ignorance (indifference prior) and a sample of size n containing x successes from the population with parameter π. When the actual prior information can be represented by a beta distribution with parameters (a, b), the same results will apply on replacing

$$\begin{aligned} x &\quad \text{by} \quad a + x \\ n &\quad \text{by} \quad a + b + n\,. \end{aligned}$$

Direct Methods (see Chap. 5 and Sec. 10-5)

The posterior distribution of π is beta with parameters $(x, n - x)$. It has

$$\text{Mean} = \frac{x}{n}\,,$$

$$\text{Variance} = \frac{x(n - x)}{n^2(n + 1)}\,,$$

$$\text{Mode} = \frac{x - 1}{n - 2}\,.$$

Tables A.14 and A.15 give percentage points and HDRs, respectively.

The posterior distributions of the difference and the ratio of two proportions π_1 and π_2 are not tabulated, but can be calculated by the method of Sec. 10-5.

Normal Approximation (see Sec. 10-4)

This is appropriate when both x and $n - x$ are at least 10. The approximate posterior distribution of π is

$$N\left(\frac{x}{n}, \frac{x(n - x)}{n^2(n + 1)}\right).$$

The corresponding posterior distribution for the difference $\pi_1 - \pi_2$ of two proportions is

$$N\left(\frac{x_1}{n_1} - \frac{x_2}{n_2}, \frac{x_1(n_1 - x_1)}{n_1^2(n_1 + 1)} + \frac{x_2(n_2 - x_2)}{n_2^2(n_2 + 1)}\right).$$

Poisson Approximation (see Sec. 10-3)

This is appropriate if $n > 10$, and $x/n < .05$ or $(n - x)/n < .05$. The approximate posterior distribution of π is $\chi^2(2x, 1/2n)$. It has

$$\text{Mean} = \frac{x}{n},$$
$$\text{Variance} = \frac{x}{n^2},$$
$$\text{Mode} = \frac{x-1}{n}.$$

Tables A.5 and A.6 give, respectively, percentage points and HDRs for the standardized chi square distribution. To find the corresponding values of π, divide by $2n$ the table entries for $2x$ degrees of freedom.

The posterior distribution of the ratio π_1/π_2 of two porportions is $F(2x_1, 2x_2, 2n_1, 2n_2)$. To find percentage points, obtain the corresponding points of the standardized F distribution on $(2x_1, 2x_2)$ degrees of freedom, using Table A.13, and multiply them by n_2x_1/n_1x_2.

Arcsine Transformation (see Sec. 10-1)

This is appropriate when $x(1 - x/n) > 5$. The posterior distribution of $\gamma = \sin^{-1}\sqrt{\pi}$ is $N[g, (4n + 2)^{-1}]$, where

$$g = \sin^{-1}\sqrt{\frac{x + \frac{3}{8}}{n + \frac{3}{4}}}.$$

Table A.18 facilitates making the transformation from the data (x, n) to g, and the reverse transformation from percentage points of γ to percentage points of π.

The posterior distribution of the difference $\gamma_1 - \gamma_2$ is

$$N[g_1 - g_2, (4n_1 + 2)^{-1} + (4n_2 + 2)^{-1}],$$

but this cannot be translated into a distribution on $\pi_1 - \pi_2$.

Log-Odds Transformation (see Sec. 10-2)

This is appropriate when both x and $n - x$ are at least 5. The posterior distribution of $\delta = \ln[\pi/(1 - \pi)]$ is (approximately)

$$N\left[\ln\frac{x - \frac{1}{2}}{n - x - \frac{1}{2}}, \frac{n}{x(n - x)}\right].$$

Table A.19(*b*) facilitates the transformation of percentage points for δ into percentage points for π.

The posterior distribution of the difference $\delta_1 - \delta_2$, which is the logarithm of the ratio of the odds in the two populations, is

$$N\left[\ln\left(\frac{x_1 - \frac{1}{2}}{x_2 - \frac{1}{2}}\,\frac{n_2 - x_2 - \frac{1}{2}}{n_1 - x_1 - \frac{1}{2}}\right), \frac{n_1}{x_1(n_1 - x_1)} + \frac{n_2}{x_2(n_2 - x_2)}\right],$$

but this cannot be translated into a distribution on $\pi_1 - \pi_2$.

10-7 BAYESIAN ANALYSIS OF THE MULTICATEGORY MODEL

All our work in Chap. 5 and so far in this chapter relates to the binary model where observations can be classified into two categories traditionally called successes and failures. In many educational situations, however, we are interested not only in dichotomies such as pass-fail but also in classification into several categories such as college grades.

Of course, such classification can always be reduced to a series of dichotomies. For example, when estimating the probability that students with a given test score will obtain an *A* grade at a certain college, we can regard the data as consisting of "grade *A* students" and "the rest". Turning to the estimation for grade *B*, we reshuffle our data to consist of "grade *B* students" and "the rest", the latter category now having a different meaning from previously.

There are situations in which this procedure may be workable, particularly if the number of observations is large compared with the number of categories. However, it can also produce unacceptable outcomes. For example, the estimated probabilities for grades *A*, *B*, *C*, *D*, and *F* might add up to more than unity. One way of avoiding this is to consider a sequence of states, A, $B|\bar{A}$, $C|\bar{A}\bar{B}$, $D|\bar{A}\bar{B}\bar{C}$, and their associated probabilities.

For a general treatment of the multicategory situation, we suppose that there are s categories C_j, indexed by the subscript j, $j = 1, 2, \ldots, s$. In the binary case, $s = 2$. We suppose also that sample members independently have probability π_j of belonging to category C_j. In many applications, π_j will be most naturally thought of as a proportion in some population from which we are drawing a random sample. We must, of course, have $\sum_{j=1}^{s} \pi_j = 1$.

A full description of a sample in this situation will be a listing, in order, of the categories to which its members belong. Thus, a sample of 10 college students might have grades *B*, *C*, *B*, *A*, *F*, *B*, *D*, *C*, *A*, and *A*. To reduce this to our standard notation, we let $A = C_1$, $B = C_2$, $C = C_3$, $D = C_4$, and $F = C_5$. Since in a random sample each member is an independent "event", the probability of the above sample, in the order in which it is listed, is

$$\pi_2\pi_3\pi_2\pi_1\pi_5\pi_2\pi_4\pi_3\pi_1\pi_1 = \pi_1^3\pi_2^3\pi_3^2\pi_4\pi_5 .$$

It is clear from this example that in the general case where the sample contains x_j members in category C_j ($j = 1, 2, \ldots, s$), the probability of this sample, in the order in which it is listed, is

$$m_{\boldsymbol{\pi}}(\mathbf{x}) \propto \pi_1^{x_1}\pi_2^{x_2} \cdots \pi_s^{x_s} . \qquad (10\text{-}7.1)$$

The total sample size here is $n = \Sigma x_j$.

The reader will recall that in Sec. 5-2 the binomial distribution was derived by counting the number of samples, different in the order in which their members occur, which contain exactly x successes and $(n - x)$ failures. In the same way, if we wish to know the probability that our sample will contain x_1 members in C_1, x_2 in C_2, and so on, *irrespective* of the order in which they occur, we must multiply (10-7.1) by the number of different orderings of a sample with this makeup. This is known to be

$$\frac{n!}{x_1!\,x_2!\,\ldots\,x_s!} . \qquad (10\text{-}7.2)$$

The product of (10-7.2) and (10-7.1) is the density function of a *multinomial distribution.* It reduces to the binomial distribution when $s = 2$ since we then have $\pi_2 = 1 - \pi_1$, $x_2 = n - x_1$.

However, for a Bayesian analysis, we do not need the factor (10-7.2). The expression (10-7.1) is the likelihood of our sample in the order in which it was obtained. The fact that we do not need to know the order of the observations to compute (10-7.1), merely the total number in each category, is just another way of saying that $x_1, x_2, \ldots, x_s$ are (jointly) sufficient statistics (recall that their total gives us n). We may, therefore, denote a sample by a vector $(x_1, x_2, \ldots, x_s)$, giving the totals in each category. From (10-7.1), it can be shown that the maximum-likelihood estimates of the π_j are the sample proportions x_j/n.

A conjugate prior for the π_j will have the form

$$b(\pi_1, \pi_2, \ldots, \pi_s) \propto \pi_1^{a_1 - 1}\pi_2^{a_2 - 1} \ldots \pi_s^{a_s - 1} , \qquad (10\text{-}7.3)$$

where $\sum_{j=1}^{s} \pi_j \leq 1$, and $a_j > 0$, $j = 1, 2, \ldots, s$. The exponent is taken as $a_j - 1$ rather than a_j for the sake of consistency with the beta distribution. On multiplying (10-7.3) by the likelihood (10-7.1), we obtain a posterior distribution of the same form with $a_j + x_j$ replacing a_j. A distribution of type (10-7.3) is called a Dirichlet distribution—named for the French mathematician who first discovered how to integrate it (in our context, how to determine the constant of proportionality).

The formal Bayesian analysis is now complete. What remains is to discuss the properties of the Dirichlet distribution, to consider a specification of indifference in the multicategory model, and to indicate methods of incorporating prior information.

The mathematical treatment of the distribution is complicated by the need to bear in mind the constraint $\Sigma\pi_j = 1$. Were it not for this constraint, (10-7.3) could be broken up into factors $\pi_j^{a_j - 1}$, each involving only one of the π_j; and so the π_j would be independent. This is certainly not the case. In the binary model, we explicitly introduced the constraint into the density by writing $\pi_1 = \pi, \pi_2 = 1 - \pi$. Many authors do the same in our present model, writing $\pi_s = 1 - \pi_1 - \pi_2 \ldots - \pi_{s-1}$. We have not done this because we shall not discuss mathematical derivations, and because to do so introduces an apparent asymmetry into the Bayes densities (prior and posterior) which has no counterpart in the real-life situation we are modeling. The existence of the constraint must, however, be borne in mind. It is precisely its presence in the multinomial-Dirichlet analysis which prevents us from obtaining the unacceptable estimates we noted might arise if we consider each category separately.

Consider first the joint distribution of all the π_j in the general form (10-7.3). The distribution is proper, provided $a_j > 0$ for all j. The joint mean is the point

$$\left(\frac{a_1}{A}, \frac{a_2}{A}, \ldots, \frac{a_s}{A}\right), \quad (10\text{-}7.4)$$

where

$$A = \sum_{j=1}^{s} a_j .$$

The joint mode is the point

$$\left(\frac{a_1 - 1}{A - s}, \frac{a_2 - 1}{A - s}, \ldots, \frac{a_s - 1}{A - s}\right), \quad (10\text{-}7.5)$$

provided $a_j > 1$ for all j. Note that if we think of (10-7.4) and (10-7.5) as point estimates of the π_j, each set is coherent in the everyday sense that the sum of the estimates is unity. Note also that if A is only moderately large compared with s, the estimates may differ noticeably. For example, if there are three categories and $a_1 = 2$, $a_2 = 3$, $a_3 = 4$, giving $A = 9$, then the mean vector is (.22,.33,.44) whereas the mode vector is (.17,.33,.50).

We hasten to point out that in most applications, we should not be faced with quite so large a discrepancy. Even in the evaluation solely of prior information, we shall typically require a value of A much larger than 9 and thus, on the average, the values of the a_i will be much greater than those given above. Then, of course, we are most concerned with point estimates, a posteriori, where A is transformed to $A + n$ and a_j to $a_j + x_j$.

Suppose we have $A = 18$ with $a_1 = 4$, $a_2 = 6$, and $a_3 = 8$; and suppose that we observe a sample of size $n = 21$ with observation vector $(x_1, x_2, x_3) = (5, 4, 12)$. Then, a posteriori, we have a Dirichlet density with parameters (9,10,20) with $A = 39$. The mean vector is (.231,.256,.513), and the mode vector is (.222,.250,.528). These differences between the elements of the mean vector and of the mode vector are unlikely to be of importance.

Next suppose that we are interested only in a subset of the categories, say the first t of them. The natural way to handle this is to retain the categories $C_1, C_2, \ldots, C_t$ as before and define a new category D as "the rest", with corresponding parameter

$$\begin{aligned} \kappa &= \pi_{t+1} + \pi_{t+2} + \cdots + \pi_s \\ &= 1 - \pi_1 - \pi_2 - \cdots - \pi_t \,. \end{aligned} \tag{10-7.6}$$

A feature of the Dirichlet distribution is that the parameters associated with a reduced set of categories also have a Dirichlet distribution with density

$$b(\pi_1, \pi_2, \ldots, \pi_t) \propto \pi_1^{a_1 - 1} \pi_2^{a_2 - 1} \cdots \pi_t^{a_t - 1} \kappa^{(a_{t+1} + a_{t+2} + \cdots + a_s - 1)} \,. \tag{10-7.7}$$

The joint mean of the distribution (10-7.7) gives the same estimates as before for the parameters, namely, a_j/A ($j = 1, 2, \ldots, t$). This would be true whatever the distribution. It is simply a generalization of the result we have already met in the bivariate case that the components of a joint mean are the same as the marginal means.

If we turn to the joint mode, however, we find our estimates have been affected by the reduction in the number of categories considered. The new estimates are

$$\frac{a_j - 1}{A - t - 1} \qquad j = 1, 2, \ldots, t \tag{10-7.8}$$

and are, therefore, smaller than before (the denominator is larger).

A special case of the results for subsets of categories arises when we focus attention on a single category only, say C_j. The marginal distribution of π_j is then beta, with parameters $(a_j, A - a_j)$. Its mean is a_j/A, as we know it must be. Its mode is $(a_j - 1)/(A - 2)$, as can be seen by putting $t = 1$ in (10-7.8) or from our previous knowledge about beta–Eq. (5-5.4). Note that the modal estimate is smallest when we consider the marginal distribution of that parameter alone rather than take the joint mode with other parameters.

The fact that the mean estimates remain static whereas the modal ones change as we vary the number of categories under consideration might be taken as a reason for preferring the mean as an estimate, if we have no specific loss function in mind. The reason for the changes which occur in the modal estimates is, of course, that zero-one loss applied to the full set of π_j is not the same thing as zero-one loss applied to a subset of them.

Next let us consider the specification of prior distributions and, in particular, the expression of prior ignorance. Considerations of symmetry require that such ignorance should be expressed by giving each a_j in (10-7.3) the same value. The indifference prior is obtained by putting $a_j = 0$; all j, corresponding to no hypothetical prior observations, giving

$$b(\pi_1, \pi_2, \ldots, \pi_s) \propto \pi_1^{-1}\pi_2^{-1} \cdots \pi_s^{-1} . \quad (10\text{-}7.9)$$

If we use this prior and recall that the sample increases the prior a_j value to $a_j + x_j$, the posterior is seen to be of the form (10-7.3) with x_j in place of a_j. Thus, the mean estimates will be simply the sample proportions x_j/n and the joint modal estimates will be $(x_j - 1)/(n - s)$, provided in each case the posterior distribution is proper.

An attractive feature of the indifference prior is that, as is clear from (10-7.7) with all the a_j equal to zero, it will imply a prior of the same form no matter how we combine or subdivide categories. Indeed, it is the *only* form of prior which has this property. To some people, the fact that the posterior mean estimate is the sample proportion will also be appealing. Others find this a reason for rejecting it. An interesting feature is that the posterior distribution remains improper until we have observed at least one sample member in each category. (Hence, if the posterior is proper, n is not less than s, and so the modal estimates as we stated them can not turn out to be negative!) Even when the posterior is proper, the modal estimate for any category in which there is a single observation will be zero.

An alternative specification of ignorance is to generalize Bayes' postulate and take a uniform distribution. This is equivalent to putting $a_j = 1$ for all j in (10-7.3). The posterior will then be of the same form with $x_j + 1$ in place of a_j. The mean estimates are

$$\frac{x_j + 1}{n + s} = \frac{n(x_j/n) + s(1/s)}{n + s} , \quad (10\text{-}7.10)$$

and the modal estimates are now the sample proportions x_j/n.

A difficulty affecting the uniform prior is that, if we decide to combine or subdivide some categories, it will be incoherent to take a uniform prior on the reduced (increased) set of parameters. For example, suppose we combine the last three categories into one. The implied prior on the new set of parameters is given by (10-7.7), with $a_j = 1$ for all j. It is proportional to

$$\kappa^2 = (1 - \pi_1 \cdots - \pi_{s-3})^2$$

and is certainly not uniform.

One way to gain some insight into this phenomenon, which on first acquaintance seems disturbing, is to study the alternative expression for the posterior mean given on the right-hand side of Eq. (10-7.10). This expresses the mean as a weighted average of the sample proportion and the value s^{-1}, the weights being the sample size and the number of categories, respectively. Now on a number of previous occasions, we have been able to express a posterior mean as a weighted average of the maximum-likelihood estimate and the prior mean [e.g., Eq. (6-3.2)] ; and on reflection, it is clear that this is what is happening here. Any expression of symmetric prior knowledge about the π_j must imply that we think each to be somewhere around $1/s$. The only question to be settled is how much weight we give to this belief. By going to the indifference prior, we give it zero weight but encounter the difficulties already mentioned. The uniform prior gives it the weight of s observations, which may be uncomfortably large. One suggestion is to give it the weight of a single observation by putting each $a_j = s^{-1}$ in (10-7.3).

As usual, in the presence of any substantial amount of data, the precise value of a_j chosen in the range $0 \leq a_j \leq 1$ will not matter. This is true even in the most aesthetically disturbing case when we use the indifference prior, observe a single success in a particular category, and come up with a modal estimate of zero for the corresponding π_j. The difference between an estimate of zero and an estimate (using the uniform prior) of $1/n$ with n large is unlikely to be of *practical* importance provided we do not make the mistake of confusing an estimate with the true value (a point we discussed at the end of Sec. 8-2).

Finally, we may note that the difficulty of specifying prior ignorance is not simply a mathematical fiction but reflects the realities of the situation. In truth, there can be no such thing as total ignorance in the multicategory situation. The very fact that one lists 10 categories rather than 5 implies that one expects to find some observations falling in the additional categories—at least if one is a scientific investigator and not an incorrigible bureaucrat. If this expectation is symmetric over the categories one has listed, one's prior point estimate must be one-tenth in the 10-category case, and one-fifth in the 5-category case. If it is not symmetric, it follows that one has even more prior information; and if this seems likely to be important, one should quantify it by assigning higher a_j values to those categories in which one expects to have the higher probabilities.

When prior information is substantial, the hypothetical sample method will be extremely valuable for quantifying it. The exact prior taken to represent ignorance will now be unimportant, so we may as well take the indifference prior (10-7.9). We then equate our prior knowledge, as accurately as we can, to a hypothetical sample of size m with proportion p_j in the jth category, bearing in mind that larger values of m imply more precise prior knowledge. Alternatively, we may think in terms of the numbers of observations in each category of our hypothetical sample, say $w_j = mp_j$, where the total $m = \Sigma w_j$ represents the precision of our knowledge. As a check, we can then look at credibility intervals from the implied marginal distributions of the π_j, which are beta with parameters $(w_j, m - w_j)$. When we have arrived at a satisfactory set of w_j, these are just the values a_j needed in the prior (10-7.3). Equivalently, we can add the w_j to the actual observations x_j and use the indifference prior with the combined sample.

A summary of the properties of the Dirichlet distribution is given in Table 10-7.1.

Consider the data in Table 2-1.4. Suppose we wish to estimate the percentage of students in each ACT category who have a GPA of 3.0 to 4.0. Let π_1 represent the percentage of students with GPA of 3.0 to 4.0 who have an ACT score of 0 to 15; π_2, an ACT score of 16 to 21; π_3, an ACT score of 22 to 25; and π_4, an ACT score of 26 to 36.

Assume our prior mean estimates of π_1, π_2, π_3, and π_4 are

$$\tilde{\pi}_1 = .02, \quad \tilde{\pi}_2 = .12, \quad \tilde{\pi}_3 = .36, \quad \tilde{\pi}_4 = .50,$$

worth a total of $A = \Sigma a_j = 50$ observations. Then

$$a_1 = 1, \quad a_2 = 6, \quad a_3 = 18, \quad a_4 = 25.$$

Table 10-7.1 SUMMARY OF PROPERTIES OF THE DIRICHLET DISTRIBUTION

Density:

$$b(\pi) \propto \pi_1^{a_1 - 1} \pi_2^{a_2 - 1} \cdots \pi_s^{a_s - 1},$$

where $\Sigma \pi_j = 1$,

$a_j > 0, \; j = 1, 2, \ldots, s$

Joint mean:

$$\left(\frac{a_1}{A}, \frac{a_2}{A}, \ldots, \frac{a_s}{A}\right) \quad \text{where } A = \sum_{j=1}^{s} a_j$$

Joint mode:

$$\left(\frac{a_1 - 1}{A - s}, \frac{a_2 - 1}{A - s}, \ldots, \frac{a_s - 1}{A - s}\right)$$

Marginal mean:

$$\frac{a_j}{A}$$

Marginal mode:

$$\frac{a_j - 1}{A - 2}$$

Marginal variance:

$$\frac{a_j(A - a_j)}{A^2(A + 1)}$$

Correlation between π_j and π_k:

$$\rho(\pi_j, \pi_k) = -\sqrt{\frac{a_j a_k}{(A - a_j)(A - a_k)}}$$

The joint prior distribution for π_1, π_2, π_3, and π_4 is a Dirichlet distribution with parameters (1,6,18,25). The joint mode is

$$\left(\frac{a_1 - 1}{A - 4}, \frac{a_2 - 1}{A - 4}, \frac{a_3 - 1}{A - 4}, \frac{a_4 - 1}{A - 4}\right) = \left(\frac{0}{46}, \frac{5}{46}, \frac{17}{46}, \frac{24}{46}\right)$$
$$= (.00, .11, .37, .52) .$$

The prior marginal distribution for π_1 is $\beta(1,49)$ with mean = 1/50 = .02, mode = 0/48 = .00, and variance = $1(49)/(50)^2(51)$ = .00038; for π_2, $\beta(6,44)$ with mean of .12, mode of .10, and variance of .00207; for π_3, $\beta(18,32)$ with mean of .36, mode of .35, and variance of .00452; and for π_4, $\beta(25,25)$ with mean of .50, mode of .50, and variance of .00490.

The sample data are

$$x_1 = 0, \quad x_2 = 24, \quad x_3 = 92, \quad x_4 = 118, \quad n = 234 .$$

The joint posterior distribution for π_1, π_2, π_3, and π_4 is a Dirichlet distribution with parameters $(a_1 + x_1, a_2 + x_2, a_3 + x_3, a_4 + x_4) = (1, 30, 110, 143)$. The joint mean is

$$\left(\frac{a_1 + x_1}{A + n}, \frac{a_2 + x_2}{A + n}, \frac{a_3 + x_3}{A + n}, \frac{a_4 + x_4}{A + n}\right) = \left(\frac{1}{284}, \frac{30}{284}, \frac{110}{284}, \frac{143}{284}\right)$$
$$= (.0035, .1057, .3873, .5035) ;$$

the joint mode is

$$\left(\frac{a_1 + x_1 - 1}{A + n - 4}, \frac{a_2 + x_2 - 1}{A + n - 4}, \frac{a_3 + x_3 - 1}{A + n - 4}, \frac{a_4 + x_4 - 1}{A + n - 4}\right)$$
$$= \left(\frac{0}{280}, \frac{29}{280}, \frac{109}{280}, \frac{142}{280}\right)$$
$$= (.0000, .1036, .3893, .5071).$$

The posterior marginal distribution for π_1 is $\beta(1,283)$ with mean = 1/284 = .0035, mode = 0/282 = .0000, and variance = $1(283)/(284)^2(285)$ = .00001; for π_2, $\beta(30,254)$ with mean of .1057, mode of .1028, and variance of .00033; for π_3, $\beta(110,174)$ with mean of .3873, mode of .3865, and variance of .00083; and for π_4, $\beta(143,141)$ with mean of .5035, mode of .5035, and variance of .00088.

10-8 REGRESSED ESTIMATES OF PROPORTIONS

Suppose we are interested in the proportion of students in each of m similar colleges passing or failing a particular course or program. We observe in each of the m colleges that a proportion p_i of students have passed, and we are interested in estimating the true pass rate π_i for that college. The situation here is identical to that in Sec. 9-5 except that we are now interested in estimating proportions rather than means.

Making the usual assumption that our observations are a random sample of size n_i from the population of interest, the distribution of p_i is binomial with mean π_i and variance $n_i^{-1}\pi_i\kappa_i$, where $\kappa_i = 1 - \pi_i$, the true proportion of failures. The transformation

$$g_i = \sin^{-1}\sqrt{\frac{x_i + \frac{3}{8}}{n_i + \frac{3}{4}}} = \sin^{-1}\sqrt{\frac{p_i + \dfrac{3}{8n_i}}{1 + \dfrac{3}{4n_i}}} \tag{10-8.1}$$

results in an "observation" g_i which is more symmetrically distributed than p_i and has approximate mean

$$\gamma_i = \sin^{-1}\sqrt{\pi_i} \tag{10-8.2}$$

and approximate variance

$$\frac{1}{4n_i + 2}. \tag{10-8.3}$$

We noted in Sec. 10-1 that the transformation (10-8.1) is preferable, both in regard to the closeness of its mean to the value (10-8.2) and in regard to variance stabilization, to the simpler transformation $\sin^{-1}\sqrt{p_i}$. Then, by assuming the γ_i to be independently distributed with common mean μ_Γ and variance σ_Γ^2, we obtain a Kelley-type regressed estimate of γ_i

$$\hat{\gamma}_i = R(\Gamma_i|g_i) = \frac{\hat{\sigma}_\Gamma^2 g_i + (4n_i + 2)^{-1}\hat{\mu}_\Gamma}{\hat{\sigma}_\Gamma^2 + (4n_i + 2)^{-1}} \tag{10-8.4}$$

similar to that obtained in Sec. 9-5. Here

$$\hat{\sigma}_\Gamma^2 = (m - 1)^{-1}\Sigma(g_i - g_\bullet)^2 - m^{-1}\Sigma(4n_i + 2)^{-1} \tag{10-8.5}$$

where $g_\bullet = m^{-1}\Sigma g_i$, and

$$\hat{\mu}_\Gamma = \frac{\Sigma w_i g_i}{\Sigma w_i} \tag{10-8.6}$$

where

$$w_i = \left[\hat{\sigma}_\Gamma^2 + \frac{1}{4n_i + 2}\right]^{-1}$$

From (10-8.2), we finally obtain the regressed estimate of π_i,

$$\tilde{\pi}_i = \sin^2\hat{\gamma}_i\,. \tag{10-8.7}$$

We could, of course, have worked with the observed failure rates $q_i = 1 - p_i$ and the corresponding true failure rates κ_i. For the method presented here to be useful, we require that if $\tilde{\kappa}_i$ is the estimate analogous to (10-8.7), then

$$\tilde{\pi}_i + \tilde{\kappa}_i = 1 . \qquad (10\text{-}8.8)$$

It is possible to show that this consistency property holds for a binomial model but does not hold for the case of more than two categories.

Suppose available data for 11 schools are as follows: (n_i, x_i) = (15,10), (21,13), (16,5), (17,10), (15,6), (17,11), (18,9), (20,15), (30,12), (19,8), (14,7). The observed proportions are thus .67, .62, .31, .59, .40, .65, .50, .75, .40, .42, .50 while the regressed estimates are .56, .55, .48, .54, .50, .55, .52, .59, .49, .50, .52, suggesting much lesser variation among the true proportions than the observed proportions would indicate.

10-9 A SMOOTHING OF A CONTINGENCY TABLE

A small college in Iowa was preparing a handbook which would be distributed to high school counselors. It was deemed necessary to include among the data a comparison of ACT composite scaled score and college grade-point average. The following table was obtained from the *previous* year's freshmen.

GPA/ACT	0-15	16-21	22-25	26-36	Row totals
3.0-4.0	0 (.00)	24 (.06)	92 (.15)	118 (.39)	234
2.0-2.9	31 (.22)	130 (.31)	299 (.48)	133 (.44)	593
1.0-1.9	62 (.44)	184 (.45)	157 (.25)	41 (.13)	444
0.0-0.9	49 (.34)	75 (.18)	75 (.12)	12 (.04)	211
Column totals	142	413	623	304	1,482

The entries in parentheses are column proportions. They are typically interpreted as probabilities of attaining the GPA category given the ACT category. Since the data in this table were gathered from only a single year, it was felt that more stable estimates should be attained before the table was printed. One major reason for this decision was the zero in the first cell (with ACT score of 0 to 15 and GPA of 3.0 to 4.0). Using this table as given, someone might think that the probability was zero of attaining a GPA of 3.0 to 4.0 given an ACT score from 0 to 15. However, this would not be true.

The contingency table on the following page of first-year GPA given ACT scaled composite score was obtained from the five freshmen classes preceding the last freshmen class. The total number of students represented by this table was 6,000. It was felt that this table was only worth 1,000 observations because of recent changes in the admissions policy. During the years when these data were gathered, there were fewer applicants to the college than in the past year. Therefore, the admissions and grading standards were

GPA/ACT	0-15	16-21	22-25	26-36	Row totals
3.0-4.0	90	588	366	186	1,230
2.0-2.9	246	2,034	342	90	2,712
1.0-1.9	426	858	66	24	1,374
0.0-0.9	222	432	18	12	684
Column totals	984	3,912	792	312	6,000

lower in those years than in the past year. The increase in applications was believed a consequence of the winding down of the Vietnam war and lack of jobs. A revised prior contingency table, based on 1,000 hypothetical observations, is as follows.

GPA/ACT	0-15	16-21	22-25	26-36	
3.0-4.0	15	98	61	31	
2.0-2.9	41	339	57	15	
1.0-1.9	71	143	11	4	
0.0-0.9	37	72	3	2	
Column totals	164	652	132	52	1,000

This revised prior contingency table was obtained by dividing all entries in the original table by 6. This table was then converted into the following prior expectancy table.

GPA/ACT	0-15	16-21	22-25	26-36	
3.0-4.0	.091	.150	.462	.596	
2.0-2.9	.250	.520	.432	.288	
1.0-1.9	.433	.219	.083	.077	
0.0-0.9	.226	.110	.023	.038 .	
Column weights	164	652	132	52	1,000

The values given in the above table do not seem entirely satisfactory when interpreted as probabilities and thus some adjustments seem in order. Therefore, a new table was formed by modifying the above table in the direction suggested by the changed admissions and grading policies.

GPA/ACT	0-15	16-21	22-25	26-36	
3.0-4.0	.043	.132	.432	.596	
2.0-2.9	.159	.383	.462	.308	
1.0-1.9	.512	.322	.083	.077	
0.0-0.9	.287	.163	.023	.019	
Column weights	164	652	132	52	1,000

It can be seen that it was felt to be more difficult now for a person in the lower two ACT categories to get at least a C average (2.0 or better) than in the past. Also, it can be noted that in the third ACT category it was felt to be slightly more difficult to achieve a B average (3.0 or better). The expectancy table was then converted back to a contingency table by multiplying the percentages in each column by the appropriate column weight. The following table is the final prior contingency table of hypothetical prior observations.

GPA/ACT	0-15	16-21	22-25	26-36	
3.0-4.0	7	86	57	31	
2.0-2.9	26	250	61	16	
1.0-1.9	84	210	11	4	
0.0-0.9	47	106	3	1	
Column totals	164	652	132	52	1,000

Given the prior contingency table as adjusted, the joint prior distribution for each column is a Dirichlet distribution with the following parameters.

Column 1 (7,26,84,47)
Column 2 (86,250,210,106)
Column 3 (57,61,11,3)
Column 4 (31,16,4,1)

The following notation is used in the remainder of this example:

a_i, $1 \leq i \leq 4$, corresponds to the entry in the ith row of the column being described.

$A = \sum_{i=1}^{4} a_i$ corresponds to the column weight.

S = the number of columns in the table = 4.

The prior joint means are $\left(\dfrac{a_1}{A}, \dfrac{a_2}{A}, \dfrac{a_3}{A}, \dfrac{a_4}{A}\right)$.

Column 1 $\left(\dfrac{7}{164}, \dfrac{26}{164}, \dfrac{84}{164}, \dfrac{47}{164}\right) = (.043, .159, .512, .287)$

Column 2 $\left(\dfrac{86}{652}, \dfrac{250}{652}, \dfrac{210}{652}, \dfrac{106}{652}\right) = (.132, .383, .322, .163)$

Column 3 $\left(\dfrac{57}{132}, \dfrac{61}{132}, \dfrac{11}{132}, \dfrac{3}{132}\right) = (.432, .462, .083, .023)$

Column 4 $\left(\dfrac{31}{52}, \dfrac{16}{52}, \dfrac{4}{52}, \dfrac{1}{52}\right) = (.596, .308, .077, .019)$

The prior joint modes are $\left(\dfrac{a_1 - 1}{A - S}, \dfrac{a_2 - 1}{A - S}, \dfrac{a_3 - 1}{A - S}, \dfrac{a_4 - 1}{A - S}\right)$.

Column 1 $\left(\dfrac{6}{160}, \dfrac{25}{160}, \dfrac{83}{160}, \dfrac{46}{160}\right) = (.038, .156, .519, .288)$

Column 2 $\left(\dfrac{85}{648}, \dfrac{249}{648}, \dfrac{209}{648}, \dfrac{105}{648}\right) = (.131, .384, .323, .162)$

Column 3 $\quad (\frac{56}{128}, \frac{60}{128}, \frac{10}{128}, \frac{2}{128}) = (.438, .469, .078, .016)$

Column 4 $\quad (\frac{30}{48}, \frac{15}{48}, \frac{3}{48}, \frac{0}{48}) = (.625, .313, .063, .000)$

The prior marginal distributions ($\pi_{\text{row, column}}$) are

	Mean $\frac{a_{ij}}{A_j}$	Mode $\frac{a_{ij} - 1}{A_j - 2}$	Standard deviation $\sqrt{\frac{a_{ij}(A_j - a_{ij})}{A_j^2(A_j + 1)}}$
$\pi_{1,1}$ $\beta(7,157)$	.043	.037	.0157
$\pi_{2,1}$ $\beta(26,138)$	.159	.154	.0284
$\pi_{3,1}$ $\beta(84,80)$	.512	.512	.0389
$\pi_{4,1}$ $\beta(47,117)$	.287	.284	.0352
$\pi_{1,2}$ $\beta(86,566)$	.132	.131	.0132
$\pi_{2,2}$ $\beta(250,402)$	.383	.383	.0190
$\pi_{3,2}$ $\beta(210,442)$	.322	.322	.0183
$\pi_{4,2}$ $\beta(106,546)$	.163	.162	.0144
$\pi_{1,3}$ $\beta(57,75)$	.432	.431	.0430
$\pi_{2,3}$ $\beta(61,71)$	.462	.462	.0432
$\pi_{3,3}$ $\beta(11,121)$	.083	.077	.0240
$\pi_{4,3}$ $\beta(3,129)$	.023	.015	.0129
$\pi_{1,4}$ $\beta(31,21)$	.596	.600	.0674
$\pi_{2,4}$ $\beta(16,36)$	.308	.300	.0634
$\pi_{3,4}$ $\beta(4,48)$	.077	.060	.0366
$\pi_{4,4}$ $\beta(1,51)$	.019	.000	.0189

None of these distributions or their properties seems disturbingly unrealistic. The marginal distribution for $\pi_{4,4}$ is not exactly what we would want it to be, but it does seem tolerable. Therefore, we accept the "revised contingency table" as reflecting our prior beliefs, based in part on real prior data, but also in part on our judgment of the changes that have occurred in the college environment. In some applications, there may be a great deal of hard prior data and little postulated change in the system. In other situations, it may be necessary to construct a "prior contingency table" based almost entirely on informal observation. The problems of specification and coherence checking would be identical. In the former case, a relatively high prior sample number (as in this example) would be appropriate. In the latter case, a much smaller number would be indicated, perhaps something of the order of 100 or 200 or possibly even less. But again, marginal distributions would need to be checked.

Using the grades of the previous year's freshman class as sample data, the joint posterior distributions for the columns are Dirichlet distributions with the following parameters:

Column 1 (7,57,146,96)
Column 2 (110,380,394,181)
Column 3 (149,360,168,78)
Column 4 (149,149,45,13)

The joint means are $\left(\frac{a_1}{A}, \frac{a_2}{A}, \frac{a_3}{A}, \frac{a_4}{A}\right)$.

Column 1 $\left(\frac{7}{306}, \frac{57}{306}, \frac{146}{306}, \frac{96}{306}\right) = (.023, .186, .477, .314)$

Column 2 $\left(\frac{110}{1065}, \frac{380}{1065}, \frac{394}{1065}, \frac{181}{1065}\right) = (.103, .357, .370, .170)$

Column 3 $\frac{149}{755}, \frac{360}{755}, \frac{168}{755}, \frac{78}{755}) = (.197, .477, .223, .103)$

Column 4 $\left(\frac{149}{356}, \frac{149}{356}, \frac{45}{356}, \frac{13}{356}\right) = (.419, .419, .126, .037)$

The joint modes are $\left(\frac{a_1 - 1}{A - S}, \frac{a_2 - 1}{A - S}, \frac{a_3 - 1}{A - S}, \frac{a_4 - 1}{A - S}\right)$.

Column 1 $\left(\frac{6}{302}, \frac{56}{302}, \frac{145}{302}, \frac{95}{302}\right) = (.020, .185, .480, .315)$

Column 2 $\left(\frac{109}{1061}, \frac{379}{1061}, \frac{393}{1061}, \frac{180}{1061}\right) = (.103, .357, .370, .170)$

Column 3 $\left(\frac{148}{751}, \frac{359}{751}, \frac{167}{751}, \frac{77}{751}\right) = (.197, .478, .222, .103)$

Column 4 $\left(\frac{148}{352}, \frac{148}{352}, \frac{44}{352}, \frac{12}{352}\right) = (.420, .420, .125, .034)$

The posterior marginal distributions ($\pi_{\text{row, column}}$) are

		Mean $\frac{a_{ij}}{A_j}$	Mode $\frac{a_{ij} - 1}{A_j - 2}$	Standard deviation $\sqrt{\frac{a_{ij}(A_j - a_{ij})}{A_j^2(A_j + 1)}}$
$\pi_{1.1}$	$\beta(7,299)$	.023	.020	.0085
$\pi_{2,1}$	$\beta(57,249)$	.186	.184	.0222
$\pi_{3,1}$	$\beta(146,160)$	.477	.477	.0285
$\pi_{4,1}$	$\beta(96,210)$	.314	.313	.0265
$\pi_{1,2}$	$\beta(110,955)$	.103	.103	.0093
$\pi_{2,2}$	$\beta(380,685)$	.357	.357	.0147
$\pi_{3,2}$	$\beta(394,671)$	.370	.370	.0148
$\pi_{4.2}$	$\beta(181,884)$	.170	.169	.0115
$\pi_{1,3}$	$\beta(149,606)$	.197	.197	.0145
$\pi_{2,3}$	$\beta(360,395)$	.477	.477	.0182
$\pi_{3,3}$	$\beta(168,587)$	.223	.222	.0151
$\pi_{4.3}$	$\beta(78,677)$	.103	.102	.0111
$\pi_{1,4}$	$\beta(149,207)$	.419	.418	.0261
$\pi_{2,4}$	$\beta(149,207)$	.419	.418	.0261
$\pi_{3,4}$	$\beta(45,311)$	.126	.124	.0176
$\pi_{4,4}$	$\beta(13,343)$	.037	.034	.0099

It is seen that there is little difference between the marginal means and the marginal modes. We recall also that the marginal medians lie between these two values. Therefore, the choice of the precise value to be reported will depend largely on rounding up conveniently, which we have done in the following table.

GPA/ACT	0-15	16-21	22-25	26-36
3.0-4.0	.02	.10	.20	.42
2.0-2.9	.19	.36	.48	.42
1.0-1.9	.48	.37	.22	.12
0.0-0.9	.31	.17	.10	.04

The technique we have demonstrated here is not particularly sophisticated and it is certainly not the best way of smoothing a contingency table. Also, one would probably want to look rather more closely at the top entry in the first column to decide whether a prior estimate of .01, .02, .03, or .04 might be most defensible, and of course, it may well be that a hypothetical prior sample size of 1,000 may well be too large if any substantial change in admissions and grading procedures has taken place.

As a final check, it is probably a good idea to verify that the relationship between predicted GPA (y) and ACT composite scaled score (x) is strictly increasing. To do this, we look at Prob ($Y \geq y|x$). For $y = 3.0$, these values are given in the top row of the table, and indeed, these values are strictly increasing in x. For Prob ($Y \geq 2.0|x$), we do *not* look at the entries in the second row. These entries are not and need not be strictly increasing. To make the appropriate check, we must add up the probabilities in the top two rows for each value of x. These values are .209, .460, .674, and .838 and are thus strictly increasing. We can now skip to the bottom row, which indicates that Prob ($Y < 1.0|x$) is also decreasing.

As a final exercise, the reader may wish to consider again Table 2-1.8 and construct an expectancy table from these data. Presumably with smoothing, some rather fine gradation of ACT scores will be possible. For this example, we give no real prior information but ask each reader to create his own scenario.

APPENDIX CONTENTS

APPENDIX STATISTICAL TABLES

In order to do serious statistical work, it is necessary to have access to numerous values of certain standard distributions. Extensive tables of the normal, t, chi square, F, beta, and other distributions are readily available. These largely satisfy the needs of those doing classical statistical inference emphasizing tests of point hypotheses at the .05 and .01 level and with associated confidence intervals. The Bayesian statistician is typically concerned with additional percentage points of these distributions and also with other distributions such as the inverse-chi and the Behrens. He is also interested in HDRs for all of these distributions.

The tables given in this Appendix constitute what we judge to be a convenient compilation of tables for readers of this book and for some working statisticians. All tables were specifically calculated for presentation here and compared to previously published tables to the extent that the values we calculated existed in previous tables. The only discrepancy found was in the Behrens-Fisher table where a difference of .01 was found between some of our values and those given by Sukatme. We believe that the refinements we used on Sukatme's method account for this discrepancy.

Even a casual look through our tables should cause the reader to think that we have done some rather peculiar things. It may be useful to explain why we made certain decisions. In Table A.5, we do not tabulate percentage points of chi square for 1, 2, or 3 degrees of freedom. Why? There are two reasons. First, a Bayesian will probably never need these values. As a prior distribution of a Poisson mean parameter, a chi square on 1, 2, or 3 degrees of freedom will almost always be too diffuse. We have strongly advocated the careful fitting of prior distributions in this book, and if the unavailability of a tabulated value makes it difficult to select an unrealistically diffuse prior, that probably isn't too bad. The determined statistician can defeat our purpose, however, simply by using an appropriate uniform prior (corresponding to zero degrees of freedom) as detailed in the text. Second, including tabulations for small degrees of freedom values for chi square and certain other variables completely destroys the alignment of tabled values. If tables are to be used with ease, decimal points must be aligned and this cannot be done without great loss of space when even one entry is several orders of magnitude different from other tabled entries. Look carefully at Table A.5 and imagine how the ease of use of this table would be destroyed by adding a line for degrees of freedom = 1 with values such as .000039 and .00016. A brief description of how to use each table immediately precedes the table. More detailed examples can be found in the text by use of the Index.

TABLE A.1

THE NORMAL CUMULATIVE DISTRIBUTION FUNCTION

The quantity tabulated is the cumulative distribution function of the standardized normal distribution for values of the argument z = 0.00(.01)2.59. The integer and first decimal place of z are given in the left column and the second decimal in the top row. Linear interpolation will be adequate throughout the table. Thus, the value of the cumulative distribution function for z = 1.205 is .5(.8869 + .8849) = .8859 . Since the density function for z is symmetric, the value of the CDF for negative z can be obtained by subtracting from unity the value of the CDF for −z . Thus, for z = −1.205 the value of the CDF is 1 − .8859 = .1141 .

z=	.00	.01	.02	.03	.04	.05	.06	.07	.08	.09
.00	.5000	.5040	.5080	.5120	.5160	.5199	.5239	.5279	.5319	.5359
.10	.5398	.5438	.5478	.5517	.5557	.5596	.5636	.5675	.5714	.5753
.20	.5793	.5832	.5871	.5910	.5948	.5987	.6026	.6064	.6103	.6141
.30	.6179	.6217	.6255	.6293	.6331	.6368	.6406	.6443	.6480	.6517
.40	.6554	.6591	.6628	.6664	.6700	.6736	.6772	.6808	.6844	.6879
.50	.6915	.6950	.6985	.7019	.7054	.7088	.7123	.7157	.7190	.7224
.60	.7257	.7291	.7324	.7357	.7389	.7422	.7454	.7486	.7517	.7549
.70	.7580	.7611	.7642	.7673	.7704	.7734	.7764	.7794	.7823	.7852
.80	.7881	.7910	.7939	.7967	.7995	.8023	.8051	.8078	.8106	.8133
.90	.8159	.8186	.8212	.8238	.8264	.8289	.8315	.8340	.8365	.8389
1.00	.8413	.8438	.8461	.8485	.8508	.8531	.8554	.8577	.8599	.8621
1.10	.8643	.8665	.8686	.8708	.8729	.8749	.8770	.8790	.8810	.8830
1.20	.8849	.8869	.8888	.8907	.8925	.8944	.8962	.8980	.8997	.9015
1.30	.9032	.9049	.9066	.9082	.9099	.9115	.9131	.9147	.9162	.9177
1.40	.9192	.9207	.9222	.9236	.9251	.9265	.9279	.9292	.9306	.9319
1.50	.9332	.9345	.9357	.9370	.9382	.9394	.9406	.9418	.9429	.9441
1.60	.9452	.9463	.9474	.9484	.9495	.9505	.9515	.9525	.9535	.9545
1.70	.9554	.9564	.9573	.9582	.9591	.9599	.9608	.9616	.9625	.9633
1.80	.9641	.9649	.9656	.9664	.9671	.9678	.9686	.9693	.9699	.9706
1.90	.9713	.9719	.9726	.9732	.9738	.9744	.9750	.9756	.9761	.9767
2.00	.9772	.9778	.9783	.9788	.9793	.9798	.9803	.9808	.9812	.9817
2.10	.9821	.9826	.9830	.9834	.9838	.9842	.9846	.9850	.9854	.9857
2.20	.9861	.9864	.9868	.9871	.9875	.9878	.9881	.9884	.9887	.9890
2.30	.9893	.9896	.9898	.9901	.9904	.9906	.9909	.9911	.9913	.9916
2.40	.9918	.9920	.9922	.9925	.9927	.9929	.9931	.9932	.9934	.9936
2.50	.9938	.9940	.9941	.9943	.9945	.9946	.9948	.9949	.9951	.9952

TABLE A.2

PERCENTAGE POINTS OF THE NORMAL DISTRIBUTION

The quantities tabulated are the percentage points of the standardized normal variable corresponding to values P(z) = 75%, 80%, 85%, 87.5%, 90%, 95%, 97.5%, 99%, 99.5%. For example, a value of z = 1.6448 is required to obtain a CDF value of .95. Values of z required to obtain CDF values of .005, .01, .025, .05, .10, .125, .150, .20, and .25 can also be obtained because of the symmetry of the normal distribution. Thus, a value of z = −.6745 will give a CDF value of P = 100% − 75% = 25%.

P(z) =	75%	80%	85%	87.5%	90%	95%	97.5%	99%	99.5%
z =	.6745	.8416	1.0364	1.1503	1.2816	1.6448	1.9600	2.3263	2.5758

TABLE A.3

THE CUMULATIVE STUDENT "t" DISTRIBUTION

The format of this table is identical to that for the Cumulative Normal Distribution which, in fact, is Student "t" with infinitely many degrees of freedom. Where a table for a particular ν is not given, linear interpolation between tables will be generally adequate. For ν greater than 60, interpolation using the reciprocal of the degrees of freedom will be necessary.

For example: To find the probability $t \leq .8$ where t has a Student distribution on 100 degrees of freedom. We invert the degrees of freedom and find that $\nu = 100$ lies $\frac{\frac{1}{60} - \frac{1}{100}}{\frac{1}{60} - \frac{1}{\infty}} = \frac{.01667 - .0100}{.01667 - 0} = .400$ of the way between the value for $\nu = 60$ and $\nu = \infty$ [N(0, 1)]. Thus, the desired value is $.7866 + .400(.7881 - .7866) = .7872$.

The Cumulative Student "t" Distribution $\nu = 6$

t	.00	.01	.02	.03	.04	.05	.06	.07	.08	.09
.0	.5000	.5038	.5077	.5115	.5153	.5191	.5229	.5268	.5306	.5344
.10	.5382	.5420	.5458	.5496	.5534	.5572	.5609	.5647	.5685	.5722
.20	.5760	.5797	.5834	.5871	.5908	.5945	.5982	.6019	.6056	.6092
.30	.6129	.6165	.6201	.6237	.6273	.6309	.6344	.6380	.6415	.6450
.40	.6485	.6520	.6554	.6589	.6623	.6657	.6691	.6725	.6759	.6792
.50	.6826	.6859	.6892	.6924	.6957	.6989	.7021	.7053	.7085	.7116
.60	.7148	.7179	.7210	.7240	.7271	.7301	.7331	.7361	.7391	.7420
.70	.7449	.7478	.7507	.7536	.7564	.7592	.7620	.7647	.7675	.7702
.80	.7729	.7756	.7782	.7808	.7835	.7860	.7886	.7911	.7936	.7961
.90	.7986	.8010	.8035	.8059	.8082	.8106	.8129	.8152	.8175	.8198
1.00	.8220	.8243	.8265	.8286	.8308	.8329	.8350	.8371	.8392	.8412
1.10	.8433	.8453	.8472	.8492	.8511	.8530	.8549	.8568	.8587	.8605
1.20	.8623	.8641	.8659	.8676	.8694	.8711	.8728	.8744	.8761	.8777
1.30	.8793	.8809	.8825	.8841	.8856	.8871	.8886	.8901	.8916	.8930
1.40	.8945	.8959	.8973	.8987	.9000	.9014	.9027	.9040	.9053	.9066
1.50	.9079	.9091	.9103	.9116	.9128	.9139	.9151	.9163	.9174	.9185
1.60	.9196	.9207	.9218	.9229	.9239	.9250	.9260	.9270	.9280	.9290
1.70	.9300	.9309	.9319	.9328	.9337	.9347	.9356	.9364	.9373	.9382
1.80	.9390	.9399	.9407	.9415	.9423	.9431	.9439	.9447	.9454	.9462
1.90	.9469	.9476	.9484	.9491	.9498	.9505	.9512	.9518	.9525	.9531
2.00	.9538	.9544	.9550	.9557	.9563	.9569	.9575	.9581	.9586	.9592
2.10	.9598	.9603	.9609	.9614	.9619	.9624	.9630	.9635	.9640	.9645
2.20	.9649	.9654	.9659	.9664	.9668	.9673	.9677	.9682	.9686	.9690
2.30	.9694	.9699	.9703	.9707	.9711	.9715	.9719	.9722	.9726	.9730
2.40	.9734	.9737	.9741	.9744	.9748	.9751	.9754	.9758	.9761	.9764
2.50	.9767	.9770	.9774	.9777	.9780	.9783	.9785	.9788	.9791	.9794

TABLE A.3 (continued)

The Cumulative Student "t" Distribution ν = 7

t	.00	.01	.02	.03	.04	.05	.06	.07	.08	.09
.0	.5000	.5038	.5077	.5115	.5154	.5192	.5231	.5269	.5308	.5346
.10	.5384	.5423	.5461	.5499	.5537	.5575	.5613	.5651	.5689	.5726
.20	.5764	.5802	.5839	.5877	.5914	.5951	.5988	.6025	.6062	.6099
.30	.6136	.6172	.6208	.6245	.6281	.6317	.6353	.6388	.6424	.6459
.40	.6495	.6530	.6565	.6599	.6634	.6668	.6703	.6737	.6771	.6804
.50	.6838	.6871	.6905	.6937	.6970	.7003	.7035	.7068	.7100	.7131
.60	.7163	.7194	.7226	.7257	.7287	.7318	.7348	.7378	.7408	.7438
.70	.7467	.7497	.7526	.7555	.7583	.7611	.7640	.7668	.7695	.7723
.80	.7750	.7777	.7804	.7830	.7857	.7883	.7909	.7934	.7960	.7985
.90	.8010	.8035	.8059	.8083	.8107	.8131	.8155	.8178	.8201	.8224
1.00	.8247	.8269	.8292	.8314	.8335	.8357	.8378	.8399	.8420	.8441
1.10	.8461	.8482	.8502	.8521	.8541	.8560	.8580	.8599	.8617	.8636
1.20	.8654	.8672	.8690	.8708	.8725	.8743	.8760	.8777	.8793	.8810
1.30	.8826	.8842	.8858	.8874	.8889	.8905	.8920	.8935	.8950	.8964
1.40	.8979	.8993	.9007	.9021	.9035	.9048	.9062	.9075	.9088	.9101
1.50	.9114	.9126	.9138	.9151	.9163	.9175	.9186	.9198	.9209	.9221
1.60	.9232	.9243	.9254	.9264	.9275	.9285	.9296	.9306	.9316	.9326
1.70	.9335	.9345	.9354	.9364	.9373	.9382	.9391	.9400	.9409	.9417
1.80	.9426	.9434	.9442	.9450	.9458	.9466	.9474	.9482	.9489	.9497
1.90	.9504	.9511	.9518	.9525	.9532	.9539	.9546	.9553	.9559	.9566
2.00	.9572	.9578	.9584	.9590	.9596	.9602	.9608	.9614	.9620	.9625
2.10	.9631	.9636	.9641	.9647	.9652	.9657	.9662	.9667	.9672	.9677
2.20	.9681	.9686	.9691	.9695	.9700	.9704	.9708	.9713	.9717	.9721
2.30	.9725	.9729	.9733	.9737	.9741	.9745	.9748	.9752	.9756	.9759
2.40	.9763	.9766	.9770	.9773	.9776	.9779	.9783	.9786	.9789	.9792
2.50	.9795	.9798	.9801	.9804	.9807	.9809	.9812	.9815	.9818	.9820

The Cumulative Student "t" Distribution ν = 8

t	.00	.01	.02	.03	.04	.05	.06	.07	.08	.09
.0	.5000	.5039	.5077	.5116	.5155	.5193	.5232	.5270	.5309	.5348
.10	.5386	.5424	.5463	.5501	.5539	.5578	.5616	.5654	.5692	.5730
.20	.5768	.5805	.5843	.5881	.5918	.5956	.5993	.6030	.6067	.6104
.30	.6141	.6178	.6214	.6251	.6287	.6323	.6359	.6395	.6431	.6466
.40	.6502	.6537	.6572	.6607	.6642	.6677	.6711	.6745	.6780	.6814
.50	.6847	.6881	.6914	.6947	.6981	.7013	.7046	.7078	.7111	.7143
.60	.7174	.7206	.7237	.7269	.7300	.7330	.7361	.7391	.7422	.7451
.70	.7481	.7511	.7540	.7569	.7598	.7626	.7655	.7683	.7711	.7738
.80	.7766	.7793	.7820	.7847	.7874	.7900	.7926	.7952	.7977	.8003
.90	.8028	.8053	.8078	.8102	.8126	.8150	.8174	.8198	.8221	.8244
1.00	.8267	.8290	.8312	.8334	.8356	.8378	.8400	.8421	.8442	.8463
1.10	.8483	.8504	.8524	.8544	.8564	.8583	.8603	.8622	.8641	.8659
1.20	.8678	.8696	.8714	.8732	.8749	.8767	.8784	.8801	.8818	.8835
1.30	.8851	.8867	.8883	.8899	.8915	.8930	.8945	.8960	.8975	.8990
1.40	.9005	.9019	.9033	.9047	.9061	.9074	.9088	.9101	.9114	.9127
1.50	.9140	.9153	.9165	.9177	.9189	.9201	.9213	.9225	.9236	.9248
1.60	.9259	.9270	.9281	.9291	.9302	.9312	.9323	.9333	.9343	.9353
1.70	.9362	.9372	.9381	.9391	.9400	.9409	.9418	.9427	.9435	.9444
1.80	.9452	.9461	.9469	.9477	.9485	.9493	.9500	.9508	.9515	.9523
1.90	.9530	.9537	.9544	.9551	.9558	.9565	.9572	.9578	.9585	.9591
2.00	.9597	.9604	.9610	.9616	.9622	.9627	.9633	.9639	.9644	.9650
2.10	.9655	.9661	.9666	.9671	.9676	.9681	.9686	.9691	.9696	.9700
2.20	.9705	.9710	.9714	.9719	.9723	.9727	.9731	.9736	.9740	.9744
2.30	.9748	.9752	.9755	.9759	.9763	.9767	.9770	.9774	.9777	.9781
2.40	.9784	.9787	.9791	.9794	.9797	.9800	.9803	.9806	.9809	.9812
2.50	.9815	.9818	.9821	.9824	.9826	.9829	.9832	.9834	.9837	.9839

TABLE A.3 (continued)

The Cumulative Student "t" Distribution $\nu = 9$

t	.00	.01	.02	.03	.04	.05	.06	.07	.08	.09
.0	.5000	.5039	.5078	.5116	.5155	.5194	.5233	.5271	.5310	.5349
.10	.5387	.5426	.5464	.5503	.5541	.5580	.5618	.5656	.5694	.5732
.20	.5770	.5808	.5846	.5884	.5921	.5959	.5996	.6034	.6071	.6108
.30	.6145	.6182	.6219	.6255	.6292	.6328	.6364	.6400	.6436	.6472
.40	.6508	.6543	.6578	.6613	.6648	.6683	.6718	.6752	.6787	.6821
.50	.6855	.6888	.6922	.6955	.6988	.7021	.7054	.7087	.7119	.7151
.60	.7183	.7215	.7247	.7278	.7309	.7340	.7371	.7402	.7432	.7462
.70	.7492	.7522	.7551	.7580	.7609	.7638	.7667	.7695	.7723	.7751
.80	.7778	.7806	.7833	.7860	.7887	.7913	.7939	.7965	.7991	.8017
.90	.8042	.8067	.8092	.8117	.8141	.8165	.8189	.8213	.8237	.8260
1.00	.8283	.8306	.8328	.8351	.8373	.8395	.8416	.8438	.8459	.8480
1.10	.8501	.8521	.8541	.8562	.8581	.8601	.8621	.8640	.8659	.8678
1.20	.8696	.8714	.8733	.8751	.8768	.8786	.8803	.8820	.8837	.8854
1.30	.8870	.8887	.8903	.8919	.8935	.8950	.8965	.8981	.8996	.9010
1.40	.9025	.9039	.9053	.9067	.9081	.9095	.9109	.9122	.9135	.9148
1.50	.9161	.9173	.9186	.9198	.9210	.9222	.9234	.9246	.9257	.9269
1.60	.9280	.9291	.9302	.9312	.9323	.9333	.9344	.9354	.9364	.9374
1.70	.9383	.9393	.9402	.9412	.9421	.9430	.9439	.9447	.9456	.9465
1.80	.9473	.9481	.9489	.9498	.9505	.9513	.9521	.9529	.9536	.9543
1.90	.9551	.9558	.9565	.9572	.9578	.9585	.9592	.9598	.9605	.9611
2.00	.9617	.9623	.9629	.9635	.9641	.9647	.9653	.9658	.9664	.9669
2.10	.9674	.9680	.9685	.9690	.9695	.9700	.9705	.9709	.9714	.9719
2.20	.9723	.9728	.9732	.9737	.9741	.9745	.9749	.9753	.9757	.9761
2.30	.9765	.9769	.9773	.9776	.9780	.9783	.9787	.9790	.9794	.9797
2.40	.9801	.9804	.9807	.9810	.9813	.9816	.9819	.9822	.9825	.9828
2.50	.9831	.9833	.9836	.9839	.9841	.9844	.9847	.9849	.9852	.9854

The Cumulative Student "t" Distribution $\nu = 10$

t	.00	.01	.02	.03	.04	.05	.06	.07	.08	.09
.0	.5000	.5039	.5078	.5117	.5156	.5194	.5233	.5272	.5311	.5350
.10	.5388	.5427	.5466	.5504	.5543	.5581	.5620	.5658	.5696	.5734
.20	.5773	.5811	.5849	.5886	.5924	.5962	.5999	.6037	.6074	.6111
.30	.6148	.6185	.6222	.6259	.6296	.6332	.6368	.6405	.6441	.6476
.40	.6512	.6548	.6583	.6618	.6654	.6688	.6723	.6758	.6792	.6826
.50	.6861	.6894	.6928	.6962	.6995	.7028	.7061	.7094	.7126	.7159
.60	.7191	.7223	.7254	.7286	.7317	.7348	.7379	.7410	.7440	.7471
.70	.7501	.7530	.7560	.7589	.7618	.7647	.7676	.7704	.7733	.7761
.80	.7788	.7816	.7843	.7870	.7897	.7924	.7950	.7976	.8002	.8028
.90	.8054	.8079	.8104	.8129	.8153	.8177	.8202	.8225	.8249	.8272
1.00	.8296	.8318	.8341	.8364	.8386	.8408	.8430	.8451	.8472	.8494
1.10	.8514	.8535	.8556	.8576	.8596	.8615	.8635	.8654	.8673	.8692
1.20	.8711	.8729	.8748	.8766	.8784	.8801	.8819	.8836	.8853	.8870
1.30	.8886	.8903	.8919	.8935	.8951	.8966	.8981	.8997	.9012	.9027
1.40	.9041	.9056	.9070	.9084	.9098	.9112	.9125	.9138	.9152	.9165
1.50	.9177	.9190	.9203	.9215	.9227	.9239	.9251	.9263	.9274	.9285
1.60	.9297	.9308	.9318	.9329	.9340	.9350	.9360	.9371	.9381	.9390
1.70	.9400	.9410	.9419	.9428	.9438	.9447	.9455	.9464	.9473	.9481
1.80	.9490	.9498	.9506	.9514	.9522	.9530	.9537	.9545	.9552	.9560
1.90	.9567	.9574	.9581	.9588	.9595	.9601	.9608	.9614	.9621	.9627
2.00	.9633	.9639	.9645	.9651	.9657	.9662	.9668	.9674	.9679	.9684
2.10	.9690	.9695	.9700	.9705	.9710	.9715	.9719	.9724	.9729	.9733
2.20	.9738	.9742	.9747	.9751	.9755	.9759	.9763	.9767	.9771	.9775
2.30	.9779	.9782	.9786	.9790	.9793	.9797	.9800	.9804	.9807	.9810
2.40	.9813	.9817	.9820	.9823	.9826	.9829	.9832	.9834	.9837	.9840
2.50	.9843	.9845	.9848	.9851	.9853	.9856	.9858	.9861	.9863	.9865

TABLE A.3 (continued)

The Cumulative Student "t" Distribution $\nu = 12$

t	.00	.01	.02	.03	.04	.05	.06	.07	.08	.09
.0	.5000	.5039	.5078	.5117	.5156	.5195	.5234	.5273	.5312	.5351
.10	.5390	.5429	.5468	.5506	.5545	.5584	.5622	.5661	.5699	.5738
.20	.5776	.5814	.5852	.5890	.5928	.5966	.6004	.6041	.6079	.6116
.30	.6153	.6191	.6228	.6265	.6301	.6338	.6374	.6411	.6447	.6483
.40	.6519	.6555	.6590	.6626	.6661	.6696	.6731	.6766	.6801	.6835
.50	.6869	.6903	.6937	.6971	.7005	.7038	.7071	.7104	.7137	.7169
.60	.7202	.7234	.7266	.7297	.7329	.7360	.7391	.7422	.7453	.7483
.70	.7514	.7544	.7573	.7603	.7632	.7661	.7690	.7719	.7747	.7776
.80	.7804	.7831	.7859	.7886	.7913	.7940	.7967	.7993	.8019	.8045
.90	.8071	.8096	.8122	.8146	.8171	.8196	.8220	.8244	.8268	.8291
1.00	.8315	.8338	.8361	.8383	.8406	.8428	.8450	.8472	.8493	.8514
1.10	.8535	.8556	.8577	.8597	.8617	.8637	.8657	.8676	.8696	.8715
1.20	.8734	.8752	.8770	.8789	.8807	.8824	.8842	.8859	.8876	.8893
1.30	.8910	.8926	.8943	.8959	.8975	.8990	.9006	.9021	.9036	.9051
1.40	.9066	.9080	.9095	.9109	.9123	.9137	.9150	.9164	.9177	.9190
1.50	.9203	.9215	.9228	.9240	.9252	.9264	.9276	.9288	.9300	.9311
1.60	.9322	.9333	.9344	.9355	.9365	.9376	.9386	.9396	.9406	.9416
1.70	.9426	.9435	.9445	.9454	.9463	.9472	.9481	.9489	.9498	.9507
1.80	.9515	.9523	.9531	.9539	.9547	.9555	.9562	.9570	.9577	.9584
1.90	.9591	.9598	.9605	.9612	.9619	.9625	.9632	.9638	.9644	.9651
2.00	.9657	.9663	.9669	.9674	.9680	.9686	.9691	.9697	.9702	.9707
2.10	.9712	.9717	.9722	.9727	.9732	.9737	.9741	.9746	.9751	.9755
2.20	.9759	.9764	.9768	.9772	.9776	.9780	.9784	.9788	.9792	.9795
2.30	.9799	.9803	.9806	.9810	.9813	.9816	.9820	.9823	.9826	.9829
2.40	.9832	.9835	.9838	.9841	.9844	.9847	.9850	.9853	.9855	.9858
2.50	.9860	.9863	.9865	.9868	.9870	.9873	.9875	.9877	.9880	.9882

The Cumulative Student "t" Distribution $\nu = 14$

t	.00	.01	.02	.03	.04	.05	.06	.07	.08	.09
.0	.5000	.5039	.5078	.5118	.5157	.5196	.5235	.5274	.5313	.5352
.10	.5391	.5430	.5469	.5508	.5547	.5585	.5624	.5663	.5701	.5740
.20	.5778	.5817	.5855	.5893	.5931	.5969	.6007	.6045	.6082	.6120
.30	.6157	.6194	.6232	.6269	.6305	.6342	.6379	.6415	.6452	.6488
.40	.6524	.6560	.6596	.6631	.6667	.6702	.6737	.6772	.6807	.6841
.50	.6876	.6910	.6944	.6978	.7012	.7045	.7078	.7111	.7144	.7177
.60	.7210	.7242	.7274	.7306	.7337	.7369	.7400	.7431	.7462	.7493
.70	.7523	.7553	.7583	.7613	.7642	.7672	.7701	.7730	.7758	.7786
.80	.7815	.7843	.7870	.7893	.7925	.7952	.7979	.8005	.8031	.8057
.90	.8083	.8109	.8134	.8159	.8184	.8209	.8233	.8257	.8281	.8305
1.00	.8329	.8352	.8375	.8398	.8420	.8442	.8465	.8486	.8508	.8529
1.10	.8551	.8571	.8592	.8613	.8633	.8653	.8673	.8692	.8712	.8731
1.20	.8750	.8768	.8787	.8805	.8823	.8841	.8859	.8876	.8893	.8910
1.30	.8927	.8944	.8960	.8976	.8992	.9008	.9023	.9039	.9054	.9069
1.40	.9084	.9098	.9113	.9127	.9141	.9155	.9168	.9182	.9195	.9208
1.50	.9221	.9234	.9246	.9259	.9271	.9283	.9295	.9306	.9318	.9329
1.60	.9340	.9351	.9362	.9373	.9384	.9394	.9404	.9414	.9424	.9434
1.70	.9444	.9453	.9463	.9472	.9481	.9490	.9499	.9508	.9516	.9525
1.80	.9533	.9541	.9549	.9557	.9565	.9572	.9580	.9587	.9595	.9602
1.90	.9609	.9616	.9623	.9629	.9636	.9643	.9649	.9655	.9661	.9668
2.00	.9674	.9679	.9685	.9691	.9697	.9702	.9708	.9713	.9718	.9723
2.10	.9728	.9733	.9738	.9743	.9748	.9752	.9757	.9761	.9766	.9770
2.20	.9774	.9779	.9783	.9787	.9791	.9795	.9799	.9802	.9806	.9810
2.30	.9813	.9817	.9820	.9824	.9827	.9830	.9833	.9837	.9840	.9843
2.40	.9846	.9849	.9851	.9854	.9857	.9860	.9862	.9865	.9868	.9870
2.50	.9873	.9875	.9877	.9880	.9882	.9884	.9887	.9889	.9891	.9893

TABLE A.3 (continued)

The Cumulative Student "t" Distribution $\nu = 16$

t	.00	.01	.02	.03	.04	.05	.06	.07	.08	.09
.0	.5000	.5039	.5079	.5118	.5157	.5196	.5236	.5275	.5314	.5353
.10	.5392	.5431	.5470	.5509	.5548	.5587	.5626	.5664	.5703	.5742
.20	.5780	.5818	.5857	.5895	.5933	.5971	.6009	.6047	.6085	.6122
.30	.6160	.6197	.6234	.6272	.6309	.6345	.6382	.6419	.6455	.6492
.40	.6528	.6564	.6600	.6635	.6671	.6706	.6741	.6777	.6811	.6846
.50	.5881	.6915	.6949	.6983	.7017	.7050	.7084	.7117	.7150	.7183
.60	.7215	.7248	.7280	.7312	.7344	.7375	.7407	.7438	.7469	.7500
.70	.7530	.7560	.7590	.7620	.7650	.7679	.7708	.7737	.7766	.7795
.80	.7823	.7851	.7879	.7906	.7934	.7961	.7988	.8014	.8041	.8067
.90	.8093	.8118	.8144	.8169	.8194	.8219	.8243	.8268	.8292	.8315
1.00	.8339	.8362	.8385	.8408	.8431	.8453	.8476	.8498	.8519	.8541
1.10	.8562	.8583	.8604	.8624	.8645	.8665	.8685	.8704	.8724	.8743
1.20	.8762	.8781	.8799	.8818	.8836	.8854	.8871	.8889	.8906	.8923
1.30	.8940	.8957	.8973	.8989	.9005	.9021	.9037	.9052	.9067	.9082
1.40	.9097	.9112	.9126	.9140	.9154	.9168	.9182	.9195	.9209	.9222
1.50	.9235	.9247	.9260	.9272	.9284	.9297	.9308	.9320	.9332	.9343
1.60	.9354	.9365	.9376	.9387	.9397	.9408	.9418	.9428	.9438	.9448
1.70	.9458	.9467	.9476	.9486	.9495	.9504	.9512	.9521	.9530	.9538
1.80	.9546	.9554	.9562	.9570	.9578	.9586	.9593	.9601	.9608	.9615
1.90	.9622	.9629	.9636	.9642	.9649	.9655	.9662	.9668	.9674	.9680
2.00	.9586	.9692	.9698	.9703	.9709	.9714	.9720	.9725	.9730	.9735
2.10	.9740	.9745	.9750	.9755	.9759	.9764	.9769	.9773	.9777	.9782
2.20	.9786	.9790	.9794	.9798	.9802	.9806	.9809	.9813	.9817	.9820
2.30	.9824	.9827	.9831	.9834	.9837	.9840	.9843	.9847	.9850	.9852
2.40	.9855	.9858	.9861	.9864	.9866	.9869	.9872	.9874	.9877	.9879
2.50	.9882	.9884	.9886	.9889	.9891	.9893	.9895	.9897	.9899	.9901

The Cumulative Student "t" Distribution $\nu = 18$

t	.00	.01	.02	.03	.04	.05	.06	.07	.08	.09
.0	.5000	.5039	.5079	.5118	.5157	.5197	.5236	.5275	.5314	.5354
.10	.5393	.5432	.5471	.5510	.5549	.5588	.5627	.5665	.5704	.5743
.20	.5781	.5820	.5858	.5897	.5935	.5973	.6011	.6049	.6087	.6124
.30	.6162	.6199	.6237	.6274	.6311	.6348	.6385	.6421	.6458	.6494
.40	.6531	.6567	.6603	.6639	.6674	.6710	.6745	.6780	.6815	.6850
.50	.6884	.6919	.6953	.6987	.7021	.7055	.7088	.7121	.7154	.7187
.60	.7220	.7253	.7285	.7317	.7349	.7380	.7412	.7443	.7474	.7505
.70	.7536	.7566	.7596	.7626	.7656	.7685	.7715	.7744	.7772	.7801
.80	.7829	.7857	.7885	.7913	.7940	.7968	.7995	.8021	.8048	.8074
.90	.8100	.8126	.8151	.8177	.8202	.8227	.8251	.8275	.8300	.8324
1.00	.8347	.8371	.8394	.8417	.8439	.8462	.8484	.8506	.8528	.8550
1.10	.8571	.8592	.8613	.8633	.8654	.8674	.8694	.8714	.8733	.8752
1.20	.8772	.8790	.8809	.8827	.8846	.8863	.8881	.8899	.8916	.8933
1.30	.8950	.8967	.8983	.8999	.9015	.9031	.9047	.9062	.9078	.9093
1.40	.9107	.9122	.9137	.9151	.9165	.9179	.9192	.9206	.9219	.9232
1.50	.9245	.9258	.9271	.9283	.9295	.9307	.9319	.9331	.9342	.9354
1.60	.9365	.9376	.9387	.9398	.9408	.9419	.9429	.9439	.9449	.9459
1.70	.9468	.9478	.9487	.9496	.9505	.9514	.9523	.9532	.9540	.9549
1.80	.9557	.9565	.9573	.9581	.9588	.9596	.9603	.9611	.9618	.9625
1.90	.9632	.9639	.9646	.9652	.9659	.9665	.9672	.9678	.9684	.9690
2.00	.9696	.9702	.9707	.9713	.9718	.9724	.9729	.9734	.9740	.9745
2.10	.9750	.9754	.9759	.9764	.9768	.9773	.9777	.9782	.9786	.9790
2.20	.9794	.9799	.9802	.9806	.9810	.9814	.9818	.9821	.9825	.9828
2.30	.9832	.9835	.9839	.9842	.9845	.9848	.9851	.9854	.9857	.9860
2.40	.9863	.9866	.9868	.9871	.9874	.9876	.9879	.9881	.9884	.9886
2.50	.9888	.9891	.9893	.9895	.9897	.9899	.9902	.9904	.9906	.9908

TABLE A.3 (continued)

The Cumulative Student "t" Distribution $\nu = 20$

t	.00	.01	.02	.03	.04	.05	.06	.07	.08	.09
0.0	0.5000	0.5039	0.5079	0.5118	0.5158	0.5197	0.5236	0.5276	0.5315	0.5354
0.10	0.5393	0.5432	0.5472	0.5511	0.5550	0.5589	0.5628	0.5666	0.5705	0.5744
0.20	0.5782	0.5821	0.5859	0.5898	0.5936	0.5974	0.6012	0.6050	0.6088	0.6126
0.30	0.6164	0.6201	0.6239	0.6276	0.6313	0.6350	0.6387	0.6424	0.6460	0.6497
0.40	0.6533	0.6569	0.6605	0.6641	0.6677	0.6712	0.6748	0.6783	0.6818	0.6853
0.50	0.6887	0.6922	0.6956	0.6990	0.7024	0.7058	0.7092	0.7125	0.7158	0.7191
0.60	0.7224	0.7256	0.7289	0.7321	0.7353	0.7385	0.7416	0.7447	0.7478	0.7509
0.70	0.7540	0.7570	0.7601	0.7631	0.7661	0.7690	0.7719	0.7749	0.7777	0.7806
0.80	0.7834	0.7863	0.7891	0.7918	0.7946	0.7973	0.8000	0.8027	0.8053	0.8080
0.90	0.8106	0.8132	0.8157	0.8183	0.8208	0.8233	0.8257	0.8282	0.8306	0.8330
1.00	0.8354	0.8377	0.8400	0.8423	0.8446	0.8469	0.8491	0.8513	0.8535	0.8557
1.10	0.8578	0.8599	0.8620	0.8641	0.8661	0.8681	0.8701	0.8721	0.8741	0.8760
1.20	0.8779	0.8798	0.8817	0.8835	0.8853	0.8871	0.8889	0.8907	0.8924	0.8941
1.30	0.8958	0.8975	0.8991	0.9008	0.9024	0.9040	0.9055	0.9071	0.9086	0.9101
1.40	0.9116	0.9130	0.9145	0.9159	0.9173	0.9187	0.9201	0.9214	0.9228	0.9241
1.50	0.9254	0.9267	0.9279	0.9292	0.9304	0.9316	0.9328	0.9339	0.9351	0.9362
1.60	0.9374	0.9385	0.9396	0.9406	0.9417	0.9427	0.9437	0.9448	0.9457	0.9467
1.70	0.9477	0.9486	0.9496	0.9505	0.9514	0.9523	0.9532	0.9540	0.9549	0.9557
1.80	0.9565	0.9573	0.9581	0.9589	0.9597	0.9604	0.9612	0.9619	0.9626	0.9633
1.90	0.9640	0.9647	0.9654	0.9660	0.9667	0.9673	0.9680	0.9686	0.9692	0.9698
2.00	0.9704	0.9709	0.9715	0.9721	0.9726	0.9731	0.9737	0.9742	0.9747	0.9752
2.10	0.9757	0.9762	0.9766	0.9771	0.9776	0.9780	0.9785	0.9789	0.9793	0.9797
2.20	0.9801	0.9805	0.9809	0.9813	0.9817	0.9821	0.9824	0.9828	0.9831	0.9835
2.30	0.9838	0.9842	0.9845	0.9848	0.9851	0.9854	0.9857	0.9860	0.9863	0.9866
2.40	0.9869	0.9871	0.9874	0.9877	0.9879	0.9882	0.9884	0.9887	0.9889	0.9892
2.50	0.9894	0.9896	0.9898	0.9900	0.9903	0.9905	0.9907	0.9909	0.9911	0.9912

The Cumulative Student "t" Distribution $\nu = 22$

t	.00	.01	.02	.03	.04	.05	.06	.07	.08	.09
.0	.5000	.5039	.5079	.5118	.5158	.5197	.5237	.5276	.5315	.5354
.10	.5394	.5433	.5472	.5511	.5550	.5589	.5628	.5667	.5706	.5745
.20	.5783	.5822	.5861	.5899	.5937	.5975	.6014	.6052	.6090	.6127
.30	.6165	.6203	.6240	.6277	.6315	.6352	.6389	.6425	.6462	.6499
.40	.6535	.6571	.6607	.6643	.6679	.6714	.6750	.6785	.6820	.6855
.50	.6890	.6924	.6959	.6993	.7027	.7061	.7094	.7128	.7161	.7194
.60	.7227	.7259	.7292	.7324	.7356	.7388	.7419	.7451	.7482	.7513
.70	.7544	.7574	.7604	.7635	.7664	.7694	.7723	.7753	.7781	.7810
.80	.7839	.7867	.7895	.7923	.7950	.7978	.8005	.8032	.8058	.8085
.90	.8111	.8137	.8162	.8188	.8213	.8238	.8263	.8287	.8311	.8335
1.00	.8359	.8383	.8406	.8429	.8452	.8474	.8497	.8519	.8541	.8562
1.10	.8584	.8605	.8626	.8647	.8667	.8688	.8708	.8727	.8747	.8766
1.20	.8785	.8804	.8823	.8842	.8860	.8878	.8896	.8913	.8931	.8948
1.30	.8965	.8981	.8998	.9014	.9030	.9046	.9062	.9077	.9093	.9108
1.40	.9123	.9137	.9152	.9166	.9180	.9194	.9208	.9221	.9235	.9248
1.50	.9261	.9274	.9286	.9299	.9311	.9323	.9335	.9347	.9358	.9369
1.60	.9381	.9392	.9403	.9413	.9424	.9434	.9444	.9455	.9464	.9474
1.70	.9484	.9493	.9503	.9512	.9521	.9530	.9538	.9547	.9556	.9564
1.80	.9572	.9580	.9588	.9596	.9603	.9611	.9618	.9626	.9633	.9640
1.90	.9647	.9654	.9660	.9667	.9673	.9680	.9686	.9692	.9698	.9704
2.00	.9710	.9716	.9721	.9727	.9732	.9738	.9743	.9748	.9753	.9758
2.10	.9763	.9768	.9772	.9777	.9782	.9786	.9790	.9795	.9799	.9803
2.20	.9807	.9811	.9815	.9819	.9822	.9826	.9830	.9833	.9837	.9840
2.30	.9843	.9847	.9850	.9853	.9856	.9859	.9862	.9865	.9868	.9871
2.40	.9874	.9876	.9879	.9881	.9884	.9886	.9889	.9891	.9894	.9896
2.50	.9898	.9900	.9903	.9905	.9907	.9909	.9911	.9913	.9915	.9916

TABLE A.3 (continued)

The Cumulative Student "t" Distribution ν = 24

t	.00	.01	.02	.03	.04	.05	.06	.07	.08	.09
.0	.5000	.5039	.5079	.5118	.5158	.5197	.5237	.5276	.5315	.5355
.10	.5394	.5433	.5473	.5512	.5551	.5590	.5629	.5668	.5707	.5745
.20	.5784	.5823	.5861	.5900	.5938	.5976	.6015	.6053	.6091	.6128
.30	.6166	.6204	.6241	.6279	.6316	.6353	.6390	.6427	.6464	.6500
.40	.6537	.6573	.6609	.6645	.6681	.6716	.6752	.6787	.6822	.6857
.50	.6892	.6926	.6961	.6995	.7029	.7063	.7097	.7130	.7163	.7196
.60	.7229	.7262	.7294	.7327	.7359	.7391	.7422	.7454	.7485	.7516
.70	.7547	.7577	.7608	.7638	.7668	.7697	.7727	.7756	.7785	.7814
.80	.7842	.7871	.7899	.7926	.7954	.7981	.8009	.8035	.8062	.8088
.90	.8115	.8141	.8166	.8192	.8217	.8242	.8267	.8291	.8316	.8340
1.00	.8364	.8387	.8410	.8434	.8456	.8479	.8502	.8524	.8546	.8567
1.10	.8589	.8610	.8631	.8652	.8672	.8693	.8713	.8733	.8752	.8772
1.20	.8791	.8810	.8828	.8847	.8865	.8883	.8901	.8919	.8936	.8953
1.30	.8970	.8987	.9004	.9020	.9036	.9052	.9068	.9083	.9098	.9114
1.40	.9128	.9143	.9158	.9172	.9186	.9200	.9214	.9227	.9241	.9254
1.50	.9267	.9280	.9292	.9305	.9317	.9329	.9341	.9352	.9364	.9375
1.60	.9387	.9398	.9408	.9419	.9430	.9440	.9450	.9460	.9470	.9480
1.70	.9490	.9499	.9508	.9518	.9527	.9536	.9544	.9553	.9561	.9570
1.80	.9578	.9586	.9594	.9602	.9609	.9617	.9624	.9631	.9638	.9646
1.90	.9652	.9659	.9666	.9672	.9679	.9685	.9691	.9698	.9704	.9709
2.00	.9715	.9721	.9727	.9732	.9737	.9743	.9748	.9753	.9758	.9763
2.10	.9768	.9773	.9777	.9782	.9786	.9791	.9795	.9799	.9804	.9808
2.20	.9812	.9816	.9819	.9823	.9827	.9831	.9834	.9838	.9841	.9844
2.30	.9848	.9851	.9854	.9857	.9860	.9863	.9866	.9869	.9872	.9875
2.40	.9877	.9880	.9883	.9885	.9888	.9890	.9893	.9895	.9897	.9900
2.50	.9902	.9904	.9906	.9908	.9910	.9912	.9914	.9916	.9918	.9920

The Cumulative Student "t" Distribution ν = 26

t	.00	.01	.02	.03	.04	.05	.06	.07	.08	.09
.0	.5000	.5040	.5079	.5119	.5158	.5197	.5237	.5276	.5316	.5355
.10	.5394	.5434	.5473	.5512	.5551	.5590	.5629	.5668	.5707	.5746
.20	.5785	.5823	.5862	.5901	.5939	.5977	.6015	.6054	.6092	.6129
.30	.5167	.6205	.6242	.6280	.6317	.6354	.6391	.6428	.6465	.6501
.40	.6538	.6574	.6610	.6646	.6682	.6718	.6753	.6789	.6824	.6859
.50	.6894	.6928	.6963	.6997	.7031	.7065	.7099	.7132	.7165	.7199
.60	.7231	.7264	.7297	.7329	.7361	.7393	.7425	.7456	.7487	.7518
.70	.7549	.7580	.7610	.7640	.7670	.7700	.7730	.7759	.7788	.7817
.80	.7845	.7874	.7902	.7930	.7957	.7985	.8012	.8039	.8065	.8092
.90	.8118	.8144	.8170	.8195	.8221	.8246	.8271	.8295	.8319	.8344
1.00	.8367	.8391	.8414	.8438	.8460	.8483	.8506	.8528	.8550	.8571
1.10	.8593	.8614	.8635	.8656	.8677	.8697	.8717	.8737	.8757	.8776
1.20	.8795	.8814	.8833	.8851	.8870	.8888	.8906	.8923	.8941	.8958
1.30	.8975	.8992	.9008	.9025	.9041	.9057	.9072	.9088	.9103	.9118
1.40	.9133	.9148	.9163	.9177	.9191	.9205	.9219	.9232	.9246	.9259
1.50	.9272	.9284	.9297	.9310	.9322	.9334	.9346	.9357	.9369	.9380
1.60	.9392	.9403	.9413	.9424	.9435	.9445	.9455	.9465	.9475	.9485
1.70	.9495	.9504	.9513	.9523	.9532	.9540	.9549	.9558	.9566	.9574
1.80	.9583	.9591	.9599	.9606	.9614	.9621	.9629	.9636	.9643	.9650
1.90	.9657	.9664	.9671	.9677	.9683	.9690	.9696	.9702	.9708	.9714
2.00	.9720	.9725	.9731	.9736	.9742	.9747	.9752	.9757	.9762	.9767
2.10	.9772	.9777	.9781	.9786	.9790	.9795	.9799	.9803	.9807	.9812
2.20	.9816	.9819	.9823	.9827	.9831	.9834	.9838	.9841	.9845	.9848
2.30	.9851	.9855	.9858	.9861	.9864	.9867	.9870	.9873	.9875	.9878
2.40	.9881	.9883	.9886	.9888	.9891	.9893	.9896	.9898	.9900	.9903
2.50	.9905	.9907	.9909	.9911	.9913	.9915	.9917	.9919	.9921	.9922

TABLE A.3(continued)

The Cumulative Student "t" Distribution $\nu = 28$

t	.00	.01	.02	.03	.04	.05	.06	.07	.08	.09
.0	.5000	.5040	.5079	.5119	.5158	.5198	.5237	.5277	.5316	.5355
.10	.5395	.5434	.5473	.5513	.5552	.5591	.5630	.5669	.5708	.5747
.20	.5785	.5824	.5863	.5901	.5940	.5978	.6016	.6054	.6092	.6130
.30	.6168	.6206	.6243	.6281	.6318	.6355	.6392	.6429	.6466	.6503
.40	.6539	.6575	.6612	.6648	.6683	.6719	.6755	.6790	.6825	.6860
.50	.6895	.6930	.6964	.6999	.7033	.7067	.7100	.7134	.7167	.7200
.60	.7233	.7266	.7299	.7331	.7363	.7395	.7427	.7458	.7490	.7521
.70	.7551	.7582	.7613	.7643	.7673	.7702	.7732	.7761	.7790	.7819
.80	.7848	.7876	.7904	.7932	.7960	.7987	.8015	.8042	.8068	.8095
.90	.8121	.8147	.8173	.8198	.8224	.8249	.8274	.8298	.8323	.8347
1.00	.8371	.8394	.8418	.8441	.8464	.8487	.8509	.8531	.8553	.8575
1.10	.8596	.8618	.8639	.8660	.8680	.8701	.8721	.8741	.8760	.8780
1.20	.8799	.8818	.8837	.8855	.8874	.8892	.8910	.8927	.8945	.8962
1.30	.8979	.8996	.9012	.9029	.9045	.9061	.9077	.9092	.9107	.9123
1.40	.9138	.9152	.9167	.9181	.9195	.9209	.9223	.9236	.9250	.9263
1.50	.9276	.9289	.9301	.9314	.9326	.9338	.9350	.9362	.9373	.9385
1.60	.9396	.9407	.9418	.9428	.9439	.9449	.9460	.9470	.9480	.9489
1.70	.9499	.9508	.9518	.9527	.9536	.9545	.9553	.9562	.9570	.9579
1.80	.9587	.9595	.9603	.9610	.9618	.9626	.9633	.9640	.9647	.9654
1.90	.9661	.9668	.9675	.9681	.9687	.9694	.9700	.9706	.9712	.9718
2.00	.9724	.9729	.9735	.9740	.9746	.9751	.9756	.9761	.9766	.9771
2.10	.9776	.9780	.9785	.9790	.9794	.9798	.9803	.9807	.9811	.9815
2.20	.9819	.9823	.9827	.9830	.9834	.9838	.9841	.9844	.9848	.9851
2.30	.9854	.9858	.9861	.9864	.9867	.9870	.9873	.9875	.9878	.9881
2.40	.9884	.9886	.9889	.9891	.9894	.9896	.9898	.9901	.9903	.9905
2.50	.9907	.9909	.9911	.9913	.9915	.9917	.9919	.9921	.9923	.9925

The Cumulative Student "t" Distribution $\nu = 30$

t	.00	.01	.02	.03	.04	.05	.06	.07	.08	.09
.0	.5000	.5040	.5079	.5119	.5158	.5198	.5237	.5277	.5316	.5356
.10	.5395	.5434	.5474	.5513	.5552	.5591	.5630	.5669	.5708	.5747
.20	.5786	.5825	.5863	.5902	.5940	.5979	.6017	.6055	.6093	.6131
.30	.6169	.6206	.6244	.6282	.6319	.6356	.6393	.6430	.6467	.6504
.40	.6540	.6576	.6613	.6649	.6685	.6720	.6756	.6791	.6826	.6862
.50	.6896	.6931	.6966	.7000	.7034	.7068	.7102	.7135	.7169	.7202
.60	.7235	.7268	.7300	.7333	.7365	.7397	.7429	.7460	.7491	.7523
.70	.7553	.7584	.7615	.7645	.7675	.7705	.7734	.7763	.7792	.7821
.80	.7850	.7878	.7907	.7935	.7962	.7990	.8017	.8044	.8071	.8097
.90	.8124	.8150	.8175	.8201	.8226	.8251	.8276	.8301	.8325	.8350
1.00	.8373	.8397	.8421	.8444	.8467	.8489	.8512	.8534	.8556	.8578
1.10	.8600	.8621	.8642	.8663	.8683	.8704	.8724	.8744	.8764	.8783
1.20	.8802	.8821	.8840	.8859	.8877	.8895	.8913	.8931	.8948	.8965
1.30	.8982	.8999	.9016	.9032	.9048	.9064	.9080	.9096	.9111	.9126
1.40	.9141	.9156	.9170	.9185	.9199	.9213	.9227	.9240	.9254	.9267
1.50	.9280	.9292	.9305	.9318	.9330	.9342	.9354	.9365	.9377	.9388
1.60	.9400	.9411	.9422	.9432	.9443	.9453	.9463	.9473	.9483	.9493
1.70	.9503	.9512	.9521	.9530	.9539	.9548	.9557	.9566	.9574	.9582
1.80	.9590	.9598	.9606	.9614	.9622	.9629	.9636	.9644	.9651	.9658
1.90	.9665	.9671	.9678	.9684	.9691	.9697	.9703	.9709	.9715	.9721
2.00	.9727	.9733	.9738	.9743	.9749	.9754	.9759	.9764	.9769	.9774
2.10	.9779	.9783	.9788	.9793	.9797	.9801	.9806	.9810	.9814	.9818
2.20	.9822	.9826	.9829	.9833	.9837	.9840	.9844	.9847	.9851	.9854
2.30	.9857	.9860	.9863	.9866	.9869	.9872	.9875	.9878	.9881	.9883
2.40	.9886	.9889	.9891	.9894	.9896	.9898	.9901	.9903	.9905	.9907
2.50	.9909	.9912	.9914	.9916	.9917	.9919	.9921	.9923	.9925	.9927

TABLE A.3(continued)

The Cumulative Student "t" Distribution $\nu = 40$

t	.00	.01	.02	.03	.04	.05	.06	.07	.08	.09
.0	.5000	.5040	.5079	.5119	.5159	.5198	.5238	0.5277	.5317	.5356
.10	.5396	.5435	.5475	.5514	.5553	.5592	.5632	0.5671	.5710	.5749
.20	.5788	.5826	.5865	.5904	.5942	.5981	.6019	0.6057	.6095	.6133
.30	.6171	.6209	.6247	.6284	.6322	.6359	.6396	0.6433	.6470	.6507
.40	.6544	.6580	.6616	.6652	.6688	.6724	.6760	0.6795	.6831	.6866
.50	.6901	.6936	.6970	.7005	.7039	.7073	.7107	0.7141	.7174	.7207
.60	.7241	.7273	.7306	.7339	.7371	.7403	.7435	0.7466	.7498	.7529
.70	.7560	.7591	.7621	.7652	.7682	.7712	.7741	0.7771	.7800	.7829
.80	.7858	.7886	.7915	.7943	.7970	.7998	.8025	0.8053	.8079	.8106
.90	.8132	.8159	.8185	.8210	.8236	.8261	.8286	0.8311	.8335	.8359
1.00	.8383	.8407	.8431	.8454	.8477	.8500	.8522	0.8545	.8567	.8589
1.10	.8610	.8632	.8653	.8674	.8695	.8715	.8735	0.8755	.8775	.8795
1.20	.8814	.8833	.8852	.8871	.8889	.8907	.8925	0.8943	.8960	.8978
1.30	.8995	.9012	.9028	.9045	.9061	.9077	.9093	0.9108	.9124	.9139
1.40	.9154	.9169	.9183	.9198	.9212	.9226	.9239	0.9253	.9266	.9280
1.50	.9293	.9305	.9318	.9331	.9343	.9355	.9367	0.9379	.9390	.9401
1.60	.9413	.9424	.9435	.9445	.9456	.9466	.9476	0.9486	.9496	.9506
1.70	.9516	.9525	.9534	.9543	.9552	.9561	.9570	0.9578	.9587	.9595
1.80	.9603	.9611	.9619	.9626	.9634	.9641	.9649	0.9656	.9663	.9670
1.90	.9677	.9683	.9690	.9696	.9703	.9709	.9715	0.9721	.9727	.9733
2.00	.9738	.9744	.9749	.9755	.9760	.9765	.9770	0.9775	.9780	.9785
2.10	.9790	.9794	.9799	.9803	.9807	.9812	.9816	0.9820	.9824	.9828
2.20	.9832	.9836	.9839	.9843	.9846	.9850	.9853	0.9857	.9860	.9863
2.30	.9866	.9869	.9872	.9875	.9878	.9881	.9884	0.9887	.9889	.9892
2.40	.9894	.9897	.9899	.9902	.9904	.9906	.9908	0.9911	.9913	.9915
2.50	.9917	.9919	.9921	.9923	.9925	.9926	.9928	0.9930	.9932	.9933

The Cumulative Student "t" Distribution $\nu = 50$

t	.00	.01	.02	.03	.04	.05	.06	.07	.08	.09
.0	.5000	.5040	.5079	.5119	.5159	.5198	.5238	.5278	.5317	.5357
.10	.5396	.5436	.5475	.5515	.5554	.5593	.5632	.5672	.5711	.5750
.20	.5789	.5827	.5866	.5905	.5943	.5982	.6020	.6059	.6097	.6135
.30	.6173	.6211	.6248	.6286	.6324	.6361	.6398	.6435	.6472	.6509
.40	.6546	.6582	.6619	.6655	.6691	.6727	.6762	.6798	.6833	.6869
.50	.6904	.6939	.6973	.7008	.7042	.7076	.7110	.7144	.7177	.7211
.60	.7244	.7277	.7310	.7342	.7375	.7407	.7439	.7470	.7502	.7533
.70	.7564	.7595	.7626	.7656	.7686	.7716	.7746	.7775	.7805	.7834
.80	.7863	.7891	.7919	.7948	.7975	.8003	.8031	.8058	.8085	.8111
.90	.8138	.8164	.8190	.8216	.8241	.8267	.8292	.8316	.8341	.8365
1.00	.8389	.8413	.8437	.8460	.8483	.8506	.8529	.8551	.8573	.8595
1.10	.8617	.8638	.8660	.8681	.8701	.8722	.8742	.8762	.8782	.8802
1.20	.8821	.8840	.8859	.8878	.8896	.8914	.8932	.8950	.8968	.8985
1.30	.9002	.9019	.9036	.9052	.9068	.9085	.9100	.9116	.9131	.9147
1.40	.9162	.9176	.9191	.9205	.9219	.9233	.9247	.9261	.9274	.9287
1.50	.9300	.9313	.9326	.9338	.9351	.9363	.9375	.9386	.9398	.9409
1.60	.9421	.9432	.9442	.9453	.9464	.9474	.9484	.9494	.9504	.9514
1.70	.9523	.9533	.9542	.9551	.9560	.9569	.9577	.9586	.9594	.9602
1.80	.9611	.9618	.9626	.9634	.9641	.9649	.9656	.9663	.9670	.9677
1.90	.9684	.9691	.9697	.9704	.9710	.9716	.9722	.9728	.9734	.9740
2.00	.9745	.9751	.9756	.9762	.9767	.9772	.9777	.9782	.9787	.9791
2.10	.9796	.9801	.9805	.9809	.9814	.9818	.9822	.9826	.9830	.9834
2.20	.9838	.9841	.9845	.9849	.9852	.9856	.9859	.9862	.9865	.9869
2.30	.9872	.9875	.9878	.9881	.9883	.9886	.9889	.9892	.9894	.9897
2.40	.9899	.9902	.9904	.9906	.9909	.9911	.9913	.9915	.9917	.9919
2.50	.9921	.9923	.9925	.9927	.9929	.9931	.9932	.9934	.9936	.9937

TABLE A.3 (continued)

The Cumulative Student "t" Distribution $\nu = 60$

t	.00	.01	.02	.03	.04	.05	.06	.07	.08	.09
.0	.5000	.5040	.5079	.5119	.5159	.5199	.5238	.5278	.5317	.5357
.10	.5397	.5436	.5476	.5515	.5554	.5594	.5633	.5672	.5711	.5750
.20	.5789	.5828	.5867	.5906	.5944	.5983	.6021	.6060	.6098	.6136
.30	.6174	.6212	.6250	.6287	.6325	.6362	.6399	.6437	.6474	.6510
.40	.6547	.6584	.6620	.6656	.6692	.6728	.6764	.6800	.6835	.6870
.50	.6905	.6940	.6975	.7010	.7044	.7078	.7112	.7146	.7180	.7213
.60	.7246	.7279	.7312	.7345	.7377	.7409	.7441	.7473	.7504	.7536
.70	.7567	.7598	.7628	.7659	.7689	.7719	.7749	.7778	.7808	.7837
.80	.7866	.7894	.7923	.7951	.7979	.8006	.8034	.8061	.8088	.8115
.90	.8141	.8168	.8194	.8220	.8245	.8270	.8295	.8320	.8345	.8369
1.00	.8393	.8417	.8441	.8464	.8487	.8510	.8533	.8555	.8578	.8600
1.10	.8621	.8643	.8664	.8685	.8706	.8726	.8747	.8767	.8787	.8806
1.20	.8826	.8845	.8864	.8883	.8901	.8919	.8937	.8955	.8973	.8990
1.30	.9007	.9024	.9041	.9057	.9074	.9090	.9105	.9121	.9136	.9152
1.40	.9167	.9181	.9196	.9210	.9225	.9239	.9252	.9266	.9279	.9293
1.50	.9306	.9319	.9331	.9344	.9356	.9368	.9380	.9392	.9403	.9415
1.60	.9426	.9437	.9448	.9458	.9469	.9479	.9489	.9499	.9509	.9519
1.70	.9528	.9538	.9547	.9556	.9565	.9574	.9582	.9591	.9599	.9607
1.80	.9616	.9623	.9631	.9639	.9646	.9654	.9661	.9668	.9675	.9682
1.90	.9689	.9695	.9702	.9703	.9715	.9721	.9727	.9733	.9739	.9744
2.00	.9750	.9755	.9761	.9765	.9771	.9776	.9781	.9786	.9791	.9796
2.10	.9800	.9805	.9809	.9814	.9818	.9822	.9826	.9830	.9834	.9838
2.20	.9842	.9845	.9849	.9852	.9856	.9859	.9863	.9866	.9869	.9872
2.30	.9875	.9878	.9881	.9884	.9887	.9890	.9892	.9895	.9897	.9900
2.40	.9902	.9905	.9907	.9909	.9912	.9914	.9916	.9918	.9920	.9922
2.50	.9924	.9926	.9928	.9930	.9932	.9933	.9935	.9937	.9938	.9940

TABLE A.4

PERCENTAGE POINTS OF THE STUDENT "t" DISTRIBUTION

The format for this table is similar to that for the percentage points for the normal distribution with each row here referring to a "t" distribution with the stated degrees of freedom. It should be noted that the function tabulated is the standardized t, $t(\nu, 0, \nu)$ and that the corresponding percentage point for $t(\nu, \zeta, \kappa)$ is $\zeta + (\frac{\kappa}{\nu})^{\frac{1}{2}} t$. For example, to find the 75th percentile for t(10, 5, 160), we find from the table that the 75th percentile for t(10) = .6998. Thus, the 75th percentile for t(10, 5, 160) is $5 + (\frac{160}{10})^{\frac{1}{2}}(.6998) = 5 + 4(.6998) = 7.7992$.

P(T) = ν =	75%	80%	85%	87.5%	90%	95%	97.5%	99%	99.5%
1	1.0000	1.3764	1.9626	2.4142	3.0777	6.3137	12.706	31.821	63.657
2	.8165	1.0607	1.3862	1.6036	1.8856	2.9200	4.3026	6.9649	9.9248
3	.7649	.9785	1.2498	1.4226	1.6377	2.3534	3.1824	4.5406	5.8411
4	.7407	.9410	1.1896	1.3444	1.5332	2.1318	2.7764	3.7470	4.6043
5	.7267	.9195	1.1558	1.3010	1.4759	2.0150	2.5706	3.3649	4.0321
6	.7176	.9057	1.1342	1.2733	1.4398	1.9432	2.4469	3.1427	3.7075
7	.7111	.8960	1.1192	1.2543	1.4149	1.8946	2.3646	2.9980	3.4996
8	.7064	.8889	1.1081	1.2403	1.3968	1.8595	2.3060	2.8965	3.3554
9	.7027	.8834	1.0997	1.2297	1.3830	1.8331	2.2622	2.8214	3.2497
10	.6998	.8791	1.0931	1.2213	1.3722	1.8125	2.2281	2.7637	3.1693
12	.6955	.8726	1.0832	1.2089	1.3562	1.7823	2.1788	2.6810	3.0546
14	.6924	.8681	1.0763	1.2001	1.3450	1.7613	2.1448	2.6245	2.9768
16	.6901	.8647	1.0711	1.1937	1.3368	1.7459	2.1199	2.5835	2.9207
18	.6884	.8621	1.0672	1.1887	1.3304	1.7341	2.1009	2.5524	2.8784
20	.6870	.8600	1.0640	1.1848	1.3253	1.7247	2.0860	2.5280	2.8454
22	.6858	.8583	1.0615	1.1815	1.3212	1.7171	2.0739	2.5084	2.8187
24	.6849	.8569	1.0593	1.1789	1.3178	1.7109	2.0639	2.4921	2.7969
26	.6840	.8557	1.0575	1.1766	1.3150	1.7056	2.0555	2.4786	2.7787
28	.6834	.8546	1.0560	1.1747	1.3125	1.7011	2.0484	2.4672	2.7633
30	.6828	.8538	1.0547	1.1731	1.3104	1.6973	2.0423	2.4572	2.7500
40	.6807	.8507	1.0500	1.1673	1.3031	1.6839	2.0211	2.4233	2.7044
50	.6794	.8489	1.0473	1.1639	1.2987	1.6759	2.0086	2.4033	2.6777
60	.6786	.8476	1.0455	1.1616	1.2958	1.6706	2.0003	2.3901	2.6603
∞	.6745	.8416	1.0364	1.1503	1.2816	1.6448	1.9600	2.3263	2.5758

TABLE A.5

PERCENTAGE POINTS OF THE CHI-SQUARE DISTRIBUTION

The values are tabulated for the χ^2 distribution with scale factor 1 commonly written $\chi^2(\nu)$, or in the notation of section 7.2, $\chi^2(\nu, 1)$ To find the percentage point for $\chi^2(\nu, \omega)$, $\omega \neq 1$, multiply the tabulated value for $\chi^2(\nu, 1)$ by ω. For example, to find the 10% point for $\chi^2(20, 10)$, we first note that the 10% point for $\chi^2(20, 1) = 29.05$. Thus, the desired value is $10(29.05) = 290.5$.

P(x) = / ν =	.5%	1%	2.5%	5%	10%	12.5%	25%	50%	75%	87.5%	90%	95%	97.5%	99%	99.5%
4	.2070	.2971	.4844	.7107	1.064	1.219	1.923	3.357	5.385	7.214	7.779	9.488	11.14	13.28	14.86
5	.4117	.5543	.8312	1.145	1.610	1.808	2.675	4.351	6.626	8.625	9.236	11.07	12.83	15.09	16.75
6	.6758	.8721	1.237	1.635	2.204	2.441	3.455	5.348	7.841	9.992	10.64	12.59	14.45	16.81	18.55
7	.9892	1.239	1.690	2.167	2.833	3.106	4.255	6.346	9.037	11.33	12.02	14.07	16.01	18.48	20.28
8	1.344	1.647	2.180	2.733	3.490	3.797	5.071	7.344	10.22	12.64	13.36	15.51	17.53	20.09	21.96
9	1.735	2.088	2.700	3.325	4.168	4.507	5.899	8.343	11.39	13.93	14.68	16.92	19.02	21.67	23.59
10	2.156	2.558	3.247	3.940	4.865	5.234	6.737	9.342	12.55	15.20	15.99	18.31	20.48	23.21	25.19
11	2.603	3.053	3.816	4.575	5.578	5.975	7.584	10.34	13.70	16.46	17.28	19.68	21.92	24.72	26.76
12	3.074	3.571	4.404	5.226	6.304	6.729	8.438	11.34	14.85	17.70	18.55	21.03	23.34	26.22	28.30
13	3.565	4.107	5.009	5.892	7.042	7.493	9.299	12.34	15.98	18.94	19.81	22.36	24.74	27.69	29.82
14	4.075	4.660	5.629	6.571	7.790	8.266	10.17	13.34	17.12	20.17	21.06	23.68	26.12	29.14	31.32
15	4.601	5.229	6.262	7.261	8.547	9.048	11.04	14.34	18.25	21.38	22.31	25.00	27.49	30.58	32.80
16	5.142	5.812	6.908	7.962	9.312	9.837	11.91	15.34	19.37	22.59	23.54	26.30	28.85	32.00	34.27
17	5.697	6.408	7.564	8.672	10.09	10.63	12.79	16.34	20.49	23.80	24.77	27.59	30.19	33.41	35.72
18	6.265	7.015	8.231	9.390	10.86	11.43	13.68	17.34	21.60	25.00	25.99	28.87	31.53	34.81	37.16
19	6.844	7.633	8.907	10.12	11.65	12.24	14.56	18.34	22.72	26.19	27.20	30.14	32.85	36.19	38.58
20	7.434	8.260	9.591	10.85	12.44	13.06	15.45	19.34	23.83	27.38	28.41	31.41	34.17	37.57	40.00
21	8.034	8.897	10.28	11.59	13.24	13.87	16.34	20.34	24.93	28.56	29.62	32.67	35.48	38.93	41.40
22	8.643	9.542	10.98	12.34	14.04	14.69	17.24	21.34	26.04	29.74	30.81	33.92	36.78	40.29	42.80
23	9.261	10.20	11.69	13.09	14.85	15.52	18.14	22.34	27.14	30.91	32.01	35.17	38.08	41.64	44.18
24	9.886	10.86	12.40	13.85	15.66	16.35	19.04	23.34	28.24	32.08	33.20	36.42	39.36	42.98	45.56
25	10.52	11.52	13.12	14.61	16.47	17.18	19.94	24.34	29.34	33.25	34.38	37.65	40.65	44.31	46.93
26	11.16	12.20	13.84	15.38	17.29	18.02	20.84	25.34	30.43	34.41	35.56	38.89	41.92	45.64	48.29
27	11.81	12.88	14.57	16.15	18.11	18.86	21.75	26.34	31.53	35.57	36.74	40.11	43.19	46.96	49.64
28	12.46	13.56	15.31	16.93	18.94	19.70	22.66	27.34	32.62	36.73	37.92	41.34	44.46	48.28	50.99
29	13.12	14.26	16.05	17.71	19.77	20.55	23.57	28.34	33.71	37.88	39.09	42.56	45.72	49.59	52.34
30	13.79	14.95	16.79	18.49	20.60	21.40	24.48	29.34	34.80	39.03	40.26	43.77	46.98	50.89	53.67
40	20.71	22.16	24.43	26.51	29.05	30.01	33.66	39.34	45.62	50.42	51.81	55.76	59.34	63.69	66.77
50	27.99	29.71	32.36	34.76	37.69	38.78	42.94	49.33	56.33	61.65	63.17	67.50	71.42	76.15	79.49
60	35.53	37.48	40.48	43.19	46.46	47.68	52.29	59.33	66.98	72.75	74.40	79.08	83.30	88.38	91.95
70	43.28	45.44	48.76	51.74	55.33	56.67	61.70	69.33	77.58	83.77	85.53	90.53	95.02	100.4	104.2
80	51.17	53.54	57.15	60.39	64.28	65.72	71.14	79.33	88.13	94.71	96.58	101.9	106.6	112.3	116.3
90	59.20	61.75	65.65	69.13	73.29	74.84	80.62	89.33	98.65	105.6	107.6	113.1	118.1	124.1	128.3
100	67.33	70.06	74.22	77.93	82.36	84.00	90.13	99.33	109.1	116.4	118.5	124.3	129.6	135.8	140.2

TABLE A.6

TABLE OF HIGHEST DENSITY REGIONS (50%, 75%, 90%, 95%, 99%) FOR THE CHI-SQUARE DISTRIBUTION FOR ν EQUAL 6(1)30

This table gives Highest Density Regions for Chi-Square **variables** with scale factor 1, $\chi^2(\nu, 1)$. It is used in a similar fashion to Table A.5. When the variable under consideration is $\chi^2(\nu, \omega)$ $\omega \neq 1$, the endpoints of the interval for $\chi^2(\nu, 1)$ should be multiplied by ω. For example, to find the 90% HDR for a $\chi^2(16, 4)$, we find from the table that the endpoints for a $\chi^2(16, 1)$ 90% HDR are (10.69, 17.93). Multiplying both endpoints by 4, we get the desired interval (42.76, 71.72).

	Content of Region									
	50%		75%		90%		95%		99%	
ν=										
6	2.327	6.330	1.493	8.405	0.8827	10.96	0.6070	12.80	0.2641	16.90
7	3.107	7.540	2.118	9.753	1.355	12.44	0.9893	14.37	0.4964	18.62
8	3.907	8.732	2.779	11.08	1.875	13.89	1.425	15.90	0.7855	20.30
9	4.724	9.911	3.465	12.38	2.431	15.31	1.903	17.39	1.122	21.93
10	5.552	11.08	4.174	13.66	3.017	16.71	2.414	18.86	1.498	23.53
11	6.391	12.24	4.899	14.92	3.628	18.09	2.953	20.30	1.907	25.10
12	7.238	13.39	5.639	16.18	4.258	19.45	3.516	21.73	2.345	26.65
13	8.093	14.53	6.391	17.42	4.906	20.79	4.099	23.13	2.807	28.18
14	8.954	15.67	7.155	18.65	5.569	22.12	4.700	24.52	3.291	29.69
15	9.820	16.80	7.928	19.88	6.246	23.44	5.317	25.90	3.795	31.17
16	10.69	17.93	8.709	21.09	6.935	24.74	5.948	27.26	4.316	32.64
17	11.57	19.05	9.497	22.30	7.634	26.04	6.591	28.61	4.853	34.10
18	12.45	20.17	10.29	23.50	8.343	27.33	7.245	29.96	5.404	35.54
19	13.33	21.29	11.09	24.70	9.060	28.60	7.910	31.29	5.968	36.97
20	14.22	22.40	11.90	25.89	9.786	29.88	8.584	32.61	6.545	38.39
21	15.11	23.51	12.71	27.08	10.52	31.14	9.267	33.92	7.131	39.80
22	16.00	24.62	13.53	28.26	11.26	32.40	9.958	35.23	7.730	41.19
23	16.90	25.72	14.35	29.44	12.00	33.65	10.66	36.53	8.336	42.58
24	17.79	26.82	15.18	30.61	12.76	34.90	11.36	37.82	8.950	43.97
25	18.69	27.92	16.01	31.78	13.51	36.14	12.07	39.10	9.576	45.34
26	19.60	29.02	16.84	32.94	14.28	37.37	12.79	40.38	10.21	46.71
27	20.50	30.11	17.68	34.11	15.04	38.60	13.51	41.66	10.85	48.06
28	21.41	31.21	18.52	35.27	15.82	39.83	14.24	42.93	11.49	49.42
29	22.32	32.30	19.36	36.42	16.59	41.05	14.98	44.19	12.14	50.76
30	23.22	33.39	20.21	37.57	17.37	42.27	15.72	45.45	12.80	52.10

TABLE A.7

PERCENTAGE POINTS OF THE INVERSE CHI-SQUARE DISTRIBUTION

This table giving percentage points for an inverse chi-square variable with scale factor 1, $\chi^{-2}(\nu, 1)$, is used in an identical manner to Table A.5.

P(φ) = / ν =	.5%	1%	2.5%	5%	10%	12.5%	25%	50%	75%	87.5%	90%	95%	97.5%	99%	99.5%
2	.09437	.1086	.1355	.1669	.2171	.2404	.3607	.7213	1.738	3.744	4.746	9.748	19.75	49.75	99.75
3	.07789	.08815	.1070	.1280	.1600	.1742	.2434	.4227	.8247	1.444	1.711	2.842	4.634	8.708	13.94
4	.06729	.07532	.08974	.1054	.1285	.1386	.1857	.2979	.5201	.8205	.9402	1.407	2.064	3.366	4.831
5	.05970	.06629	.07793	.09033	.1083	.1159	.1509	.2298	.3739	.5530	.6210	.8730	1.203	1.804	2.429
6	.05391	.05948	.06921	.07942	.09394	.1001	.1275	.1870	.2895	.4097	.4537	.6115	.8082	1.147	1.480
7	.04932	.05413	.06245	.07109	.08321	.08829	.1107	.1576	.2350	.3219	.3530	.4614	.5918	.8071	1.011
8	.04555	.04977	.05703	.06449	.07484	.07914	.09786	.1362	.1972	.2634	.2866	.3659	.4588	.6073	.7438
9	.04239	.04616	.05257	.05911	.06810	.07181	.08781	.1199	.1695	.2219	.2399	.3007	.3703	.4790	.5764
10	.03970	.04309	.04882	.05462	.06255	.06580	.07969	.1070	.1484	.1911	.2055	.2538	.3080	.3909	.4638
11	.03737	.04044	.04562	.05083	.05789	.06076	.07299	.09670	.1319	.1674	.1793	.2186	.2621	.3275	.3842
12	.03534	.03814	.04285	.04756	.05391	.05649	.06736	.08818	.1185	.1486	.1586	.1913	.2271	.2801	.3253
13	.03354	.03612	.04043	.04472	.05047	.05280	.06256	.08104	.1075	.1335	.1420	.1697	.1996	.2435	.2805
14	.03193	.03432	.03829	.04222	.04747	.04959	.05842	.07497	.09837	.1210	.1284	.1522	.1777	.2146	.2454
15	.03049	.03270	.03638	.04001	.04483	.04676	.05481	.06974	.09061	.1105	.1170	.1377	.1597	.1912	.2173
16	.02918	.03125	.03467	.03803	.04243	.04426	.05163	.06520	.08395	.1017	.1074	.1256	.1448	.1720	.1945
17	.02800	.02993	.03312	.03625	.04037	.04202	.04381	.06121	.07817	.09405	.09916	.1153	.1322	.1561	.1755
18	.02691	.02873	.03172	.03464	.03848	.04000	.04629	.05768	.07312	.08745	.09204	.1065	.1215	.1426	.1596
19	.02592	.02763	.03044	.03317	.03676	.03818	.04402	.05453	.06867	.08168	.08583	.09884	.1123	.1310	.1461
20	.02500	.02662	.02927	.03184	.03520	.03653	.04197	.05171	.06472	.07660	.08037	.09216	.1043	.1211	.1345
21	.02415	.02569	.02819	.03061	.03377	.03502	.04010	.04917	.06118	.07208	.07553	.08627	.09725	.1124	.1245
22	.02337	.02482	.02719	.02948	.03245	.03363	.03840	.04687	.05801	.06805	.07122	.08105	.09106	.1048	.1157
23	.02263	.02402	.02626	.02843	.03124	.03235	.03684	.04477	.05514	.06443	.06735	.07639	.08555	.09808	.1080
24	.02195	.02327	.02540	.02746	.03012	.03117	.03541	.04285	.05253	.06116	.06386	.07221	.08064	.09211	.1012
25	.02131	.02257	.02460	.02656	.02909	.03008	.03408	.04109	.05015	.05819	.06070	.06844	.07622	.08678	.09506
26	.02071	.02191	.02385	.02572	.02812	.02906	.03286	.03947	.04798	.05549	.05783	.06502	.07223	.08198	.08960
27	.02014	.02129	.02315	.02493	.02722	.02811	.03172	.03797	.04598	.05302	.05521	.06191	.06862	.07765	.08469
28	.01961	.02071	.02249	.02419	.02637	.02723	.03066	.03658	.04414	.05075	.05280	.05907	.06533	.07372	.08025
29	.01911	.02017	.02187	.02350	.02558	.02640	.02966	.03529	.04243	.04866	.05059	.05647	.06232	.07014	.07621
30	.01863	.01965	.02129	.02285	.02484	.02562	.02874	.03409	.04085	.04673	.04855	.05408	.05956	.06687	.07253
40	.01498	.01570	.01685	.01793	.01930	.01983	.02192	.02542	.02971	.03332	.03442	.03772	.04093	.04512	.04829
50	.01258	.01313	.01400	.01481	.01583	.01622	.01775	.02027	.02329	.02578	.02653	.02877	.03090	.03366	.03573
60	.01088	.01131	.01201	.01265	.01344	.01375	.01493	.01685	.01912	.02097	.02152	.02315	.02470	.02668	.02814

TABLE A.8

TABLE OF HIGHEST DENSITY REGIONS (50%, 75%, 90%, 95%, 99%) FOR THE INVERSE CHI-SQUARE DISTRIBUTIONS FOR ν EQUAL 6(1)30

This table giving the endpoints for Inverse Chi-Square distributions with scale factor of 1, $\chi^{-2}(\nu, 1)$, is used in an identical manner to Table A.6.

	Content of Region									
	50%		75%		90%		95%		99%	
ν =										
6	.08193	.2044	.06351	.2994	.05032	.4598	.04397	.6160	.03461	1.149
7	.07548	.1732	.05953	.2442	.04778	.3586	.04203	.4657	.03342	.8097
8	.06988	.1502	.05591	.2056	.04537	.2919	.04014	.3700	.03221	.6098
9	.06501	.1326	.05264	.1773	.04313	.2449	.03835	.3046	.03102	.4814
10	.06074	.1187	.04970	.1556	.04107	.2102	.03668	.2574	.02988	.3933
11	.05699	.1073	.04705	.1385	.03917	.1836	.03512	.2219	.02880	.3297
12	.05367	.09797	.04466	.1246	.03743	.1627	.03368	.1945	.02778	.2821
13	.05071	.09009	.04249	.1133	.03583	.1458	.03234	.1727	.02682	.2454
14	.04806	.08336	.04052	.1037	.03435	.1319	.03110	.1550	.02592	.2165
15	.04567	.07756	.03872	.09561	.03299	.1204	.02995	.1404	.02508	.1930
16	.04351	.07250	.03708	.08864	.03173	.1106	.02888	.1281	.02429	.1737
17	.04154	.06805	.03557	.08260	.03057	.1022	.02789	.1177	.02355	.1577
18	.03974	.06411	.03418	.07730	.02949	.09489	.02696	.1088	.02284	.1441
19	.03810	.06059	.03289	.07262	.02848	.08854	.02609	.1010	.02219	.1325
20	.03659	.05744	.03170	.06846	.02754	.08295	.02528	.09423	.02156	.1225
21	.03519	.05459	.03059	.06473	.02666	.07798	.02451	.08825	.02097	.1138
22	.03390	.05200	.02956	.06138	.02584	.07356	.02380	.08294	.02042	.1061
23	.03270	.04965	.02860	.05835	.02506	.06959	.02312	.07821	.01989	.09934
24	.03158	.04750	.02770	.05560	.02433	.06600	.02248	.07395	.01939	.09332
25	.03054	.04552	.02686	.05308	.02365	.06276	.02188	.07011	.01892	.08792
26	.02956	.04370	.02606	.05078	.02300	.05980	.02131	.06663	.01847	.08310
27	.02865	.04201	.02532	.04867	.02239	.05709	.02077	.06345	.01804	.07872
28	.02779	.04045	.02461	.04671	.02181	.05462	.02026	.06056	.01763	.07476
29	.02698	.03900	.02394	.04491	.02126	.05233	.01977	.05790	.01724	.07115
30	.02622	.03765	.02331	.04323	.02074	.05023	.01931	.05546	.01687	.06784

TABLE A.9

PERCENTAGE POINTS OF THE INVERSE-CHI DISTRIBUTION

This table which tabulates the percentage points for the inverse chi distribution with scale factor 1, $\chi^{-1}(\nu, 1)$, is used in an identical manner to Table A.5.

$P(\phi^{\frac{1}{2}})$ =	.5%	1%	2.5%	5%	10%	12.5%	25%	50%	75%	87.5%	90%	95%	97.5%	99%	99.5%
ν =															
2	.3072	.3295	.3682	.4085	.4660	.4904	.6006	.8493	1.318	1.935	2.178	3.122	4.444	7.054	9.987
3	.2791	.2969	.3271	.3577	.4000	.4174	.4934	.6501	.9081	1.202	1.308	1.686	2.153	2.951	3.734
4	.2594	.2744	.2996	.3247	.3585	.3723	.4309	.5458	.7212	.9058	.9696	1.186	1.437	1.835	2.198
5	.2443	.2575	.2792	.3005	.3290	.3405	.3885	.4794	.6115	.7437	.7880	.9343	1.097	1.343	1.558
6	.2322	.2439	.2631	.2818	.3065	.3164	.3571	.4324	.5380	.6400	.6736	.7820	.8990	1.071	1.216
7	.2221	.2327	.2499	.2666	.2885	.2971	.3326	.3970	.4848	.5674	.5941	.6793	.7693	.8984	1.005
8	.2134	.2231	.2388	.2539	.2736	.2813	.3128	.3690	.4441	.5132	.5353	.6049	.6773	.7793	.8625
9	.2059	.2148	.2293	.2431	.2610	.2680	.2963	.3462	.4117	.4710	.4898	.5484	.6085	.6921	.7592
10	.1993	.2076	.2210	.2337	.2501	.2565	.2823	.3272	.3853	.4371	.4534	.5038	.5550	.6252	.6811
11	.1933	.2011	.2136	.2254	.2406	.2465	.2702	.3110	.3631	.4091	.4234	.4675	.5119	.5723	.6198
12	.1880	.1953	.2070	.2181	.2322	.2377	2595	.2970	.3442	.3855	.3983	.4374	.4765	.5292	.5704
13	.1831	.1900	.2011	.2115	.2247	.2298	.2501	.2847	.3279	.3653	.3768	.4120	.4468	.4934	.5296
14	.1787	.1852	.1957	.2055	.2179	.2227	.2417	.2738	.3136	.3478	.3583	.3901	.4215	.4632	.4954
15	.1746	.1808	.1907	.2000	.2117	.2162	.2341	.2641	.3010	.3324	.3421	.3711	.3996	.4373	.4662
16	.1708	.1768	.1862	.1950	.2061	.2104	.2272	.2553	.2897	.3188	.3277	.3544	.3805	.4148	.4410
17	.1673	.1730	.1820	.1904	.2009	.2050	.2209	.2474	.2796	.3067	.3149	.3396	.3636	.3950	.4190
18	.1641	.1695	.1781	.1861	.1962	.2000	.2151	.2402	.2704	.2957	.3034	.3263	.3486	.3776	.3995
19	.1610	.1662	.1745	.1821	.1917	.1954	.2098	.2335	.2621	.2858	.2930	.3144	.3351	.3620	.3822
20	.1581	.1632	.1711	.1784	.1876	.1911	.2049	.2274	.2544	.2768	.2835	.3036	.3229	.3479	.3668
21	.1554	.1603	.1679	.1750	.1838	.1871	.2003	.2217	.2474	.2685	.2748	.2937	.3118	.3353	.3528
22	.1529	.1575	.1649	.1717	.1801	.1834	.1960	.2165	.2408	.2609	.2669	.2847	.3018	.3237	.3402
23	.1504	.1550	.1621	.1686	.1768	.1799	.1919	.2116	.2348	.2538	.2595	.2764	.2925	.3132	.3286
24	.1482	.1525	.1594	.1657	.1736	.1766	.1882	.2070	.2292	.2473	.2527	.2687	.2840	.3035	.3180
25	.1460	.1502	.1569	.1630	.1705	.1734	.1846	.2027	.2239	.2412	.2464	.2616	.2761	.2946	.3083
26	.1439	.1480	.1544	.1604	.1677	.1705	.1813	.1987	.2190	.2356	.2405	.2550	.2688	.2863	.2993
27	.1419	.1459	.1522	.1579	.1650	.1677	.1781	.1949	.2144	.2303	.2350	.2488	.2620	.2787	.2910
28	.1400	.1439	.1500	.1555	.1624	.1650	.1751	.1913	.2101	.2253	.2298	.2431	.2556	.2715	.2833
29	.1382	.1420	.1479	.1533	.1599	.1625	.1722	.1879	.2060	.2206	.2249	.2376	.2496	.2648	.2761
30	.1365	.1402	.1459	.1511	.1576	.1601	.1695	.1846	.2021	.2162	.2203	.2325	.2440	.2586	.2693
40	.1224	.1253	.1298	.1339	.1389	.1408	.1481	.1594	.1724	.1826	.1855	.1942	.2023	.2124	.2198
50	.1122	.1146	.1183	.1217	.1258	.1274	.1332	.1424	.1526	.1606	.1629	.1696	.1758	.1835	.1890
60	.1043	.1064	.1096	.1125	.1159	.1172	.1222	.1298	.1383	.1448	.1467	.1522	.1572	.1633	.1678

TABLE A.10

TABLE OF HIGHEST DENSITY REGIONS (50%, 75%, 90%, 95%, 99%) FOR THE

INVERSE-CHI DISTRIBUTION FOR ν EQUAL 6(1)30

This table which gives the endpoints of Highest Density regions for Inverse Chi distributions with a scale factor of 1, $\chi^{-1}(\nu, 1)$, is used in an identical manner to Table A.6.

Content of Region

ν=	50%		75%		90%		95%		99%	
6	.3113	.4724	.2756	.5639	.2456	.6912	.2294	.7961	.2030	1.080
7	.2956	.4333	.2638	.5086	.2368	.6105	.2220	.6925	.1976	.9075
8	.2820	.4023	.2534	.4661	.2288	.5506	.2152	.6174	.1925	.7879
9	.2702	.3770	.2442	.4322	.2215	.5042	.2089	.5601	.1878	.7003
10	.2597	.3558	.2359	.4044	.2149	.4668	.2031	.5148	.1833	.6330
11	.2505	.3377	.2284	.3810	.2088	.4361	.1978	.4780	.1791	.5797
12	.2421	.3220	.2216	.3611	.2033	.4103	.1929	.4474	.1753	.5363
13	.2346	.3083	.2154	.3439	.1982	.3883	.1884	.4214	.1716	.5002
14	.2277	.2962	.2097	.3288	.1934	.3692	.1842	.3991	.1682	.4697
15	.2214	.2853	.2044	.3154	.1890	.3524	.1803	.3797	.1650	.4435
16	.2157	.2755	.1996	.3034	.1850	.3376	.1766	.3626	.1620	.4207
17	.2103	.2666	.1951	.2927	.1811	.3244	.1731	.3475	.1592	.4008
18	.2054	.2585	.1909	.2829	.1776	.3125	.1699	.3339	.1565	.3831
19	.2008	.2511	.1869	.2741	.1742	.3017	.1668	.3217	.1539	.3673
20	.1965	.2443	.1832	.2659	.1710	.2919	.1640	.3106	.1515	.3531
21	.1924	.2380	.1798	.2585	.1680	.2829	.1612	.3005	.1492	.3402
22	.1886	.2321	.1765	.2516	.1652	.2747	.1586	.2913	.1471	.3286
23	.1851	.2267	.1734	.2451	.1625	.2671	.1562	.2827	.1450	.3179
24	.1817	.2216	.1705	.2392	.1600	.2600	.1538	.2749	.1430	.3080
25	.1785	.2168	.1677	.2336	.1575	.2535	.1516	.2676	.1411	.2990
26	.1755	.2123	.1650	.2284	.1552	.2474	.1495	.2608	.1393	.2906
27	.1727	.2081	.1625	.2235	.1530	.2416	.1474	.2544	.1375	.2828
28	.1699	.2041	.1601	.2189	.1509	.2363	.1455	.2485	.1358	.2756
29	.1673	.2003	.1578	.2146	.1489	.2312	.1436	.2430	.1342	.2688
30	.1648	.1967	.1556	.2104	.1469	.2265	.1418	.2377	.1327	.2625

TABLE A.11

THE PERCENTAGE POINTS OF THE BEHRENS-FISHER DISTRIBUTION

The quantity tabulated is the percentage point u of the Behrens-Fisher distribution for P(u) = 75%, 90%, 95%, 97.5%, 99% with ν_1, ν_2 = 6, 8, 12, 24, ∞, and x = 0°(15°)45°. For example, a value of u = 2.18 is required to obtain a CDF value of 97.5% with ν_1, ν_2 = 12 and ψ = 15°. The values for ψ = 60°, 75°, and 90° are the same as those for ψ = 30°, 15°, and 0° with ν_1 and ν_2 interchanged.

ψ = 0°

ν_2	75%	90%	95%	97.5%	99%
			ν_1 = 6		
6	.72	1.44	1.94	2.45	3.14
8	.71	1.40	1.86	2.31	2.90
12	.70	1.36	1.78	2.18	2.68
24	.68	1.32	1.71	2.06	2.49
∞	.67	1.28	1.64	1.96	2.33
			ν_1 = 8		
6	.72	1.44	1.94	2.45	3.14
8	.71	1.40	1.86	2.31	2.90
12	.70	1.36	1.78	2.18	2.68
24	.68	1.32	1.71	2.06	2.49
∞	.67	1.28	1.64	1.96	2.33
			ν_1 = 12		
6	.72	1.44	1.94	2.45	3.14
8	.71	1.40	1.86	2.31	2.90
12	.70	1.36	1.78	2.18	2.68
24	.68	1.32	1.71	2.06	2.49
∞	.67	1.28	1.64	1.96	2.33
			ν_1 = 24		
6	.72	1.44	1.94	2.45	3.14
8	.71	1.40	1.86	2.31	2.90
12	.70	1.36	1.78	2.18	2.68
24	.68	1.32	1.71	2.06	2.49
∞	.67	1.28	1.64	1.96	2.33
			ν_1 = ∞		
6	.72	1.44	1.94	2.45	3.14
8	.71	1.40	1.86	2.31	2.90
12	.69	1.36	1.78	2.18	2.68
24	.68	1.32	1.71	2.06	2.49
∞	.67	1.28	1.64	1.96	2.33

ψ = 15°

ν_2	75%	90%	95%	97.5%	99%
			ν_1 = 6		
6	.73	1.45	1.95	2.44	3.11
8	.72	1.41	1.87	2.31	2.88
12	.71	1.37	1.80	2.19	2.69
24	.69	1.34	1.73	2.09	2.51
∞	.68	1.30	1.67	1.99	2.37
			ν_1 = 8		
6	.73	1.45	1.94	2.43	3.10
8	.71	1.41	1.86	2.30	2.87
12	.70	1.37	1.79	2.18	2.67
24	.69	1.33	1.72	2.08	2.50
∞	.68	1.29	1.66	1.98	2.35
			ν_1 = 12		
6	.72	1.44	1.93	2.42	3.09
8	.71	1.40	1.86	2.29	2.86
12	.70	1.36	1.78	2.17	2.67
24	.69	1.32	1.72	2.07	2.49
∞	.68	1.29	1.66	1.97	2.34
			ν_1 = 24		
6	.72	1.44	1.93	2.42	3.09
8	.71	1.40	1.85	2.29	2.86
12	.70	1.36	1.78	2.17	2.66
24	.69	1.32	1.71	2.06	2.48
∞	.68	1.29	1.65	1.97	2.33
			ν_1 = ∞		
6	.72	1.43	1.92	2.41	3.08
8	.71	1.39	1.85	2.28	2.85
12	.70	1.35	1.77	2.16	2.65
24	.68	1.32	1.71	2.06	2.48
∞	.67	1.28	1.64	1.96	2.33

TABLE A.11 (continued)

THE PERCENTAGE POINTS OF THE BEHRENS-FISHER DISTRIBUTION

ψ = 30°

ν_2	75%	90%	95%	97.5%	99%
			ν_1 = 6		
6	.75	1.48	1.96	2.43	3.05
8	.74	1.44	1.90	2.33	2.88
12	.72	1.41	1.84	2.24	2.73
24	.71	1.37	1.78	2.15	2.60
∞	.70	1.34	1.73	2.08	2.50
			ν_1 = 8		
6	.74	1.46	1.94	2.40	3.01
8	.73	1.42	1.87	2.29	2.83
12	.72	1.39	1.81	2.20	2.68
24	.71	1.36	1.76	2.12	2.55
∞	.69	1.32	1.71	2.04	2.44
			ν_1 = 12		
6	.73	1.44	1.91	2.37	2.97
8	.72	1.41	1.85	2.26	2.79
12	.71	1.37	1.79	2.17	2.64
24	.70	1.34	1.73	2.09	2.51
∞	.69	1.31	1.68	2.01	2.40
			ν_1 = 24		
6	.73	1.43	1.89	2.34	2.94
8	.71	1.39	1.83	2.24	2.76
12	.70	1.36	1.77	2.14	2.60
24	.69	1.33	1.71	2.06	2.47
∞	.68	1.29	1.66	1.98	2.36
			ν_1 = ∞		
6	.72	1.41	1.87	2.32	2.92
8	.71	1.38	1.81	2.21	2.73
12	.70	1.34	1.75	2.12	2.58
24	.69	1.31	1.70	2.03	2.44
∞	.67	1.28	1.64	1.96	2.33

ψ = 45°

ν_2	75%	90%	95%	97.5%	99%
			ν_1 = 6		
6	.76	1.49	1.97	2.43	3.03
8	.75	1.46	1.92	2.36	2.92
12	.74	1.43	1.88	2.30	2.83
24	.73	1.41	1.84	2.24	2.76
∞	.72	1.38	1.81	2.20	2.70
			ν_1 = 8		
6	.75	1.46	1.93	2.36	2.93
8	.74	1.43	1.88	2.29	2.81
12	.72	1.40	1.83	2.23	2.72
24	.71	1.38	1.80	2.17	2.64
∞	.70	1.36	1.76	2.13	2.58
			ν_1 = 12		
6	.74	1.43	1.88	2.30	2.84
8	.73	1.40	1.83	2.23	2.72
12	.71	1.38	1.79	2.17	2.63
24	.70	1.35	1.75	2.11	2.54
∞	.69	1.33	1.72	2.06	2.48
			ν_1 = 24		
6	.73	1.41	1.84	2.25	2.76
8	.71	1.38	1.80	2.18	2.64
12	.70	1.35	1.75	2.11	2.54
24	.69	1.33	1.71	2.06	2.46
∞	.68	1.30	1.68	2.01	2.40
			ν_1 = ∞		
6	.72	1.38	1.81	2.20	2.70
8	.70	1.36	1.76	2.13	2.58
12	.69	1.33	1.72	2.06	2.48
24	.68	1.30	1.68	2.01	2.40
∞	.67	1.28	1.64	1.96	2.33

TABLE A.12

TABLE OF ARCTAN $\sqrt{x}$

The values tabled are given in degrees and decimal fractions of a degree.

x	.00	.01	.02	.03	.04	.05	.06	.07	.08	.09
.0	0.0000	5.7106	8.0495	9.8264	11.3099	12.6044	13.7635	14.8195	15.7932	16.6992
.1	17.5484	18.3487	19.1066	19.8270	20.5141	21.1713	21.8014	22.4069	22.9898	23.5519
.2	24.0948	24.6200	25.1285	25.6216	26.1001	26.5651	27.0171	27.4571	27.8856	28.3032
.3	28.7105	29.1080	29.4962	29.8755	30.2463	30.6089	30.9638	31.3112	31.6514	31.9848
.4	32.3115	32.6319	32.9462	33.2546	33.5573	33.8545	34.1464	34.4332	34.7150	34.9920
.5	35.2644	35.5323	35.7958	36.0550	36.3102	36.5614	36.8087	37.0522	37.2921	37.5284
.6	37.7612	37.9907	38.2169	38.4399	38.6598	38.8767	39.0905	39.3015	39.5097	39.7151
.7	39.9179	40.1180	40.3155	40.5106	40.7032	40.8934	41.0813	41.2668	41.4502	41.6313
.8	41.8103	41.9872	42.1621	42.3349	42.5057	42.6746	42.8417	43.0068	43.1702	43.3317
.9	43.4915	43.6496	43.8060	43.9607	44.1138	44.2654	44.4153	44.5637	44.7106	44.8560

TABLE A.13

PERCENTAGE POINTS OF THE F-DISTRIBUTION

This table gives percentage points for the F-distribution $F(\nu_1, \nu_2)$. ν_1 is the number of degrees of freedom of the numerator, and ν_2 is the number of degrees of freedom of the denominator. To find the p% point where p is less than 50%, take the inverse of the 100-p% point found by entering the table with ν_1 and ν_2 reversed. For example, to find the 25% point for F(16, 19), we note that the 100% - 25% = 75% point for F(19, 16) is 1.401. Inverting, we find the desired 25% point for F(16, 19) is $\frac{1}{1.401} = .0714$.

$\nu_1=3$

$\nu_2=$	50%	75%	90%	95%	99%
3	1.0000	2.356	5.391	9.277	29.46
4	.9405	2.047	4.191	6.591	16.69
5	.9071	1.884	3.619	5.409	12.06
6	.8858	1.784	3.289	4.757	9.780
7	.8709	1.717	3.074	4.347	8.452
8	.8600	1.668	2.924	4.066	7.591
9	.8517	1.632	2.813	3.863	6.992
10	.8451	1.603	2.728	3.708	6.552
11	.8397	1.580	2.660	3.587	6.217
12	.8353	1.561	2.606	3.490	5.952
13	.8316	1.545	2.560	3.411	5.739
14	.8284	1.532	2.522	3.344	5.564
15	.8257	1.520	2.490	3.287	5.417
16	.8233	1.510	2.462	3.239	5.292
17	.8212	1.502	2.437	3.197	5.185
18	.8194	1.494	2.416	3.160	5.092
19	.8177	1.487	2.397	3.127	5.010
20	.8162	1.481	2.380	3.098	4.938
21	.8149	1.475	2.365	3.072	4.874
22	.8137	1.470	2.351	3.049	4.817
23	.8125	1.466	2.339	3.028	4.765
24	.8115	1.462	2.327	3.009	4.718
25	.8106	1.458	2.317	2.991	4.675
26	.8097	1.454	2.307	2.975	4.637
27	.8089	1.451	2.299	2.960	4.601
28	.8082	1.448	2.291	2.947	4.568
29	.8075	1.445	2.283	2.934	4.538
30	.8069	1.443	2.276	2.922	4.510
40	.8023	1.424	2.226	2.839	4.313
50	.7995	1.413	2.197	2.790	4.199
60	.7977	1.405	2.177	2.758	4.126
70	.7964	1.400	2.164	2.736	4.074
80	.7954	1.396	2.154	2.719	4.036
90	.7947	1.393	2.146	2.706	4.007
100	.7941	1.391	2.139	2.696	3.984

$\nu_1=4$

$\nu_2=$	50%	75%	90%	95%	99%
3	1.063	2.390	5.343	9.117	28.71
4	1.0000	2.064	4.107	6.388	15.98
5	.9646	1.893	3.520	5.192	11.39
6	.9419	1.787	3.181	4.534	9.148
7	.9262	1.716	2.961	4.120	7.847
8	.9146	1.664	2.806	3.838	7.006
9	.9058	1.625	2.693	3.633	6.422
10	.8988	1.595	2.605	3.478	5.994
11	.8932	1.570	2.536	3.357	5.668
12	.8885	1.550	2.480	3.259	5.412
13	.8845	1.534	2.434	3.179	5.205
14	.8812	1.519	2.395	3.112	5.035
15	.8783	1.507	2.361	3.056	4.893
16	.8758	1.497	2.333	3.007	4.773
17	.8736	1.487	2.308	2.965	4.669
18	.8716	1.479	2.286	2.928	4.579
19	.8699	1.472	2.266	2.895	4.500
20	.8683	1.465	2.249	2.866	4.431
21	.8669	1.459	2.233	2.840	4.369
22	.8656	1.454	2.219	2.817	4.313
23	.8644	1.449	2.207	2.796	4.264
24	.8633	1.445	2.195	2.776	4.218
25	.8624	1.441	2.184	2.759	4.177
26	.8615	1.437	2.174	2.743	4.140
27	.8606	1.433	2.165	2.728	4.106
28	.8598	1.430	2.157	2.714	4.074
29	.8591	1.427	2.149	2.701	4.045
30	.8584	1.424	2.142	2.690	4.018
40	.8536	1.404	2.091	2.606	3.828
50	.8507	1.393	2.061	2.557	3.719
60	.8487	1.385	2.041	2.525	3.649
70	.8474	1.379	2.027	2.503	3.600
80	.8463	1.375	2.016	2.486	3.563
90	.8455	1.372	2.008	2.473	3.535
100	.8449	1.369	2.002	2.463	3.513

$\nu_1=5$

$\nu_2=$	50%	75%	90%	95%	99%
3	1.102	2.409	5.309	9.013	28.24
4	1.037	2.072	4.051	6.256	15.52
5	1.0000	1.895	3.453	5.050	10.97
6	.9765	1.785	3.108	4.387	8.746
7	.9603	1.711	2.883	3.972	7.460
8	.9483	1.658	2.726	3.688	6.632
9	.9392	1.617	2.611	3.482	6.057
10	.9319	1.585	2.522	3.326	5.636
11	.9261	1.560	2.451	3.204	5.316
12	.9212	1.539	2.394	3.106	5.064
13	.9172	1.521	2.347	3.025	4.862
14	.9137	1.507	2.307	2.958	4.695
15	.9107	1.494	2.273	2.901	4.556
16	.9081	1.483	2.244	2.852	4.437
17	.9058	1.473	2.218	2.810	4.336
18	.9038	1.464	2.196	2.773	4.248
19	.9020	1.457	2.176	2.740	4.171
20	.9004	1.450	2.158	2.711	4.103
21	.8989	1.444	2.142	2.685	4.042
22	.8976	1.438	2.128	2.661	3.988
23	.8964	1.433	2.115	2.640	3.939
24	.8953	1.428	2.103	2.621	3.895
25	.8942	1.424	2.092	2.603	3.855
26	.8933	1.420	2.082	2.587	3.818
27	.8924	1.417	2.073	2.572	3.785
28	.8916	1.413	2.064	2.558	3.754
29	.8909	1.410	2.057	2.545	3.725
30	.8902	1.407	2.049	2.534	3.699
40	.8852	1.386	1.997	2.449	3.514
50	.8822	1.374	1.966	2.400	3.408
60	.8802	1.366	1.946	2.368	3.339
70	.8787	1.360	1.931	2.346	3.291
80	.8777	1.355	1.921	2.329	3.255
90	.8769	1.352	1.912	2.316	3.228
100	.8762	1.349	1.906	2.305	3.206

TABLE A.13 (continued)

PERCENTAGE POINTS OF THE F-DISTRIBUTION

	$\nu_1=6$				
$\nu_2=$	50%	75%	90%	95%	99%
3	1.129	2.422	5.285	8.941	27.91
4	1.062	2.077	4.010	6.163	15.21
5	1.024	1.894	3.405	4.950	10.67
6	1.0000	1.782	3.055	4.284	8.466
7	.9833	1.706	2.827	3.866	7.191
8	.9711	1.651	2.668	3.581	6.371
9	.9617	1.609	2.551	3.374	5.802
10	.9544	1.576	2.461	3.217	5.386
11	.9484	1.550	2.389	3.095	5.069
12	.9434	1.529	2.331	2.996	4.821
13	.9393	1.511	2.283	2.915	4.620
14	.9357	1.495	2.243	2.848	4.456
15	.9327	1.482	2.208	2.790	4.318
16	.9300	1.471	2.178	2.741	4.202
17	.9277	1.460	2.152	2.699	4.102
18	.9256	1.452	2.130	2.661	4.015
19	.9238	1.444	2.109	2.628	3.939
20	.9221	1.437	2.091	2.599	3.871
21	.9206	1.430	2.075	2.573	3.812
22	.9192	1.424	2.060	2.549	3.758
23	.9180	1.419	2.047	2.528	3.710
24	.9169	1.414	2.035	2.508	3.667
25	.9158	1.410	2.024	2.490	3.627
26	.9149	1.406	2.014	2.474	3.591
27	.9140	1.402	2.005	2.459	3.558
28	.9132	1.399	1.996	2.445	3.528
29	.9124	1.395	1.988	2.432	3.499
30	.9117	1.392	1.980	2.421	3.474
40	.9065	1.371	1.927	2.336	3.291
50	.9035	1.358	1.895	2.286	3.186
60	.9014	1.349	1.875	2.254	3.119
70	.9000	1.343	1.860	2.231	3.071
80	.8989	1.338	1.849	2.214	3.036
90	.8981	1.335	1.841	2.201	3.009
100	.8974	1.332	1.834	2.191	2.988

	$\nu_1=7$				
$\nu_2=$	50%	75%	90%	95%	99%
3	1.148	2.430	5.266	8.887	27.67
4	1.080	2.079	3.979	6.094	14.98
5	1.041	1.894	3.368	4.876	10.46
6	1.017	1.779	3.014	4.207	8.260
7	1.0000	1.701	2.785	3.787	6.993
8	.9876	1.645	2.624	3.500	6.178
9	.9781	1.602	2.505	3.293	5.613
10	.9705	1.569	2.414	3.135	5.200
11	.9645	1.542	2.342	3.012	4.886
12	.9594	1.520	2.283	2.913	4.640
13	.9552	1.501	2.234	2.832	4.441
14	.9516	1.485	2.193	2.764	4.278
15	.9485	1.472	2.158	2.707	4.142
16	.9458	1.460	2.128	2.657	4.026
17	.9434	1.450	2.102	2.614	3.927
18	.9413	1.441	2.079	2.577	3.841
19	.9394	1.432	2.058	2.544	3.765
20	.9378	1.425	2.040	2.514	3.699
21	.9362	1.419	2.023	2.488	3.640
22	.9349	1.413	2.008	2.464	3.587
23	.9336	1.407	1.995	2.442	3.539
24	.9325	1.402	1.983	2.423	3.496
25	.9314	1.398	1.971	2.405	3.457
26	.9304	1.393	1.961	2.388	3.421
27	.9295	1.390	1.952	2.373	3.388
28	.9287	1.386	1.943	2.359	3.358
29	.9279	1.383	1.935	2.346	3.330
30	.9272	1.380	1.927	2.334	3.304
40	.9220	1.357	1.873	2.249	3.124
50	.9189	1.344	1.840	2.199	3.020
60	.9168	1.335	1.819	2.167	2.953
70	.9153	1.329	1.804	2.143	2.906
80	.9142	1.324	1.793	2.126	2.871
90	.9134	1.320	1.785	2.113	2.845
100	.9127	1.317	1.778	2.103	2.823

	$\nu_1=8$				
$\nu_2=$	50%	75%	90%	95%	99%
3	1.163	2.436	5.252	8.845	27.49
4	1.093	2.080	3.955	6.041	14.80
5	1.055	1.892	3.339	4.818	10.29
6	1.030	1.776	2.983	4.147	8.102
7	1.013	1.697	2.752	3.726	6.840
8	1.0000	1.640	2.589	3.438	6.029
9	.9904	1.596	2.469	3.230	5.467
10	.9828	1.562	2.377	3.072	5.057
11	.9766	1.535	2.304	2.948	4.745
12	.9715	1.512	2.245	2.849	4.499
13	.9672	1.493	2.195	2.767	4.302
14	.9636	1.477	2.154	2.699	4.140
15	.9605	1.463	2.119	2.641	4.005
16	.9577	1.451	2.088	2.591	3.890
17	.9553	1.441	2.061	2.548	3.791
18	.9532	1.431	2.038	2.510	3.705
19	.9513	1.423	2.017	2.477	3.631
20	.9496	1.415	1.999	2.447	3.564
21	.9481	1.409	1.982	2.420	3.506
22	.9467	1.402	1.967	2.397	3.453
23	.9454	1.397	1.953	2.375	3.406
24	.9442	1.392	1.941	2.355	3.363
25	.9432	1.387	1.929	2.337	3.324
26	.9422	1.383	1.919	2.321	3.288
27	.9413	1.379	1.909	2.305	3.256
28	.9404	1.375	1.900	2.291	3.226
29	.9396	1.372	1.892	2.278	3.198
30	.9389	1.369	1.884	2.266	3.173
40	.9336	1.345	1.829	2.180	2.993
50	.9305	1.332	1.796	2.130	2.890
60	.9284	1.323	1.775	2.097	2.823
70	.9269	1.316	1.760	2.074	2.776
80	.9258	1.311	1.748	2.056	2.742
90	.9249	1.307	1.739	2.043	2.715
100	.9242	1.304	1.732	2.032	2.694

TABLE A.13 (continued)

PERCENTAGE POINTS OF THE F-DISTRIBUTION

$\nu_1=9$

$\nu_2=$	50%	75%	90%	95%	99%
3	1.174	2.441	5.240	8.812	27.34
4	1.104	2.081	3.936	5.999	14.66
5	1.065	1.891	3.316	4.772	10.16
6	1.040	1.773	2.958	4.099	7.976
7	1.022	1.693	2.725	3.677	6.719
8	1.010	1.635	2.561	3.388	5.911
9	1.0000	1.591	2.440	3.179	5.351
10	.9923	1.556	2.347	3.020	4.942
11	.9861	1.528	2.274	2.896	4.632
12	.9810	1.505	2.214	2.796	4.388
13	.9767	1.486	2.164	2.714	4.191
14	.9730	1.470	2.122	2.646	4.030
15	.9698	1.456	2.086	2.588	3.895
16	.9670	1.443	2.055	2.538	3.780
17	.9646	1.433	2.028	2.494	3.682
18	.9625	1.423	2.005	2.456	3.597
19	.9606	1.414	1.984	2.423	3.522
20	.9588	1.407	1.965	2.393	3.457
21	.9573	1.400	1.948	2.366	3.398
22	.9559	1.394	1.933	2.342	3.346
23	.9546	1.388	1.919	2.320	3.299
24	.9534	1.383	1.906	2.300	3.256
25	.9523	1.378	1.895	2.282	3.217
26	.9513	1.374	1.884	2.265	3.182
27	.9504	1.370	1.874	2.250	3.149
28	.9496	1.366	1.865	2.236	3.120
29	.9488	1.362	1.857	2.223	3.092
30	.9480	1.359	1.849	2.211	3.067
40	.9427	1.335	1.793	2.124	2.888
50	.9395	1.321	1.760	2.073	2.785
60	.9374	1.312	1.738	2.040	2.718
70	.9359	1.305	1.723	2.017	2.672
80	.9348	1.300	1.711	1.999	2.637
90	.9339	1.296	1.702	1.986	2.611
100	.9332	1.293	1.695	1.975	2.590

$\nu_1=10$

$\nu_2=$	50%	75%	90%	95%	99%
3	1.183	2.445	5.230	8.786	27.23
4	1.113	2.082	3.920	5.964	14.55
5	1.073	1.890	3.297	4.735	10.05
6	1.048	1.771	2.937	4.060	7.874
7	1.030	1.690	2.703	3.637	6.620
8	1.018	1.631	2.538	3.347	5.814
9	1.008	1.586	2.416	3.137	5.257
10	1.0000	1.551	2.323	2.978	4.849
11	.9937	1.523	2.248	2.854	4.539
12	.9886	1.500	2.188	2.753	4.296
13	.9842	1.480	2.138	2.671	4.100
14	.9805	1.463	2.095	2.602	3.939
15	.9773	1.449	2.059	2.544	3.805
16	.9745	1.437	2.028	2.494	3.691
17	.9721	1.426	2.001	2.450	3.593
18	.9699	1.416	1.977	2.412	3.508
19	.9680	1.407	1.956	2.378	3.434
20	.9663	1.399	1.937	2.348	3.368
21	.9647	1.392	1.920	2.321	3.310
22	.9633	1.386	1.904	2.297	3.258
23	.9620	1.380	1.890	2.275	3.211
24	.9608	1.375	1.877	2.255	3.168
25	.9597	1.370	1.866	2.236	3.129
26	.9587	1.366	1.855	2.220	3.094
27	.9578	1.361	1.845	2.204	3.062
28	.9569	1.358	1.836	2.190	3.032
29	.9561	1.354	1.827	2.177	3.005
30	.9554	1.351	1.819	2.165	2.979
40	.9500	1.327	1.763	2.077	2.801
50	.9468	1.312	1.729	2.026	2.698
60	.9447	1.303	1.707	1.993	2.632
70	.9432	1.296	1.691	1.969	2.585
80	.9421	1.291	1.680	1.951	2.551
90	.9412	1.287	1.670	1.938	2.524
100	.9405	1.283	1.663	1.927	2.503

$\nu_1=11$

$\nu_2=$	50%	75%	90%	95%	99%
3	1.191	2.448	5.222	8.763	27.13
4	1.120	2.082	3.907	5.936	14.45
5	1.080	1.889	3.282	4.704	9.963
6	1.054	1.769	2.920	4.027	7.789
7	1.037	1.687	2.684	3.603	6.538
8	1.024	1.627	2.519	3.313	5.734
9	1.014	1.582	2.396	3.102	5.178
10	1.006	1.547	2.302	2.943	4.771
11	1.0000	1.518	2.227	2.818	4.462
12	.9948	1.495	2.166	2.717	4.220
13	.9904	1.475	2.116	2.635	4.025
14	.9867	1.458	2.073	2.565	3.864
15	.9835	1.443	2.037	2.507	3.730
16	.9807	1.431	2.005	2.456	3.616
17	.9782	1.420	1.978	2.413	3.519
18	.9760	1.410	1.954	2.374	3.434
19	.9741	1.401	1.932	2.340	3.360
20	.9724	1.393	1.913	2.310	3.294
21	.9708	1.386	1.896	2.283	3.236
22	.9694	1.379	1.880	2.259	3.184
23	.9681	1.374	1.866	2.236	3.137
24	.9669	1.368	1.853	2.216	3.094
25	.9658	1.363	1.841	2.198	3.056
26	.9648	1.359	1.830	2.181	3.020
27	.9638	1.354	1.820	2.166	2.988
28	.9630	1.350	1.811	2.151	2.959
29	.9622	1.347	1.802	2.138	2.931
30	.9614	1.343	1.794	2.126	2.906
40	.9560	1.319	1.737	2.038	2.727
50	.9528	1.304	1.703	1.986	2.625
60	.9507	1.294	1.680	1.952	2.559
70	.9492	1.287	1.665	1.928	2.512
80	.9480	1.282	1.653	1.910	2.478
90	.9471	1.278	1.643	1.897	2.451
100	.9464	1.275	1.636	1.886	2.430

TABLE A.13 (continued)

PERCENTAGE POINTS OF THE F-DISTRIBUTION

$\nu_2=$	$\nu_1=12$ 50%	75%	90%	95%	99%
3	1.197	2.450	5.216	8.745	27.05
4	1.126	2.083	3.896	5.912	14.37
5	1.085	1.888	3.268	4.678	9.888
6	1.060	1.767	2.905	4.000	7.719
7	1.042	1.684	2.668	3.575	6.469
8	1.029	1.624	2.502	3.284	5.667
9	1.019	1.579	2.379	3.073	5.111
10	1.012	1.543	2.284	2.913	4.706
11	1.005	1.514	2.209	2.788	4.397
12	1.0000	1.490	2.147	2.687	4.155
13	.9956	1.470	2.097	2.604	3.960
14	.9919	1.453	2.054	2.534	3.800
15	.9886	1.438	2.017	2.475	3.666
16	.9858	1.425	1.985	2.425	3.553
17	.9833	1.414	1.958	2.381	3.455
18	.9812	1.404	1.933	2.342	3.371
19	.9792	1.395	1.912	2.308	3.297
20	.9775	1.387	1.892	2.278	3.231
21	.9759	1.380	1.875	2.250	3.173
22	.9744	1.374	1.859	2.226	3.121
23	.9731	1.368	1.845	2.204	3.074
24	.9719	1.362	1.832	2.183	3.032
25	.9708	1.357	1.820	2.165	2.993
26	.9698	1.352	1.809	2.148	2.958
27	.9689	1.348	1.799	2.132	2.926
28	.9680	1.344	1.790	2.118	2.896
29	.9672	1.340	1.781	2.104	2.868
30	.9665	1.337	1.773	2.092	2.843
40	.9610	1.312	1.715	2.003	2.665
50	.9578	1.297	1.680	1.952	2.562
60	.9557	1.287	1.657	1.917	2.496
70	.9541	1.280	1.641	1.893	2.450
80	.9530	1.275	1.629	1.875	2.415
90	.9521	1.270	1.620	1.861	2.389
100	.9514	1.267	1.612	1.850	2.368

$\nu_2=$	$\nu_1=13$ 50%	75%	90%	95%	99%
3	1.203	2.452	5.210	8.729	26.98
4	1.131	2.083	3.886	5.891	14.31
5	1.090	1.887	3.257	4.655	9.825
6	1.065	1.765	2.892	3.976	7.657
7	1.047	1.682	2.654	3.550	6.410
8	1.034	1.622	2.488	3.259	5.609
9	1.024	1.576	2.364	3.048	5.055
10	1.016	1.540	2.269	2.887	4.650
11	1.010	1.510	2.193	2.761	4.342
12	1.004	1.486	2.131	2.660	4.100
13	1.0000	1.466	2.080	2.577	3.905
14	.9962	1.449	2.037	2.507	3.745
15	.9930	1.434	2.000	2.448	3.611
16	.9902	1.421	1.968	2.397	3.498
17	.9877	1.409	1.940	2.353	3.401
18	.9855	1.399	1.916	2.314	3.316
19	.9835	1.390	1.894	2.280	3.242
20	.9818	1.382	1.875	2.250	3.177
21	.9802	1.375	1.857	2.222	3.119
22	.9787	1.368	1.841	2.197	3.067
23	.9774	1.362	1.827	2.175	3.020
24	.9762	1.357	1.814	2.155	2.977
25	.9751	1.352	1.802	2.136	2.939
26	.9741	1.347	1.790	2.119	2.904
27	.9732	1.342	1.780	2.103	2.871
28	.9723	1.338	1.771	2.089	2.842
29	.9715	1.335	1.762	2.075	2.814
30	.9707	1.331	1.754	2.063	2.789
40	.9653	1.306	1.695	1.974	2.611
50	.9620	1.291	1.660	1.921	2.508
60	.9599	1.280	1.637	1.887	2.442
70	.9584	1.273	1.621	1.863	2.395
80	.9572	1.268	1.609	1.845	2.361
90	.9563	1.263	1.599	1.830	2.334
100	.9556	1.260	1.592	1.819	2.313

$\nu_2=$	$\nu_1=14$ 50%	75%	90%	95%	99%
3	1.207	2.454	5.205	8.715	26.92
4	1.135	2.083	3.878	5.873	14.25
5	1.094	1.886	3.247	4.636	9.770
6	1.069	1.764	2.881	3.956	7.605
7	1.051	1.680	2.643	3.529	6.359
8	1.038	1.619	2.475	3.237	5.559
9	1.028	1.573	2.351	3.025	5.005
10	1.020	1.537	2.255	2.865	4.601
11	1.013	1.507	2.179	2.739	4.293
12	1.008	1.483	2.117	2.637	4.052
13	1.004	1.462	2.066	2.554	3.857
14	1.0000	1.445	2.022	2.484	3.698
15	.9967	1.430	1.985	2.424	3.564
16	.9939	1.417	1.953	2.373	3.451
17	.9914	1.405	1.925	2.329	3.353
18	.9892	1.395	1.900	2.290	3.269
19	.9872	1.386	1.878	2.256	3.195
20	.9855	1.378	1.859	2.225	3.130
21	.9839	1.370	1.841	2.197	3.072
22	.9824	1.364	1.825	2.173	3.019
23	.9811	1.357	1.811	2.150	2.973
24	.9799	1.352	1.797	2.130	2.930
25	.9788	1.347	1.785	2.111	2.892
26	.9778	1.342	1.774	2.094	2.857
27	.9769	1.337	1.764	2.078	2.824
28	.9760	1.333	1.754	2.064	2.795
29	.9752	1.330	1.745	2.050	2.767
30	.9744	1.326	1.737	2.037	2.742
40	.9689	1.300	1.678	1.948	2.563
50	.9657	1.285	1.643	1.895	2.461
60	.9635	1.274	1.619	1.860	2.394
70	.9620	1.267	1.603	1.836	2.348
80	.9608	1.262	1.590	1.817	2.313
90	.9599	1.257	1.581	1.803	2.286
100	.9592	1.254	1.573	1.792	2.265

TABLE A.13 (continued)

PERCENTAGE POINTS OF THE F-DISTRIBUTION

ν_2 =	ν_1=15 50%	75%	90%	95%	99%
3	1.211	2.455	5.200	8.703	26.87
4	1.139	2.083	3.870	5.858	14.20
5	1.098	1.885	3.238	4.619	9.722
6	1.072	1.762	2.871	3.938	7.559
7	1.054	1.678	2.632	3.511	6.314
8	1.041	1.617	2.464	3.218	5.515
9	1.031	1.570	2.340	3.006	4.962
10	1.023	1.534	2.244	2.845	4.558
11	1.017	1.504	2.167	2.719	4.251
12	1.012	1.480	2.105	2.617	4.010
13	1.007	1.459	2.053	2.533	3.815
14	1.003	1.441	2.010	2.463	3.656
15	1.0000	1.426	1.972	2.403	3.522
16	.9972	1.413	1.940	2.352	3.409
17	.9947	1.401	1.912	2.308	3.312
18	.9924	1.391	1.887	2.269	3.227
19	.9905	1.382	1.865	2.234	3.153
20	.9887	1.374	1.845	2.203	3.088
21	.9871	1.366	1.827	2.176	3.030
22	.9857	1.359	1.811	2.151	2.978
23	.9843	1.353	1.796	2.128	2.931
24	.9831	1.347	1.783	2.108	2.889
25	.9820	1.342	1.771	2.089	2.850
26	.9810	1.337	1.760	2.072	2.815
27	.9800	1.333	1.749	2.056	2.783
28	.9792	1.329	1.740	2.041	2.753
29	.9784	1.325	1.731	2.027	2.726
30	.9776	1.321	1.722	2.015	2.700
40	.9721	1.295	1.662	1.924	2.522
50	.9688	1.280	1.627	1.871	2.419
60	.9667	1.269	1.603	1.836	2.352
70	.9651	1.262	1.587	1.812	2.306
80	.9640	1.256	1.574	1.793	2.271
90	.9631	1.252	1.564	1.779	2.244
100	.9624	1.248	1.557	1.768	2.223

ν_2 =	ν_1=16 50%	75%	90%	95%	99%
3	1.215	2.456	5.196	8.692	26.83
4	1.142	2.083	3.864	5.844	14.15
5	1.101	1.884	3.230	4.604	9.680
6	1.075	1.761	2.863	3.922	7.518
7	1.057	1.676	2.623	3.494	6.275
8	1.044	1.615	2.455	3.202	5.477
9	1.034	1.568	2.330	2.989	4.924
10	1.026	1.531	2.233	2.828	4.520
11	1.020	1.501	2.156	2.701	4.213
12	1.014	1.477	2.094	2.599	3.972
13	1.010	1.456	2.042	2.515	3.778
14	1.006	1.438	1.998	2.445	3.619
15	1.003	1.423	1.961	2.385	3.485
16	1.0000	1.410	1.928	2.333	3.372
17	.9975	1.398	1.900	2.289	3.275
18	.9953	1.388	1.875	2.250	3.190
19	.9933	1.378	1.852	2.215	3.116
20	.9915	1.370	1.833	2.184	3.051
21	.9899	1.362	1.815	2.156	2.993
22	.9885	1.355	1.798	2.131	2.941
23	.9871	1.349	1.784	2.109	2.894
24	.9859	1.343	1.770	2.088	2.852
25	.9848	1.338	1.758	2.069	2.813
26	.9838	1.333	1.747	2.052	2.778
27	.9828	1.329	1.736	2.036	2.746
28	.9820	1.325	1.726	2.021	2.716
29	.9811	1.321	1.717	2.007	2.689
30	.9804	1.317	1.709	1.995	2.663
40	.9749	1.291	1.649	1.904	2.484
50	.9716	1.275	1.613	1.850	2.382
60	.9694	1.264	1.589	1.815	2.315
70	.9679	1.257	1.572	1.790	2.268
80	.9667	1.251	1.559	1.772	2.233
90	.9658	1.246	1.550	1.757	2.206
100	.9651	1.243	1.542	1.746	2.185

ν_2 =	ν_1=17 50%	75%	90%	95%	99%
3	1.218	2.458	5.193	8.683	26.79
4	1.145	2.083	3.858	5.832	14.11
5	1.104	1.884	3.223	4.590	9.643
6	1.078	1.760	2.855	3.908	7.483
7	1.060	1.675	2.615	3.480	6.240
8	1.047	1.613	2.446	3.187	5.442
9	1.037	1.566	2.320	2.974	4.890
10	1.029	1.529	2.224	2.812	4.487
11	1.022	1.499	2.147	2.685	4.180
12	1.017	1.474	2.084	2.583	3.939
13	1.012	1.453	2.032	2.499	3.745
14	1.009	1.435	1.988	2.428	3.586
15	1.005	1.420	1.950	2.368	3.452
16	1.003	1.407	1.917	2.317	3.339
17	1.000	1.395	1.889	2.272	3.242
18	.9978	1.384	1.864	2.233	3.158
19	.9958	1.375	1.841	2.198	3.084
20	.9940	1.367	1.821	2.167	3.018
21	.9924	1.359	1.803	2.139	2.960
22	.9909	1.352	1.787	2.114	2.908
23	.9896	1.346	1.772	2.091	2.861
24	.9884	1.340	1.759	2.070	2.819
25	.9873	1.335	1.746	2.051	2.780
26	.9863	1.330	1.735	2.034	2.745
27	.9853	1.325	1.724	2.018	2.713
28	.9844	1.321	1.715	2.003	2.683
29	.9836	1.317	1.705	1.989	2.655
30	.9828	1.313	1.697	1.976	2.630
40	.9773	1.286	1.636	1.885	2.451
50	.9740	1.270	1.600	1.831	2.348
60	.9719	1.260	1.576	1.796	2.281
70	.9703	1.252	1.559	1.771	2.234
80	.9692	1.246	1.546	1.752	2.199
90	.9683	1.242	1.536	1.737	2.172
100	.9675	1.238	1.528	1.726	2.151

TABLE A.13 (continued)

PERCENTAGE POINTS OF THE F-DISTRIBUTION

ν_2	$\nu_1=18$ 50%	75%	90%	95%	99%
3	1.220	2.459	5.190	8.675	26.75
4	1.147	2.083	3.853	5.821	14.08
5	1.106	1.883	3.217	4.579	9.609
6	1.080	1.759	2.848	3.896	7.451
7	1.062	1.674	2.607	3.467	6.209
8	1.049	1.612	2.438	3.173	5.412
9	1.039	1.564	2.312	2.960	4.860
10	1.031	1.527	2.215	2.798	4.457
11	1.025	1.497	2.138	2.671	4.150
12	1.019	1.472	2.075	2.568	3.909
13	1.015	1.451	2.023	2.484	3.716
14	1.011	1.433	1.979	2.413	3.556
15	1.008	1.417	1.941	2.353	3.423
16	1.005	1.404	1.908	2.302	3.310
17	1.002	1.392	1.879	2.257	3.212
18	1.000	1.381	1.854	2.217	3.128
19	.9980	1.372	1.831	2.182	3.054
20	.9962	1.363	1.811	2.151	2.989
21	.9946	1.356	1.793	2.123	2.931
22	.9932	1.349	1.777	2.098	2.879
23	.9918	1.342	1.762	2.075	2.832
24	.9906	1.337	1.748	2.054	2.789
25	.9895	1.331	1.736	2.035	2.751
26	.9885	1.326	1.724	2.018	2.715
27	.9875	1.322	1.714	2.002	2.683
28	.9866	1.317	1.704	1.987	2.653
29	.9858	1.313	1.695	1.973	2.626
30	.9850	1.310	1.686	1.960	2.600
40	.9795	1.283	1.625	1.868	2.421
50	.9762	1.266	1.588	1.814	2.318
60	.9740	1.255	1.564	1.778	2.251
70	.9725	1.248	1.547	1.753	2.204
80	.9713	1.242	1.534	1.734	2.169
90	.9704	1.237	1.524	1.720	2.142
100	.9697	1.234	1.516	1.708	2.120

ν_2	$\nu_1=19$ 50%	75%	90%	95%	99%
3	1.223	2.459	5.187	8.667	26.72
4	1.150	2.083	3.848	5.811	14.05
5	1.109	1.882	3.212	4.568	9.580
6	1.083	1.758	2.842	3.884	7.422
7	1.064	1.672	2.601	3.455	6.181
8	1.051	1.610	2.431	3.161	5.384
9	1.041	1.563	2.305	2.948	4.833
10	1.033	1.525	2.208	2.785	4.430
11	1.027	1.495	2.130	2.658	4.123
12	1.021	1.470	2.067	2.555	3.883
13	1.017	1.449	2.014	2.471	3.689
14	1.013	1.431	1.970	2.400	3.529
15	1.010	1.415	1.932	2.340	3.396
16	1.007	1.401	1.899	2.288	3.283
17	1.004	1.389	1.870	2.243	3.186
18	1.002	1.379	1.845	2.203	3.101
19	1.000	1.369	1.822	2.168	3.027
20	.9982	1.361	1.802	2.137	2.962
21	.9966	1.353	1.784	2.109	2.904
22	.9951	1.346	1.768	2.084	2.852
23	.9938	1.339	1.753	2.061	2.805
24	.9926	1.333	1.739	2.040	2.762
25	.9915	1.328	1.726	2.021	2.724
26	.9904	1.323	1.715	2.003	2.688
27	.9895	1.318	1.704	1.987	2.656
28	.9886	1.314	1.694	1.972	2.626
29	.9878	1.310	1.685	1.958	2.599
30	.9870	1.306	1.676	1.945	2.573
40	.9815	1.279	1.615	1.853	2.394
50	.9782	1.263	1.578	1.798	2.290
60	.9760	1.252	1.553	1.763	2.223
70	.9744	1.244	1.536	1.737	2.176
80	.9733	1.238	1.523	1.718	2.141
90	.9723	1.233	1.513	1.703	2.114
100	.9716	1.229	1.505	1.691	2.092

ν_2	$\nu_1=20$ 50%	75%	90%	95%	99%
3	1.225	2.460	5.184	8.660	26.69
4	1.152	2.083	3.844	5.803	14.02
5	1.111	1.882	3.207	4.558	9.553
6	1.084	1.757	2.836	3.874	7.396
7	1.066	1.671	2.595	3.445	6.155
8	1.053	1.609	2.425	3.150	5.359
9	1.043	1.561	2.298	2.936	4.808
10	1.035	1.523	2.201	2.774	4.405
11	1.028	1.493	2.123	2.646	4.099
12	1.023	1.468	2.060	2.544	3.858
13	1.019	1.447	2.007	2.459	3.665
14	1.015	1.428	1.962	2.388	3.505
15	1.011	1.413	1.924	2.328	3.372
16	1.009	1.399	1.891	2.276	3.259
17	1.006	1.387	1.862	2.230	3.161
18	1.004	1.376	1.837	2.191	3.077
19	1.002	1.367	1.814	2.155	3.003
20	1.000	1.358	1.794	2.124	2.938
21	.9984	1.350	1.776	2.096	2.880
22	.9969	1.343	1.759	2.071	2.827
23	.9956	1.337	1.744	2.048	2.781
24	.9944	1.331	1.730	2.027	2.738
25	.9932	1.325	1.718	2.007	2.699
26	.9922	1.320	1.706	1.990	2.664
27	.9912	1.315	1.695	1.974	2.632
28	.9904	1.311	1.685	1.959	2.602
29	.9895	1.307	1.676	1.945	2.574
30	.9888	1.303	1.667	1.932	2.549
40	.9832	1.276	1.605	1.839	2.369
50	.9799	1.259	1.568	1.784	2.265
60	.9777	1.248	1.543	1.748	2.198
70	.9762	1.240	1.526	1.722	2.150
80	.9750	1.234	1.513	1.703	2.115
90	.9741	1.229	1.503	1.688	2.088
100	.9734	1.226	1.494	1.676	2.067

TABLE A.13 (continued)

PERCENTAGE POINTS OF THE F-DISTRIBUTION

ν_2	$\nu_1=21$ 50%	75%	90%	95%	99%
3	1.227	2.461	5.182	8.654	26.66
4	1.154	2.083	3.841	5.795	13.99
5	1.112	1.881	3.202	4.549	9.528
6	1.086	1.756	2.831	3.865	7.372
7	1.068	1.670	2.589	3.435	6.132
8	1.055	1.608	2.419	3.140	5.336
9	1.045	1.560	2.292	2.926	4.785
10	1.037	1.522	2.194	2.764	4.383
11	1.030	1.491	2.117	2.636	4.077
12	1.025	1.466	2.053	2.533	3.836
13	1.020	1.445	2.000	2.448	3.643
14	1.016	1.426	1.955	2.377	3.483
15	1.013	1.411	1.917	2.316	3.350
16	1.010	1.397	1.884	2.264	3.237
17	1.008	1.385	1.855	2.219	3.139
18	1.005	1.374	1.829	2.179	3.055
19	1.003	1.364	1.807	2.144	2.981
20	1.002	1.356	1.786	2.112	2.916
21	1.000	1.348	1.768	2.084	2.857
22	.9985	1.341	1.751	2.059	2.805
23	.9972	1.334	1.736	2.036	2.758
24	.9960	1.328	1.722	2.015	2.716
25	.9948	1.323	1.710	1.995	2.677
26	.9938	1.318	1.698	1.978	2.642
27	.9929	1.313	1.687	1.961	2.609
28	.9920	1.308	1.677	1.946	2.579
29	.9911	1.304	1.668	1.932	2.552
30	.9904	1.301	1.659	1.919	2.526
40	.9848	1.273	1.596	1.826	2.346
50	.9815	1.256	1.559	1.771	2.242
60	.9793	1.245	1.534	1.735	2.175
70	.9777	1.237	1.517	1.709	2.127
80	.9766	1.231	1.503	1.689	2.092
90	.9757	1.226	1.493	1.674	2.065
100	.9749	1.222	1.485	1.663	2.043

ν_2	$\nu_1=22$ 50%	75%	90%	95%	99%
3	1.229	2.462	5.180	8.648	26.64
4	1.155	2.083	3.837	5.787	13.97
5	1.114	1.881	3.198	4.541	9.506
6	1.088	1.755	2.827	3.856	7.350
7	1.070	1.669	2.584	3.426	6.111
8	1.056	1.606	2.414	3.131	5.316
9	1.046	1.558	2.287	2.917	4.765
10	1.038	1.520	2.189	2.754	4.363
11	1.032	1.490	2.111	2.626	4.057
12	1.026	1.464	2.047	2.523	3.816
13	1.022	1.443	1.994	2.438	3.622
14	1.018	1.425	1.949	2.367	3.463
15	1.015	1.409	1.911	2.306	3.330
16	1.012	1.395	1.877	2.254	3.216
17	1.009	1.383	1.848	2.208	3.119
18	1.007	1.372	1.823	2.168	3.035
19	1.005	1.362	1.800	2.133	2.961
20	1.003	1.353	1.779	2.102	2.895
21	1.001	1.345	1.761	2.073	2.837
22	1.000	1.338	1.744	2.048	2.785
23	.9987	1.332	1.729	2.025	2.738
24	.9974	1.326	1.715	2.003	2.695
25	.9963	1.320	1.702	1.984	2.657
26	.9953	1.315	1.690	1.966	2.621
27	.9943	1.310	1.680	1.950	2.589
28	.9934	1.306	1.669	1.935	2.559
29	.9926	1.302	1.660	1.921	2.531
30	.9918	1.298	1.651	1.908	2.506
40	.9863	1.270	1.588	1.814	2.325
50	.9830	1.253	1.551	1.759	2.221
60	.9808	1.242	1.526	1.722	2.153
70	.9792	1.234	1.508	1.696	2.106
80	.9780	1.227	1.495	1.677	2.070
90	.9771	1.223	1.484	1.662	2.043
100	.9764	1.219	1.476	1.650	2.021

ν_2	$\nu_1=23$ 50%	75%	90%	95%	99%
3	1.231	2.462	5.178	8.643	26.62
4	1.157	2.083	3.834	5.780	13.95
5	1.116	1.881	3.194	4.534	9.485
6	1.089	1.755	2.822	3.849	7.331
7	1.071	1.668	2.580	3.418	6.092
8	1.058	1.605	2.409	3.123	5.297
9	1.048	1.557	2.282	2.908	4.746
10	1.040	1.519	2.183	2.745	4.344
11	1.033	1.488	2.105	2.617	4.038
12	1.028	1.463	2.041	2.514	3.798
13	1.023	1.441	1.988	2.429	3.604
14	1.019	1.423	1.943	2.357	3.445
15	1.016	1.407	1.905	2.297	3.311
16	1.013	1.393	1.871	2.244	3.198
17	1.010	1.381	1.842	2.199	3.101
18	1.008	1.370	1.816	2.159	3.016
19	1.006	1.360	1.793	2.123	2.942
20	1.004	1.351	1.773	2.092	2.877
21	1.003	1.343	1.754	2.063	2.818
22	1.001	1.336	1.737	2.038	2.766
23	1.000	1.330	1.722	2.014	2.719
24	.9988	1.323	1.708	1.993	2.676
25	.9976	1.318	1.695	1.974	2.638
26	.9966	1.313	1.684	1.956	2.602
27	.9956	1.308	1.673	1.940	2.570
28	.9948	1.304	1.662	1.924	2.540
29	.9939	1.299	1.653	1.910	2.512
30	.9932	1.296	1.644	1.897	2.486
40	.9876	1.267	1.581	1.803	2.306
50	.9843	1.250	1.543	1.748	2.202
60	.9821	1.239	1.518	1.711	2.134
70	.9805	1.231	1.500	1.685	2.086
80	.9793	1.224	1.487	1.665	2.050
90	.9784	1.220	1.476	1.650	2.023
100	.9777	1.216	1.468	1.638	2.001

TABLE A.13 (continued)

PERCENTAGE POINTS OF THE F-DISTRIBUTION

$\nu_2=$	$\nu_1=24$ 50%	75%	90%	95%	99%
3	1.232	2.463	5.176	8.639	26.60
4	1.158	2.083	3.831	5.774	13.93
5	1.117	1.880	3.190	4.527	9.467
6	1.091	1.754	2.818	3.841	7.313
7	1.072	1.667	2.575	3.410	6.074
8	1.059	1.604	2.404	3.115	5.279
9	1.049	1.556	2.277	2.900	4.729
10	1.041	1.518	2.178	2.737	4.327
11	1.034	1.487	2.100	2.609	4.021
12	1.029	1.461	2.036	2.505	3.781
13	1.024	1.440	1.983	2.420	3.587
14	1.020	1.421	1.938	2.349	3.427
15	1.017	1.405	1.899	2.288	3.294
16	1.014	1.391	1.866	2.235	3.181
17	1.012	1.379	1.836	2.190	3.083
18	1.009	1.368	1.810	2.150	2.999
19	1.007	1.358	1.787	2.114	2.925
20	1.006	1.349	1.767	2.082	2.859
21	1.004	1.341	1.748	2.054	2.801
22	1.003	1.334	1.731	2.028	2.749
23	1.001	1.327	1.716	2.005	2.702
24	1.000	1.321	1.702	1.984	2.659
25	.9989	1.316	1.689	1.964	2.620
26	.9978	1.311	1.677	1.946	2.585
27	.9969	1.306	1.666	1.930	2.552
28	.9960	1.301	1.656	1.915	2.522
29	.9951	1.297	1.647	1.901	2.495
30	.9944	1.293	1.638	1.887	2.469
40	.9888	1.265	1.574	1.793	2.288
50	.9855	1.248	1.536	1.737	2.183
60	.9833	1.236	1.511	1.700	2.115
70	.9817	1.228	1.493	1.674	2.067
80	.9805	1.222	1.479	1.654	2.032
90	.9796	1.217	1.468	1.639	2.004
100	.9789	1.213	1.460	1.627	1.983

$\nu_2=$	$\nu_1=25$ 50%	75%	90%	95%	99%
3	1.234	2.463	5.175	8.634	26.58
4	1.160	2.083	3.828	5.769	13.91
5	1.118	1.880	3.187	4.521	9.449
6	1.092	1.753	2.815	3.835	7.296
7	1.074	1.667	2.571	3.404	6.058
8	1.060	1.603	2.400	3.108	5.263
9	1.050	1.555	2.272	2.893	4.713
10	1.042	1.517	2.174	2.730	4.311
11	1.035	1.486	2.095	2.601	4.005
12	1.030	1.460	2.031	2.498	3.765
13	1.026	1.438	1.978	2.412	3.571
14	1.022	1.420	1.933	2.341	3.412
15	1.018	1.404	1.894	2.280	3.278
16	1.015	1.390	1.860	2.227	3.165
17	1.013	1.377	1.831	2.181	3.068
18	1.011	1.366	1.805	2.141	2.983
19	1.009	1.356	1.782	2.106	2.909
20	1.007	1.348	1.761	2.074	2.843
21	1.005	1.340	1.742	2.045	2.785
22	1.004	1.332	1.726	2.020	2.733
23	1.002	1.326	1.710	1.996	2.686
24	1.001	1.319	1.696	1.975	2.643
25	1.000	1.314	1.683	1.955	2.604
26	.9990	1.309	1.671	1.938	2.569
27	.9980	1.304	1.660	1.921	2.536
28	.9971	1.299	1.650	1.906	2.506
29	.9963	1.295	1.640	1.891	2.478
30	.9955	1.291	1.632	1.878	2.453
40	.9899	1.263	1.568	1.783	2.271
50	.9866	1.245	1.529	1.727	2.167
60	.9844	1.234	1.504	1.690	2.098
70	.9828	1.225	1.486	1.664	2.050
80	.9816	1.219	1.472	1.644	2.015
90	.9807	1.214	1.461	1.629	1.987
100	.9800	1.210	1.453	1.616	1.965

$\nu_2=$	$\nu_1=26$ 50%	75%	90%	95%	99%
3	1.235	2.464	5.173	8.630	26.56
4	1.161	2.083	3.826	5.763	13.89
5	1.119	1.880	3.184	4.515	9.433
6	1.093	1.753	2.811	3.829	7.280
7	1.075	1.666	2.568	3.397	6.043
8	1.061	1.602	2.396	3.102	5.248
9	1.051	1.554	2.268	2.886	4.698
10	1.043	1.516	2.170	2.723	4.296
11	1.037	1.485	2.091	2.594	3.990
12	1.031	1.459	2.027	2.491	3.750
13	1.027	1.437	1.973	2.405	3.556
14	1.023	1.418	1.928	2.333	3.397
15	1.019	1.402	1.889	2.272	3.264
16	1.016	1.388	1.855	2.220	3.150
17	1.014	1.376	1.826	2.174	3.053
18	1.012	1.365	1.800	2.134	2.968
19	1.010	1.355	1.777	2.098	2.894
20	1.008	1.346	1.756	2.066	2.829
21	1.006	1.338	1.737	2.037	2.770
22	1.005	1.330	1.720	2.012	2.718
23	1.003	1.324	1.705	1.988	2.671
24	1.002	1.318	1.691	1.967	2.628
25	1.001	1.312	1.678	1.947	2.589
26	1.000	1.307	1.666	1.929	2.554
27	.9990	1.302	1.655	1.913	2.521
28	.9981	1.297	1.644	1.897	2.491
29	.9973	1.293	1.635	1.883	2.463
30	.9965	1.289	1.626	1.870	2.437
40	.9910	1.260	1.562	1.775	2.256
50	.9876	1.243	1.523	1.718	2.151
60	.9854	1.231	1.498	1.681	2.083
70	.9838	1.223	1.479	1.654	2.034
80	.9827	1.216	1.465	1.634	1.999
90	.9818	1.211	1.455	1.619	1.971
100	.9810	1.207	1.446	1.607	1.949

TABLE A.13 (continued)

PERCENTAGE POINTS OF THE F-DISTRIBUTION

ν_2=	ν_1=27 50%	75%	90%	95%	99%
3	1.236	2.464	5.172	8.626	26.55
4	1.162	2.083	3.823	5.759	13.88
5	1.121	1.879	3.181	4.510	9.418
6	1.094	1.752	2.808	3.823	7.266
7	1.076	1.665	2.564	3.391	6.029
8	1.062	1.602	2.392	3.095	5.234
9	1.052	1.553	2.265	2.880	4.684
10	1.044	1.515	2.166	2.716	4.283
11	1.038	1.483	2.087	2.588	3.977
12	1.032	1.458	2.022	2.484	3.736
13	1.028	1.436	1.969	2.398	3.543
14	1.024	1.417	1.923	2.326	3.383
15	1.020	1.401	1.885	2.265	3.250
16	1.017	1.387	1.851	2.213	3.137
17	1.015	1.374	1.821	2.167	3.039
18	1.013	1.363	1.795	2.126	2.955
19	1.011	1.353	1.772	2.090	2.880
20	1.009	1.344	1.751	2.059	2.815
21	1.007	1.336	1.732	2.030	2.756
22	1.006	1.329	1.715	2.004	2.704
23	1.004	1.322	1.700	1.981	2.657
24	1.003	1.316	1.686	1.959	2.614
25	1.002	1.310	1.672	1.940	2.575
26	1.001	1.305	1.660	1.921	2.540
27	1.000	1.300	1.649	1.905	2.507
28	.9991	1.295	1.639	1.889	2.477
29	.9983	1.291	1.630	1.875	2.449
30	.9975	1.287	1.621	1.862	2.423
40	.9919	1.258	1.556	1.766	2.242
50	.9886	1.241	1.517	1.710	2.136
60	.9864	1.229	1.492	1.672	2.068
70	.9848	1.220	1.473	1.646	2.019
80	.9836	1.214	1.459	1.626	1.983
90	.9827	1.209	1.448	1.610	1.956
100	.9820	1.205	1.440	1.598	1.934

ν_2=	ν_1=28 50%	75%	90%	95%	99%
3	1.237	2.464	5.171	8.623	26.53
4	1.163	2.083	3.821	5.754	13.86
5	1.122	1.879	3.179	4.505	9.404
6	1.095	1.752	2.805	3.818	7.253
7	1.077	1.665	2.561	3.386	6.016
8	1.063	1.601	2.389	3.090	5.222
9	1.053	1.552	2.261	2.874	4.672
10	1.045	1.514	2.162	2.710	4.270
11	1.038	1.482	2.083	2.582	3.964
12	1.033	1.456	2.019	2.478	3.724
13	1.028	1.435	1.965	2.392	3.530
14	1.025	1.416	1.919	2.320	3.371
15	1.021	1.400	1.880	2.259	3.237
16	1.018	1.385	1.847	2.206	3.124
17	1.016	1.373	1.817	2.160	3.026
18	1.014	1.362	1.791	2.119	2.942
19	1.012	1.352	1.767	2.084	2.868
20	1.010	1.343	1.746	2.052	2.802
21	1.008	1.335	1.728	2.023	2.743
22	1.007	1.327	1.711	1.997	2.691
23	1.005	1.321	1.695	1.973	2.644
24	1.004	1.314	1.681	1.952	2.601
25	1.003	1.309	1.668	1.932	2.562
26	1.002	1.303	1.656	1.914	2.526
27	1.001	1.298	1.645	1.898	2.494
28	1.000	1.294	1.634	1.882	2.464
29	.9992	1.290	1.625	1.868	2.436
30	.9984	1.286	1.616	1.854	2.410
40	.9928	1.256	1.551	1.759	2.228
50	.9895	1.239	1.512	1.702	2.123
60	.9872	1.227	1.486	1.664	2.054
70	.9857	1.218	1.467	1.637	2.005
80	.9845	1.212	1.453	1.617	1.969
90	.9836	1.207	1.442	1.601	1.942
100	.9828	1.203	1.434	1.589	1.919

ν_2=	ν_1=29 50%	75%	90%	95%	99%
3	1.238	2.465	5.169	8.620	26.52
4	1.164	2.082	3.819	5.750	13.85
5	1.122	1.879	3.176	4.500	9.391
6	1.096	1.751	2.803	3.813	7.240
7	1.078	1.664	2.558	3.381	6.003
8	1.064	1.600	2.386	3.084	5.209
9	1.054	1.551	2.258	2.869	4.660
10	1.046	1.513	2.159	2.705	4.258
11	1.039	1.481	2.080	2.576	3.952
12	1.034	1.455	2.015	2.472	3.712
13	1.029	1.433	1.961	2.386	3.518
14	1.025	1.415	1.916	2.314	3.359
15	1.022	1.398	1.876	2.253	3.225
16	1.019	1.384	1.843	2.200	3.112
17	1.017	1.372	1.813	2.154	3.014
18	1.014	1.360	1.787	2.113	2.930
19	1.012	1.350	1.763	2.077	2.856
20	1.011	1.341	1.742	2.045	2.790
21	1.009	1.333	1.723	2.016	2.731
22	1.007	1.326	1.706	1.990	2.679
23	1.006	1.319	1.691	1.967	2.632
24	1.005	1.313	1.676	1.945	2.589
25	1.004	1.307	1.663	1.926	2.550
26	1.003	1.302	1.651	1.907	2.514
27	1.002	1.297	1.640	1.891	2.481
28	1.001	1.292	1.630	1.875	2.451
29	1.000	1.288	1.620	1.861	2.423
30	.9992	1.284	1.611	1.847	2.398
40	.9936	1.255	1.546	1.751	2.215
50	.9903	1.237	1.507	1.694	2.110
60	.9881	1.225	1.481	1.656	2.041
70	.9865	1.216	1.462	1.629	1.992
80	.9853	1.210	1.448	1.609	1.956
90	.9844	1.205	1.437	1.593	1.928
100	.9837	1.200	1.428	1.581	1.906

TABLE A.13 (continued)

PERCENTAGE POINTS OF THE F-DISTRIBUTION

$\nu_2=$	$\nu_1=30$ 50%	75%	90%	95%	99%
3	1.239	2.465	5.168	8.617	26.50
4	1.165	2.082	3.817	5.746	13.84
5	1.123	1.878	3.174	4.496	9.379
6	1.097	1.751	2.800	3.808	7.228
7	1.079	1.663	2.555	3.376	5.992
8	1.065	1.600	2.383	3.079	5.198
9	1.055	1.551	2.255	2.864	4.648
10	1.047	1.512	2.155	2.700	4.247
11	1.040	1.481	2.076	2.570	3.941
12	1.035	1.454	2.011	2.466	3.701
13	1.030	1.432	1.958	2.380	3.507
14	1.026	1.414	1.912	2.308	3.348
15	1.023	1.397	1.873	2.247	3.214
16	1.020	1.383	1.839	2.194	3.101
17	1.017	1.370	1.809	2.148	3.003
18	1.015	1.359	1.783	2.107	2.919
19	1.013	1.349	1.759	2.071	2.844
20	1.011	1.340	1.738	2.039	2.778
21	1.010	1.332	1.719	2.010	2.720
22	1.008	1.324	1.702	1.984	2.667
23	1.007	1.318	1.686	1.961	2.620
24	1.006	1.311	1.672	1.939	2.577
25	1.005	1.306	1.659	1.919	2.538
26	1.003	1.300	1.647	1.901	2.503
27	1.003	1.295	1.636	1.884	2.470
28	1.002	1.291	1.625	1.869	2.440
29	1.001	1.286	1.616	1.854	2.412
30	1.000	1.282	1.606	1.841	2.386
40	.9944	1.253	1.541	1.744	2.203
50	.9911	1.235	1.502	1.687	2.098
60	.9888	1.223	1.476	1.649	2.028
70	.9873	1.214	1.457	1.622	1.980
80	.9861	1.208	1.443	1.602	1.944
90	.9852	1.202	1.432	1.586	1.916
100	.9844	1.198	1.423	1.573	1.893

$\nu_2=$	$\nu_1=40$ 50%	75%	90%	95%	99%
3	1.246	2.467	5.160	8.594	26.41
4	1.172	2.082	3.804	5.717	13.74
5	1.130	1.876	3.157	4.464	9.291
6	1.103	1.748	2.781	3.774	7.143
7	1.085	1.659	2.535	3.340	5.909
8	1.071	1.595	2.361	3.043	5.116
9	1.061	1.545	2.232	2.826	4.567
10	1.053	1.506	2.132	2.661	4.165
11	1.046	1.474	2.052	2.531	3.860
12	1.041	1.447	1.986	2.426	3.619
13	1.036	1.425	1.931	2.339	3.425
14	1.032	1.405	1.885	2.266	3.266
15	1.029	1.389	1.845	2.204	3.132
16	1.026	1.374	1.811	2.151	3.018
17	1.023	1.361	1.781	2.104	2.920
18	1.021	1.350	1.754	2.063	2.835
19	1.019	1.339	1.730	2.026	2.761
20	1.017	1.330	1.708	1.994	2.695
21	1.015	1.322	1.689	1.965	2.636
22	1.014	1.314	1.671	1.938	2.583
23	1.013	1.307	1.655	1.914	2.535
24	1.011	1.300	1.641	1.892	2.492
25	1.010	1.294	1.627	1.872	2.453
26	1.009	1.289	1.615	1.853	2.417
27	1.008	1.284	1.603	1.836	2.384
28	1.007	1.279	1.592	1.820	2.354
29	1.006	1.275	1.583	1.806	2.325
30	1.006	1.270	1.573	1.792	2.299
40	1.000	1.240	1.506	1.693	2.114
50	.9966	1.221	1.465	1.634	2.007
60	.9944	1.208	1.437	1.594	1.936
70	.9928	1.199	1.418	1.566	1.886
80	.9916	1.192	1.403	1.545	1.849
90	.9907	1.186	1.391	1.528	1.820
100	.9900	1.182	1.382	1.515	1.797

$\nu_2=$	$\nu_1=50$ 50%	75%	90%	95%	99%
3	1.251	2.469	5.155	8.581	26.35
4	1.176	2.082	3.795	5.699	13.69
5	1.134	1.875	3.147	4.444	9.238
6	1.107	1.746	2.770	3.754	7.092
7	1.088	1.657	2.523	3.319	5.858
8	1.075	1.591	2.348	3.020	5.065
9	1.064	1.541	2.218	2.803	4.517
10	1.056	1.502	2.117	2.637	4.115
11	1.050	1.469	2.036	2.507	3.810
12	1.044	1.443	1.970	2.401	3.569
13	1.039	1.420	1.915	2.314	3.375
14	1.036	1.400	1.869	2.241	3.215
15	1.032	1.383	1.828	2.178	3.081
16	1.029	1.369	1.793	2.124	2.968
17	1.027	1.355	1.763	2.077	2.869
18	1.024	1.344	1.736	2.035	2.784
19	1.022	1.333	1.711	1.999	2.709
20	1.020	1.324	1.690	1.966	2.643
21	1.019	1.315	1.670	1.936	2.584
22	1.017	1.307	1.652	1.909	2.531
23	1.016	1.300	1.636	1.885	2.483
24	1.015	1.293	1.621	1.863	2.439
25	1.014	1.287	1.607	1.842	2.400
26	1.013	1.282	1.594	1.823	2.364
27	1.012	1.276	1.583	1.806	2.330
28	1.011	1.271	1.572	1.790	2.300
29	1.010	1.267	1.562	1.775	2.271
30	1.009	1.263	1.552	1.761	2.245
40	1.003	1.231	1.483	1.660	2.058
50	1.000	1.212	1.441	1.599	1.949
60	.9978	1.198	1.413	1.559	1.877
70	.9962	1.189	1.392	1.530	1.826
80	.9950	1.181	1.377	1.508	1.788
90	.9941	1.176	1.365	1.491	1.759
100	.9933	1.171	1.355	1.477	1.735

TABLE A.14

PERCENTAGE POINTS OF THE BETA DISTRIBUTION

This table gives percentage points for the Beta distribution $\beta(p,q)$ p,q = 2(1)25 $p \leq q$. To find a p% point where $p > q$, enter the table with p and q reversed and subtract the 100-p% point from 1. For example, to find the 95% point for a $\beta(10,2)$ distribution, note that the 100% - 95% = 5% point for a $\beta(10,2)$ distribution is .03332. Thus, the desired point is 1 - .03332 = .96668.

p=2	.5%	1%	5%	10%	25%	50%	75%	90%	95%	99%	99.5%
q=2	.04140	.05890	.1353	.1958	.3264	.5000	.6736	.8042	.8647	.9411	.9586
3	.02944	.04199	.09761	.1426	.2430	.3857	.5437	.6795	.7514	.8591	.8892
4	.02288	.03268	.07645	.1122	.1938	.3138	.4542	.5839	.6574	.7780	.8149
5	.01872	.02676	.06285	.09259	.1612	.2645	.3895	.5103	.5818	.7057	.7461
6	.01584	.02267	.05338	.07883	.1380	.2285	.3407	.4526	.5207	.6433	.6848
7	.01373	.01965	.04639	.06863	.1206	.2011	.3027	.4062	.4707	.5900	.6316
8	.01212	.01736	.04102	.06077	.1072	.1796	.2723	.3684	.4291	.5441	.5850
9	.01085	.01553	.03677	.05453	.09641	.1623	.2474	.3369	.3942	.5044	.5442
10	.009819	.01407	.03332	.04945	.08761	.1480	.2266	.3102	.3643	.4698	.5085
11	.008967	.01285	.03046	.04524	.08029	.1360	.2091	.2875	.3387	.4396	.4771
12	.008252	.01183	.02805	.04169	.07410	.1258	.1941	.2678	.3163	.4128	.4490
13	.007642	.01096	.02600	.03866	.06879	.1170	.1810	.2507	.2967	.3891	.4241
14	.007116	.01020	.02422	.03604	.06419	.1094	.1697	.2356	.2794	.3679	.4016
15	.006658	.009544	.02268	.03375	.06017	.1027	.1596	.2222	.2639	.3489	.3813
16	.006255	.008965	.02132	.03173	.05663	.09678	.1507	.2102	.2501	.3317	.3630
17	.005899	.008453	.02011	.02995	.05348	.09151	.1427	.1995	.2377	.3160	.3463
18	.005581	.008003	.01903	.02835	.05066	.08678	.1355	.1898	.2264	.3018	.3311
19	.005295	.007591	.01807	.02691	.04812	.08251	.1291	.1810	.2161	.2888	.3171
20	.005037	.007225	.01719	.02562	.04583	.07864	.1232	.1729	.2067	.2769	.3043
21	.004803	.006889	.01640	.02444	.04374	.07512	.1178	.1656	.1981	.2659	.2925
22	.004590	.006584	.01567	.02337	.04184	.07191	.1128	.1588	.1902	.2557	.2815
23	.004395	.006302	.01501	.02238	.04009	.06895	.1083	.1526	.1829	.2462	.2712
24	.004216	.006046	.01440	.02148	.03849	.06623	.1041	.1469	.1761	.2375	.2617
25	.004051	.005810	.01384	.02065	.03700	.06372	.1002	.1415	.1698	.2293	.2529

TABLE A.14 (continued)

PERCENTAGE POINTS OF THE BETA DISTRIBUTION

p=3	.5%	1%	5%	10%	25%	50%	75%	90%	95%	99%	99.5%
q=3	.08283	.1056	.1893	.2466	.3594	.5000	.6406	.7534	.8107	.8943	.9171
4	.06628	.08472	.1532	.2009	.2969	.4214	.5532	.6668	.7287	.8269	.8564
5	.05530	.07080	.1288	.1696	.2531	.3641	.4861	.5962	.6588	.7637	.7970
6	.04749	.06085	.1111	.1469	.2206	.3205	.4332	.5382	.5997	.7068	.7422
7	.04156	.05334	.09775	.1295	.1955	.2862	.3905	.4901	.5497	.6563	.6926
8	.03699	.04752	.08727	.1158	.1756	.2586	.3554	.4496	.5069	.6117	.6482
9	.03333	.04282	.07882	.1048	.1593	.2358	.3261	.4152	.4701	.5723	.6084
10	.03033	.03897	.07187	.09565	.1459	.2167	.3012	.3855	.4381	.5374	.5730
11	.02783	.03577	.06605	.08800	.1345	.2004	.2798	.3598	.4101	.5062	.5410
12	.02570	.03305	.06110	.08147	.1247	.1865	.2612	.3372	.3854	.4783	.5123
13	.02390	.03073	.05685	.07586	.1163	.1743	.2450	.3173	.3634	.4531	.4863
14	.02231	.02870	.05315	.07097	.1090	.1637	.2306	.2996	.3438	.4305	.4628
15	.02092	.02692	.04990	.06667	.1025	.1542	.2178	.2837	.3262	.4099	.4413
16	.01971	.02536	.04703	.06286	.09677	.1458	.2064	.2694	.3103	.3912	.4216
17	.01862	.02396	.04446	.05946	.09163	.1383	.1961	.2565	.2958	.3740	.4037
18	.01764	.02271	.04217	.05642	.08701	.1315	.1867	.2448	.2826	.3583	.3871
19	.01677	.02159	.04010	.05367	.08284	.1253	.1783	.2340	.2706	.3439	.3718
20	.01598	.02057	.03822	.05117	.07904	.1197	.1705	.2242	.2595	.3305	.3577
21	.01526	.01964	.03651	.04890	.07558	.1146	.1634	.2152	.2493	.3181	.3446
22	.01459	.01880	.03495	.04682	.07241	.1099	.1569	.2068	.2398	.3066	.3324
23	.01399	.01802	.03352	.04491	.06950	.1055	.1509	.1991	.2310	.2959	.3210
24	.01343	.01730	.03220	.04316	.06681	.1015	.1453	.1920	.2229	.2859	.3104
25	.01291	.01664	.03098	.04153	.06432	.09781	.1401	.1853	.2153	.2766	.3004

p=4	.5%	1%	5%	10%	25%	50%	75%	90%	95%	99%	99.5%
q=4	.1177	.1423	.2253	.2786	.3788	.5000	.6212	.7214	.7747	.8577	.8823
5	.09985	.1210	.1929	.2397	.3291	.4402	.5555	.6554	.7108	.8018	.8303
6	.08679	.1053	.1687	.2104	.2910	.3931	.5020	.5994	.6551	.7500	.7809
7	.07678	.09320	.1500	.1876	.2608	.3551	.4577	.5517	.6066	.7029	.7351
8	.06885	.08368	.1351	.1692	.2364	.3238	.4205	.5108	.5644	.6604	.6934
9	.06238	.07590	.1228	.1542	.2162	.2976	.3888	.4753	.5273	.6222	.6553
10	.05707	.06946	.1127	.1416	.1991	.2753	.3615	.4443	.4947	.5878	.6206
11	.05261	.06403	.1040	.1309	.1846	.2561	.3377	.4170	.4657	.5566	.5891
12	.04877	.05939	.09666	.1218	.1720	.2394	.3169	.3928	.4398	.5285	.5605
13	.04547	.05539	.09026	.1138	.1611	.2247	.2985	.3712	.4166	.5029	.5344
14	.04254	.05188	.08464	.1068	.1514	.2118	.2821	.3519	.3956	.4796	.5104
15	.04004	.04880	.07970	.1006	.1429	.2002	.2674	.3344	.3767	.4583	.4884
16	.03778	.04605	.07529	.09514	.1353	.1899	.2541	.3186	.3594	.4387	.4681
17	.03577	.04361	.07135	.09021	.1284	.1805	.2421	.3042	.3437	.4207	.4495
18	.03394	.04141	.06781	.08577	.1222	.1721	.2312	.2910	.3292	.4041	.4321
19	.03232	.03943	.06460	.08175	.1166	.1644	.2212	.2789	.3159	.3887	.4161
20	.03082	.03763	.06168	.07808	.1115	.1573	.2120	.2678	.3036	.3745	.4011
21	.02948	.03598	.05901	.07473	.1068	.1509	.2036	.2575	.2923	.3612	.3872
22	.02823	.03447	.05656	.07166	.1024	.1449	.1958	.2480	.2817	.3488	.3743
23	.02710	.03308	.05431	.06883	.09845	.1394	.1886	.2392	.2719	.3372	.3621
24	.02603	.03180	.05223	.06622	.09477	.1343	.1819	.2309	.2627	.3264	.3507
25	.02509	.03062	.05031	.06379	.09135	.1296	.1756	.2232	.2542	.3162	.3400

TABLE A.14 (continued)

PERCENTAGE POINTS OF THE BETA DISTRIBUTION

p=5

	.5%	1%	5%	10%	25%	50%	75%	90%	95%	99%	99.5%
q=5	.1460	.1710	.2514	.3010	.3920	.5000	.6080	.6990	.7486	.8290	.8540
6	.1283	.1505	.2224	.2673	.3507	.4517	.5555	.6458	.6965	.7817	.8091
7	.1145	.1344	.1996	.2405	.3173	.4119	.5111	.5995	.6502	.7378	.7668
8	.1034	.1215	.1810	.2187	.2898	.3785	.4731	.5590	.6091	.6976	.7275
9	.09424	.1108	.1657	.2005	.2668	.3502	.4403	.5234	.5726	.6609	.6913
10	.08661	.1019	.1527	.1851	.2471	.3258	.4117	.4920	.5400	.6274	.6580
11	.08008	.09436	.1417	.1720	.2301	.3045	.3865	.4640	.5107	.5969	.6273
12	.07452	.08783	.1321	.1606	.2154	.2859	.3642	.4389	.4844	.5690	.5991
13	.06970	.08215	.1238	.1506	.2024	.2694	.3444	.4164	.4605	.5434	.5732
14	.06543	.07718	.1164	.1418	.1909	.2547	.3265	.3960	.4389	.5199	.5493
15	.06171	.07278	.1099	.1339	.1806	.2415	.3105	.3775	.4191	.4983	.5271
16	.05835	.06885	.1041	.1269	.1714	.2297	.2959	.3607	.4010	.4783	.5066
17	.05533	.06531	.09885	.1206	.1631	.2189	.2826	.3452	.3844	.4598	.4875
18	.05261	.06213	.09411	.1149	.1556	.2091	.2705	.3310	.3691	.4426	.4698
19	.05017	.05925	.08981	.1097	.1487	.2001	.2593	.3180	.3549	.4267	.4534
20	.04791	.05661	.08588	.1050	.1424	.1919	.2491	.3059	.3418	.4118	.4380
21	.04590	.05421	.08229	.1006	.1366	.1843	.2396	.2947	.3296	.3979	.4236
22	.04401	.05200	.07899	.09661	.1313	.1773	.2308	.2842	.3182	.3849	.4099
23	.04230	.04997	.07594	.09292	.1264	.1709	.2226	.2745	.3076	.3727	.3972
24	.04068	.04810	.07311	.08950	.1218	.1648	.2150	.2655	.2977	.3613	.3853
25	.03918	.04636	.07050	.08632	.1175	.1592	.2079	.2570	.2884	.3505	.3740

p=6

	.5%	1%	5%	10%	25%	50%	75%	90%	95%	99%	99.5%
q=6	.1693	.1940	.2712	.3177	.4016	.5000	.5984	.6823	.7288	.8060	.8307
7	.1522	.1746	.2453	.2882	.3663	.4595	.5547	.6377	.6848	.7651	.7915
8	.1383	.1588	.2240	.2637	.3368	.4251	.5167	.5982	.6452	.7271	.7546
9	.1267	.1457	.2061	.2432	.3117	.3954	.4835	.5631	.6096	.6920	.7202
10	.1169	.1346	.1909	.2256	.2902	.3697	.4543	.5317	.5775	.6597	.6882
11	.1086	.1251	.1778	.2104	.2714	.3470	.4283	.5035	.5483	.6299	.6584
12	.1014	.1168	.1664	.1972	.2549	.3270	.4051	.4701	.5219	.6025	.6310
13	.09509	.1096	.1563	.1855	.2404	.3092	.3843	.4550	.4978	.5772	.6055
14	.08948	.1032	.1475	.1751	.2274	.2932	.3655	.4341	.4758	.5538	.5818
15	.08453	.09753	.1396	.1659	.2157	.2788	.3484	.4149	.4556	.5321	.5598
16	.08014	.09247	.1324	.1575	.2052	.2657	.3329	.3973	.4370	.5120	.5393
17	.07611	.08789	.1260	.1500	.1956	.2538	.3187	.3812	.4198	.4933	.5201
18	.07251	.08374	.1202	.1432	.1870	.2430	.3056	.3663	.4039	.4758	.5022
19	.06927	.07999	.1149	.1369	.1790	.2330	.2936	.3525	.3891	.4595	.4855
20	.06625	.07654	.1101	.1312	.1717	.2238	.2824	.3397	.3754	.4443	.4697
21	.06351	.07339	.1056	.1260	.1650	.2153	.2721	.3277	.3626	.4300	.4550
22	.06097	.07050	.1015	.1211	.1588	.2074	.2625	.3166	.3506	.4166	.4412
23	.05865	.06781	.09769	.1166	.1530	.2001	.2536	.3062	.3394	.4039	.4280
24	.05649	.06531	.09415	.1125	.1476	.1933	.2452	.2965	.3289	.3920	.4156
25	.05447	.06300	.09087	.1086	.1426	.1869	.2374	.2874	.3190	.3808	.4041

TABLE A.14 (continued)

PERCENTAGE POINTS OF THE BETA DISTRIBUTION

p=7	.5%	1%	5%	10%	25%	50%	75%	90%	95%	99%	99.5%
q=7	.1887	.2129	.2870	.3309	.4090	.5000	.5910	.6691	.7130	.7871	.8113
8	.1724	.1947	.2636	.3046	.3782	.4651	.5535	.6309	.6750	.7512	.7766
9	.1587	.1794	.2437	.2822	.3518	.4348	.5204	.5965	.6404	.7177	.7439
10	.1471	.1664	.2267	.2629	.3289	.4082	.4909	.5654	.6090	.6866	.7133
11	.1371	.1552	.2119	.2461	.3088	.3847	.4646	.5374	.5803	.6577	.6846
12	.1284	.1454	.1990	.2314	.2910	.3637	.4409	.5118	.5540	.6309	.6578
13	.1207	.1368	.1875	.2183	.2752	.3449	.4195	.4886	.5300	.6060	.6329
14	.1139	.1292	.1773	.2067	.2610	.3279	.4000	.4673	.5078	.5829	.6096
15	.1078	.1223	.1682	.1962	.2482	.3126	.3823	.4477	.4874	.5613	.5879
16	.1024	.1162	.1599	.1867	.2366	.2986	.3660	.4297	.4685	.5412	.5674
17	.09741	.1107	.1525	.1782	.2260	.2858	.3511	.4131	.4510	.5225	.5483
18	.09296	.1056	.1457	.1703	.2164	.2741	.3373	.3976	.4347	.5049	.5304
19	.08887	.1010	.1395	.1632	.2075	.2632	.3246	.3833	.4195	.4884	.5135
20	.08514	.09680	.1338	.1566	.1994	.2532	.3128	.3700	.4053	.4729	.4977
21	.08173	.09293	.1285	.1505	.1918	.2440	.3018	.3575	.3921	.4584	.4828
22	.07855	.08936	.1237	.1449	.1848	.2354	.2915	.3459	.3797	.4446	.4687
23	.07562	.08603	.1192	.1397	.1784	.2274	.2819	.3349	.3680	.4317	.4553
24	.07294	.08298	.1150	.1348	.1723	.2199	.2730	.3247	.3570	.4195	.4427
25	.07037	.08011	.1111	.1303	.1666	.2128	.2646	.3150	.3466	.4080	.4308

p=8	.5%	1%	5%	10%	25%	50%	75%	90%	95%	99%	99.5%
q=8	.2052	.2288	.3000	.3415	.4150	.5000	.5850	.6585	.7000	.7712	.7948
9	.1897	.2117	.2786	.3178	.3877	.4694	.5522	.6250	.6666	.7393	.7638
10	.1764	.1971	.2601	.2973	.3638	.4423	.5229	.5945	.6360	.7094	.7344
11	.1649	.1844	.2440	.2792	.3427	.4182	.4964	.5667	.6078	.6814	.7068
12	.1549	.1733	.2297	.2633	.3239	.3966	.4725	.5413	.5819	.6553	.6809
13	.1460	.1634	.2171	.2491	.3071	.3771	.4507	.5180	.5580	.6309	.6566
14	.1381	.1547	.2057	.2363	.2920	.3594	.4308	.4966	.5359	.6082	.6338
15	.1310	.1468	.1956	.2248	.2783	.3433	.4126	.4768	.5155	.5869	.6123
16	.1246	.1396	.1863	.2144	.2658	.3286	.3959	.4586	.4964	.5669	.5922
17	.1188	.1332	.1780	.2049	.2544	.3151	.3804	.4416	.4787	.5482	.5731
18	.1135	.1273	.1703	.1962	.2440	.3027	.3661	.4258	.4622	.5306	.5553
19	.1086	.1219	.1633	.1883	.2344	.2912	.3528	.4111	.4468	.5140	.5385
20	.1042	.1170	.1568	.1809	.2255	.2806	.3405	.3974	.4323	.4984	.5226
21	.1002	.1125	.1508	.1741	.2172	.2707	.3290	.3845	.4187	.4838	.5076
22	.09637	.1083	.1453	.1678	.2096	.2614	.3182	.3725	.4060	.4698	.4934
23	.09290	.1044	.1402	.1620	.2024	.2528	.3081	.3611	.3940	.4567	.4799
24	.08966	.1007	.1354	.1565	.1958	.2447	.2986	.3505	.3826	.4443	.4670
25	.08661	.09735	.1309	.1514	.1895	.2372	.2897	.3404	.3719	.4325	.4550

TABLE A.14 (continued)

PERCENTAGE POINTS OF THE BETA DISTRIBUTION

p = 9

	.5%	1%	5%	10%	25%	50%	75%	90%	95%	99%	99.5%
q = 9	.2192	.2422	.3108	.3504	.4199	.5000	.5801	.6496	.6892	.7578	.7808
10	.2047	.2263	.2912	.3288	.3954	.4727	.5510	.6198	.6594	.7290	.7526
11	.1919	.2123	.2739	.3098	.3736	.4483	.5246	.5925	.6319	.7020	.7261
12	.1807	.2001	.2587	.2929	.3541	.4263	.5006	.5673	.6064	.6766	.7009
13	.1707	.1891	.2450	.2778	.3366	.4063	.4787	.5442	.5828	.6528	.6772
14	.1617	.1793	.2327	.2642	.3207	.3881	.4585	.5228	.5609	.6304	.6549
15	.1537	.1705	.2216	.2518	.3062	.3715	.4400	.5029	.5405	.6094	.6338
16	.1465	.1625	.2116	.2406	.2931	.3562	.4229	.4845	.5214	.5897	.6140
17	.1399	.1553	.2024	.2303	.2810	.3422	.4071	.4673	.5036	.5710	.5952
18	.1339	.1487	.1940	.2209	.2698	.3292	.3924	.4513	.4870	.5535	.5775
19	.1283	.1426	.1862	.2122	.2596	.3171	.3787	.4364	.4714	.5370	.5608
20	.1232	.1370	.1791	.2042	.2500	.3059	.3660	.4224	.4567	.5214	.5449
21	.1185	.1318	.1725	.1968	.2412	.2955	.3540	.4092	.4429	.5067	.5299
22	.1142	.1270	.1663	.1899	.2329	.2858	.3428	.3968	.4299	.4927	.5156
23	.1102	.1225	.1606	.1834	.2253	.2766	.3323	.3852	.4177	.4794	.5021
24	.1064	.1184	.1553	.1774	.2181	.2681	.3224	.3742	.4061	.4668	.4891
25	.1029	.1145	.1503	.1718	.2113	.2600	.3131	.3638	.3951	.4548	.4769

p = 10

	.5%	1%	5%	10%	25%	50%	75%	90%	95%	99%	99.5%
q = 10	.2316	.2540	.3201	.3579	.4241	.5000	.5759	.6421	.6799	.7460	.7684
11	.2178	.2390	.3020	.3382	.4018	.4754	.5498	.6152	.6531	.7199	.7428
12	.2054	.2256	.2858	.3205	.3818	.4531	.5258	.5905	.6281	.6953	.7185
13	.1946	.2138	.2713	.3046	.3637	.4329	.5039	.5675	.6048	.6721	.6954
14	.1848	.2031	.2582	.2903	.3472	.4143	.4836	.5462	.5832	.6501	.6737
15	.1759	.1935	.2464	.2772	.3322	.3973	.4649	.5264	.5629	.6295	.6531
16	.1678	.1848	.2356	.2653	.3184	.3816	.4476	.5079	.5439	.6100	.6335
17	.1605	.1768	.2257	.2544	.3058	.3671	.4315	.4907	.5262	.5916	.6150
18	.1538	.1694	.2166	.2443	.2941	.3537	.4165	.4746	.5095	.5742	.5974
19	.1477	.1627	.2082	.2350	.2833	.3412	.4025	.4594	.4938	.5578	.5808
20	.1420	.1565	.2005	.2264	.2732	.3296	.3895	.4452	.4790	.5422	.5651
21	.1367	.1500	.1933	.2104	.2638	.3187	.3772	.4319	.4651	.5275	.5500
22	.1318	.1454	.1866	.2110	.2551	.3086	.3657	.4193	.4519	.5134	.5358
23	.1273	.1404	.1804	.2040	.2469	.2990	.3548	.4074	.4395	.5001	.5222
24	.1230	.1358	.1746	.1975	.2393	.2900	.3446	.3961	.4276	.4874	.5093
25	.1191	.1315	.1691	.1914	.2321	.2816	.3350	.3855	.4164	.4753	.4969

TABLE A.14 (continued)

PERCENTAGE POINTS OF THE BETA DISTRIBUTION

p=11

	.5%	1%	5%	10%	25%	50%	75%	90%	95%	99%	99.5%
q=11	.2424	.2642	.3281	.3644	.4277	.5000	.5723	.6356	.6719	.7358	.7576
12	.2294	.2501	.3113	.3462	.4073	.4776	.5486	.6112	.6475	.7119	.7340
13	.2175	.2374	.2961	.3297	.3887	.4572	.5267	.5885	.6246	.6892	.7117
14	.2070	.2260	.2823	.3148	.3718	.4384	.5064	.5674	.6032	.6678	.6904
15	.1974	.2156	.2699	.3011	.3564	.4211	.4877	.5477	.5832	.6476	.6702
16	.1887	.2062	.2584	.2886	.3421	.4051	.4702	.5293	.5643	.6284	.6510
17	.1807	.1976	.2479	.2771	.3290	.3903	.4539	.5120	.5466	.6102	.6328
18	.1733	.1896	.2383	.2665	.3169	.3765	.4388	.4958	.5300	.5930	.6155
19	.1666	.1823	.2293	.2567	.3056	.3637	.4246	.4806	.5143	.5767	.5991
20	.1603	.1755	.2211	.2476	.2951	.3517	.4112	.4663	.4994	.5612	.5834
21	.1545	.1693	.2134	.2391	.2853	.3405	.3987	.4528	.4854	.5464	.5685
22	.1492	.1634	.2062	.2312	.2761	.3299	.3869	.4400	.4721	.5325	.5543
23	.1442	.1580	.1995	.2238	.2675	.3200	.3758	.4279	.4595	.5191	.5408
24	.1395	.1529	.1932	.2168	.2594	.3107	.3653	.4165	.4476	.5064	.5278
25	.1351	.1481	.1873	.2103	.2518	.3019	.3554	.4056	.4363	.4943	.5155

p=12

	.5%	1%	5%	10%	25%	50%	75%	90%	95%	99%	99.5%
q=12	.2521	.2733	.3351	.3701	.4308	.5000	.5692	.6299	.6649	.7267	.7479
13	.2396	.2599	.3194	.3532	.4120	.4795	.5475	.6076	.6424	.7047	.7262
14	.2284	.2479	.3051	.3377	.3947	.4605	.5273	.5867	.6214	.6837	.7054
15	.2181	.2369	.2921	.3236	.3789	.4431	.5085	.5671	.6016	.6639	.6857
16	.2087	.2268	.2801	.3106	.3643	.4268	.4910	.5488	.5829	.6450	.6669
17	.2002	.2176	.2691	.2987	.3508	.4118	.4746	.5316	.5654	.6271	.6490
18	.1923	.2091	.2589	.2876	.3383	.3978	.4593	.5154	.5488	.6101	.6320
19	.1851	.2013	.2495	.2773	.3266	.3846	.4450	.5001	.5331	.5939	.6157
20	.1783	.1940	.2408	.2678	.3157	.3724	.4315	.4857	.5182	.5786	.6002
21	.1720	.1873	.2326	.2589	.3055	.3609	.4188	.4721	.5042	.5639	.5854
22	.1662	.1810	.2250	.2505	.2960	.3500	.4068	.4592	.4909	.5499	.5713
23	.1608	.1751	.2179	.2427	.2870	.3398	.3954	.4470	.4782	.5366	.5577
24	.1556	.1696	.2112	.2354	.2786	.3302	.3847	.4354	.4661	.5239	.5449
25	.1509	.1644	.2049	.2285	.2707	.3211	.3746	.4244	.4547	.5117	.5325

p=13

	.5%	1%	5%	10%	25%	50%	75%	90%	95%	99%	99.5%
q=13	.2607	.2814	.3414	.3751	.4335	.5000	.5665	.6249	.6586	.7186	.7393
14	.2489	.2687	.3266	.3593	.4161	.4810	.5464	.6043	.6379	.6982	.7191
15	.2380	.2572	.3131	.3448	.4000	.4634	.5277	.5849	.6184	.6787	.6998
16	.2281	.2466	.3007	.3314	.3851	.4471	.5102	.5667	.6000	.6602	.6814
17	.2191	.2369	.2893	.3191	.3713	.4318	.4938	.5496	.5825	.6426	.6638
18	.2107	.2280	.2787	.3076	.3584	.4176	.4784	.5334	.5661	.6258	.6470
19	.2029	.2197	.2688	.2970	.3464	.4043	.4640	.5182	.5504	.6098	.6310
20	.1957	.2119	.2597	.2870	.3352	.3918	.4503	.5037	.5356	.5945	.6156
21	.1890	.2047	.2511	.2777	.3247	.3800	.4375	.4901	.5216	.5800	.6010
22	.1827	.1980	.2431	.2690	.3149	.3690	.4253	.4771	.5082	.5661	.5869
23	.1769	.1918	.2356	.2608	.3056	.3585	.4138	.4648	.4955	.5528	.5735
24	.1714	.1859	.2285	.2532	.2969	.3486	.4029	.4531	.4834	.5401	.5607
25	.1663	.1803	.2219	.2459	.2886	.3393	.3926	.4420	.4719	.5280	.5483

TABLE A.14 (continued)
PERCENTAGE POINTS OF THE BETA DISTRIBUTION

p=14

	.5%	1%	5%	10%	25%	50%	75%	90%	95%	99%	99.5%
q=14	.2686	.2887	.3470	.3796	.4360	.5000	.5640	.6204	.6530	.7113	.7314
15	.2572	.2767	.3331	.3648	.4197	.4824	.5454	.6013	.6338	.6923	.7126
16	.2468	.2657	.3203	.3511	.4046	.4659	.5280	.5832	.6156	.6741	.6946
17	.2373	.2555	.3085	.3384	.3905	.4506	.5116	.5662	.5984	.6567	.6772
18	.2285	.2461	.2975	.3266	.3774	.4362	.4962	.5501	.5820	.6402	.6608
19	.2203	.2374	.2873	.3156	.3652	.4227	.4817	.5349	.5665	.6244	.6450
20	.2126	.2292	.2778	.3053	.3537	.4100	.4679	.5205	.5518	.6093	.6299
21	.2056	.2217	.2688	.2957	.3430	.3981	.4550	.5068	.5378	.5949	.6154
22	.1989	.2146	.2605	.2867	.3328	.3868	.4427	.4938	.5244	.5811	.6014
23	.1927	.2079	.2527	.2782	.3233	.3762	.4311	.4815	.5117	.5679	.5881
24	.1869	.2017	.2453	.2702	.3143	.3661	.4201	.4697	.4995	.5552	.5753
25	.1814	.1958	.2383	.2627	.3058	.3565	.4096	.4585	.4880	.5431	.5631

p=15

	.5%	1%	5%	10%	25%	50%	75%	90%	95%	99%	99.5%
q=15	.2756	.2953	.3520	.3837	.4382	.5000	.5618	.6163	.6480	.7047	.7244
16	.2649	.2839	.3389	.3697	.4229	.4835	.5445	.5985	.6301	.6868	.7067
17	.2549	.2733	.3267	.3567	.4087	.4681	.5281	.5816	.6130	.6698	.6898
18	.2456	.2635	.3154	.3447	.3954	.4536	.5127	.5657	.5968	.6535	.6735
19	.2371	.2545	.3049	.3334	.3829	.4400	.4982	.5505	.5814	.6379	.6580
20	.2291	.2460	.2951	.3228	.3712	.4272	.4844	.5361	.5668	.6230	.6429
21	.2216	.2380	.2858	.3129	.3602	.4151	.4714	.5225	.5528	.6087	.6287
22	.2146	.2306	.2772	.3036	.3499	.4037	.4591	.5095	.5395	.5950	.6149
23	.2081	.2236	.2691	.2949	.3401	.3929	.4474	.4971	.5268	.5819	.6017
24	.2019	.2171	.2614	.2866	.3309	.3826	.4362	.4853	.5147	.5693	.5890
25	.1961	.2109	.2541	.2788	.3221	.3729	.4256	.4740	.5031	.5573	.5768

p=16

	.5%	1%	5%	10%	25%	50%	75%	90%	95%	99%	99.5%
q=16	.2821	.3014	.3566	.3873	.4401	.5000	.5599	.6127	.6434	.6986	.7179
17	.2719	.2905	.3441	.3741	.4258	.4845	.5436	.5960	.6266	.6819	.7013
18	.2622	.2803	.3326	.3618	.4123	.4700	.5282	.5801	.6106	.6658	.6853
19	.2533	.2709	.3218	.3503	.3997	.4563	.5137	.5651	.5953	.6505	.6699
20	.2450	.2621	.3117	.3395	.3878	.4434	.4999	.5508	.5808	.6357	.6553
21	.2372	.2538	.3022	.3294	.3767	.4312	.4869	.5371	.5669	.6216	.6411
22	.2299	.2461	.2932	.3198	.3661	.4197	.4745	.5241	.5536	.6080	.6274
23	.2230	.2388	.2848	.3108	.3562	.4087	.4627	.5117	.5410	.5950	.6144
24	.2166	.2320	.2769	.3023	.3467	.3983	.4515	.4999	.5289	.5825	.6018
25	.2104	.2255	.2694	.2943	.3378	.3884	.4408	.4886	.5172	.5705	.5897

TABLE A.14 (continued)

PERCENTAGE POINTS OF THE BETA DISTRIBUTION

p=17	.5%	1%	5%	10%	25%	50%	75%	90%	95%	99%	99.5%
q=17	.2881	.3069	.3607	.3906	.4419	.5000	.5581	.6094	.6393	.6931	.7119
18	.2782	.2965	.3489	.3781	.4284	.4854	.5428	.5937	.6234	.6773	.6962
19	.2689	.2867	.3379	.3664	.4156	.4717	.5283	.5787	.6083	.6622	.6812
20	.2603	.2776	.3275	.3554	.4036	.4587	.5145	.5645	.5939	.6476	.6666
21	.2523	.2692	.3178	.3451	.3923	.4464	.5015	.5509	.5801	.6336	.6526
22	.2446	.2611	.3087	.3353	.3816	.4348	.4890	.5379	.5669	.6202	.6392
23	.2375	.2536	.3000	.3261	.3714	.4237	.4772	.5256	.5543	.6073	.6262
24	.2308	.2465	.2918	.3174	.3618	.4132	.4659	.5137	.5422	.5949	.6138
25	.2244	.2397	.2841	.3091	.3527	.4032	.4552	.5024	.5306	.5829	.6017

p=18	.5%	1%	5%	10%	25%	50%	75%	90%	95%	99%	99.5%
q=18	.2936	.3120	.3646	.3937	.4436	.5000	.5564	.6063	.6354	.6880	.7064
19	.2841	.3020	.3533	.3818	.4307	.4862	.5420	.5915	.6205	.6731	.6915
20	.2751	.2927	.3428	.3706	.4186	.4732	.5283	.5773	.6062	.6587	.6772
21	.2668	.2839	.3328	.3601	.4072	.4609	.5152	.5638	.5925	.6449	.6635
22	.2590	.2756	.3235	.3502	.3963	.4492	.5028	.5509	.5794	.6316	.6501
23	.2516	.2679	.3146	.3408	.3861	.4380	.4909	.5386	.5669	.6188	.6373
24	.2446	.2605	.3062	.3319	.3763	.4274	.4796	.5268	.5548	.6065	.6250
25	.2380	.2535	.2983	.3234	.3670	.4173	.4688	.5154	.5433	.5947	.6131

p=19	.5%	1%	5%	10%	25%	50%	75%	90%	95%	99%	99.5%
q=19	.2987	.3167	.3681	.3965	.4451	.5000	.5549	.6035	.6319	.6833	.7013
20	.2896	.3071	.3574	.3852	.4329	.4870	.5412	.5895	.6178	.6691	.6873
21	.2809	.2982	.3472	.3745	.4213	.4746	.5282	.5760	.6042	.6555	.6736
22	.2728	.2897	.3377	.3644	.4104	.4628	.5158	.5632	.5912	.6423	.6605
23	.2653	.2817	.3287	.3549	.4000	.4516	.5039	.5509	.5787	.6297	.6478
24	.2581	.2741	.3201	.3458	.3901	.4410	.4926	.5391	.5667	.6175	.6356
25	.2512	.2669	.3120	.3372	.3808	.4308	.4818	.5278	.5552	.6057	.6238

p=20	.5%	1%	5%	10%	25%	50%	75%	90%	95%	99%	99.5%
q=20	.3034	.3211	.3714	.3991	.4465	.5000	.5535	.6009	.6286	.6789	.6966
21	.2946	.3119	.3611	.3883	.4349	.4876	.5405	.5876	.6152	.6654	.6832
22	.2863	.3032	.3514	.3781	.4238	.4758	.5281	.5748	.6023	.6525	.6702
23	.2785	.2950	.3422	.3684	.4134	.4646	.5163	.5626	.5899	.6399	.6577
24	.2711	.2873	.3335	.3592	.4034	.4538	.5050	.5508	.5780	.6278	.6456
25	.2640	.2799	.3252	.3504	.3939	.4436	.4941	.5396	.5665	.6161	.6339

TABLE A.14 (continued)

PERCENTAGE POINTS OF THE BETA DISTRIBUTION

p=21

	.5%	1%	5%	10%	25%	50%	75%	90%	95%	99%	99.5%
q=21	.3079	.3252	.3744	.4015	.4478	.5000	.5522	.5985	.6256	.6748	.6921
22	.2993	.3163	.3645	.3912	.4367	.4882	.5399	.5858	.6128	.6620	.6794
23	.2913	.3080	.3552	.3814	.4261	.4769	.5280	.5736	.6005	.6496	.6670
24	.2837	.3000	.3464	.3720	.4161	.4662	.5167	.5620	.5887	.6376	.6550
25	.2766	.2925	.3380	.3632	.4065	.4559	.5059	.5507	.5773	.6260	.6434

p=22

	.5%	1%	5%	10%	25%	50%	75%	90%	95%	99%	99.5%
q=22	.3120	.3290	.3772	.4038	.4490	.5000	.5510	.5962	.6228	.6710	.6880
23	.3038	.3205	.3678	.3939	.4384	.4887	.5392	.5841	.6106	.6588	.6758
24	.2960	.3124	.3588	.3844	.4283	.4779	.5279	.5725	.5988	.6469	.6640
25	.2886	.3047	.3503	.3754	.4186	.4676	.5171	.5613	.5875	.6354	.6525

p=23

	.5%	1%	5%	10%	25%	50%	75%	90%	95%	99%	99.5%
q=23	.3158	.3326	.3799	.4059	.4501	.5000	.5499	.5941	.6201	.6674	.6842
24	.3079	.3243	.3708	.3963	.4400	.4892	.5386	.5826	.6085	.6557	.6725
25	.3004	.3165	.3621	.3873	.4302	.4789	.5278	.5714	.5972	.6443	.6611

p=24

	.5%	1%	5%	10%	25%	50%	75%	90%	95%	99%	99.5%
q=24	.3195	.3359	.3824	.4078	.4512	.5000	.5488	.5922	.6176	.6641	.6805
25	.3118	.3280	.3736	.3987	.4414	.4897	.5380	.5811	.6065	.6528	.6693

p=25

	.5%	1%	5%	10%	25%	50%	75%	90%	95%	99%	99.5%
q=25	.3229	.3391	.3847	.4097	.4522	.5000	.5478	.5903	.6153	.6609	.6771

TABLE A.15

TABLES OF THE HIGHEST DENSITY REGIONS (50%, 75%, 90%, 95%, 99%) FOR BETA DISTRIBUTIONS WITH INDICES $p,q = 4(1)\ 25,\ p \leq q$

To find an HDR for β (p,q) distribution, $p > q$, we find the corresponding interval for a β(q,p) distribution and then reverse the endpoints after subtracting them from 1. For example, to find the 75% HDR for β (18,7) distribution, we first find that the 75% interval for a β (7,18) distribution is (.2040, .3237). Then reversing the endpoints and subtracting them from 1, we get (1 - .3237, 1 - .2040) = (.6763, .7960) which is the desired interval.

p=4

q =	50%		75%		90%		95%		99%	
4	.3788	.6212	.2992	.7008	.2253	.7747	.1840	.8160	.1177	.8823
5	.3181	.5441	.2477	.6236	.1839	.7008	.1488	.7459	.09338	.8227
6	.2740	.4839	.2111	.5612	.1549	.6388	.1245	.6854	.07692	.7679
7	.2406	.4356	.1838	.5100	.1337	.5863	.1068	.6332	.06517	.7185
8	.2144	.3961	.1627	.4673	.1175	.5416	.09337	.5880	.05644	.6740
9	.1934	.3632	.1459	.4311	.1047	.5030	.08288	.5485	.04968	.6344
10	.1760	.3353	.1322	.4001	.09440	.4695	.07448	.5138	.04433	.5987
11	.1616	.3114	.1208	.3732	.08591	.4400	.06759	.4832	.03998	.5667
12	.1493	.2906	.1112	.3497	.07881	.4141	.06185	.4559	.03640	.5376
13	.1387	.2725	.1030	.3290	.07278	.3909	.05700	.4315	.03341	.5113
14	.1295	.2565	.09598	.3106	.06760	.3703	.05285	.4095	.03085	.4874
15	.1215	.2422	.08982	.2941	.06310	.3516	.04925	.3897	.02865	.4655
16	.1144	.2295	.08440	.2793	.05916	.3348	.04611	.3716	.02675	.4455
17	.1081	.2180	.07959	.2659	.05568	.3194	.04334	.3551	.02507	.4271
18	.1024	.2077	.07530	.2537	.05258	.3055	.04088	.3401	.02359	.4101
19	.09736	.1982	.07144	.2426	.04981	.2926	.03868	.3262	.02226	.3944
20	.09274	.1896	.06796	.2324	.04731	.2809	.03671	.3134	.02109	.3799
21	.08855	.1817	.06480	.2231	.04505	.2700	.03492	.3016	.02003	.3663
22	.08471	.1745	.06193	.2145	.04300	.2599	.03330	.2906	.01907	.3537
23	.08120	.1678	.05929	.2065	.04112	.2505	.03182	.2804	.01819	.3419
24	.07796	.1616	.05687	.1991	.03940	.2418	.03047	.2709	.01740	.3308
25	.07497	.1558	.05464	.1921	.03782	.2337	.02923	.2620	.01666	.3205

p=5

q =	50%		75%		90%		95%		99%	
5	.3920	.6080	.3199	.6801	.2514	.7486	.2120	.7880	.1460	.8540
6	.3437	.5483	.2780	.6199	.2165	.6901	.1816	.7316	.1237	.8039
7	.3060	.4992	.2457	.5691	.1899	.6393	.1586	.6818	.1071	.7577
8	.2758	.4581	.2201	.5259	.1691	.5951	.1407	.6377	.09424	.7156
9	.2509	.4232	.1993	.4886	.1524	.5564	.1263	.5987	.08408	.6773
10	.2302	.3932	.1821	.4563	.1386	.5223	.1146	.5640	.07586	.6424
11	.2126	.3672	.1676	.4279	.1271	.4921	.1048	.5329	.06908	.6107
12	.1976	.3444	.1552	.4028	.1173	.4650	.09657	.5049	.06338	.5817
13	.1845	.3243	.1445	.3804	.1090	.4408	.08952	.4797	.05853	.5553
14	.1730	.3063	.1352	.3604	.1017	.4189	.08341	.4568	.05438	.5310
15	.1629	.2903	.1270	.3424	.09531	.3991	.07808	.4360	.05075	.5087
16	.1539	.2758	.1198	.3261	.08970	.3810	.07338	.4170	.04759	.4880
17	.1458	.2628	.1133	.3113	.08469	.3645	.06921	.3995	.04479	.4690
18	.1385	.2509	.1075	.2978	.08022	.3494	.06549	.3834	.04229	.4514
19	.1320	.2400	.1022	.2853	.07619	.3354	.06214	.3686	.04006	.4350
20	.1260	.2300	.09746	.2739	.07255	.3225	.05912	.3548	.03805	.4197
21	.1205	.2209	.09313	.2634	.06924	.3106	.05638	.3420	.03622	.4055
22	.1155	.2124	.08916	.2536	.06621	.2995	.05388	.3301	.03456	.3921
23	.1109	.2046	.08551	.2445	.06344	.2892	.05159	.3190	.03305	.3796
24	.1066	.1973	.08215	.2361	.06089	.2796	.04949	.3086	.03167	.3679
25	.1027	.1905	.07905	.2282	.05854	.2705	.04755	.2989	.03039	.3569

TABLE A.15 (continued)

TABLES OF HIGHEST DENSITY REGIONS FOR THE BETA DISTRIBUTION

p=6	50%		75%		90%		95%		99%	
q=										
6	.4016	.5984	.3353	.6647	.2712	.7288	.2338	.7662	.1693	.8307
7	.3615	.5498	.2999	.6154	.2411	.6803	.2070	.7191	.1488	.7877
8	.3287	.5083	.2712	.5727	.2169	.6374	.1856	.6768	.1326	.7480
9	.3014	.4726	.2475	.5354	.1971	.5993	.1682	.6388	.1195	.7112
10	.2783	.4416	.2277	.5025	.1806	.5654	.1537	.6045	.1087	.6775
11	.2584	.4144	.2107	.4734	.1666	.5349	.1415	.5736	.09970	.6464
12	.2412	.3903	.1961	.4474	.1546	.5075	.1311	.5455	.09201	.6179
13	.2262	.3688	.1834	.4242	.1442	.4827	.1221	.5200	.08542	.5917
14	.2129	.3496	.1723	.4031	.1351	.4602	.1142	.4967	.07972	.5674
15	.2011	.3323	.1624	.3841	.1271	.4396	.1073	.4754	.07470	.5449
16	.1905	.3166	.1536	.3668	.1200	.4208	.1012	.4557	.07027	.5242
17	.1810	.3023	.1457	.3509	.1136	.4035	.09573	.4376	.06635	.5048
18	.1724	.2893	.1385	.3364	.1079	.3875	.09082	.4209	.06282	.4868
19	.1645	.2773	.1320	.3230	.1027	.3728	.08638	.4054	.05968	.4699
20	.1574	.2663	.1261	.3106	.09800	.3591	.08236	.3909	.05680	.4543
21	.1508	.2561	.1208	.2992	.09370	.3464	.07869	.3775	.05421	.4395
22	.1448	.2467	.1158	.2885	.08977	.3345	.07534	.3649	.05183	.4257
23	.1392	.2379	.1112	.2786	.08615	.3235	.07226	.3531	.04965	.4127
24	.1341	.2297	.1070	.2694	.08281	.3131	.06941	.3421	.04764	.4005
25	.1293	.2221	.1031	.2607	.07972	.3034	.06678	.3317	.04580	.3889

p=7	50%		75%		90%		95%		99%	
q=										
7	.4090	.5910	.3473	.6527	.2870	.7130	.2513	.7487	.1887	.8113
8	.3747	.5499	.3166	.6110	.2604	.6717	.2274	.7082	.1698	.7738
9	.3458	.5141	.2909	.5741	.2383	.6346	.2075	.6715	.1542	.7388
10	.3210	.4827	.2691	.5414	.2197	.6012	.1909	.6381	.1413	.7063
11	.2995	.4548	.2503	.5120	.2037	.5710	.1767	.6076	.1303	.6762
12	.2807	.4300	.2340	.4857	.1899	.5435	.1644	.5798	.1209	.6483
13	.2642	.4077	.2196	.4619	.1778	.5105	.1538	.5543	.1127	.6224
14	.2494	.3876	.2070	.4402	.1672	.4957	.1444	.5309	.1055	.5984
15	.2363	.3694	.1957	.4205	.1578	.4747	.1361	.5093	.09928	.5760
16	.2244	.3528	.1855	.4025	.1493	.4554	.1287	.4894	.09368	.5552
17	.2137	.3376	.1764	.3860	.1418	.4376	.1220	.4709	.08867	.5358
18	.2040	.3237	.1681	.3707	.1349	.4211	.1160	.4537	.08418	.5176
19	.1951	.3109	.1606	.3566	.1287	.4058	.1106	.4377	.08012	.5005
20	.1870	.2990	.1537	.3435	.1230	.3916	.1056	.4228	.07644	.4845
21	.1795	.2880	.1474	.3314	.1179	.3783	.1011	.4089	.07305	.4696
22	.1726	.2778	.1415	.3200	.1131	.3659	.09696	.3958	.06998	.4554
23	.1662	.2683	.1362	.3094	.1087	.3542	.09314	.3836	.06713	.4421
24	.1602	.2595	.1312	.2995	.1046	.3433	.08960	.3720	.06451	.4295
25	.1547	.2511	.1265	.2902	.1008	.3330	.08632	.3612	.06208	.4176

TABLE A.15 (continued)

TABLES OF HIGHEST DENSITY REGIONS FOR THE BETA DISTRIBUTION

p=8 q=	50%		75%		90%		95%		99%	
8	.4150	.5850	.3570	.6430	.3000	.7000	.2659	.7341	.2051	.7949
9	.3850	.5495	.3299	.6069	.2762	.6641	.2442	.6988	.1876	.7616
10	.3591	.5181	.3067	.5745	.2558	.6315	.2258	.6664	.1728	.7304
11	.3365	.4899	.2865	.5453	.2383	.6017	.2099	.6366	.1601	.7013
12	.3165	.4647	.2688	.5188	.2230	.5745	.1961	.6092	.1492	.6741
13	.2988	.4419	.2532	.4948	.2096	.5496	.1841	.5839	.1396	.6488
14	.2830	.4212	.2393	.4728	.1977	.5266	.1734	.5606	.1312	.6251
15	.2687	.4024	.2268	.4527	.1870	.5055	.1639	.5389	.1238	.6030
16	.2559	.3852	.2156	.4342	.1775	.4859	.1554	.5189	.1171	.5823
17	.2442	.3694	.2054	.4172	.1689	.4678	.1477	.5002	.1111	.5629
18	.2335	.3548	.1962	.4014	.1610	.4510	.1407	.4828	.1057	.5447
19	.2237	.3413	.1877	.3868	.1539	.4353	.1344	.4665	.1008	.5276
20	.2147	.3288	.1800	.3732	.1474	.4206	.1286	.4513	.09636	.5114
21	.2064	.3172	.1728	.3605	.1414	.4069	.1233	.4370	.09224	.4963
22	.1988	.3064	.1662	.3486	.1358	.3941	.1184	.4236	.08849	.4819
23	.1916	.2963	.1601	.3375	.1307	.3820	.1138	.4110	.08502	.4684
24	.1850	.2868	.1544	.3271	.1260	.3706	.1097	.3991	.08180	.4556
25	.1788	.2779	.1492	.3173	.1216	.3599	.1058	.3878	.07883	.4434

p=9 q=	50%		75%		90%		95%		99%	
9	.4199	.5801	.3651	.6349	.3108	.6892	.2781	.7219	.2193	.7807
10	.3933	.5489	.3408	.6031	.2893	.6574	.2583	.6905	.2030	.7509
11	.3698	.5208	.3196	.5742	.2705	.6282	.2412	.6615	.1889	.7228
12	.3490	.4954	.3009	.5479	.2540	.6014	.2261	.6346	.1766	.6964
13	.3305	.4723	.2842	.5238	.2394	.5767	.2129	.6097	.1659	.6717
14	.3138	.4513	.2693	.5017	.2265	.5539	.2011	.5866	.1564	.6484
15	.2987	.4321	.2559	.4814	.2148	.5327	.1905	.5651	.1478	.6267
16	.2850	.4144	.2438	.4627	.2043	.5131	.1810	.5450	.1402	.6062
17	.2725	.3981	.2328	.4453	.1948	.4948	.1724	.5263	.1333	.5869
18	.2611	.3830	.2227	.4292	.1861	.4778	.1646	.5088	.1271	.5688
19	.2505	.3691	.2135	.4141	.1781	.4618	.1575	.4924	.1214	.5517
20	.2408	.3561	.2049	.4001	.1708	.4469	.1509	.4769	.1162	.5355
21	.2319	.3440	.1971	.3870	.1641	.4329	.1449	.4624	.1114	.5203
22	.2235	.3327	.1898	.3748	.1579	.4197	.1393	.4488	.1070	.5058
23	.2158	.3221	.1831	.3632	.1522	.4073	.1342	.4359	.1030	.4921
24	.2085	.3121	.1768	.3524	.1468	.3956	.1294	.4237	.09922	.4791
25	.2018	.3028	.1709	.3422	.1418	.3846	.1249	.4122	.09570	.4668

TABLE A.15 (continued)

TABLES OF HIGHEST DENSITY REGIONS FOR THE BETA DISTRIBUTION

p=10

q=	50%		75%		90%		95%		99%	
10	.4241	.5759	.3720	.6280	.3201	.6799	.2886	.7114	.2316	.7684
11	.4001	.5480	.3500	.5996	.3004	.6514	.2704	.6831	.2164	.7413
12	.3787	.5227	.3305	.5736	.2830	.6251	.2544	.6569	.2030	.7157
13	.3595	.4996	.3130	.5496	.2675	.6007	.2401	.6324	.1912	.6917
14	.3421	.4784	.2973	.5276	.2536	.5781	.2274	.6096	.1807	.6690
15	.3264	.4589	.2832	.5072	.2411	.5570	.2160	.5883	.1712	.6476
16	.3120	.4409	.2703	.4883	.2297	.5374	.2056	.5684	.1628	.6274
17	.2989	.4243	.2585	.4707	.2194	.5191	.1962	.5497	.1551	.6083
18	.2868	.4089	.2477	.4543	.2100	.5019	.1877	.5322	.1481	.5904
19	.2757	.3945	.2378	.4391	.2014	.4859	.1798	.5157	.1417	.5733
20	.2654	.3811	.2287	.4248	.1934	.4708	.1726	.5002	.1358	.5572
21	.2558	.3686	.2202	.4114	.1860	.4566	.1659	.4855	.1304	.5419
22	.2469	.3569	.2123	.3988	.1792	.4432	.1597	.4717	.1254	.5274
23	.2386	.3459	.2050	.3869	.1729	.4305	.1540	.4586	.1208	.5137
24	.2309	.3356	.1982	.3758	.1670	.4186	.1487	.4463	.1165	.5006
25	.2236	.3259	.1918	.3652	.1615	.4073	.1437	.4345	.1125	.4882

p=11

q=	50%		75%		90%		95%		99%	
11	.4277	.5723	.3779	.6221	.3281	.6719	.2978	.7022	.2425	.7575
12	.4059	.5472	.3578	.5965	.3099	.6461	.2809	.6766	.2281	.7328
13	.3862	.5241	.3397	.5727	.2937	.6221	.2659	.6526	.2154	.7094
14	.3683	.5028	.3234	.5508	.2791	.5998	.2524	.6302	.2041	.6872
15	.3521	.4832	.3086	.5304	.2659	.5789	.2402	.6092	.1938	.6663
16	.3372	.4651	.2951	.5115	.2538	.5594	.2291	.5894	.1846	.6464
17	.3235	.4482	.2827	.4938	.2429	.5411	.2190	.5708	.1762	.6276
18	.3109	.4326	.2714	.4773	.2328	.5239	.2098	.5534	.1685	.6098
19	.2993	.4179	.2609	.4619	.2235	.5078	.2013	.5369	.1615	.5929
20	.2885	.4043	.2512	.4474	.2150	.4926	.1935	.5213	.1550	.5769
21	.2784	.3915	.2422	.4337	.2071	.4782	.1862	.5066	.1490	.5616
22	.2690	.3794	.2338	.4209	.1997	.4647	.1795	.4927	.1435	.5471
23	.2603	.3681	.2260	.4088	.1929	.4519	.1733	.4795	.1384	.5334
24	.2521	.3575	.2186	.3974	.1865	.4398	.1674	.4670	.1336	.5202
25	.2443	.3474	.2118	.3866	.1805	.4283	.1620	.4551	.1291	.5077

TABLE A.15 (continued)

TABLES OF HIGHEST DENSITY REGIONS FOR THE BETA DISTRIBUTION

p=12

q=	50%		75%		90%		95%		99%	
12	.4308	.5692	.3830	.6170	.3351	.6649	.3059	.6941	.2521	.7479
13	.4108	.5463	.3645	.5936	.3183	.6413	.2902	.6707	.2386	.7251
14	.3926	.5251	.3477	.5718	.3031	.6193	.2760	.6487	.2265	.7035
15	.3759	.5055	.3324	.5515	.2893	.5986	.2632	.6279	.2156	.6830
16	.3606	.4872	.3184	.5326	.2767	.5793	.2515	.6084	.2057	.6635
17	.3465	.4702	.3055	.5149	.2651	.5611	.2408	.5900	.1966	.6450
18	.3335	.4544	.2937	.4984	.2545	.5439	.2310	.5727	.1884	.6274
19	.3214	.4396	.2827	.4828	.2447	.5278	.2219	.5562	.1808	.6107
20	.3102	.4257	.2725	.4682	.2357	.5126	.2136	.5407	.1737	.5948
21	.2997	.4127	.2630	.4544	.2272	.4982	.2058	.5260	.1672	.5796
22	.2899	.4004	.2542	.4414	.2194	.4845	.1986	.5120	.1612	.5652
23	.2808	.3888	.2460	.4292	.2121	.4716	.1919	.4988	.1556	.5515
24	.2722	.3779	.2382	.4175	.2053	.4594	.1856	.4861	.1504	.5383
25	.2641	.3676	.2310	.4065	.1989	.4477	.1797	.4742	.1455	.5258

p=13

q=	50%		75%		90%		95%		99%	
13	.4335	.5665	.3876	.6124	.3414	.6586	.3131	.6869	.2607	.7393
14	.4151	.5454	.3704	.5909	.3257	.6369	.2983	.6654	.2480	.7182
15	.3981	.5258	.3547	.5708	.3114	.6166	.2850	.6450	.2365	.6981
16	.3825	.5076	.3403	.5520	.2983	.5974	.2728	.6257	.2260	.6790
17	.3681	.4905	.3270	.5344	.2863	.5794	.2615	.6075	.2164	.6608
18	.3547	.4746	.3147	.5178	.2752	.5623	.2512	.5903	.2076	.6435
19	.3423	.4596	.3033	.5022	.2649	.5462	.2417	.5740	.1994	.6270
20	.3307	.4456	.2928	.4875	.2554	.5310	.2329	.5585	.1919	.6112
21	.3199	.4324	.2829	.4736	.2466	.5166	.2247	.5438	.1849	.5962
22	.3097	.4199	.2737	.4605	.2383	.5029	.2170	.5299	.1784	.5819
23	.3002	.4082	.2650	.4481	.2306	.4899	.2099	.5166	.1724	.5682
24	.2913	.3970	.2569	.4363	.2234	.4776	.2032	.5039	.1668	.5550
25	.2828	.3865	.2493	.4251	.2166	.4658	.1969	.4918	.1615	.5425

p=14

q=	50%		75%		90%		95%		99%	
14	.4360	.5640	.3916	.6084	.3470	.6530	.3195	.6805	.2686	.7314
15	.4188	.5446	.3756	.5885	.3323	.6330	.3057	.6605	.2565	.7118
16	.4030	.5263	.3609	.5698	.3188	.6140	.2930	.6415	.2455	.6931
17	.3883	.5093	.3473	.5522	.3063	.5962	.2814	.6236	.2354	.6752
18	.3746	.4933	.3346	.5357	.2949	.5793	.2706	.6065	.2260	.6582
19	.3619	.4783	.3229	.5201	.2842	.5632	.2606	.5903	.2175	.6419
20	.3500	.4642	.3120	.5054	.2743	.5481	.2514	.5750	.2095	.6263
21	.3389	.4508	.3018	.4915	.2651	.5337	.2428	.5603	.2021	.6114
22	.3285	.4382	.2922	.4783	.2564	.5200	.2348	.5464	.1953	.5972
23	.3187	.4263	.2832	.4658	.2483	.5070	.2272	.5331	.1888	.5836
24	.3094	.4150	.2748	.4539	.2408	.4946	.2202	.5204	.1828	.5706
25	.3007	.4043	.2669	.4426	.2336	.4827	.2136	.5083	.1772	.5580

TABLE A.15(continued)

TABLES OF HIGHEST DENSITY REGIONS FOR THE BETA DISTRIBUTION

p=15

q=	50%		75%		90%		95%		99%	
15	.4382	.5618	.3953	.6047	.3520	.6480	.3253	.6747	.2757	.7243
16	.4221	.5437	.3803	.5862	.3382	.6293	.3123	.6560	.2642	.7060
17	.4072	.5267	.3664	.5688	.3254	.6116	.3002	.6383	.2537	.6884
18	.3934	.5107	.3535	.5523	.3136	.5949	.2891	.6215	.2439	.6717
19	.3804	.4957	.3415	.5368	.3026	.5790	.2788	.6054	.2349	.6557
20	.3683	.4815	.3303	.5221	.2923	.5639	.2692	.5902	.2266	.6403
21	.3570	.4681	.3198	.5081	.2828	.5495	.2602	.5756	.2188	.6255
22	.3463	.4554	.3099	.4949	.2738	.5359	.2518	.5618	.2115	.6115
23	.3362	.4433	.3006	.4823	.2654	.5228	.2440	.5485	.2047	.5979
24	.3267	.4319	.2919	.4704	.2575	.5104	.2366	.5359	.1984	.5849
25	.3178	.4211	.2837	.4590	.2501	.4986	.2297	.5238	.1924	.5725

p=16

q=	50%		75%		90%		95%		99%	
16	.4401	.5599	.3986	.6014	.3566	.6434	.3306	.6694	.2821	.7179
17	.4251	.5429	.3845	.5841	.3435	.6260	.3183	.6519	.2712	.7006
18	.4111	.5270	.3714	.5678	.3314	.6094	.3068	.6353	.2611	.6842
19	.3980	.5119	.3591	.5523	.3201	.5936	.2962	.6195	.2518	.6683
20	.3856	.4977	.3476	.5376	.3096	.5786	.2862	.6043	.2430	.6532
21	.3741	.4842	.3369	.5237	.2997	.5643	.2770	.5899	.2349	.6386
22	.3632	.4715	.3268	.5104	.2905	.5507	.2683	.5761	.2273	.6247
23	.3529	.4594	.3173	.4978	.2818	.5377	.2601	.5629	.2202	.6112
24	.3432	.4479	.3083	.4858	.2736	.5253	.2524	.5503	.2135	.5984
25	.3340	.4369	.2998	.4744	.2659	.5134	.2452	.5382	.2072	.5860

p=17

q=	50%		75%		90%		95%		99%	
17	.4419	.5581	.4016	.5984	.3607	.6393	.3354	.6646	.2881	.7119
18	.4278	.5422	.3883	.5822	.3484	.6229	.3237	.6482	.2777	.6957
19	.4145	.5272	.3758	.5668	.3368	.6073	.3128	.6325	.2680	.6801
20	.4021	.5129	.3642	.5522	.3261	.5924	.3026	.6175	.2590	.6652
21	.3903	.4995	.3532	.5383	.3159	.5782	.2930	.6032	.2505	.6508
22	.3793	.4867	.3429	.5250	.3064	.5646	.2841	.5895	.2426	.6370
23	.3688	.4745	.3332	.5124	.2975	.5517	.2757	.5764	.2352	.6237
24	.3589	.4629	.3240	.5004	.2891	.5393	.2677	.5638	.2282	.6109
25	.3496	.4519	.3153	.4889	.2811	.5274	.2602	.5518	.2217	.5987

TABLE A.15 (continued)

TABLES OF HIGHEST DENSITY REGIONS FOR THE BETA DISTRIBUTION

p=18

q=	50%		75%		90%		95%		99%	
18	.4436	.5564	.4044	.5956	.3646	.6354	.3399	.6601	.2936	.7064
19	.4302	.5415	.3918	.5804	.3528	.6200	.3287	.6446	.2836	.6911
20	.4176	.5273	.3799	.5658	.3418	.6052	.3183	.6298	.2743	.6764
21	.4058	.5138	.3688	.5520	.3315	.5911	.3085	.6157	.2656	.6622
22	.3946	.5010	.3583	.5388	.3218	.5777	.2993	.6021	.2574	.6486
23	.3840	.4888	.3484	.5262	.3126	.5648	.2906	.5890	.2497	.6354
24	.3739	.4772	.3390	.5142	.3040	.5524	.2825	.5765	.2425	.6227
25	.3644	.4661	.3301	.5027	.2958	.5406	.2747	.5645	.2357	.6106

p=19

q=	50%		75%		90%		95%		99%	
19	.4451	.5549	.4069	.5931	.3681	.6319	.3440	.6560	.2987	.7013
20	.4324	.5408	.3949	.5787	.3569	.6173	.3333	.6414	.2891	.6868
21	.4205	.5273	.3836	.5649	.3464	.6033	.3233	.6273	.2802	.6728
22	.4091	.5145	.3730	.5518	.3365	.5899	.3139	.6139	.2718	.6593
23	.3984	.5023	.3629	.5392	.3271	.5771	.3051	.6009	.2638	.6463
24	.3882	.4907	.3534	.5272	.3183	.5648	.2967	.5885	.2564	.6338
25	.3786	.4796	.3443	.5157	.3099	.5530	.2888	.5766	.2493	.6217

p=20

q=	50%		75%		90%		95%		99%	
20	.4465	.5535	.4092	.5908	.3714	.6286	.3478	.6522	.3034	.6966
21	.4344	.5401	.3978	.5771	.3607	.6148	.3376	.6383	.2942	.6828
22	.4230	.5273	.3871	.5640	.3506	.6015	.3280	.6250	.2856	.6695
23	.4122	.5151	.3769	.5515	.3411	.5888	.3190	.6122	.2775	.6566
24	.4019	.5035	.3672	.5395	.3321	.5766	.3104	.5998	.2698	.6442
25	.3922	.4923	.3580	.5280	.3235	.5648	.3023	.5880	.2625	.6322

=21

q=	50%		75%		90%		95%		99%	
21	.4478	.5522	.4114	.5886	.3744	.6256	.3513	.6487	.3078	.6922
22	.4363	.5395	.4005	.5756	.3642	.6124	.3416	.6355	.2990	.6790
23	.4254	.5273	.3902	.5631	.3545	.5998	.3324	.6228	.2907	.6663
24	.4150	.5157	.3804	.5512	.3454	.5876	.3236	.6105	.2828	.6541
25	.4052	.5045	.3711	.5397	.3367	.5760	.3154	.5987	.2753	.6422

TABLE A.15 (continued)

TABLES OF HIGHEST DENSITY REGIONS FOR THE BETA DISTRIBUTION

p=22, q=	50%		75%		90%		95%		99%	
22	.4490	.5510	.4135	.5865	.3772	.6228	.3546	.6454	.3120	.6880
23	.4380	.5389	.4030	.5742	.3674	.6102	.3453	.6328	.3035	.6755
24	.4276	.5272	.3931	.5623	.3582	.5982	.3364	.6206	.2954	.6634
25	.4177	.5161	.3837	.5509	.3493	.5865	.3280	.6089	.2878	.6516

p=23, q=	50%		75%		90%		95%		99%	
23	.4501	.5499	.4154	.5846	.3799	.6201	.3577	.6423	.3159	.6841
24	.4396	.5383	.4054	.5728	.3705	.6081	.3487	.6302	.3076	.6722
25	.4296	.5272	.3959	.5615	.3615	.5966	.3402	.6186	.2999	.6605

p=24, q=	50%		75%		90%		95%		99%	
24	.4512	.5488	.4171	.5829	.3824	.6176	.3606	.6394	.3195	.6805
25	.4411	.5377	.4075	.5716	.3733	.6062	.3520	.6278	.3115	.6690

p=25, q=	50%		75%		90%		95%		99%	
25	.4522	.5478	.4188	.5812	.3847	.6153	.3634	.6366	.3229	.6771

TABLE A.16

TABLE OF THE PROBABILITY THAT ONE BETA VARIABLE IS LARGER THAN A SECOND BETA VARIABLE

The values tabled are Prob $(\pi_1 \geq \pi_2)$ where π_i: $\beta(p_i, q_i) i = 1, 2$, $p_1 + q_1 = p_2 + q_2 = N$. For values not tabled, the following relationships may be used:

a) Prob $(\pi_2 \geq \pi_1) = 1 -$ Prob $(\pi_1 \geq \pi_2)$

Example: In finding the probability that a $\beta(6, 10)$ variable is greater than a $\beta(9, 7)$ variable, we note that there is no entry for $P_1 = 6$, $P_2 = 9$, $N = 16$. However, employing the above relationship, we find the value..86385. Subtracting this from 1 (1 - .86385 = .13615), we obtain the desired value.

b) Let π_1 be distributed as $\beta(p_i, q_i)$ $i = 1, 2$

then,

Prob $(\pi_1 \geq \pi_2) =$ Prob $(\pi_2' \geq \pi_1')$

Example: To find the probability that a β (16, 4) variable, we first note that there is no entry for $p_1 = 16$, $p_2 = 14$, $N = 20$. Using the relationship above, we look under $p_1 = 6$, $p_2 = 4$, $N = 20$, and obtain..77648 as the desired value.

TABLE A.16 (continued)

TABLE OF PROB($\pi_2 < \pi_1$)

N= 3

$p_1 \backslash p_2$	1
2	.83333

N= 4

$p_1 \backslash p_2$	1
2	.80000
3	.95000

N= 5

$p_1 \backslash p_2$	1	2
2	.78571	
3	.92857	.75714
4	.98571	

N= 6

$p_1 \backslash p_2$	1	2
2	.77778	
3	.91667	.73810
4	.97619	.89683
5	.99603	

N= 7

$p_1 \backslash p_2$	1	2	3
2	.77273		
3	.90909	.72727	
4	.96970	.87879	.71645
5	.99242	.95996	
6	.99892		

N= 8

$p_1 \backslash p_2$	1	2	3
2	.76923		
3	.90385	.72028	
4	.96503	.86713	.70396
5	.98951	.94872	.85693
6	.99767	.98543	
7	.99971		

N= 9

$p_1 \backslash p_2$	1	2	3	4
2	.76667			
3	.90000	.71538		
4	.96154	.85897	.69580	
5	.98718	.94056	.84266	.69037
6	.99650	.97972	.93403	
7	.99930	.99495		
8	.99992			

N= 10

$p_1 \backslash p_2$	1	2	3	4
2	.76471			
3	.89706	.71176		
4	.95882	.85294	.69005	
5	.98529	.93439	.83258	.68141
6	.99548	.97511	.92328	.82653
7	.99887	.99239	.97166	
8	.99979	.99831		
9	.99998			

N= 11

$p_1 \backslash p_2$	1	2	3	4	5
2	.76316				
3	.89474	.70898			
4	.95666	.84830	.68576		
5	.98375	.92957	.82508	.67504	
6	.99458	.97136	.91510	.81508	.67186
7	.99845	.99012	.96511	.91055	
8	.99964	.99726	.98849		
9	.99994	.99945			
10	.99999				

N= 12

$p_1 \backslash p_2$	1	2	3	4	5
2	.76190				
3	.89286	.70677			
4	.95489	.84461	.68244		
5	.98246	.92570	.81927	.67028	
6	.99381	.96827	.90867	.80650	.66504
7	.99807	.98813	.95975	.90081	.80257
8	.99948	.99624	.98501	.95695	
9	.99989	.99905	.99554		
10	.99998	.99983			
11	1.00000				

TABLE OF PROB($\pi_2 < \pi_1$) (continued)

N= 13

$p_1 \backslash p_2$	1	2	3	4	5	6
2	.76087					
3	.89130	.70497				
4	.95342	.84161	.67980			
5	.98137	.92252	.81465	.66658		
6	.99314	.96568	.90349	.79984	.65991	
7	.99771	.98640	.95531	.89312	.79318	.65786
8	.99933	.99529	.98196	.95023	.88983	
9	.99983	.99862	.99386	.98044		
10	.99997	.99968	.99834			
11	1.00000	.99995				
12	1.00000					

N= 14

$p_1 \backslash p_2$	1	2	3	4		
2	.76000					
3	.89000	.70348				
4	.95217	.83913	.67764			
5	.98043	.91988	.81087	.66362		
6	.99255	.96348	.89922	.79451	.65592	
7	.99739	.98490	.95158	.88690	.78585	.65245
8	.99918	.99442	.97930	.94465	.88113	.78312
9	.99977	.99820	.99229	.97641	.94238	
10	.99995	.99951	.99758	.99153		
11	.99999	.99989	.99940			
12	1.00000	.99998				
13	1.00000					

N= 15

$p_1 \backslash p_2$	1	2	3	4	5	6	7
2	.75926						
3	.88889	.70222					
4	.95111	.83704	.67585				
5	.97963	.91763	.80773	.66119			
6	.99203	.96159	.89565	.79014	.65271		
7	.99710	.98357	.94841	.88177	.77996	.64822	
8	.99903	.99362	.97696	.93994	.87407	.77526	.64680
9	.99971	.99779	.99085	.97288	.93583	.87160	
10	.99992	.99933	.99684	.98935	.97151		
11	.99998	.99983	.99908	.99649			
12	1.00000	.99997	.99979				
13	1.00000	1.00000					
14	1.00000						

N= 16

$p_1 \backslash p_2$	1	2	3	4	5	6	7
2	.75862						
3	.88793	.70115					
4	.95019	.83525	.67433				
5	.97893	.91571	.80508	.65917			
6	.99157	.95996	.89262	.78651	.65007		
7	.99684	.98241	.94568	.87746	.77514	.64481	
8	.99890	.99290	.97491	.93593	.86823	.76893	.64238
9	.99965	.99740	.98953	.96978	.93029	.86385	.76695
10	.99990	.99915	.99611	.98734	.96720	.92844	
11	.99998	.99976	.99875	.99539	.98658		
12	.99999	.99994	.99966	.99859			
13	1.00000	.99999	.99993				
14	1.00000	1.00000					
15	1.00000						

N= 17

$p_1 \backslash p_2$	1	2	3	4	5	6	7	8
2	.75806							
3	.88710	.70022						
4	.94939	.83370	.67303					
5	.97831	.91404	.80281	.65746				
6	.99116	.95853	.89001	.78343	.64787			
7	.99660	.98137	.94331	.87379	.77110	.64201		
8	.99878	.99225	.97310	.93247	.86332	.76373	.63880	
9	.99959	.99704	.98833	.96705	.92556	.85742	.76026	.63778
10	.99988	.99897	.99543	.98550	.96341	.92219	.85551	
11	.99997	.99968	.99841	.99433	.98402	.96220		
12	.99999	.99991	.99952	.99808	.99394			
13	1.00000	.99998	.99988	.99945				
14	1.00000	1.00000	.99998					
15	1.00000	1.00000						
16	1.00000							

N= 18

$p_1 \backslash p_2$	1	2	3	4	5	6	7	8
2	.75758							
3	.88636	.69941						
4	.94868	.83236	.67191					
5	.97776	.91258	.80084	.65599				
6	.99080	.95728	.88775	.78078	.64601			
7	.99638	.98045	.94123	.87063	.76768	.63966		
8	.99866	.99166	.97149	.92946	.85912	.75937	.63586	
9	.99954	.99670	.98725	.96464	.92147	.85200	.75474	.63407
10	.99985	.99880	.99478	.98382	.96007	.91684	.84859	.75325
11	.99996	.99961	.99807	.99332	.98168	.95779	.91532	
12	.99999	.99988	.99937	.99755	.99254	.98096		
13	1.00000	.99997	.99982	.99922	.99737			
14	1.00000	.99999	.99996	.99979				
15	1.00000	1.00000	.99999					
16	1.00000	1.00000						
17	1.00000							

TABLE A.16 (continued)

TABLE OF PROB($\pi_2 < \pi_1$)

N= 19

$p_1 \backslash p_2$	1	2	3	4	5	6	7	8	9
2	.75714								
3	.88571	.69870							
4	.94805	.83117	.67093						
5	.97727	.91129	.79912	.65472					
6	.99047	.95616	.88576	.77849	.64440				
7	.99619	.97962	.93940	.86788	.76474	.63766			
8	.99855	.99112	.97005	.92682	.85551	.75566	.63339		
9	.99948	.99638	.98625	.96248	.91791	.84737	.75010	.63101	
10	.99983	.99864	.99418	.98229	.95710	.91221	.84274	.74746	.63024
11	.99995	.99953	.99774	.99237	.97954	.95389	.90943	.84123	
12	.99999	.99985	.99921	.99703	.99120	.97814	.95283		
13	1.00000	.99996	.99975	.99898	.99665	.99080			
14	1.00000	.99999	.99993	.99969	.99889				
15	1.00000	1.00000	.99999	.99992					
16	1.00000	1.00000	1.00000						
17	1.00000	1.00000							
18	1.00000								

N= 20

$p_1 \backslash p_2$	1	2	3	4	5	6	7	8	9
2	.75676								
3	.88514	.69807							
4	.94749	.83012	.67006						
5	.97683	.91014	.79760	.65360					
6	.99017	.95516	.88401	.77648	.64301				
7	.99601	.97888	.93777	.86547	.76218	.63595			
8	.99845	.99062	.96875	.92449	.85235	.75247	.63129		
9	.99943	.99609	.98535	.96055	.91478	.84336	.74616	.62843	
10	.99980	.99848	.99362	.98090	.95445	.90816	.83773	.74259	.62707
11	.99994	.99945	.99743	.99148	.97759	.95043	.90432	.83501	.74144
12	.99998	.99982	.99905	.99653	.98994	.97557	.94843	.90306	
13	.99999	.99995	.99969	.99873	.99593	.98915	.97489		
14	1.00000	.99999	.99991	.99958	.99854	.99572			
15	1.00000	1.00000	.99998	.99988	.99955				
16	1.00000	1.00000	.99999	.99997					
17	1.00000	1.00000	1.00000						
18	1.00000	1.00000							
19	1.00000								

TABLE A.16 (continued)

TABLE OF PROB($\pi_2 < \pi_1$)

N= 21

$P_1 \backslash P_2$	1	2	3	4	5	6	7	8	9	10
2	.75641									
3	.88462	.69751								
4	.94699	.82918	.66929							
5	.97644	.90912	.79626	.65262						
6	.98990	.95426	.88244	.77471	.64179					
7	.99584	.97820	.93631	.86333	.75994	.63445				
8	.99836	.99017	.96758	.92241	.84958	.74970	.62947			
9	.99939	.99582	.98452	.95882	.91200	.83987.	.74276	.62624		
10	.99978	.99833	.99309	.97963	.95208	.90460	.83339	.73845	.62441	
11	.99993	.99938	.99713	.99065	.97581	.94733	.89986	.82968	.73637	.62381
12	.99998	.99978	.99890	.99604	.98876	.97322	.94452	.89754	.82847	
13	.99999	.99993	.99961	.99847	.99523	.98758	.97192	.94358		
14	1.00000	.99998	.99988	.99947	.99818	.99481	.98718			
15	1.00000	.99999	.99997	.99984	.99938	.99808				
16	1.00000	1.00000	.99999	.99996	.99982					
17	1.00000	1.00000	1.00000	.99999						
18	1.00000	1.00000	1.00000							
19	1.00000	1.00000								
20	1.00000									

N= 22

$P_1 \backslash P_2$	1	2	3	4	5	6	7	8	9	10
2	.75610									
3	.88415	.69700								
4	.94653	.82833	.66860							
5	.97608	.90819	.79505	.65174						
6	.98966	.95345	.88104	.77314	.64071					
7	.99569	.97759	.93499	.86142	.75796	.63314				
8	.99828	.98976	.96652	.92054	.84712	.74726	.62789			
9	.99934	.99557	.98377	.95725	.90953	.83679	.73980	.62434		
10	.99976	.99819	.99261	.97846	.94994	.90145	.82960	.73487	.62213	
11	.99992	.99930	.99685	.98987	.97419	.94455	.89592	.82506	.73205	.62107
12	.99997	.99975	.99875	.99558	.98766	.97108	.94101	.89270	.82285	.73113
13	.99999	.99992	.99954	.99822	.99456	.98611	.96920	.93926	.89164	
14	1.00000	.99997	.99985	.99935	.99782	.99391	.98532	.96857		
15	1.00000	.99999	.99995	.99978	.99921	.99760	.99369			
16	1.00000	1.00000	.99999	.99994	.99975	.99916				
17	1.00000	1.00000	1.00000	.99998	.99993					
18	1.00000	1.00000	1.00000	1.00000						
19	1.00000	1.00000	1.00000							
20	1.00000	1.00000								
21	1.00000									

TABLE A.16 (continued)

TABLE OF PROB $(\pi_2 < \pi_1)$

N= 23

$p_1 \backslash p_2$	1	2	3	4	5	6	7	8	9	10	11
2	.75581										
3	.88372	.69654									
4	.94611	.82757	.66798								
5	.97575	.90736	.79397	.65096							
6	.98943	.95271	.87978	.77172	.63974						
7	.99555	.97703	.93380	.85971	.75620	.63198					
8	.99820	.98938	.96556	.91886	.84492	.74511	.62651				
9	.99930	.99533	.98307	.95583	.90731	.83406	.73720	.62269			
10	.99974	.99805	.99215	.97740	.94800	.89863	.82626	.73175	.62016		
11	.99991	.99923	.99658	.98915	.97269	.94204	.89242	.82101	.72831	.61872	
12	.99997	.99972	.99860	.99514	.98662	.96911	.93787	.88843	.81798	.72665	.61825
13	.99999	.99990	.99947	.99798	.99392	.98473	.96671	.93540	.88647	.81699	
14	1.00000	.99997	.99981	.99922	.99746	.99305	.98357	.96550	.93458		
15	1.00000	.99999	.99994	.99973	.99903	.99712	.99260	.98317			
16	1.00000	1.00000	.99998	.99991	.99967	.99892	.99700				
17	1.00000	1.00000	1.00000	.99998	.99990	.99964					
18	1.00000	1.00000	1.00000	.99999	.99997						
19	1.00000	1.00000	1.00000	1.00000							
20	1.00000	1.00000	1.00000								
21	1.00000	1.00000									
22	1.00000										

N= 24

$p_1 \backslash p_2$	1	2	3	4	5	6	7	8	9	10	11
2	.75556										
3	.88333	.69612									
4	.94574	.82687	.66742								
5	.97545	.90660	.79299	.65025							
6	.98922	.95204	.87863	.77045	.63888						
7	.99542	.97651	.93272	.85817	.75462	.63094					
8	.99812	.98902	.96468	.91734	.84295	.74318	.62528				
9	.99926	.99511	.98243	.95453	.90531	.83161	.73489	.62124			
10	.99972	.99793	.99173	.97641	.94625	.89609	.82329	.72900	.61845		
11	.99990	.99917	.99632	.98848	.97132	.93977	.88930	.81744	.72505	.61669	
12	.99997	.99968	.99846	.99472	.98566	.96731	.93503	.88463	.81371	.72278	.61584
13	.99999	.99989	.99940	.99774	.99331	.98345	.96442	.93192	.88191	.81189	.72204
14	1.00000	.99996	.99978	.99910	.99710	.99222	.98193	.96269	.93038	.88101	
15	1.00000	.99999	.99993	.99967	.99884	.99664	.99155	.98116	.96212		
16	1.00000	1.00000	.99998	.99989	.99958	.99867	.99639	.99132			
17	1.00000	1.00000	.99999	.99997	.99986	.99953	.99861				
18	1.00000	1.00000	1.00000	.99999	.99996	.99985					
19	1.00000	1.00000	1.00000	1.00000	.99999						
20	1.00000	1.00000	1.00000	1.00000							
21	1.00000	1.00000	1.00000								
22	1.00000	1.00000									
23	1.00000										

TABLE OF PROB. ($\pi_2 < \pi_1$)

N= 25

$p_1 \backslash p_2$	1	2	3	4	5	6	7	8	9	10	11	12
2	.75532											
3	.88298	.69574										
4	.94539	.82624	.66691									
5	.97518	.90590	.79210	.64961								
6	.98903	.95143	.87759	.76930	.63810							
7	.99530	.97604	.93174	.85677	.75319	.63002						
8	.99805	.98870	.96387	.91595	.84117	.74146	.62418					
9	.99922	.99490	.98184	.95335	.90349	.82942	.73284	.61995				
10	.99970	.99781	.99133	.97550	.94464	.89381	.82064	.72656	.61694			
11	.99989	.99910	.99608	.98785	.97006	.93771	.88649	.81427	.72218	.61492		
12	.99996	.99965	.99832	.99432	.98476	.96565	.93245	.88124	.80994	.71939	.61376	
13	.99999	.99987	.99933	.99751	.99273	.98224	.96233	.92877	.87784	.80742	.71804	.61338
14	1.00000	.99996	.99975	.99898	.99676	.99144	.98039	.96011	.92660	.87618	.80660	
15	1.00000	.99999	.99991	.99961	.99866	.99617	.99053	.97927	.95901	.92588		
16	1.00000	1.00000	.99997	.99986	.99949	.99842	.99579	.99007	.97889			
17	1.00000	1.00000	.99999	.99996	.99982	.99941	.99830	.99566				
18	1.00000	1.00000	1.00000	.99999	.99994	.99980	.99938					
19	1.00000	1.00000	1.00000	1.00000	.99998	.99994						
20	1.00000	1.00000	1.00000	1.00000	1.00000							
21	1.00000	1.00000	1.00000	1.00000								
22	1.00000	1.00000	1.00000									
23	1.00000	1.00000										
24	1.00000											

N= 26

$p_1 \backslash p_2$	1	2	3	4	5	6	7	8	9	10	11	12
2	.75510											
3	.88265	.69540										
4	.94507	.82566	.66645									
5	.97492	.90527	.79129	.64903								
6	.98886	.95086	.87664	.76825	.63740							
7	.99519	.97560	.93083	.85549	.75190	.62918						
8	.99799	.98839	.96312	.91469	.83955	.73990	.62319					
9	.99918	.99471	.98129	.95226	.90184	.82743	.73099	.61879				
10	.99968	.99769	.99096	.97466	.94317	.89173	.81825	.72439	.61559			
11	.99988	.99904	.99585	.98726	.96889	.93582	.88395	.81142	.71963	.61336		
12	.99996	.99962	.99819	.99394	.98392	.96412	.93011	.87818	.80658	.71641	.61193	
13	.99999	.99986	.99926	.99728	.99217	.98112	.96040	.92592	.87420	.80347	.71454	.61124
14	1.00000	.99995	.99971	.99885	.99642	.99069	.97896	.95774	.92318	.87187	.80195	.71393
15	1.00000	.99998	.99990	.99955	.99847	.99571	.98957	.97750	.95616	.92182	.87110	
16	1.00000	.99999	.99996	.99983	.99940	.99817	.99520	.98888	.97676	.95563		
17	1.00000	1.00000	.99999	.99994	.99978	.99928	.99797	.99494	.98865			
18	1.00000	1.00000	1.00000	.99998	.99993	.99974	.99922	.99790				
19	1.00000	1.00000	1.00000	1.00000	.99998	.99992	.99973					
20	1.00000	1.00000	1.00000	1.00000	.99999	.99998						
21	1.00000	1.00000	1.00000	1.00000	1.00000							
22	1.00000	1.00000	1.00000	1.00000								
23	1.00000	1.00000	1.00000									
24	1.00000	1.00000										
25	1.00000											

TABLE A.16 (continued)
TABLE OF PROB ($\pi_2 < \pi_1$)

N= 27

$p_1 \backslash p_2$	1	2	3	4	5	6	7	8	9	10	11	12	13
2	.75490												
3	.88235	.69508											
4	.94478	.82513	.66602										
5	.97469	.90468	.79054	.64850									
6	.98869	.95034	.87577	.76730	.63676								
7	.99508	.97520	.93000	.85433	.75072	.62842							
8	.99792	.98811	.96243	.91353	.83808	.73849	.62230						
9	.99915	.99453	.98077	.95125	.90032	.82563	.72932	.61776					
10	.99966	.99759	.99062	.97339	.94182	.88984	.81609	.72243	.61439				
11	.99987	.99898	.99563	.98671	.96781	.93409	.88165	.80886	.71735	.61197			
12	.99995	.99959	.99807	.99358	.98314	.96270	.92796	.87542	.80357	.71376	.61033		
13	.99998	.99984	.99919	.99707	.99165	.98007	.95861	.92332	.87093	.79995	.71146	.60937	
14	.99999	.99994	.99968	.99873	.99610	.98997	.97762	.95556	.92007	.86802	.79783	.71034	.60906
15	1.00000	.99998	.99988	.99949	.99829	.99527	.98865	.97584	.95353	.91815	.86658	.79714	
16	1.00000	.99999	.99996	.99981	.99930	.99791	.99463	.98774	.97476	.95252	.91751		
17	1.00000	1.00000	.99999	.99993	.99973	.99915	.99764	.99423	.98728	.97440			
18	1.00000	1.00000	1.00000	.99998	.99991	.99968	.99905	.99750	.99409				
19	1.00000	1.00000	1.00000	.99999	.99997	.99989	.99965	.99901					
20	1.00000	1.00000	1.00000	1.00000	.99999	.99997	.99988						
21	1.00000	1.00000	1.00000	1.00000	1.00000	.99999							
22	1.00000	1.00000	1.00000	1.00000	1.00000								
23	1.00000	1.00000	1.00000	1.00000									
24	1.00000	1.00000	1.00000										
25	1.00000	1.00000											
26	1.00000												

N= 28

$p_1 \backslash p_2$	1	2	3	4	5	6	7	8	9	10	11	12	13
2	.75472												
3	.88208	.69478											
4	.94451	.82464	.66563										
5	.97447	.90414	.78986	.64801									
6	.98854	.94986	.87496	.76642	.63617								
7	.99499	.97482	.92923	.85325	.74965	.62773							
8	.99787	.98785	.96180	.91246	.83673	.73721	.62150						
9	.99912	.99436	.98030	.95032	.89894	.82399	.72780	.61682					
10	.99965	.99748	.99029	.97316	.94058	.88811	.81412	.72067	.61331				
11	.99986	.99892	.99543	.98620	.96681	.93250	.87954	.80655	.71530	.61072			
12	.99995	.99956	.99795	.99325	.98240	.96139	.92600	.87291	.80086	.71138	.60889		
13	.99998	.99983	.99912	.99636	.99115	.97909	.95697	.92094	.86796	.79679	.70871	.60772	
14	.99999	.99994	.99964	.99852	.99579	.98930	.97636	.95354	.91724	.86454	.79417	.70716	.60715
15	1.00000	.99998	.99986	.99943	.99811	.99484	.98778	.97429	.95111	.91481	.86253	.79288	.70665
16	1.00000	.99999	.99995	.99978	.99921	.99766	.99407	.98665	.97289	.94966	.91361	.86187	
17	1.00000	1.00000	.99998	.99992	.99969	.99901	.99731	.99353	.98596	.97219	.94918		
18	1.00000	1.00000	.99999	.99997	.99989	.99961	.99887	.99709	.99325	.98573			
19	1.00000	1.00000	1.00000	.99999	.99996	.99986	.99956	.99880	.99701				
20	1.00000	1.00000	1.00000	1.00000	.99999	.99995	.99985	.99955					
21	1.00000	1.00000	1.00000	1.00000	1.00000	.99999	.99995						
22	1.00000	1.00000	1.00000	1.00000	1.00000	1.00000							
23	1.00000	1.00000	1.00000	1.00000	1.00000								
24	1.00000	1.00000	1.00000	1.00000									
25	1.00000	1.00000	1.00000										
26	1.00000	1.00000											
27	1.00000												

TABLE A.16 (continued)

TABLE OF PROB($\pi_2 < \pi_1$)

N= 29

$p_1 \backslash p_2$	1	2	3	4	5	6	7	8	9	10	11	12	13	14
2	.75455													
3	.88182	.69451												
4	.94425	.82419	.66527											
5	.97427	.90364	.78922	.64756										
6	.98840	.94941	.87422	.76561	.63563									
7	.99489	.97447	.92852	.85227	.74866	.62709								
8	.99781	.98760	.96120	.91147	.83549	.73603	.62076							
9	.99909	.99420	.97985	.94946	.89766	.82248	.72642	.61597						
10	.99963	.99739	.98998	.97249	.93942	.88652	.81233	.71906	.61234					
11	.99986	.99887	.99523	.98571	.96587	.93104	.87762	.80444	.71344	.60961				
12	.99995	.99953	.99783	.99293	.98171	.96017	.92419	.87062	.79840	.70925	.60761			
13	.99998	.99981	.99906	.99666	.99068	.97817	.95544	.91876	.86527	.79394	.70626	.60625		
14	.99999	.99993	.99961	.99851	.99550	.98866	.97519	.95168	.91464	.86139	.79088	.70434	.60546	
15	1.00000	.99997	.99985	.99937	.99794	.99443	.98695	.97284	.94888	.91176	.85887	.78908	.70339	.60520
16	1.00000	.99999	.99994	.99975	.99911	.99742	.99353	.98562	.97114	.94702	.91006	.85763	.78849	
17	1.00000	1.00000	.99998	.99990	.99964	.99888	.99699	.99285	.98471	.97012	.94610	.90949		
18	1.00000	1.00000	.99999	.99997	.99986	.99954	.99869	.99669	.99244	.98426	.96978			
19	1.00000	1.00000	1.00000	.99999	.99995	.99983	.99947	.99857	.99653	.99230				
20	1.00000	1.00000	1.00000	1.00000	.99998	.99994	.99981	.99944	.99853					
21	1.00000	1.00000	1.00000	1.00000	1.00000	.99998	.99993	.99980						
22	1.00000	1.00000	1.00000	1.00000	1.00000	.99999	.99998							
23	1.00000	1.00000	1.00000	1.00000	1.00000	1.00000								
24	1.00000	1.00000	1.00000	1.00000	1.00000									
25	1.00000	1.00000	1.00000	1.00000										
26	1.00000	1.00000	1.00000											
27	1.00000	1.00000												
28	1.00000													

N= 30

$p_1 \backslash p_2$	1	2	3	4	5	6	7	8	9	10	11	12	13	14
2	.75439													
3	.88158	.69426												
4	.94402	.82376	.66494											
5	.97408	.90318	.78864	.64715										
6	.98826	.94899	.87353	.76487	.63514									
7	.99481	.97415	.92786	.85136	.74775	.62651								
8	.99776	.98737	.96065	.91056	.83435	.73495	.62009							
9	.99906	.99405	.97944	.94866	.89648	.82110	.72516	.61520						
10	.99962	.99730	.98970	.97186	.93835	.88506	.81069	.71760	.61145					
11	.99985	.99882	.99505	.98526	.96500	.92968	.87585	.80251	.71176	.60859				
12	.99994	.99950	.99772	.99262	.98106	.95904	.92252	.86851	.79617	.70732	.60646			
13	.99998	.99980	.99900	.99648	.99024	.97730	.95402	.91675	.86280	.79136	.70405	.60494		
14	.99999	.99992	.99958	.99840	.99521	.98805	.97409	.94994	.91226	.85853	.78791	.70181	.60396	
15	1.00000	.99997	.99983	.99931	.99777	.99403	.98616	.97148	.94680	.90897	.85556	.78567	.70049	.60348
16	1.00000	.99999	.99994	.99971	.99902	.99718	.99301	.98464	.96950	.94458	.90681	.85381	.78457	.70006
17	1.00000	1.00000	.99998	.99989	.99959	.99874	.99667	.99220	.98352	.96818	.94325	.90574	.85324	
18	1.00000	1.00000	.99999	.99996	.99984	.99947	.99851	.99629	.99165	.98285	.96752	.94281		
19	1.00000	1.00000	1.00000	.99999	.99994	.99979	.99938	.99835	.99604	.99136	.98262			
20	1.00000	1.00000	1.00000	1.00000	.99998	.99993	.99976	.99932	.99826	.99596				
21	1.00000	1.00000	1.00000	1.00000	.99999	.99998	.99991	.99974	.99930					
22	1.00000	1.00000	1.00000	1.00000	1.00000	.99999	.99997	.99991						
23	1.00000	1.00000	1.00000	1.00000	1.00000	1.00000	.99999							
24	1.00000	1.00000	1.00000	1.00000	1.00000	1.00000								
25	1.00000	1.00000	1.00000	1.00000	1.00000									
26	1.00000	1.00000	1.00000	1.00000										
27	1.00000	1.00000	1.00000											
28	1.00000	1.00000												
29	1.00000													

TABLE A.16 (continued)

TABLE OF PROB($\pi_2 < \pi_1$)

N= 31

$p_1 \backslash p_2$	1	2	3	4	5	6	7	8	9	10	11	12	13	14	15
2	.75424														
3	.88136	.69402													
4	.94380	.82337	.66463												
5	.97391	.90275	.78810	.64677											
6	.98814	.94861	.87289	.76418	.63468										
7	.99473	.97384	.92725	.85051	.74691	.62598									
8	.99771	.98715	.96014	.90971	.83329	.73395	.61947								
9	.99903	.99391	.97905	.94792	.89538	.81982	.72400	.61449							
10	.99960	.99721	.98943	.97127	.93736	.88370	.80917	.71626	.61064						
11	.99984	.99877	.99488	.98483	.96419	.92842	.87422	.80075	.71022	.60767					
12	.99994	.99947	.99762	.99233	.98045	.95798	.92097	.86658	.79412	.70556	.60541				
13	.99998	.99978	.99894	.99630	.98931	.97649	.95269	.91489	.86054	.78901	.70205	.60375			
14	.99999	.99992	.99955	.99829	.99494	.98747	.97305	.94833	.91007	.85591	.78522	.69952	.60261		
15	1.00000	.99997	.99981	.99925	.99761	.99365	.98541	.97020	.94488	.90641	.85254	.78259	.69790	.60195	
16	1.00000	.99999	.99993	.99968	.99892	.99695	.99251	.98370	.96796	.94231	.90384	.85035	.78105	.69710	.60173
17	1.00000	1.00000	.99997	.99987	.99954	.99861	.99636	.99157	.98239	.96636	.94062	.90232	.84927	.78054	
18	1.00000	1.00000	.99999	.99995	.99982	.99940	.99834	.99589	.99088	.98150	.96540	.93977	.90182		
19	1.00000	1.00000	1.00000	.99998	.99993	.99976	.99928	.99812	.99557	.99045	.98106	.96508			
20	1.00000	1.00000	1.00000	.99999	.99998	.99991	.99971	.99920	.99799	.99540	.99031				
21	1.00000	1.00000	1.00000	1.00000	.99999	.99997	.99989	.99968	.99915	.99794					
22	1.00000	1.00000	1.00000	1.00000	1.00000	.99999	.99996	.99988	.99967						
23	1.00000	1.00000	1.00000	1.00000	1.00000	1.00000	.99999	.99996							
24	1.00000	1.00000	1.00000	1.00000	1.00000	1.00000	1.00000								
25	1.00000	1.00000	1.00000	1.00000	1.00000	1.00000									
26	1.00000	1.00000	1.00000	1.00000	1.00000										
27	1.00000	1.00000	1.00000	1.00000											
28	1.00000	1.00000	1.00000												
29	1.00000	1.00000													
30	1.00000														

TABLE A.16 (continued)

TABLE OF PROB($\pi_2 < \pi_1$)

N= 32

P_1 \ P_2	1	2	3	4	5	6	7	8	9	10	11	12	13	14	15
2	.75410														
3	.88115	.69380													
4	.94360	.82301	.66434												
5	.97374	.90234	.78759	.64641											
6	.98802	.94824	.87230	.76354	.63425										
7	.99465	.97356	.92668	.84972	.74613	.62548									
8	.99767	.98695	.95966	.90892	.83231	.73303	.61889								
9	.99901	.99377	.97868	.94722	.89436	.81864	.72293	.61384							
10	.99959	.99713	.98917	.97071	.93643	.88244	.80778	.71502	.60990						
11	.99983	.99872	.99471	.98443	.96343	.92724	.87270	.79912	.70881	.60683					
12	.99993	.99945	.99751	.99206	.97988	.95699	.91953	.86480	.79225	.70395	.60446				
13	.99998	.99977	.99888	.99612	.98941	.97572	.95146	.91317	.85847	.78686	.70022	.60268			
14	.99999	.99991	.99951	.99819	.99468	.98692	.97208	.94683	.90804	.85351	.78276	.69746	.60140		
15	1.00000	.99996	.99980	.99919	.99745	.99329	.98470	.96900	.94309	.90404	.84978	.77980	.69555	.60057	
16	1.00000	.99999	.99992	.99965	.99883	.99672	.99203	.98282	.96652	.94021	.90111	.84719	.77787	.69444	.60016
17	1.00000	1.00000	.99997	.99986	.99949	.99848	.99606	.99097	.98132	.96465	.93818	.89918	.84566	.77692	.69407
18	1.00000	1.00000	.99999	.99995	.99979	.99933	.99816	.99551	.99014	.98023	.96341	.93696	.89823	.84516	
19	1.00000	1.00000	1.00000	.99998	.99992	.99972	.99919	.99789	.99509	.98957	.97957	.96278	.93656		
20	1.00000	1.00000	1.00000	.99999	.99997	.99989	.99966	.99907	.99771	.99484	.98928	.97935			
21	1.00000	1.00000	1.00000	1.00000	.99999	.99996	.99987	.99962	.99900	.99761	.99475				
22	1.00000	1.00000	1.00000	1.00000	1.00000	.99999	.99995	.99986	.99960	.99898					
23	1.00000	1.00000	1.00000	1.00000	1.00000	1.00000	.99998	.99995	.99985						
24	1.00000	1.00000	1.00000	1.00000	1.00000	1.00000	1.00000	.99998							
25	1.00000	1.00000	1.00000	1.00000	1.00000	1.00000	1.00000								
26	1.00000	1.00000	1.00000	1.00000	1.00000	1.00000									
27	1.00000	1.00000	1.00000	1.00000	1.00000										
28	1.00000	1.00000	1.00000	1.00000											
29	1.00000	1.00000	1.00000												
30	1.00000	1.00000													
31	1.00000														

TABLE A.17

TABLE OF LOGFACTORIALS

Natural logarithm of n factorial

The values tabled are $\ell n(n!)$ for n = 0(1)499.

n	0	1	2	3	4	5	6	7	8	9
0	0.	0.	.6931	1.7918	3.1781	4.7875	6.5793	8.5252	10.6046	12.80
10	15.1044	17.5023	19.9872	22.5522	25.1912	27.8993	30.6719	33.5051	36.3954	39.34
20	42.3356	45.3801	48.4712	51.6067	54.7847	58.0036	61.2617	64.5575	67.8897	71.26
30	74.6582	78.0922	81.5580	85.0545	88.5808	92.1362	95.7197	99.3306	102.9682	106.63
40	110.3206	114.0342	117.7719	121.5331	125.3173	129.1239	132.9526	136.8027	140.6739	144.57
50	148.4778	152.4096	156.3608	160.3311	164.3201	168.3274	172.3528	176.3958	180.4563	184.53
60	188.6282	192.7390	196.8662	201.0093	205.1682	209.3426	213.5322	217.7369	221.9564	226.19
70	230.4390	234.7017	238.9784	243.2688	247.5729	251.8904	256.2211	260.5649	264.9216	269.29
80	273.6731	278.0676	282.4743	286.8931	291.3240	295.7666	300.2209	304.6869	309.1642	313.65
90	318.1526	322.6635	327.1853	331.7179	336.2612	340.8151	345.3794	349.9541	354.5391	359.13
100	363.7394	368.3545	372.9795	377.6142	382.2586	386.9125	391.5760	396.2488	400.9309	405.62
110	410.3228	415.0323	419.7508	424.4782	429.2144	433.9593	438.7129	443.4751	448.2458	453.02
120	457.8124	462.6082	467.4122	472.2244	477.0447	481.8730	486.7093	491.5534	496.4055	501.27
130	506.1328	511.0080	515.8908	520.7812	525.6790	530.5843	535.4969	540.4169	545.3442	550.28
140	555.2203	560.1691	565.1249	570.0877	575.0575	580.0343	585.0179	590.0083	595.0055	600.01
150	605.0201	610.0374	615.0613	620.0917	625.1287	630.1721	635.2219	640.2782	645.3408	650.41
160	655.4849	660.5663	665.6539	670.7476	675.8475	680.9534	686.0654	691.1834	696.3074	701.44
170	706.5731	711.7147	716.8622	722.0155	727.1746	732.3394	737.5098	742.6860	747.8678	753.06
180	758.2481	763.4466	768.6506	773.8601	779.0750	784.2954	789.5211	794.7522	799.9887	805.23
190	810.4775	815.7297	820.9872	826.2499	831.5178	836.7908	842.0689	847.3521	852.6404	857.93
200	863.2320	868.5353	873.8436	879.1568	884.4749	889.7979	895.1258	900.4585	905.7960	911.14
210	916.4855	921.8373	927.1939	932.5552	937.9212	943.2918	948.6671	954.0470	959.4315	964.82
220	970.2142	975.6124	981.0150	986.4222	991.8338	997.2499	1002.6705	1008.0954	1013.5248	1018.96
230	1024.3966	1029.8390	1035.2857	1040.7368	1046.1921	1051.6517	1057.1155	1062.5836	1068.0558	1073.53
240	1079.0129	1084.4977	1089.9867	1095.4797	1100.9769	1106.4782	1111.9835	1117.4929	1123.0063	1128.52
250	1134.0452	1139.5707	1145.1001	1150.6335	1156.1708	1161.7121	1167.2573	1172.8064	1178.3593	1183.92
260	1189.4768	1195.0413	1200.6097	1206.1818	1211.7578	1217.3375	1222.9210	1228.5083	1234.0993	1239.69
270	1245.2924	1250.8945	1256.5003	1262.1098	1267.7229	1273.3397	1278.9601	1284.5841	1290.2117	1295.84
280	1301.4777	1307.1161	1312.7580	1318.4034	1324.0524	1329.7049	1335.3609	1341.0204	1346.6833	1352.35
290	1358.0196	1363.6930	1369.3697	1375.0499	1380.7335	1386.4204	1392.1108	1397.8045	1403.5016	1409.20
300	1414.9058	1420.6130	1426.3234	1432.0371	1437.7541	1443.4745	1449.1980	1454.9249	1460.6550	1466.39
310	1472.1249	1477.8647	1483.6077	1489.3539	1495.1033	1500.8559	1506.6116	1512.3705	1518.1326	1523.90
320	1529.6661	1535.4375	1541.2121	1546.9897	1552.7705	1558.5543	1564.3412	1570.1311	1575.9242	1581.72
330	1587.5193	1593.3214	1599.1266	1604.9347	1610.7459	1616.5600	1622.3771	1628.1972	1634.0202	1639.85
340	1645.6752	1651.5070	1657.3419	1663.1796	1669.0202	1674.8638	1680.7102	1686.5595	1692.4117	1698.27
350	1704.1247	1709.9855	1715.8492	1721.7156	1727.5849	1733.4570	1739.3320	1745.2097	1751.0902	1756.97
360	1762.8597	1768.7486	1774.6402	1780.5346	1786.4318	1792.3316	1798.2343	1804.1396	1810.0477	1815.96
370	1821.8720	1827.7882	1833.7071	1839.6287	1845.5530	1851.4799	1857.4095	1863.3417	1869.2766	1875.21
380	1881.1543	1887.0971	1893.0425	1898.9906	1904.9412	1910.8945	1916.8503	1922.8087	1928.7697	1934.73
390	1940.6995	1946.6682	1952.6394	1958.6132	1964.5896	1970.5685	1976.5499	1982.5338	1988.5203	1994.51
400	2000.5007	2006.4947	2012.4911	2018.4900	2024.4915	2030.4954	2036.5017	2042.5105	2048.5218	2054.54
410	2060.5517	2066.5702	2072.5913	2078.6147	2084.6406	2090.6689	2096.6995	2102.7326	2108.7681	2114.81
420	2120.8462	2126.8889	2132.9339	2138.9813	2145.0310	2151.0831	2157.1375	2163.1943	2169.2534	2175.31
430	2181.3787	2187.4448	2193.5132	2199.5839	2205.6570	2211.7323	2217.8100	2223.8899	2229.9721	2236.06
440	2242.1434	2248.2324	2254.3237	2260.4173	2266.5131	2272.6112	2278.7115	2284.8141	2290.9189	2297.03
450	2303.1352	2309.2466	2315.3603	2321.4762	2327.5943	2333.7146	2339.8371	2345.9618	2352.0886	2358.22
460	2364.3489	2370.4823	2376.6179	2382.7556	2388.8955	2395.0375	2401.1817	2407.3280	2413.4765	2419.63
470	2425.7798	2431.9347	2438.0917	2444.2508	2450.4120	2456.5753	2462.7407	2468.9082	2475.0778	2481.25
480	2487.4233	2493.5992	2499.7771	2505.9572	2512.1392	2518.3234	2524.5096	2530.6979	2536.8882	2543.08
490	2549.2750	2555.4714	2561.6699	2567.8704	2574.0729	2580.2775	2586.4841	2592.6926	2598.9032	2605.12

TABLES A.18 (a and b) --THE ARC-SINE TRANSFORM AND ITS INVERSE

TABLE A.18 (a): **This table gives arcsin $\sqrt{p}$ in radians for p = .000(.001).999.**

p	.000	.001	.002	.003	.004	.005	.006	.007	.008	.009
0.	0.	.0316	.0447	.0548	.0633	.0708	.0775	.0838	.0896	.0950
.01	.1002	.1051	.1098	.1143	.1186	.1228	.1268	.1308	.1346	.1383
.02	.1419	.1454	.1489	.1522	.1555	.1588	.1620	.1651	.1681	.1711
.03	.1741	.1770	.1799	.1827	.1855	.1882	.1909	.1936	.1962	.1988
.04	.2014	.2039	.2064	.2089	.2113	.2138	.2162	.2185	.2209	.2232
.05	.2255	.2278	.2301	.2323	.2345	.2367	.2389	.2411	.2432	.2454
.06	.2475	.2496	.2516	.2537	.2558	.2578	.2598	.2618	.2638	.2658
.07	.2678	.2697	.2717	.2736	.2755	.2774	.2793	.2812	.2830	.2849
.08	.2868	.2886	.2904	.2922	.2940	.2958	.2976	.2994	.3012	.3029
.09	.3047	.3064	.3082	.3099	.3116	.3133	.3150	.3167	.3184	.3201
.10	.3218	.3234	.3251	.3267	.3284	.3300	.3316	.3332	.3349	.3365
.11	.3381	.3397	.3412	.3428	.3444	.3460	.3475	.3491	.3507	.3522
.12	.3537	.3553	.3568	.3583	.3599	.3614	.3629	.3644	.3659	.3674
.13	.3689	.3703	.3718	.3733	.3748	.3762	.3777	.3792	.3806	.3821
.14	.3835	.3849	.3864	.3878	.3892	.3906	.3921	.3935	.3949	.3963
.15	.3977	.3991	.4005	.4019	.4033	.4047	.4060	.4074	.4088	.4102
.16	.4115	.4129	.4142	.4156	.4169	.4183	.4196	.4210	.4223	.4237
.17	.4250	.4263	.4276	.4290	.4303	.4316	.4329	.4342	.4355	.4368
.18	.4381	.4394	.4407	.4420	.4433	.4446	.4459	.4472	.4485	.4498
.19	.4510	.4523	.4536	.4548	.4561	.4574	.4586	.4599	.4611	.4624
.20	.4636	.4649	.4661	.4674	.4686	.4699	.4711	.4723	.4736	.4748
.21	.4760	.4773	.4785	.4797	.4809	.4821	.4834	.4846	.4858	.4870
.22	.4882	.4894	.4906	.4918	.4930	.4942	.4954	.4966	.4978	.4990
.23	.5002	.5014	.5026	.5037	.5049	.5061	.5073	.5085	.5096	.5108
.24	.5120	.5131	.5143	.5155	.5166	.5178	.5190	.5201	.5213	.5224
.25	.5236	.5248	.5259	.5271	.5282	.5294	.5305	.5316	.5328	.5339
.26	.5351	.5362	.5373	.5385	.5396	.5408	.5419	.5430	.5441	.5453
.27	.5464	.5475	.5487	.5498	.5509	.5520	.5531	.5543	.5554	.5565
.28	.5576	.5587	.5598	.5609	.5620	.5632	.5643	.5654	.5665	.5676
.29	.5687	.5698	.5709	.5720	.5731	.5742	.5753	.5764	.5775	.5785
.30	.5796	.5807	.5818	.5829	.5840	.5851	.5862	.5873	.5883	.5894
.31	.5905	.5916	.5927	.5937	.5948	.5959	.5970	.5980	.5991	.6002
.32	.6013	.6023	.6034	.6045	.6055	.6066	.6077	.6087	.6098	.6109
.33	.6119	.6130	.6141	.6151	.6162	.6172	.6183	.6194	.6204	.6215
.34	.6225	.6236	.6246	.6257	.6267	.6278	.6289	.6299	.6310	.6320
.35	.6331	.6341	.6351	.6362	.6372	.6383	.6393	.6404	.6414	.6425
.36	.6435	.6445	.6456	.6466	.6477	.6487	.6497	.6508	.6518	.6529
.37	.6539	.6549	.6560	.6570	.6580	.6591	.6601	.6611	.6622	.6632
.38	.6642	.6652	.6663	.6673	.6683	.6694	.6704	.6714	.6724	.6735
.39	.6745	.6755	.6765	.6776	.6786	.6796	.6806	.6817	.6827	.6837
.40	.6847	.6857	.6868	.6878	.6888	.6898	.6908	.6919	.6929	.6939
.41	.6949	.6959	.6969	.6980	.6990	.7000	.7010	.7020	.7030	.7040
.42	.7051	.7061	.7071	.7081	.7091	.7101	.7111	.7121	.7131	.7142
.43	.7152	.7162	.7172	.7182	.7192	.7202	.7212	.7222	.7232	.7242
.44	.7253	.7263	.7273	.7283	.7293	.7303	.7313	.7323	.7333	.7343
.45	.7353	.7363	.7373	.7383	.7393	.7403	.7413	.7423	.7433	.7444
.46	.7454	.7464	.7474	.7484	.7494	.7504	.7514	.7524	.7534	.7544
.47	.7554	.7564	.7574	.7584	.7594	.7604	.7614	.7624	.7634	.7644
.48	.7654	.7664	.7674	.7684	.7694	.7704	.7714	.7724	.7734	.7744
.49	.7754	.7764	.7774	.7784	.7794	.7804	.7814	.7824	.7834	.7844

TABLE A.18(a) (continued)

TABLE OF THE ARC-SINE TRANSFORM

p	.000	.001	.002	.003	.004	.005	.006	.007	.008	.009
.50	.7854	.7864	.7874	.7884	.7894	.7904	.7914	.7924	.7934	.7944
.51	.7954	.7964	.7974	.7984	.7994	.8004	.8014	.8024	.8034	.8044
.52	.8054	.8064	.8074	.8084	.8094	.8104	.8114	.8124	.8134	.8144
.53	.8154	.8164	.8174	.8184	.8194	.8204	.8214	.8224	.8234	.8244
.54	.8254	.8264	.8274	.8285	.8295	.8305	.8315	.8325	.8335	.8345
.55	.8355	.8365	.8375	.8385	.8395	.8405	.8415	.8425	.8435	.8445
.56	.8455	.8466	.8476	.8486	.8496	.8506	.8516	.8526	.8536	.8546
.57	.8556	.8566	.8576	.8587	.8597	.8607	.8617	.8627	.8637	.8647
.58	.8657	.8668	.8678	.8688	.8698	.8708	.8718	.8728	.8739	.8749
.59	.8759	.8769	.8779	.8789	.8800	.8810	.8820	.8830	.8840	.8851
.60	.8861	.8871	.8881	.8891	.8902	.8912	.8922	.8932	.8943	.8953
.61	.8963	.8973	.8984	.8994	.9004	.9014	.9025	.9035	.9045	.9056
.62	.9066	.9076	.9086	.9097	.9107	.9117	.9128	.9138	.9148	.9159
.63	.9169	.9179	.9190	.9200	.9211	.9221	.9231	.9242	.9252	.9263
.64	.9273	.9283	.9294	.9304	.9315	.9325	.9336	.9346	.9356	.9367
.65	.9377	.9388	.9398	.9409	.9419	.9430	.9440	.9451	.9462	.9472
.66	.9483	.9493	.9504	.9514	.9525	.9535	.9546	.9557	.9567	.9578
.67	.9589	.9599	.9610	.9621	.9631	.9642	.9653	.9663	.9674	.9685
.68	.9695	.9706	.9717	.9728	.9738	.9749	.9760	.9771	.9781	.9792
.69	.9803	.9814	.9825	.9835	.9846	.9857	.9868	.9879	.9890	.9901
.70	.9912	.9922	.9933	.9944	.9955	.9966	.9977	.9988	.9999	1.0010
.71	1.0021	1.0032	1.0043	1.0054	1.0065	1.0076	1.0088	1.0099	1.0110	1.0121
.72	1.0132	1.0143	1.0154	1.0165	1.0177	1.0188	1.0199	1.0210	1.0221	1.0233
.73	1.0244	1.0255	1.0267	1.0278	1.0289	1.0300	1.0312	1.0323	1.0334	1.0346
.74	1.0357	1.0369	1.0380	1.0392	1.0403	1.0414	1.0426	1.0437	1.0449	1.0460
.75	1.0472	1.0484	1.0495	1.0507	1.0518	1.0530	1.0542	1.0553	1.0565	1.0577
.76	1.0588	1.0600	1.0612	1.0623	1.0635	1.0647	1.0659	1.0671	1.0682	1.0694
.77	1.0706	1.0718	1.0730	1.0742	1.0754	1.0766	1.0778	1.0790	1.0802	1.0814
.78	1.0826	1.0838	1.0850	1.0862	1.0874	1.0887	1.0899	1.0911	1.0923	1.0935
.79	1.0948	1.0960	1.0972	1.0985	1.0997	1.1009	1.1022	1.1034	1.1047	1.1059
.80	1.1071	1.1084	1.1097	1.1109	1.1122	1.1134	1.1147	1.1160	1.1172	1.1185
.81	1.1198	1.1210	1.1223	1.1236	1.1249	1.1262	1.1275	1.1288	1.1301	1.1313
.82	1.1326	1.1340	1.1353	1.1366	1.1379	1.1392	1.1405	1.1418	1.1432	1.1445
.83	1.1458	1.1471	1.1485	1.1498	1.1512	1.1525	1.1539	1.1552	1.1566	1.1579
.84	1.1593	1.1606	1.1620	1.1634	1.1648	1.1661	1.1675	1.1689	1.1703	1.1717
.85	1.1731	1.1745	1.1759	1.1773	1.1787	1.1801	1.1816	1.1830	1.1844	1.1859
.86	1.1873	1.1887	1.1902	1.1916	1.1931	1.1946	1.1960	1.1975	1.1990	1.2004
.87	1.2019	1.2034	1.2049	1.2064	1.2079	1.2094	1.2109	1.2125	1.2140	1.2155
.88	1.2171	1.2186	1.2201	1.2217	1.2233	1.2248	1.2264	1.2280	1.2295	1.2311
.89	1.2327	1.2343	1.2359	1.2376	1.2392	1.2408	1.2424	1.2441	1.2457	1.2474
.90	1.2490	1.2507	1.2524	1.2541	1.2558	1.2575	1.2592	1.2609	1.2626	1.2644
.91	1.2661	1.2679	1.2696	1.2714	1.2732	1.2750	1.2767	1.2786	1.2804	1.2822
.92	1.2840	1.2859	1.2877	1.2896	1.2915	1.2934	1.2953	1.2972	1.2991	1.3011
.93	1.3030	1.3050	1.3070	1.3090	1.3110	1.3130	1.3150	1.3171	1.3192	1.3212
.94	1.3233	1.3254	1.3276	1.3297	1.3319	1.3341	1.3363	1.3385	1.3407	1.3430
.95	1.3453	1.3476	1.3499	1.3523	1.3546	1.3570	1.3595	1.3619	1.3644	1.3669
.96	1.3694	1.3720	1.3746	1.3772	1.3799	1.3826	1.3853	1.3881	1.3909	1.3938
.97	1.3967	1.3997	1.4027	1.4057	1.4088	1.4120	1.4153	1.4186	1.4219	1.4254
.98	1.4289	1.4325	1.4362	1.4400	1.4440	1.4480	1.4522	1.4565	1.4610	1.4657
.99	1.4706	1.4758	1.4812	1.4870	1.4933	1.5000	1.5075	1.5160	1.5261	1.5392

TABLE A.18 (b) : TABLE OF $p = \mathrm{SIN}^2\ \gamma,\ \gamma = 0(.001)\,1.499$

p	.000	.001	.002	.003	.004	.005	.006	.007	.008	.009
0.	0.	.0000	.0000	.0000	.0000	.0000	.0000	.0000	.0001	.0001
.01	.0001	.0001	.0001	.0002	.0002	.0002	.0003	.0003	.0003	.0004
.02	.0004	.0004	.0005	.0005	.0006	.0006	.0007	.0007	.0008	.0008
.03	.0009	.0010	.0010	.0011	.0012	.0012	.0013	.0014	.0014	.0015
.04	.0016	.0017	.0018	.0018	.0019	.0020	.0021	.0022	.0023	.0024
.05	.0025	.0026	.0027	.0028	.0029	.0030	.0031	.0032	.0034	.0035
.06	.0036	.0037	.0038	.0040	.0041	.0042	.0043	.0045	.0046	.0048
.07	.0049	.0050	.0052	.0053	.0055	.0056	.0058	.0059	.0061	.0062
.08	.0064	.0065	.0067	.0069	.0070	.0072	.0074	.0075	.0077	.0079
.09	.0081	.0083	.0084	.0086	.0088	.0090	.0092	.0094	.0096	.0098
.10	.0100	.0102	.0104	.0106	.0108	.0110	.0112	.0114	.0116	.0118
.11	.0121	.0123	.0125	.0127	.0129	.0132	.0134	.0136	.0139	.0141
.12	.0143	.0146	.0148	.0151	.0153	.0155	.0158	.0160	.0163	.0165
.13	.0168	.0171	.0173	.0176	.0178	.0181	.0184	.0187	.0189	.0192
.14	.0195	.0197	.0200	.0203	.0206	.0209	.0212	.0215	.0217	.0220
.15	.0223	.0226	.0229	.0232	.0235	.0238	.0241	.0244	.0248	.0251
.16	.0254	.0257	.0260	.0263	.0267	.0270	.0273	.0276	.0280	.0283
.17	.0286	.0290	.0293	.0296	.0300	.0303	.0307	.0310	.0314	.0317
.18	.0321	.0324	.0328	.0331	.0335	.0338	.0342	.0346	.0349	.0353
.19	.0357	.0360	.0364	.0368	.0372	.0375	.0379	.0383	.0387	.0391
.20	.0395	.0399	.0403	.0406	.0410	.0414	.0418	.0422	.0426	.0430
.21	.0435	.0439	.0443	.0447	.0451	.0455	.0459	.0464	.0468	.0472
.22	.0476	.0481	.0485	.0489	.0493	.0498	.0502	.0506	.0511	.0515
.23	.0520	.0524	.0529	.0533	.0538	.0542	.0547	.0551	.0556	.0560
.24	.0565	.0570	.0574	.0579	.0584	.0588	.0593	.0598	.0603	.0607
.25	.0612	.0617	.0622	.0627	.0631	.0636	.0641	.0646	.0651	.0656
.26	.0661	.0666	.0671	.0676	.0681	.0686	.0691	.0696	.0701	.0706
.27	.0711	.717	.0722	.0727	.0732	.0737	.0743	.0748	.0753	.0758
.28	.0764	.0769	.0774	.0780	.0785	.0790	.0796	.0801	.0807	.0812
.29	.0818	.0823	.0829	.0834	.0840	.0845	.0851	.0856	.0862	.0868
.30	.0873	.0879	.0885	.0890	.0896	.0902	.0907	.0913	.0919	.0925
.31	.0931	.0936	.0942	.0948	.0954	.0960	.0966	.0972	.0978	.0984
.32	.0990	.0996	.1001	.1008	.1014	.1020	.1026	.1032	.1038	.1044
.33	.1050	.1056	.1062	.1069	.1075	.1081	.1087	.1093	.1100	.1106
.34	.1112	.1118	.1125	.1131	.1137	.1144	.1150	.1157	.1163	.1169
.35	.1176	.1182	.1189	.1195	.1202	.1208	.1215	.1221	.1228	.1234
.36	.1241	.1248	.1254	.1261	.1267	.1274	.1281	.1287	.1294	.1301
.37	.1308	.1314	.1321	.1328	.1335	.1342	.1348	.1355	.1362	.1369
.38	.1376	.1383	.1390	.1397	.1403	.1410	.1417	.1424	.1431	.1438
.39	.1445	.1452	.1460	.1467	.1474	.1481	.1488	.1495	.1502	.1509
.40	.1516	.1524	.1531	.1538	.1545	.1553	.1560	.1567	.1574	.1582
.41	.1589	.1596	.1604	.1611	.1618	.1626	.1633	.1640	.1648	.1655
.42	.1663	.1670	.1678	.1685	.1693	.1700	.1708	.1715	.1723	.1730
.43	.1738	.1745	.1753	.1761	.1768	.1776	.1784	.1791	.1799	.1807
.44	.1814	.1822	.1830	.1837	.1845	.1853	.1861	.1869	.1876	.1884
.45	.1892	.1900	.1908	.1916	.1923	.1931	.1939	.1947	.1955	.1963
.46	.1971	.1979	.1987	.1995	.2003	.2011	.2019	.2027	.2035	.2043
.47	.2051	.2059	.2067	.2075	.2083	.2092	.2100	.2108	.2116	.2124
.48	.2132	.2141	.2149	.2157	.2165	.2174	.2182	.2190	.2198	.2207
.49	.2215	.2223	.2232	.2240	.2248	.2257	.2265	.2273	.2282	.2290

TABLE A.18(b) (continued)

TABLE OF $SIN^2 \gamma$

P	.000	.001	.002	.003	.004	.005	.006	.007	.008	.009
.50	.2298	.2307	.2315	.2324	.2332	.2341	.2349	.2358	.2366	.2375
.51	.2383	.2392	.2400	.2409	.2417	.2426	.2434	.2443	.2452	.2460
.52	.2469	.2478	.2486	.2495	.2503	.2512	.2521	.2530	.2538	.2547
.53	.2556	.2564	.2573	.2582	.2591	.2599	.2608	.2617	.2626	.2635
.54	.2643	.2652	.2661	.2670	.2679	.2688	.2696	.2705	.2714	.2723
.55	.2732	.2741	.2750	.2759	.2768	.2777	.2786	.2795	.2804	.2813
.56	.2822	.2831	.2840	.2849	.2858	.2867	.2876	.2885	.2894	.2903
.57	.2912	.2921	.2930	.2939	.2948	.2958	.2967	.2976	.2985	.2994
.58	.3003	.3012	.3022	.3031	.3040	.3049	.3058	.3068	.3077	.3086
.59	.3095	.3105	.3114	.3123	.3132	.3142	.3151	.3160	.3170	.3179
.60	.3188	.3198	.3207	.3216	.3226	.3235	.3244	.3254	.3263	.3272
.61	.3282	.3291	.3301	.3310	.3319	.3329	.3338	.3348	.3357	.3367
.62	.3376	.3385	.3395	.3404	.3414	.3423	.3433	.3442	.3452	.3461
.63	.3471	.3480	.3490	.3500	.3509	.3519	.3528	.3538	.3547	.3557
.64	.3566	.3576	.3586	.3595	.3605	.3614	.3624	.3634	.3643	.3653
.65	.3663	.3672	.3682	.3691	.3701	.3711	.3720	.3730	.3740	.3749
.66	.3759	.3769	.3779	.3788	.3798	.3808	.3817	.3827	.3837	.3847
.67	.3856	.3866	.3876	.3885	.3895	.3905	.3915	.3924	.3934	.3944
.68	.3954	.3964	.3973	.3983	.3993	.4003	.4013	.4022	.4032	.4042
.69	.4052	.4062	.4071	.4081	.4091	.4101	.4111	.4121	.4130	.4140
.70	.4150	.4160	.4170	.4180	.4190	.4199	.4209	.4219	.4229	.4239
.71	.4249	.4259	.4269	.4279	.4288	.4298	.4308	.4318	.4328	.4338
.72	.4348	.4358	.4368	.4378	.4388	.4397	.4407	.4417	.4427	.4437
.73	.4447	.4457	.4467	.4477	.4487	.4497	.4507	.4517	.4527	.4537
.74	.4547	.4557	.4567	.4577	.4586	.4596	.4606	.4616	.4626	.4636
.75	.4646	.4656	.4666	.4676	.4686	.4696	.4706	.4716	.4726	.4736
.76	.4746	.4756	.4766	.4776	.4786	.4796	.4806	.4816	.4826	.4836
.77	.4846	.4856	.4866	.4876	.4886	.4896	.4906	.4916	.4926	.4936
.78	.4946	.4956	.4966	.4976	.4986	.4996	.5006	.5016	.5026	.5036
.79	.5046	.5056	.5066	.5076	.5086	.5096	.5106	.5116	.5126	.5136
.80	.5146	.5156	.5166	.5176	.5186	.5196	.5206	.5216	.5226	.5236
.81	.5246	.5256	.5266	.5276	.5286	.5296	.5306	.5316	.5326	.5336
.82	.5346	.5356	.5366	.5376	.5386	.5396	.5406	.5416	.5426	.5435
.83	.5445	.5455	.5465	.5475	.5485	.5495	.5505	.5515	.5525	.5535
.84	.5545	.5555	.5565	.5575	.5585	.5595	.5605	.5614	.5624	.5634
.85	.5644	.5654	.5664	.5674	.5684	.5694	.5704	.5714	.5723	.5733
.86	.5743	.5753	.5763	.5773	.5783	.5793	.5803	.5812	.5822	.5832
.87	.5842	.5852	.5862	.5872	.5881	.5891	.5901	.5911	.5921	.5931
.88	.5940	.5950	.5960	.5970	.5980	.5989	.5999	.6009	.6019	.6029
.89	.6038	.6048	.6058	.6068	.6077	.6087	.6097	.6107	.6117	.6126
.90	.6136	.6146	.6155	.6165	.6175	.6185	.6194	.6204	.6214	.6223
.91	.6233	.6243	.6253	.6262	.6272	.6282	.6291	.6301	.6311	.6320
.92	.6330	.6339	.6349	.6359	.6368	.6378	.6388	.6397	.6407	.6416
.93	.6426	.6436	.6445	.6455	.6464	.6474	.6483	.6493	.6502	.6512
.94	.6522	.6531	.6541	.6550	.6560	.6569	.6579	.6588	.6598	.6607
.95	.6616	.6626	.6635	.6645	.6654	.6664	.6673	.6683	.6692	.6701
.96	.6711	.6720	.6730	.6739	.6748	.6758	.6767	.6776	.6786	.6795
.97	.6804	.6814	.6823	.6832	.6842	.6851	.6860	.6869	.6879	.6888
.98	.6897	.6907	.6916	.6925	.6934	.6943	.6953	.6962	.6971	.6980
.99	.6989	.6999	.7008	.7017	.7026	.7035	.7044	.7053	.7063	.7072

TABLE A.18(b) (continued)

TABLE OF $SIN^2 \gamma$

P	.000	.001	.002	.003	.004	.005	.006	.007	.008	.009
1.00	.7081	.7090	.7099	.7108	.7117	.7126	.7135	.7144	.7153	.7162
1.01	.7171	.7180	.7189	.7198	.7207	.7216	.7225	.7234	.7243	.7252
1.02	.7261	.7270	.7279	.7288	.7296	.7305	.7314	.7323	.7332	.7341
1.03	.7350	.7358	.7367	.7376	.7385	.7394	.7402	.7411	.7420	.7429
1.04	.7437	.7446	.7455	.7464	.7472	.7481	.7490	.7498	.7507	.7516
1.05	.7524	.7533	.7541	.7550	.7559	.7567	.7576	.7584	.7593	.7602
1.06	.7610	.7619	.7627	.7636	.7644	.7653	.7661	.7669	.7678	.7686
1.07	.7695	.7703	.7712	.7720	.7728	.7737	.7745	.7754	.7762	.7770
1.08	.7778	.7787	.7795	.7803	.7812	.7820	.7828	.7836	.7845	.7853
1.09	.7861	.7869	.7877	.7886	.7894	.7902	.7910	.7918	.7926	.7934
1.10	.7943	.7951	.7959	.7967	.7975	.7983	.7991	.7999	.8007	.8015
1.11	.8023	.8031	.8039	.8047	.8055	.8062	.8070	.8078	.8086	.8094
1.12	.8102	.8110	.8117	.8125	.8133	.8141	.8149	.8156	.8164	.8172
1.13	.8180	.8187	.8195	.8203	.8210	.8218	.8226	.8233	.8241	.8249
1.14	.8256	.8264	.8271	.8279	.8286	.8294	.8301	.8309	.8316	.8324
1.15	.8331	.8339	.8346	.8354	.8361	.8368	.8376	.8383	.8391	.8398
1.16	.8405	.8413	.8420	.8427	.8434	.8442	.8449	.8456	.8463	.8471
1.17	.8478	.8485	.8492	.8499	.8506	.8514	.8521	.8528	.8535	.8542
1.18	.8549	.8556	.8563	.8570	.8577	.8584	.8591	.8598	.8605	.8612
1.19	.8619	.8626	.8632	.8639	.8646	.8653	.8660	.8667	.8673	.8680
1.20	.8687	.8694	.8700	.8707	.8714	.8721	.8727	.8734	.8741	.8747
1.21	.8754	.8760	.8767	.8774	.8780	.8787	.8793	.8800	.8806	.8813
1.22	.8819	.8826	.8832	.8838	.8845	.8851	.8858	.8864	.8870	.8877
1.23	.8883	.8889	.8895	.8902	.8908	.8914	.8920	.8927	.8933	.8939
1.24	.8945	.8951	.8957	.8963	.8970	.8976	.8982	.8988	.8994	.9000
1.25	.9006	.9012	.9018	.9024	.9030	.9035	.9041	.9047	.9053	.9059
1.26	.9065	.9071	.9076	.9082	.9088	.9094	.9099	.9105	.9111	.9117
1.27	.9122	.9128	.9133	.9139	.9145	.9150	.9156	.9161	.9167	.9172
1.28	.9178	.9183	.9189	.9194	.9200	.9205	.9211	.9216	.9221	.9227
1.29	.9232	.9237	.9243	.9248	.9253	.9258	.9264	.9269	.9274	.9279
1.30	.9284	.9290	.9295	.9300	.9305	.9310	.9315	.9320	.9325	.9330
1.31	.9335	.9340	.9345	.9350	.9355	.9360	.9365	.9370	.9374	.9379
1.32	.9384	.9389	.9394	.9398	.9403	.9408	.9413	.9417	.9422	.9427
1.33	.9431	.9436	.9441	.9445	.9450	.9454	.9459	.9463	.9468	.9472
1.34	.9477	.9481	.9486	.9490	.9494	.9499	.9503	.9507	.9512	.9516
1.35	.9520	.9525	.9529	.9533	.9537	.9542	.9546	.9550	.9554	.9558
1.36	.9562	.9566	.9570	.9574	.9578	.9582	.9586	.9590	.9594	.9598
1.37	.9602	.9606	.9610	.9614	.9618	.9622	.9625	.9629	.9633	.9637
1.38	.9640	.9644	.9648	.9651	.9655	.9659	.9662	.9666	.9670	.9673
1.39	.9677	.9680	.9684	.9687	.9691	.9694	.9698	.9701	.9704	.9708
1.40	.9711	.9714	.9718	.9721	.9724	.9728	.9731	.9734	.9737	.9740
1.41	.9744	.9747	.9750	.9753	.9756	.9759	.9762	.9765	.9768	.9771
1.42	.9774	.9777	.9780	.9783	.9786	.9789	.9792	.9795	.9797	.9800
1.43	.9803	.9806	.9809	.9811	.9814	.9817	.9819	.9822	.9825	.9827
1.44	.9830	.9832	.9835	.9838	.9840	.9843	.9845	.9848	.9850	.9852
1.45	.9855	.9857	.9860	.9862	.9864	.9867	.9869	.9871	.9873	.9876
1.46	.9878	.9880	.9882	.9884	.9886	.9888	.9891	.9893	.9895	.9897
1.47	.9899	.9901	.9903	.9905	.9907	.9909	.9910	.9912	.9914	.9916
1.48	.9918	.9920	.9921	.9923	.9925	.9927	.9928	.9930	.9932	.9933
1.49	.9935	.9936	.9938	.9940	.9941	.9943	.9944	.9946	.9947	.9949

TABLE A.19 (a and b) – TABLES OF THE LOG-ODDS AND INVERSE LOG-ODDS TRANSFORM

TABLE A.19 (a): Table of the Log-Odds Transform

The quantity tabulated is for $\lambda = \ln[\pi/(1 - \pi)]$ as a function of π, for $\pi = .5(.001).999$. For values of $\pi = .001(.001).5$, the corresponding value of $\lambda = \lambda(\pi)$ can be obtained using the relation $\lambda(1 - \pi) = -\lambda(\pi)$. Thus, for $\pi = .2$, $\lambda(\pi) = -\lambda(1 - \pi) = -\lambda(.8) = -1.3863$. If π is given to more than three decimal places linear interpolation will be adequate in the range $.05 \leq \pi \leq .95$.

λ(π)	.000	.001	.002	.003	.004	.005	.006	.007	.008	.009
.50	.0000	.0040	.0080	.0120	.0160	.0200	.0240	.0280	.0320	.0360
.51	.0400	.0440	.0480	.0520	.0560	.0600	.0640	.0680	.0720	.0760
.52	.0800	.0840	.0881	.0921	.0961	.1001	.1041	.1081	.1121	.1161
.53	.1201	.1242	.1282	.1322	.1362	.1402	.1442	.1483	.1523	.1563
.54	.1603	.1644	.1684	.1724	.1765	.1805	.1845	.1886	.1926	.1966
.55	.2007	.2047	.2088	.2128	.2168	.2209	.2249	.2290	.2330	.2371
.56	.2412	.2452	.2493	.2533	.2574	.2615	.2655	.2696	.2737	.2778
.57	.2819	.2859	.2900	.2941	.2982	.3023	.3064	.3105	.3146	.3187
.58	.3228	.3269	.3310	.3351	.3392	.3433	.3475	.3516	.3557	.3598
.59	.3640	.3681	.3722	.3764	.3805	.3847	.3888	.3930	.3971	.4013
.60	.4055	.4096	.4138	.4180	.4222	.4263	.4305	.4347	.4389	.4431
.61	.4473	.4515	.4557	.4599	.4642	.4684	.4726	.4768	.4811	.4853
.62	.4895	.4938	.4980	.5023	.5066	.5108	.5151	.5194	.5236	.5279
.63	.5322	.5365	.5408	.5451	.5494	.5537	.5580	.5624	.5667	.5710
.64	.5754	.5797	.5841	.5884	.5928	.5971	.6015	.6059	.6103	.6146
.65	.6190	.6234	.6278	.6323	.6367	.6411	.6455	.6500	.6544	.6588
.66	.6633	.6678	.6722	.6767	.6812	.6857	.6901	.6946	.6992	.7037
.67	.7082	.7127	.7172	.7218	.7263	.7309	.7354	.7400	.7446	.7492
.68	.7538	.7584	.7630	.7676	.7722	.7768	.7815	.7861	.7908	.7954
.69	.8001	.8048	.8095	.8142	.8189	.8236	.8283	.8331	.8378	.8425
.70	.8473	.8521	.8568	.8616	.8664	.8712	.8760	.8809	.8857	.8905
.71	.8954	.9002	.9051	.9100	.9149	.9198	.9247	.9296	.9346	.9395
.72	.9445	.9494	.9544	.9594	.9644	.9694	.9744	.9795	.9845	.9896
.73	.9946	.9997	1.0048	1.0099	1.0150	1.0201	1.0253	1.0304	1.0356	1.0408
.74	1.0460	1.0512	1.0564	1.0616	1.0669	1.0721	1.0774	1.0827	1.0880	1.0933
.75	1.0986	1.1040	1.1093	1.1147	1.1201	1.1255	1.1309	1.1363	1.1417	1.1472
.76	1.1527	1.1582	1.1637	1.1692	1.1747	1.1803	1.1859	1.1914	1.1971	1.2027
.77	1.2083	1.2140	1.2196	1.2253	1.2310	1.2368	1.2425	1.2483	1.2540	1.2598
.78	1.2657	1.2715	1.2774	1.2832	1.2891	1.2950	1.3010	1.3069	1.3129	1.3189
.79	1.3249	1.3310	1.3370	1.3431	1.3492	1.3553	1.3615	1.3676	1.3738	1.3801
.80	1.3863	1.3926	1.3988	1.4052	1.4115	1.4178	1.4242	1.4306	1.4371	1.4435
.81	1.4500	1.4565	1.4631	1.4696	1.4762	1.4828	1.4895	1.4962	1.5029	1.5096
.82	1.5163	1.5231	1.5300	1.5368	1.5437	1.5506	1.5575	1.5645	1.5715	1.5786
.83	1.5856	1.5927	1.5999	1.6070	1.6142	1.6215	1.6288	1.6361	1.6434	1.6508
.84	1.6582	1.6657	1.6732	1.6807	1.6883	1.6959	1.7036	1.7113	1.7190	1.7268
.85	1.7346	1.7425	1.7504	1.7583	1.7663	1.7744	1.7825	1.7906	1.7988	1.8070
.86	1.8153	1.8236	1.8320	1.8404	1.8489	1.8575	1.8660	1.8747	1.8834	1.8921
.87	1.9010	1.9098	1.9188	1.9277	1.9368	1.9459	1.9551	1.9643	1.9736	1.9830
.88	1.9924	2.0019	2.0115	2.0212	2.0309	2.0407	2.0505	2.0605	2.0705	2.0806
.89	2.0907	2.1010	2.1113	2.1218	2.1323	2.1429	2.1535	2.1643	2.1752	2.1862
.90	2.1972	2.2084	2.2196	2.2310	2.2425	2.2541	2.2657	2.2775	2.2895	2.3015
.91	2.3136	2.3259	2.3383	2.3508	2.3635	2.3763	2.3892	2.4023	2.4155	2.4288
.92	2.4423	2.4560	2.4698	2.4838	2.4980	2.5123	2.5268	2.5415	2.5564	2.5714
.93	2.5867	2.6022	2.6178	2.6337	2.6498	2.6662	2.6827	2.6995	2.7166	2.7339
.94	2.7515	2.7694	2.7876	2.8060	2.8248	2.8439	2.8633	2.8830	2.9031	2.9236
.95	2.9444	2.9657	2.9874	3.0095	3.0320	3.0550	3.0786	3.1026	3.1272	3.1523
.96	3.1781	3.2044	3.2314	3.2591	3.2876	3.3168	3.3468	3.3777	3.4095	3.4423
.97	3.4761	3.5110	3.5472	3.5845	3.6233	3.6636	3.7054	3.7490	3.7945	3.8420
.98	3.8918	3.9441	3.9992	4.0574	4.1190	4.1846	4.2546	4.3297	4.4108	4.4988
.99	4.5951	4.7015	4.8203	4.9548	5.1100	5.2933	5.5175	5.8061	6.2126	6.9068

TABLE A.19 (b) : TABLE OF INVERSE LOG-ODDS TRANSFORM

The quantity tabulated is $\pi = e^{\lambda}/(1 + e^{\lambda})$ as a function of λ, for $\lambda = 0(.01)4.99$. For values of $\lambda = -4.99(.01)0$, the corresponding value of $\pi = \pi(\lambda)$ can be obtained using the relation $\pi(\lambda) = 1 - \pi(-\lambda)$. Thus, for $\lambda = -.2$, $\pi(\lambda) = 1 - \pi(.2) = 1 - .5498 = .4501$.

$\pi(\lambda)$	.00	.01	.02	.03	.04	.05	.06	.07	.08	.09
0.0	.5000	.5025	.5050	.5075	.5100	.5125	.5150	.5175	.5200	.5225
0.1	.5250	.5275	.5300	.5325	.5349	.5374	.5399	.5424	.5449	.5474
0.2	.5498	.5523	.5548	.5572	.5597	.5622	.5646	.5671	.5695	.5720
0.3	.5744	.5769	.5793	.5818	.5842	.5866	.5890	.5915	.5939	.5963
0.4	.5987	.6011	.6035	.6059	.6083	.6106	.6130	.6154	.6177	.6201
0.5	.6225	.6248	.6271	.6295	.6318	.6341	.6365	.6388	.6411	.6434
0.6	.6457	.6479	.6502	.6525	.6548	.6570	.6593	.6615	.6637	.6660
0.7	.6682	.6704	.6726	.6748	.6770	.6792	.6814	.6835	.6857	.6878
0.8	.6900	.6921	.6942	.6964	.6985	.7006	.7027	.7047	.7068	.7089
0.9	.7109	.7130	.7150	.7171	.7191	.7211	.7231	.7251	.7271	.7291
1.0	.7311	.7330	.7350	.7369	.7389	.7408	.7427	.7446	.7465	.7484
1.1	.7503	.7521	.7540	.7558	.7577	.7595	.7613	.7631	.7649	.7667
1.2	.7685	.7703	.7721	.7738	.7756	.7773	.7790	.7807	.7824	.7841
1.3	.7858	.7875	.7892	.7908	.7925	.7941	.7958	.7974	.7990	.8006
1.4	.8022	.8038	.8053	.8069	.8085	.8100	.8115	.8131	.8146	.8161
1.5	.8176	.8191	.8205	.8220	.8235	.8249	.8264	.8278	.8292	.8306
1.6	.8320	.8334	.8348	.8362	.8375	.8389	.8402	.8416	.8429	.8442
1.7	.8455	.8468	.8481	.8494	.8507	.8520	.8532	.8545	.8557	.8569
1.8	.8581	.8594	.8606	.8618	.8629	.8641	.8653	.8665	.8676	.8688
1.9	.8699	.8710	.8721	.8732	.8744	.8754	.8765	.8776	.8787	.8797
2.0	.8808	.8818	.8829	.8839	.8849	.8859	.8870	.8880	.8889	.8899
2.1	.8909	.8919	.8928	.8938	.8947	.8957	.8966	.8975	.8984	.8993
2.2	.9002	.9011	.9020	.9029	.9038	.9047	.9055	.9064	.9072	.9080
2.3	.9089	.9097	.9105	.9113	.9121	.9129	.9137	.9145	.9153	.9161
2.4	.9168	.9176	.9183	.9191	.9198	.9206	.9213	.9220	.9227	.9234
2.5	.9241	.9248	.9255	.9262	.9269	.9276	.9282	.9289	.9296	.9302
2.6	.9309	.9315	.9321	.9328	.9334	.9340	.9346	.9352	.9358	.9364
2.7	.9370	.9376	.9382	.9388	.9393	.9399	.9405	.9410	.9416	.9421
2.8	.9427	.9432	.9437	.9443	.9448	.9453	.9458	.9463	.9468	.9473
2.9	.9478	.9483	.9488	.9493	.9498	.9503	.9507	.9512	.9517	.9521
3.0	.9526	.9530	.9535	.9539	.9543	.9548	.9552	.9556	.9561	.9565
3.1	.9569	.9573	.9577	.9581	.9585	.9589	.9593	.9597	.9601	.9605
3.2	.9608	.9612	.9616	.9619	.9623	.9627	.9630	.9634	.9637	.9641
3.3	.9644	.9648	.9651	.9654	.9658	.9661	.9664	.9668	.9671	.9674
3.4	.9677	.9680	.9683	.9686	.9689	.9692	.9695	.9698	.9701	.9704
3.5	.9707	.9710	.9713	.9715	.9718	.9721	.9723	.9726	.9729	.9731
3.6	.9734	.9737	.9739	.9742	.9744	.9747	.9749	.9752	.9754	.9756
3.7	.9759	.9761	.9763	.9766	.9768	.9770	.9772	.9775	.9777	.9779
3.8	.9781	.9783	.9785	.9788	.9790	.9792	.9794	.9796	.9798	.9800
3.9	.9802	.9804	.9805	.9807	.9809	.9811	.9813	.9815	.9817	.9818
4.0	.9820	.9822	.9824	.9825	.9827	.9829	.9830	.9832	.9834	.9835
4.1	.9837	.9839	.9840	.9842	.9843	.9845	.9846	.9848	.9849	.9851
4.2	.9852	.9854	.9855	.9857	.9858	.9859	.9861	.9862	.9863	.9865
4.3	.9866	.9867	.9869	.9870	.9871	.9873	.9874	.9875	.9876	.9878
4.4	.9879	.9880	.9881	.9882	.9883	.9885	.9886	.9887	.9888	.9889
4.5	.9890	.9891	.9892	.9893	.9894	.9895	.9896	.9897	.9898	.9899
4.6	.9900	.9901	.9902	.9903	.9904	.9905	.9906	.9907	.9908	.9909
4.7	.9910	.9911	.9912	.9913	.9913	.9914	.9915	.9916	.9917	.9918
4.8	.9918	.9919	.9920	.9921	.9922	.9922	.9923	.9924	.9925	.9925
4.9	.9926	.9927	.9928	.9928	.9929	.9930	.9930	.9931	.9932	.9932

TABLE A.20 (a and b) – TABLES OF FISHER z-TRANSFORMATION AND ITS INVERSE

TABLE A.20 (a) : TABLE OF THE FISHER z-TRANSFORMATION

z-transformation of the correlation coefficient

$z = \tanh^{-1}(r)$ $\quad r = 0.0(.001).999$

r	.000	.001	.002	.003	.004	.005	.006	.007	.008	.009
.000	.000000	.001000	.002000	.003000	.004000	.005000	.006000	.007000	.008000	.009000
.010	.01000	.01100	.01200	.01300	.01400	.01500	.01600	.01700	.01800	.01900
.020	.02000	.02100	.02200	.02300	.02400	.02501	.02601	.02701	.02801	.02901
.030	.03001	.03101	.03201	.03301	.03401	.03501	.03602	.03702	.03802	.03902
.040	.04002	.04102	.04202	.04303	.04403	.04503	.04603	.04703	.04804	.04904
.050	.05004	.05104	.05205	.05305	.05405	.05506	.05606	.05706	.05807	.05907
.060	.06007	.06108	.06208	.06308	.06409	.06509	.06610	.06710	.06811	.06911
.070	.07011	.07112	.07212	.07313	.07414	.07514	.07615	.07715	.07816	.07916
.080	.08017	.08118	.08218	.08319	.08420	.08521	.08621	.08722	.08823	.08924
.090	.09024	.09125	.09226	.09327	.09428	.09529	.09630	.09731	.09832	.09933
.100	.1003	.1013	.1024	.1034	.1044	.1054	.1064	.1074	.1084	.1094
.110	.1104	.1115	.1125	.1135	.1145	.1155	.1165	.1175	.1186	.1196
.120	.1206	.1216	.1226	.1236	.1246	.1257	.1267	.1277	.1287	.1297
.130	.1307	.1318	.1328	.1338	.1348	.1358	.1368	.1379	.1389	.1399
.140	.1409	.1419	.1430	.1440	.1450	.1460	.1471	.1481	.1491	.1501
.150	.1511	.1522	.1532	.1542	.1552	.1563	.1573	.1583	.1593	.1604
.160	.1614	.1624	.1634	.1645	.1655	.1665	.1676	.1686	.1696	.1706
.170	.1717	.1727	.1737	.1748	.1758	.1768	.1779	.1789	.1799	.1809
.180	.1820	.1830	.1841	.1851	.1861	.1872	.1882	.1892	.1903	.1913
.190	.1923	.1934	.1944	.1955	.1965	.1975	.1986	.1996	.2007	.2017
.200	.2027	.2038	.2048	.2059	.2069	.2079	.2090	.2100	.2111	.2121
.210	.2132	.2142	.2153	.2163	.2174	.2184	.2195	.2205	.2216	.2226
.220	.2237	.2247	.2258	.2268	.2279	.2289	.2300	.2310	.2321	.2331
.230	.2342	.2352	.2363	.2374	.2384	.2395	.2405	.2416	.2427	.2437
.240	.2448	.2458	.2469	.2480	.2490	.2501	.2512	.2522	.2533	.2543
.250	.2554	.2565	.2575	.2586	.2597	.2608	.2618	.2629	.2640	.2650
.260	.2661	.2672	.2683	.2693	.2704	.2715	.2726	.2736	.2747	.2758
.270	.2769	.2779	.2790	.2801	.2812	.2823	.2833	.2844	.2855	.2866
.280	.2877	.2888	.2899	.2909	.2920	.2931	.2942	.2953	.2964	.2975
.290	.2986	.2997	.3008	.3018	.3029	.3040	.3051	.3062	.3073	.3084
.300	.3095	.3106	.3117	.3128	.3139	.3150	.3161	.3172	.3183	.3194
.310	.3205	.3217	.3228	.3239	.3250	.3261	.3272	.3283	.3294	.3305
.320	.3316	.3328	.3339	.3350	.3361	.3372	.3383	.3395	.3406	.3417
.330	.3428	.3440	.3451	.3462	.3473	.3484	.3496	.3507	.3518	.3530
.340	.3541	.3552	.3564	.3575	.3586	.3598	.3609	.3620	.3632	.3643
.350	.3654	.3666	.3677	.3689	.3700	.3712	.3723	.3734	.3746	.3757
.360	.3769	.3780	.3792	.3803	.3815	.3826	.3838	.3850	.3861	.3873
.370	.3884	.3896	.3907	.3919	.3931	.3942	.3954	.3966	.3977	.3989
.380	.4001	.4012	.4024	.4036	.4047	.4059	.4071	.4083	.4094	.4106
.390	.4118	.4130	.4142	.4153	.4165	.4177	.4189	.4201	.4213	.4225
.400	.4236	.4248	.4260	.4272	.4284	.4296	.4308	.4320	.4332	.4344
.410	.4356	.4368	.4380	.4392	.4404	.4416	.4428	.4441	.4453	.4465
.420	.4477	.4489	.4501	.4513	.4526	.4538	.4550	.4562	.4574	.4587
.430	.4599	.4611	.4624	.4636	.4648	.4660	.4673	.4685	.4698	.4710
.440	.4722	.4735	.4747	.4760	.4772	.4784	.4797	.4809	.4822	.4834
.450	.4847	.4860	.4872	.4885	.4897	.4910	.4922	.4935	.4948	.4960
.460	.4973	.4986	.4999	.5011	.5024	.5037	.5049	.5062	.5075	.5088
.470	.5101	.5114	.5126	.5139	.5152	.5165	.5178	.5191	.5204	.5217
.480	.5230	.5243	.5256	.5269	.5282	.5295	.5308	.5321	.5334	.5347
.490	.5361	.5374	.5387	.5400	.5413	.5427	.5440	.5453	.5466	.5480
.500	.5493	.5506	.5520	.5533	.5547	.5560	.5573	.5587	.5600	.5614

TABLE A.20(a) (continued)

TABLE OF FISHER z-TRANSFORMATION

r	.000	.001	.002	.003	.004	.005	.006	.007	.008	.009
.510	.5627	.5641	.5654	.5668	.5682	.5695	.5709	.5722	.5736	.5750
.520	.5763	.5777	.5791	.5805	.5818	.5832	.5846	.5860	.5874	.5888
.530	.5901	.5915	.5929	.5943	.5957	.5971	.5985	.5999	.6013	.6027
.540	.6042	.6056	.6070	.6084	.6098	.6112	.6127	.6141	.6155	.6169
.550	.6184	.6198	.6213	.6227	.6241	.6256	.6270	.6285	.6299	.6314
.560	.6328	.6343	.6358	.6372	.6387	.6401	.6416	.6431	.6446	.6460
.570	.6475	.6490	.6505	.6520	.6535	.6550	.6565	.6580	.6595	.6610
.580	.6625	.6640	.6655	.6670	.6685	.6700	.6716	.6731	.6746	.6761
.590	.6777	.6792	.6807	.6823	.6838	.6854	.6869	.6885	.6900	.6916
.600	.6931	.6947	.6963	.6978	.6994	.7010	.7026	.7042	.7057	.7073
.610	.7089	.7105	.7121	.7137	.7153	.7169	.7185	.7201	.7218	.7234
.620	.7250	.7266	.7283	.7299	.7315	.7332	.7348	.7365	.7381	.7398
.630	.7414	.7431	.7447	.7464	.7481	.7498	.7514	.7531	.7548	.7565
.640	.7582	.7599	.7616	.7633	.7650	.7667	.7684	.7701	.7718	.7736
.650	.7753	.7770	.7788	.7805	.7823	.7840	.7858	.7875	.7893	.7910
.660	.7928	.7946	.7964	.7981	.7999	.8017	.8035	.8053	.8071	.8089
.670	.8107	.8126	.8144	.8162	.8180	.8199	.8217	.8236	.8254	.8273
.680	.8291	.8310	.8328	.8347	.8366	.8385	.8404	.8423	.8441	.8460
.690	.8480	.8499	.8518	.8537	.8556	.8576	.8595	.8614	.8634	.8653
.700	.8673	.8693	.8712	.8732	.8752	.8772	.8792	.8812	.8832	.8852
.710	.8872	.8892	.8912	.8933	.8953	.8973	.8994	.9014	.9035	.9056
.720	.9076	.9097	.9118	.9139	.9160	.9181	.9202	.9223	.9245	.9266
.730	.9287	.9309	.9330	.9352	.9373	.9395	.9417	.9439	.9461	.9483
.740	.9505	.9527	.9549	.9571	.9594	.9616	.9639	.9661	.9684	.9707
.750	.9730	.9752	.9775	.9798	.9822	.9845	.9868	.9892	.9915	.9939
.760	.9962	.9986	1.001	1.003	1.006	1.008	1.011	1.013	1.015	1.018
.770	1.020	1.023	1.025	1.028	1.030	1.033	1.035	1.038	1.040	1.043
.780	1.045	1.048	1.050	1.053	1.056	1.058	1.061	1.064	1.066	1.069
.790	1.071	1.074	1.077	1.079	1.082	1.085	1.088	1.090	1.093	1.096
.800	1.099	1.101	1.104	1.107	1.110	1.113	1.116	1.118	1.121	1.124
.810	1.127	1.130	1.133	1.136	1.139	1.142	1.145	1.148	1.151	1.154
.820	1.157	1.160	1.163	1.166	1.169	1.172	1.175	1.179	1.182	1.185
.830	1.188	1.191	1.195	1.198	1.201	1.204	1.208	1.211	1.214	1.218
.840	1.221	1.225	1.228	1.231	1.235	1.238	1.242	1.245	1.249	1.253
.850	1.256	1.260	1.263	1.267	1.271	1.274	1.278	1.282	1.286	1.290
.860	1.293	1.297	1.301	1.305	1.309	1.313	1.317	1.321	1.325	1.329
.870	1.333	1.337	1.341	1.346	1.350	1.354	1.358	1.363	1.367	1.371
.880	1.376	1.380	1.385	1.389	1.394	1.398	1.403	1.408	1.412	1.417
.890	1.422	1.427	1.432	1.437	1.442	1.447	1.452	1.457	1.462	1.467
.900	1.472	1.478	1.483	1.488	1.494	1.499	1.505	1.510	1.516	1.522
.910	1.528	1.533	1.539	1.545	1.551	1.557	1.564	1.570	1.576	1.583
.920	1.589	1.596	1.602	1.609	1.616	1.623	1.630	1.637	1.644	1.651
.930	1.658	1.666	1.673	1.681	1.689	1.697	1.705	1.713	1.721	1.730
.940	1.738	1.747	1.756	1.764	1.774	1.783	1.792	1.802	1.812	1.822
.950	1.832	1.842	1.853	1.863	1.874	1.886	1.897	1.909	1.921	1.933
.960	1.946	1.959	1.972	1.986	2.000	2.014	2.029	2.044	2.060	2.076
.970	2.092	2.109	2.127	2.146	2.165	2.185	2.205	2.227	2.249	2.273
.980	2.298	2.323	2.351	2.380	2.410	2.443	2.477	2.515	2.555	2.599
.990	2.647	2.700	2.759	2.826	2.903	2.994	3.106	3.250	3.453	3.800

TABLE A.20 (b) : INVERSE OF FISHER z-TRANSFORMATION

r = tanh(z)   z = 0.0(.01)4.99

z	.00	.01	.02	.03	.04	.05	.06	.07	.08	.09
.0	.0000	.0100	.0200	.0300	.0400	.0500	.0599	.0699	.0798	.0898
.1	.0997	.1096	.1194	.1293	.1391	.1489	.1586	.1684	.1781	.1877
.2	.1974	.2070	.2165	.2260	.2355	.2449	.2543	.2636	.2729	.2821
.3	.2913	.3004	.3095	.3185	.3275	.3364	.3452	.3540	.3627	.3714
.4	.3799	.3885	.3969	.4053	.4136	.4219	.4301	.4382	.4462	.4542
.5	.4621	.4699	.4777	.4854	.4930	.5005	.5080	.5154	.5227	.5299
.6	.5370	.5441	.5511	.5581	.5649	.5717	.5784	.5850	.5915	.5980
.7	.6044	.6107	.6169	.6231	.6291	.6351	.6411	.6469	.6527	.6584
.8	.6640	.6696	.6751	.6805	.6858	.6911	.6963	.7014	.7064	.7114
.9	.7163	.7211	.7259	.7306	.7352	.7398	.7443	.7487	.7531	.7574
1.0	.7616	.7658	.7699	.7739	.7779	.7818	.7857	.7895	.7932	.7969
1.1	.8005	.8041	.8076	.8110	.8144	.8178	.8210	.8243	.8275	.8306
1.2	.8337	.8367	.8397	.8426	.8455	.8483	.8511	.8538	.8565	.8591
1.3	.8617	.8643	.8668	.8692	.8717	.8741	.8764	.8787	.8810	.8832
1.4	.8854	.8875	.8896	.8917	.8937	.8957	.8977	.8996	.9015	.9033
1.5	.9051	.9069	.9087	.9104	.9121	.9138	.9154	.9170	.9186	.9201
1.6	.9217	.9232	.9246	.9261	.9275	.9289	.9302	.9316	.9329	.9341
1.7	.9354	.9366	.9379	.9391	.9402	.9414	.9425	.9436	.9447	.9458
1.8	.9468	.9478	.9488	.9498	.9508	.9517	.9527	.9536	.9545	.9554
1.9	.9562	.9571	.9579	.9587	.9595	.9603	.9611	.9618	.9626	.9633
2.0	.9640	.9647	.9654	.9661	.9667	.9674	.9680	.9687	.9693	.9699
2.1	.9705	.9710	.9716	.9721	.9727	.9732	.9737	.9743	.9748	.9753
2.2	.9757	.9762	.9767	.9771	.9776	.9780	.9785	.9789	.9793	.9797
2.3	.9801	.9805	.9809	.9812	.9816	.9820	.9823	.9827	.9830	.9833
2.4	.9837	.9840	.9843	.9846	.9849	.9852	.9855	.9858	.9861	.9863
2.5	.9866	.9869	.9871	.9874	.9876	.9879	.9881	.9884	.9886	.9888
2.6	.9890	.9892	.9895	.9897	.9899	.9901	.9903	.9905	.9906	.9908
2.7	.9910	.9912	.9914	.9915	.9917	.9919	.9920	.9922	.9923	.9925
2.8	.9926	.9928	.9929	.9931	.9932	.9933	.9935	.9936	.9937	.9938
2.9	.9940	.9941	.9942	.9943	.9944	.9945	.9946	.9947	.9949	.9950
3.0	.9951	.9952	.9952	.9953	.9954	.9955	.9956	.9957	.9958	.9959
3.1	.9959	.9960	.9961	.9962	.9963	.9963	.9964	.9965	.9965	.9966
3.2	.9967	.9967	.9968	.9969	.9969	.9970	.9971	.9971	.9972	.9972
3.3	.9973	.9973	.9974	.9974	.9975	.9975	.9976	.9976	.9977	.9977
3.4	.9978	.9978	.9979	.9979	.9979	.9980	.9980	.9981	.9981	.9981
3.5	.9982	.9982	.9982	.9983	.9983	.9984	.9984	.9984	.9984	.9985
3.6	.9985	.9985	.9986	.9986	.9986	.9986	.9987	.9987	.9987	.9988
3.7	.9988	.9988	.9988	.9988	.9989	.9989	.9989	.9989	.9990	.9990
3.8	.9990	.9990	.9990	.9991	.9991	.9991	.9991	.9991	.9991	.9992
3.9	.9992	.9992	.9992	.9992	.9992	.9993	.9993	.9993	.9993	.9993
4.0	.9993	.9993	.9994	.9994	.9994	.9994	.9994	.9994	.9994	.9994
4.1	.9995	.9995	.9995	.9995	.9995	.9995	.9995	.9995	.9995	.9995
4.2	.9996	.9996	.9996	.9996	.9996	.9996	.9996	.9996	.9996	.9996
4.3	.9996	.9996	.9996	.9997	.9997	.9997	.9997	.9997	.9997	.9997
4.4	.9997	.9997	.9997	.9997	.9997	.9997	.9997	.9997	.9997	.9997
4.5	.9998	.9998	.9998	.9998	.9998	.9998	.9998	.9998	.9998	.9998
4.6	.9998	.9998	.9998	.9998	.9998	.9998	.9998	.9998	.9998	.9998
4.7	.9998	.9998	.9998	.9998	.9998	.9999	.9999	.9999	.9999	.9999
4.8	.9999	.9999	.9999	.9999	.9999	.9999	.9999	.9999	.9999	.9999
4.9	.9999	.9999	.9999	.9999	.9999	.9999	.9999	.9999	.9999	.9999

TABLE A.21

TABLE OF e^{-x}

In the second and third sections of the table multiply the tabled value by the constant preceding that section.

x	0.0	0.1	0.2	0.3	0.4	0.5	0.6	0.7	0.8	0.9
0	1.000000000	.904837418	.818730753	.740818221	.670320046	.606530660	.548811636	.496585304	.449328964	.406569660
1	.367879441	.332871084	.301194212	.272531793	.246596964	.223130160	.201896518	.182683524	.165298888	.149568619
2	.135335283	.122456428	.110803158	.100258844	.090717953	.082084999	.074273578	.067205513	.060810063	.055023220
3	.049787068	.045049202	.040762204	.036883167	.033373270	.030197383	.027323722	.024723526	.022370772	.020241911
4	.018315639	.016572675	.014995577	.013568559	.012277340	.011108997	.010051836	.009095277	.008229747	.007446583
5	.006737947	.006096747	.005516564	.004991594	.004516581	.004086771	.003697864	.003345965	.003027555	.002739445
6	.002478752	.002242868	.002029431	.001836305	.001661557	.001503439	.001360368	.001230912	.001113775	.001007785
7	.000911882	.000825105	.000746586	.000675539	.000611253	.000553084	.000500451	.000452827	.000409735	.000370744
8	.000335463	.000303539	.000274654	.000248517	.000224867	.000203468	.000184106	.000166586	.000150733	.000136389
9	.000123410	.000111666	.000101039	.000091424	.000082724	.000074852	.000067729	.000061283	.000055452	.000050175
10	.000045400	.000041080	.000037170	.000033633	.000030432	.000027536	.000024916	.000022545	.000020400	.000018458
					multiply all entries by 10^{-5}					
11	1.670170079	1.511232382	1.367419607	1.237292426	1.119548484	1.013009360	.916608774	.829381916	.750455792	.679040481
12	.614421235	.555951324	.503045561	.455174446	.411858871	.372665317	.337201523	.305112556	.276077257	.249805033
13	.226032941	.204523062	.185060120	.167449321	.151514411	.137095909	.124049508	.112244637	.101563147	.091898136
14	.083152872	.075239830	.068079813	.061601163	.055739037	.050434766	.045635264	.041292494	.037362994	.033807435
15	.030590232	.027679187	.025045164	.022661801	.020505246	.018553914	.016788275	.015190660	.013745077	.012437060
16	.011253517	.010182604	.009213601	.008336811	.007543458	.006825603	.006176061	.005588331	.005056531	.004575339
17	.004139938	.003745971	.003389494	.003066941	.002775083	.002510999	.002272046	.002055832	.001860194	.001683173
18	.001522998	.001378066	.001246925	.001128265	.001020896	.000923745	.000835839	.000756298	.000684327	.000619205
19	.000560280	.000506962	.000458718	.000415065	.000375567	.000339827	.000307488	.000278227	.000251750	.000227793
20	.000206115	.000186501	.000168753	.000152694	.000138163	.000125015	.000113119	.000102354	.000092614	.000083800
21	.000075826	.000068610	.000062081	.000056173	.000050827	.000045991	.000041614	.000037654	.000034071	.000030828
22	.000027895	.000025240	.000022838	.000020665	.000018698	.000016919	.000015309	.000013852	.000012534	.000011341
					multiply all entries by 10^{-10}					
23	1.026187963	.928533267	.840171644	.760218741	.687874363	.622414462	.563183895	.509589861	.461095974	.417216891
24	.377513454	.341588299	.309081875	.279668846	.253054836	.228973485	.207183777	.187467633	.169627729	.153485517
25	.138879439	.125663313	.113704867	.102884419	.093093672	.084234638	.076218652	.068965488	.062402554	.056464166
26	.051090890	.046228949	.041829683	.037849062	.034247248	.030988191	.028039275	.025370985	.022956617	.020772006
27	.018795288	.017006680	.015388280	.013923892	.012598858	.011399919	.010315073	.009333464	.008445267	.007641594
28	.006914400	.006256408	.005661032	.005122314	.004634861	.004193796	.003794703	.003433589	.003106840	.002811185
29	.002543666	.002301604	.002082577	.001884394	.001705070	.001542811	.001395993	.001263147	.001142943	.001034177
30	.000935762	.000846713	.000766137	.000693230	.000627260	.000567569	.000513557	.000464686	.000420465	.000380453
31	.000344248	.000311488	.000281846	.000255025	.000230756	.000208797	.000188927	.000170948	.000154680	.000139961
32	.000126642	.000114590	.000103685	.000093818	.000084890	.000076812	.000069502	.000062888	.000056904	.000051489
33	.000046589	.000042155	.000038144	.000034514	.000031229	.000028258	.000025569	.000023135	.000020934	.000018942

TABLE A.22

TABLE OF NATURAL LOGARITHMS

This table gives the natural logarithms for the interval $1 \leq x \leq 10$. These are defined by the relationship $e^{\ln(x)} = x$. To find logarithms for values outside the range of the table, add or subtract the proper constant from the foot of the table to shift the decimal point right or left to the desired position.

Examples: $\ln(45.3) = \ln(4.53) + \ln(10^1) = 1.5107 + 2.3026 = 3.8133$

$\ln(.0453) = \ln(4.53) - \ln(10^2) = 1.5107 - 4.6052 = -3.0945$

To find the antilogrithm of a number:

a) If the number lies between 0 and 2.3016, find a row in the table where the number falls between entries in two adjacent columns. The antilog is equal to the sum of the heading to the left of the row, plus the value at the top of the first of the two adjacent columns, plus .01 times the ratio of the difference between the number and the entry in the left column and the difference between the entries in the two columns.

Example: find the antilog of 1.2075.

$$3.30 + .04 + \frac{1.2075 - 1.2060}{1.2090 - 1.2060} = 3.345.$$

b) If the number falls outside the bounds of the table, add or subtract from the number a constant chosen from those at the foot of the table, so that the result will be within the bounds of the table. Proceed as in part (a), and finally, shift the decimal place left or right the number of places corresponding to the constant used. Shift left if you added and right if you subtracted.

Example: find the antilog of -.5056.

1) $-.5056 + 2.3026 = 1.7970$

2) find antilog 1.7970

$$6.00 + .03 + .01 \frac{1.7970 - 1.7967}{1.7984 - 1.7967} = 6.032$$

3) shift the decimal left one place.

The answer is .6032.

TABLE A.22 (continued)

TABLE OF NATURAL LOGARITHMS

x	.00	.01	.02	.03	.04	.05	.06	.07	.08	.09
1.00	.0000	.0100	.0198	.0296	.0392	.0488	.0583	.0677	.0770	.0862
1.10	.0953	.1044	.1133	.1222	.1310	.1398	.1484	.1570	.1655	.1740
1.20	.1823	.1906	.1989	.2070	.2151	.2231	.2311	.2390	.2469	.2546
1.30	.2624	.2700	.2776	.2852	.2927	.3001	.3075	.3148	.3221	.3293
1.40	.3365	.3436	.3507	.3577	.3646	.3716	.3784	.3853	.3920	.3988
1.50	.4055	.4121	.4187	.4253	.4318	.4383	.4447	.4511	.4574	.4637
1.60	.4700	.4762	.4824	.4886	.4947	.5008	.5068	.5128	.5188	.5247
1.70	.5306	.5365	.5423	.5481	.5539	.5596	.5653	.5710	.5766	.5822
1.80	.5878	.5933	.5988	.6043	.6098	.6152	.6206	.6259	.6313	.6366
1.90	.6419	.6471	.6523	.6575	.6627	.6678	.6729	.6780	.6831	.6881
2.00	.6931	.6981	.7031	.7080	.7129	.7178	.7227	.7275	.7324	.7372
2.10	.7419	.7467	.7514	.7561	.7608	.7655	.7701	.7747	.7793	.7839
2.20	.7885	.7930	.7975	.8020	.8065	.8109	.8154	.8198	.8242	.8286
2.30	.8329	.8372	.8416	.8459	.8502	.8544	.8587	.8629	.8671	.8713
2.40	.8755	.8796	.8838	.8879	.8920	.8961	.9002	.9042	.9083	.9123
2.50	.9163	.9203	.9243	.9282	.9322	.9361	.9400	.9439	.9478	.9517
2.60	.9555	.9594	.9632	.9670	.9708	.9746	.9783	.9821	.9858	.9895
2.70	.9933	.9969	1.0006	1.0043	1.0080	1.0116	1.0152	1.0188	1.0225	1.0260
2.80	1.0296	1.0332	1.0367	1.0403	1.0438	1.0473	1.0508	1.0543	1.0578	1.0613
2.90	1.0647	1.0682	1.0716	1.0750	1.0784	1.0818	1.0852	1.0886	1.0919	1.0953
3.00	1.0986	1.1019	1.1053	1.1086	1.1119	1.1151	1.1184	1.1217	1.1249	1.1282
3.10	1.1314	1.1346	1.1378	1.1410	1.1442	1.1474	1.1506	1.1537	1.1569	1.1600
3.20	1.1632	1.1663	1.1694	1.1725	1.1756	1.1787	1.1817	1.1848	1.1878	1.1909
3.30	1.1939	1.1969	1.2000	1.2030	1.2060	1.2090	1.2119	1.2149	1.2179	1.2208
3.40	1.2238	1.2267	1.2296	1.2326	1.2355	1.2384	1.2413	1.2442	1.2470	1.2499
3.50	1.2528	1.2556	1.2585	1.2613	1.2641	1.2669	1.2698	1.2726	1.2754	1.2782
3.60	1.2809	1.2837	1.2865	1.2892	1.2920	1.2947	1.2975	1.3002	1.3029	1.3056
3.70	1.3083	1.3110	1.3137	1.3164	1.3191	1.3218	1.3244	1.3271	1.3297	1.3324
3.80	1.3350	1.3376	1.3403	1.3429	1.3455	1.3481	1.3507	1.3533	1.3558	1.3584
3.90	1.3610	1.3635	1.3661	1.3686	1.3712	1.3737	1.3762	1.3788	1.3813	1.3838
4.00	1.3863	1.3888	1.3913	1.3938	1.3962	1.3987	1.4012	1.4036	1.4061	1.4085
4.10	1.4110	1.4134	1.4159	1.4183	1.4207	1.4231	1.4255	1.4279	1.4303	1.4327
4.20	1.4351	1.4375	1.4398	1.4422	1.4446	1.4469	1.4493	1.4516	1.4540	1.4563
4.30	1.4586	1.4609	1.4633	1.4656	1.4679	1.4702	1.4725	1.4748	1.4770	1.4793
4.40	1.4816	1.4839	1.4861	1.4884	1.4907	1.4929	1.4951	1.4974	1.4996	1.5019
4.50	1.5041	1.5063	1.5085	1.5107	1.5129	1.5151	1.5173	1.5195	1.5217	1.5239
4.60	1.5261	1.5282	1.5304	1.5326	1.5347	1.5369	1.5390	1.5412	1.5433	1.5454
4.70	1.5476	1.5497	1.5518	1.5539	1.5560	1.5581	1.5602	1.5623	1.5644	1.5665
4.80	1.5686	1.5707	1.5728	1.5748	1.5769	1.5790	1.5810	1.5831	1.5851	1.5872
4.90	1.5892	1.5913	1.5933	1.5953	1.5974	1.5994	1.6014	1.6034	1.6054	1.6074
5.00	1.6094	1.6114	1.6134	1.6154	1.6174	1.6194	1.6214	1.6233	1.6253	1.6273
5.10	1.6292	1.6312	1.6332	1.6351	1.6371	1.6390	1.6409	1.6429	1.6448	1.6467
5.20	1.6487	1.6506	1.6525	1.6544	1.6563	1.6582	1.6601	1.6620	1.6639	1.6658
5.30	1.6677	1.6696	1.6715	1.6734	1.6752	1.6771	1.6790	1.6808	1.6827	1.6845
5.40	1.6864	1.6882	1.6901	1.6919	1.6938	1.6956	1.6974	1.6993	1.7011	1.7029
5.50	1.7047	1.7066	1.7084	1.7102	1.7120	1.7138	1.7156	1.7174	1.7192	1.7210

TABLE A.22 (continued)

TABLE OF NATURAL LOGARITHMS

x	.00	.01	.02	.03	.04	.05	.06	.07	.08	.09
5.60	1.7228	1.7246	1.7263	1.7281	1.7299	1.7317	1.7334	1.7352	1.7370	1.7387
5.70	1.7405	1.7422	1.7440	1.7457	1.7475	1.7492	1.7509	1.7527	1.7544	1.7561
5.80	1.7579	1.7596	1.7613	1.7630	1.7647	1.7664	1.7681	1.7699	1.7716	1.7733
5.90	1.7750	1.7766	1.7783	1.7800	1.7817	1.7834	1.7851	1.7867	1.7884	1.7901
6.00	1.7918	1.7934	1.7951	1.7967	1.7984	1.8001	1.8017	1.8034	1.8050	1.8066
6.10	1.8083	1.8099	1.8116	1.8132	1.8148	1.8165	1.8181	1.8197	1.8213	1.8229
6.20	1.8245	1.8262	1.8278	1.8294	1.8310	1.8326	1.8342	1.8358	1.8374	1.8390
6.30	1.8405	1.8421	1.8437	1.8453	1.8469	1.8485	1.8500	1.8516	1.8532	1.8547
6.40	1.8563	1.8579	1.8594	1.8610	1.8625	1.8641	1.8656	1.8672	1.8687	1.8703
6.50	1.8718	1.8733	1.8749	1.8764	1.8779	1.8795	1.8810	1.8825	1.8840	1.8856
6.60	1.8871	1.8886	1.8901	1.8916	1.8931	1.8946	1.8961	1.8976	1.8991	1.9006
6.70	1.9021	1.9036	1.9051	1.9066	1.9081	1.9095	1.9110	1.9125	1.9140	1.9155
6.80	1.9169	1.9184	1.9199	1.9213	1.9228	1.9242	1.9257	1.9272	1.9286	1.9301
6.90	1.9315	1.9330	1.9344	1.9359	1.9373	1.9387	1.9402	1.9416	1.9430	1.9445
7.00	1.9459	1.9473	1.9488	1.9502	1.9516	1.9530	1.9544	1.9559	1.9573	1.9587
7.10	1.9601	1.9615	1.9629	1.9643	1.9657	1.9671	1.9685	1.9699	1.9713	1.9727
7.20	1.9741	1.9755	1.9769	1.9782	1.9796	1.9810	1.9824	1.9838	1.9851	1.9865
7.30	1.9879	1.9892	1.9906	1.9920	1.9933	1.9947	1.9961	1.9974	1.9988	2.0001
7.40	2.0015	2.0028	2.0042	2.0055	2.0069	2.0082	2.0096	2.0109	2.0122	2.0136
7.50	2.0149	2.0162	2.0176	2.0189	2.0202	2.0215	2.0229	2.0242	2.0255	2.0268
7.60	2.0281	2.0295	2.0308	2.0321	2.0334	2.0347	2.0360	2.0373	2.0386	2.0399
7.70	2.0412	2.0425	2.0438	2.0451	2.0464	2.0477	2.0490	2.0503	2.0516	2.0528
7.80	2.0541	2.0554	2.0567	2.0580	2.0592	2.0605	2.0618	2.0631	2.0643	2.0656
7.90	2.0669	2.0681	2.0694	2.0707	2.0719	2.0732	2.0744	2.0757	2.0769	2.0782
8.00	2.0794	2.0807	2.0819	2.0832	2.0844	2.0857	2.0869	2.0882	2.0894	2.0906
8.10	2.0919	2.0931	2.0943	2.0956	2.0968	2.0980	2.0992	2.1005	2.1017	2.1029
8.20	2.1041	2.1054	2.1066	2.1078	2.1090	2.1102	2.1114	2.1126	2.1138	2.1150
8.30	2.1163	2.1175	2.1187	2.1199	2.1211	2.1223	2.1235	2.1247	2.1258	2.1270
8.40	2.1282	2.1294	2.1306	2.1318	2.1330	2.1342	2.1353	2.1365	2.1377	2.1389
8.50	2.1401	2.1412	2.1424	2.1436	2.1448	2.1459	2.1471	2.1483	2.1494	2.1506
8.60	2.1518	2.1529	2.1541	2.1552	2.1564	2.1576	2.1587	2.1599	2.1610	2.1622
8.70	2.1633	2.1645	2.1656	2.1668	2.1679	2.1691	2.1702	2.1713	2.1725	2.1736
8.80	2.1748	2.1759	2.1770	2.1782	2.1793	2.1804	2.1815	2.1827	2.1838	2.1849
8.90	2.1861	2.1872	2.1883	2.1894	2.1905	2.1917	2.1928	2.1939	2.1950	2.1961
9.00	2.1972	2.1983	2.1994	2.2006	2.2017	2.2028	2.2039	2.2050	2.2061	2.2072
9.10	2.2083	2.2094	2.2105	2.2116	2.2127	2.2138	2.2148	2.2159	2.2170	2.2181
9.20	2.2192	2.2203	2.2214	2.2225	2.2235	2.2246	2.2257	2.2268	2.2279	2.2289
9.30	2.2300	2.2311	2.2322	2.2332	2.2343	2.2354	2.2364	2.2375	2.2386	2.2396
9.40	2.2407	2.2418	2.2428	2.2439	2.2450	2.2460	2.2471	2.2481	2.2492	2.2502
9.50	2.2513	2.2523	2.2534	2.2544	2.2555	2.2565	2.2576	2.2586	2.2597	2.2607
9.60	2.2618	2.2628	2.2638	2.2649	2.2659	2.2670	2.2680	2.2690	2.2701	2.2711
9.70	2.2721	2.2732	2.2742	2.2752	2.2762	2.2773	2.2783	2.2793	2.2803	2.2814
9.80	2.2824	2.2834	2.2844	2.2854	2.2865	2.2875	2.2885	2.2895	2.2905	2.2915
9.90	2.2925	2.2935	2.2946	2.2956	2.2966	2.2976	2.2986	2.2996	2.3006	2.3016

10^1	10^2	10^3	10^4	10^5	10^6	10^7	10^8	10^9	10^{10}
2.3026	4.6052	6.9078	9.2103	11.5129	13.8155	16.1181	18.4207	20.7233	23.0259

TABLE A.23

TABLE OF PERCENTAGE POINTS OF THE POSTERIOR DISTRIBUTION OF THE CORRELATION COEFFICIENT. N = 30(1) 50(5) 100, r = 0(0.5) .90.

For observed correlations less than zero, use the negative of the entry for the 100-p% point for -r.

For example: To find the 75% point when N = 35 and r = -.3 find the 100 - 75 = 25% point for N = 35 and r = -(-.3) = .3. By inspection, this value is .1932. The desired value is then -.1932.

For values of N greater than 100 using an hyperbolic tangent transform should result in errors no greater than 5 units in the 3rd decimal place.

N = 30

r	0.0100	0.0250	0.0500	0.1000	0.2500	0.5000	0.7500	0.9000	0.9500	0.9750	0.9900
0.0	-0.4226	-0.3610	-0.3061	-0.2407	-0.1281	0.0000	0.1281	0.2407	0.3061	0.3610	0.4226
0.05	-0.3798	-0.3159	-0.2592	-0.1922	-0.0777	0.0509	0.1778	0.2881	0.3515	0.4045	0.4635
0.10	-0.3352	-0.2691	-0.2108	-0.1425	-0.0266	0.1018	0.2269	0.3343	0.3955	0.4464	0.5027
0.15	-0.2885	-0.2205	-0.1609	-0.0914	0.0251	0.1526	0.2753	0.3794	0.4382	0.4868	0.5403
0.20	-0.2396	-0.1699	-0.1093	-0.0392	0.0774	0.2034	0.3230	0.4234	0.4795	0.5257	0.5764
0.25	-0.1884	-0.1174	-0.0561	0.0144	0.1304	0.2542	0.3701	0.4663	0.5197	0.5634	0.6110
0.30	-0.1348	-0.0628	-0.0011	0.0694	0.1841	0.3049	0.4166	0.5082	0.5586	0.5997	0.6442
0.35	-0.0785	-0.0059	0.0558	0.1257	0.2384	0.3555	0.4624	0.5491	0.5964	0.6348	0.6762
0.40	-0.0193	0.0533	0.1146	0.1835	0.2933	0.4060	0.5075	0.5889	0.6331	0.6687	0.7070
0.45	0.0428	0.1149	0.1753	0.2427	0.3489	0.4564	0.5520	0.6279	0.6687	0.7015	0.7365
0.50	0.1081	0.1792	0.2381	0.3034	0.4051	0.5067	0.5959	0.6659	0.7033	0.7332	0.7650
0.55	0.1769	0.2461	0.3031	0.3656	0.4620	0.5568	0.6391	0.7030	0.7369	0.7639	0.7925
0.60	0.2493	0.3160	0.3703	0.4294	0.5194	0.6068	0.6817	0.7392	0.7695	0.7935	0.8189
0.65	0.3257	0.3889	0.4399	0.4948	0.5775	0.6567	0.7237	0.7746	0.8013	0.8223	0.8444
0.70	0.4064	0.4650	0.5118	0.5618	0.6361	0.7063	0.7650	0.8091	0.8321	0.8501	0.8690
0.75	0.4917	0.5445	0.5863	0.6305	0.6954	0.7558	0.8057	0.8428	0.8620	0.8771	0.8928
0.80	0.5818	0.6276	0.6634	0.7008	0.7552	0.8051	0.8458	0.8758	0.8912	0.9032	0.9157
0.85	0.6773	0.7145	0.7432	0.7729	0.8156	0.8542	0.8852	0.9079	0.9195	0.9285	0.9379
0.90	0.7785	0.8054	0.8258	0.8468	0.8765	0.9030	0.9241	0.9394	0.9471	0.9532	0.9595

TABLE A.23 (continued)

TABLE OF PERCENTAGE POINTS OF THE POSTERIOR DISTRIBUTION OF THE CORRELATION COEFFICIENT

N = 31

r	0.0100	0.0250	0.0500	0.1000	0.2500	0.5000	0.7500	0.9000	0.9500	0.9750	0.9900
0.0	-0.4158	-0.3550	-0.3009	-0.2366	-0.1256	0.0000	0.1256	0.2366	0.3009	0.3550	0.4158
0.05	-0.3728	-0.3098	-0.2539	-0.1880	-0.0755	0.0509	0.1756	0.2840	0.3464	0.3987	0.4570
0.10	-0.3279	-0.2628	-0.2055	-0.1382	-0.0244	0.1017	0.2247	0.3304	0.3906	0.4408	0.4965
0.15	-0.2810	-0.2140	-0.1554	-0.0872	0.0272	0.1525	0.2731	0.3755	0.4335	0.4814	0.5344
0.20	-0.2320	-0.1634	-0.1038	-0.0349	0.0796	0.2033	0.3209	0.4197	0.4751	0.5207	0.5708
0.25	-0.1806	-0.1108	-0.0506	0.0187	0.1325	0.2540	0.3680	0.4627	0.5154	0.5586	0.6057
0.30	-0.1269	-0.0562	0.0044	0.0736	0.1861	0.3047	0.4146	0.5048	0.5546	0.5952	0.6393
0.35	-0.0705	0.0007	0.0612	0.1298	0.2403	0.3553	0.4604	0.5458	0.5926	0.6306	0.6716
0.40	-0.0114	0.0598	0.1199	0.1875	0.2952	0.4058	0.5057	0.5859	0.6296	0.6648	0.7027
0.45	0.0506	0.1213	0.1805	0.2465	0.3507	0.4562	0.5503	0.6251	0.6654	0.6979	0.7326
0.50	0.1158	0.1854	0.2432	0.3071	0.4068	0.5064	0.5942	0.6633	0.7003	0.7299	0.7615
0.55	0.1844	0.2522	0.3079	0.3691	0.4635	0.5566	0.6376	0.7006	0.7342	0.7609	0.7893
0.60	0.2566	0.3217	0.3748	0.4326	0.5208	0.6066	0.6803	0.7371	0.7671	0.7909	0.8161
0.65	0.3326	0.3943	0.4441	0.4977	0.5787	0.6564	0.7224	0.7727	0.7991	0.8199	0.8420
0.70	0.4128	0.4699	0.5156	0.5644	0.6372	0.7061	0.7639	0.8075	0.8302	0.8481	0.8669
0.75	0.4974	0.5489	0.5896	0.6328	0.6963	0.7556	0.8047	0.8414	0.8605	0.8754	0.8910
0.80	0.5868	0.6313	0.6662	0.7028	0.7559	0.8049	0.8450	0.8746	0.8899	0.9018	0.9143
0.85	0.6814	0.7175	0.7454	0.7745	0.8162	0.8540	0.8846	0.9071	0.9186	0.9275	0.9368
0.90	0.7815	0.8075	0.8274	0.8479	0.8769	0.9029	0.9237	0.9388	0.9465	0.9525	0.9588

N = 32

r	0.0100	0.0250	0.0500	0.1000	0.2500	0.5000	0.7500	0.9000	0.9500	0.9750	0.9900
0.0	-0.4093	-0.3494	-0.2960	-0.2327	-0.1237	0.0000	0.1237	0.2327	0.2960	0.3494	0.4093
0.05	-0.3661	-0.3039	-0.2489	-0.1840	-0.0733	0.0508	0.1734	0.2802	0.3417	0.3932	0.4508
0.10	-0.3210	-0.2568	-0.2003	-0.1342	-0.0223	0.1016	0.2225	0.3266	0.3860	0.4355	0.4905
0.15	-0.2739	-0.2079	-0.1503	-0.0831	0.0293	0.1524	0.2710	0.3719	0.4290	0.4764	0.5287
0.20	-0.2247	-0.1572	-0.0986	-0.0309	0.0816	0.2032	0.3188	0.4161	0.4708	0.5159	0.5654
0.25	-0.1732	-0.1046	-0.0453	0.0227	0.1345	0.2539	0.3660	0.4594	0.5113	0.5540	0.6007
0.30	-0.1194	-0.0499	0.0096	0.0775	0.1880	0.3045	0.4126	0.5016	0.5507	0.5909	0.6346
0.35	-0.0630	0.0069	0.0664	0.1337	0.2422	0.3551	0.4586	0.5428	0.5890	0.6265	0.6672
0.40	-0.0039	0.0660	0.1250	0.1912	0.2969	0.4056	0.5039	0.5830	0.6262	0.6610	0.6986
0.45	0.0581	0.1274	0.1855	0.2502	0.3523	0.4560	0.5486	0.6224	0.6623	0.6944	0.7289
0.50	0.1232	0.1913	0.2479	0.3105	0.4083	0.5062	0.5926	0.6608	0.6974	0.7267	0.7581
0.55	0.1916	0.2579	0.3125	0.3724	0.4649	0.5564	0.6361	0.6983	0.7315	0.7580	0.7862
0.60	0.2635	0.3272	0.3791	0.4357	0.5221	0.6064	0.6789	0.7350	0.7647	0.7883	0.8134
0.65	0.3391	0.3993	0.4480	0.5005	0.5799	0.6562	0.7212	0.7709	0.7970	0.8177	0.8396
0.70	0.4188	0.4746	0.5192	0.5670	0.6382	0.7059	0.7628	0.8059	0.8284	0.8462	0.8649
0.75	0.5028	0.5530	0.5928	0.6350	0.6972	0.7554	0.8038	0.8401	0.8590	0.8738	0.8893
0.80	0.5915	0.6349	0.6689	0.7046	0.7567	0.8048	0.8442	0.8736	0.8887	0.9006	0.9130
0.85	0.6852	0.7203	0.7475	0.7759	0.8167	0.8539	0.8841	0.9063	0.9177	0.9265	0.9358
0.90	0.7842	0.8095	0.8289	0.8489	0.8773	0.9028	0.9233	0.9383	0.9459	0.9519	0.9581

TABLE A.23 (continued)

TABLE OF PERCENTAGE POINTS OF THE POSTERIOR DISTRIBUTION OF THE CORRELATION COEFFICIENT

N = 33

r	0.0100	0.0250	0.0500	0.1000	0.2500	0.5000	0.7500	0.9000	0.9500	0.9750	0.9900
0.0	-0.4032	-0.3440	-0.2913	-0.2289	-0.1217	0.0000	0.1217	0.2289	0.2913	0.3440	0.4032
0.05	-0.3597	-0.2984	-0.2441	-0.1802	-0.0713	0.0508	0.1714	0.2765	0.3371	0.3880	0.4448
0.10	-0.3144	-0.2511	-0.1955	-0.1304	-0.0203	0.1016	0.2205	0.3230	0.3816	0.4305	0.4849
0.15	-0.2671	-0.2021	-0.1454	-0.0793	0.0313	0.1524	0.2690	0.3684	0.4248	0.4716	0.5233
0.20	-0.2178	-0.1513	-0.0937	-0.0270	0.0835	0.2031	0.3169	0.4128	0.4667	0.5113	0.5603
0.25	-0.1662	-0.0986	-0.0404	0.0265	0.1364	0.2538	0.3641	0.4561	0.5075	0.5496	0.5958
0.30	-0.1123	-0.0439	0.0146	0.0813	0.1898	0.3044	0.4108	0.4985	0.5471	0.5868	0.6301
0.35	-0.0558	0.0129	0.0713	0.1374	0.2439	0.3549	0.4568	0.5399	0.5855	0.6227	0.6630
0.40	0.0033	0.0719	0.1298	0.1948	0.2986	0.4054	0.5022	0.5803	0.6229	0.6574	0.6947
0.45	0.0652	0.1332	0.1901	0.2536	0.3539	0.4558	0.5470	0.6198	0.6593	0.6911	0.7253
0.50	0.1302	0.1970	0.2524	0.3138	0.4098	0.5060	0.5911	0.6584	0.6946	0.7237	0.7548
0.55	0.1983	0.2633	0.3168	0.3755	0.4663	0.5562	0.6347	0.6962	0.7290	0.7553	0.7833
0.60	0.2700	0.3323	0.3832	0.4386	0.5233	0.6062	0.6777	0.7331	0.7625	0.7859	0.8108
0.65	0.3453	0.4041	0.4518	0.5032	0.5810	0.6560	0.7200	0.7691	0.7950	0.8155	0.8373
0.70	0.4245	0.4790	0.5226	0.5693	0.6392	0.7057	0.7618	0.8044	0.8267	0.8443	0.8629
0.75	0.5079	0.5569	0.5958	0.6370	0.6980	0.7553	0.8029	0.8388	0.8575	0.8722	0.8877
0.80	0.5959	0.6382	0.6714	0.7063	0.7573	0.8046	0.8435	0.8725	0.8876	0.8993	0.9117
0.85	0.6887	0.7230	0.7495	0.7772	0.8172	0.8538	0.8835	0.9055	0.9168	0.9256	0.9348
0.90	0.7868	0.8114	0.8303	0.8498	0.8776	0.9027	0.9229	0.9377	0.9453	0.9512	0.9575

N = 34

r	0.0100	0.0250	0.0500	0.1000	0.2500	0.5000	0.7500	0.9000	0.9500	0.9750	0.9900
0.0	-0.3972	-0.3388	-0.2869	-0.2254	-0.1197	0.0000	0.1197	0.2254	0.2869	0.3388	0.3972
0.05	-0.3536	-0.2930	-0.2396	-0.1766	-0.0694	0.0508	0.1695	0.2730	0.3328	0.3830	0.4392
0.10	-0.3081	-0.2457	-0.1908	-0.1267	-0.0184	0.1015	0.2186	0.3196	0.3774	0.4257	0.4794
0.15	-0.2607	-0.1966	-0.1407	-0.0756	0.0332	0.1523	0.2671	0.3651	0.4207	0.4669	0.5181
0.20	-0.2112	-0.1457	-0.0890	-0.0234	0.0854	0.2030	0.3150	0.4096	0.4628	0.5068	0.5554
0.25	-0.1595	-0.0930	-0.0357	0.0301	0.1382	0.2537	0.3623	0.4530	0.5038	0.5455	0.5912
0.30	-0.1055	-0.0382	0.0193	0.0849	0.1916	0.3043	0.4090	0.4955	0.5435	0.5828	0.6257
0.35	-0.0490	0.0185	0.0759	0.1409	0.2456	0.3548	0.4551	0.5371	0.5822	0.6190	0.6589
0.40	0.0101	0.0775	0.1343	0.1982	0.3002	0.4052	0.5006	0.5777	0.6198	0.6540	0.6910
0.45	0.0719	0.1387	0.1946	0.2569	0.3554	0.4556	0.5454	0.6174	0.6564	0.6879	0.7219
0.50	0.1368	0.2023	0.2567	0.3170	0.4112	0.5058	0.5897	0.6562	0.6920	0.7208	0.7517
0.55	0.2048	0.2684	0.3209	0.3785	0.4676	0.5560	0.6334	0.6941	0.7266	0.7526	0.7805
0.60	0.2761	0.3372	0.3870	0.4414	0.5245	0.6060	0.6764	0.7312	0.7603	0.7835	0.8083
0.65	0.3511	0.4087	0.4553	0.5057	0.5821	0.6558	0.7189	0.7675	0.7931	0.8135	0.8351
0.70	0.4299	0.4831	0.5258	0.5716	0.6402	0.7055	0.7608	0.8029	0.8251	0.8425	0.8610
0.75	0.5128	0.5606	0.5986	0.6390	0.6988	0.7551	0.8021	0.8376	0.8562	0.8707	0.8861
0.80	0.6001	0.6414	0.6738	0.7080	0.7580	0.8045	0.8428	0.8715	0.8864	0.8981	0.9104
0.85	0.6921	0.7255	0.7514	0.7785	0.8177	0.8537	0.8830	0.9047	0.9159	0.9247	0.9339
0.90	0.7892	0.8132	0.8316	0.8507	0.8780	0.9027	0.9226	0.9372	0.9448	0.9506	0.9569

TABLE A.23 (continued)

TABLE OF PERCENTAGE POINTS OF THE POSTERIOR DISTRIBUTION OF THE CORRELATION COEFFICIENT

N = 35

r	0.0100	0.0250	0.0500	0.1000	0.2500	0.5000	0.7500	0.9000	0.9500	0.9750	0.9900
0.0	-0.3916	-0.3338	-0.2826	-0.2220	-0.1179	0.0000	0.1179	0.2220	0.2826	0.3338	0.3916
0.05	-0.3477	-0.2880	-0.2352	-0.1732	-0.0675	0.0508	0.1676	0.2697	0.3286	0.3782	0.4337
0.10	-0.3021	-0.2405	-0.1864	-0.1232	-0.0166	0.1015	0.2168	0.3163	0.3734	0.4211	0.4742
0.15	-0.2545	-0.1913	-0.1362	-0.0721	0.0350	0.1522	0.2653	0.3619	0.4168	0.4625	0.5132
0.20	-0.2049	-0.1403	-0.0844	-0.0199	0.0871	0.2029	0.3133	0.4065	0.4591	0.5026	0.5507
0.25	-0.1531	-0.0876	-0.0311	0.0336	0.1399	0.2535	0.3606	0.4501	0.5002	0.5414	0.5868
0.30	-0.0990	-0.0328	0.0238	0.0883	0.1932	0.3041	0.4074	0.4927	0.5402	0.5790	0.6215
0.35	-0.0425	0.0239	0.0804	0.1442	0.2472	0.3546	0.4535	0.5344	0.5790	0.6154	0.6551
0.40	0.0166	0.0828	0.1387	0.2015	0.3017	0.4051	0.4990	0.5752	0.6168	0.6507	0.6874
0.45	0.0784	0.1439	0.1988	0.2600	0.3568	0.4554	0.5440	0.6150	0.6536	0.6849	0.7186
0.50	0.1431	0.2074	0.2608	0.3200	0.4125	0.5057	0.5883	0.6540	0.6895	0.7180	0.7487
0.55	0.2109	0.2733	0.3247	0.3813	0.4688	0.5558	0.6321	0.6921	0.7243	0.7501	0.7777
0.60	0.2820	0.3418	0.3907	0.4440	0.5257	0.6058	0.6753	0.7294	0.7582	0.7813	0.8058
0.65	0.3566	0.4130	0.4587	0.5081	0.5831	0.6557	0.7179	0.7659	0.7913	0.8115	0.8330
0.70	0.4350	0.4871	0.5289	0.5738	0.6410	0.7054	0.7599	0.8015	0.8235	0.8408	0.8592
0.75	0.5174	0.5641	0.6013	0.6409	0.6996	0.7549	0.8013	0.8364	0.8548	0.8693	0.8846
0.80	0.6040	0.6443	0.6761	0.7095	0.7586	0.8043	0.8422	0.8706	0.8854	0.8970	0.9092
0.85	0.6953	0.7279	0.7532	0.7797	0.8182	0.8535	0.8825	0.9040	0.9151	0.9239	0.9330
0.90	0.7915	0.8149	0.8329	0.8516	0.8783	0.9026	0.9222	0.9367	0.9442	0.9501	0.9562

N = 36

r	0.0100	0.0250	0.0500	0.1000	0.2500	0.5000	0.7500	0.9000	0.9500	0.9750	0.9900
0.0	-0.3862	-0.3291	-0.2785	-0.2187	-0.1161	0.0000	0.1161	0.2187	0.2785	0.3291	0.3862
0.05	-0.3421	-0.2831	-0.2310	-0.1699	-0.0658	0.0507	0.1659	0.2665	0.3247	0.3736	0.4285
0.10	-0.2963	-0.2355	-0.1822	-0.1199	-0.0148	0.1015	0.2150	0.3132	0.3695	0.4166	0.4692
0.15	-0.2486	-0.1862	-0.1319	-0.0688	0.0367	0.1522	0.2636	0.3589	0.4131	0.4583	0.5084
0.20	-0.1988	-0.1352	-0.0801	-0.0166	0.0888	0.2028	0.3116	0.4036	0.4555	0.4986	0.5461
0.25	-0.1469	-0.0824	-0.0268	0.0369	0.1415	0.2534	0.3590	0.4473	0.4968	0.5376	0.5825
0.30	-0.0928	-0.0277	0.0280	0.0915	0.1948	0.3040	0.4058	0.4900	0.5369	0.5754	0.6175
0.35	-0.0363	0.0291	0.0846	0.1474	0.2487	0.3545	0.4520	0.5318	0.5760	0.6120	0.6513
0.40	0.0227	0.0879	0.1428	0.2046	0.3032	0.4049	0.4976	0.5727	0.6140	0.6475	0.6839
0.45	0.0845	0.1489	0.2028	0.2630	0.3582	0.4553	0.5426	0.6128	0.6510	0.6819	0.7154
0.50	0.1491	0.2122	0.2647	0.3228	0.4138	0.5055	0.5870	0.6519	0.6870	0.7153	0.7458
0.55	0.2167	0.2780	0.3284	0.3840	0.4700	0.5556	0.6309	0.6902	0.7221	0.7477	0.7751
0.60	0.2875	0.3462	0.3942	0.4465	0.5268	0.6056	0.6742	0.7277	0.7563	0.7791	0.8035
0.65	0.3618	0.4171	0.4619	0.5104	0.5841	0.6555	0.7169	0.7643	0.7895	0.8096	0.8309
0.70	0.4398	0.4908	0.5318	0.5758	0.6419	0.7052	0.7590	0.8002	0.8220	0.8392	0.8575
0.75	0.5217	0.5675	0.6039	0.6427	0.7003	0.7548	0.8006	0.8353	0.8535	0.8679	0.8832
0.80	0.6078	0.6472	0.6782	0.7110	0.7592	0.8042	0.8416	0.8697	0.8843	0.8959	0.9080
0.85	0.6983	0.7301	0.7550	0.7809	0.8186	0.8534	0.8820	0.9033	0.9144	0.9230	0.9321
0.90	0.7936	0.8165	0.8341	0.8524	0.8786	0.9025	0.9219	0.9363	0.9437	0.9495	0.9556

TABLE A.23 (continued)

TABLE OF PERCENTAGE POINTS OF THE POSTERIOR DISTRIBUTION OF THE CORRELATION COEFFICIENT

N = 37

r	0.0100	0.0250	0.0500	0.1000	0.2500	0.5000	0.7500	0.9000	0.9500	0.9750	0.9900
0.0	-0.3810	-0.3246	-0.2746	-0.2156	-0.1144	0.0000	0.1144	0.2156	0.2746	0.3246	0.3810
0.05	-0.3368	-0.2784	-0.2271	-0.1667	-0.0641	0.0507	0.1642	0.2634	0.3209	0.3692	0.4235
0.10	-0.2908	-0.2307	-0.1781	-0.1167	-0.0132	0.1014	0.2134	0.3102	0.3658	0.4124	0.4644
0.15	-0.2429	-0.1814	-0.1278	-0.0656	0.0383	0.1521	0.2620	0.3560	0.4096	0.4542	0.5038
0.20	-0.1930	-0.1303	-0.0760	-0.0134	0.0904	0.2027	0.3100	0.4008	0.4521	0.4947	0.5418
0.25	-0.1411	-0.0775	-0.0227	0.0400	0.1431	0.2533	0.3574	0.4446	0.4935	0.5339	0.5784
0.30	-0.0869	-0.0227	0.0321	0.0946	0.1963	0.3039	0.4042	0.4875	0.5338	0.5719	0.6137
0.35	-0.0304	0.0340	0.0886	0.1505	0.2502	0.3544	0.4505	0.5294	0.5731	0.6088	0.6477
0.40	0.0286	0.0928	0.1468	0.2075	0.3046	0.4048	0.4962	0.5704	0.6113	0.6445	0.6806
0.45	0.0903	0.1537	0.2067	0.2659	0.3595	0.4551	0.5413	0.6106	0.6484	0.6791	0.7123
0.50	0.1548	0.2169	0.2684	0.3255	0.4151	0.5053	0.5858	0.6499	0.6847	0.7127	0.7430
0.55	0.2222	0.2824	0.3320	0.3865	0.4712	0.5555	0.6297	0.6884	0.7200	0.7453	0.7726
0.60	0.2928	0.3504	0.3975	0.4489	0.5278	0.6055	0.6731	0.7260	0.7543	0.7770	0.8012
0.65	0.3668	0.4211	0.4650	0.5126	0.5850	0.6553	0.7159	0.7629	0.7878	0.8077	0.8290
0.70	0.4444	0.4944	0.5346	0.5778	0.6427	0.7051	0.7582	0.7989	0.8205	0.8376	0.8558
0.75	0.5258	0.5707	0.6063	0.6444	0.7010	0.7547	0.7999	0.8343	0.8523	0.8666	0.8818
0.80	0.6113	0.6499	0.6803	0.7124	0.7598	0.8041	0.8410	0.8688	0.8834	0.8948	0.9069
0.85	0.7012	0.7323	0.7566	0.7820	0.8191	0.8533	0.8816	0.9027	0.9136	0.9222	0.9313
0.90	0.7957	0.8180	0.8352	0.8531	0.8789	0.9024	0.9216	0.9358	0.9432	0.9489	0.9550

N = 38

r	0.0100	0.0250	0.0500	0.1000	0.2500	0.5000	0.7500	0.9000	0.9500	0.9750	0.9900
0.0	-0.3760	-0.3202	-0.2709	-0.2126	-0.1128	0.0000	0.1128	0.2126	0.2709	0.3202	0.3760
0.05	-0.3316	-0.2740	-0.2232	-0.1637	-0.0625	0.0507	0.1626	0.2605	0.3172	0.3650	0.4187
0.10	-0.2855	-0.2262	-0.1743	-0.1137	-0.0116	0.1014	0.2118	0.3073	0.3623	0.4083	0.4598
0.15	-0.2375	-0.1767	-0.1239	-0.0626	0.0399	0.1520	0.2604	0.3532	0.4061	0.4503	0.4994
0.20	-0.1875	-0.1256	-0.0721	-0.0103	0.0920	0.2027	0.3084	0.3981	0.4488	0.4910	0.5376
0.25	-0.1355	-0.0727	-0.0188	0.0430	0.1446	0.2533	0.3559	0.4420	0.4904	0.5304	0.5744
0.30	-0.0812	-0.0180	0.0361	0.0976	0.1978	0.3038	0.4028	0.4850	0.5308	0.5686	0.6099
0.35	-0.0247	0.0387	0.0925	0.1534	0.2516	0.3543	0.4491	0.5270	0.5702	0.6056	0.6442
0.40	0.0343	0.0974	0.1506	0.2104	0.3059	0.4047	0.4948	0.5682	0.6086	0.6415	0.6773
0.45	0.0959	0.1582	0.2104	0.2686	0.3608	0.4550	0.5400	0.6085	0.6460	0.6764	0.7093
0.50	0.1602	0.2213	0.2720	0.3281	0.4162	0.5052	0.5846	0.6480	0.6824	0.7102	0.7403
0.55	0.2275	0.2866	0.3354	0.3890	0.4722	0.5553	0.6286	0.6866	0.7179	0.7431	0.7702
0.60	0.2979	0.3544	0.4007	0.4512	0.5288	0.6053	0.6721	0.7244	0.7525	0.7750	0.7991
0.65	0.3716	0.4248	0.4679	0.5147	0.5859	0.6552	0.7150	0.7615	0.7862	0.8060	0.8271
0.70	0.4488	0.4978	0.5373	0.5796	0.6435	0.7049	0.7574	0.7977	0.8191	0.8361	0.8542
0.75	0.5298	0.5737	0.6087	0.6460	0.7016	0.7545	0.7992	0.8332	0.8511	0.8653	0.8804
0.80	0.6147	0.6525	0.6823	0.7138	0.7603	0.8040	0.8404	0.8680	0.8824	0.8938	0.9058
0.85	0.7039	0.7343	0.7581	0.7831	0.8195	0.8533	0.8811	0.9020	0.9129	0.9215	0.9305
0.90	0.7977	0.8194	0.8363	0.8539	0.8792	0.9024	0.9213	0.9354	0.9427	0.9484	0.9544

TABLE A.23 (continued)

TABLE OF PERCENTAGE POINTS OF THE POSTERIOR DISTRIBUTION OF THE CORRELATION COEFFICIENT.

N = 39

r	0.0100	0.0250	0.0500	0.1000	0.2500	0.5000	0.7500	0.9000	0.9500	0.9750	0.9900
0.0	-0.3712	-0.3160	-0.2673	-0.2097	-0.1113	0.0000	0.1113	0.2097	0.2673	0.3160	0.3712
0.05	-0.3266	-0.2697	-0.2196	-0.1608	-0.0610	0.0507	0.1611	0.2577	0.3137	0.3609	0.4141
0.10	-0.2804	-0.2218	-0.1705	-0.1107	-0.0101	0.1013	0.2102	0.3046	0.3589	0.4044	0.4554
0.15	-0.2322	-0.1723	-0.1201	-0.0596	0.0414	0.1520	0.2589	0.3505	0.4029	0.4465	0.4952
0.20	-0.1822	-0.1211	-0.0683	-0.0074	0.0934	0.2026	0.3069	0.3955	0.4457	0.4874	0.5336
0.25	-0.1301	-0.0682	-0.0150	0.0459	0.1460	0.2532	0.3544	0.4395	0.4874	0.5269	0.5706
0.30	-0.0758	-0.0135	0.0398	0.1005	0.1992	0.3037	0.4014	0.4826	0.5280	0.5653	0.6064
0.35	-0.0193	0.0432	0.0962	0.1562	0.2529	0.3541	0.4477	0.5248	0.5675	0.6026	0.6409
0.40	0.0397	0.1018	0.1542	0.2131	0.3072	0.4045	0.4935	0.5661	0.6061	0.6387	0.6742
0.45	0.1012	0.1626	0.2139	0.2712	0.3620	0.4548	0.5388	0.6065	0.6436	0.6738	0.7065
0.50	0.1655	0.2255	0.2753	0.3306	0.4174	0.5051	0.5834	0.6461	0.6802	0.7078	0.7376
0.55	0.2326	0.2907	0.3386	0.3913	0.4733	0.5552	0.6275	0.6849	0.7159	0.7409	0.7678
0.60	0.3027	0.3583	0.4037	0.4534	0.5297	0.6052	0.6711	0.7229	0.7507	0.7730	0.7970
0.65	0.3762	0.4284	0.4708	0.5167	0.5867	0.6551	0.7141	0.7601	0.7846	0.8043	0.8252
0.70	0.4530	0.5011	0.5398	0.5814	0.6443	0.7048	0.7566	0.7965	0.8177	0.8346	0.8526
0.75	0.5335	0.5766	0.6109	0.6476	0.7023	0.7544	0.7985	0.8322	0.8500	0.8641	0.8791
0.80	0.6179	0.6549	0.6841	0.7151	0.7608	0.8039	0.8399	0.8672	0.8815	0.8928	0.9048
0.85	0.7065	0.7363	0.7596	0.7841	0.8199	0.8532	0.8807	0.9014	0.9122	0.9207	0.9297
0.90	0.7995	0.8208	0.8373	0.8546	0.8794	0.9023	0.9210	0.9349	0.9422	0.9478	0.9538

N = 40

r	0.0100	0.0250	0.0500	0.1000	0.2500	0.5000	0.7500	0.9000	0.9500	0.9750	0.9900
0.0	-0.3665	-0.3120	-0.2638	-0.2070	-0.1098	0.0000	0.1098	0.2070	0.2638	0.3120	0.3665
0.05	-0.3219	-0.2655	-0.2160	-0.1580	-0.0595	0.0507	0.1596	0.2550	0.3103	0.3570	0.4096
0.10	-0.2754	-0.2176	-0.1670	-0.1079	-0.0086	0.1013	0.2088	0.3020	0.3556	0.4006	0.4511
0.15	-0.2272	-0.1680	-0.1165	-0.0568	0.0429	0.1519	0.2574	0.3480	0.3997	0.4429	0.4911
0.20	-0.1771	-0.1168	-0.0647	-0.0046	0.0949	0.2025	0.3055	0.3930	0.4426	0.4839	0.5297
0.25	-0.1249	-0.0638	-0.0114	0.0487	0.1474	0.2531	0.3530	0.4371	0.4845	0.5236	0.5669
0.30	-0.0706	-0.0091	0.0434	0.1032	0.2005	0.3036	0.4000	0.4803	0.5252	0.5622	0.6029
0.35	-0.0141	0.0475	0.0997	0.1588	0.2542	0.3540	0.4464	0.5226	0.5649	0.5996	0.6377
0.40	0.0449	0.1061	0.1577	0.2157	0.3084	0.4044	0.4923	0.5640	0.6036	0.6360	0.6712
0.45	0.1063	0.1667	0.2173	0.2737	0.3632	0.4547	0.5376	0.6046	0.6414	0.6713	0.7037
0.50	0.1705	0.2295	0.2786	0.3330	0.4185	0.5049	0.5823	0.6444	0.6782	0.7055	0.7351
0.55	0.2374	0.2946	0.3417	0.3936	0.4743	0.5550	0.6265	0.6833	0.7140	0.7388	0.7655
0.60	0.3074	0.3619	0.4066	0.4555	0.5307	0.6050	0.6702	0.7214	0.7490	0.7712	0.7949
0.65	0.3805	0.4318	0.4734	0.5186	0.5876	0.6549	0.7133	0.7588	0.7831	0.8026	0.8234
0.70	0.4570	0.5042	0.5422	0.5832	0.6450	0.7047	0.7558	0.7954	0.8164	0.8332	0.8511
0.75	0.5371	0.5793	0.6130	0.6491	0.7029	0.7543	0.7979	0.8313	0.8489	0.8629	0.8776
0.80	0.6210	0.6573	0.6859	0.7164	0.7613	0.8038	0.8394	0.8664	0.8806	0.8918	0.9037
0.85	0.7090	0.7381	0.7610	0.7851	0.8203	0.8531	0.8803	0.9008	0.9115	0.9200	0.9290
0.90	0.8013	0.8221	0.8383	0.8552	0.8797	0.9022	0.9207	0.9345	0.9417	0.9473	0.9532

TABLE A.23 (continued)

TABLE OF PERCENTAGE POINTS OF THE POSTERIOR DISTRIBUTION OF THE CORRELATION COEFFICIENT

N = 41

r	0.0100	0.0250	0.0500	0.1000	0.2500	0.5000	0.7500	0.9000	0.9500	0.9750	0.9900
0.0	-0.3621	-0.3081	-0.2605	-0.2043	-0.1084	0.0000	0.1084	0.2043	0.2605	0.3081	0.3621
0.05	-0.3173	-0.2616	-0.2126	-0.1553	-0.0581	0.0506	0.1581	0.2524	0.3071	0.3533	0.4053
0.10	-0.2707	-0.2135	-0.1635	-0.1052	-0.0072	0.1013	0.2074	0.2994	0.3524	0.3970	0.4469
0.15	-0.2224	-0.1639	-0.1130	-0.0541	0.0442	0.1519	0.2560	0.3455	0.3966	0.4394	0.4871
0.20	-0.1722	-0.1126	-0.0612	-0.0019	0.0962	0.2025	0.3041	0.3906	0.4397	0.4806	0.5259
0.25	-0.1199	-0.0597	-0.0079	0.0514	0.1487	0.2530	0.3517	0.4348	0.4817	0.5205	0.5634
0.30	-0.0656	-0.0049	0.0469	0.1058	0.2018	0.3035	0.3987	0.4781	0.5226	0.5592	0.5996
0.35	-0.0090	0.0517	0.1032	0.1614	0.2554	0.3539	0.4452	0.5205	0.5624	0.5968	0.6345
0.40	0.0499	0.1102	0.1610	0.2182	0.3096	0.4043	0.4911	0.5621	0.6013	0.6333	0.6683
0.45	0.1112	0.1707	0.2205	0.2761	0.3643	0.4546	0.5364	0.6028	0.6392	0.6688	0.7010
0.50	0.1753	0.2334	0.2817	0.3353	0.4195	0.5048	0.5813	0.6427	0.6761	0.7033	0.7327
0.55	0.2421	0.2983	0.3447	0.3958	0.4753	0.5549	0.6255	0.6817	0.7122	0.7368	0.7633
0.60	0.3118	0.3655	0.4094	0.4575	0.5316	0.6049	0.6693	0.7200	0.7474	0.7693	0.7930
0.65	0.3847	0.4351	0.4760	0.5205	0.5884	0.6548	0.7125	0.7575	0.7817	0.8010	0.8217
0.70	0.4608	0.5072	0.5445	0.5848	0.6457	0.7046	0.7551	0.7943	0.8152	0.8318	0.8496
0.75	0.5405	0.5820	0.6151	0.6505	0.7035	0.7542	0.7973	0.8303	0.8478	0.8618	0.8766
0.80	0.6239	0.6595	0.6877	0.7175	0.7618	0.8037	0.8389	0.8656	0.8797	0.8909	0.9028
0.85	0.7113	0.7399	0.7624	0.7860	0.8207	0.8530	0.8799	0.9003	0.9109	0.9193	0.9282
0.90	0.8030	0.8234	0.8393	0.8559	0.8799	0.9022	0.9204	0.9341	0.9412	0.9468	0.9526

N = 42

r	0.0100	0.0250	0.0500	0.1000	0.2500	0.5000	0.7500	0.9000	0.9500	0.9750	0.9900
0.0	-0.3578	-0.3044	-0.2573	-0.2018	-0.1070	0.0000	0.1070	0.2018	0.2573	0.3044	0.3578
0.05	-0.3128	-0.2577	-0.2094	-0.1527	-0.0567	0.0506	0.1568	0.2499	0.3039	0.3496	0.4011
0.10	-0.2662	-0.2096	-0.1602	-0.1026	-0.0058	0.1012	0.2060	0.2970	0.3494	0.3935	0.4430
0.15	-0.2177	-0.1599	-0.1097	-0.0515	0.0456	0.1518	0.2547	0.3431	0.3937	0.4360	0.4833
0.20	-0.1674	-0.1086	-0.0578	0.0007	0.0975	0.2024	0.3028	0.3883	0.4369	0.4773	0.5223
0.25	-0.1151	-0.0556	-0.0045	0.0540	0.1500	0.2529	0.3504	0.4326	0.4790	0.5174	0.5599
0.30	-0.0608	-0.0009	0.0502	0.1084	0.2031	0.3034	0.3975	0.4760	0.5200	0.5563	0.5963
0.35	-0.0042	0.0557	0.1064	0.1639	0.2566	0.3538	0.4440	0.5185	0.5600	0.5941	0.6315
0.40	0.0546	0.1141	0.1642	0.2206	0.3107	0.4042	0.4899	0.5602	0.5990	0.6308	0.6655
0.45	0.1160	0.1746	0.2236	0.2784	0.3654	0.4545	0.5354	0.6010	0.6371	0.6665	0.6985
0.50	0.1799	0.2371	0.2847	0.3375	0.4205	0.5047	0.5802	0.6410	0.6742	0.7011	0.7303
0.55	0.2465	0.3018	0.3475	0.3978	0.4762	0.5548	0.6246	0.6802	0.7104	0.7348	0.7612
0.60	0.3160	0.3688	0.4121	0.4594	0.5324	0.6048	0.6684	0.7186	0.7458	0.7676	0.7911
0.65	0.3886	0.4382	0.4785	0.5222	0.5891	0.6547	0.7117	0.7563	0.7803	0.7995	0.8201
0.70	0.4645	0.5100	0.5468	0.5864	0.6463	0.7044	0.7544	0.7932	0.8139	0.8305	0.8481
0.75	0.5438	0.5845	0.6170	0.6519	0.7041	0.7541	0.7967	0.8294	0.8468	0.8606	0.8754
0.80	0.6268	0.6616	0.6893	0.7187	0.7623	0.8036	0.8384	0.8649	0.8789	0.8900	0.9018
0.85	0.7136	0.7416	0.7637	0.7869	0.8210	0.8529	0.8796	0.8997	0.9103	0.9186	0.9275
0.90	0.8046	0.8246	0.8402	0.8565	0.8802	0.9021	0.9202	0.9337	0.9408	0.9463	0.9520

TABLE A.23 (continued)

TABLE OF PERCENTAGE POINTS OF THE POSTERIOR DISTRIBUTION OF THE CORRELATION COEFFICIENT

N = 43

r	0.0100	0.0250	0.0500	0.1000	0.2500	0.5000	0.7500	0.9000	0.9500	0.9750	0.9900
0.0	-0.3536	-0.3008	-0.2542	-0.1993	-0.1057	0.0000	0.1057	0.1993	0.2542	0.3008	0.3536
0.05	-0.3085	-0.2540	-0.2062	-0.1502	-0.0554	0.0506	0.1555	0.2474	0.3009	0.3461	0.3971
0.10	-0.2618	-0.2058	-0.1570	-0.1001	-0.0045	0.1012	0.2047	0.2946	0.3465	0.3901	0.4391
0.15	-0.2133	-0.1561	-0.1065	-0.0490	0.0469	0.1518	0.2534	0.3408	0.3909	0.4328	0.4796
0.20	-0.1629	-0.1048	-0.0546	0.0032	0.0988	0.2023	0.3016	0.3861	0.4341	0.4742	0.5188
0.25	-0.1105	-0.0518	-0.0013	0.0564	0.1513	0.2529	0.3492	0.4304	0.4764	0.5144	0.5566
0.30	-0.0561	0.0030	0.0534	0.1108	0.2042	0.3033	0.3963	0.4739	0.5175	0.5535	0.5932
0.35	0.0004	0.0595	0.1096	0.1663	0.2578	0.3537	0.4428	0.5165	0.5577	0.5915	0.6286
0.40	0.0592	0.1179	0.1673	0.2229	0.3118	0.4041	0.4888	0.5583	0.5968	0.6283	0.6628
0.45	0.1205	0.1783	0.2266	0.2807	0.3664	0.4544	0.5343	0.5993	0.6350	0.6642	0.6959
0.50	0.1843	0.2407	0.2876	0.3396	0.4215	0.5046	0.5793	0.6394	0.6723	0.6990	0.7280
0.55	0.2508	0.3053	0.3502	0.3998	0.4771	0.5547	0.6237	0.6788	0.7087	0.7329	0.7591
0.60	0.3201	0.3721	0.4146	0.4613	0.5332	0.6047	0.6676	0.7173	0.7442	0.7659	0.7892
0.65	0.3925	0.4412	0.4808	0.5239	0.5899	0.6546	0.7109	0.7551	0.7789	0.7980	0.8184
0.70	0.4680	0.5128	0.5489	0.5879	0.6470	0.7043	0.7538	0.7922	0.8127	0.8292	0.8467
0.75	0.5469	0.5869	0.6189	0.6532	0.7046	0.7540	0.7961	0.8286	0.8458	0.8596	0.8742
0.80	0.6294	0.6637	0.6909	0.7198	0.7627	0.8035	0.8379	0.8642	0.8781	0.8891	0.9009
0.85	0.7158	0.7433	0.7649	0.7878	0.8214	0.8529	0.8792	0.8992	0.9097	0.9180	0.9268
0.90	0.8061	0.8257	0.8411	0.8571	0.8804	0.9020	0.9199	0.9333	0.9403	0.9458	0.9514

N = 44

r	0.0100	0.0250	0.0500	0.1000	0.2500	0.5000	0.7500	0.9000	0.9500	0.9750	0.9900
0.0	-0.3496	-0.2973	-0.2512	-0.1970	-0.1044	0.0000	0.1044	0.1970	0.2512	0.2973	0.3496
0.05	-0.3044	-0.2505	-0.2032	-0.1478	-0.0541	0.0506	0.1542	0.2451	0.2980	0.3427	0.3933
0.10	-0.2575	-0.2022	-0.1539	-0.0977	-0.0033	0.1012	0.2034	0.2923	0.3436	0.3868	0.4354
0.15	-0.2089	-0.1524	-0.1034	-0.0466	0.0481	0.1517	0.2521	0.3386	0.3881	0.4296	0.4761
0.20	-0.1585	-0.1010	-0.0515	0.0056	0.1000	0.2023	0.3003	0.3839	0.4315	0.4712	0.5154
0.25	-0.1061	-0.0480	0.0018	0.0588	0.1524	0.2528	0.3480	0.4284	0.4738	0.5116	0.5534
0.30	-0.0517	0.0067	0.0565	0.1131	0.2054	0.3032	0.3951	0.4719	0.5151	0.5508	0.5902
0.35	0.0049	0.0632	0.1126	0.1686	0.2589	0.3537	0.4417	0.5147	0.5554	0.5889	0.6257
0.40	0.0637	0.1215	0.1703	0.2251	0.3129	0.4040	0.4878	0.5565	0.5947	0.6259	0.6602
0.45	0.1249	0.1818	0.2295	0.2828	0.3674	0.4543	0.5333	0.5976	0.6330	0.6620	0.6935
0.50	0.1885	0.2441	0.2904	0.3417	0.4224	0.5045	0.5783	0.6379	0.6705	0.6970	0.7258
0.55	0.2549	0.3086	0.3529	0.4017	0.4780	0.5546	0.6228	0.6773	0.7070	0.7311	0.7571
0.60	0.3240	0.3752	0.4171	0.4630	0.5340	0.6046	0.6668	0.7161	0.7427	0.7642	0.7874
0.65	0.3961	0.4441	0.4831	0.5256	0.5906	0.6545	0.7102	0.7540	0.7776	0.7965	0.8169
0.70	0.4714	0.5154	0.5510	0.5894	0.6476	0.7042	0.7531	0.7912	0.8116	0.8279	0.8454
0.75	0.5499	0.5892	0.6207	0.6545	0.7052	0.7539	0.7955	0.8277	0.8448	0.8585	0.8731
0.80	0.6320	0.6657	0.6924	0.7208	0.7632	0.8034	0.8375	0.8635	0.8773	0.8883	0.9000
0.85	0.7178	0.7448	0.7661	0.7866	0.8217	0.8528	0.8789	0.8987	0.9091	0.9173	0.9261
0.90	0.8076	0.8268	0.8419	0.8576	0.8806	0.9020	0.9197	0.9330	0.9399	0.9453	0.9509

TABLE A.23 (continued)

TABLE OF PERCENTAGE POINTS OF THE POSTERIOR DISTRIBUTION OF THE CORRELATION COEFFICIENT

N = 45

r	0.0100	0.0250	0.0500	0.1000	0.2500	0.5000	0.7500	0.9000	0.9500	0.9750	0.9900
0.0	-0.3457	-0.2940	-0.2483	-0.1947	-0.1032	0.0000	0.1032	0.1947	0.2483	0.2940	0.3457
0.05	-0.3004	-0.2470	-0.2003	-0.1455	-0.0529	0.0506	0.1530	0.2429	0.2952	0.3395	0.3895
0.10	-0.2534	-0.1987	-0.1510	-0.0954	-0.0020	0.1012	0.2022	0.2901	0.3409	0.3837	0.4318
0.15	-0.2047	-0.1489	-0.1004	-0.0443	0.0493	0.1517	0.2509	0.3364	0.3855	0.4266	0.4726
0.20	-0.1542	-0.0975	-0.0485	0.0079	0.1012	0.2022	0.2991	0.3818	0.4290	0.4683	0.5121
0.25	-0.1018	-0.0444	0.0048	0.0611	0.1536	0.2527	0.3468	0.4264	0.4714	0.5088	0.5503
0.30	-0.0474	0.0103	0.0594	0.1154	0.2065	0.3032	0.3940	0.4700	0.5128	0.5482	0.5872
0.35	0.0092	0.0667	0.1155	0.1708	0.2599	0.3536	0.4406	0.5128	0.5532	0.5864	0.6230
0.40	0.0679	0.1250	0.1732	0.2272	0.3139	0.4039	0.4867	0.5548	0.5926	0.6236	0.6576
0.45	0.1291	0.1853	0.2323	0.2849	0.3683	0.4542	0.5323	0.5960	0.6311	0.6598	0.6912
0.50	0.1926	0.2475	0.2930	0.3436	0.4233	0.5044	0.5774	0.6364	0.6687	0.6950	0.7237
0.55	0.2588	0.3117	0.3554	0.4036	0.4788	0.5545	0.6219	0.6760	0.7054	0.7293	0.7552
0.60	0.3278	0.3782	0.4195	0.4648	0.5348	0.6045	0.6660	0.7148	0.7413	0.7626	0.7857
0.65	0.3997	0.4469	0.4853	0.5271	0.5912	0.6544	0.7095	0.7529	0.7763	0.7951	0.8153
0.70	0.4746	0.5179	0.5529	0.5908	0.6482	0.7041	0.7525	0.7903	0.8105	0.8267	0.8441
0.75	0.5528	0.5915	0.6224	0.6557	0.7057	0.7538	0.7950	0.8269	0.8439	0.8575	0.8720
0.80	0.6345	0.6676	0.6939	0.7219	0.7636	0.8033	0.8370	0.8629	0.8766	0.8875	0.8991
0.85	0.7198	0.7463	0.7673	0.7894	0.8220	0.8527	0.8785	0.8982	0.9085	0.9167	0.9255
0.90	0.8090	0.8279	0.8427	0.8582	0.8808	0.9019	0.9194	0.9326	0.9395	0.9448	0.9503

N = 46

r	0.0100	0.0250	0.0500	0.1000	0.2500	0.5000	0.7500	0.9000	0.9500	0.9750	0.9900
0.0	-0.3420	-0.2907	-0.2455	-0.1925	-0.1020	0.0000	0.1020	0.1925	0.2455	0.2907	0.3420
0.05	-0.2966	-0.2437	-0.1974	-0.1433	-0.0517	0.0506	0.1518	0.2407	0.2925	0.3363	0.3859
0.10	-0.2495	-0.1953	-0.1481	-0.0932	-0.0009	0.1011	0.2010	0.2880	0.3383	0.3806	0.4283
0.15	-0.2007	-0.1454	-0.0975	-0.0420	0.0505	0.1517	0.2498	0.3344	0.3829	0.4237	0.4693
0.20	-0.1501	-0.0940	-0.0456	0.0101	0.1023	0.2022	0.2980	0.3798	0.4265	0.4655	0.5089
0.25	-0.0977	-0.0410	0.0077	0.0633	0.1547	0.2527	0.3457	0.4244	0.4690	0.5061	0.5473
0.30	-0.0432	0.0137	0.0623	0.1176	0.2076	0.3031	0.3929	0.4682	0.5106	0.5456	0.5844
0.35	0.0133	0.0702	0.1184	0.1729	0.2610	0.3535	0.4396	0.5111	0.5511	0.5840	0.6203
0.40	0.0721	0.1284	0.1759	0.2293	0.3149	0.4038	0.4857	0.5532	0.5906	0.6214	0.6551
0.45	0.1331	0.1886	0.2350	0.2869	0.3693	0.4541	0.5314	0.5945	0.6293	0.6578	0.6889
0.50	0.1966	0.2507	0.2956	0.3455	0.4242	0.5043	0.5765	0.6349	0.6670	0.6931	0.7216
0.55	0.2626	0.3148	0.3579	0.4054	0.4796	0.5543	0.6211	0.6747	0.7039	0.7276	0.7533
0.60	0.3314	0.3811	0.4218	0.4664	0.5355	0.6044	0.6652	0.7136	0.7399	0.7611	0.7840
0.65	0.4031	0.4496	0.4874	0.5287	0.5919	0.6543	0.7088	0.7518	0.7750	0.7937	0.8139
0.70	0.4777	0.5204	0.5549	0.5921	0.6488	0.7040	0.7519	0.7893	0.8094	0.8255	0.8428
0.75	0.5556	0.5936	0.6241	0.6569	0.7062	0.7537	0.7945	0.8261	0.8430	0.8565	0.8709
0.80	0.6369	0.6694	0.6953	0.7229	0.7640	0.8033	0.8366	0.8622	0.8758	0.8867	0.8982
0.85	0.7217	0.7478	0.7684	0.7901	0.8223	0.8527	0.8782	0.8977	0.9079	0.9161	0.9248
0.90	0.8103	0.8289	0.8434	0.8587	0.8810	0.9019	0.9192	0.9323	0.9390	0.9443	0.9497

TABLE A.23 (continued)

TABLE OF PERCENTAGE POINTS OF THE POSTERIOR DISTRIBUTION OF THE CORRELATION COEFFICIENT

N = 47

r	0.0100	0.0250	0.0500	0.1000	0.2500	0.5000	0.7500	0.9000	0.9500	0.9750	0.9900
0.0	-0.3384	-0.2876	-0.2429	-0.1903	-0.1008	0.0000	0.1008	0.1903	0.2429	0.2876	0.3384
0.05	-0.2923	-0.2405	-0.1947	-0.1411	-0.0506	0.0506	0.1506	0.2386	0.2899	0.3333	0.3824
0.10	-0.2457	-0.1920	-0.1453	-0.0910	0.0003	0.1011	0.1999	0.2859	0.3357	0.3777	0.4249
0.15	-0.1968	-0.1421	-0.0947	-0.0398	0.0516	0.1516	0.2487	0.3324	0.3805	0.4208	0.4661
0.20	-0.1462	-0.0906	-0.0428	0.0123	0.1034	0.2021	0.2969	0.3779	0.4241	0.4627	0.5058
0.25	-0.0937	-0.0376	0.0105	0.0655	0.1558	0.2526	0.3446	0.4226	0.4668	0.5035	0.5444
0.30	-0.0392	0.0171	0.0651	0.1197	0.2086	0.3030	0.3919	0.4664	0.5084	0.5432	0.5816
0.35	0.0173	0.0735	0.1211	0.1750	0.2620	0.3534	0.4386	0.5094	0.5490	0.5817	0.6178
0.40	0.0760	0.1317	0.1786	0.2313	0.3158	0.4037	0.4848	0.5516	0.5887	0.6192	0.6527
0.45	0.1370	0.1917	0.2376	0.2888	0.3702	0.4540	0.5305	0.5929	0.6275	0.6557	0.6867
0.50	0.2004	0.2537	0.2981	0.3474	0.4250	0.5042	0.5756	0.6335	0.6654	0.6913	0.7195
0.55	0.2663	0.3177	0.3602	0.4071	0.4804	0.5543	0.6203	0.6734	0.7024	0.7259	0.7514
0.60	0.3349	0.3838	0.4240	0.4680	0.5362	0.6043	0.6645	0.7125	0.7385	0.7596	0.7824
0.65	0.4063	0.4521	0.4895	0.5301	0.5925	0.6542	0.7082	0.7508	0.7738	0.7924	0.8124
0.70	0.4807	0.5227	0.5567	0.5934	0.6494	0.7040	0.7513	0.7884	0.8084	0.8244	0.8416
0.75	0.5583	0.5957	0.6257	0.6580	0.7066	0.7536	0.7940	0.8254	0.8421	0.8555	0.8699
0.80	0.6392	0.6711	0.6966	0.7238	0.7644	0.8032	0.8362	0.8616	0.8751	0.8859	0.8974
0.85	0.7235	0.7492	0.7694	0.7909	0.8226	0.8526	0.8779	0.8972	0.9074	0.9155	0.9242
0.90	0.8116	0.8299	0.8442	0.8592	0.8812	0.9018	0.9190	0.9319	0.9386	0.9439	0.9492

N = 48

r	0.0100	0.0250	0.0500	0.1000	0.2500	0.5000	0.7500	0.9000	0.9500	0.9750	0.9900
0.0	-0.3348	-0.2845	-0.2403	-0.1883	-0.0997	0.0000	0.0997	0.1883	0.2403	0.2845	0.3348
0.05	-0.2892	-0.2374	-0.1920	-0.1391	-0.0494	0.0505	0.1495	0.2366	0.2873	0.3303	0.3790
0.10	-0.2419	-0.1889	-0.1426	-0.0889	0.0014	0.1011	0.1938	0.2839	0.3332	0.3748	0.4216
0.15	-0.1930	-0.1389	-0.0920	-0.0377	0.0527	0.1516	0.2476	0.3304	0.3781	0.4181	0.4629
0.20	-0.1423	-0.0874	-0.0401	0.0144	0.1045	0.2021	0.2958	0.3760	0.4218	0.4601	0.5029
0.25	-0.0898	-0.0343	0.0132	0.0675	0.1563	0.2525	0.3436	0.4208	0.4646	0.5010	0.5415
0.30	-0.0353	0.0203	0.0678	0.1217	0.2096	0.3030	0.3909	0.4647	0.5063	0.5408	0.5790
0.35	0.0212	0.0767	0.1237	0.1769	0.2629	0.3533	0.4376	0.5077	0.5470	0.5795	0.6152
0.40	0.0799	0.1348	0.1812	0.2332	0.3167	0.4036	0.4838	0.5500	0.5869	0.6171	0.6504
0.45	0.1408	0.1948	0.2401	0.2906	0.3710	0.4539	0.5296	0.5915	0.6257	0.6538	0.6845
0.50	0.2041	0.2567	0.3005	0.3491	0.4258	0.5041	0.5748	0.6322	0.6638	0.6895	0.7176
0.55	0.2699	0.3206	0.3625	0.4088	0.4811	0.5542	0.6196	0.6721	0.7009	0.7243	0.7497
0.60	0.3383	0.3865	0.4261	0.4696	0.5369	0.6042	0.6638	0.7113	0.7372	0.7581	0.7808
0.65	0.4095	0.4546	0.4914	0.5315	0.5932	0.6541	0.7075	0.7498	0.7727	0.7911	0.8110
0.70	0.4836	0.5250	0.5585	0.5947	0.6499	0.7039	0.7508	0.7876	0.8074	0.8233	0.8404
0.75	0.5608	0.5977	0.6273	0.6591	0.7071	0.7536	0.7935	0.8246	0.8413	0.8546	0.8689
0.80	0.6413	0.6728	0.6979	0.7247	0.7648	0.8031	0.8358	0.8610	0.8744	0.8852	0.8966
0.85	0.7253	0.7505	0.7705	0.7916	0.8229	0.8526	0.8776	0.8967	0.9069	0.9149	0.9236
0.90	0.8129	0.8308	0.8449	0.8597	0.8814	0.9018	0.9187	0.9316	0.9382	0.9434	0.9486

TABLE A.23 (continued)

TABLE OF PERCENTAGE POINTS OF THE POSTERIOR DISTRIBUTION OF THE CORRELATION COEFFICIENT

N = 49

r	0.0100	0.0250	0.0500	0.1000	0.2500	0.5000	0.7500	0.9000	0.9500	0.9750	0.9900
0.0	-0.3314	-0.2816	-0.2377	-0.1863	-0.0987	0.0000	0.0987	0.1863	0.2377	0.2816	0.3314
0.05	-0.2857	-0.2344	-0.1895	-0.1370	-0.0484	0.0505	0.1465	0.2346	0.2848	0.3274	0.3757
0.10	-0.2384	-0.1858	-0.1400	-0.0869	0.0024	0.1011	0.1977	0.2820	0.3308	0.3720	0.4185
0.15	-0.1894	-0.1358	-0.0894	-0.0357	0.0537	0.1516	0.2465	0.3285	0.3757	0.4154	0.4599
0.20	-0.1386	-0.0843	-0.0374	0.0164	0.1055	0.2020	0.2948	0.3742	0.4196	0.4575	0.4999
0.25	-0.0860	-0.0312	0.0158	0.0695	0.1578	0.2525	0.3426	0.4190	0.4624	0.4985	0.5388
0.30	-0.0316	0.0235	0.0703	0.1237	0.2106	0.3029	0.3899	0.4630	0.5042	0.5385	0.5764
0.35	0.0250	0.0798	0.1263	0.1789	0.2639	0.3533	0.4367	0.5061	0.5451	0.5773	0.6128
0.40	0.0836	0.1379	0.1836	0.2351	0.3176	0.4036	0.4829	0.5485	0.5850	0.6151	0.6481
0.45	0.1444	0.1978	0.2425	0.2924	0.3719	0.4538	0.5287	0.5901	0.6241	0.6519	0.6824
0.50	0.2076	0.2596	0.3028	0.3508	0.4266	0.5040	0.5740	0.6309	0.6622	0.6878	0.7157
0.55	0.2733	0.3233	0.3647	0.4104	0.4819	0.5541	0.6188	0.6709	0.6995	0.7227	0.7479
0.60	0.3415	0.3891	0.4282	0.4711	0.5376	0.6041	0.6631	0.7103	0.7359	0.7567	0.7792
0.65	0.4125	0.4570	0.4933	0.5329	0.5938	0.6540	0.7069	0.7488	0.7715	0.7899	0.8097
0.70	0.4864	0.5272	0.5602	0.5959	0.6504	0.7038	0.7502	0.7867	0.8064	0.8222	0.8392
0.75	0.5633	0.5996	0.6288	0.6601	0.7076	0.7535	0.7931	0.8239	0.8404	0.8537	0.8679
0.80	0.6435	0.6745	0.6992	0.7256	0.7651	0.8031	0.8354	0.8604	0.8738	0.8844	0.8958
0.85	0.7270	0.7518	0.7714	0.7923	0.8232	0.8525	0.8773	0.8963	0.9064	0.9144	0.9229
0.90	0.8141	0.8317	0.8456	0.8602	0.8816	0.9017	0.9185	0.9312	0.9379	0.9430	0.9481

N = 50

r	0.0100	0.0250	0.0500	0.1000	0.2500	0.5000	0.7500	0.9000	0.9500	0.9750	0.9900
0.0	-0.3281	-0.2787	-0.2353	-0.1843	-0.0976	0.0000	0.0976	0.1843	0.2353	0.2787	0.3281
0.05	-0.2823	-0.2314	-0.1870	-0.1351	-0.0473	0.0505	0.1474	0.2327	0.2824	0.3247	0.3725
0.10	-0.2349	-0.1828	-0.1375	-0.0849	0.0034	0.1010	0.1967	0.2801	0.3285	0.3693	0.4154
0.15	-0.1858	-0.1328	-0.0868	-0.0337	0.0547	0.1515	0.2455	0.3267	0.3735	0.4128	0.4569
0.20	-0.1350	-0.0812	-0.0349	0.0184	0.1065	0.2020	0.2938	0.3724	0.4174	0.4550	0.4971
0.25	-0.0824	-0.0282	0.0183	0.0715	0.1588	0.2524	0.3416	0.4173	0.4603	0.4962	0.5361
0.30	-0.0279	0.0265	0.0728	0.1256	0.2115	0.3028	0.3889	0.4614	0.5023	0.5362	0.5738
0.35	0.0286	0.0828	0.1287	0.1807	0.2648	0.3532	0.4357	0.5046	0.5432	0.5752	0.6104
0.40	0.0872	0.1408	0.1861	0.2369	0.3185	0.4035	0.4821	0.5470	0.5833	0.6131	0.6459
0.45	0.1479	0.2007	0.2448	0.2942	0.3727	0.4537	0.5279	0.5887	0.6224	0.6501	0.6804
0.50	0.2110	0.2624	0.3050	0.3525	0.4274	0.5039	0.5732	0.6296	0.6607	0.6861	0.7138
0.55	0.2766	0.3260	0.3668	0.4119	0.4826	0.5540	0.6181	0.6698	0.6981	0.7211	0.7462
0.60	0.3447	0.3916	0.4302	0.4725	0.5382	0.6040	0.6625	0.7092	0.7347	0.7553	0.7777
0.65	0.4155	0.4594	0.4952	0.5342	0.5943	0.6539	0.7063	0.7479	0.7704	0.7886	0.8083
0.70	0.4891	0.5293	0.5618	0.5971	0.6509	0.7037	0.7497	0.7859	0.8054	0.8211	0.8381
0.75	0.5657	0.6015	0.6302	0.6612	0.7080	0.7534	0.7926	0.8232	0.8396	0.8528	0.8670
0.80	0.6455	0.6760	0.7004	0.7264	0.7655	0.8030	0.8351	0.8599	0.8731	0.8837	0.8951
0.85	0.7286	0.7531	0.7724	0.7929	0.8235	0.8524	0.8770	0.8959	0.9059	0.9138	0.9223
0.90	0.8152	0.8326	0.8462	0.8606	0.8818	0.9017	0.9183	0.9309	0.9375	0.9425	0.9475

TABLE A.23 (continued)

TABLE OF PERCENTAGE POINTS OF THE POSTERIOR DISTRIBUTION OF THE CORRELATION COEFFICIENT

N = 55

r	0.0100	0.0250	0.0500	0.1000	0.2500	0.5000	0.7500	0.9000	0.9500	0.9750	0.9900
0.0	-0.3129	-0.2656	-0.2241	-0.1755	-0.0929	0.0000	0.0929	0.1755	0.2241	0.2656	0.3129
0.05	-0.2667	-0.2181	-0.1756	-0.1261	-0.0426	0.0505	0.1427	0.2240	0.2715	0.3119	0.3578
0.10	-0.2189	-0.1692	-0.1260	-0.0759	0.0081	0.1009	0.1920	0.2716	0.3178	0.3570	0.4012
0.15	-0.1696	-0.1190	-0.0753	-0.0247	0.0593	0.1514	0.2409	0.3184	0.3632	0.4009	0.4433
0.20	-0.1186	-0.0674	-0.0233	0.0273	0.1110	0.2018	0.2893	0.3644	0.4075	0.4436	0.4841
0.25	-0.0658	-0.0143	0.0299	0.0803	0.1632	0.2522	0.3372	0.4095	0.4508	0.4853	0.5238
0.30	-0.0113	0.0403	0.0843	0.1343	0.2158	0.3026	0.3846	0.4539	0.4932	0.5258	0.5622
0.35	0.0451	0.0965	0.1400	0.1892	0.2689	0.3529	0.4316	0.4975	0.5346	0.5654	0.5995
0.40	0.1035	0.1543	0.1970	0.2451	0.3224	0.4032	0.4781	0.5403	0.5752	0.6040	0.6358
0.45	0.1640	0.2137	0.2554	0.3021	0.3764	0.4534	0.5241	0.5824	0.6149	0.6416	0.6710
0.50	0.2266	0.2750	0.3152	0.3600	0.4309	0.5035	0.5697	0.6238	0.6537	0.6783	0.7052
0.55	0.2916	0.3380	0.3765	0.4190	0.4858	0.5536	0.6143	0.6644	0.6917	0.7140	0.7384
0.60	0.3589	0.4030	0.4392	0.4791	0.5412	0.6036	0.6594	0.7043	0.7289	0.7489	0.7707
0.65	0.4287	0.4699	0.5035	0.5402	0.5970	0.6535	0.7036	0.7436	0.7654	0.7830	0.8022
0.70	0.5012	0.5388	0.5693	0.6025	0.6533	0.7034	0.7473	0.7821	0.8010	0.8163	0.8328
0.75	0.5765	0.6099	0.6368	0.6658	0.7100	0.7531	0.7906	0.8200	0.8359	0.8487	0.8625
0.80	0.6547	0.6831	0.7059	0.7303	0.7671	0.8027	0.8334	0.8573	0.8701	0.8804	0.8915
0.85	0.7360	0.7587	0.7767	0.7960	0.8247	0.8522	0.8757	0.8939	0.9035	0.9113	0.9195
0.90	0.8204	0.8365	0.8492	0.8627	0.8826	0.9015	0.9174	0.9294	0.9357	0.9405	0.9451

N = 60

r	0.0100	0.0250	0.0500	0.1000	0.2500	0.5000	0.7500	0.9000	0.9500	0.9750	0.9900
0.0	-0.2997	-0.2542	-0.2144	-0.1678	-0.0888	0.0000	0.0888	0.1678	0.2144	0.2542	0.2997
0.05	-0.2531	-0.2064	-0.1657	-0.1184	-0.0385	0.0504	0.1386	0.2164	0.2620	0.3008	0.3449
0.10	-0.2050	-0.1574	-0.1160	-0.0681	0.0122	0.1009	0.1879	0.2642	0.3086	0.3462	0.3888
0.15	-0.1555	-0.1070	-0.0652	-0.0170	0.0634	0.1513	0.2368	0.3112	0.3541	0.3904	0.4314
0.20	-0.1043	-0.0553	-0.0133	0.0351	0.1150	0.2017	0.2853	0.3573	0.3988	0.4336	0.4727
0.25	-0.0515	-0.0023	0.0398	0.0880	0.1670	0.2520	0.3333	0.4028	0.4425	0.4757	0.5129
0.30	0.0030	0.0523	0.0942	0.1418	0.2195	0.3024	0.3809	0.4474	0.4852	0.5168	0.5520
0.35	0.0594	0.1083	0.1497	0.1966	0.2724	0.3526	0.4280	0.4913	0.5271	0.5568	0.5899
0.40	0.1176	0.1658	0.2065	0.2523	0.3258	0.4029	0.4746	0.5345	0.5681	0.5959	0.6268
0.45	0.1778	0.2250	0.2646	0.3089	0.3797	0.4531	0.5209	0.5769	0.6083	0.6341	0.6627
0.50	0.2400	0.2858	0.3240	0.3665	0.4339	0.5032	0.5666	0.6187	0.6476	0.6714	0.6976
0.55	0.3044	0.3484	0.3848	0.4251	0.4886	0.5533	0.6119	0.6597	0.6861	0.7078	0.7315
0.60	0.3711	0.4127	0.4470	0.4848	0.5437	0.6033	0.6568	0.7001	0.7239	0.7433	0.7646
0.65	0.4401	0.4789	0.5106	0.5454	0.5993	0.6532	0.7013	0.7398	0.7609	0.7780	0.7967
0.70	0.5116	0.5470	0.5758	0.6071	0.6553	0.7031	0.7452	0.7788	0.7971	0.8120	0.8281
0.75	0.5857	0.6171	0.6424	0.6698	0.7117	0.7528	0.7888	0.8172	0.8327	0.8451	0.8586
0.80	0.6625	0.6892	0.7106	0.7337	0.7685	0.8025	0.8319	0.8550	0.8675	0.8775	0.8884
0.85	0.7422	0.7635	0.7804	0.7986	0.8258	0.8520	0.8745	0.8921	0.9015	0.9089	0.9168
0.90	0.8248	0.8399	0.8518	0.8645	0.8833	0.9013	0.9165	0.9281	0.9341	0.9387	0.9429

TABLE A.23 (continued)

TABLE OF PERCENTAGE POINTS OF THE POSTERIOR DISTRIBUTION OF THE CORRELATION COEFFICIENT

N = 65

r	0.0100	0.0250	0.0500	0.1000	0.2500	0.5000	0.7500	0.9000	0.9500	0.9750	0.9900
0.0	-0.2880	-0.2441	-0.2058	-0.1610	-0.0852	0.0000	0.0852	0.1610	0.2058	0.2441	0.2880
0.05	-0.2411	-0.1962	-0.1571	-0.1115	-0.0349	0.0504	0.1350	0.2097	0.2536	0.2910	0.3335
0.10	-0.1928	-0.1470	-0.1073	-0.0612	0.0158	0.1008	0.1844	0.2576	0.3004	0.3366	0.3778
0.15	-0.1430	-0.0965	-0.0564	-0.0101	0.0669	0.1512	0.2333	0.3048	0.3462	0.3812	0.4208
0.20	-0.0918	-0.0448	-0.0045	0.0419	0.1184	0.2015	0.2818	0.3511	0.3911	0.4247	0.4626
0.25	-0.0389	0.0083	0.0486	0.0947	0.1704	0.2519	0.3299	0.3968	0.4351	0.4672	0.5033
0.30	0.0156	0.0627	0.1028	0.1484	0.2228	0.3022	0.3776	0.4417	0.4782	0.5087	0.5428
0.35	0.0719	0.1186	0.1582	0.2030	0.2756	0.3524	0.4248	0.4858	0.5204	0.5492	0.5813
0.40	0.1299	0.1760	0.2148	0.2565	0.3288	0.4027	0.4716	0.5293	0.5618	0.5888	0.6188
0.45	0.1898	0.2348	0.2726	0.3149	0.3825	0.4528	0.5180	0.5721	0.6024	0.6275	0.6552
0.50	0.2517	0.2953	0.3317	0.3722	0.4366	0.5030	0.5639	0.6142	0.6422	0.6653	0.6908
0.55	0.3156	0.3574	0.3920	0.4305	0.4911	0.5530	0.6094	0.6556	0.6812	0.7022	0.7253
0.60	0.3817	0.4212	0.4538	0.4857	0.5460	0.6030	0.6545	0.6963	0.7194	0.7383	0.7590
0.65	0.4499	0.4867	0.5169	0.5499	0.6013	0.6530	0.6992	0.7364	0.7569	0.7736	0.7919
0.70	0.5206	0.5541	0.5813	0.6111	0.6571	0.7028	0.7434	0.7759	0.7937	0.8081	0.8239
0.75	0.5937	0.6233	0.6473	0.6734	0.7132	0.7526	0.7872	0.8148	0.8297	0.8419	0.8551
0.80	0.6693	0.6945	0.7147	0.7366	0.7698	0.8023	0.8306	0.8530	0.8651	0.8749	0.8855
0.85	0.7476	0.7676	0.7836	0.8008	0.8267	0.8518	0.8735	0.8905	0.8996	0.9068	0.9144
0.90	0.8286	0.8428	0.8540	0.8660	0.8840	0.9011	0.9158	0.9270	0.9328	0.9371	0.9411

N = 70

r	0.0100	0.0250	0.0500	0.1000	0.2500	0.5000	0.7500	0.9000	0.9500	0.9750	0.9900
0.0	-0.2776	-0.2352	-0.1982	-0.1550	-0.0820	0.0000	0.0820	0.1550	0.1982	0.2352	0.2776
0.05	-0.2304	-0.1870	-0.1493	-0.1055	-0.0317	0.0504	0.1318	0.2038	0.2461	0.2822	0.3234
0.10	-0.1819	-0.1377	-0.0995	-0.0552	0.0189	0.1007	0.1812	0.2518	0.2931	0.3281	0.3680
0.15	-0.1320	-0.0872	-0.0486	-0.0040	0.0700	0.1511	0.2302	0.2991	0.3391	0.3730	0.4114
0.20	-0.0806	-0.0354	0.0034	0.0479	0.1215	0.2014	0.2788	0.3456	0.3843	0.4168	0.4536
0.25	-0.0277	0.0176	0.0564	0.1006	0.1734	0.2517	0.3269	0.3915	0.4285	0.4597	0.4947
0.30	0.0268	0.0720	0.1105	0.1542	0.2257	0.3020	0.3747	0.4366	0.4719	0.5015	0.5347
0.35	0.0829	0.1277	0.1657	0.2087	0.2784	0.3523	0.4220	0.4810	0.5145	0.5424	0.5736
0.40	0.1408	0.1849	0.2221	0.2640	0.3315	0.4025	0.4689	0.5247	0.5562	0.5824	0.6116
0.45	0.2004	0.2435	0.2796	0.3202	0.3850	0.4526	0.5154	0.5678	0.5972	0.6216	0.6486
0.50	0.2620	0.3036	0.3384	0.3772	0.4389	0.5028	0.5615	0.6101	0.6373	0.6598	0.6846
0.55	0.3255	0.3653	0.3984	0.4352	0.4933	0.5528	0.6072	0.6519	0.6768	0.6972	0.7198
0.60	0.3910	0.4286	0.4597	0.4941	0.5480	0.6028	0.6525	0.6930	0.7154	0.7338	0.7540
0.65	0.4586	0.4936	0.5223	0.5539	0.6031	0.6528	0.6973	0.7335	0.7534	0.7696	0.7875
0.70	0.5284	0.5603	0.5863	0.6147	0.6587	0.7026	0.7418	0.7733	0.7906	0.8047	0.8201
0.75	0.6006	0.6287	0.6516	0.6764	0.7146	0.7524	0.7858	0.8126	0.8271	0.8390	0.8519
0.80	0.6752	0.6991	0.7183	0.7391	0.7709	0.8021	0.8295	0.8512	0.8630	0.8725	0.8829
0.85	0.7523	0.7712	0.7864	0.8028	0.8276	0.8517	0.8726	0.8891	0.8979	0.9049	0.9122
0.90	0.8319	0.8453	0.8560	0.8674	0.8845	0.9010	0.9152	0.9260	0.9317	0.9358	0.9397

TABLE A.23 (continued)

TABLE OF PERCENTAGE POINTS OF THE POSTERIOR DISTRIBUTION OF THE CORRELATION COEFFICIENT

N = 75

r	0.0100	0.0250	0.0500	0.1000	0.2500	0.5000	0.7500	0.9000	0.9500	0.9750	0.9900
0.0	-0.2682	-0.2272	-0.1914	-0.1457	-0.0791	-0.0000	0.0791	0.1497	0.1914	0.2272	0.2682
0.05	-0.2208	-0.1789	-0.1424	-0.1001	-0.0289	0.0503	0.1289	0.1985	0.2394	0.2744	0.3143
0.10	-0.1721	-0.1294	-0.0925	-0.0457	0.0218	0.1007	0.1783	0.2466	0.2865	0.3205	0.3592
0.15	-0.1221	-0.0788	-0.0416	0.0014	0.0728	0.1510	0.2274	0.2940	0.3328	0.3656	0.4029
0.20	-0.0707	-0.0271	0.0104	0.0533	0.1242	0.2013	0.2760	0.3407	0.3781	0.4097	0.4454
0.25	-0.0177	0.0260	0.0633	0.1060	0.1760	0.2516	0.3242	0.3867	0.4226	0.4528	0.4869
0.30	0.0367	0.0803	0.1173	0.1595	0.2283	0.3019	0.3721	0.4320	0.4663	0.4950	0.5273
0.35	0.0928	0.1359	0.1724	0.2138	0.2809	0.3521	0.4195	0.4766	0.5091	0.5363	0.5667
0.40	0.1505	0.1929	0.2286	0.2689	0.3339	0.4023	0.4665	0.5206	0.5512	0.5767	0.6051
0.45	0.2099	0.2513	0.2859	0.3249	0.3873	0.4525	0.5131	0.5639	0.5925	0.6162	0.6426
0.50	0.2711	0.3111	0.3444	0.3817	0.4411	0.5026	0.5594	0.6065	0.6330	0.6549	0.6791
0.55	0.3342	0.3724	0.4041	0.4394	0.4952	0.5526	0.6052	0.6486	0.6727	0.6927	0.7147
0.60	0.3992	0.4353	0.4651	0.4980	0.5498	0.6026	0.6506	0.6900	0.7118	0.7298	0.7495
0.65	0.4663	0.4997	0.5272	0.5575	0.6048	0.6526	0.6957	0.7308	0.7501	0.7660	0.7835
0.70	0.5354	0.5658	0.5907	0.6179	0.6601	0.7024	0.7403	0.7709	0.7878	0.8016	0.8166
0.75	0.6068	0.6336	0.6554	0.6792	0.7158	0.7522	0.7846	0.8106	0.8248	0.8364	0.8491
0.80	0.6804	0.7031	0.7215	0.7414	0.7719	0.8020	0.8284	0.8495	0.8610	0.8703	0.8804
0.85	0.7564	0.7744	0.7889	0.8046	0.8283	0.8515	0.8718	0.8878	0.8964	0.9032	0.9103
0.90	0.8349	0.8476	0.8577	0.8686	0.8851	0.9009	0.9145	0.9252	0.9307	0.9348	0.9386

N = 80

r	0.0100	0.0250	0.0500	0.1000	0.2500	0.5000	0.7500	0.9000	0.9500	0.9750	0.9900
0.0	-0.2597	-0.2199	-0.1852	-0.1448	-0.0765	0.0000	0.0765	0.1448	0.1852	0.2199	0.2597
0.05	-0.2122	-0.1715	-0.1362	-0.0952	-0.0263	0.0503	0.1263	0.1937	0.2334	0.2673	0.3060
0.10	-0.1633	-0.1220	-0.0862	-0.0448	0.0243	0.1006	0.1758	0.2419	0.2806	0.3136	0.3512
0.15	-0.1132	-0.0713	-0.0353	0.0063	0.0753	0.1509	0.2248	0.2894	0.3270	0.3589	0.3951
0.20	-0.0617	-0.0195	0.0167	0.0581	0.1267	0.2012	0.2735	0.3362	0.3725	0.4033	0.4380
0.25	-0.0087	0.0335	0.0696	0.1108	0.1784	0.2515	0.3218	0.3824	0.4173	0.4467	0.4798
0.30	0.0457	0.0877	0.1235	0.1642	0.2306	0.3017	0.3697	0.4278	0.4612	0.4891	0.5206
0.35	0.1017	0.1432	0.1784	0.2183	0.2831	0.3520	0.4172	0.4726	0.5043	0.5307	0.5604
0.40	0.1592	0.2000	0.2345	0.2733	0.3360	0.4022	0.4643	0.5168	0.5466	0.5714	0.5992
0.45	0.2184	0.2582	0.2916	0.3291	0.3893	0.4523	0.5111	0.5603	0.5882	0.6113	0.6371
0.50	0.2793	0.3178	0.3499	0.3858	0.4430	0.5024	0.5574	0.6032	0.6290	0.6503	0.6740
0.55	0.3420	0.3787	0.4093	0.4432	0.4970	0.5525	0.6034	0.6455	0.6691	0.6886	0.7101
0.60	0.4066	0.4412	0.4698	0.5015	0.5514	0.6025	0.6490	0.6872	0.7085	0.7260	0.7454
0.65	0.4731	0.5052	0.5316	0.5607	0.6062	0.6524	0.6942	0.7283	0.7472	0.7627	0.7798
0.70	0.5416	0.5707	0.5946	0.6207	0.6614	0.7023	0.7390	0.7688	0.7852	0.7987	0.8135
0.75	0.6123	0.6379	0.6588	0.6817	0.7169	0.7521	0.7835	0.8087	0.8226	0.8340	0.8464
0.80	0.6850	0.7068	0.7244	0.7435	0.7728	0.8018	0.8275	0.8480	0.8592	0.8683	0.8780
0.85	0.7601	0.7773	0.7912	0.8062	0.8290	0.8514	0.8711	0.8866	0.8950	0.9017	0.9085
0.90	0.8375	0.8496	0.8593	0.8698	0.8855	0.9009	0.9142	0.9245	0.9299	0.9340	0.9378

TABLE A.23 (continued)

TABLE OF PERCENTAGE POINTS OF THE POSTERIOR DISTRIBUTION OF THE CORRELATION COEFFICIENT

N = 85

r	0.0100	0.0250	0.0500	0.1000	0.2500	0.5000	0.7500	0.9000	0.9500	0.9750	0.9900
0.0	-0.2520	-0.2133	-0.1796	-0.1404	-0.0742	0.0000	0.0742	0.1404	0.1796	0.2133	0.2520
0.05	-0.2043	-0.1648	-0.1305	-0.0907	-0.0239	0.0503	0.1240	0.1894	0.2279	0.2608	0.2985
0.10	-0.1553	-0.1152	-0.0805	-0.0404	0.0266	0.1006	0.1735	0.2376	0.2752	0.3073	0.3438
0.15	-0.1051	-0.0645	-0.0295	0.0107	0.0776	0.1509	0.2225	0.2852	0.3218	0.3528	0.3881
0.20	-0.0535	-0.0127	0.0224	0.0625	0.1289	0.2012	0.2713	0.3322	0.3675	0.3974	0.4312
0.25	-0.0006	0.0403	0.0752	0.1151	0.1806	0.2514	0.3196	0.3784	0.4124	0.4410	0.4734
0.30	0.0538	0.0945	0.1291	0.1684	0.2327	0.3016	0.3676	0.4240	0.4565	0.4838	0.5145
0.35	0.1097	0.1499	0.1839	0.2225	0.2852	0.3518	0.4152	0.4690	0.4998	0.5256	0.5546
0.40	0.1671	0.2065	0.2398	0.2773	0.3380	0.4020	0.4624	0.5134	0.5424	0.5667	0.5938
0.45	0.2261	0.2645	0.2967	0.3330	0.3912	0.4522	0.5092	0.5571	0.5843	0.6068	0.6320
0.50	0.2867	0.3238	0.3548	0.3894	0.4447	0.5023	0.5557	0.6003	0.6254	0.6462	0.6694
0.55	0.3491	0.3845	0.4139	0.4466	0.4986	0.5523	0.6018	0.6428	0.6658	0.6848	0.7059
0.60	0.4133	0.4466	0.4741	0.5047	0.5529	0.6023	0.6475	0.6847	0.7055	0.7227	0.7416
0.65	0.4793	0.5101	0.5355	0.5636	0.6075	0.6523	0.6929	0.7261	0.7445	0.7597	0.7765
0.70	0.5472	0.5752	0.5981	0.6233	0.6625	0.7021	0.7378	0.7669	0.7829	0.7961	0.8106
0.75	0.6172	0.6418	0.6619	0.6839	0.7179	0.7520	0.7825	0.8071	0.8207	0.8318	0.8440
0.80	0.6892	0.7100	0.7269	0.7453	0.7736	0.8017	0.8266	0.8466	0.8575	0.8664	0.8758
0.85	0.7634	0.7799	0.7932	0.8076	0.8296	0.8513	0.8704	0.8856	0.8938	0.9003	0.9071
0.90	0.8398	0.8514	0.8608	0.8708	0.8860	0.9009	0.9138	0.9240	0.9293	0.9334	0.9373

N = 90

r	0.0100	0.0250	0.0500	0.1000	0.2500	0.5000	0.7500	0.9000	0.9500	0.9750	0.9900
0.0	-0.2449	-0.2072	-0.1745	-0.1364	-0.0720	0.0000	0.0720	0.1364	0.1745	0.2072	0.2449
0.05	-0.1970	-0.1586	-0.1253	-0.0867	-0.0218	0.0503	0.1219	0.1854	0.2228	0.2549	0.2916
0.10	-0.1480	-0.1089	-0.0752	-0.0363	0.0288	0.1006	0.1713	0.2337	0.2703	0.3015	0.3371
0.15	-0.0977	-0.0582	-0.0243	0.0148	0.0797	0.1508	0.2204	0.2814	0.3170	0.3472	0.3816
0.20	-0.0460	-0.0064	0.0276	0.0666	0.1310	0.2011	0.2692	0.3284	0.3628	0.3920	0.4250
0.25	0.0069	0.0465	0.0804	0.1191	0.1826	0.2513	0.3176	0.3748	0.4079	0.4358	0.4674
0.30	0.0612	0.1006	0.1342	0.1723	0.2347	0.3016	0.3656	0.4206	0.4522	0.4788	0.5088
0.35	0.1170	0.1559	0.1889	0.2263	0.2870	0.3517	0.4133	0.4657	0.4958	0.5210	0.5493
0.40	0.1743	0.2124	0.2446	0.2810	0.3398	0.4019	0.4606	0.5103	0.5386	0.5623	0.5888
0.45	0.2331	0.2702	0.3014	0.3365	0.3928	0.4520	0.5075	0.5542	0.5807	0.6027	0.6274
0.50	0.2935	0.3293	0.3592	0.3927	0.4463	0.5021	0.5541	0.5975	0.6220	0.6424	0.6651
0.55	0.3555	0.3897	0.4181	0.4498	0.5001	0.5522	0.6003	0.6403	0.6627	0.6814	0.7020
0.60	0.4193	0.4514	0.4781	0.5076	0.5543	0.6022	0.6461	0.6824	0.7027	0.7195	0.7381
0.65	0.4849	0.5146	0.5391	0.5662	0.6088	0.6521	0.6916	0.7240	0.7421	0.7570	0.7734
0.70	0.5523	0.5792	0.6013	0.6257	0.6636	0.7020	0.7367	0.7651	0.7808	0.7937	0.8080
0.75	0.6217	0.6454	0.6647	0.6859	0.7188	0.7519	0.7815	0.8056	0.8188	0.8297	0.8417
0.80	0.6930	0.7130	0.7293	0.7470	0.7743	0.8016	0.8258	0.8453	0.8560	0.8646	0.8737
0.85	0.7664	0.7822	0.7950	0.8089	0.8302	0.8513	0.8699	0.8847	0.8928	0.8992	0.9059
0.90	0.8420	0.8531	0.8621	0.8717	0.8865	0.9009	0.9135	0.9235	0.9289	0.9331	0.9373

TABLE A.23 (continued)

TABLE OF PERCENTAGE POINTS OF THE POSTERIOR DISTRIBUTION OF THE CORRELATION COEFFICIENT

N = 95

r	0.0100	0.0250	0.0500	0.1000	0.2500	0.5000	0.7500	0.9000	0.9500	0.9750	0.9900
0.0	-0.2384	-0.2017	-0.1698	-0.1327	-0.0700	0.0000	0.0700	0.1327	0.1698	0.2017	0.2384
0.05	-0.1904	-0.1530	-0.1205	-0.0829	-0.0198	0.0503	0.1199	0.1817	0.2182	0.2494	0.2852
0.10	-0.1412	-0.1032	-0.0704	-0.0326	0.0307	0.1005	0.1694	0.2301	0.2658	0.2962	0.3310
0.15	-0.0908	-0.0525	-0.0195	0.0185	0.0816	0.1508	0.2185	0.2779	0.3126	0.3421	0.3757
0.20	-0.0392	-0.0007	0.0324	0.0703	0.1329	0.2010	0.2673	0.3250	0.3586	0.3870	0.4193
0.25	0.0137	0.0523	0.0851	0.1227	0.1845	0.2513	0.3157	0.3715	0.4038	0.4311	0.4619
0.30	0.0680	0.1063	0.1388	0.1759	0.2364	0.3015	0.3638	0.4174	0.4483	0.4743	0.5036
0.35	0.1237	0.1615	0.1935	0.2298	0.2887	0.3517	0.4115	0.4627	0.4920	0.5166	0.5443
0.40	0.1808	0.2179	0.2491	0.2844	0.3414	0.4018	0.4589	0.5074	0.5350	0.5582	0.5842
0.45	0.2395	0.2754	0.3057	0.3357	0.3944	0.4519	0.5059	0.5515	0.5773	0.5989	0.6231
0.50	0.2996	0.3343	0.3633	0.3958	0.4478	0.5020	0.5526	0.5950	0.6190	0.6389	0.6612
0.55	0.3614	0.3944	0.4219	0.4526	0.5014	0.5521	0.5989	0.6379	0.6599	0.6781	0.6984
0.60	0.4248	0.4559	0.4816	0.5102	0.5555	0.6021	0.6449	0.6803	0.7002	0.7166	0.7349
0.65	0.4900	0.5187	0.5424	0.5686	0.6099	0.6520	0.6905	0.7221	0.7398	0.7544	0.7705
0.70	0.5569	0.5829	0.6043	0.6278	0.6646	0.7019	0.7358	0.7634	0.7788	0.7915	0.8055
0.75	0.6257	0.6436	0.6673	0.6876	0.7197	0.7518	0.7807	0.8041	0.8171	0.8278	0.8395
0.80	0.6964	0.7157	0.7314	0.7485	0.7750	0.8015	0.8251	0.8441	0.8545	0.8629	0.8718
0.85	0.7691	0.7844	0.7967	0.8102	0.8308	0.8512	0.8694	0.8839	0.8918	0.8982	0.9050
0.90	0.8439	0.8546	0.8633	0.8726	0.8869	0.9009	0.9133	0.9232	0.9286	0.9330	0.9378

N = 100

r	0.0100	0.0250	0.0500	0.1000	0.2500	0.5000	0.7500	0.9000	0.9500	0.9750	0.9900
0.0	-0.2324	-0.1966	-0.1654	-0.1292	-0.0682	0.0000	0.0682	0.1292	0.1654	0.1966	0.2324
0.05	-0.1843	-0.1478	-0.1161	-0.0795	-0.0180	0.0503	0.1181	0.1783	0.2139	0.2444	0.2794
0.10	-0.1350	-0.0980	-0.0660	-0.0291	0.0325	0.1005	0.1676	0.2268	0.2616	0.2913	0.3253
0.15	-0.0846	-0.0472	-0.0150	0.0219	0.0834	0.1507	0.2167	0.2746	0.3085	0.3373	0.3701
0.20	-0.0329	0.0046	0.0368	0.0737	0.1346	0.2010	0.2656	0.3218	0.3546	0.3824	0.4140
0.25	0.0200	0.0575	0.0895	0.1261	0.1862	0.2512	0.3140	0.3685	0.4000	0.4267	0.4569
0.30	0.0743	0.1115	0.1431	0.1792	0.2381	0.3014	0.3622	0.4145	0.4446	0.4701	0.4988
0.35	0.1299	0.1666	0.1977	0.2329	0.2903	0.3516	0.4099	0.4599	0.4885	0.5126	0.5398
0.40	0.1869	0.2228	0.2532	0.2874	0.3429	0.4017	0.4574	0.5047	0.5318	0.5544	0.5799
0.45	0.2453	0.2803	0.3096	0.3427	0.3958	0.4518	0.5045	0.5490	0.5743	0.5954	0.6191
0.50	0.3053	0.3389	0.3670	0.3986	0.4491	0.5019	0.5512	0.5927	0.6161	0.6357	0.6575
0.55	0.3668	0.3988	0.4255	0.4553	0.5027	0.5520	0.5976	0.6358	0.6573	0.6752	0.6951
0.60	0.4299	0.4600	0.4849	0.5127	0.5566	0.6020	0.6437	0.6784	0.6978	0.7139	0.7319
0.65	0.4947	0.5225	0.5454	0.5709	0.6109	0.6519	0.6894	0.7204	0.7377	0.7520	0.7678
0.70	0.5612	0.5863	0.6070	0.6298	0.6655	0.7018	0.7348	0.7619	0.7770	0.7895	0.8033
0.75	0.6294	0.6515	0.6696	0.6895	0.7204	0.7517	0.7798	0.8028	0.8155	0.8260	0.8374
0.80	0.6995	0.7182	0.7334	0.7500	0.7755	0.8014	0.8244	0.8430	0.8532	0.8614	0.8700
0.85	0.7716	0.7863	0.7983	0.8113	0.8313	0.8512	0.8689	0.8832	0.8911	0.8975	0.9045
0.90	0.8457	0.8560	0.8644	0.8734	0.8873	0.9010	0.9131	0.9230	0.9285	0.9332	0.9394

INDEX